Conor

CONOR

A Biography of Conor Cruise O'Brien

Donald Harman Akenson

Cornell University Press
Ithaca, New York

Library of Congress Cataloging-in-Publication Data

Akenson, Donald H.
   Conor: a biography of Conor Cruise O'Brien: narrative/Donald Harman
   Akenson.
         p.   cm.
   Includes bibliographical references (p.   ) and index.
   ISBN 0-8014-3086-0
   1. O'Brien, Conor Cruise, 1917–   . 2. Authors, Irish – 20th century –
   Biography. 3. Diplomats – Ireland – Biography. 4. Scholars – Ireland –
   Biography. I. Title.
   PR6065.B67Z53 1994
   808'.0092 – dc20
   [B]   94-22090

CONTENTS

ACKNOWLEDGMENTS   ix

PREFACE   xiii

PROLOGUE   1

PART 1   BENDING LIFE'S BOW

1 Nationalist Dublin: Not, Indeed, Joyceland   5

2 The Cruise O'Briens before Conor   40

3 His Father's Son: 1917–1936   60

PART 2   A RISING PROFESSIONAL

4 Living by His Wits: 1936–1941   85

5 A Reasonably Civil Servant: 1942–1954   113

6 To Paris, and New York, and Katanga, and Back:
   1955–1961   149

PART 3   SURVIVING THE SIXTIES

7 Reflections on a Watershed   187

8 African Academe: Ghana, 1962–1965   215

9 In the Kingdom of the New York Intellectuals:
   1965–1969   272

PART 4 AN IRISH PATRIOT
10 "Had Life Been Normal": 1969–1972   331
11 The Chains of Office: 1973–1977   385

PART 5 PARTICIPANT OBSERVER
12 Kildare Street to Fleet Street: 1977–1981   429
13 An Enviable Freedom: 1982–1992   457
    EPILOGUE   487
    NOTES   491
    INDEX   565

To The Greatest Living Irishman
and to my godson, Caleb

Acknowledgments

It is a pleasure to be able to express my gratitude to the individuals and institutions that helped me in writing this biography.

Among institutions, special thanks are due to DBA Productions, Belfast; the Grawemeyer Foundation; the curators of the Harold White Fellowship of the National Library of Australia, especially Graeme Powell; the Rockefeller Study Center, Villa Serbelloni, Bellagio, Italy; the Tyrone Guthrie Centre, Annaghmakerrig, Co. Monaghan; the archives of University College, Dublin, and of New York University; and the Social Sciences and Humanities Research Council of Canada.

Quotations from copyright material by Conor are used with his permission and, where there was any doubt about ownership, by permission of other parties involved. Quotation of Maire's poetry and correspondence is by her kind permission.

Photographs of Conor's first family were kindly provided by Mrs. George Hetherington and are reproduced with her permission. Unless otherwise indicated in the photograph's caption, all other photographs are by permission of Conor and Maire Cruise O'Brien.

For help in a wide variety of ways I am particularly grateful to

William E. Abraham
John C. Ackerman
John H. Ahtes III
Steve Anderson
David Astor
David Barnard

Richard R. Beeman
Deirdre Levinson Bergson
Isaiah Berlin
Paul Bew
Peter Braunstein
Archie and Ena Brown

Tony Brown
Andrea Ebel Brozyna
Robert Brozyna
Cindy Butts
Jeffrey Care
Philip Cercone
John M. Cole
Claire Culhane
Nancy Cutway
Paddy Devlin
Nancy di Benedetto
Martin Dillon
Noel Dorr
William Dunphy
Diane Duttle
Owen Dudley Edwards
Shula Eisner
Donald Fanger
Garret FitzGerald
David Fitzpatrick
Roy Foster
Paul Fournier
Amy Friedman Fraser
Skip and Penny Friedman
John Gamble
J. Brian Garrett
Arnold Goodman
Elaine Greene
Gerry Gregg
Brendan Halligan
Stuart Hampshire
Joan Harcourt
John Harcourt
William Burnett Harvey
Roger Haydon
Carolyn Heald
John Henshaw
Christine Foster Hetherington
John Horgan
John Hume
Mrs. Joseph Kearney
  (Kate Cruise O'Brien)

John Keith
Mark Lloyd
Bernard Loughlin
Mary Loughlin
Neil Jumonville
John V. Kelleher
Teddy Kollek
Dennis Kennedy
Alex A. Kwapong
Patrick Lynch
Susanne McAdam
Edward McCamley
Michael McDowell
Muiris MacConghail
Joan McGilvray
Christopher McGimpsey
Maurice Manning
Carol Martin
Roger Martin
Adrienne Mayor
Tom Murphy
Donall O'Morain
Donal and Rita Cruise O'Brien
Maire Cruise O'Brien
Margaret Cruise O'Brien
Patrick Cruise O'Brien
Liam O'Reagain
Ian R.K. Paisley
Kitty Quinn
Hannah Rapport
Robert and Diana Rawlinson
George Rawlyk
Barbara Rieck
Nicholas and Rachel Wheeler
  Robinson
Shane Ross
Stuart J. Saunders
Robert J. Savage
Tom Sawicki
Robert Silvers
Mrs. Nicholas Simms
  (Fedelma Cruise O'Brien)

Nicholas Simms
Peter Stansky
Saul P. Steinberg
Dorothy Thompson
the late Edward Thompson

Donald Trelford
Brian Urquhart
Brian Walker
David Welsh

PREFACE

Finding the right model for a biography of Conor Cruise O'Brien is tricky. The ideal way to tell his story would be aloud, in an old pub, as part of a good conversation. It should be done of a weekday afternoon, when the place is given over to a few rays of sunshine coming through the grimy windows, and to old men sitting in corners, conversing softly. After a couple of pints they lean forward conspiratorially. One old fellow taps another on the knee and starts to talk about "your man," whoever that might be. That's how one wants to talk about Conor, with the sense that he might be coming through the door any moment, and, by God, things around here will pick up when he does.

In written biographies, my own favorite is the cornerstone of all Irish biographical work, Adamnan's seventh-century life of St. Columba. But, consisting as it does of three books dealing with the prophecies, miracles, and angel visions of a Christian saint, it is not a useful template for the life of the first avowedly agnostic and divorced person to sit in Dail Eireann. Nor is Adamnan's example very helpful when dealing with a person whose reputation always has been contradictory, and dazzlingly so. At one time, in the early 1970s, Conor was simultaneously the most hated man in Ireland and the most admired outside of it. Those within Ireland who loathed him did so because his antiterrorism campaign went to the heart of the modern Irish identity. He forced a reexamination of Irish nationalism, and that hurt. In contrast, outside of Ireland he was highly respected for his anti-imperialist activities. And, among those in Africa, North America, and Europe who paid attention to Irish nonfiction writers, he was reckoned to be the most important of the twentieth century.

Richard Ellman's epoch-making *James Joyce* (1959) sets the standard by which all subsequent Irish biographies are to be judged, but for me to adopt it as a model would be hubris. Someday, in the next century, someone will do for Conor what Ellman did for Joyce. That, though, is many Ph.D. theses down the line. This is not to say that I have not done the homework that an Ellmanesque biographer needs to do. I have, indeed, transcribed Conor's appointment books and travel diaries, covering decades. What they prove—given that Conor lists his hobby in *Who's Who* as traveling—is that this man, who was born free, was everywhere in planes. And I have gone through his check stubs and his correspondence with bank managers over his adult lifetime, a genre of subliterature that is remarkably repetitive: the unavoidable conclusion is that the Irish government was very lucky when, early in his civil service career, Conor transferred from the Department of Finance to the Department of External Affairs. As far as managing money is concerned, Conor is not merely a Holy Innocent, but wholly innocent.

But to swamp the reader in that sort of detail would be to miss the point. And here is where the appropriate model appears. It is R. Barry O'Brien's two-volume *Life of Charles Stewart Parnell, 1846–1891*, published in 1898. This flawed, but wonderfully vibrant work, makes Parnell accessible to later generations. R. Barry O'Brien knew Parnell when he was alive and he lets us meet the man as a living and breathing being, not as a specimen under glass. Parnell's mixture of coolness and of charisma emanated from tectonic emotive forces that were controlled by a glacial outward personality. This had to be felt. Without R. Barry O'Brien, later political analysis of the great Irish nationalist leader would be arid scholasticism; and the ivy would have withered outside of Joyce's committee room, a literary curiosity preserved in amber. So it is with Conor: appreciate him alive, before analyzing him to death.

Because we are dealing with a person who is very much alive, the voices employed have to be mixed. The perpetual use of the third person, with its implied academic omniscience, is not appropriate. Sometimes, I have to talk directly to the reader and say, "I'm not sure, but I think," or, "I wonder, could it be that?" And, whenever possible, our man's own voice has to be heard. It's a good one, strong, pungent, funny.

If there is a central question in this biography, it is Where did Conor go right? This is just the opposite of what one might ask concerning, say, a criminal: where did he or she go wrong? Conor Cruise O'Brien could have become one of the great wasted talents of modern Irish history. As a young man, he was extremely bright, witty, acerbic, ambitious, drunk, and more clever by half than anyone in his generation. He easily could have been an up-market version of Brian O'Nolan (the great Irish humorist *noir*, also known as Flann O'Brien and Myles na gCopaleen): trapped, unhappy, vindictive, cramped in the civil service and increasingly crabbit and crapulous, finding only a partial outlet for his talents in Irish literary and intellectual circles. That Conor became a man on a mission, a person of immense passion in his commitment to certain humane values central to the preservation of civilization, is a small miracle, and well worth attention.

Except for a few details, this biography stops at the end of 1992, with the publication of Conor's monumental biography of Edmund Burke. That is not a matter of convenience. That book is his master achievement. He continues to work very hard (in his later seventies, he still puts in a sixty-five-hour work week, and usually more) and his subsequent publications undoubtedly will be of significance. But the Burke book is something special: one of the major biographies in Irish historiography and a summation of Conor's own life. Edmund Burke and Conor Cruise O'Brien look at each other across the centuries with, one conjectures, deep respect on both sides.

About documentation: when material from publicly accessible sources is employed, my citations are in standard historical form. With documentary material that is unsorted—such as the uncatalogued O'Brien papers in the archives of University College, Dublin, and the material stored in the O'Briens' garden shed—my citations are made as precisely as possible to the actual document, letter, or artifact. However, it would be futile to give precise locations within those collections, for the location will change when the collections are moved and recatalogued. Much of the most significant material comes from interviews undertaken between 1991 and 1994. I have spent hundreds of hours with Conor, with Maire, with members of the family and with Conor's friends and enemies. A fair bit of the information I have found useful was provided by individuals who did not want it directly attributed to them (this held not only for some of Conor's more astringent critics, but for some of his close friends, who seemed embarrassed about being too nice and about having nothing really nasty or scandalous to say). So, a judgment call is involved. Where it is important and can be done without breaking confidence, I shall identify the source of the information either in the text or in the notes. Sometimes, though, this cannot be done.

This is an authorized biography in the sense that Conor has given me unrestricted access to every piece of paper, photograph, or artifact that could possibly be relevant. He has spent hour after hour with me, discussing and remembering, while walking up and down the hill of

Howth, or sitting in a pub, or chatting over dinner; and he has put up with an endless flow of questions. He has helped me to gain access to family and friends and has pointed me in the direction of men and women who are very critical of him, but who had to be interviewed if the story was to be told whole. He has seen no part of this book before publication and he would not have it any other way. A man who has made his mark in life by looking unflinchingly at the history of his own times, wants his own life to be looked at by the same rules.

D.H.A.
Kingston, Ontario

PROLOGUE

Christmas morning, 1927, was heavily clouded, and the sunrise was more sensed than seen. A short December day in Dublin promised to be even shorter than usual.

Francis Cruise O'Brien, journalist, marched into the back garden of his rented house at 44 Leinster Road, accompanied by his ten-year-old son. Mr. O'Brien was a small man, not robust, but he moved with an avian quickness, the sort one associated with hummingbirds. He had chosen a perfect Christmas present for his son, an only child, who was just beginning to take on the interest of a young man: a handmade archery set. Father and son had strung the bow indoors and had plucked the tense string several times, as if they were muses playing on a lyre.

Outside, Francis Cruise O'Brien made ready to test the bow, his son standing back, respectful, but excited and impatient for his own moment with the new wonder to arrive. Mr. O'Brien nocked an arrow and started to pull back the string, but thought better of it: best to test the tension first. He placed the arrow on the ground and took the bow in his left hand, pulling the waxed string as hard as he could with his right. The arrowless bow formed a warrior's arc. And then, without warning, Mr. O'Brien dropped the bow; it hit the ground, the string resonating, and Mr. O'Brien collapsed near it.

Young Conor Cruise O'Brien ran into the house to fetch his mother. Soon relatives swarmed all over the house, and Conor was not permitted to see his father die.

Not long after that, the dark, low, featureless clouds descended, and throughout the British Isles heavy gales and a great blizzard raged. Two days after Christmas, snow plows were at work in London; widespread flooding caused homelessness in Canterbury; heavy gales swept the Irish Sea and several inches of snow fell as far south as Cork. This was the worst winter weather in a decade and a frightful time to hold a wake and a funeral.

All that ended in the new year. The sun came out. John McCormack gave a gala New Year's Day concert at the Theatre Royale in Dublin. He began the program with "Let Us But Rest."[1]

PART 1

BENDING LIFE'S BOW

CHAPTER 1

NATIONALIST DUBLIN: NOT, INDEED, JOYCELAND

The most important events in any of our lives occurred before we were born. Each of us is a contemporary summation of a chain of biological and social cause and effect that stretches back of time's horizon to a point beyond all possible knowing. For most of us, knowledge of what makes self is restricted to a hazy time before our birth. Conor Cruise O'Brien has put it this way:

> There is for all of us a twilit zone of time, stretching back for a generation or two before we were born, which never quite belongs to the rest of history. Our elders have talked their memories into our memories until we come to possess some sense of a continuity exceeding and traversing our own individual being. The degree in which we possess that sense of continuity, and the form it takes—national, religious, racial or social—depends on our own imagination and on the personality, opinions and garrulity of our elder relatives. Children of small and vocal communities are likely to possess it to a high degree, and if they are imaginative, have the power of incorporating into their own lives a significant span of time before their individual births.[1]

Conor's own consciousness was in considerable degree formed by his assimilation of two family traditions, those of the Sheehys (his mother's people) and those of his father, the Cruise O'Briens. (The name was never legally hyphenated, although it sometimes appears as Cruise-O'Brien in public records.) These two traditions were not symmetrical, nor were they of equal power. The Sheehys were grand (in the Irish sense of the word), but the Cruise O'Briens were wiry and witty. In

Conor's world, the Sheehys provided the unction, the Cruise O'Briens the friction.

Wisely, Conor never tried the trick equitation of the circus rider, keeping one foot on both horses while careening in circles. Instead, from the Sheehys he acquired a broad family mythology and a sense of expectation, of rightful place. But it was from his father's side that he acquired his sense of self, his immense skepticism of received wisdom— and above all, of Irish received wisdom. Conor was willing to wear the Sheehy livery at times, but, always, he rode as a Cruise O'Brien.

Conor is very much his father's son, and that is a primary key to understanding his character. The pattern, however, is not simple. Francis Cruise O'Brien died early, and from the viewpoint of a young boy, inexplicably. Much of Conor's life involved his being the son of a father who was not there, and whom he came to know, after age ten, only indirectly, mostly through reminiscences of family and friends. His father's death, so random, so wrong, haunted him, and at several times during his career as a writer and political commentator, that paternal death has found transmuted form in plays, books, and, occasionally, conspiracy theories.

• • •

The Sheehy family mythology that Conor assimilated was richly Catholic and deeply nationalistic. It effectively begins with the vaguely related martyr figure, Father Nicholas Sheehy. Of a County Limerick family that settled in Waterford, Nicholas Sheehy became parish priest of Clogheen, County Tipperary. He steps sharply into the family mythology in February 1766, as he attempts to walk out of a Dublin courtroom where he has just been cleared of a charge of inciting to riot and rebellion. This charge arose out of his alleged (and probable) association with the Whiteboys, agrarian agitators and economic rebels who resisted landlord agents and the tithe proctors of the Established Church, and who punished fellow tenant farmers who outbid them for land. Father Sheehy's sympathy with the Whiteboys may not have gone so far as to have been criminal, but he became the *bête noire* of local land agents, and also of a local cleric of the Established Church, the Rev. John Hewetson, who owned the rights to the tithes in several parishes in Counties Tipperary and Waterford. Hewetson, more than anyone else, was responsible for Father Sheehy having been charged with incitement.

Although the Dublin trial lasted only fourteen hours and resulted in an acquittal, Father Sheehy was not allowed to walk out of court a free man. His enemies, led by Hewetson, had him immediately detained on a charge of having initiated a murder by the Whiteboys. The corpse of the supposed victim was never found, but that meant little; this time no chances were taken with a Dublin jury, notably independent as they could be. Instead, Father Sheehy was taken to Clonmel, where his enemies were in complete control. The courthouse was surrounded by armed men and the intimidation was intense. Only selected observers of the right sort were permitted into the courtroom, and Sheehy's own attorney had to leave town at night, for fear of his own safety. In what the great historian W.E.H. Lecky adjudged to be one of the most scandalous trials ever known in Ireland—and that is no small condemnation—Father Sheehy was found guilty and sentenced to death. (Thus, in the later eighteenth and nineteenth centuries, the phrase "a Sheehy jury" became a vernacular term for an infamously rigged process.) On 15 March 1766, in front of Clonmel jail, Father Sheehy was hanged, drawn, and quartered. His grave became a site of pilgrimage, and Father Sheehy became an unofficial local saint: a Catholic martyr and an Irish one.[2]

Father Sheehy had a distant kinsman who watched this and related events in penal-era Ireland with great acuity: Edmund Burke. He said little publicly, outraged though he was, for Burke was too Irish and (as we now know) too closely associated with the Irish Catholics to be able to do anything, even for his Catholic relatives, without endangering himself. The ties of kinship to Father Sheehy were real, though distant—Father Sheehy's sister had married a Richard Burke who, it now appears, was a first cousin of Edmund.[3]

The intriguing tie, however, spans a considerably greater distance. Eventually, a descendant of the Limerick Sheehys, Conor Cruise O'Brien, would write a monumental biography of Edmund Burke: *The Great Melody* (1992). A reviewer of that volume, having no awareness of the distant but stout familial cord that tied Edmund Burke and Conor Cruise O'Brien, saw another, quite different, affinity. He wrote, "Serious readers of history are in for a treat: a book by the greatest living Irishman on the greatest Irishman who ever lived."[4]

The first fully formed figure in the Sheehy mythology was Conor's great-uncle, another priest, Father Eugene Sheehy (1841–1917), famous to his contemporaries as the "Land League priest." This title refers to his having been not only the sole priest to come forward to join the Land League in its formative year but, as one of his fellow agitators noted, "among the first batch of leaders" of any sort, religious or secular.[5] At that time, in 1880, he had just been appointed curate of Kilmallock, County Limerick. The Land League, which was the beginning of the achievement of a "peasant proprietorship"—meaning, effectively, the overthrow of the landlord system—was condemned by the Irish Catholic bishops. This did not stop Father Sheehy from accompanying the constitutional-nationalist leader Charles Stewart Parnell on his 1880 fund-raising tour of the United States. As a result of his continuing involvement with the Land League, Father Sheehy was arrested in August 1881. The police took him into custody at the curate's house, Kilmallock, and marched him from there to the police barracks. As Father Sheehy passed the cottages of his flock, people came out, fell on their knees, and asked for his blessing. That received, they stood up and cursed the constabulary.[6] As Brendan Behan once noted, for an Irish patriot, being in prison for a political cause is rather like an Englishman's acquiring a proper old school tie, only classier. And Father Sheehy's distinction was the classiest, since he was imprisoned along with Charles Stewart Parnell and became part of an elite of fellow prisoners known as "the Kilmainham Party."[7]

Obnoxious as Father Eugene Sheehy's political activities were to his religious superiors, he could not easily be disciplined: he was a person of considerable presence and ability and his was a very strong local family. His parents were from County Limerick families of deep roots and fairish means. He had been born at Broadford, eight miles north of the city of Limerick, and attended Mungret College and then the Irish College, Paris. The resurgence of the Catholic Church in Ireland in the nineteenth century was built on the base of rural middle-class families, such as the Sheehys, who had survived the penal laws of the eighteenth century and emerged with some resources intact. After the land agitation temporarily cooled down, Father Eugene was promoted to parish priest of Bruree, County Limerick. This did not buy his silence, however, and Father Eugene was on the edge of Irish radical politics right up to his death in 1917.[8]

His younger brother, David Sheehy (1844–1932)—Conor's grandfather on his mother's side—was deeply engaged in radical politics as a young man and later became solidly ensconced in what seemed to be the Irish nationalist establishment. Born near Broadford, as Father Eugene had been, he too was intended for the priesthood. He too attended the Irish College in Paris, but there the destinies of the two brothers divided. When a cholera epidemic struck Paris, David Sheehy was sent home. His older brother, however, stayed in Europe and continued to study for the priesthood. Once home, David Sheehy quickly became involved in radical politics. He joined the Irish Republican Brotherhood (the "Fenians"), the oath-bound secret society that intended to produce an Irish revolution. A handsome, confident young man, David Sheehy affected a striking blond beard and had an eye for the local girls. The locality now was County Cork, where his father owned a mill in Arthur's Glen, Mallow. It was there that William O'Brien, then a journalist and later a leading land agitator, came across David Sheehy and his contingent going through the manual of arms and casting bullets for the revolution.[9]

In the 1880s, David Sheehy bought a mill at Loughmore, near Templemore in County Tipperary.[10] He was a prosperous young man, but not rich. However, the mill was located near a railway line, so it did well and his property appreciated quickly in value. Simultaneously, his politics moved from revolutionary Fenianism to home-rule nationalism and land agitation. He became a devoted follower of Charles Stewart Parnell and was elected Member of Parliament for Galway South in 1885 (a seat he held until 1900; he was subsequently elected MP for Meath South from 1903 to 1918). In middle age, he became physically imposing: gray-haired, with a massive down-drooping mustache. He would have been a dominating figure in the Sheehy family tapestry even if he had not been involved in two dramatic events.[11]

The first occurred in 1887 when he was imprisoned in Tullamore jail for his radical political activities. In protest he refused to wear prison clothes. In response, the prison authorities allowed him and his fellow protestors only bread and water and left them naked all winter, with only the odd scrap of blanket to keep out the cold and damp. His hearing was permanently damaged, presumably as a result of exposure and illness.

This action, dramatic enough in itself, was outlined in the family tapestry when his brother preached a legendary sermon, based in part on David's incarceration. The occasion was the annual collection of Peter's Pence, a benefit for the Vatican. Father Eugene Sheehy was not terribly keen on this compulsory fundraising, since in the later nineteenth century neither the Vatican nor the Irish bishops were at all supportive of the idea of Irish land reform or Irish self-government. In his sermon Father Eugene first pointed to the conditions his own brother had experienced in Tullamore jail and then assured his congregation that His Holiness was in much better shape: that he lived in a splendid palace, had many servants, was free to move around as he wished. In sum, in no way did the Vatican resemble Tullamore jail. That year the appeal raised either one penny or six pence, depending on which version of the Sheehy family tradition one prefers.[12]

Rather more soundly documented was David Sheehy's part in the political downfall and subsequent death of Charles Stewart Parnell. This sequence of events, which followed upon Parnell's being named as co-respondent in a divorce, has been given epic proportions in Irish literary history—witness James Joyce's use of it in *Dubliners* and *Ulysses*, and William Butler Yeats's statement in his Nobel Prize acceptance that modern Irish literature began when Parnell died and "a disillusioned and embittered Ireland turned from parliamentary politics" and the Irish literary renaissance began.[13] Within the historical community, the tendency has been unconsciously to assume that the majority of Irish nationalist MPs who decided Parnell's fate in December 1890 by walking out on his leadership, did so with an awareness of the consequences that would ensue. They could not know how significant their decision was to be. Of course they knew it was important and they were riven with deep-felt emotion about whether or not to turn on their great leader. But they were engaged in making what they believed was an immediate and merely short-run political decision; namely, how to get their party through the next few months, while weathering the disapproval of the Irish Catholic bishops and of the English non-conformists.[14]

David Sheehy, deeply loyal to Parnell, took his leader at his word when Parnell told him and a number of other nationalist MPs that there was nothing in the charge by Captain William O'Shea, MP for Galway, that Parnell was having an affair with O'Shea's wife. According to family tradition, Parnell met the query leaning insouciantly against a mantelpiece. He coolly asked his visitors, "Gentlemen, could you believe that of me?" This was taken to be a denial and the MPs all went out to defend their leader. David Sheehy was doing just that in his constituency when his speech was interrupted by a newsboy bringing papers bearing the headline "Divorce Suit Undefended." Sheehy felt betrayed. And, according to family mythology, he was beaten physically as well: his audience had consisted in part of a band of pig-buyers from Limerick, and they attacked him so vigorously that he required six stitches in his head.[15] Thus, when the moment of decision came, David Sheehy marched out of Committee Room 15 (perhaps the most famous venue in Irish political history), along with the majority of the Irish parliamentary party. Thereafter he campaigned hard against his former leader.

As a young man, Conor was embarrassed by his grandfather's actions. How much better it might have been for him to stay at Parnell's side and to fight against the alliance of Catholic clergy and English dissenters that was savaging the Irish chief. Yet, as he grew older, Conor came to see David Sheehy's position.[16] The two arch-Parnellites—Joyce and Yeats—had so captured the public imagination, had so successfully converted the issue into a Manichean drama between the Parnellite sons of light and the anti-Parnellite sons of darkness, that the basic political realities were lost. David Sheehy and the anti-Parnellites were convinced that home rule for Ireland was less obtainable with Parnell in front than if he were gone. They made a simple political decision, tough, but merely political.

These events centering around Parnell and the Sheehys suggest that the most visible figures in the family mythology were males. (One cannot count as much of an exception Conor's great-grandmother who lived to be 106 and was still alive in the 1880s; she claimed that in her youth she had known the legendary revolutionary figure of the 1790s, Lord Edward Fitzgerald.)[17] Yet, in fact, the primary keeper of the family mythology, and the person who intended to fashion the Sheehys' past into the Sheehys' future, was female. This was the formidable Elizabeth ("Bessie") McCoy of Loughill, County Limerick. She married David Sheehy in 1876, when he was thirty-two and she was either twenty-five or twenty-seven (accounts vary).[18] David Sheehy needed domesticating—he had just returned from an extended stay in the United States where he had gone to escape prosecution for his Fenian activities—if he was not to spend his life in prison or in some far-off dominion as a wild colonial boy. Bessie took over. They had six children, four girls and two boys. The oldest, Johanna (always called Hanna), was born in May 1877, the youngest, Kathleen, in 1887. In between there were Margaret (1881), Richard (1882), Eugene (1883), and Mary (1885).[19]

In 1887, a year after David Sheehy became a nationalist Member of Parliament (much safer and seemingly holding a better future than being a Fenian revolutionary), the ménage moved from the Tipperary millsite to Dublin. They lived first in Hollybank Road, Drumcondra, and then in a fine Georgian house at 2 Belvedere Place.[20] From that command post, Bessie Sheehy ran her campaign. "My grandmother intended, quite consciously I believe, to preside over the birth of a new ruling class: those who would run the country when Home Rule was won," Conor later wrote. "It was not," he adjudged, "a fanciful ambition."[21]

The indirect indications of the force of Bessie Sheehy's personality are clear, if scattered. For example, one piece of family mythology is patently false: that, in a classic Irish elopement, she had been spirited out of a convent school as a teenaged beauty by the ardent David Sheehy. This hardly works, given that she was in her mid-twenties at the time of marriage, but no one dared let mere fact overcome romantic assertion.[22] More important was the way her daughters were raised. Of course they were intended to marry, and well, but they were brought up to have a personal assertiveness that, within the context of the times, was unusual. The girls were sent to the demanding and fashionable (if not quite top-of-the-line) Dominican Convent in Eccles Street, Dublin. There they were encouraged to compete for scholarships and monetary prizes, and they did very well. Subsequently, three of the four girls (the exception was Margaret) earned university degrees. All of them were strongly feminist (again, within the context of their time).[23]

Within the walls of 2 Belvedere Place, one could see Bessie Sheehy at her most commanding. There, in the late 1890s and in the first decade of the twentieth century, she ran a salon. Her goal was to ensure that her sons became friends with the smartest, most promising, and most ambitious young people of their generation among Dublin Catholics (no Protestants need apply), and that her daughters were given the best selection of men to sort through. These were the young people who would be running the new Ireland, and soon, Bessie believed. And despite the Metternich-like seriousness with which she proceeded, it was great fun for the young men and women who were in their late teens and twenties. "Second Sundays"—meaning fortnightly soirées—became a regular ritual and an invitation was a prize among the scions of the rising Catholic bourgeoisie.[24]

It is at this point, just when we want to peek through the windows of 2 Belvedere Place and see what a typical Second Sunday was like, that things become tricky. The Sheehy mythology, relatively straightforward thus far, suddenly becomes a maze, and this because of one of their frequent guests: James Joyce. If we are to make any real sense of the Sheehys' world and of those who passed through it, we must respectfully tip our hat to Dublin's most seductive dragoman, but not let him take us on a dizzying tour of his world, Joyceland. The Sheehys in a literary sense were inhabitants of Joyceland, but in real life Joyce was part of the kingdom of the Sheehys. It is hard to think of Joyce as just another bright undergraduate, taking tea, respectfully asking David Sheehy for his opinion on some political matter, but that is the way it was. Unless we can first take Joyce as an everyday being, then we can never see the Sheehys when they were the real thing, before their later fictional anabiosis in Joyce's writings. (The Sheehys appear as the Daniels family in *Stephen Hero* and, less clearly, in *A Portrait of the Artist as a Young Man*; members of the family seem to make cameo appearances in *Dubliners*, although this is problematical; and Bessie Sheehy has a walk-on role in *Ulysses* in a conversation with Father John Conmee, S.J.)

The greatest problem with Joyceland is that it was created by one of the world's most singular literary minds. Rarely, if ever, can a great imagination have been combined with such a consistent refusal to invent. Joyce's material, even the interior monologues, are fragments of actual events, so we are tempted to take them as being historical. But Joyce, while abhorring outright invention, changes the meaning of each wee found-fact, by the creative juxtaposition of it with others. Meaning, and especially, relationships, are thereby altered, and Joyceland becomes a cosmological triumph, an imaginary world created entirely from the found-shards of a once-tangible Dublin. So, one should not believe Joyce, but, instead, believe *in* him: let us venerate him as a cosmologist, but distrust him as historian.

The Sheehys' world was different from Joyceland. Unlike Joyceland, it was not flat. To the people invited into the Sheehys' drawing room, the times were lively and full of hope. The Irish nationalist party, reunited at the end of January 1900, once again held promise of future power. This world had its share of very bright young people; several of them of greater intellect than James Joyce, though he chose not to believe that. And, these contemporaries liked Joyce and treated him well, contrary to his later version of events.[25] If Catholic Ireland bored Joyce to tears, he had more interesting and amiable companions there than he was to have elsewhere for the rest of his life. But, as Joyce remarked in 1906 in a letter concerning *Dubliners*, "I have written it for the most part in a style of scrupulous meanness," and that style, which in his later work turned into an Olympian meanness, made a variegated and lively Dublin appear misleadingly flat.[26]

So, in, say, February 1900, let Joyce walk up to the front door of 2 Belvedere Place, just off Mountjoy Square, as just another Sunday evening guest. He is late as usual and has to bang the door knocker several times; the guests inside are arguing and laughing so loudly that he is not heard. The house on whose top step he impatiently stands is a part of an imposing Georgian row. Four stories high, plus a full basement, it easily houses live-in staff, six children, and Mr. and Mrs. Sheehy. Granite steps lead up to the front door, which is black enameled, with narrow side windows and a column on either side, surmounted by a leaded-glass fan-shaped window. The house is appropriate for a Member of Parliament.[27]

When, finally, the door is opened, it is by a plump and smiling Richard Sheehy and his younger brother Eugene. They and Joyce had been at Belvedere College. Richard calls Joyce "James-Disgusting-Joyce" and pulls him inside.[28] (Other friends call Joyce "The Hatter," as in mad-as-a, and "Dirty Jimmy"—at this stage in his life for his lack of hygiene, not for his morals.) At the doorway to the drawing room, Joyce shakes hands with David Sheehy. He considers him to be pompous and didactic, but he treats him respectfully. As quickly as he can, he seeks out Mrs. Sheehy, whom he prefers and, indeed, quite likes.[29]

Seated in a wingback chair in the corner, she is very much the empress. Joyce is one of her projects. Bessie Sheehy, round faced, with center-parted hair pulled tightly back, resembles a middle-aged version of Queen Victoria, an impression enhanced when she wears a lace shawl.[30] Usually Mrs. Sheehy surveyed her realm quietly, as if commanding the young people to be brilliant and to have a good time. She brightens visibly when Jimmy (as she calls him) enters. He has come such a long way and she largely credits herself. She started this project when Jimmy and her boys were at Belvedere, when he was withdrawn compared to the other youngsters.[31] Now he is quite at home, even a bit of a show-off. If only he would wear a clean shirt!

Bessie Sheehy, though unconsciously patronizing to young Joyce (as, in fact, were all the females in the Sheehy family), was educating him socially. Joyce's brother Stanislaus, who sometimes came along to Second Sundays, was later to note, concerning the Sheehys, that "this friendly relationship lasted some years and was practically the only experience of what might be called social life that my brother had in Dublin."[32] What Stanislaus meant, I think, was social life of the proper sort: genteel. James Joyce had plenty of social life during his Dublin years if one counts barmen, bowzies, and whores, but it was Bessie Sheehy who taught him how polite society worked and how to behave in it. Rarely did Joyce forgive anyone who did him a favor, and his etchings of the Sheehy family are done with mild acid. But one need spare no pity on Bessie Sheehy. Aside from the fact that she probably never read a word that Joyce wrote, she had been cultivating him not because of any humanitarian streak, but because he was extremely promising, a useful addition to her cadre of elite young Catholics.

What almost everyone at the Sheehys' soirées had in common, besides being Catholic, nationalist, and very promising intellectually, was that they either attended or planned on attending the Jesuit College at St. Stephen's Green. This institution was the direct descendant of the Catholic University which the Irish bishops had opened in 1854. They had placed John Henry Newman in charge, a position that sharply accelerated his understanding of the concept of purgatory. Although sometimes referred to as "the Jesuit College," or as the "St. Stephen's Green College," it was usually colloquially called "the Royal" (and in memoirs is found as "the old Royal"), because in 1882 the Royal University of Ireland was founded. This was an examining and accrediting body for the university colleges at Cork, Galway, Belfast, and Dublin. Meanwhile, the administration of the college, having proved beyond the scope of the Irish bishops, was taken over by the Jesuits in 1883.[33] (Eventually, under the Irish Universities Act of 1908, it became University College, Dublin.)

The young men at the Sheehys' salon were all active in the college's Literary and Historical Society—which they usually referred to as "the L. & H." (Only men were members, for women, though able to take Royal University degrees, were not at this time full members of the Catholic college.) The L. & H. debated everything, while pretending to debate everything but Irish politics. (The Jesuit fathers enforced the antipolitics rule very selectively.) The society met Saturday evenings in the physics theater of the college, and all the young men present at Bessie Sheehy's soirée would have been there, participating in the debate. Almost certainly on Sunday evening they would have been assaying the results, deciding who had been the cleverest and who had suffered the most devastating hit. Self-importance would not be lacking.

And, surprisingly, most of the young men at the Sheehys' (Joyce included) were members of the college's Sodality of the Blessed Virgin Mary.[34] For the Sheehy boys and for Joyce this was a continuation of their actions at Belvedere, where both Dick Sheehy and James Joyce had been officers of the sodality.[35] Since several of the leaders of the sodality later turned from the faith, in their memoirs they played down their youthful innocence or the reality of their early adhesion. No: at this time they were good Catholic lads, the best.

The most striking person present at the Sheehys' would have been Francis—"Frank"—Skeffington. At first meeting, he was a preposterous figure, a small, bearded young man, dressed in knickerbockers and a rough tweed jacket. He had an Ulster Catholic accent which cut through the cultivated modulations of the Dublin haute bourgeoisie. (Such an accent always tended to get Dublin Catholic backs up; almost always it signaled a harsh, argumentative intransigence, foreign to the educated southerner. "Not an inch" was a northern Catholic as well as northern Presbyterian characteristic.) Dead serious in manner, Skeffington was quite incandescent in belief. He was a socialist, feminist, pacifist, and food crusader and, in those days, still a good Catholic. A perpetual defender of the underdog, he once was commissioned during his university days to write half a column in the *Freeman's Journal* on the subject of rats. The editor went over it. "I really do not know what I can do with you. You have written about rats as if they were an oppressed nationality."[36] Skeffington was much more than a character; he was the moral powerhouse of the St. Stephen's Green college. He had been auditor (that is, head) of the Literary and Historical Society in 1897–98 and had in considerable part been responsible for turning a moribund society into the centerpiece of the college's social life.[37] Eugene Sheehy, in later life, said that Skeffington was one of the first to recognize the genius of James Joyce.[38] He and Joyce were to collaborate in 1901 on a joint pamphlet, privately printed, which contained essays of theirs that had been excluded from the university college's student magazine by the clerical censor, namely, Joyce's "The Day of the Rabblement," and Skeffington's argument that women should be given equal status with men in the college. Respect between the two eccentrics was reciprocal. Joyce (who re-creates Skeffington as "McCann" in several of his writings), told his own brother that Skeffington was the second cleverest man at the college. The first, of course, was himself.[39]

Most denizens of Bessie Sheehy's salon probably would have reversed the order: when Joyce ran for auditor of the L. & H. in 1900, he was defeated by nearly a two-to-one margin, an indication that he was not considered quite top flight.[40] And, almost certainly, both Skeffington and Joyce would have been dropped down the list by contemporaries behind the acknowledged star of the time, Tom Kettle.

Kettle had been auditor of the L. & H. in 1898–99 and was generally reckoned the best speaker and debater among the students of his time. Tall, darkly handsome, given to expensively tailored clothes, he, of all the young men in Bessie's salon, looked to be a certain winner. He had not only brains and presence, but money. His father was a large farmer in north County Dublin, a sometime MP, and one of the founders of the Land League. Kettle and Joyce (who paints him as "Hughes" in *Stephen Hero*) had an off-again, on-again friendship.[41]

As the young men and women sipped their madeira or sherry and talked, the one division in their ranks they all remembered was the occasion in May 1899, when William Butler Yeats's play *The Countess Cathleen* was produced in the Antient Concert Rooms. The highly abstract drama was set in a time of famine, when, according to Yeats, the souls of the people were being purchased by demon-merchants. The Countess, after giving away all her possessions to feed the starving, sells her own soul, thus saving the peasantry. The play simultaneously touched nationalist and Catholic nerves. The theological reaction was that the notion of selling one's soul, and thus saving it, was heretical. The nationalist response was that talking about the Irish peasant was *infra dig*—especially among the new Catholic middle class whose own peasant roots frequently were too recent to be discussed openly.[42]

Considerable agitation arose at the Royal and 23 students signed a letter of protest which was published in the *Freeman's Journal* of 10 May. The letter concluded, "We feel it our duty in the name and for the honour of Dublin Catholic students of the Royal University to protest against an art, even a dispassionate art, which offers as a type of our people a loathsome brood of apostates." James Joyce was not among the signers, which included Francis Skeffington, Richard Sheehy, Eugene Sheehy, and Tom Kettle. The 23 signatories were from a student body of more than 400.[43] This incident reveals something interesting about the young people who were being groomed as the elite of an independent Ireland. While acting like good militant Catholics (the play had been condemned by Cardinal Logue), they would do so under the public guise of Irish nationalism (which was the form most of the protest assumed). And their actions made clear that culture, even Irish culture, would be a gored ox if it impinged at all on their version either of Irish Catholicism or Irish nationalism.[44]

The young women of the Sheehy family mixed equally with the men on Second Sundays and they were not there to flirt, at least not in the conventional manner. They were expected to be as unrelentingly clever, as good at syllogisms, as sharp at word play, as clever at puns, as well read, as the young men. The Sheehy girls could be unnerving, especially Hanna, who was older than everyone else and had decided opinions on everything. Conor later remarked, concerning his aunt, "Hanna had intended to be a nun; she would have made a great reforming Mother Superior in a medieval order. When she took up a cause she did not let go."[45] Fortunately for the public peace, she was beginning to be attached to Frank Skeffington and the two of them increasingly formed a self-enclosed cyclone of their own.

The most vivacious of the young Sheehy women, and the handsomest, was Margaret. She was the least intellectual. Very keen on drama in an amateur way, on that cold Sunday in February 1900, she was enlivening things by discussing with anyone who would listen a play that she had written, entitled *Cupid's Confidante*. It was a mixture of high melodrama and of admonitions to buy-Irish. She convinced James Joyce to play the male lead, a seductive villain. The play was produced at the X.L. Café, Grafton Street, in March 1900, and then again at the Antient Concert Rooms in January 1901.[46] Popular—and scholarly—conventions to the contrary, it was Margaret among the Sheehy girls to whom Joyce was most attached.[47]

Voicing even such minor observations about James Joyce's affect might seem at this point to be counterproductive. After all, what I wish to emphasize is that the literary world of Joyceland and the real kingdom of the Sheehys were different places, and such notice of Joyce brings him back to center stage. Why not just rehearse the links in the Sheehy family mythology—the martyr Father Sheehy, the Land League priest Sheehy, David Sheehy, imprisoned nationalist; anti-Parnellite Sheehys, and Bessie Sheehy, impresario, filling her drawing room with the brightest and best? Why not?—because of a literary mortmain from Joyce's works which affected the view of his own family that Conor adopted in his adult years. Joyce's great dead hand wrote on time's wall, and beyond. Consider Conor's view of his Aunt Mary and of his mother Kathleen Sheehy. In each case the reports that reached him from Joyceland not only led but misled him.

Aunt Mary as a young woman was the most conventionally pretty of the Sheehy women. Of course Conor knew her personally, but in his early middle age he also mislearned about her from James Joyce's brother Stanislaus. In 1958 Stanislaus published a memoir in which he stated that "Mary Sheehy was the only girl who had ever aroused any emotional interest" in his brother James as a youth.[48] He suggested that Mary Sheehy, therefore, was the female figure in *A Portrait* who long had been unidentified, a young lady called "E.C."; in *Stephen Hero* her name is spelled out as "Emma Clery." The identification with Mary Sheehy offered a neat end to a literary puzzle and a bit of biography for Mary Sheehy. "For Mary, Joyce conceived a small, rich passion which, unsuspected by her, lasted for several years. She queened his imagination in a way that, modest and a little abashed before him as she was, she could not have believed."[49] Indeed not: for it was not Mary Sheehy he had in mind, but rather a fellow student at the Royal, one Mary Elizabeth ("Emm Eh") Cleary. This has been convincingly argued by Peter Costello in his 1992 study of Joyce's early years.[50]

Here, however, the intriguing point is that Conor, as he became acquainted with the burgeoning of Joyce studies in the late 1950s and thereafter (led, but certainly not limited to the work of the great Richard Ellman), came to believe that, in part, Joyceland was congruent with the kingdom of the Sheehys. He inserted Joyce's E.C. into his own family mythology. Thus, he assimilated the inaccurate identification of Emma with his Aunt Mary. "Joyce used to come regularly on Sunday evening to act in charades. He was attracted by the presence there of my Aunt Mary (later married to Tom Kettle). Mary Sheehy was one of the great beauties of Dublin of those days: dark, fine-boned, with classic features, high in colouring, fiery of speech and as proud as Lucifer. Joyce was in love with her for a while. For her part, she liked Joyce, but never took him seriously."[51] Conor was right about his Aunt Mary's beauty and about her not taking Joyce seriously, but not about Joyce's having been in love with her. But right or wrong is only a small matter—mythologies, after all, are only in part factual. The fascinating point is that the great magus, Joyce, could reach out from beyond the grave and through the indirect agency of later, mistaken scholarship, could still capture for Joyceland a part of Dublin that previously had not been under his rule.

Where the hand of Joyce, through the misapprehension of scholarly readers, really pinched in on Conor's consciousness, concerned his mother, Kathleen Sheehy. Until he read Ellman's authoritative biography of Joyce, he did not know that Miss Ivors in Joyce's masterpiece, "The Dead" (in *Dubliners*) was supposed to have been modeled on his mother. Miss Ivors was an aggressively nationalistic young woman, very keen on the Irish language and quite intolerant of those who did not share her enthusiasm. When asked if he had recognized the portrait of his mother at first reading, Conor replied, "It wasn't obvious to me at first reading; it wasn't obvious to me until I read Richard Ellman's book."[52]

Nor should he have recognized her, because, although there may have been just a hint of his mother there, the model almost certainly was the same Mary Elizabeth Cleary who was also the chief model for Emma Clery. She was dead keen on the Irish language, was a member of the central branch of the Gaelic League (into which she, along with George Clancey, seems to have drawn Joyce for a time), and studied Old Irish. She had visited the Aran Islands to improve her *blas* and heartily recommended going there to others.[53] Once this misidentification was made—of Kathleen Sheehy with Miss Ivors—its suggestive power was overpowering.

"Is it an acceptable portrait?" the interviewer from the *James Joyce Quarterly* asked in 1974.

"Oh yes," replied Conor, "it is, perfectly."[54]

Thus, I think we must be intentionally schizophrenic in reflecting on the Sheehy family mythology, on the mixture of historical belief and disbelief, of sense of purpose and of position, that eventually came to help shape Conor Cruise O'Brien. We must appreciate the wonders of Joyceland (who could not?) and accept the incredible power of that imagined, but not invented, land, while somehow keeping our awareness that the Sheehys had a kingdom of their own, one different, happier, more promising. The Sheehys' kingdom was small. Scale is important. Everybody knew everybody, if they were of any importance. The Sheehy domain, like Joyceland, was an unreal world. The Sheehys talked home rule for Ireland and planned on being the rulers of home rule, a fancy that was ultimately fruitless, if not entirely harmless.

• • •

Into this world rode Francis Cruise O'Brien and rode is the proper figure of speech. He was built like a hunt jockey—premature at birth, frail all his life, thin, pint-sized—yet, like a good hunt rider, he was aggressive, determined, and capable of exhibiting surprising bursts of strength and energy.

He matriculated at the St. Stephen's Green college in the autumn of 1903 after Joyce had left; he thus escaped the fate of becoming yet-another fly trapped in Joyce's creative amber. Immediately he became involved in the L. & H. and with *St. Stephen's*, the college magazine. Within a year he was one of the two arts sub-editors of the publication,[55] a post filled the following year by Richard Sheehy.[56] Cruise O'Brien was in the L. & H. at the apogee of the Sheehy brothers. Richard was inaugurated as auditor in November 1904 and his brother Eugene as the honorary secretary at the same time.[57] Cruise O'Brien mixed with the right people which, considering his own déclassé background, was an indication of his own talent: he and his sister lived alone in Leeson Street, near Morehampton Road, as both of their parents were dead.[58] He became known to his college friends as "Crusoe," and, given his independent approach to everything, the name was apposite. A contemporary has described him as follows: "Cruise O'Brien came to the college, a frail figure with long black hair and a mature mind full of interesting and often unorthodox ideas. He was widely read and had already studied Sanskrit and comparative philology."[59]

"Crusoe" was quickly admitted to the select company invited to 2 Belvedere Place and there he fit in well, playing charades with style, excelling at word games, and happily arguing about the topic of the day. Bessie Sheehy, however, kept a skeptical eye on him. Francis Cruise O'Brien (like his son Conor after him) was brilliant, the best of company, and he was trouble.

To understand the kind of trouble Francis became—and became famous for—one has to look briefly at the Jesuit College buildings at 85 and 86 St. Stephen's Green. The college was a pretentious little place, hoping to fall on good times. As mentioned earlier, the St. Stephen's Green college (and its female affiliate, St. Mary's College for Women) was a teaching body which could not grant its own degrees. Degree courses were examined and degrees were granted by the Royal University which had its headquarters in Earlsfort Terrace. The premises of the Jesuit College were woefully inadequate for its 400 students: they consisted of two buildings, door-to-door town mansions that had been taken over in 1854 and 1865. One of these, number 85, was of Palladian design, the other Rococo. Number 86 had been built by Richard Chapel Whaley (known as "Burn Chapel Whaley" for his fierce anti-Catholicism) and was associated with Buck Whaley who once walked to Jerusalem on a spur-of-the-moment bet. Two crumbling lions aptly signified the decline of the old Anglo-Irish and the capture of their world by the rising Catholic middle class. Inside these two buildings were high ceilings, ornamental plasterwork, and fine fireplaces, all of which contrasted with their new usage as offices and lecture rooms.[60]

A good example of the jerry-built nature of the place was the physics theater in number 85 where Cruise O'Brien, the Sheehy boys, Skeffington, Kettle, and Joyce played out their L. & H. debates. This had originally been the first floor salon of the old mansion. A long demonstration table dominated the room; it was cleared of physics apparatus when the L. & H. convened and covered with green baize. There, like a Roman triumvirate, sat the auditor and the chief officers. Perhaps thirty or forty members attended a Saturday evening's debate, but if more than fifty attended, the room was uncomfortably crowded. This makeshift debating arena adjoined the study of the president of the college, so that debaters were always aware of the presence of Father Delaney who, *ex officio*, was also the president of the L. & H.[61] The real educational deficiency of the St. Stephen's Green college was that it had virtually no library. Its students, therefore, used the reading room of Dublin's National Library as their preferred place of study and the semicircle of steps in front of that building became an informal clubhouse.

These inadequacies greatly vexed the Catholic authorities, not only the Jesuits, but, particularly, Archbishop Walsh of Dublin. The comparison between the riches of nearby Trinity College and the poverty of the St. Stephen's Green college was galling. The Catholic college barely survived financially and only then because of the selflessness of the Jesuits who, in essence, underwrote the institution with their labor. What the Catholic authorities wanted was, first, direct grants from the government to pay for their teaching activities and, simultaneously, safeguards against interference on the part of the state with their educational activities.

So, as part of a continuing campaign for fairness (fairness, equality, various similar words were used) the Catholic authorities played a slightly dangerous game. They agitated their students. That is, one finds the question of "university reform" (a code phrase for more money for Catholic university education) being frequently brought before the students. The matter was often debated in the L. & H., despite the supposed rule that political topics were not a matter for the society. The patron of the society, the president of the college, approved. This was a perilous strategy, however, for the students easily could get out of hand and, through bad behavior, raise governmental disapproval and thus cut down the chance of increased grants.

The moment when this dicey approach was most dangerous was at an annual event, the autumn conferring of degrees. These were given by the Royal University—the examining body that was run by the old ascendancy and therefore a tempting target for student attack. The conferrals day provided a rare chance for the Catholic students to combine Irish nationalism, defense of the faith, and old-fashioned hell-raising. The first flash in this tinderbox occurred the autumn Cruise O'Brien enrolled, on 30 October 1903. Students heckled and protested during the ceremony and during the singing of the British national anthem. Police were called into the hall to remove troublemakers. James Joyce, in one of his bravura performances before an undergraduate audience, stood on a chair outside and was wildly cheered by his fellow students as he denounced the proceedings.[62]

The next year, 1904, the college authorities, wishing to avoid the embarrassment of the previous year, announced that all members of the university, except those receiving their degrees and their friends, would be excluded from the hall. The excuse that there was not enough room was transparent, and vexing. Hordes of students massed outside and only a sturdy phalanx of police kept them from rushing the half-filled hall as the names of graduands were called. Then, cannily, a bunch of students distracted the police and the rest rushed through a gap in the police lines. Lord Meath, head of the Royal University, was in the midst of conferring degrees; he scuttled away and the remaining degrees had to be granted in absentia.[63] *St. Stephen's,* of which Francis Cruise O'Brien was now the arts sub-editor, published a satirical report based on eyewitness (and, perhaps, participant) accounts: FIERCE ENGAGEMENT ... FORT CAPTURED! ROYALISTS COMPLETELY DEFEATED.[64]

In 1905 a group of leaders—Eugene Sheehy, Thomas Madden, John E. Kennedy, and Francis Cruise O'Brien—plotted something more original than a mere riot. Despite not having proper admission tickets, they managed to sneak into seats in the upper gallery of the conferral hall. They absented themselves unobtrusively, went downstairs, and ran along a corridor until they found a door that led under the dais, where the ceremony was taking place. They climbed a steep ladder that brought them up behind, and on top of, the large pipe organ. Then, to everyone's astonishment, they jumped down onto the organ (family tradition has it that Cruise O'Brien, who was cox of the college's heavyweight crew, was the first down, lowered on a rope). The lads called out that they would not permit the singing of "God Save the King." As the authorities moved in on them, they left the hall, loudly singing "God Save Ireland."

The upshot of this burlesque was farce. Cruise O'Brien had a brief triumph as he was carried across O'Connell Bridge on the shoulders of the college heavies. The authorities of the Royal University (not of the

college) charged Madden and Kennedy for indiscipline, but they confused Cruise O'Brien with Tom Kettle and Eugene Sheehy with another student, Sarsfield Kerrigan. Hence, O'Brien and Sheehy got off
scot-free. The other defendants denied that the authorities of the Royal
University had any right to impose discipline, being, in Tom Kettle's
brief, "not a true university in the right sense of the word." Wisely, the
senate of the Royal let the matter drop. Lord Meath, dissatisfied with
this, resigned as chancellor. Not a bad result for an undergraduate
prank, and all in a higher cause as well.[65]

• • •

From whence arose this brilliant hellion, Francis Cruise O'Brien?
Certainly not from roots as grand as those of the Sheehys. The O'Briens
hailed from Ennistymon, County Clare. Like so many Irish families,
they had their traditions of how great they once were and how they had
come down in the world. These were probably better founded than
most. The family had held lands at Ennistymon and owned what is now
the Falls Hotel. Francis Cruise O'Brien was later to tell Conor with intense pride that the O'Briens of Ennistymon had clung to their Catholic
faith during the penal era of the eighteenth century, when it would have
been greatly to their advantage to renounce it.[66] (He also used to tell
his young son that Conor would be "the last of the Ennistymon
O'Briens," a title that pleased the lad until he began to wonder why he
had to be the last. Later, when he reflected that the top O'Briens were
among the earliest of the Irish nobility to jump ship and embrace loyalty
and Protestantism, he determined not to be the last of the true cantan-
kerous lot.) Compared to the Sheehy family, however, the Cruise
O'Brien family memory was thin, and because Francis Cruise O'Brien
died while Conor was still young, most of that collective memory was
lost.[67]

There are some noteworthy threads, but they are not as rich as the
Sheehy tapestry. A Miss Cruise of some wealth had married a nineteenth-century O'Brien, and her family name was carefully preserved. She claimed descent from one of the Irish "Wild Geese" who in
the seventeenth and eighteenth centuries served in various continental
armies. This individual, Thomas Lally, Baron Tollendal (1702–1766),
was executed for losing India, a distinction of sorts.[68]

John Cruise O'Brien, Francis's father and Conor's grandfather,
made the break from County Clare. He trained in Dublin and became
the clerk of a large law firm there. That is a perfectly reasonable profession and was potentially quite lucrative; solicitors' and barristers'
clerks often made more money than did many of their superiors.

However, Francis's sister—Conor's Aunt Cathleen—a terrible snob, insisted on the false story that John Cruise O'Brien had been a solicitor, and it was not until years after his own father's death that Conor found out his grandfather's real status.[69]

Thus, in contrast to the Sheehys, Francis Cruise O'Brien did not have a background or a family mythology that would give him a sense of *amour propre* or any particular advantage in life. That "Crusoe" prospered in his own peculiar way was made all the more noteworthy because of his premature birth (18 November 1885), his small size, and apparent frailness. He was tutored at home, too weak to go to elementary school with other children. For this task, the family employed a come-down-in-the-world Englishman, an educated alcoholic. Young Francis received an excellent, if slightly eccentric, elementary education, including the basics of Latin, Greek, and some Sanskrit. From the alcoholic Englishman he also acquired a preposterous accent which to his critics (such as Bessie and David Sheehy were to become) sounded affected and totally West British. Actually, it was real, just different. (The influence of this speech pattern was considerable. His son Conor Cruise O'Brien has himself been accused by opponents of affecting a toney, slightly off-key British accent of indeterminate origin; in fact, it is the accent passed on to him by his own father, who had received it from his semisodden tutor.)

During the 1890s, Francis's father turned increasingly to drink and the family began to run short of cash. They were not broke, for they still had some assets, but fees from attorneys dropped and takings for the publicans increased. So young Francis, now ready for secondary school, was sent off to the Christian Brothers School in Synge Street, the cheapest decent education available. The school's staff and student body had a deservedly tough reputation. A lad as frail as Francis, and with a strange accent, should not have had much chance of schoolyard survival. Yet, in fact, he got along famously and remembered his days at Synge Street with great affection. He survived by developing the mixture of joketelling, mimicry, and acid that characterized him for the rest of his life. Also, he had plenty of guts.[70] Sometime near the end of his secondary school career, Francis transferred to the North Richmond Street Christian Brothers School, a tonier place. (Tom Kettle and James and Stanislaus Joyce had been pupils there at one time, although they did not overlap with Cruise O'Brien.) It was from Richmond Street that Francis, after doing brilliantly in his Intermediate examination (the equivalent of the modern school leaving certificate), matriculated at the St. Stephen's Green college in the autumn of 1903.[71] Since both parents had died before he reached university age, young Francis was something of an unbridled mustang, free to run about at will.

At the Christian Brothers, Francis had received the standard late-Victorian education—lots of dead languages being the chief feature—with one major difference. The Christian Brothers were unique in the late nineteenth century in that they taught Irish history as a major subject. They used their own textbook and, implicitly, they taught Irish patriotism of a vigorous but nonviolent variety.[72] They also taught the Irish language, but the key to their formation of patriotic attitudes was in the history curriculum. And here, history itself formed one of its curious little circles. Francis Cruise O'Brien was taught history from a book entitled *The Catechism of Irish History* written in 1876 by Brother J.M. O'Brien, who had been born in 1848 and raised and educated in Ennistymon, County Clare. The author was a contemporary and probably a distant relative of Francis's own father. The *Catechism*'s central purpose was clearly stated: to help the teacher have his class "up" on Irish history. In aid of that goal, it invoked the glories of ancient Irish civilization, the horrors of the Viking and English invasions, and, most important, it emphasized what the Irish Catholics had suffered for their faith.[73] In that sense, the teaching was more Irish Catholic than Irish nationalist.

Because he was a leading figure at the St. Stephen's Green college —prominent in the L. & H. (eventually auditor), on the staff of *St. Stephen's* (eventually editor), a strong nationalist, and well-received raconteur and mimic—Francis was invited to Second Sundays at 2 Belvedere Place. There he fit in well with everyone except his host and hostess. They tolerated him, but Bessie could see that he was not good breeding stock (he might even be tubercular, mightn't he?) and David Sheehy, as a Member of Parliament, expected respect, not backchat from some gurrier from Synge Street. For the moment, however, they put up with him.

The social chemistry of 2 Belvedere Place was changing. Hanna Sheehy and Frank Skeffington were becoming closer and closer allies. Hanna took her degree with honors in 1902, Frank in the same year with honors and with the Chancellor's Gold Medal for English Prose. Frank was appointed the first lay registrar of the university college in the spring of 1903, a post that promised a stable income for life. He and Hanna were married in June 1903. They still frequented 2 Belvedere Place, but they ran their own Wednesday evening salon and in some ways became an antipole, a loyal opposition to the older, regnal couple. Both Hanna and Frank were serious feminists and as a sign of this they hyphenated their surname: Sheehy-Skeffington. Frank was so serious about this feminism that he quit his post as registrar rather than modulate for the Jesuit fathers his view that women should have full privileges in the university. Thereafter, the two of them scrimped along,

Hanna teaching part-time, Frank writing for various papers. Frank tried his hand at a novel (which was serialized, but not published in book form until after his death) and wrote a successful biography of the Irish patriot Michael Davitt. Mostly, Frank and Hanna were full-time agitators for socialism, feminism, pacifism and antismoking, food, and diet crusades.[74]

If Frank and Hanna remained as a single, somewhat erratic, constellation in the Belvedere Place solar system, James Joyce burst from orbit altogether. In the autumn of 1902, he took the examination for the honors degree in English, French, and Italian, but failed to obtain the required grade; he was awarded a pass degree as a consolation.[75] After attempting medical school for a brief time, he spent the winter in London and Paris. He filled the next year with odd bits of employment. He asked Frank Sheehy-Skeffington's help in finding a lectureship, but nothing suitable turned up. What turned up instead, in June 1904, was the sight on Nassau Street of a tall, auburn-haired woman, Nora Barnacle, with whom he quickly fell in love.[76] Thereafter, the Sheehy circle lost its attraction for him.

Meanwhile, Margaret Sheehy, the amateur actress and dramatist, the nonintellectual of the Sheehy women, was seriously looking for a husband. She settled on money, in the form of John F. Culhane, a solicitor, whose family was in trade. They were feather merchants and very successful ones. Hyper-Catholic, they displayed their religious enthusiasm and their wealth simultaneously, with a private chapel, but Bessie Sheehy would have preferred a better match for Margaret. When Margaret and Frank Culhane married in 1907, they moved away from Bessie's dominating ambition. (Frank Culhane was not physically robust and after a long illness he died early in 1916, leaving Margaret with four children.)[77]

As if in compensation, Tom Kettle, always the most promising, became the major player, the center of Bessie's hopes for a future dynasty. Kettle took his degree with second-class honors in 1902 and then studied for the bar. He was the embodiment of a successful attorney long before he actually became one. Tall, clean-shaven, handsome, he was especially particular about his clothes. The story in his circle was that he once instructed a tailor to make him a suit that would not look new and that, when it was old, would not look old.[78] In September 1905, he launched a young-ideas weekly, *The Nationist*. A tabloid of one folio (sixteen pages), it sold for a penny. Kettle's assistant editor was Frank Sheehy-Skeffington. The editorial policy was for home rule of a keen sort. Tom and Frank were helped out by the old gang, and some new additions—Eugene and Richard Sheehy, Francis Cruise O'Brien,

Padraic Colum, Oliver Gogarty, and Bulmer Hobson. The effort lasted little more than six months (the last issue was in March 1906), but, among other things, it called attention to Tom Kettle as a figure of potential political importance outside the undergraduate confines of St. Stephen's Green.[79]

This was one of the reasons that, when the death of a sitting MP forced a by-election in East Tyrone in July 1906, Tom Kettle—still only twenty-six years old—was selected as the nationalist candidate. (Among the other reasons that he was chosen was that his father had been a leading land agitator and nationalist MP and that, as will be mentioned in a moment, Kettle was involved with his college friends in a ginger group of young nationalists who operated around the edges of the nationalist party.) The constituency for which he was chosen was one of those nasty areas—now known as bandit country—where the population was split closely between the nationalists and the unionists, which is to say between Catholics and Protestants. As he started his campaign of Kettle supporters, a grizzled veteran told him, "You've a terrible road ahead of you."

"Is it full of hills?" Kettle asked innocently.

"No, it's full of Protestants."[80]

Since there were slightly more Protestants than Catholics in the constituency, he needed to pick up a few cross-over votes to win. He campaigned very well indeed and squeaked in by eighteen votes. This was joy for Bessie Sheehy, for Tom Kettle was courting Mary Sheehy. On 8 September 1909, they were married in the pro-cathedral, Dublin, the biggest send-off possible.[81]

Bessie Sheehy's joy should have been tempered slightly by the rumors that Tom was drinking a lot. He could be a convivial man, charming and witty in conversation. In 1918, Shane Leslie recalled what it was like "to spend a morning at St. Enda's School and discuss the ideals of Irish education with [Patrick] Pearse and [Thomas] MacDonagh, to catch a vivid minute with George Russell in Plunkett House, in the afternoon to see Yeats and Lady Gregory moving down the quays to rehearsal at the Abbey Theatre, and in the evening to hear a Synge play and pass a late hour with Kettle. An ambrosian night and day."[82]

The trouble was, too many late hours were passed by Kettle, and early ones too. His closest friends came to see that beneath the handsome facade there was a sad and self-destructive personality. His confidant and admirer, the essayist Robert Lynd, called him "the Hamlet of Modern Ireland" and pointed to the strain of melancholy that ran through his life: pessimism, self-doubt and, one infers, self-loathing.[83]

These problems had become clear (though not well known) while Tom Kettle was still an undergraduate. Although eligible to sit his degree examination at the end of 1900, he did not do so. He had a nervous breakdown and was sent to Europe for a year. Kettle's biographer, J.B. Lyons, shrewdly points to Kettle's rigid and highly demanding upbringing. His father was virtually impossible to please and Tom was always made to feel guilty, no matter how well he did at anything. By 1905, he already was drinking heavily.[84] He was indeed good company when drinking, but, increasingly, he appeared at public events with drink taken. "Poor drunken Kettle" began to be his sobriquet.

Meanwhile Bessie Sheehy's *bête noire*, Francis Cruise O'Brien, was becoming the best-known, most popular, and most notorious student at the university college. In the autumn of 1905 he was elected to the executive of the L. & H.; in February 1906 he became editor of *St. Stephen's*, and in May 1906, he was elected auditor for the 1906–7 session of the L. & H.[85]

"Crusoe" used his positions to conduct a war against the Rev. William Delany, S.J., president of the college. Delany was not a harsh man, but he was of a generation of Irish clerics who were totally unaccustomed to anything approaching disrespect. In 1906, he was in his seventieth year, and he was tired. Cheeky undergraduates bated him, forever addressing him as "Doctor Delany," just to hear the inevitable snap, "Don't call me Doctor, sir. I'm not an apothecary."[86] Setting him off was no problem for Cruise O'Brien, and he did so with relish. The two issues of *St. Stephen's* that were published in 1906 under O'Brien's editorship were heavily "Bolshie," a mixture of cruel satire and of frontal attacks on both the Royal University and on the authorities of the Catholic college. In response, Father Delany brought his boot down hard: he suppressed the student paper entirely.[87]

When the time came for the degree-conferring ceremony in 1906, everyone knew that there would again be some kind of a demonstration and that the L. & H., as the chief voice of student opinion, would be in the forefront. Once again, 26 October 1906, all students except degree candidates were carefully excluded. Unable to gain admission at the Earlsfort Terrace premises of the Royal University, the band of protesting students assembled near 86 St. Stephen's Green, with the intention of holding their protest on the steps of the college. Father Delany asked them to move away, but they ignored him. He responded by calling the Dublin Metropolitan Police who, at his instruction, prevented the demonstrators from reaching the college steps.

This enraged the leaders, who were also the executive committee of the L. & H., and in response, they passed a resolution of their society censuring the college president for exposing the students to insulting treatment at the hands of the police. That was a flung gauntlet indeed: students do not censure the Jesuit head of a university college, certainly not in Dublin in 1906. Peacemakers who tried to work out a compromise between Father Delany and Cruise O'Brien came close: the executive committee of the L. & H. rescinded its censure of the president, but, in a companion resolution, asserted that the society indeed had the power to invoke such a censure if it wished to do so. In response, Father Delany convened a meeting of the college discipline committee on 13 November. Cruise O'Brien was present but not allowed to speak. He was expelled from the L. & H. and rusticated from the college for twelve months.[88]

Thus began a tiny Avignon papacy. The majority of the L. & H. supported Francis Cruise O'Brien on a matter of principle, that the college's governing authorities did not have the right to expel any student from a society or to deprive an elected officer of a college society of his position. A minority, following the lead of Maurice Healy, preferred to go along with the college authorities. Cruise O'Brien's phalanx, now excluded from holding meetings on college premises, removed the society's records and held meetings at various ad hoc locations around Dublin, the University Club, the Dolphin Hotel, the Mansion House. The peripatetic L. & H. had quite a successful year. Guest speakers included Arthur Griffith, Lindsay G. Crawford, and Padraic Colum. It took two years before the schism was healed.[89]

The Sheehy family's reaction to this undergraduate turmoil varied. David Sheehy, MP, was in complete agreement with the students that "God Save the King" should not be played at degree-conferring ceremonies. In fact, on that day in late October 1906 when Father Delany turned the police on the undergraduates, he and Frank Sheehy-Skeffington were haranguing the crowd from a horse car opposite the university college building. His daughter Hanna was proudly visible in the vehicle, lending her support.[90] When the split occurred in the L. & H., both Eugene and Dick Sheehy followed Cruise O'Brien.[91] But David and Bessie Sheehy parted company with Cruise O'Brien over his disrespect for religious authority. His description of Father Delany as a "decaying old Whig" went the rounds of the college and that was only one of the epithets that flew off his raspish tongue. From Bessie's point of view, especially, this was not the sort of lad who should be paying attention to her youngest daughter, Kathleen.

The year 1908 was the final full year for the old Royal University and just as well. As an examining body, it had preserved standards effectively, but in its pretension and in its imperial customs, it had become an embarrassment. The Earlsfort Terrace building was much too grand, and when not being used for examinations, it was hired out. Oliver Gogarty and Tom Kettle once arrived at its doors. "What institution is this?" Gogarty demanded of the porter.

"You know full well it's the Royal University."

"The last time I was here," Gogarty observed, "it was a flower show."[92]

This all changed with the passage in 1908 of the Irish University Act which created a state-funded National University of Ireland with constituent colleges at Cork, Galway, and Dublin. It was to be a real university, not just an examining body. In theory, University College, Dublin (UCD), was to be secular (in fact, clerical influence continued to be very strong for the next seventy years). It has been suggested that "the *affaire* Cruise O'Brien probably played some part in determining the decision to make the new state-endowed university, of which UCD became a constituent college, a secular rather than a Catholic, and hence clerically-controlled one," but this is fanciful.[93] The pattern, in fact, was one that had been evolving through a series of governmental commissions that stretched back over two decades.[94] The real effects of "the *affaire* Cruise O'Brien" were that a very good student newspaper was killed and that Francis Cruise O'Brien took an extra year to graduate, so that he was one of the last to complete his degree in the institution he had so thoroughly entertained and sometimes tormented.

• • •

That Francis Cruise O'Brien was an Irish nationalist is manifest, but exactly of what sort was very much in flux. He was not attracted to the violent sect of Irish nationalism, so in a general sense he was within the home rule tradition. He was young, however, and still working out his ideas. Fighting against the singing of "God Save the King" was a piece of nationalist protest, certainly, but not a political philosophy. Cruise O'Brien was not particularly keen on the Irish language movement, although because Kathleen Sheehy was immersed in it he had to show a modest interest. In fact, European languages and literature interested him a great deal more.

His wide-visioned, essentially European cultural perspective makes curious two activities during his university years. The first of these was his association with D.P. Moran, who had founded in 1900 a weekly called the *Leader*. In 1905, Moran began to recruit members of the L. & H. to write for him.[95] Cruise O'Brien took this opportunity a bit later (I suspect in 1906 when Tom Kettle's *Nationist* folded and *St. Stephen's* was suppressed). He made a few shillings by writing unsigned articles but what is surprising is the association with Moran, whose vision was exactly the opposite of broad and tolerant. From 1900 to his death thirty-six years later, Moran spewed forth a stream of the most narrow-minded and hate-filled Irish nationalism. He attacked cosmopolitanism of any sort, arguing that the Irish character had to be kept distinctive. He had no time for the Irish literary renaissance, viewing it, in the words of Brian Inglis, as a "clever piece of stock-jobbing on the English market."[96] Moran had even less time for the Irish parliamentary party members (of whom David Sheehy and Tom Kettle were prominent examples). Cruise O'Brien worked for Moran off and on for several years. This doubtlessly was useful to Cruise O'Brien, who had decided to become a journalist if he could, for Moran was a good editor, and a young man had to learn the trade somewhere.[97]

Francis Cruise O'Brien may have had more than merely careerist reasons for freelancing for Moran, however. He well may have been in sympathy with some of Moran's ideas, particularly his insistence on ridiculing the Irish literary revival. This possibility is indicated by Cruise O'Brien's second rather surprising activity: in 1907 he joined the opposition to J.M. Synge's *The Playboy of the Western World*. The tale of this play's troubles are well known—Yeats, as chairman of the Abbey Theatre, called in the police to defend the actors and the playwright against demonstrators. There is no question that it is a great drama. But *The Playboy* was, moreover, one of the most prescient pieces of social observation about peasant Ireland that had been performed in public, and it hit some very raw nerves. The first of these was the Irish rural family system as it had developed after the Great Famine. The previous general pattern of subdividing farms among children stopped and, instead, a holding usually went to only one son—but not necessarily the oldest, or the youngest, or any one in particular. Marriage was not possible until a parent passed on the farm to his chosen heir. This situation gave Irish parents—and especially Irish fathers—immense and arbitrary power over their offspring. It was not at all unusual for a man to be called a "boy" until he was forty-five or fifty, because he only became a man in rural society when his father finally passed the holding on to him. Nor was it unusual for a father to play one son off against another. Custom placed no limit on paternal arbitrariness. Thus, when Synge's protagonist in *The Playboy* bursts into a shebeen on the coast of Mayo and explains that he is hiding from the Peelers because he has killed his father and his revelation makes him an immediate hero, Synge is basing his entire drama on an observation few wanted to hear: that parricide lay very close to the secret heart of the Irish peasant.

The second controversy related to sexuality. Catholic Ireland of Synge's time was well on its way to being the most sexually repressed and the least knowledgeable about sexuality of any Western culture that has yet been documented. (The zenith of this movement was probably reached in the 1930s, but the process was well in train by Synge's day.) There is mention in his play of cousins marrying (which was forbidden by Catholic canon law) and, worse, the decent god-fearing Irish peasantry are heard in *The Playboy* to use the indecent word "shift" to describe a woman's undergarment, usually known as a chemise. Such things were not permissible; the play was obscene. And, to add to his having drilled so precisely into two of Catholic and nationalist Ireland's most sensitive nerves, Synge had the beastliness to write a play that was funny. *The Playboy* is a good comedy.

A third problem, and probably the most important, was that Synge, a Trinity College, Dublin, man and a Protestant, had portrayed most accurately in *Playboy* (and *In the Shadow of the Glen* and in his essays) what the stiff-collar Dublin nationalists and Gaels knew was true but could never admit: that to actual Irish farmers and Gaelic speakers they and their ideas were totally irrelevant and had nothing to do with Irish life as it was lived.

Shortly after the performance for which Yeats called out the police, a public meeting was held at the theater. Yeats, amid much heckling, tried to defend himself. Several speakers said that the play should be banned. Included in this group were Richard Sheehy and Francis Cruise O'Brien.[98] In a sense, the situation recalled the events of 1899, when the Sheehy squad had fought against the right of Yeats's *Countess Cathleen* to be performed on a combination of nationalist and Catholic grounds. This time, Tom Kettle was engaged elsewhere and was not in the forefront, although his biographer implies that he would have approved of the opposition to Synge's play.[99] And, unlike in 1899, Frank Sheehy-Skeffington, while condemning the play as bad, protested against the demonstrators' methods.[100]

That there was a potentially ruthless edge to Francis Cruise O'Brien's nationalism became clear in his work for the Young Ireland Branch of the United Irish League (called the "Yibs" in the contemporary vernacular). This group was mooted in late 1904 and officially inaugurated a year later. Basically, it was the Literary and Historical gang in search of real political influence. The group's goal was to acquire leverage on the reunited Irish parliamentary party. As reunited in 1900 under John Redmond, the Irish party had solved successfully, if uneasily, the split between Parnellites and anti-Parnellites; however, a residue of tensions remained between an agrarian radical wing and the more traditional approach, characterized by the party's conciliatory stance toward unionist opposition and delays on matters of social reform. The agrarian wing, which had been led by William O'Brien and his United

Irish League, was subsumed, from 1900 onward, by the traditionalists, who used the United Irish League as their national political front.[101]

For an understanding of the later hatred between Francis Cruise O'Brien and the Sheehys, it is essential to realize three facts. David Sheehy had long been active in agrarian reform campaigns and had an interest in their continuance; he was very loyal to John Dillon, the anti-Parnellite leader who stepped down in 1900 to permit the reuniting of the Irish parliamentary party behind John Redmond; and in the years in question, 1904–9, David Sheehy was the organizing secretary of the United Irish League.[102]

The moving force behind the creation of the Young Ireland Branch of the United Irish League was Tom Kettle and it was he who gave the presidential address at the inaugural meeting, held in the Oak Room of the Mansion House, 14 December 1905.[103] The actual membership was made up almost entirely of L. & H. members, past and present, and when delegates were sent to the national conventions of the United Irish League, only L. & H. stalwarts were sent. The Yibs were an impressive group, many of whom became important names in the national history: James Creed Meredith and Louis Walsh (later justices), Rory O'Connor (antitreaty leader executed in 1922), Edward Kelly (later a nationalist MP), Hector Hughes (who became a Labour MP in Great Britain)—and on and on. These were in addition to Tom Kettle, Richard and Eugene Sheehy, Frank Sheehy-Skeffington (the latter combining Yib membership with being a socialist and being one of the founders of the Independent Labour party of Ireland in 1908), and Francis Cruise O'Brien. Patrick Pearse attended several of the meetings but did not formally join. Interestingly, women were permitted membership. This was an important departure from local custom (the operative paradigm was the L. & H., to whose membership Father Delany forbade the admission of women). Thus, Hanna Sheehy-Skeffington, Mary Sheehy (later Mary Kettle), and Kathleen Sheehy all were full members and at various times served on the executive committee.[104]

The older generation of Irish politicians welcomed the Yibs as a voting branch of the United Irish League. They might have hesitated a bit, had they recalled that when the notion of the group first came up, sharp critic of the nationalist party, D.P. Moran, had heartily praised the idea.[105] For a time, the Yibs were the darling of the nationalist party, and they were given the keys to the United Irish League's spacious facilities in Sackville Street (now O'Connell Street).[106]

This privilege did not last long. The Yibs did not understand that the rules of adult politics were different from the games played at college; they were arrogant and cheeky to an unbearable degree. They advised the parliamentary party to stop wasting its time on social (meaning land) reform and to concentrate all of its effort on gaining home rule for Ireland; they ridiculed the party leaders, especially Redmond and Dillon; and they let it be known that they could generally run things a whole lot better than could the veterans. Not surprisingly, the United Irish League's officers demanded the return of the office keys. Thereafter, the Yibs, still fully affiliated with the United Irish League, but no longer favorite sons, met in ad hoc quarters before finally settling down in Dawson Street. A sympathetic landlord provided the Yibs and the L. & H. (the same membership, really) with rooms and a caretaker, without charge.[107]

Having been turfed out of college in November 1906, Francis Cruise O'Brien had plenty of time to devote to his two overlapping constituencies: the L. & H., of which he was auditor, and the Yibs. In the latter organization Cruise O'Brien became the effective power, since Tom Kettle was often away as an MP in Westminster, and in any case, Kettle was trying to sound more like a serious statesman than a difficult university student. Frank Sheehy-Skeffington was Cruise O'Brien's chief ally. At the annual inaugural meeting for the year, held in late November 1907, Tom Kettle was in the chair, but it was Cruise O'Brien, now vice-president of the Yibs, who gave the keynote address. Speaking first in Irish and then in English, he rehearsed the political history of the previous twenty-five years and then advised the Irish parliamentary party to return to the policy of Parnell. With the confidence of the young, he replied to a question of what he thought of William Ewart Gladstone by paraphrasing Parnell: "I think of Mr. Gladstone and the English people what I have always thought of them—they will do what we make them do!"[108] Some idea of the vituperation that must have been integral to Cruise O'Brien's speech is indicated by the content of Tom Kettle's summing up (as part of the usual vote-of-thanks to the speaker). Kettle noted that some of the audience might have resented the speech, as it was impatient and censorious, but he himself did not resent it. The Yibs, Kettle said, represented the most advanced ideas to be found in the nationalist movement (presumably he meant the most advanced nonviolent ideas). "I think Mr. Cruise O'Brien put himself on the side of the angels, or at least of the saints."[109]

Saints? Even Kettle cannot have believed that. To established members of the Irish parliamentary party, the Yibs increasingly were demons. At a meeting in May 1908, a motion proposed by Francis Cruise O'Brien and seconded by Frank Sheehy-Skeffington called upon the Irish parliamentary party to hasten the dissolution of Parliament and thereafter to make the government of Ireland impossible. Only with great personal effort was Kettle able to have the second part of that motion withdrawn.[110]

The Yibs were running out of credit with the nationalist party. Granted, they had gained a few points when in February 1908, they had sent out an electioneering phalanx to County Leitrim to help the United Irish League fight a by-election against Sinn Fein (launched by Arthur Griffith in 1906), an effort that was successful.[111] By November 1908, however, the Irish nationalist party—of whom David Sheehy was a major broker—were fed to the teeth with the youngsters, and their suppression was being discussed.[112]

In February 1909, a national convention of the United Irish League was summoned to the Mansion House, Dublin, to discuss an impending land bill. Cruise O'Brien was now president of the Young Ireland Branch, and Sheehy-Skeffington secretary. Tom Kettle, though still a member, was distancing himself. One suspects that this was not only for political reasons but because his marriage to Mary Sheehy was planned for September and the necessity of keeping in the good books of David and Bessie Sheehy loomed large.

Besides the land issue, a wide range of policy questions were to be raised at the February 1909 convention. One of these led to the first serious split between Sheehy-Skeffington and Kettle, which had implications for the future domestic life of Francis Cruise O'Brien. The Yibs, at the request of the Irish Women's Franchise League, sponsored a resolution calling for women's suffrage. The plan was for Frank to move the motion and then Tom Kettle would add his weight as an MP by seconding it. At the last moment, Kettle reneged on his promise to do this.[113] This betrayal long rankled with Sheehy-Skeffington and predisposed him to fight Kettle on other issues when they came up later.[114]

A more public drama centered on the resolution moved by Cruise O'Brien that called on the nationalist party to give its whole attention to home rule and to engage in strenuous opposition in every way to any British government that refused to grant home rule or tried to postpone the question. Implicitly, this was a motion of no-confidence in the leadership of the nationalist party. It brought strong reaction.[115] Cruise O'Brien, Frank Sheehy-Skeffington and W.E.G. Lloyd, Yibs who tried to speak for the motion, were hollered down. They were physically attacked, and afterward the event moved into legend as "the Baton Convention."[116] The motion, of course, was defeated.

• • •

If Francis Cruise O'Brien had been trying to find a way to get on the wrong side of David and Bessie Sheehy, he could not have been more successful. As Conor himself has noted, to David Sheehy "Cruise O'Brien was one of the most obnoxious of the new intellectuals in the party organization, critical of the party leadership—including David's venerated chief, John Dillon—and rich in, if little else, the power to say wounding things in a memorable manner."[117] Of course, whether Francis was a wit or a witling, a younker or a chevalier, depended very much on one's taste. His friends were staunch to the point of fanaticism; his enemies deep and often permanent. Francis Cruise O'Brien divided people.

Significantly, the woman he courted, Kathleen Sheehy, while definitely on his side, was not one of his more trustworthy supporters, and this characteristic held throughout their married life. In part, this was because Kathleen sometimes had better judgment than Francis, in part because of a certain plasticity in her makeup. Kathleen Sheehy, the youngest of the family, was two years younger than Francis. She was known as the most "biddable" of the Sheehy girls which, in the dialect of the time, meant that she was the one most willing to do what she was told by her parents. Not that she was a cipher: she was most biddable within the context of the Sheehy family, a group each of whose members could have given a course in Assertiveness Training long before the concept was invented. Kathleen had studied on her own in the Aran Islands and was enthusiastic enough about the Irish language revival to upbraid her parents for not being committed to the language; indeed, she said, their generation had betrayed it.[118]

Kathleen and Francis must have come to know each other quite well during 1904 and 1905, for Cruise O'Brien was frequently at 2 Belvedere Place with the two Sheehy sons. However, Kathleen was away in France for almost the entire academic year 1906–7 and this bears note, because it relates both to Kathleen's character and to the features that were being built into the polite education of the Dublin intellectual class. This trip abroad involved a French connection from which not only Kathleen, Conor's mother, but Conor himself eventually benefited. It began with the marriage of the legendary land agitator, William O'Brien, in 1889 to Sophie Raffalovitch, daughter of a Russian-Jewish banker living in Paris. Sophie turned Catholic when she married William O'Brien and moved to Ireland. There she determined to help the education of Irish girls, by making it possible for at least a few of them to study in France. She approached the Dominicans at Eccles Street, and their head, Mother Peter, was taken by the idea. As it turned out, Sophie and William O'Brien lived on Mountjoy Square, close to the Sheehy family. So it was natural that the first pupil sent to France, for the school year 1904–5, was Mary Sheehy. The experiment went well, and two years later Kathleen Sheehy and a French girl exchanged places for a year.[119]

During the 1907–8 academic year Kathleen was back in Dublin and she and Cruise O'Brien became close. In June 1908, Hanna Sheehy-Skeffington wrote to Frank, who was in Cork at the time, that Kathleen and Cruise O'Brien were studying French, but she wondered where they were studying, since it certainly was not in the Sheehys' house. "No one suspects anything yet," she told Frank, and added with a touch of disapproval, "and won't of course till it's too late."[120] When, in November 1908, the Irish Women's Franchise League was founded at a meeting in the Sheehy-Skeffington's house, Kathleen was quick to join. Among the men who joined as associates (full membership was limited to women) were Cruise O'Brien (along with Thomas MacDonagh and Frank Sheehy-Skeffington).[121] And, when in the autumn of 1910 Cruise O'Brien's time as president of the Yibs was over, Kathleen asserted her continued identification with his viewpoint by accepting the vice-presidency, an action that must have displeased her parents a great deal.[122]

Such assertions of agreement with Cruise O'Brien came at great personal cost to one as sensitive as Kathleen. As it became clear that an alliance between Francis Cruise O'Brien and Kathleen was in the making, the Sheehy family drew up battle lines. Of course, the elder Sheehys, David and Bessie, were opposed. Mary Sheehy, engaged to Tom Kettle, had taken a particular dislike to Cruise O'Brien, and therefore Tom joined the elder Sheehys as opponents of the marriage. Dick Sheehy was as violently against the marriage as was Mary. Eugene and Margaret also opposed it, but less savagely. (Why the two Sheehy boys turned against the former friend, Crusoe, is a mystery.) This left only Hanna and Frank Sheehy-Skeffington on the side of the young couple. They liked the Cruise O'Briens (Frank and Francis had been allies in many a hard battle), and, in principle, they believed in a woman's right to choose her own husband. This latter argument weighed heavily with Hanna, who had originally been skeptical of Cruise O'Brien.[123]

By early 1909, Kathleen and Francis began to meet secretly, and Frank Sheehy-Skeffington took on the role of courier and adviser. When his partisanship became evident in February, Kathleen was forbidden by Bessie Sheehy to visit the Sheehy-Skeffingtons' house, even though Kathleen was giving Frank Irish lessons at the time. For a month or so, Kathleen continued his Irish lessons on the sly, but she lost courage and abandoned even this clandestine assertion of her individuality. Frank became quite upset over her refusal to endure even "a little temporary discomfort" in this fray.[124] Ten days later, after Kathleen told him tearfully that she was not strong enough to revolt openly, he wrote her a much kinder, more supportive letter. In it, he did not talk about love, or passion, or even Cruise O'Brien, but of the need for her to "attain by degrees the power of altering your own course in great things and in small, instead of drifting with surface currents."[125]

Kathleen could have gone either way. Yet, on 4 August 1909, James Joyce ran into Frank and Hanna on the street and wrote the latest gossip to his brother Stanislaus. "Kettle marries Mary Sheehy on 8 September. ... Kathleen marries Cruise O'Brien."[126] What had happened to turn things Cruise O'Brien's way?

Conor thinks that the following event was the breaking point, and the suggestion makes sense. Probably during the summer of 1909 (the date is indeterminate) at 2 Belvedere Place, Frank Sheehy-Skeffington lectured the Sheehys about the proper way to treat their youngest daughter. David Sheehy took exception and a heated argument ensued. Dick Sheehy was present. As big a man as Frank was small, Dick picked Frank up and carried him to the front door, threw him down the granite steps, and slammed the door. Frank got to his feet, brushed himself off, walked up the steps and hammered away on the big door knocker. "Force solves nothing, Dick," he said when the door was opened. He then proceeded into the house to continue the argument with David Sheehy, MP.[127] Conor believes that at that moment the senior Sheehys became unnerved, gave in, and permitted Kathleen to marry Francis Cruise O'Brien.

The facade of the years obscures the real nature of Kathleen and Francis Cruise O'Brien's attraction to each other. One doubts that it was predominantly sexual, at least on Kathleen's part. She had received the same Dominican convent education that Hanna had; and we know from Frank Sheehy-Skeffington's reports that this convent training had emphasized the shamefulness of the body. And, further, the nun who taught religious instruction at Eccles Street made it abundantly clear that the girls should feel loathing for the very idea of marriage.[128] Finally, we cannot know the hectoring, sniping, and ritual humiliation that the couple almost certainly continued to endure even after consent for their union was given; nor do we know whether or not Kathleen wavered, or if she remained steadfast. The couple was not married until 7 October 1911, which strongly implies that the Sheehys fought a rearguard action for two more years. It must have been a galling and unhappy time for both young people.[129]

What finally overcame this nastiness was Cruise O'Brien's being offered the editorship of the Wexford *Free Press*, his first full-time job. He married Kathleen, but he remembered the Sheehys' treatment of himself and his wife. "My father ... never forgave Mary, or any of the Sheehys who had opposed the marriage," recalls Conor. "He was civil to them for my mother's sake, but it was only for the Skeffingtons that he felt real liking and respect."[130]

CHAPTER 2

THE CRUISE O'BRIENS BEFORE CONOR

If Conor Cruise O'Brien had been born in, say, 1912, instead of 1917, he would have known his father better, but would have had a father less worth knowing. In the year or so after his marriage into the Sheehy flotilla, Francis Cruise O'Brien was a bitter and cruelly clever man; by the time Conor was born in 1917, he was much more generous, less mordant, much more constructive, and increasingly concerned not with straightforward political nationalism but with the well-being of other persons, considered broadly in social and economic context. Still witty, still clever with words, he became a genuinely nice person, well loved by a varied circle of friends who, later, after his death, were willing to help finance the education of his son, Conor. Kathleen, for her part, seems to have changed only slightly. She transferred much of her biddability from her parents to her husband, although on occasion she could put her foot down, hard. She still was a Sheehy and that meant she had quietly to put up with bastinadoes of advice and admonishment from them, and especially from her three older sisters, each of whom knew better than she how to go about everything she did.

The Cruise O'Briens started their married life in Wexford in 1911, where Francis was editor of the *Free Press*. Wexford promised sanctuary: distance from the Sheehys. Francis and Kathleen—her pet name for him was "Ted"—took with them to Wexford thirteen large steamer trunks full of clothes and household goods, everything needed to set up a permanent life outside the confines of the Sheehy kingdom. Running a provincial newspaper made Cruise O'Brien a significant figure in a medium-sized pond. He was good at his job, too good probably. But he did not yet understand the fundamental rule of second-line journalism, that the proprietor is the boss and that journalistic professionalism stops where the owner's check book begins.

Cruise O'Brien came unstuck when a freelancer submitted a daft, virtually demented article, about the Freemasons. The piece alleged that the Masons summoned up the devil whenever they met and that cloven hoof marks had been found on the altar in their local temple. This was not only a lunatic story, but in the context of Wexford society, where residual anti-Protestantism was very strong, it constituted a hate story. Cruise O'Brien spiked it. Having heard of the story, the proprietor came in and told O'Brien to use it. He refused and was fired. Thus, with their thirteen trunks, the couple, not long married, trailed back to Dublin, there to face the Sheehys and no job.[1]

From then on the couple was short of money. Neither Francis nor Kathleen ever had a job that paid well and, if not spendthrift, the two of them always lived beyond their means. Kathleen eventually was able to gain part-time employment as a teacher of Irish at Rathmines Technical School, where Hanna Sheehy-Skeffington also taught. (Married women could not teach full-time under the regulations that prevailed at the time.) Francis scrambled for intellectual odd-jobs. He still did the occasional piece for Moran's *Leader*, but that was only pocket money.

His great good fortune and ultimately that of his son Conor—for it changed his father's personality—was that Cruise O'Brien, through his search for a living, came under the influence of two of the most constructive personalities in early twentieth-century Ireland; this at a time when forceful nastiness flourished, hard men prospered, and constructive outlooks were very scarce on the ground.

The first of these individuals was Horace Curzon Plunkett (knighted, 1903). Plunkett at first glance seemed to be everything that Irish Catholics and nationalists abhorred: an Anglican, a unionist, and perched at the top of the land-owning class with a large establishment in the east of Counties Dublin, Louth, and Meath: the old Pale. Educated at Eton and University College, Oxford (where he was captain of the university chess team), he not only eventually became an agnostic and a constitutional nationalist, but also the apostle of a movement that aimed, in its own pacific way, to end landlordism in Ireland.

Plunkett had spent almost ten years ranching in Wyoming, where he had been sent for his health, and there had been taken with the Grange movement, a form of agrarian cooperationism. But even before that he had possessed an interest in the concept: in 1878, just out of Oxford, he had organized a co-op on his family estate. Back home from America, he investigated various cooperative societies in the British Isles and in 1889 he launched his own cooperative campaign in Ireland, at the house of Thomas Spring-Rice, Lord Monteagle. His Lordship assembled some of his neighbors and the parish priest and from that beginning came the Irish Agricultural Organisation Society (IAOS) and several related efforts.

Plunkett became a lifelong evangelist of a mode of revolution that was quiet, essentially gentle, and which not only changed matters of economics, but revolutionized the view that Irish rural men and women held of themselves and of what they could accomplish. Cooperate— club together to buy farm necessities and escape the grasp of the local gombeen man! Cooperate—join together and form your own creamery or cheese factory and defeat the landlord's agent! Cooperate and take control of your own destiny![2]

By the time that Francis Cruise O'Brien sought employment with him, Sir Horace had become head of what was a small philanthropic conglomerate. By 1908, there were 881 cooperatives in Ireland, with an annual turnover of £3.3 million. In that year the benefactors of the Irish Agricultural Organisation Society presented to Plunkett as a headquarters building one of Dublin's best Georgian houses, 84 Merrion Square. There, in the president's office were hung portraits by Dermod O'Brien of the society's holy trinity—Plunkett, founding secretary R.A. Anderson, and Lord Monteagle, founding member and keen enthusiast of cooperationism—and there Plunkett ran his benevolent empire. It was a fourfold world: the IAOS was the base; second, housed upstairs were the offices of the *Irish Homestead*, newspaper of the movement; third, Plunkett was the Ireland trustee for the Carnegie Library Trust; and, fourth, there was the Co-operative Reference Library, a considerable collection funded by the Carnegie Foundation and also housed at 84 Merrion Square.[3]

Sir Horace took to Francis Cruise O'Brien and gave him a variety of posts. One should not think about these positions the way one thinks about modern jobs—with precise job descriptions, delimitations of authority, reporting functions, and all that sort of thing. Cruise O'Brien was working for Horace Plunkett in the same way that an agent worked for a nineteenth-century landlord: he did what needed doing. For a time, Cruise O'Brien was described as a secretary to Plunkett; later he was shifted to the docket of the Carnegie Foundation and he did a report on the rural library service in Ireland that was said to be the basis for the way the Carnegie system eventually came to operate. And then he was placed in charge of the Co-Operative Reference Library, which explains why, when Conor was born in 1917, his father's occupation on the birth certificate read "librarian."[4]

Sir Horace was a pleasure to work for most of the time: he was known for his sense of humor and quiet wit. If every now and then his manner, as well as his manor, reminded one that he was of the old quality, his heart certainly was in the right place. He was a good source of information on the luminaries of the literary renaissance, as they were usually willing to listen to his cooperative theories in return for a good table and an opportunity to drink his port.[5]

As a result of Cruise O'Brien's post with Sir Horace and his freelance work, increasingly with the *Freeman's Journal*, and the additional income from Kathleen's part-time teaching, the couple was able to rent a presentable Dublin address: 44 Leinster Road, Rathmines. It was a terrace house on a quiet road, halfway between two shopping streets, Rathmines Road and Harold's Cross Road. Constance Markievicz lived three or four doors away and Lord Longford's town house was just across the road. The site was upmarket for a couple with such a small and unstable income, but considering the Sheehy factor, it was the least they could take and still keep up required appearances. Besides, they planned to have a family.

Now, the second very constructive person with whom Francis Cruise O'Brien spent time in these years was George Russell—the "AE" of the Irish literary renaissance. Russell was another one of Plunkett's retainers. He edited the cooperative movement's paper, the *Irish Homestead*, and worked in the upper floor of 84 Merrion Square where, with his own murals, he turned the walls into rivals of a Medici villa. He and Cruise O'Brien were informal friends and office collaborators, engaged, when meeting each other on the stairs, in the exchange of jokes or gossip, passing on to each other the latest pamphlet or short story and, in off hours, discussing politics (discussion, always, because with AE one never really argued; he was too gentle). AE's place in the history of the Irish renaissance and in Irish political history is impossible to document fully. He was that rare sort of person who, though big in his own time, leaves small footprints in time's sands. Everyone knew him; he is the one figure of the Irish renaissance about whom virtually everyone had good things to say. And, in fact, he had almost nothing to say but good things about his contemporaries (except, perhaps, George Moore). He was a great developer of young literary talent (stories that later appear in Joyce's *Dubliners* saw their first public light in his *Irish Homestead*). He painted, wrote poetry, edited; he swam around in Theosophy, and after leaving that group, he set up a club of spiritualists and devotees of secret (but not black) knowledge. Amazingly, when George Russell walked into the real world, he tilted not at windmills, but at real life problems, such as organizing land banks.

Russell picked up the gospel of cooperation from Horace Plunkett and became in 1897 an organizer for the Irish Agricultural Organisation Society. His view of cooperation was semimystical. Whereas Plunkett saw cooperation both as an economic lever and as a way to bind Catholics and Protestants together in a common cause, AE preached co-operation as someone who saw it as the first step toward the brother-hood of mankind. With his Ulster accent and his slight Ascendancy tone (he had begun life Church of Ireland, before migrating toward mysticism), he somehow convinced the small tenant farmers of Ballina and Belmullet and of a hundred unnamed crossroads that working to-gether was not a better way, but the only way. And, then, in 1905, he became editor of the *Irish Homestead*, a paper whose title belies its wide range and high quality.[6]

The development of Francis Cruise O'Brien under the twin influ-ence of Plunkett and Russell is clear in his writing. He became kinder and more generous, undramatic terms that refer to major virtues. Take two examples, pamphlets that he co-authored in 1914 and 1917 with Lionel Smith-Gordon, a cooperative enthusiast and novelist.[7] The first, *Ireland's Food in War-Time*, was a very prescient set of predictions: namely, that as the Great War progressed, food prices would rise. The best method of keeping prices down, Cruise O'Brien and Smith-Gordon argued, was by means of a consumers' league.[8] Of course this was the company line—the pamphlet was published by the Cooperative Reference Library—but there was a good deal of passion evident in the authors' explication of their strategy.

This passion, which was founded on a concern for the problems of the Irish urban working class, came out even more clearly in another Cruise O'Brien and Smith-Gordon product in 1917. Their three-penny, thirty-one page pamphlet was titled *Starvation in Dublin*. "Let us look at the facts," it said. "There is in Dublin at the present moment a vast number of people with insufficient food to nourish themselves and their families. This is due partially to unemployment, partly to low wages. ... And partially to their having large families."[9] (One hardly need note that this latter observation would not have gone down well with the church.) The pamphlet was laced with tables and solid data. It argued for a food controller and it praised the work of the Dublin Food Supply Society, an urban cooperative. It was earnest and deeply com-mitted, the writing of persons who had seen urban poverty and had paid attention.

The salvation that Cruise O'Brien came to believe in was entirely secular. Well before his marriage, he had become an agnostic and this was just one more item that had turned the Sheehys against him. (And it may have provided yet another reason why Hanna and Frank Sheehy-Skeffington were on his side; they had both given up the church). In 1910, Cruise O'Brien and W.E.G. Lloyd had edited a version of W.E.H. Lecky's *History of the Rise and Influence of the Spirit of Rationalism in Europe*.[10] Guy Lloyd was a former member of the L. & H. and had stood by Cruise O'Brien at the Baton Convention of 1909. He was a Protestant, unusual for someone who had attended the Jesuit college on St. Stephen's Green. In his Protestant background, however, he was not unusual among Cruise O'Brien's friends. Increasingly, as Francis grew away from his undergraduate attitudes, he found that he worked well with Protestants—Lloyd, AE, Sir Horace—and if in each case they were "lapsed Protestants," they inevitably had a great deal in common with him as a lapsed Catholic, not least a refusal to accept sectarian definitions of Irish nationalism.

In 1911, Cruise O'Brien and Lloyd edited a more cutting work of Lecky's, his *Clerical Influences*. To this the two editors added their own subtitle: *An Essay on Irish Sectarianism and English Government*. Putting out this edition was a useful service, for the first edition of Lecky's essay had been published in 1861 as part of his *Leaders of Public Opinion*, which sold only thirty-four copies. The essay had been left out of the second edition of *Leaders* and also from the 1903 edition. This nearly forgotten essay by Ireland's greatest historian possesses the elegance and the Ciceronian sentences for which he was known, but it also had a sharp edge. For example: "It is a lamentable but, we fear, an undoubted fact that if the whole people of Ireland were converted to Mohammedanism nine-tenths of the present obstacles to the prosperity of the country would be removed."[11]

Francis Cruise O'Brien's and Guy Lloyd's intention in republishing Lecky's work was to help overcome the attitude of those "who find in the existence, or the fear of sectarianism in Ireland, their strongest argument against the establishment of a national government in Ireland."[12] Their own arguments were rather less realistic than were Lecky's, for they traced the recent history of the "undoubted decay of sectarianism" in Ireland.[13] This, in 1911! Although the two editors admitted that some sectarianism still existed, they argued that "the establishment of National Self-Government in Ireland is the surest means of destroying sectarian ill-feeling can hardly be doubted by anyone who weighs impartially the arguments put forward in the Essay."[14] "A national government, by creating an Irish public opinion irrespective of religious differences, and by bringing together, in the administration of the country, people who now belong to the unionist minority, most of which is Protestant, and people who belong to the nationalist majority, most of which is Catholic, will obliterate the line upon which politics and religion coincide in Ireland."[15] Except for George Bernard Shaw's writings (97 percent wrong, 100 percent self-assured), it is hard to conceive of a less realistic, more inaccurate, set of predictions about Ireland's future or of a less prescient view of how the Ulster unionists would act should Ireland become self-governing. This fantasy, however, at least is a benevolent one, quite the opposite of the self-dramatizing desire for immolation so many of the same generation later came to espouse.

In reflecting on his own life, Conor frequently has stated that he is himself a child of the Enlightenment, because his own father was a person of the Enlightenment.[16] With Francis Cruise O'Brien, however, the key question is which Enlightenment? The one that was caustic, negative and destroyed without replacing, or the benign Enlightenment, the one predicated upon inherent human rights, combined with a devotion to rational thought? In his days as an unholy terror at University College, and as the head hellion of the Yibs, Cruise O'Brien was of the first tradition. As he grew older (not much older, just enough), he turned to the second form of the Enlightenment. His work with Plunkett and his associates involved the use of rational means and the harnessing of human potential to ease the pain of the urban and rural poor, and was very much in the tradition of the gentler Enlightenment.

And Francis Cruise O'Brien was an Enlightenment person in that the Enlightenment was the first time we know of in modern human history that anyone stepped back from religion and looked at it with a candid eye. Cruise O'Brien, however naive he might be about some things, believed that if there were any place on earth where that exercise would improve everyday life, it was Ireland.

• • •

For the Sheehys, for their extended family, and for everyone with any political interest in Ireland, the years 1911–17—the time between Kathleen and Francis's marriage and the birth of Conor—were immensely confusing. For the Sheehys, nothing went right; even though individual members of the clan acted nobly, the collective effort was disastrous and, by 1918, the Sheehys as a political power were done.

The case of Tom Kettle is sad, but instructive. Stage by stage in its mixture of superficial success and ultimate demise, his life is virtually isomorphic with the prestige and power of the Sheehys as a clan. Kettle was apparently in command of his life: a nationalist Member of Parliament, he married Mary Sheehy in September 1909 and then, in late October of the same year, he was appointed the first (and, as it turned out, the last) "professor of national economics" at University College, Dublin, a constituent of the new National University of Ireland that replaced the old Royal.[17] Kettle's intention was to keep his seat in the House of Commons at Westminster, and to do his work at UCD as well. When a general election was called for 28 January 1910, Kettle not only held his seat, but slightly increased his majority in his religiously split constituency.[18] This seemed to promise a brilliant political future, for the Irish nationalist party was once again in the position it wanted—namely, holding the balance of power in the U.K. House of Commons. Because the general election of 1906 had given the liberal party a large electoral majority, its leaders had been able to ignore their longstanding pledge to the Irish nationalists. Then, in 1909–10, the liberals came into conflict with the House of Lords over David Lloyd George's famous "people's budget." An election was called for January 1910 and after the liberals' majority slipped away, they made a simple bargain with the Irish nationalists: if the Irish would help the liberals to strangle the House of Lords, they, in turn, would pass a home rule statute for Ireland. Tom Kettle, his father-in-law David Sheehy, and the entire nationalist party believed they were in sight of the promised land: home rule for Ireland, Dublin once again a capital city, and they, of course, in charge.

Strangely, Kettle turned his back. Soon after his appointment was announced, one of his colleagues, the medieval historian and nationalist Alice Stopford-Green, had raised with him (and presumably with others) the propriety of his holding a seat in Parliament and simultaneously being a full-time professor. He replied that he had already explained to his East Tyrone constituents that he could not attend Parliament regularly and that his first duty would always be to the university. He argued that, in any case, in the immediate year ahead he really had very little to do at UCD, as the transition from the old Royal University had yet to be completed.[19] Although this sort of thing would be deemed a conflict of interest in most present-day universities, one should not be anachronistic. It was common for full-time UCD staff to hold outside posts—as leader writers (that is, editorialists) for Dublin newspapers, or as board members of private and public corporations—at least up to the 1960s. By the standards of the time, Tom Kettle was not unethical or terribly greedy. Yet, when Parliament was again dissolved on 28 November 1910 and another general election announced (one in which the British liberals and their Irish nationalist allies clearly held the whip hand), Kettle unexpectedly wrote to John Redmond, head of the nationalist party, announcing that he would not run.[20] The Sheehys, especially Bessie, must have gone into shock, for Tom Kettle was their best hope.

Why Tom Kettle retired from Parliament is not known. There is a strong suggestion in his letter to John Redmond that he would stay on if he could find an uncontested nationalist constituency to replace the sectarian cockpit that he represented. One of his close friends, Arthur Clery, has suggested that Kettle expected the party to do something that would allow him to withdraw his resignation (such as to offer him a safe seat), but that he was outmaneuvred; he had in fact gone out on a limb and, unintentionally, sawn it off.[21] Perhaps. There is force, however, in his biographer's observation that Kettle was suffering from an "affective disorder." He was melancholy, doom-obsessed, and a serious alcoholic. With epigrams, wit, and false high spirits he fought against the constant depression that beclouded his life.[22] In this context, quitting Parliament was not so much an affirmation of an allegiance to his new professorial post, so much as a retreat, one that took him a step closer to the brink.

Tom Kettle became a sham professor: not irresponsible, not a complete fake, but close to it. Today he would be known as a "telly don," someone willing to comment publicly on anything, with real competence in nothing. When he accepted the post, Kettle had no illusions about his competence in the discipline of economics,[23] and yet he never troubled to acquire any. His writing reveals that he was not conversant with the work of the major British economists of his time, let alone in touch with the ideas of the continental school. He simply knew no economics in the technical sense. As a teacher this made his classes a pleasant ride. As George O'Brien (who became professor of economics in UCD in 1926) recalled, Kettle would take his class out to St. Stephen's Green on a sunny spring morning and there not so much lecture them as just talk. "Kettle did not pretend to be a profound student of economic theory," O'Brien remembered. "He was a 'professor of things in general' from whom I learned a great deal about history and literature."[24] In print, Kettle wrote pamphlets concerning economic nationalism that showed the economic sophistication of a counting house clerk,[25] translations of continental thinkers, done without serious commentary,[26] and an assortment of lightweight essays and editions.[27]

In the years immediately preceding the Great War, Tom Kettle had two opportunities to show that there still was marrow beneath his mouldering carapace. The first of these occurred in August 1912, during what turned out to be James Joyce's last visit to Ireland. Joyce was having a terrible time with George Roberts, the managing director of the Dublin publishing house of Maunsel and Company, who, for increasingly flimsy reasons, kept putting off publishing *Dubliners*. In fact, Roberts disapproved of several of the stories from a moral, not a literary perspective. So, Joyce called upon Kettle who himself had been published by Maunsel. This was a sensible tactic, as Kettle had recommended Maunsel to the newly funded University College, Dublin, as their official printer and publisher. It was also a perfectly reasonable request to make of Tom Kettle, for he and Joyce were old friends. Joyce had attended Kettle's bachelor dinner and a few days later, after spending more hours drinking with Kettle, had written to Nora Barnacle that Kettle was the best friend he had in Ireland and that Kettle had done him great service. On their honeymoon Tom and Mary Kettle had spent a day or two with Joyce and Barnacle in Trieste.[28] Thus, it was a terrible slap in the face when Kettle read Joyce's manuscript and sided entirely with the publisher. "I'll slate that book," Kettle declared, meaning that he would review it savagely in the public press. Kettle was entirely put off by the two boys meeting with the pederast in "An Encounter."[29] The failing here was not that he should have shown a recognition of Joyce's originality and of the quality of the writing—writing in quite a new mode and from an attitude alien to what would have seemed natural to Kettle—but that he neither instinctively backed his friend Joyce (on the Irish principle that sins against faith are greater than sins against morals) nor faced down Joyce on the issue.

His second opportunity to show mettle came in 1913–14, and this occasion provided an interesting contrast with the actions of his old friend and recent opponent Frank Sheehy-Skeffington. This event was the great Dublin strike of 1913. On one side was William Martin Murphy, the biggest mercantile capitalist in the south of Ireland. Sixty-nine years old in 1913, still handsome and forceful, adamant against trade unions, he resembled the capitalist of caricature. The strike, led by James Larkin, pioneer Irish labor leader, began on 26 August 1913 when the tramway drivers struck against one of Murphy's many holdings, his street railway company. A lockout ensued, then violence, and then near-starvation for the workers. For a time, Dublin seemed on the edge of a genuine social revolution, not just a change in management, as promised by the home rule movement.

David Sheehy denounced James Larkin as an anarchist "who would tear down all and build nothing."[30] Tom Kettle attempted to steer a middle course between capital and labor. He wrote a series of articles for the *Freeman's Journal* that were quite hard on Murphy. His major energy, however, was focused on the foundation of a "peace committee," which he chaired. This was intended to represent neither side but to be the force of disinterested public opinion. Among others, Eugene Sheehy, Osborn Bergin, Thomas MacDonagh, and Kettle's wife Mary joined him on the platform at the first meeting.[31] In fact, the peace committee did nothing effective and at its last meeting on 11 November, Kettle, as chairman, appeared half an hour late. He arrived obviously having drink taken, with blood streaming from a cut on his face, a bunch of carnations in one hand and a bag of oysters in the other. The meeting became a shambles.[32]

In contrast, Frank and Hanna Sheehy-Skeffington were deeply involved in support of the workers. When a fraternal offer of support was made by English trade unionists to take the children of the Dublin strikers into English homes, the Catholic clergy of Ireland denounced the plan as exposing the children of Ireland to the dangers of Protestantism: better to be malnourished in Dublin than spiritually starved in London. Both Frank and Hanna supported the plan and tried to circumvent the Catholic priests' vigilant watch on the ports of east coast Ireland. For his troubles, Frank was physically attacked while helping to get children out.[33]

Francis Cruise O'Brien did not take a prominent part in the fray. The family tradition that he was strongly opposed to Murphy and the employers almost certainly is correct. George Russell, now Cruise O'Brien's friend and colleague, was one of the most outspoken opponents of capital. The analogy between landlords and capitalists was clear, as was that between rural cooperative farmers and urban trade unionists, and cooperationism is where Cruise O'Brien's heart now was.[34]

• • •

One of the reasons for paying attention to how Tom Kettle, on the one hand, and Frank Sheehy-Skeffington, on the other, responded to pivotal events is that these two men defined a spectrum of behavior within whose boundaries Francis and Kathleen Cruise O'Brien lived.

For a brief time, it seemed as if the home rule movement, on which David and Bessie Sheehy pinned their hopes for the future, would indeed win. The British liberals overcame the House of Lords in August

1911 and in the spring of 1912, Prime Minister Herbert Asquith began to pay his political debts to the Irish. This took the form of the "third home rule bill." It passed its third reading in the Commons by 367 votes to 357. Under the new constitutional rules it had to be repassed twice, in successive sessions, before becoming law. Finally, in 1914, the bill was law. Ireland would have its own parliament.

But before the act could come into effect, it was suspended until after the European war, which had just begun. So, instead of embracing a triumphal future, the young people of the Sheehy world had to make a terrible decision: how were they to react to the war? That question was difficult enough for young people who lived in Great Britain. For the Irish nationalists, it was infinitely harder, for they were pulled by two opposing forces. Was the evil of the Kaiser's Germany such a threat to Western civilization that helping the British was justified? And this in addition to the perennial question—is war itself ever justified?

When the news of the breakout of hostilities reached Tom Kettle, he was not in Dublin. He was in Belgium, buying arms for the Irish Volunteers.[35] The Volunteers, founded in November 1913, were headed by the relatively moderate nationalist Professor Eoin MacNeill, but many of the ranking Volunteers were members of the Irish Republican Brotherhood (the "Fenians"), the secret oath-bound, militant body. What exactly the constitutional nationalists, such as Tom Kettle, thought they were doing in obtaining arms is anybody's guess. In an inchoate situation, people act strangely. (For instance, Frank Sheehy-Skeffington joined for a short time a rival organization, the Irish Citizen Army, before quitting it as a violation of his principles.) Probably Kettle was engaged in buying arms for coastal defense, John Redmond having obtained customs clearance for such importation.

Did these young people know what guns were all about? One doubts it. Guns were fun, adventure. Kettle's arms-buying mission was in fact a follow-up to a dramatic arms delivery affected in July 1914 by young people with whom the Sheehys (and, especially, Francis Cruise O'Brien) were close friends. This was the delivery of two yacht-loads of arms. One vessel was the *Asgard*, skippered by Erskine Childers. Among his crew were his wife and Mary Spring-Rice, daughter of one of the main patrons of cooperationism, Lord Monteagle, and herself a keen believer in that movement. This yacht off-loaded at Howth. The second vessel, the *Kelpie*, landed at Kilcoole, County Wicklow. It was skippered by Conor O'Brien who was a well-known long distance sailor and who was also a step-brother of Dermod O'Brien, the noted painter and nephew of Lord Monteagle.[36] Conor O'Brien not only was a very close friend of Francis Cruise O'Brien, but reckoned that he and Cruise O'Brien were distantly related. (This seemingly spidery family relationship was later to affect the as-yet-unborn Conor Cruise O'Brien.)

When the Great War gave the children the chance to play with guns for real, how did they respond? Tom Kettle stayed on for a time in Belgium as a war correspondent. For the *Daily News* he chronicled the plight of the Belgian refugees and came to identify very strongly with the victims of German aggression.[37] When he returned home, he joined the army and as a lieutenant for the Ninth Dublin Fusiliers, became a recruiter. He made the equivalent of political stump-speeches throughout the country, encouraging young men to sign up for service. There is no doubt that on a conscious level Kettle was absolutely sincere in believing that the best way to defend the cause of Irish nationalism was to defend the small nations of Europe. His war writings show an idealism that is heart-rending in its transparent sincerity.[38] Yet, there is a sense beneath the surface that something more was going on, that the Great War offered Tom Kettle an honorable way to escape the life that increasingly was an ill-made suit of clothes, one that looked new when new, and old when old, and which he hated.

The antipole to Kettle was Frank Sheehy-Skeffington who opposed having anything to do with the war not (as, for example, Patrick Pearse) on the grounds that one should never serve the imperial master, but from deeply held pacifist beliefs. Frank became the arch-antirecruiter. He managed to deliver forty antirecruiting and anticonscription speeches before he was arrested in May 1915. (Hanna had already spent jail-time for her feminist activities.) He was held in Mountjoy prison and eventually sentenced to six months hard labor and six additional months in default of bail. His reaction was to go on a hunger strike. He told the magistrate that he would be out of prison dead or alive before the expiration of his sentence. At the end of June 1915 he was let out under the "Cat and Mouse Act," which was specifically designed to deal with hunger strikers: one was let out, became healthy, and then was clapped back inside where, presumably, one starved oneself, was let out, became healthy ... and on and on. He went on a lecture tour of the United States where he covered his favorite issues: feminism, socialism, Irish nationalism, and pacifism. There was a certain amount of nod-and-wink about his leaving the country (he could easily have been stopped, but why not let him leave and make his trouble elsewhere?). When he returned in mid-December 1915, he was only minimally harassed: after all, there really was a Great War on.[39]

Between the two extremes, Tom and Frank, what happened? Eugene Sheehy joined the Dublin Fusiliers and served with the heavy artillery.

The immediate reaction of Francis Cruise O'Brien to the invasion of Belgium was to become keen on the war, keen as mustard gas. Now there was no chance of Cruise O'Brien's being allowed to sign up, because of his physical demerits, but he wanted to make recruiting speeches. In judging this ambition, one should not forget the extraordinary impact of the story of the sack of Belgium, especially when heightened artfully by the British propaganda agencies. Francis wanted to help. Kathleen, who still could be a Sheehy when she needed to be, said, "No," and that was that.[40] This was just as well. It was one thing in post independence Ireland for the Sheehys to have been associated with the ultimately unsuccessful parliamentary party, but had Cruise O'Brien spent the war years recruiting for the imperial military, there would have been scant place for him and his family in Ireland after 1921.

• • •

If knowing how to respond to the Great War was a difficult problem for the young people of Dublin's intellectual elite, the question of how to respond to the Easter Rising was even harder. Ultimately, the Easter Rising of 1916 sealed the doom of the Irish parliamentary party, of which David Sheehy was a venerated elder. That, though, was not clear at the time. Then, the young people (now all in their thirties, but young still, as if in prolonged adolescence) had to react to a patriotic event that was gnomic in its meaning and which energized conflicting synapses in their cultural awareness.

The Easter Rising of 1916 is the one event in Irish history which is well known to the informed public throughout the English-speaking world, and its drama and heroism need no emphasis. Three comments are in order, however. First, the 1916 Rising should not be interpreted primarily as a military episode, but as a symbolic event. Although the Irish Republican Brotherhood was defeated in the streets, it won the hearts of a new generation of Irish nationalists. Second, despite their ultimate success, it is hard to say what the republicans thought they were achieving. Their proclamation was impressive in its fervor but extremely vague in content. And there was even some serious talk among the leaders, most notably Patrick Pearse, of placing a German prince upon an Irish throne, which, in some unexplained way, would serve to prevent a British reconquest of Ireland.[41] Indeed, in the last analysis it is impossible to discover whether or not the republican leaders expected the rising to succeed militarily or even if they wished it to succeed. Third, the desire for self-immolation was strong among several of the leaders.

The reaction to the Rising of Frank Sheehy-Skeffington was the most eirenic and, ultimately, the most tragic. When the Rising was in full spate, Hanna went to the General Post Office, to see if she could be of help in running messages. Frank tried to organize a citizens' defense force to stop the looting. The Rising itself was widely unpopular among the Dublin working class (let alone among their betters) and the response of the workers and the unemployed was to trash and to loot. This bothered Frank immensely, but his efforts were of little effect.

On the Tuesday evening of Easter Week, Frank was arrested as he passed Portobello Barracks. That is hardly surprising, given that he had been the most visible leader of the anti-enlistment campaign. Still, there was no real reason to arrest him and, in fact, the charge sheet that was later produced at the investigation into the affair said simply "no charge." He was detained, however, as a hostage.

Sheehy-Skeffington was handed over to a new watch commander, Captain J.C. Bowen-Colthurst, and he was taken along as hostage with a counterinsurgency party. The party traversed Rathmines, and outside Rathmines church, grabbed a young lad named Coade who said he was coming from mass. Young Coade was whipped in the jaw by the butt-end of a rifle, apparently on Bowen-Colthurst's orders. The captain then shot him. Sheehy-Skeffington protested and was told to say his prayers. In fact, Captain Bowen-Colthurst said his own prayers and reflected on the Bible, for guidance. He was a staunch sort of literal Protestant and he found a text that spoke to him: "But those of mine enemies which would not that I should reign over them, bring hither, and slay them before me" (Luke 19:27). The Lord having spoken, at ten o'clock on Wednesday morning, Frank Sheehy-Skeffington was shot.[42] "In Sheehy-Skeffington, and not in [James] Connolly, fell the first martyr to Irish socialism," Sean O'Casey later declared. He referred to Sheehy-Skeffington as the Gandhi of Ireland.[43]

The news of Frank's death was brought to Francis Cruise O'Brien by Sir Horace Plunkett. In his diary for Thursday, 27 April, Plunkett records his having been in the suburbs and returning to central Dublin: "Communications are badly interrupted. I got back about 7 to find Cruise O'Brien. ... I had to tell him that his wife's brother-in-law Sheehy-Skeffington had been shot."[44] The news for Francis and Kathleen must have been terribly wrenching. Their best and strongest ally was gone. But we have no record of that pain.

Instead, we have only a pale, semi-autonomous record in a public newspaper. This record arises because, in addition to being the librarian of the Cooperative Reference Library and general factotum to Sir Horace Plunkett, Cruise O'Brien had also found a part-time position as a writer of leaders for the *Freeman's Journal*. This newspaper was controlled completely by the Irish parliamentary party, with John Redmond at its head and David Sheehy as one of its pillars. Francis Cruise O'Brien was twinned with Professor Robert Donovan of the English department of UCD as chief editorial writers. The *Freeman's Journal* office was heavily damaged during the 1916 Rising and the paper did not appear until 5 May. (Easter was very late in 1916—23 April—less than two weeks' production was lost.) This hiatus was a break for the editorial writers; they had the advantage of not having to comment on the Easter Rising as it took place. When Cruise O'Brien and Donovan started commenting, they shrewdly avoided as much as possible directly addressing the issue of the Rising, but instead attacked rival newspapers: the *Irish Times* for implicitly sanctioning Ulster unionism and thus leading to the Rising; the *Irish Independent* (owned by William Martin Murphy, no revolutionary) for having flirted with extreme nationalism. Their own position? It was threefold: that the Rising would not have happened if the Irish had been granted home rule instead of having it postponed for the duration of the war; that the Irish nationalist party still was the best hope of the Irish people; and that the executions should stop. This was after fifteen executions had taken place; James Connolly was still alive. What this very indirect evidence implies is that Francis Cruise O'Brien was not very enthusiastic about the Rising. Certainly he was willing to keep earning a useful part of his living by working for the home rule newspaper. One suspects (given some of his later political positions) that at this time he still believed sincerely that home rule was the most practical and, therefore, most desirable form of Irish independence.[45]

Tom Kettle, with his labile emotions, responded to Easter Week like an affective flare. To him the Rising was a source of deep anger. Mary Kettle later recalled that it made him furious, and he would bitterly repeat his view that the rebellion had spoiled the chance of a free and united Ireland coming into being in a free Europe.[46] His close friend and admirer, Robert Lynd, believed that the murder of Frank Sheehy-Skeffington "cast another shadow over his imagination from which he never recovered."[47] In fact, the whole Rising was traumatic. Of the men court-martialed and shot for their part in the rebellion, Thomas MacDonagh was a colleague (an assistant lecturer) at University College, Dublin, and Patrick Pearse an old friend. Kettle, now a captain in the United Kingdom military, gave evidence for Eoin MacNeill at his court martial.[48]

The toll on Kettle was terrible, the more so because he was twisted by grief at the loss of his friends and an equally great grief for the

loss—he believed—of Irish freedom. Thus, Kettle could testify for
MacNeill and memorialize the greatness of MacDonagh, and still feel
hatred for the Rising and those men executed who were not his friends.
Drunkenly, he described how Major John MacBride, who had fought
for the Boers in South Africa, had talked to the firing squad on the
morning of his execution.

"Fire away. I've been looking down the barrels of rifles all my life.'"

"That was a lie," Kettle said, "but a magnificent lie." Then, he added,
"He had been looking down the neck of porter bottles all his life."[49]

Tom Kettle, unable to stand life in the Dublin of 1916 or to contemplate the Ireland of the future, asked for a transfer to active duty. He
sailed from Dublin on 14 July.

It is no dishonor to Tom Kettle to label his decision to go on active
duty as intentional suicide, but there is some reluctance to make such
a suggestion in a Catholic country. Robert Lynd, who spent a fair
amount of time with the drunken and disturbed Kettle in the period
after Easter Week, clearly interpreted Kettle's grand gesture in that
manner. However else does one deal with a man who wrote lines such
as "There is only one journey, as it seems to me ... in which we attain
our ideal of going away and going home at the same time. Death, normally encountered, has all the attractions of suicide without any of its
horrors." And this: "Since life has been a constant slipping from one
good-by to another, why should we fear that sole good-by which prom-
ises to cancel all its forerunnings?"[50]

Kettle knew full well what he was doing. Just before departing for the
trenches, he gave his collection of economic books to the Cooperative
Reference Library.[51] And finally at the Somme—that four-and-a-half-
month-long bloodbath that became a hallowed time in the mythology
of Ulster unionists, for there most of the Ulster Volunteer Force was
sacrificed—Tom Kettle received a bullet in the chest. The date was 9
September 1916 and the shot was fired by one of the Prussian Guards,
but neither the date nor the source are important: Tom Kettle had decided to die; the rest was just a matter of detail.[52]

• • •

What had once promised to be the kingdom of the Sheehys was fast
turning into a necropolis. Three of the four Sheehy daughters now were
widows (Margaret's husband, John F. Culhane, had died early in the
same year). The widows all had children and financial problems.
Margaret Sheehy Culhane was supported largely by her in-laws, the
feather merchants whom Bessie Sheehy had once looked down upon.[53]
Father Eugene Sheehy, the Land League priest, died in mid-July 1917,

and Bessie Sheehy in January 1918. Both she and David had been living
with Margaret Culhane for some time before her death, which means,
in effect, that they were living on the charity of the Culhane family.
From his wife's death onward, David Sheehy ceased to be a patriarch
and increasingly became an old man, not fully able to cope.[54]

The two central figures in the Sheehy mythology now became Tom
Kettle and Frank Sheehy-Skeffington, each of whom had left a widow
who was committed to keeping his memory alive. Each of these women
had played a major role in the life of Francis and Kathleen Cruise
O'Brien, and how the men's memory was preserved had a direct impact
on young Conor Cruise O'Brien.

Conor recalls being roughly age seven when his mother told him the
story of his two uncles. They both were honorable and the memory of
both was to be revered. It was clearly implied, though, that Tom Kettle
had been mistaken. Honorable, yes, but in some sense he had not died
directly for Ireland. Frank, on the other hand, had.[55] Yet, Conor was
also to learn while still quite young that they both were wrong—in
the perception of the nationalist mind that prevailed in Dublin in his
youth. Conor recalled that, puzzling as were the Kettle and Sheehy-
Skeffington deaths when he was told about them by his mother, things
were even more confusing when he talked to outsiders:

> I got a little more puzzled as I got a little older. I found that people who were
> shot in 1916 were held in high esteem. My two uncles had indubitably been
> shot in 1916. But it seemed they had not been shot in quite the right way.
> Uncle Frank, indeed, had been shot in the right way, to the extent that he
> had been shot by the British who had become the right people to have been
> shot by. All the same, he didn't really qualify, because he hadn't been shoot-
> ing at the British before they shot him.

As for Kettle,

> The case of my Uncle Tom was far worse. He had been shot, in 1916, by
> Germans, who had become altogether the wrong people to have been shot
> by, back then. The Germans were the "gallant allies in Europe" of whom the
> Easter Proclamation spoke.

Therefore:

> It was wrong, on Uncle Frank's part, *not* to have been shooting at the people
> who shot him. But it was much worse, on Uncle Tom's part, to *have been*
> shooting at the people who shot him. My uncles couldn't do anything right,

it seems, by the standards which came to prevail in Ireland just after their deaths.[56]

These words are written in the later voice of a world-weary adult, but even then the reedy worries, the confusion of a youth, still are discernible.

• • •

For the Cruise O'Briens the great stabilizer in the post-Rising period was the cooperative movement and the personality of Sir Horace Plunkett. From 1912 onward, it had been clear that the Ulster unionists would not accept home rule as defined by the third home rule bill; and, after 1916, the physical-force nationalists would not accept it either. The operative question was whether or not a sufficiently broad middle group could be constructed so as to isolate the two opposite extremes. David Lloyd George, who became prime minister of the United Kingdom in December 1916, wanted out of the problem, and badly. His idea was to have an "Irish convention" called, to represent, if possible, all branches of opinion, but in any case sufficiently broadly based and prestigious so that anything the convention agreed on would carry the day both in Ireland and in the halls of Westminster.[57]

This idea was not new with Lloyd George, and had its backers even before he publicly announced it in May 1917. By the middle of July the convention was in operation. The start-up was so swift largely because the government shrewdly chose a spine of moderates—Horace Plunkett, Edward MacLysaght, and George Russell—who succeeded in convincing most of the major interested parties to send representatives. The Ulster unionists yielded grudging participation and only Sinn Fein of the significant parties did not take a seat, but even their viewpoint was represented by Irish nationalists who were in touch with Sinn Fein. In getting things set up quickly, informal help came from both Lord Monteagle and his son, Tom Spring-Rice, the latter having good contacts with Sinn Fein.

When the convention met in July, the first job was to elect a chairman. A ten-person committee was struck to do this and had, by a vote of six to four, chosen Viscount Midleton, a southern unionist, when George Russell declared that if Horace Plunkett were not made chairman, he would himself take the issue to the full convention for a floor fight. Midleton, under pressure from John Redmond, thereupon withdrew and Plunkett became chairman. He turned out to be a competent, if eccentric chair, but it was in this public forum that his one personal weakness was most evident: he was a terrible public speaker and frequently made gaffes. For instance, in his valedictory speech he included

in his peroration the phrase "Gentlemen ... never despair of the republic!" The classical reference was lost in a welter of contemporary connotations; the unionists were aghast.

Significantly, Plunkett found places in the secretariat of the Irish
convention for Dermot Coffey (who had been a crew member on
Conor O'Brien's *Kelpie* when it delivered arms to Kilcoole in 1914)[58]
and Sir Horace's general retainer, Francis Cruise O'Brien. The plenary
session of the convention commissioned seven different plans for the future government of Ireland. One of these was written pseudonymously,
by "Two Irishmen"—Francis Cruise O'Brien and Coffey. The plan
they put forward was for dominion self-government. That is, for
Ireland to be a wholly self-governing dominion within the British
Empire, with this exception: the London government would still control defense. There would no longer be any Irish representation at
Westminster. As for Ulster, Cruise O'Brien and Coffey suggested that
there should in Ireland be two provincial councils: one for the historic
province of Ulster (as distinct from the modern six counties) and another for the rest of the country. Each of these two councils was to have
power to initiate direct taxation for education, local government, police,
public works, and health. These provincial councils were to nest under
an all-Ireland parliament and, in effect, would produce a form of home
rule for Ulster. Cruise O'Brien and Coffey suggested a major conces-
sion to the Ulster unionists: if an act of the all-Ireland parliament were
rejected by a two-thirds majority of a provincial council, then it would
not be operative. This clearly was intended as an effective answer to the
charge that home rule would be Rome rule: that Protestant civil liberties would not be safeguarded in a state whose majority was Roman
Catholic.[59]

This is the closest insight we have into Francis Cruise O'Brien's personal political views. The ideas that he and Dermot Coffey put forward
were intended to convince a specific audience, but that does not mean
there was anything contrived or meretricious about them. Essentially,
Francis Cruise O'Brien wanted for Ireland in 1917 what the dominion
of Canada obtained in the 1920s and the twenty-six counties obtained
in 1937, and without Partition. It was a slightly advanced position, but
not violent, and certainly not republican.

During July, August, and September the convention met frequently
and Cruise O'Brien was kept busy. The convention recessed for
October and November, and that is just as well, for he had other things
on his mind: Kathleen was pregnant, and due soon.

On 3 November 1917, the only child of Kathleen and Francis Cruise
O'Brien was born.

CHAPTER 3

HIS FATHER'S SON: 1917–1936

As was usual in Ireland of the time, the Cruise O'Briens chose to have their child born at home. What was unusual was that, in addition to a midwife, a gynecologist was present at the birth. This was Bethel Solomons, considered to be the best in Ireland and one of the best in the British Isles. He was a friend of Francis (a well-known Dublin figure, Solomons had been capped ten times for Ireland as a rugby fullback in the years 1908–10 and was the fulcrum of a famous rugby story: a Dublin cabby picked up an English newspaperman who asked "How is the Irish team doing?" "Irish team?!" came the incredulous reply. "What fuckin' chance could they have—fourteen fuckin' Protestants and one fuckin' Jew").[1] It was well that Dr. Solomons was present, for the delivery was a difficult one and his help was required.

When Bethel Solomons came downstairs after the birth, he took a cup of tea in the drawing room with Francis's sister Cathleen (who was known in the family as "Tiny"). As usual, she was being very grand. Bethel Solomons was a man of sly wit. He picked up a miniature from a table, a picture of Francis's late mother, she of the Lally family, which could trace itself back to one of the Wild Geese (seventeenth- and eighteenth-century emigrés), who had won for himself a French barony before losing India for the French and then, understandably, his own head. Solomons held up the miniature, smiled broadly, and then put it down.

"I see," he said, "One of us."

"Good God, no!" cried Conor's aunt. Some horrors could not even be imagined.

This story was preserved for two reasons. One is that Bethel

Solomons thought it immensely funny and, since Francis Cruise
O'Brien agreed, it was built into the O'Brien family's collective memory. And, second, it was incorporated into Conor's own sense of self. In
a way, the story is a predictive item: not causal, but predictive, for
Conor spent a great deal of his time with Jews, something very unusual
for an Irish person for simple demographic reasons. In later life, Conor
came to identify with them directly and intensely. In fact, in the late
1970s, he focused an *Observer* column on Bethel Solomons's joke and
chose to suggest that maybe the good doctor was right. "Did one of my
Lally forebears make off, in one way or another, with a *Jewish* heiress?
I don't know, but unlike my aunt, I am inclined to accept Dr. Solomons'
ethnic Eureka!"² Now, indeed, this may have been wishful thinking but
Conor, in later life, wanted to be Jewish and was willing to suspend
disbelief.

Though Francis Cruise O'Brien was an agnostic, Conor was christened in the Rathmines parish church. (This was in contrast to Owen,
the son of Frank and Hanna Sheehy-Skeffington, who, by virtue of both
his parents being nonbelievers, was never formally baptized—but since
every believing relative and child-minder practiced the rite of private
baptism on him, just to be sure, he became one of the most baptized
children in Ireland.)³ It was intended that Conor should be christened
Donal Conor Cruise O'Brien. Donal is a traditional O'Brien name. The
"Conor" was in honor of one of his two godfathers, Conor O'Brien,
who was himself a grandson of William Smith O'Brien, one of the leaders of the 1848 rising. As mentioned earlier, Conor O'Brien was a good
friend of Francis and they had worked out that they were some kind of
blood relations (the exact details of which have been lost). Conor
O'Brien was one of the Foynes O'Briens, who were also the Inchiquin
O'Briens and the Monteagle O'Briens, very wealthy Protestant families.
Conor O'Brien, like so many of Francis's friends, was a man of character and also a Dublin character. He was a wonderful sailor and later
wrote a brilliant book about his long-distance cruise from Dublin to
Melbourne and back.⁴ In Dublin folklore, he was known for his patriotism (he had landed arms at Kilcoole in 1914) and for his vile and violent temper. He looked rather like a large member of the monkey
family, which makes his most famous outburst appropriate: incensed by
a visiting English journalist who referred to the simian appearance of
the Irish people, he ambushed the man and horsewhipped him on the
steps of one of Dublin's most exclusive addresses, the Kildare Street
Club.

The other godfather was Richard Sheehy. (That Francis not only
permitted his son to be christened, but allowed one of the chief oppo-

nents to his marriage to stand as a godfather, indicates that he was willing to go a long way to maintain peace with his wife's people.) Richard Sheehy, whose part it was to give the child's name to the priest, was not at all happy with this particular cleric. The same priest had caused Richard's family some difficulties by refusing to christen Richard's daughter "Frances Eugenie"; he spelled the first name with an "i" and refused to have anything to do with the second. So, when the moment came to name the infant Cruise O'Brien, Richard was heard to chant out a whole line of names: Donal Conor David Dermot Donat Francis Cruise O'Brien. "Francis" did not make it to the official birth certificate, but the other names did. Almost immediately the wee bairn became known either as Donal or as Conor, a brevity for which he has always been grateful.[5]

Conor's father was a good father by the standards of his society and time. He paid the bills, kept a roof over the family's head, and was not violent or abusive. But an Irish father of his generation was not expected to spend much time with young children, save for ritually bouncing the infant on his knee when visitors called of a Sunday. Also, Francis's work as a part-time journalist (and, later, a full-time one) meant that he often toiled until the early hours of the morning. As a result, Conor was raised for the first four or five years of his life entirely by his mother and other women.

There is no doubt that Kathleen spoiled Conor. He was an only child and, further, the physics of her own family pushed his mother in that direction. The physics were classically Newtonian: her sisters Hanna, Margaret, and especially Mary were constantly after her, with advice and criticism. They told Kathleen she spoiled the infant. She responded by seeming to agree with them, and then spoiling Conor rotten when they were not around. (That pattern has lasted throughout life: Conor has never done so much as a day's manual labor, nor can he so much as cook an egg; everything always has been done for him.) From the beginning, Kathleen worried about Conor's soul. She was never as easy with Francis's agnosticism as she pretended. Once Conor was old enough to sit still in church, she took him to mass weekly at the Rathmines church, accompanied by her sister Mary Kettle.[6]

Part of spoiling Conor, as well as keeping up social pretenses, was to hire a nanny, one Sadie Franklin.[7] Such expenditure was way out of line with the Cruise O'Briens' actual resources, but it points to a silent and continuing problem in the family: the tastes and attitudes of both Kathleen and Francis outran their income. Francis continually scrambled to earn more money, but he eventually began going to the money-lenders, and by the time of his death in 1927, the family was deep in debt, just one step ahead of the bailiffs.

Francis's employment was not all that secure. The Irish convention met for the last time on 5 April 1918 and reported on the twelfth, so that source of income disappeared. He continued to work for Plunkett as librarian of the Cooperative Reference Library, and he wrote leaders for the *Freeman's Journal*. With his old partner Lionel Smith-Gordon (who was now chairman of the National Land Bank in Dublin), Francis wrote two small books for the Cooperative Union of England. These were a history of cooperation in Ireland and one on cooperation in Denmark, a country that Francis had never visited and whose language he did not speak or read.[8]

These were risky times for a man trying to make his living by his wits, especially a writer in the political field. The rules were changing fast. Sinn Fein in 1917 had become the front for all branches of "advanced" nationalism and the enemy of home rule politics and of the old nationalist party. Inadvertently, David Lloyd George, prime minister of the United Kingdom, had guaranteed Sinn Fein's future and, simultaneously, destroyed the old nationalist party when, in the spring of 1918, he introduced the Conscription Act making Irishmen liable for compulsory service in the U.K. military. This was the one move that would unite all sections of Irish nationalist opinion. Members of the Irish parliamentary party (David Sheehy included) stomped out of Westminster and returned to Dublin to join the opposition. They joined with Labour and Sinn Fein in a conference summoned by the Lord Mayor of Dublin. This Mansion House Conference denied the right of the U.K. government to impose compulsory military service on the Irish people against the general will of that people. The passing of the Conscription Act was regarded as an act of war upon the Irish nation, and Irishmen were called upon to resist by all means at their disposal. To this impressive degree of unity among laymen was added the backing of the Roman Catholic bishops, a surprising fact since most of the bishops had been unenthusiastic heretofore about the nationalist cause. The nationalists could only have been pleased to read the section of the bishops' manifesto stating that in view of the historical relations between the two countries, conscription was an oppressive and inhuman law, which the Irish people had a right to resist by all means consonant with the law of God. But the bishops then went on to explain what they meant by consonant with the law of God. They advised the people to attend more fervently to their religious duties and to secure domestic peace through a national novena in honor of Our Lady of Lourdes—hardly the thing the Irish Republican Brotherhood had in mind. Instead, Sinn Fein and the parliamentary nationalists were drawn together with the election of Eamon de Valera as president of the Irish Volunteers. The IRB continued to have a strong independent influence on the Volunteers, but Sinn Fein and the Volunteers were united at least nominally.

Sinn Fein now was ready to move forward. The election of December 1918 was a golden opportunity. The truce between Sinn Fein and the Irish parliamentary party had proved to be temporary, and Sinn Fein went out to win seats at the price of their former allies. The Sinn Fein election manifesto was the old pre-1917 Sinn Fein policy with a republican veneer. Sinn Fein, the manifesto said, aimed at establishing the republic through the withdrawal of Irish representatives from Westminster and by creating an Irish constituent assembly as the supreme national authority. The present Irish MPs, the manifesto flatly stated, stood in the way of that goal. In line with the Sinn Fein constitution of 1917 the manifesto promised an appeal to the Peace Conference at Versailles for its recognition of Ireland as an independent nation. Fervent republicans were kept happy by the affirmation that a republic—undefined as always—was the national goal and that every available means was to be used to render British rule nugatory. It was a splendid manifesto, and the election campaign was a success, even though the majority of Sinn Fein candidates were either in jail or fleeing arrest (the government had moved against Sinn Fein leaders in May). Sinn Fein won 73 of the 105 Irish seats, with the Irish parliamentary party maintaining only 6. David Sheehy lost his seat. He could not fathom what had happened. In January 1919, the newly elected Sinn Fein MPs met in Dublin and formed their own constituent assembly, Dail Eireann. The Irish war of independence was on.

With the mixture of guileless optimism and shrewdness that were his trademarks, Sir Horace Plunkett tried one last time to bend events toward an agreed solution. He did this by founding the Irish Dominion League in June 1919, which pressed for dominion status for Ireland. Plunkett's naive optimism was indicated by his refusal to see that the violent wing of the nationalist movement would not accept any imperial ties, no matter how light, and therefore would veto any solution that implied a continued connection to the United Kingdom. On the other hand, his shrewdness was shown by his recognizing something that the Sinn Fein leaders did not: unless some concessions were made to the northern Protestants, the partition of Ireland was inevitable. A weekly journal, the *Irish Statesman* (modeled on the London *Statesman*) was launched in June 1919 to support the Irish Dominion League. The paper's quality was very high, with strong political and literary columns. The editor was Warre B. Wells, an Englishman who had edited the *Irish Times*, and its two deputy editors were George O'Brien (best known as a professor of economics at University College, Dublin, and for his pioneering economic history of Ireland) and Francis Cruise O'Brien.[9]

This was the perfect job for Francis. The paper published contributions from some of the best of the second rank of Irish letters: Erskine Childers, James Stephens, Jack Yeats, Lennox Robinson, Shane Leslie, and Stephen Gwynn. Through the paper, Francis was working himself into a position of influence and making a decent living. The trouble was, the politics that inspired Plunkett to create the newspaper had no future. The world belonged to the hard men, the no-compromise set. After Dail Eireann was proclaimed an illegal organization in mid-September 1919, all the hard men were forced underground, and they made their important decisions while on the run. The *Irish Statesman* lasted just one full year. During what turned out to be its last months, the editors became convinced that a radical solution to Ireland's political problems was necessary, something that would be beyond dominion status. Sir Horace believed that the paper "was flirting with Sinn Fein and turned off the financial tap."[10] Francis, therefore, went back to being a librarian and picking up whatever freelance work he could get, most often with the *Freeman's Journal*.

• • •

More than once, Conor has said that the first sound he can recall as a child was the bark of small arms fire and the shudder of light artillery about 4:00 on the morning of 28 June 1922.[11] The new provisional government of the Irish Free State was attacking the Four Courts building on the quays in Dublin, where a group of diehard "republicans" held out. They opposed the peace treaty that had been signed between southern Ireland and the United Kingdom and were willing to fight their fellow Irishmen, on the way to maintaining the holy war against the old enemy, Great Britain. The guns being used by the Free State military had been provided by the United Kingdom. These weapons only a few months before had been employed against the Irish.

This was not the way it was supposed to be.

Nothing was.

Conor's first aural memory is singularly apt, for it alerts us to a set of interrelated troubles, which took the form of slowly down-spinning spirals. In the 1920s the new Irish government, the Sheehy family in its extended definition, and the Cruise O'Briens as a nuclear unit were all locked into a downtailing multiple helix of bad luck and diminished fortune.

The Irish civil war of 1922–23, much more than the war of independence of 1919–21, determined the character of the state and the society that prevailed for the next half century. The independence movement gave the hope (naive though it may have been) of a thirty-two-county Ireland and of unity within the Catholic sector of society. After the civil war there was a double division, seemingly permanent: Northern Ireland was split from the rest of the country and, more important for everyday life, a divide, fratricidal and blood-deep, arose between those who supported the Anglo-Irish treaty and, consequently, the government of the new Irish Free State, and those who did not.

The same months wherein the Irish independence movement was spinning into near self-immolation also saw the acceleration of the decline of the house of Sheehy. Here the symbolic figure is Margaret Sheehy Culhane. Since 1916 a widow with four children, she lived mostly on the financial kindness of her in-laws. Her parents, David and (up to her death in 1918) Bessie, lived with her. David required emotional care in the period after the destruction of the Irish parliamentary party and the loss of his own seat. He still had his strong moments, but mostly he was at sea on a globe he did not understand.

Margaret, age forty-two in 1921, began a flirtation and then an affair with a twenty-one-year-old poet, Michael Thomas Casey, who also happened to be her godson. She fell deeply in love and, late in 1921, she became pregnant. In Catholic Ireland that was not on. As her condition became unavoidably obvious, she was cut off financially by the Culhane family, very devout Catholics indeed. Her Sheehy brothers and sister turned on her as well and, as her eldest son Gary Culhane recalled, Margaret and the poet Casey decided to "get the hell out of the country." Margaret dumped the children on the Culhanes, and she and the poet moved to Montreal, where, in mid-August 1922, a son, Ronan, was born. (Later, Gary was shipped over to join them. Eventually, Margaret became prominent in Montreal Irish circles and her husband gave up verse and became harbour master of Montreal.)[12]

That degree of public humiliation probably would have broken David Sheehy's remaining courage, but a further blow came within the next year. In 1923, Dick Sheehy, a promising barrister on the Munster circuit and a rising law teacher at University College, Galway, died. It must have been more than David Sheehy, once-proud patriarch, could take. He had moved in with his daughter Mary Kettle when Margaret decamped, and Mary bullied him. He took to going to mass six times daily, once for each of his six children.[13] The only Sheehy who did modestly well in post independence Ireland was Conor's uncle, Eugene Sheehy. He was strongly pro-treaty, and therefore supported Cumann na nGaedheal (the pro-treaty party), and became a circuit court judge.

For Francis and Kathleen Cruise O'Brien, life was a series of reverses. First, Francis's patron, Sir Horace Plunkett, was effectively run out of the new Ireland. In late January 1923, "Kilteragh," his home in Foxrock, then an undeveloped suburb south of Dublin, was torched by the "republicans" (that is, anti-treaty, anti-Free State irregulars). The reasons are not hard to surmise. Plunkett was Protestant and avowedly pro-treaty. The burning of his house was hard on Plunkett's spirit, the more so because the cooperative movement, which he had always proposed as an antidote to sectarian animosity, was in the process of itself being partitioned. Given that the funds for the central administration of the cooperative movement came in considerable part from the central government, the partitioning of Ireland made the partitioning of the movement inevitable. Increasingly, Plunkett believed that the new Ireland had gained a world, but lost its soul. In October 1923 he departed for Weybridge, Surrey, where he made a new home. He maintained his ties with the Irish cooperative movement until his death in 1932, but for his retainers, such as Francis Cruise O'Brien, it was as if a noble lord had suddenly been called from a banquet hall. Nothing was ever quite right again.[14]

A second, related, setback was that the Cooperative Reference Library was moved from Dublin to London. What happened was that one of the paid organizers for the Carnegie library system, Lennox Robinson, of Irish theater fame, got into a battle with the Irish Catholic authorities about a story he had written. The authorities labeled it blasphemous (it was about a devout girl who was raped, but being devout, she believed that her child would be born of a Christmas day, and, indeed, her baby was thus born). When Robinson in the face of the clerical pressure refused to resign, the Carnegie trustees for the British Isles decided to shift all of their Irish operation to Scotland. Purely as a side effect, they required that the Cooperative Reference Library, for which they had been paying most of the running costs, be removed from Ireland as well.[15]

As if this were not enough, a third misfortune hit the Cruise O'Briens. The *Freeman's Journal*, which now was Francis's sole source of regular income, ceased publication. In recent years, the grand old lady of Irish journalism (whose first issue had appeared on 10 September 1763) had taken more than her fair share of bruising. The *Freeman's* offices had been heavily damaged in the Easter Rising; its offices were destroyed by "republicans" in late March 1922, and, finally, they burned out the paper.[16] The last issue appeared on 19 December 1924.

Francis Cruise O'Brien had to take the only opportunity there was: he joined the opposition—the *Irish Independent*—and from a journalistic point of view, the rest of his life was one of frustration. The paper was owned by William Martin Murphy, of 1913 strike fame. It always had been strongly favorable to Timothy Healy, former nationalist MP, first governor-general of the Irish Free State and, not incidentally, front man for the employers during the 1913 strike. (The Healyite sympathy was particularly galling for Francis, for a scion of the family, Maurice Healy, had ratted on Francis when, as auditor of the L. & H., he had fought against Father Delany.) The *Irish Independent* strove to be the paper of the upcoming Catholic middle class and the rising businessman.[17]

Francis Cruise O'Brien was kept on a very short rein. He was told what to say in editorials, or to write the obituary of a bishop in so many words. He knew how to do these things; he was a professional. But this level of journalism brought him no joy, even when the subject of an obit was a late prelate. He made a modest living, but this was a big fall in status and intrinsic interest from the days when as a deputy editor of the *Irish Statesman* he had worked with the clever people of Dublin and had written about ideas, not recent burials.

• • •

It was just at this time, when Conor was seven or eight, that his father began to take an interest in him. Even if his career had been going well, he probably would have done so—Irish fathers of that time began to recognize the existence of their male children at about the age they became little men—but undoubtedly his professional unhappiness sent him in search of new sources of comfort. Francis—"Daddy," in what was both good West British usage, and the common term for father in many English-speaking rural areas—taught Conor to play chess and began him on Greek. Francis gave him a book that Conor prized more than anything else. It was a wonderfully illustrated volume of Celtic-based young people's stories by Padraic Colum entitled *The King of Ireland's Son*.[18] The volume was significant in part because of its title, and also for the way it permanently impressed itself upon Conor's memory: the daughter of the "Enchanter" in the book is named Fedelma, and that became the name of Conor's own first-born daughter. This book was subsequently lost when the bailiffs seized much of the O'Briens' goods after his father's death, but Conor had the inscription by heart. He recites it today, in his seventies, as if holding the book before him: "To my dear Conor. That he may get to know the literature of his native land as well as that of his spiritual home, which is Greece." That is a very unusual inscription for an Irish father to write. In "Lebor Gabala," the Irish version of pre-Christian history, most of the invading peoples are depicted as coming from Greece, or they at least touch Greece in the course of their long peregrinations. Needless to say, this is far from what Conor's father had in mind in the inscription.

That book brings up a tension, fourfold in nature, that ran between Francis and Kathleen concerning their son Conor. Between the two of them there were, first, basic mother-father tensions stemming from power issues. Francis parachuted late into the parenting game; before Conor was seven or eight, Francis made some major decisions but he left the day–to–day management of the bairn to Kathleen. From age seven or eight onward, the parental power struggle became serious. Second, this struggle, as we shall see, came to focus to a considerable degree on religion and, especially on whether Conor should be raised as a strict Roman Catholic or not. Third, there was a major cultural divergence. Francis looked toward the world of Europe, Kathleen to Ireland. Finally, there was the elusive, but real, matter of style. Was Conor to grow up closer to the eccentric, slightly flamboyant character of his father or to the somewhat more reserved and more serious demeanor of his mother? In the actual event, on every issue, Conor became his father's son.

This is not to imply that Kathleen Sheehy Cruise O'Brien was a weak person either in character or intellect. She was not. Indeed her own achievements were impressive. Besides teaching Irish part-time at Rathmines Technical School, Kathleen developed an Irish language version of Gregg shorthand, and wrote *A First Irish Book* for language students.[19] She also wrote plays, and one of these, *Apartments*, a farce, was good enough to be performed at the Abbey in September 1923 (under the pseudonym of "Fand O'Grady").[20] She maintained the cultural legacy of the Sheehy family which she directly passed on to Conor. Kathleen was very conscious of who she was even if, in Conor's recollection, she was usually willing to give in on most matters to her husband. (The Dominican sisters had been clear on this; marriage might be a repugnant state, but obedience to one's husband was divinely commanded.)

Where Kathleen only partially gave in to Francis, and then most unwillingly, was on the matter of Conor's schooling—which really meant his religious training. Education and religious training were inseparable in Ireland in the 1920s. This was no small matter. The Irish Free State after independence gave to the Catholic Church a power over education equaled in no other modern state. And the Irish bishops made very clear in 1927 what education's purpose was: "the training and development of the whole man ... for the purpose not merely of fitting him for a career of usefulness and honour in this life, but also and still more for the purpose of guiding him to attain the high and happy destiny designed for him in the life to come."[21] Who was to determine the proper education for service in this world and salvation in the next? Under natural law theory the responsibility for the child's welfare lay in the first instance with the parent, but, as the following statement made in the 1940s by John Charles McQuaid, archbishop of Dublin, indicates, parental powers in education were subsumed by the church:

> Parents have a most serious duty to secure a fully Catholic upbringing for their children in all that concerns the instruction of their minds, the training of their wills to virtue, their bodily welfare and the preparation for their life as citizens.
>
> Only the church is competent to declare what is a fully Catholic upbringing; for, to the church alone, which He established, our divine Lord, Jesus Christ, has given the mission to teach mankind to observe all things whatsoever He has commanded. ... Accordingly, in the education of Catholics every branch of human training is subject to the guidance of the church, and those schools alone which the church approves are capable of providing a fully Catholic education.[22]

And the state? The encyclical of Pius XI, promulgated in 1929, emphasized that the role of the state in education was only to serve as an auxiliary to the family and to the church. The duty of the state was "to protect the prior right which the parents possess to give their children a Christian education, and therefore also to respect the supernatural right of the church over such Christian education."[23]

Thus, when Francis Cruise O'Brien told Kathleen that he wanted a non-Catholic education for their son, he was asking her to break not only with her family tradition and her own religious sense, but also with the dominant educational ideology of a very tight and inward-pressing society. It was a lot to ask.

Conor's first formal schooling, from age five to seven, was at Miss Haines, a Protestant preparatory school in the English sense of the term: preparing children of the middle and upper-middle classes for a boarding education. It was very small, fee-paying, and decidedly toney. As Conor approached the age for the one nearly universal rite of passage in post independence Ireland, first communion, he was transferred to the Muckross Convent in Marlborough Road, a school of about 300 pupils. A decided step above the average Irish national school (that is, primary school), it was run by Dominican nuns, and a very harsh world for a sheltered child. It was there that Conor experienced the only corporal punishment that he was to undergo during his education. One of the lay teachers had the habit of hitting the children across the knuckles with a ruler for virtually any educational shortcoming or disciplinary infraction. Conor in later life laughs as he says, "This contributed to my distaste for Catholic education: Pavlovian conditioning!" In fact, he was lucky. The use of physical force, sometimes to a degree that permanently injured the child, was common in Irish primary schools in the years 1920–60. This followed not from any particular predilection for force on the part of individual teachers, but derived, as in a syllogism, from an ideology of education that postulated the child suffered from Original Sin and that overcoming this great defect was the first, indeed, the primary, aim of schooling. It followed that the aim of education was, contrary to the "progressive" theories of John Dewey and Maria Montessori, to help a child overcome his imperfections of behavior and belief and so to preserve his immortal soul unto eternal life. The Irish distrust of theories of human nature that presented children in a rosy light is well represented in the authoritative statement made in 1942 by Archbishop John Charles McQuaid: "In violent contrast to our system and with the sane [scholastic] philosophy, stand those types of the so-called New or Active School (such as the materialist system of ... Montessori ... wherein, because the child is supposed to be his own end or to be physiologically predetermined or to make his own truth), the task of the educator is practically reduced to observing the spontaneous activities of the general and individual needs of the children."[24] Thus it followed that all necessary means, including physical force, should be used to kill the beast that lurked within each child.

Once Conor had taken first communion, Francis pulled him from the Dominicans and suddenly, at age nine, Conor was in a different world. Sandford Park School in Ranelagh had roughly 100 boys and half a dozen masters. The school was located on eight-and-a-half acres with good sports fields. It was Church of Ireland (that is, Anglican) in tone, but mixed in its upper-middle-class composition: roughly one-third Protestants, one-third Catholics, and one-third Jews. The head boy in 1926–27 was Conor's cousin, Owen Sheehy-Skeffington, son of Hanna and of the late Frank Sheehy-Skeffington.[25]

Conor's entry to Sandford Park intersected with another plane of his parents' tug-of-war, this one cultural. Although his parents had promised him that he could study both Greek and Irish, they found that the subjects clashed on the timetable. The O'Briens were told that a choice must be made. Kathleen asserted herself: Conor would learn Irish. This decision may have made good sense within the moral economy of the family (after all, Kathleen was permitting her son to attend a non-Catholic school; at least he could learn the national language), but it was hard for a young boy to see it that way. He wanted to follow his father and learn Greek. "I am afraid this choice somewhat damaged my relationship with my mother," Conor now says. "And damaged my relationship with the Irish language as well."[26] Later, as a teenager, Conor spent two summers in the Ring Gaeltacht, and one in Ballyvourney, West Muskerry, County Cork, and became a fluent Irish speaker.[27]

Nevertheless, a signal resonance in this early learned resentment of his mother's forcing him to learn Irish when he would have preferred Greek points to something crucial in Conor's mature relationship to the culture of post independence Ireland. Irish as the "mother tongue" came to have mystical, nearly magical properties, and after 1922, the government of southern Ireland institutionalized the Irish language revival. The common thread binding almost all the Irish language revivalists was an equation of national identity with the ethnic language. Listen to a few statements. The President of the Executive Council, W.T. Cosgrave: "The possession of a cultivated national language is known by every people who have it to be a secure guarantee of the national future."[28] Eamon de Valera told the Gaelic League: "It is my opinion that Ireland with its language and without freedom is preferable to Ireland with freedom and without its language."[29] Eoin MacNeill, first minister for education of the Irish Free State, declared that for the members of the government to abandon the attempt to revive Irish would be to abandon their own nation.[30]

Conor, in his preteen resentment of mother and mother tongue, began a relationship with Irish official culture that was always uneasy. In return for this continual unease, he gained a certain freedom and this is directly traceable to his father's cultural values. In embracing both ancient classical culture and also that of the Enlightenment, Francis Cruise O'Brien was attempting to radiate out into an orbit that was not merely parochial. Because of the marvelous achievements of the Irish literary renaissance in the preindependence years, it is easy to forget the cultural narrowing that occurred after independence. Southern Ireland as a society was engaged in an attempt to build cultural walls between itself and the outside world. One example of the many-sided cultural implosion was censorship, which was institutionalized in the 1920s. Lay and clerical leaders worried a great deal about foreign ideas, especially those from Great Britain, where a secular view of family and society was becoming prevalent. The central point about censorship as it developed in independent Ireland was that it was not imposed by the church upon the people, but was viewed by them as necessary and desirable. When the British left southern Ireland there were a number of statutes on the books containing provisions for protection against indecency, but it was the southern Irish themselves who, in 1929, created their own thorough censorship legislation. Undeniably, the Catholic Church was the chief force behind passage of the censorship measure, but the censorship campaign was as much a lay as a clerical movement. The bishops did not force censorship upon the people: the people wanted it, the politicians were strong Catholics, and the men in power in the 1920s had memories of ill treatment by the press and by book publishers, and actively distrusted unregulated publishing activities. Under the 1929 act (which remained in force until 1946), a five-man board was appointed to recommend to the minister for justice the books and periodicals which should be banned. Not only were pornographic books and pictures prohibited, but no book or periodical that advocated the use of contraceptives was permitted. Among the books by well-known authors banned as indecent under the 1929 censorship act were Sherwood Anderson, *Horses and Men*; Giovanni Boccacio, *Pasquerella and Madonna Babetta*; Erskine Caldwell, *God's Little Acre*; Noel Coward, *To Step Aside*; James T. Farrell, *Studs Lonigan*; William Faulkner, *Sanctuary*; Sinclair Lewis, *Elmer Gantry*; Somerset Maugham, *Cakes and Ale*; Sean O'Faolain, *Midsummer Night Madness*; and George Bernard Shaw, *Adventures of the Black Girl in Her Search for God.*[31]

Behind these specific pieces of attempted thought control was a deep distrust of the contemporary world outside of southern Ireland. One clerical contributor to the *Irish Ecclesiastical Record*, a publication sponsored by the Irish bishops, summed things up in 1923, when he stated that he had come into contact with the men and books which were the typical products of the educational systems of England, France, Germany, and other countries, and that the experience had convinced him that if Ireland were to "avoid the mistakes which have led to the deformation of the intelligence, and through the intelligence the literature and institutions of these countries, especially in relation to the supernatural order, we must aim to return to the sane education idea of the Middle Ages."[32] One could multiply such quotations, by both clerics and laymen, by the score. The point is that in the Irish Free State of the 1920s and 1930s, medieval theology, nineteenth-century economic orthodoxy, linguistic nationalism, and dominant social conventions all led toward the same result: a cultural implosion. This pinched most tightly upon the schools. Francis Cruise O'Brien, in refusing to send his son to a template school, in insisting on a non-Catholic education, was fighting the battle against the cultural contraction on behalf of his son.

What is hardest to capture in all of this, is the way that Francis, in fighting the battle against the official culture on several fronts, carried on living with a continuing impishness. The fight may have been serious, but Francis Cruise O'Brien still was fun to be around. He was a founding member of the United Arts Club of Dublin, a set of intellectuals, artists, and others who were in various ways out of sympathy with the new order: persons such as R.M. Smyllie, of the *Irish Times* who later gave Conor a job that helped him make it through university, and W.B. Yeats, increasingly unhappy with the mess of potage that was Irish independence. Francis Cruise O'Brien was a social catalyst, a good raconteur, and a gifted mimic. One of his famous skits at the club was to put up a screen between himself and his audience and then to impersonate various well-known figures—Yeats was one of his best turns.[33] Conor, after he entered Sandford Park, was just old enough for his father to take him around and introduce him to his friends. They once met Yeats, an occurrence that did not make a great impression on the young lad. Later, Conor solemnly told an American interviewer, hungry for any scrap of Irish renaissance lore, "I was then a very small boy and he was a very big one."[34]

The family power struggle, Conor's education, the question of cultural perspective, and matters of personal style, all these were issues that seemed to be moving toward Francis's end of the spectrum, toward the male, the non-Catholic, the Enlightenment, and effervescence. Then, on Christmas Day, 1927, Francis Cruise O'Brien's tuberculosis felled him, and every issue became again new.

• • •

The pressures that Kathleen Cruise O'Brien experienced after her husband's sudden death were nearly crushing. One aspect was financial. The family was deeply in debt to money-lenders and for the rest of her life she never was able to fight clear. Kathleen gained a full-time teaching post at the Rathmines Technical School (as a widow she was no longer restricted to part-time teaching), but the bailiffs were in and out of the house from Francis's death onward. The public shame of these seizures of chattels must have been deeply humiliating, especially for a Sheehy.

Worse, though, were religious pressures, some internally generated, others externally applied. Francis Cruise O'Brien had died an agnostic and without benefit of a priest. Kathleen accepted the presumption that Francis would eventually go to heaven, because he had lived a good life, but the indeterminacy of the length of time before he got there tortured her. Purgatory, according to Catholic dogma at the time, was a state of temporary punishment (temporary, but of long duration—on occasion, a millennium or two) where persons who had died under God's grace, but who still had mortal or venial sins that were unforgiven, were warehoused before going to heaven. The church's doctrine, as taught by St. Thomas Aquinas, was that the smallest pain in purgatory was greater than any pain on earth. The day Francis died, Kathleen started praying, and praying hard. In early January 1928, young Conor noted for the first time at her bedside a devotional manual, *In Heaven We Know Our Own*, by the suitably named Father Blot, S.J.[35]

More direct pressure came from clergy and well-meant devout Catholic laity: take your son out of that sinful Protestant school. And here the mechanics of the doctrine of purgatory cut into Kathleen like medieval torture. The church's teaching at the time was that the amount of time someone spent in purgatory would be shortened or lengthened, according to the actions of persons still living. Private devotions, prayer, and paying for special masses shortened the time, but if the person practicing any of these devotions was an unrepentant sinner, then the stay of the person in purgatory (Francis in this case) would be extended. This Kathleen knew from her religious instruction classes at the Dominican convent, and she probably had it forcibly recalled to her attention in any case. Conor remembers that about the same time as his father's death, the mother of a contemporary of his at Sandford Park, also a Catholic, was warned by a priest that every day the boy stayed at the school lengthened her late husband's agonies in purgatory. She capitulated. Conor believes that his mother received the same advice.[36] Yet, "the poor thing sweated it out and kept me at that school, though she was being mentally tortured by those people."[37]

The next stage was for the local parish priest in Rathmines to refuse to confirm Conor, on the grounds that he was being educated at a non-Catholic school, in direct disobedience of the orders of the archbishop of Dublin against "mixed education." Kathleen was put through the humiliation of petitioning the parish priest of Rathmines from outside the presbytery door on a cold winter evening; the priest, refusing to open the door more than a crack, spoke to her gruffly from inside. However, he did give in and eventually Conor was confirmed.[38] Conor for his part was unimpressed. As he said later, "I never believed any part of it."[39]

That Kathleen Cruise O'Brien honored Francis's wishes concerning Conor's education was undeniably heroic. One does not diminish that heroism by noting that there were very unusual pressures on her that somewhat countervailed those of the church. One of these was Hanna

Sheehy-Skeffington, the strongest personality among the remaining Sheehys and a woman of intense beliefs: agnostic, anticlerical, no longer pacifist but now republican (opposed to the government of the Irish Free State), anti-Irish (in the sense that she believed that the Irish language revival had become a bureaucrat's ramp), and keen on Sandford Park, where her son Owen had done very well. Hanna at this time was at the height of her Valkyrie-like powers. She had in 1926 led the agitation against Sean O'Casey's *The Plough and the Stars*, and she, more than any other single person, drove him from Ireland.[40] So when Hanna pushed her baby sister to honor the late Francis's wish that Conor be kept on at Sandford Park, it was a voice every bit as formidable as that of the average Irish bishop.

Kathleen's best excuse for removing Conor from Sandford Park would have been financial. She was well and truly broke. Sandford Park, however, gave concessionary rates to the sons of widows.[41] More important, a group of Francis's old friends clubbed together to pay for the education of his son, the one stipulation being that the money be used to pay fees at Sandford Park. These old friends made a surprise presentation to Kathleen in the autumn of 1928. The list of subscribers is now lost, but the range of contributors must have been wide, for James Joyce on the continent was canvassed and responded with a contribution.[42] The chief trustee for the fund was a Presbyterian accountant named Tulloch, something of a deterrent to any attempt to switch the funds' disbursements to, say, Belvedere College.[43]

If the origin and details of the Conor Cruise O'Brien Education Fund are tantalizingly lost, a much more intriguing and mysterious item was the proposal that Conor be adopted into the family of Lord Monteagle. This is not quite as outré as it at first sounds, and if the details are not at present available, that does not mean the project was not a real possibility at the time. The idea was based on three strands of relationships. The first was that, as indicated earlier, Conor O'Brien (Francis's good friend and one of Conor's godfathers) had worked out that he and Francis were somehow related; his O'Briens, the Foynes O'Briens, were intermarried with the Monteagles of Brandon, a family of wealthy Protestant land owners. Second, recall that in the circle of philanthropy and cooperativism around Sir Horace Plunkett, the Monteagle family—Mary Spring-Rice, Tom Spring-Rice, and Lord Monteagle himself—were included. And the players had other overlapping interests: for instance, Mary Spring-Rice had been a crew member on one of the yachts that ran guns in 1914; Tom Spring-Rice and his father Lord Monteagle had been supporters of the Irish convention, for which Francis had worked as a secretary. So, a whole variety of things had brought the Monteagles into contact with Francis Cruise O'Brien, and not just casual contact, but often as fellow workers, fellow believers.

Third, the Monteagle family needed an heir if the title Baron Monteagle of Brandon was not to pass to a collateral line. The second Lord Monteagle, enthusiastic cooperator and patron of Sir Horace Plunkett, was buried at Foynes, County Limerick, not far from his family home, "Mount Trenchard," just after Christmas in 1926. His first son and heir apparent had died unmarried at age twenty-two in 1900. His sole surviving son and his heir was Thomas Aubrey Spring-Rice, a career diplomat. He was unmarried, and, born in 1883, was in the same age-bracket as Francis Cruise O'Brien had been. When Tom Spring-Rice succeeded to the title in late 1926, he had the desire to extend his family line but, apparently, no interest in doing so through marriage. Adoption of a bright and formable son was therefore attractive. The adoption would have been complicated from a legal viewpoint, but not impossible, and would have extended the hereditary line of his family of large County Limerick and Kerry land owners.[44]

The proposal was direct and concrete. Dora Knox, secretary to Lord Monteagle, was the intermediary to Kathleen Cruise O'Brien. Conor's mother seriously considered for a time accepting the proposal. Negotiations went so far as to discuss details such as how often she would be able to see Conor.[45] Eventually, Kathleen said "No." Thus passed the opportunity for Conor to have become the fourth Baron Monteagle of Brandon before his seventeenth birthday: Tom Spring-Rice died childless in 1934 and the title passed to an uncle, a retired Royal Navy commander.[46] (Conor's not assuming the title was probably a bigger loss to the House of Lords than to himself. The next Lord Monteagle of Brandon took his seat in the Lords in 1947 and did not utter a word in debate for four-and-a-half decades. He was finally moved to speech by a debate on the subject of water shortages.)

These days must have been a crushing, twisting, force for Kathleen Cruise O'Brien. That she would even be tempted to permit the adoption of her son indicates just how desperate her financial straits were and, also, how committed she was to her son's long-term well-being. After declining the Monteagle offer, she felt she had to permit Conor to continue to attend Sandford Park; at least that benison from friends had to be accepted.

It may be that Kathleen's was merely the path of emotional least resistance. To my mind, her real heroism was not in sending Conor to Sandford Park but in keeping herself in one piece, so that she could function as a mother, when everything around her was conspiring to shred her. Courage and heroism often are far removed from our outside perception; they look different from inside.

• • •

Given the emotional turmoil that surrounded Conor's attending Sandford Park, his actual school days were remarkable chiefly for their being a happy and successful time. No English public school stories here, of blighted sensibilities and covert physical abuse: Conor loved the place. As he told a later headmaster, in 1965, he had "nothing but affectionate memories of Sandford Park school."[47] There he received a good, if slightly eccentric and somewhat limited education, and he was an academic stand-out.

Sandford Park, partly by inadvertence and accident, reinforced strongly the nature of the culture that Conor already had picked up. Simply put, Conor had been raised entirely as a word-person. He had not been taught to appreciate or, indeed, experience either music or the visual arts to any significant degree; this is a set of blind and deaf spots that exist to the present day. Everything was words: word play, languages, word games, reading, telling stories, playing charades, always words. In one sense that was a handicap for so much of the world was lost, but, as occurs when one or more of the physical senses are missing, the remaining sense was heightened. Conor became one of the most verbally gifted individuals of his generation in the English-speaking world and this was the foundation on which his literary achievement, as the most important Irish nonfiction writer of the twentieth century, was based.

Sandford Park's staff taught neither music nor art with any seriousness. Instead, there was a lazy sporting life and a curriculum that was very free, considering the time and place. Conor took to sports with more enthusiasm than ability. He hit puberty late, he was smaller than most of the lads, and there was always a touch of porcelain about him. Yet he was willing to try any sport. The school had two first-class cricketers on its staff and cricket was his best game, but he also played rugby and boxed, "just to see if I could do it."[48] That became a theme in his later life: he several times has taken physical risks and been beaten up, and he seems to have undergone these adult mortifications with the same attitude that he showed when taking up boxing as a schoolboy.

The school's curriculum was sometimes free-form to the point of parody, though not from any belief in child-centred education, but because of a sensible toleration of staff eccentricity on the part of successive headmasters. Freedom was possible because the school did not tie itself to the Irish school-leaving examinations. The assumption was that Sandford Park pupils would either enter into careers that required no such vulgar certificates or would go to places that had their own entrance examinations—Trinity College, Dublin; Oxbridge; and the British and Irish civil services.

Thus, one year Conor's English master was a gifted ham actor by the name of Fitzgerald who refused to teach anything but Shakespeare. This he did superbly. Every class was Shakespeare: reading, explicating, and, most important, memorizing great gobs of the bard and putting on scenes and sometimes whole plays. Class participation was very high. The man loved and understood his subject and the students adored it.

For most of Conor's time at Sandford Park, the headmaster was S.B. Gordon Mack. He was a very good classical teacher and through him, Conor received a strong foundation in Latin. To schoolboy eyes, Mack was a dashing chap. He played badminton internationally and would sometimes go about the school dressed in his whites. He had a bit of dash in his personal life as well. He took to having luncheon on many days at Jammets, at that time the most expensive restaurant in Dublin, and he ran up heavy personal debts. Finally, he absconded abroad with the wife of a dentist whose children were at Sandford Park.

He was replaced by a man who made the elementary error of not understanding schoolboy loyalties. The new headmaster began by denouncing Mack as a dishonorable person who had let the school down. Some of the lads, with Conor as the leading spirit, found this deplorable and determined to make the new head's life pure hell. They applied themselves with success, chiefly by breaking up the intermediate mathematics class which the new head taught. What they did not notice was that they were risking turning themselves into mathematical idiots. Indeed, Conor's mathematical education ended at this point. He never gained facility in intermediate maths, and, therefore, he was unable to do any of the hard sciences that were taught in the senior school years.[49]

That is one of those tiny, accidental points on which the formation of an individual mind often pivots. Latin, French, Irish, English literature, the school taught those subjects well, but Conor was destined to leave Sandford Park without the ability to read or discuss quantitative matters at the level of even the average university entrant. As time went on, any quantitative sense that Conor ever had atrophied. In his adult years he showed a vague awareness of the concepts of "more" and of "less," but the ability to use numbers as adjectives, to evaluate quantitative data, to deal with the conceptual models that underlie modern economics and other social sciences is totally lacking. Yet, this, like his being essentially tone deaf and color blind, tightened the focus even more on what he does superbly: play with words.

Sandford Park also reinforced another aspect of Conor's earlier upbringing: his sense of being socially and culturally different from the bulk of the Irish people and, unlike them, aware of the pluralisms that exist in any modern society.

> Actually, the school I went to—and which I liked—was not exactly a Protestant school. It was a liberal, nondenominational school, but of mainly Protestant ethos, attended by Catholics, Protestants and Jews in approximately equal numbers. We were conscious of the differences between us, but also conscious of a bond between us, as boys whose parents chose to send us to that school, so untypical of the new and overwhelmingly Catholic State—then called the Irish Free State—in which we were being brought up. All around us was the ocean—as it seemed to us—of our contemporaries, all good Catholics going to good Catholic schools, and being indoctrinated like mad. From our tiny island of Enlightenment ... we could peer out into that possibly enviable fog. And to be at that distance from the religion was to be at a corresponding distance from the nation, not in theory, but in feeling.
>
> As I said, these things form a certain bond. I knew, for example, that if I heard a Catholic priest or layman referring to Jews in a hostile manner, that person would be likely to be no friend, either, to our family—to my father, as a lapsed Catholic; to my mother, as a disobedient Catholic; and to myself, attending a non-Catholic school, along with Jews as well as Protestants. So a chance anti-semitic remark could be a red light to me too. That is to say, I had to possess something of the same kind of wary alertness that Jews have always had to have within a Gentile society.[50]

• • •

Conor was a day student at the school, so he went home every night. His mother, after teaching, would provide him with his tea; they would chat, and he would do his school work. It must have been a strange life: a large, nearly empty house and everywhere around him widowhood: Aunt Hanna, Aunt Mary, and his mother, all wearing black, if not literally, certainly in their minds. Grandfather David Sheehy, now living with Mary at 3 Belgrave Park, Rathmines, was increasingly doddering and religiously obsessed. He died in 1932, and the last great figure from the great days of the house of Sheehy was gone.

Sepulchral hues, however, should not tint our view of Conor's school days. Besides success during the academic year, he spent (thanks, in part, to the generosity of Uncle Eugene)[51] holidays in the Ring

Gaeltacht and Ballyvourney, and then, at about age sixteen, he spent the first of three summer holidays in France. The latter was part of the ongoing French connection that stretched back to Sophie Raffalovitch, wife of William O'Brien. The exchange program that she had set up continued to motor along of its own momentum. The French girl from Amiens with whom Conor's mother exchanged for the 1906–7 academic year was, in the 1930s, a mother of three children with a substantial home. Conor's cousin, Owen Sheehy-Skeffington, had spent a summer in Amiens as part of this ménage.[52] Conor followed. The time he spent living with the French family completed his facility in French. To this day, he frequently does his thinking in that language, a habit that makes conversation with him at times linguistically demanding.

Nor should one see Conor's intersection with the adult world during his teenage years as being essentially somber. He found adults interesting, for he was treated as one himself, as only children frequently are. The Sheehy widows—Mary Kettle, Hanna Sheehy-Skeffington, and Kathleen Cruise O'Brien—met most Sundays at 44 Leinster Road for dinner. Dinner was confined to family members, but guests were welcome for tea and they would all sit around the long mahogany table and do what the Sheehys always did: play word games, talk, argue, and tell stories.[53] In 1932, Conor's mother surprised everyone by abandoning the family political tradition and supporting Eamon de Valera in the general election of that year. That was cause for more than passing comment. The Sheehy family allegiance (and that of Francis Cruise O'Brien) had been for the treaty and Dev was the arch-antitreatyite. (Hanna, an exception as usual, was also opposed to Dev, because she objected to his leading Fianna Fail into the Dail and thereby implicitly recognizing the Irish Free State.) Exactly what pulled Kathleen Cruise O'Brien in de Valera's direction is not clear, but it was relevant that as a young man in Bruree, County Limerick, de Valera had been a parishioner of Father Eugene Sheehy.[54]

And there were always some odd and fascinating characters passing through, especially in the company of Aunt Hanna. For instance, Conor remembers how the legendary Maude Gonne—muse to W.B. Yeats and widow of the 1916 martyr John MacBride—appeared in the 1930s: "She was the most striking figure I have ever seen, very tall and thin and straight, with a face like an ancient eagle and dressed entirely in flowing black."[55] She and Aunt Hanna worked on various "republican" causes, mainly the Release the Prisoners campaign. And whether or not she was a histrionic, rather comic, figure in her old age, one had to be fascinated by someone who, on her honeymoon, had come up with a plan to assassinate the king and queen of England on a state visit to Spain.

The real character, the one with force, however, was Owen Sheehy-Skeffington, the only child of Frank and Hanna. Eight-and-a-half years older than Conor, Owen became Conor's big brother and, for a time, a quasi-father figure. Having been head boy at Sandford Park, he now was at Trinity College, Dublin, where he later became a lecturer in French. Owen had his parents' affinity for taking the unpopular course, but without their shrillness, or the self-righteous hardness that Hanna acquired after Frank's murder. A socialist, antifascist, humanist, secularist, and anticlericalist, Owen was hero-worshipped by Conor. The key to Owen, however, was that he was also immensely kind. He was genuinely concerned with the welfare of his younger cousin and did not patronize him, but spent time with him as one human being with another. Conor recalls how Owen once brought a light to his childhood bedroom, to deal with the darkness after the adults had decreed lights-out.[56] With the help of Owen, of the masters of Sandford Park, and by the peculiar courage of his mother, Conor, who at age ten was still a child frightened by the dark, had by the age of eighteen become a confident young man. His persona took on many of the characteristics of that most singular figure, Francis Cruise O'Brien.

PART 2

A Rising Professional

CHAPTER 4

LIVING BY HIS WITS:
1936–1941

Conor entered Trinity College, Dublin (TCD), in the autumn of 1936
with a sizarship (that is, a modest scholarship) earned by taking a competitive examination in the Irish language.

Trinity in the 1930s was in a bad way, but it had its charms. The college resembled an old lady of once-classical beauty, a former debutante,
now aged and fallen on hard times. From a distance, she still looked
good and her conversation, if stilted, was excellent. But her hands on the
teacup, delicately held, shook, not least because she was lacing the tea
with cooking sherry. Up close, her face, heavily made-up, had a craque-
lure that testified to a lot of experience and, unless something changed,
not much future.

Trinity College's problems in the years between Irish independence
and the conclusion of World War II were simple of definition, if difficult of solution: it was in straitened circumstances and did not know
where it was located.

Just before the end of the war of Irish independence, the Trinity authorities had made an arrangement with the U.K. government for a siz-
able annual grant, plus a lump sum for capital expenditures. This fell
through as southern Ireland became independent and Trinity had to
settle for markedly smaller sums from the Irish authorities. From 1923
until 1945, Trinity's leaders kept their heads down, avoiding governmental attention to the institution. The university looked inward and
came to resemble a rundown family business, whose partners kept to
themselves and quietly hoped the old firm would not go bankrupt.

The second problem was one of cultural location. Mostly Protestant
and mostly unionist before 1922, after independence Trinity either had
to adapt to the new dispensation or become a sojourner in an alien land.

Gradually, the college came to accept reality. It still was British in self-identity, but the Union Jack was flown officially for the last time in 1935 (for the jubilee of George V). "God Save the King" still was played at all degree-granting ceremonies as late as 1939 and drinking to the king's health at formal occasions continued throughout the 1930s and early 1940s, with, however, increasing protest from nationalist students (including Conor). The king was toasted for the last time in 1945.[1]

Within its walls, and when not vexed by the question of royal emblems, Trinity still had a charm of the sort that only genuine old age can give. If the college maintained few traces of its Elizabethan origins, the eighteenth century still was about. Edmund Burke was a palpable presence, not least because the most influential undergraduate organization, the College Historical Society, was directly traceable to the debating society Burke had founded. Trinity had an attractive air of foppish solemnity. As at Oxford and Cambridge, students wore gowns, meals were preceded by Latin graces, and the elaborate bad manners of an ancient English public school prevailed. The three yearly terms—Michaelmas (1 October to 11 December), Hilary (10 January to 22 March), and Trinity (20 April to 5 July)—harked back to a time before the secular calendar had displaced ecclesiastical reckonings.[2] There was a Trinity style, and Conor captured its essence in a description of a fellow undergraduate of his time, Henry McAdoo, who became the Protestant archbishop of Dublin, and as an undergraduate blended "the pompous and the dashing in a disconcertingly agreeable way."[3]

Why Conor attended Trinity rather than University College, Dublin, is not complex. His cousin Owen Sheehy-Skeffington had gone from Sandford Park to Trinity and, after taking a Ph.D. in French, he had in June 1936 obtained a permanent appointment as lecturer.[4] Going from Sandford Park to Trinity continued the pattern of non-Catholic education that Conor's father had set down for him. Trinity in those years was vaguely Protestant, but there were no doctrinal tests and Catholic students were not required to attend any religious exercise that offended their conscience.

Of course, in attending Trinity, Conor (and his mother) further called down the disapproval of the Catholic clerical authorities. However, after the torsion they had experienced on the Sandford Park issue, this was minor. The Catholic bishops as early as the Synod of Thurles of 1850 had warned the faithful of the dangers of "mixed education"—by which they meant parents' allowing Catholic children to sit in the same classroom as Protestants, unless the institution in question was entirely under the control of Catholic authorities. As far as Trinity was concerned, however, an equilibrium seemed to have developed by the 1930s, whereby if Catholic parents presented a reasonable case for sending their son or daughter to Trinity, the local parish priest usually gave his permission. Neither Conor nor his mother sought the permission of the parish priest of Rathmines and, given his past record, it is unlikely that he would have given it. There, as far as Conor's undergraduate years are concerned, the matter ended. But, because Conor eventually took a Trinity Ph.D., it is relevant that in December 1940, John Charles McQuaid, the most forceful Irish prelate since Cardinal Cullen of the mid-nineteenth century, assumed the see of Dublin and within two years he had begun the infamous "Trinity ban." Everyone within his archdiocese was forbidden to attend Trinity, unless they had a dispensation from him and him alone (which he almost never granted). To ignore his ban on Trinity was to commit a mortal sin.[5] Interestingly, the ban applied only to those within his jurisdiction; elsewhere the older, more permissive, rules prevailed. Thus, the ban on Trinity became the only regional mortal sin in the Catholic world, unless one counts the ban on mixed bathing in the diocese of Galway in the 1940s. (The proportion of Catholics in the Trinity student body was about 8 percent in 1937, Conor's second year.)[6]

In the mid-1930s, there were three ways to gain admission as a student to Trinity. Most entered by passing the college's own matriculation examination, or with a British-standard school certificate. A few entered, as Conor did, by taking the competitive examinations for junior exhibitionships. If the candidates performed at a sufficiently high level (whether or not they won a scholarship), admission followed.[7]

The course for both the ordinary arts degree (called a pass degree in most universities of the period) and for the honors degree was four years. Trinity had its own terms for these years: junior freshman, senior freshman, junior sophister, and senior sophister. Someone taking an honors degree was said to be taking a "moderatorship."

Trinity in the inter-war years was gradually effecting two changes: the transition from a period when most undergraduates took a pass degree to one in which honors prevailed. And, simultaneously, a metamorphosis from a period when most of the students' work was part of a prescribed and quite general curriculum to one in which a substantial degree of specialization prevailed. In Conor's era, the compulsory part of the curriculum was completed at the end of the second year by a set of examinations known as the "Little-go." Most of the Little-go exam was a *vive voce* test. Two or three weeks of hard work were usually sufficient for an average student to pass, and the entire process had an expired, charnel air about it. The *viva* was given in a large hall with several subjects and several students being examined at the same time.[8] Having chosen to do modern languages and literature (French and Irish), Conor also had to satisfy the examiners in English composition, logic, mathematics, and chemistry. He failed both mathematics and chemistry in the Michaelmas term 1939, but passed both in Hilary term.[9]

The quality of the college's staff was crucial. Trinity in this period was becoming a real university, with departmental structure, and serious research expected of its personnel. By the 1930s there were professorships and academic departments in most areas of the humanities and in several sciences.[10] However, the real power rested with the fellows of Trinity College, who might or might not hold academic appointment in a specific department. To become a fellow of TCD in the interwar years, one took both a written and an oral examination and, if lucky, won a lifetime stipend. In theory, fellows could be elected for a distinguished published work, but only one fellow was so elected (in 1941).[11] Manifestly, this method of choosing the inner circle of power brokers affected the tone of the entire college, and it is hard to see how choosing individuals on the basis of the impression they made in a written and oral examination can have resulted in the selection of persons with much depth of scholarship. In defense of this procedure, a historical account of Trinity argues, after reviewing the life's work of the fourteen fellows appointed between 1920 and 1939, that all "published some original work, and at least half of them a very respectable corpus."[12] Certainly, there was no pressure on academic staff members to be serious scholars, although there was an expectation that an air of great knowledge would be projected. All of Trinity's geese were expected to preen like swans.[13]

Conor's chosen specialty, French and Irish languages and literature, required extensive study and also a minimal amount of work in English literature. Lectures on both French and Irish were overwhelmingly in the English language. Examinations were held each term, except during the fourth year when, if one were in honors, one was expected to study full-time for one's moderatorship examinations. In Irish, Conor performed strongly, but without much enthusiasm. Irish was taught by Eamonn O'Toole, a scholar of no great distinction. However, in 1938, the young David W. Greene, who was to become a very distinguished scholar indeed, was appointed lecturer in Celtic languages.[14]

In his junior freshman year, Conor was required to take English literature, and in that subject too he obtained a first. This course was under the tutelage of W.F. Trench, a competent Shakespeare scholar who had written a book on the bard, but then became intellectually blocked. "He found extraordinary difficulty in clothing his thoughts in words. His lectures and much of his conversation were filled with agonized pauses during which his limbs and his body went through strange contortions in search of the right word, and presumably a similar blockage impeded his pen."[15]

Conor's real intellectual interest was in French. Modern languages was the largest humanities department and French attracted even more students than did English literature. A considerable majority of the students in the French course were women which was unusual, considering that Trinity was overwhelmingly male.[16] Conor, his contemporaries agree, got along easily with women, being neither frightened nor excessively forward. This is not the usual case for someone who has experienced a good secondary school education on the English model—a cultural benefit from which it frequently takes a lifetime to recover—but, then, Conor had been a day boy at Sandford Park and had been part of a family in which women predominated.

French language and literature was under the control of T.B. Rudmose-Brown—"Ruddy" to his friends and acolytes, but not to his face—who had been appointed chair of Romance languages in 1909. (The chair changed to French in 1937.)[17] Rudmose-Brown was the son of a Danish noblewoman and a Scottish diplomat who, in middle age, converted to Islam. Ruddy sent his own son to Patrick Pearse's St. Enda's school, an unusual choice for a Trinity professor. A medievalist, in later life he became a convert to the Catholic church.[18] Slightly stooped, white-haired, and balding, he looked the professor, but intellectually, "he was a difficult man to estimate, for his undoubted literary sensitivity and awareness of contemporary French poetry was masked by a partly assumed cynicism and an all too genuine laziness."[19] His courses were fairly straightforward. For example, his senior French examination in Hilary term, 1940, required four translations of quite difficult verses, and then required the student to give third-person singular present indicatives for verbs underlined in the test question.[20] The required reading for that term comprised five and a half volumes in French, including works by Balzac and Victor Hugo. The course was no gift.[21]

Rudmose-Brown had a good eye for talent: he had, for example, spotted Samuel Beckett, who taught for him for a time. "He may never do anything—but he's a genius!" was his judgment, long before Beckett became known outside of Trinity.[22] Ruddy was capable, in his bad moments, of combining his habitual laziness with an impressive rudeness. Conor recalls an incident in a Provençal class, in which a senior professor in one of Trinity's science departments was auditing the course in order to keep up his own knowledge of the language. The scientist politely asked Rudmose-Brown the meaning of a certain locution. Ruddy looked at him with an aristocratic air and said, "I don't know what that means. If you want to know what words mean, you look them up in the dictionary!" Students either had to get along with Rudmose-Brown and the way he did things or get out: Trinity was too small for any student to remain anonymous.

Conor's position in the department was made easier by his cousin Owen's holding the lectureship in French. That not only gave Conor social entry, but coaching when required. Owen, who in 1935 had married Andrée, a daughter of the Amiens family with whom the Sheehys had exchanged student visits, was taken ill with tuberculosis and had to take the year 1937–38 off. There was no insurance scheme at Trinity in those days for the loss of work through disability, but Rudmose-Brown with considerable kindness and good sense convinced the Trinity board that Andrée should take Owen's place until he recovered.[23] So, Conor had another relative on the staff of the department in which he was studying.

Even so, Conor almost came a cropper, because he was nearly caught in one of Trinity's nasty little internecine battles. Conor had come to be very much identified as a find of Rudmose-Brown, a favorite son academically. He wanted, however, to learn Catalan, which was under the jurisdiction of Walter Starkie, fellow of TCD, lecturer in Italian literature, and professor of Spanish. Starkie was an anecdotal lecturer and writer—his accounts of his searches for Gypsy lore were popular, and he was a director of the Abbey Theatre and a prominent figure in the literary salons of Dublin. He frequently was away during term time and he therefore sought and obtained permission from the Trinity board to appoint an unnamed "native woman speaker" in his place, while away. It was later found that this person was Italia Augusta Starkie, his wife.[24]

When Conor decided to try Catalan, he was caught in the middle of a long-lasting range war between Starkie and Rudmose-Brown. They disliked each other on every possible personal and intellectual ground and now, in the late 1930s, was added geopolitics: Rudmose-Brown was passionately anti-Franco and Starkie was for the fascists. Conor was well known in Trinity circles for being anti-Franco. Given that he was the only student taking the course in Catalan, he was in trouble. Starkie had a general policy of not allowing anyone who was a student of Rudmose-Brown to have access to the Catalan books, which he controlled. Conor finally got permission to consult them, but he did not make great progress. The exam paper that Starkie set for him involved the mastering of several hundred years of Catalan history and the first question was "Outline, with a sketch map, the tactics employed for the reduction of the citadel of Minorca." Conor could only fill the space with virtual nonsense, and much the same held for the other questions, each difficult enough for a doctoral examination. Starkie easily could have failed him, but, having made his point, that one of Rudmose-Brown's star students was not in Starkie's own supernal league, he backed off: Conor was given a poorish first, but still a first.[25]

Despite all the children's games played by grown men in academic gowns, Conor received a first-rate education. His facility in spoken and written Irish was refined and he became bilingual in French and English. Most important, his European sense was confirmed. His cultural interests and values were not primarily Irish; his perspective was very broad. This characteristic was later misread. When Conor talked and argued in later life as a European, he was sometimes criticized as being pro-British. This occurred because of the residual effects of empire-and-revolution: anything non-Irish was believed to be pro-British. Conor, in his singular way, from his Trinity days onward was strongly loyal to his "little platoon"—a phrase of Burke's he came to cherish—but he loved his Irish platoon well and not blindly. The Trinity education affirmed what his father's Enlightenment vision had already taught him: that to be truly Irish, one cannot be merely Irish.

• • •

Any good undergraduate institution teaches more outside its classroom than within. Trinity was an especially challenging experience for Conor because he literally had to live by his wits, since his mother had very limited financial resources. Conor received a small allowance from his uncle Eugene Sheehy, but that was hardly sufficient to keep him at university. Fortunately, Trinity had a large and totally unsystematic series of prizes for which undergraduates could compete. What a needy (or ambitious) student did was, first, to discover the terms of a given award (not always easy to do) and then mug up for the written examination or oral interview that was required under the terms of the prize. For Conor, living by his wits meant winning as many of these prizes as possible, not for the glory, but for the money, in order that he could stay at university. This was long before the American practice of working one's way through college crossed the Atlantic. It was a nerve-wracking process, given that Conor needed more than an occasional success if he were not to be forced to withdraw.

His first award, the sizarship in Irish that he won out of Sandford Park, covered most of his first year's expenses. It reduced his one-time entrance fee from £15 to £1.1s and 3d, and exempted him from the 20 guineas annual tuition fee.[26] Since Conor lived at home for the first year, living expenses were taken care of. He filled in the missing bits by winning £8 for obtaining first-class honors in four of his term examinations.[27]

Conor's great triumph in his first year, however, was to win a Foundation Scholarship, a rare achievement by a junior freshman. Limited to seventy of the approximately 1,600 students in the entire university, these scholarships were valuable indeed. Arts students who won a Foundation Scholarship paid only one guinea per quarter. They could hold the scholarship for five years (this eventually became important to Conor). And Foundation scholars had rooms in the college at half rate and were provided with free meals.[28] This allowed Conor to live in college from his second year on and to experience an entirely different range of college life than he otherwise would have done.

He also continued to pick up prizes for first-class examination results: £20 in his senior freshman year and £12 in his junior sophister year. Conor padded these amounts out with a bit of cash from being a "waiter," that is, one of the ten or so Foundation scholars who were annually appointed to memorize and repeat before and after meals in the dining hall a Latin grace. For acquiring this useful social skill and aid to digestion, each waiter was paid £10 per annum.[29]

All this allowed Conor not only to keep up his academic education, but to function socially without great handicap. Trinity, despite its reputation within Ireland of its time as being an aristocratic haven, was in fact solidly middle class. A study of the class that entered in 1944 (the closest we have to Conor's cohort) shows that only a total of 20 percent of the students had fathers in farming, land-owning, or land agencies, and some of the farmers were tenants with modest acreages. Nearly 40 percent had fathers who were in finance or business.[30] There were a few rich young men in Trinity, but probably no more than at Trinity's rival, University College, Dublin. Trinity, during the 1930s, was a place where "most of the students were able to enjoy an upper middle-class way of life on a lower middle-class income."[31]

What this meant for the 300 or so men for whom there was accommodation in college chambers (women were housed elsewhere) was that they had the privilege of having a "skip" (the Trinity name for college servant) occasionally clean their room and perform, for tips, incidental tasks. The rooms were primitive, without running water (although there was water in each entryway). They were ill-lighted (electricity had not entirely replaced gas) and some rooms had cavernous old-fashioned fireplaces.[32]

Conor shared a double room with Vivian Mercier, whom he had met in first year. In the language of the time, one did not have a roommate,

LIVING BY HIS WITS   93

one had a "wife." Vivian and Conor became lifelong, if slightly distant, friends. Superficially they had little in common, except that they competed for many of the same prizes and the difference between them in those competitions was needle thin.[33] Vivian, two years younger than Conor, had been reared at Clara, County Offaly. He had been educated at a national school and Portora Royal School. His family was Church of Ireland, his mother being from a significant Anglican clerical family, the Abbots. Vivian was as sober as Conor was irreverent, and at one time made a serious attempt to teach Conor the virtue of thrift, a concept previously unknown to him. Vivian did this by lending Conor five pounds and by insisting that he pay it back. He made it clear, Conor recalls, that this was for the good of the borrower's soul. The Mercier family was friendly to Conor, who found Vivian's mother, who had a bitter tongue, especially entertaining. The Merciers had Conor and his mother visit for a weekend. Kathleen Cruise O'Brien, who probably had never stayed at the house of a Protestant before, found it all very interesting and amusing.

In the winter of 1937–38, Kathleen had a stroke. After an illness that was brief, but deeply troubling to Conor, she died on 12 February 1938. Conor, who was with her when she died, ran from the room. He grabbed hold of the banisters and doubled up, sobbing.[34] That was deep, healthy grief. It was succeeded by something less healthy, but characteristic of the way Conor dealt with most serious emotional matters for the rest of his life: by numbness, and then denial. Thus, two years later, Conor reflected on his mother's death and wrote in his commonplace book, "Much of me has forgotten her already." He had, he wrote, been happy since her death. Why? "Because there is no one now whose death could hurt me. No news at all to fear from telephone or wire or face of servant at the door."[35] That not only is denial, but mannered denial, a portrait of the young artist denying that he has feelings.

Conor displaced a lot of his pain by transforming it into dissatisfaction with the rest of his family. Roughly a year after his mother's death, he wrote of his Aunt Hanna: "She has just written an article of characteristic ungraciousness. She is a howling bitch." He added, "I dislike most of my family, most of the time."[36]

Conor both feared his own emotions and feared for his own future. The latter was perfectly sensible: anyone who does not worry about whether or not his life will be a waste, especially if he is on a historical cusp, as Conor was, between an economic depression and a world war, is certifiable. The interesting thing is the way Conor, when talking in private to himself (in his undergraduate commonplace book), used the figure of his father as the chief mode by which he could express his own fears. In February 1939, Conor wrote about looking over a looseleaf notebook kept by his father. His father had written the words, "failed to set a single straw ablaze," which, in Conor's view summarized his dad's life. His father's notebook was embarrassing, Conor felt. In it were "various occasional verses, some sugared, some poisonous. ... Mostly the book was a waste of topical allusions and Swinburnian imagination." But then, the next day, Conor softened: "I wonder, would my own son find anything better after my death?"[37] He meant, among other things, would my life, like my father's, be a frustration and ultimately a waste?

Conor dealt for the most part with his inchoate feelings by fleeing from them in two ways, methods of emotional management that were to work for him the rest of his life. He became a bit of a wild man, an undergraduate character (which means that, among other things, he became very drunk now and then and fell down) and, more important, he worked hard, very hard. One of the poses that undergraduates, especially bright ones, frequently adopt is that they do little or no work and Conor tried this one on. Yet winning first-honors prizes, term after term, is not done without consistent application. A good indication of his long-term, continuous concentration was his winning the Dr. Henry Hutchinson Stewart Literary Scholarship, a great plum—worth £25 a year for three years. It was awarded on the basis of the honors examinations held each term for the first three years of undergraduate studies, in modern languages and English literature. The results were cumulative. Conor, over nine terms, covering three years, was in a neck-and-neck competition with Vivian Mercier, who did not need the money but who relished the potential honor. Therein lies a nice story. At one of the last sets of exams, part of Conor's examination paper slipped to the floor while he was on the way to hand it in. Vivian, also on his way out, saw what had happened, picked up the missing paper, and gave it to the proctor. This was a formidable piece of old school decency. Conor, reflecting on this, says, "I'm not sure that I would have done the same thing. I think I would; I hope I would, but he actually did." Conor took the Stewart prize, but in his way, Vivian won the palm.[38] (Conor also won the Vice-Chancellor's Prize in English Verse for 1939–40.)[39]

His financing of his university education largely through the winning of prizes left Conor with two legacies. One was a lifelong naiveté about examinations: a belief that they actually are a just way of distributing rewards. Never mind that an overwhelming body of systematic evidence indicates that examinations tell us as much about the examiner as about the candidate and that subjective exams in the humanities have virtually no reliability. More important, Conor gained the confidence that he could make his living by his wits. This, later in life, gave him enormous freedom. At times he has thrown over jobs that were either boring or ethically compromising and just walked away, confident that something would show up. His ability to make a solid living as a freelance writer from the 1980s onward is not merely an intellectual matter, but an indication of confidence and, ultimately, of character. Trinity gave him that confidence.

Conor probably could have survived on his mixture of scholarships, prizes, and Uncle Eugene's modest allowance, but he has always been very good at spending, just as his father had been. Thus, in his upper-class years, Conor took to "giving grinds," that is, tutoring other undergraduates for examinations. This was an honorable pursuit—the college authorities did not care how a student learned the syllabus, just so he or she attended class. And the students Conor tutored were not all losers; some of them were on the borderline between degree classes, such as an upper-second student who wanted to take a first. At least two of the men Conor tutored were major winners in Irish life. One was Douglas Gageby who, as editor of the *Irish Times*, was reckoned among the very best newspaper editors in the British Isles.[40] The other, Roy Bradford, became a Northern Ireland cabinet minister and, later, a commentator on Irish politics.[41]

Conor also gained appointment as the *Irish Times* Trinity College correspondent in 1938. This not only gave him considerable prestige around the college, but started a motif that, like a stone skipped across a pond, keeps cropping up at intervals in his life: his association with newspaper journalism. The *Irish Times* paid him a pound a column, usually weekly, during term time. That was a lot of money for a bit of spare-time work, considering that at this time a custom-made suit could be had at Switzers for seven guineas; and that Conor's cousin Owen, as a full-time permanent lecturer at Trinity was being paid £350 a year.[42]

The post gave Conor entry to the Dickensian world of one of the British Isles' best newspapers.[43] The *Irish Times* was housed in a rabbit warren made up of three old, interconnected houses, forming a triangle at Westmoreland, Fleet, and d'Olier streets. The main entrance on Westmoreland had a well-known clock that was a standard rendezvous point in Dublin. The paper was run by one of the last genuinely independent editors, Robert Maire Smyllie, a bad-tempered, idealistic, pear-shaped man, whose whiskey-red round face featured circular horn-rimmed glasses and blood-shot eyes. Smyllie, who did most of his managing of the paper in the nearby Palace Bar, never let the owners of the paper (the Arnott family) have any influence over his editorial policies.

In his curious way, Smyllie had done more than anyone else to bring southern Protestants into a grudging concordat (or, at least, détente) with the government of independent Ireland.

Why Conor got the job is impossible to say, but Smyllie's having been a friend of Francis Cruise O'Brien in the United Arts Club undoubtedly was relevant, as was Conor's stellar record at Trinity. In any case, Conor was given a fearsome half-hour's instruction on writing for the *Irish Times*—in a dark office that smelled equally of damp newsprint, tobacco, and alcohol, and that would not have passed the inspection of a purblind fire marshal—and then was told to go forth and write.

What Conor was not told was how to fill eighteen column inches (about 900 words) a week. Anyone reading his weekly column can almost feel the vulture of desperation sitting on his shoulder: how to fill all that space, when there was not much to talk about except the new squash courts, the Dixon Memorial Hall Mission, and the register of senate electors from TCD? How indeed? By shameless padding, diversionary asides, parentheses, and through an arch, word-wasting style. Here is one example, taken from the *Irish Times* of 6 May 1939:

> Examinations are now over for most people, and lectures have begun. Scholarship candidates are waiting for Trinity Monday—which falls this year on the fifth of June—to know whether they will be provided with the Scholar's Dinner that evening or whether they will have to console themselves as best they can on their own account. Many Little-go candidates on the other hand are waiting anxiously for the twenty-fourth of May, the date on which Re-Examinations in Arts for all classes occurs—to see if at last they will be able to scrape through in Mechanics and thus save their year.

In other words, he really had nothing to report. Nevertheless, Conor hirpled onward:

> Meanwhile lectures are being attended, bread is being thrown to the birds in the New Square; societies are beginning to stir to life.

What else is happening?

> The Japanese maple tree has turned ochre; the Reading Room is moderately full; tennis and cricket are being played by those "white clad figures" so dear to the columnists. ...

And on and on.

> In short, as some readers may have guessed, the ordinary summer life of College is, to coin a phrase, in full swing.

This, admittedly, was professional journalism, for one has to be paid, and quite well, to write that badly.

• • •

Under the influence of Owen Sheehy-Skeffington—whose middle name, appropriately, was Lancelot—Conor learned the joy of tilting furiously with the establishment. This was great fun as long as one pretended it was not and kept a straight face. Conor joined the Fabian Society (of which Owen was the patron), and the Irish Labour party, of which Owen was a leading member at TCD. When Owen went on sick leave for 1937–38, it was just at the time when General Franco was in the midst of his suppression of Spanish democracy. The government of Eamon de Valera adopted a policy of nonintervention, and the Irish Catholic bishops favored Franco. The Irish Labour party was very conservative, for it had been most successful in winning rural seats. In addition, its urban sector was dominated by the Irish Transport and General Workers' Union, which was largely nonideological. So the Labour party wished to avoid taking a stand.

Conor, in his senior freshman year, was elected one of the delegates of the Trinity Labour party to the annual national conference of the Irish Labour party. This was held in Dublin at the Teachers' Club, 36 Parnell Square. In response to a resolution by William O'Brien (member of the Dail [TD] for Tipperary) condemning imperialist aggression, but not naming Franco specifically, Conor stood up and broke procedural rules by talking directly about Franco's aggression. (Since Spain was not mentioned in the original resolution, this technically was out of order.) He was heckled by several delegates (shades of his father and the Yibs at the Baton Convention come to mind), but he kept on. When they jibed at him for being from Trinity College, Conor spiritedly replied that "all the progressive movements in the country for the past 150 years had their origin in Trinity College." Rather stretching a point, he instanced Wolfe Tone, Thomas Emmet, and Thomas Davis (who certainly had not learned their nationalist politics as part of the TCD curricula). Turning to William Davin (TD for Leix-Offaly, and the source of especially offensive remarks about Trinity), Conor stated that if he had "gone out with [James] Connolly's citizen army in 1916, he would know that the body had its origins in a room in Trinity College."⁴⁴ That was kick-in-the-groin street fighting on Conor's part, and showed a willingness to besmirch an opponent by implying that he was not really patriotic—an effective, if not entirely ethical, ploy.

Conor continued amid a mixture of applause and catcalls. He lauded the Labour party for its refusal, alone among Irish political parties, to accept the recognition of the Italian seizure of Abyssinia by fascist Italy.

Since that time, he said, Austria had been absorbed into Hitler's empire. Jews were being beaten up and radicals and labor organizations suppressed. "In that more controversial country, Spain, a clique of fascist generals was wantonly waging a civil war against the people for its own ends." He added that "every country which valued its freedom had a duty to hold out against the forces of fascism in all their forms."[45] Although Conor had broken the rules by talking directly about Spain when it had not been mentioned in the original motion, he carried the day in the sense that the national press picked up the story.[46] The Labour party, which had wished to gloss over the fact that in its heart it was at odds with the Catholic hierarchy on this issue, no longer could do so. Conor caught a tongue lashing from his aunt, Mary Kettle, for this, but Owen, recovering from tuberculosis in a continental sanitarium, was delighted when he learned of Conor's stand.[47]

That, though, was the end of Conor's Labour party politics. He was not chosen as a delegate for Trinity in subsequent years, and he turned his attention to other extracurricular activities. This brings up the question, how far and how sincerely leftist was Conor in his undergraduate years? The question is worth posing now, because it will have to be asked again, during his other seemingly radical period, the 1960s. As far as his undergraduate years are concerned, the picture is blurred. His friends of the period remember him as being terribly leftist and both Marxist and socialist. Yet, I think this was more impression than reality. In his commonplace book and in his student writings, there is little hint of political commitment. He read a bit of Marx and talked socialism, and was pleased to be known as a lefty, but when it counted, he was regular army: he took the exams, crammed for the prizes, and in his public writing was undergraduate-arch, not radical. Conor's socialism in his TCD days was like his father's nationalism in Francis's UCD days—a way of raising hell and grabbing the high moral ground at the same time. Conor's adolescent thrall to his cousin Owen was over by the spring of 1940. In May of that year, one finds Conor noting that he had once thought Owen right about everything. "I no longer feel this, but his manner continues to acerb, particularly his lecture room manner."[48]

Where Conor was able to meld his two dominant tendencies—iconoclastic verbal performances and respect for traditional academic forms—was in the Trinity College Historical Society. This—the equivalent of the L. & H. where his father had starred—was the direct descendant of the seven-member debating society that Edmund Burke had founded in his rooms in Trinity in April 1747. The "Hist" was open to any male undergraduate for a modest fee (all its members were male because in the 1930s women still were required to be out of college by 6:00 P.M.. The Hist had its own chambers and these served as a club room, library, and debating arena. In the 1930s, there were five debates in Michaelmas term and seven in each of the other two terms. Debates ranged from extremely serious world topics to satirical questions, and speeches ran from cheap bavardage to orotund nineteenth-century-type oratory to genuinely reflective argument. Conor made the *Irish Times* for a speech that he gave against Franco.[49] Like its counterpart at UCD, the Hist frequently had outside heavyweights take part.

The debates were only a part of the Hist. It also had a conversation area, where, by a large fire and a biggin of postprandial coffee, undergraduate politics, cricket club tactics, and local intrigues could be analyzed. It was a good place for the young gentlemen to play at being young gentlemen.[50] The Hist also sponsored several intellectual competitions and in these Conor did characteristically well, gaining honor and prizes that could be turned into cash. In his junior freshman year, 1936–37, he won the Hist book prize for composition, which is to say that he came third, behind the gold and silver medalists, not bad for a fresher.[51] The next year he won the silver (behind Vivian Mercier who took the gold) for composition and he was joint winner of the gold medal for oratory.[52] Despite his achievement in the Hist, he was not elected auditor. As he today explains, "I was regarded as arrogant." He adds, laughing, "I cannot imagine why!"

Conor did the straight intellectual act as well. He was in 1938–39 chair of the Dublin University Modern Language Society, which held general meetings and weekly teas on Tuesday afternoons. Since virtually the entire teaching staffs of the modern language departments were vice-presidents of the society, this bit of careerism can scarcely have hurt Conor's chances when it came to examinations.[53]

Not all was careerism, however. Conor learned to play lawn tennis tolerably well and was good at the gamesmanship. And, with drink taken, he played the wild boy equally well. In late April 1939, he attracted a town and gown crowd by climbing to the top of the roof of the Abbey Theatre. There, in a formidable alcoholic roar, he informed the crowd, "There is no bloody God." Then, ever the scholar, he cited his authority. "This is the voice of Trinity College!"[54]

As for Trinity's discipline of its students, the local mortal sins were damage to property or to young women, in that order. Everything else was largely a matter of taste. Conor recalls his own tutor, an overtly gay chap named John Norton Greene, telling him about his own experience with the college's counseling. Greene went to see the junior dean (the person at Trinity in overall charge of discipline of undergraduates, and a decided homophobe).

"I'm thinking of going to London, sir."

"Oh, excellent, Greene. Excellent!"

Greene continued. "Or perhaps to Shanghai, sir."

"Oh, even better, Greene!"

The only time that Conor crossed the junior dean was a very mild instance. In 1939, Conor and his "wife" received a stiff letter from the dean, noting that they had had a lady in their rooms without the permission of the lady registrar and that they were improperly dressed on this occasion (that is, in casual garb). Normally, the dean would have imposed a fine, but as they were Scholars, they were instead to attend nightly roll call for a week.[55]

• • •

T.C.D.: A College Miscellany, founded in 1895, was a combination student newspaper, literary magazine, and bulletin board, published every Thursday during term. Conor wrote for it and, eventually, in the autumn of 1939, became editor for a term. (Here again, the parallel with his father, who edited *St. Stephen's*, is striking.) Conor's editorship was no different than anyone else's, however; the template was set and he followed it.

What is of interest is the way Conor's contributions to *T.C.D.* relate to his development as a writer. Mostly, they show that he did well to abandon his first interest, poetry. In writing about Abraham Lincoln, one of the least recognized, but most important masters of nonfiction prose of the nineteenth century, Garry Wills has noted, "Lincoln, like most writers of great prose, began by writing bad poetry." Wills continued: "Economy of words, grip, precision come later."[56] That fits Conor perfectly. Conor probably would have taken up poetry in any case—he was studying modern languages and literature and he was in Ireland, where poets within living memory had had a pretty good run—but he was directly encouraged by Leslie Daiken, one of Owen Sheehy-Skeffington's circle. Jewish (his full name was Leslie Yodaiken, and he was known as "Yod" to his friends), Yod thought Conor's work excellent.[57] Further, Conor's roommate, Vivian Mercier, also aspired to write poetry, so there was a natural community of poetic interest.[58] The results were not wonderful. Conor in the mid-1980s referred to "absolutely awful poetry, which I blush to recall."[59]

For the most part the verse was facile, arch, and hypereducated. (Conor mostly wrote under the pseudonym "Donat," one of his string of middle names and one he later extended to "Donat O'Donnell" when, as an Irish civil servant, he could not write under his own name.) A good example of his undergraduate style was the start to a piece entitled "Said to Me Francis Winterbotham":

> The whiskered men who stand in Capel Street
>> Selling used tram tickets,
> Are driving bargains with Dravidian merchants
>> All the wet morning.[60]

Rather a sharper hit was "Sir Horace: A Ballad," which tore a strip off Horace Porter, an undergraduate a year ahead of Conor, known for his pomposity and for being head of the TCD branch of Fine Gael. This is one of its thirteen stanzas:

> The Constitution to expose
>> And Dev. himself defame
> In lucid lines of mordant prose
>> Was *Horace's* proud aim.[61]

That was good enough to result in a libel action being taken against *T.C.D.* It eventually was dropped, but among undergraduates it became a feather in Conor's cap.

With rare exceptions, Conor's more serious efforts from his undergraduate days should not be read on an empty stomach. Consider this, the centerpiece of a poetical triptych entitled "In County Wicklow, Now":

> But rags of the garment of Yeats
>> hang on every Wicklow bog
> And a crowd invented by Joyce
>> still drifts in Dublin fog.
>
> So an Irish acre yields
> More verse than English fields,
> And Genius, weed in England rare,
> Runs wild in Irish air!
>
> Our Dublin's small municipality
> Has far more literary quality
>> Than Manchester for all its masses,
> And *Eire* now can claim to be —
> Where Everyman's his own M.P. —
>> The Rotten Borough of Parnassus.[62]

Conor was serious enough about his poetry to record in his commonplace book, "Intense jealousy at hearing another person's poetry praised; fury at being advised to write light satiric verse."[63] This was in a period of deep intellectual self-involvement. The preceding entry in the same journal had speculated that Conor was experiencing "a degeneration of the intellectual tissue" through having to write the Trinity notes for the *Irish Times*.[64]

In fact, the suggestion that he limit himself to light verse was halfway right. The other half came when Leslie Daiken showed some of Conor's poetry to Sean O'Faolain, who, as editor of *The Bell*, was the most influential editor on the Irish literary scene. He told Conor to give up poetry. "He wrote me a letter which was like a kick in the teeth, best kick in the teeth I ever got. I needed to be told and he told me."[65]

Curiously, there was one area in which Conor could write poetry very well and this was in the French set forms. These are complex word games and require special linguistic facility, but no deep human experience. A bravura performance, a double dizaine, was titled "Poisson d'Avril" and "Poisson d'Autrui" (see Selection 1 in the Anthology). The first title, meaning April Fool, is a play on a story well-known to Irish readers; a piece of Somerville and Ross, concerning a salmon that goes astray while being carried on one of the Irish railway lines.[66]

Conor at this stage wrote good academic prose (and, as will be discussed in the next chapter, he soon moved from good to truly excellent), but when his writing touched real life, he had as yet no voice of his own. Certainly there were plenty of real-world problems to write about and in *T.C.D.* he had a ready platform. The European conflict that became World War II pinched in hard on his generation; fascism was a great and recognizable evil; what an Irish person should do in this situation deserved pondering and in print. The Irish situation was particularly ambiguous and worth reflection, because the Irish government under Eamon de Valera remained neutral. It put in place a set of state-of-emergency regulations which covered almost every area of daily life (from thence, the southern Ireland term for the era of World War II: "the Emergency"). At Trinity, "the majority of staff and students alike adopted the attitude of heart-felt and anxious, but somewhat impotent, sympathy with the allied cause."[67] In October 1939, less than two months after the full outbreak of war, Conor wrote a long unsigned editorial in *T.C.D.* which showed that he could not yet switch from playing word games to using words to shape attitudes and actions. It began:

> "*England with bare and bloody feet*
> *Climbs the steep road of wide Empire.*"
> Oscar Wilde, circa 1880.

God forbid that the climbing down be as painful as the steep ascent. May it come, when it does come, with as little blood as possible; may the new conquerors, when they come, be much more merciful than the old. May the transfer of power come easily and lead to better things.[68]

The opening gave no hint of what was to follow or indeed what the editorial actually was about. The next paragraph referred to the war and claimed that the people of Ireland "can take in more of the real world than can eyes in England or in Germany." Conor then argued that Germany, as a young and expanding country, was in the same stage England had been in the early days of its imperialist expansion. The British Empire would come to an end, war or not; no predictions were made concerning Germany. Conor ended on this note:

> Those who are not glad to be in neutral Ireland will, we hope, speedily depart to help whichever belligerent they favour. Most of us, however, are heartily glad to be outside, if only just outside, the tremendous futile catastrophe. We may be able, while reviving what is valuable in our own Gaelic culture, to retain those few good gifts of England which England herself, at least for a time, must lose. That scepticism, that spirit of fearless enquiry to which we have referred, has from the day of Swift been part of our intellectual heritage in Trinity College. May we keep it alive, when it is gone in Britain, before it comes in Germany; may we defend it bitterly against the forces that threaten it here and now in Ireland.[69]

Besides being a confusing argument, the editorial contained only one hit of the sort for which he later became famous. He suggested that many people on the English side would fight for democracy, free speech, and liberty of the individual, but might find that they "in reality fight and die for *The New Statesman and Nation.*"[70]

Perhaps the topic was just too big for an undergraduate, no matter how book-smart. Looking back at Trinity in the early war years, the woman who became Conor's first wife says, with sad wisdom: "It was doom-shaped; we all knew that."[71] The shape of the doom, however, varied, person by person, day by day. In late May 1940, Conor wrote in his commonplace book, "The Germans are in Bologne today. This is awkward as it will probably prevent me getting the Dirb edition of the works of Proust. I ordered them from Paris three weeks ago."[72] Such self-involvement metamorphosed into an admixture of self-pity and fear of *Weltuntergang* a few weeks later. "Surrender of France. Invasion of Ireland seems certain now. ... We can only wait until we become a battleground. Twenty-three years of training. I am now ready to take my place in a liberal democracy. Too late again." Then: "It's all up with England, it's all up with us, it's all up."[73]

With the world going to hell around him, Conor coped in his usual way: he swam into books and into hard work. He spent the summer of 1940 in a strict regimen of preparation for his moderatorship examination, which was scheduled to start on the first day of October. He did extremely well, gaining a first-class moderatorship (that is, a first-class B.A. with honors) in modern languages and literature (French and Irish). For this achievement he was also awarded a gold medal, good, as these things always were, for cash at a local jewelers.[74]

That academic success is why one finds Conor, on 11 December 1940, standing amid several rows of degree candidates in Trinity College's public theater as the commencement procession enters:

> We have the opening procession led by the Porter bearing the ancient Proctors' Book with its clasps of brass: after him follow the Masters, the Doctors, the Mace, the Senior Master Non-Regent, the Provost, and the Chancellor. The Chancellor bids the proceedings begin: "*Comitia fiant in nomine Dei.*" The Registrar reads the Latin minutes. The Proctors supplicate in Latin and the Chancellor asks the consent of the Senate to the degrees. "*Placetne vobis, domini doctores?*" "*Placetne vobis, domini magistri?*" The answer comes—"*Placet,*" and the Chancellor announces "*Placet omnibus.*"[75]

Thereafter, the candidates come forward and the various degrees are conferred upon them.

What this does not explain is why Conor, when he comes forward, is, save for a pair of shoes, naked beneath a raincoat which in turn is only in small part covered by his academic gown. The reason for this is chemistry, which, though he took two tries to pass on his Little-go, Conor worked on experimentally and experientially. He had been frightfully drunk the night before and had passed out in his old room in college. Vivian Mercier woke him at the last moment, took him downstairs and threw him into a shower. Conor then took his place at commencement in the only attire he could manage.[76]

• • •

If Conor was immensely productive one moment, badly troubled the next, it was nothing pathologic. He had both great talent and real-life problems. Not only did the war seriously narrow his world, cutting down employment opportunities and reducing the chance to travel abroad, especially to France, but he also was trying to work out his approach to some major human issues, not least those of sex and, potentially, family responsibilities.

Probably the most striking woman of the class that entered Trinity in 1936 was Christine Foster. A year and a half younger than Conor,

Christine was very bright and easily took her degree with honors. By early 1938, she and Conor were engaged, at least in their own way. Both of them were virgins and serious sex was a revelation. Sometime that year at a cottage they slept together. Conor, still moved by the wonder of the event two years later, wrote a personal poem in his commonplace book, entitled "Christine." Here is the third stanza (the entire poem is found in the Anthology, Selection 2):

> Then to the cottage come, serious as children.
> Chop the sullen wood, light an unwelcoming fire
> In the trough between efforts then, sat as men do
> On half-climbed mountain, silent and anxious.
> Next doors are shut against winds inquisitiveness
> And curtains drawn against mocking sleet
>
> Your body naked, beautiful in the curving firelight
> Given
> And taken.
>
>   Oh shout and stand you flames,
> Tall candles, triumph taut, ring of the frost,
> Joy, holy inexhaustible joy
> Tears like bells of Christmas, laughter
> Like winter blown from the skies, knife edge
> Of ecstasy poised and enduring,
> And the blankets thrown from the bed, and clothes
> Thrown to four corners, and standing
> Flame-roaring bare-bodies, twining to the ceiling.
> Earth spurned. Wind cowed.

Conor by mid-summer was deeply in love, or lust, or both. In his commonplace book, he wrote: "To hold a pen is unpleasant. To hold train tickets is unbearable. The scraping of unlubricated surfaces haunts me."[77]

Christine's background was something that Conor, surrounded by the ramparts of nationalist Dublin, had not previously encountered. She was a northern Protestant (turned agnostic) and she brought with her a set of cultural attitudes and social contacts that were new to him. Her mother's people were Lynds—northern liberal Protestant intellectuals. (Robert Lynd, the essayist, had been a close friend of Tom Kettle.) Annie Lynd, Christine's mother, was the daughter of a Belfast clergyman who had held one of Ulster's premier pulpits, the May Street

Church. He had been moderator of the Presbyterian General Assembly as well. He was one of the old Presbyterian liberals, most of whom had disappeared by 1912. His son (Robert Lynd) favored home rule, and Annie Lynd and three of her sisters (Christine's aunts) for a time belonged to the Gaelic League. They were, therefore, northern Protestants of a strange sort.[78]

Christine, though raised in Belfast, had been born in Derry, where her father Alec Foster (1890–1972) was a teacher at Foyle College. Alec Foster was a compelling figure, who swerved all over the Irish landscape, like the rugby international he had been, in the era of Bethel Solomons. He was capped for Ireland seventeen times between 1910 and 1921 and captained Ireland twice and later became president of the Ulster branch of the Irish Rugby Union. A Derry man at heart, he somehow avoided contracting the ghetto mentality of the Derry Protestants. He was at home anyplace in Ireland. After receiving a first-class honors degree at the Queen's University of Belfast, Alec Foster entered teaching, first as a classics master at Foyle College and then at the Royal Belfast Academical Institution. In 1923, at the quite young age of thirty-three, he was appointed head of the Belfast Royal Academy, a post he held until 1943.[79]

Not least among the qualities that made Alec Foster an unusual man was his recognition that if his daughter was going to fall in love with a slightly weedy, very bright, forever-skint Dubliner, he would be a fool to stand in the way. Thus, in the spring of 1939, Conor took a couple of months off from Trinity and assumed a post as a substitute teacher at the Belfast Royal Academy.[80] Conor, who could navigate easily through France, had never been in the North and, like most southerners, was surprised to learn that they speak a very different language there. Alec Foster was a virtual nationalist, but the BRA staff and pupils were almost entirely strongly unionist. Belfast Royal Academic was not the greatest school in Ulster—the students from "Inst" and "Methody" frequently did the homework of the BRA lads on the bus or train home, helping out the less gifted as it were—but the experience for Conor was a revelation, for he learned of another world: Irish, but very different than Dublin.[81]

In turn, Conor was a revelation to his students, many of whom had not dealt previously with a southern Catholic (for, in Ulster terms, that is what he was, whatever his theological nonbeliefs). He taught history for the most part, and some English and languages. Conor marched into the folklore of the school when, at his first teaching session, he silenced the class and then demanded, "Hands up, those of you who would die for your country."[82] It was a good way to get to serious issues quickly.

And it is an indication of how far Alec Foster was from the run-of-the-mill Belfast headmasters that he allowed Conor to deal with this, the most sensitive of Ulster issues, in a classroom. Conor at one point assigned his class of fourteen-year-olds an essay topic, namely, "Ireland." That was the entire question. One of his students wrote that he enjoyed living in Ireland because of the beautiful scenery. And, he added, "mebbe because I get satisfaction out of having an enemy in the South."[83]

If the North was something new to Conor, so was Alec Foster. This was the first time that Conor really came to know a fully formed adult male, other than his cousin Owen. The fact that older men have their own personalities, often strangely shaped, sometimes weird, sometimes funny, occasionally heroic, is something that a young man can learn only by experience. Alec and Conor took to each other, the older man abusing Conor in his dry Ulster way, Conor catching on quickly not to laugh at Alec's jokes; for, in the North, laughing indicates that you really *don't* understand the joke. "Would you have a match?" Foster would ask Conor, who did not smoke. "And you expect to marry my daughter," he would say, shaking his head at the extreme poverty of this jackeen. When he was on beam, Alec Foster was a man of enormous charm and intelligence, but when he was off, though he was still highly entertaining, he was a bit of a menace. The Belfast schoolboy gossip of the time (and not that solely of BRA, but of the other schools) was that Foster drank a lot, sometimes in the middle of the school day. Perhaps he did—he was a great frequenter of pubs and loved talking to strangers and getting involved if possible in a ballad session—but that was not his real problem. He was manic-depressive in an era before the chemical modulation of that disease was known. This made him frequently difficult. Conor and Christine went with him to France in 1939, before they were married, and he disappeared altogether. They finally found him in Tours. When they found him, he had organized the local street sweepers into two rival teams and was teaching them to play the game of rugby. His mood alterations, combined with his being a less-than-convinced Ulster unionist, kept him in hot water with his board of governors until he was induced to resign in 1943. Conor came to love his father-in-law, mood swings and all. (See his "Appreciation" of Foster in the Anthology, Selection 31.) They remained good friends until Alec's death in 1972.[84]

Conor and Christine were married on 20 September 1939 at the registry office in Dublin. They came back to Trinity to do their fourth year as married undergraduates, a rarity in those days. Having been married outside the Christian church (both of them were agnostics) gave them even greater chic. So, too, did the story, which they enjoyed telling, of their having satisfied the legal requirements that their banns be published in a newspaper by having it done in the *Irish Times* in the Irish language—a procedure usually employed when someone wanted to sneak a particularly outrageous planning variance through without their neighbors knowing it. The young Cruise O'Briens settled down at 92 Upper Leeson Street where they had a flat. There was a lot of tension between the couple and the owner of the house, an elderly spinster. They threw loud parties and made sport of her with the callow cruelty that undergraduates frequently find natural and later, in memory, find cringe-worthy.[85]

Yet, Conor was not the insensate coxcomb that he sometimes appeared in public. In October 1939, he wrote a lengthy editorial in the college paper arguing that women should be made full members of the college through removal of the rule prohibiting them in college after 6:00 each evening.[86]

In private, he had a lot more doubts, fears, and unsettling emotions than he previously had encountered. There is a break in his commonplace book, roughly six months long, for the second half of 1939; this spans the months just before and just after his marriage. When he takes up his pen again in mid-January 1940, he begins with a notable flatness, "I suppose it is necessary to note that I have become married since the last entry."[87] This emotional monotone is caused not by any dislike of marriage, nor by his falling out of love with Christine, but by something he cannot quite understand. "Since this [my marriage, I] have met myself so little, being most of the time dual, that I don't know what to say to myself anymore. I have for fourteen years talked more to myself than to anyone else, and now [am] stammering in my own presence." He concludes, "Is there any happiness except duality? ... A couple is permanent, more than any other group, more integrated on different levels."[88] That entry is very intellectual and very frightened. What Conor really wanted to do, I think, was to scream, "What, dear God, is going on with my life and my feelings?!" But he had been trained so long and so well to be rational, cool, repressed, that he could not do so.

As the year 1940 progressed, Conor studied hard for his moderatorship, while fighting through an emotional slough. He acted out some of his personal distress by being destructive. In May 1940, he and some friends went to the Phibsboro carnival and there tore down the hoardings "that disfigure the Grand Canal," lighted them and watched as two fire engines came to put out the blaze.[89] He also claimed that "disguised as a clerical student," he stole Jacques Maritain's *The Degrees of Knowledge* from a Catholic bookshop.[90]

Conor, writing for himself, launched into a self-pitying, but artificial and mannered threnody. "Old friends disappearing on their divergent courses," he noted, but instead of admitting the sadness that parting with old friends led to, he dramatized: "Friends seem to have grown gravely older, forcing me to a flippancy of aggression. ... Vivian could go to America tomorrow [Mercier had an American fiancée], Flann [Campbell, son of Joseph Campbell] could be drowned, Victor [Craig] mangled by machinery, Jack [unidentified] blown to pieces in London, without extracting from me more than conventional regret. ... These were my most intimate friends."[91]

In mid-July, swotting hard for his moderatorship, Conor was confused and tired: "Work for degree is idea like bombs and enclitic pronouns mixed up and whirling around." And then, in a brief, hard sentence, his fears crystallized and were faced. "Possibilities are closing down: a very narrow opening for a schoolmaster and his family."[92] He had seen one of his possible futures, and it terrified him.

In that fear, Conor was dealing with reality head-on. There were very few good positions for young graduates in southern Ireland at any time after independence and, during the Emergency, there were even fewer than usual. Conor's great hope was that he could gain entry to the Irish civil service and then be chosen for admission to the Department of External Affairs. After his moderatorship examinations, Conor felt he had done very well, and he was right: he earned a first. He therefore was confident when he took the civil service entrance examination. To his "intense surprise and consternation" he did not do well enough to be offered entry.[93] This was the first time in his life (except for compulsory science and mathematics examinations) that he had ever received second-line results and he defined his performance as failure. In fact, the issue is not so much that he failed as that other candidates did better. Still, it added up to a failure in the sense that he now had no immediate hope of being respectably employed.

Conor and Christine regrouped quickly. He could have gone into schoolmastering, but, instead, they decided that he would take the civil service examination again next autumn and would fill his time by improving his qualifications. They decided that he would take a second honors degree, a moderatorship in modern history.

This was a very courageous decision and a big gamble. In late fall of 1940, Christine was pregnant. That should not have come as a great surprise, but apparently it did. Becoming pregnant was what married people did in southern Ireland. The import and sale of contraceptive devices were illegal and information related to birth control was kept out of the country by the customs authorities, acting in concert with the censorship of publications board. Even relatively sophisticated young people, such as the Cruise O'Briens, did not know a great deal about family limitation. Basically, in southern Ireland, if a couple had sex very often, they had children; that was how Vatican roulette worked.

The combination of Conor's failing the civil service entrance exams and Christine's pregnancy threatened to doom the couple to the uncertainties of schoolkeeping. Almost all of the secondary schools in Ireland, north and south, were identifiably either Catholic or Protestant. Conor had no hope of being employed in any Catholic school, because of his religious opinions and his non-Catholic educational background; and, he had a wife who, though now an agnostic, bore the social label of Protestant. As for Protestant schools, in the North he had no hope of employment except perhaps in Alec Foster's school, for Conor was labeled as a southern nationalist and a Catholic. Only in a few elite Protestant schools in the south of Ireland had he any chance of a post, and such vacancies were scarce.

Conor and Christine's big gamble was possible in part because Christine was able to earn money by substitute teaching in Protestant schools until she became noticeably pregnant, and Conor still had his annual £25 Stewart Literary Scholarship, his remission of tuition through his Foundation Scholarship, plus his odd jobs. It was a tough year. The couple moved to a cheaper flat, a basement at 106 Pembroke Road. It was there they were living when their first child, Donal Bryan Cruise O'Brien, was born on 4 July 1941.

It would be an error to romanticize the bad patch Conor and Christine went through in 1940–41. The sense of having almost no future, the prospect of perpetual lower-middle-class shabbiness, the sense of limitless possibilities harshly dashed, creased their marriage permanently. They never really got over the bad times.

Conor's extra year at Trinity was very productive intellectually. He mastered the contents of the honors course in history within a single year, and he learned a whole new way of thinking. Previously, in the modern language curriculum, he had been taught two sorts of thought: paradigmatic patterns, based on grammar; and, when interpreting literature, tangential thinking, working from one allusion to another, moving in great sweeping curves. Now, the Modern History Department taught him the more prosaic, straight-ahead, fact-based way of working, and in so doing, provided him with a keel to balance his sail. This balance is what in later life made Conor such a devastating opponent. Unlike most persons interested in the everyday world—historians, political scientists, politicians—Conor knows how to read literature. And, unlike most litterateurs, he understands how to use fact-based logic.

Trinity's History Department at this time was on the rise. Walter A. Phillips had just retired. He was a moderately able scholar, an Englishman, who with some distaste came over to Trinity for lectures and examinations and then went home to the mainland.[94] Theodore W. Moody—destined to become the god-professor of Irish historical scholarship—had just been named a fellow of the college and his effect already was being felt. Conor at this point did not study with Moody, although later he did a Ph.D. under him.

The real key to Conor's historical education was R.B. McDowell, a young lecturer, already in the early 1940s on his way to becoming a legendary Dublin character. McDowell, sometimes said to be the cheapest man in Dublin, wore an old gabardine overcoat most of the year and rarely changed his clothes. An undergraduate rhyme went:

> That foul
> Row'll
> Be
> McDowell.[95]

When expounding an idea, McDowell's voice would frequently pop into another, higher, register. And when working in a library, he would twitch and emit squeaks at frequent, but devastatingly irregular intervals. One either became accustomed to him or stayed out of his path. Despite all his eccentricities, McDowell possessed a first-rate mind of the lint-collecting variety, and when he applied himself to eighteenth- and early nineteenth-century Irish and English history, he collected sufficient detritus to pound into enough fulled cloth to form several books. He was in his way a man of considerable kindness and his agreeing to take Conor through four years of an honors history degree in a single year was over and beyond the call of duty. Conor, in the beginning of his biography of Edmund Burke (1992), acknowledges that it was McDowell who taught him to read history and who also led him to Burke.[96]

They also became friends. Conor loved the skittering rapidity of McDowell's mind, the way it picked up seemingly disparate events and personalities and put them in a pattern. And he especially loved McDowell's sense of word play.

"Tell me, do you ever pray?" Conor once asked his teacher.

"Only on the defenceless," McDowell replied instantly.[97] And McDowell, like Conor, was willing to take on the heavies in defense of individual rights. When, in June 1940, an African student had been forced to leave the Hilary term "At Home" of the Dublin University

Boat Club, solely on the basis of race, McDowell, Conor, and seven others lodged a protest against this "amazing case of race prejudice and bad manners."[98] McDowell and Conor worked well together, and in the October 1941 moderatorship examinations, Conor took a first in modern history.

Would the gamble pay off? His year learning modern history was not merely a matter of marking time, waiting for the next year's entry exams for the civil service. The year also improved Conor's chances. Impressive as was his background in modern languages, questions on Provençal grammar or Catalan literature were not apt to crop up on an examination designed to determine top-grade entry for the entire Irish civil service. That year in modern history taught Conor the common vocabulary and working culture of the sort of person who ran the civil service (and hence, who constructed the exams). The TCD honors program in modern history was not designed to be exam-cramming for the civil service, but it had that beneficial side effect.

Conor took the examination in late autumn 1941 and this time he was well up on the list, placing third nationally.[99] Suddenly he, Christine, and infant Donal had a future.

CHAPTER 5

A REASONABLY CIVIL
SERVANT: 1942–1954

There were two plum departments in the Irish civil service: foreign affairs and finance. Conor wanted the former and was assigned to the latter. That may seem surprising, given that he was exceptionally well qualified for foreign affairs and hardly qualified at all for finance: he had almost no quantitative sense and his own financial affairs were perpetually out of control. However, the appointment makes sense within the context of Ireland at the time. The "Emergency"—World War II—forced a redefinition of the way the Irish government operated. The Department of Finance which had been run up to 1939 on the tight and narrow British model, was effectively changed into a ministry of economic planning. It came to have powers previously unknown within the Irish civil service. One of the results of this transformation was that the Department of Finance needed increased manpower, even as other departments shrank. Conor, therefore, being high on the list of new recruits to the management stream, was sent to finance which had first pick of new entrants.[1]

The Irish civil service did not have a staff-training program for its young management entrants. They were just plunked down at a desk and someone looked over their shoulders as they were given the simpler tasks to perform. Conor's first day on the job provides a good indication of what this could lead to. The one thing that he was taught on his first day was what was done with a file: "PA" was marked on it—"Put Away"—and it went back to the registry. He did that with a few items. About six months later it came to light that one of these was a document urgently required to be tabled before both houses of the Oireachtas, the

Irish legislature. Thus, eventually, Conor was called before the head of this section, a gruff Yorkshireman left over from the British days.

"Are these your initials, Mr. Cruise O'Brien?"

Indeed they were. The head of section listened to Conor's explanation with the kind of quiet understanding usually reserved for the seriously impaired, and finally said, "Well, old son, I wouldn't worry about it too much. It's a mistake *almost anybody* might have made."[2]

That "almost anybody" classified Conor permanently. He was not going anyplace in the Department of Finance and not just because of that little incident. He just was not cut out for finance. He was assigned to low-level jobs, such as checking law charges in contested cases and going over the expenses of expert witnesses.[3]

The one good thing about Conor's years in finance—aside from teaching him, as his former wife notes, to date his letters, something that had not occurred to him previously—was that he met his lifelong friend, Patrick Lynch. Lynch had entered the Department of Finance in 1941 and was immediately starred for rapid promotion. In many ways, Paddy Lynch has a position in Irish history in the second half of the twentieth century that parallels that of George Russell (AE) in the first half. That is, he is a person of considerable influence on the course of important events but who has left tracks on the historical record much fainter than his influence deserves. He rose quickly in finance and then became assistant secretary to the government which meant that he was one of the closest civil servants to successive taoiseachs. In 1952 he became a lecturer in economics at University College, Dublin, and chairman of the board of Aer Lingus. Later, in the 1960s and 1970s he served as an associate professor at UCD and held a large handful of significant directorships as well as seats on government commissions. Successive taoiseachs phoned him when they wanted honest advice. But he was no power-monger. Like his earlier counterpart, AE, he was that rare being, a constructive personality. And, as was the case with AE, it is hard to find anyone who has anything bad to say about him. Conversely, Paddy is genuinely appreciative of the virtues and abilities of others, rather than, as is the usual Irish mode, a curator of their vices. Conor went through his friends quickly, but Paddy Lynch was there for life.

It was probably Paddy who made the initial arrangements that led to Conor's translation from the Department of Finance to the one he wanted, external affairs. (One says probably, because Paddy has always insisted on doing his good deeds secretly.) Conor was called for an interview designed to check his suitability for external affairs. This event was in a style more appropriate for, say, Britain's MI5, than for the Irish diplomatic service. It was conducted in secret at the private house of Joseph Hone who, among his other talents, was the early biographer of William Butler Yeats.[4] At the interview was the assistant secretary of the department, Frederick ("Freddie") H. Boland. He was one of the two main power brokers in the department and he liked what he saw. Conor was in.

That the interview was conducted in a private house was neither accidental nor normal. At this time, the Department of External Affairs was a strange, semi-Ruritanian establishment. The taoiseach, Eamon de Valera, insisted on personally filling the post of minister for external affairs. Therefore, the real locus of power was outside the department. Within the department, from the late 1930s onward, there had been a rivalry between Freddie Boland and Joseph P. Walshe, his superior, the secretary of the department (that is, the administrative head). Walshe was hyper-Catholic—he had served thirteen years as a Jesuit novice before ill health forced him to give up—and he was strongly pro-Axis. Like many Irish ecclesiastics whom he admired (not least, the Catholic bishops), he approved of Mussolini. In fact, Il Duce was Walshe's great hero and he hoped to see Ireland join what he believed were its natural political and spiritual allies: Mussolini's Italy, Franco's Spain, and Salazar's Portugal. Boland, in contrast, was pro-Allies and was rather less enthusiastic about his religious beliefs.[5]

So, when Boland, as assistant secretary of the department, became intrigued by Paddy Lynch's idea of transferring the multilingual Cruise O'Brien to his department, he had to proceed very discreetly, lest Walshe veto Conor's appointment on the basis of his non-Catholic education and outright agnosticism. Fortunately, by 1944, the Nazis and their allies clearly were going to lose the war, and thus Walshe's star was on the wane. Boland now had de Valera's ear. Conor believes (and he is almost certainly correct) that Eamon de Valera personally approved the appointment. That is not as strange as it might appear: de Valera made foreign affairs, and hence the diplomatic service, his personal concern. Ireland, one must constantly emphasize, was a very small country and in those days the people in power were a small, interconnected, and often interrelated, group. And—here genealogy becomes very important—during his youth, growing up in Bruree, County Limerick, de Valera had been kindly treated and strongly influenced by the local parish priest, Father Eugene Sheehy. This was a debt he never forgot.[6]

So, as third secretary—the lowest level of the management grade— Conor moved to Iveagh House on St. Stephen's Green. This was a great labyrinth of a mansion, given to the state by the Guinness family. The upper stories were cut into small rooms and the third secretaries shared cramped quarters. As one moved up the ladder in external affairs—from third secretary to second and to first and then to counselor—one descended from the top floor and was given more and more office space. An office of one's own on the first floor meant one had arrived. Conor's first office was shared with three others. And there was not, in fact, a lot to do.[7]

The reason for this was, first, that all the important business was done by de Valera and his staff out of the taoiseach's office. And, second, the biggest responsibility of the Department of External Affairs in these years was merely to make excuses. This is a segment of Irish history that neither successive Irish governments nor the Irish public generally have faced squarely. The fact is that Ireland in the first four years of World War II was betting on both sides at once. The Irish government was neutral between the Axis and the Allied powers and, as the two figures who were the custodians of the Irish foreign service indicate—Joe Walshe, pro-fascist and Freddie Boland, pro-Allies—the country was positioned diplomatically to go either way, depending on who won the war. This was simple self-interest. Ireland was watching out for itself. De Valera, in 1957, stated that Ireland kept out of World War II because "the terms on which the war would be ended would not be the terms we would have wished for but the terms which would suit the interests of the large powers engaged in the war."[8]

This unbending self-interest is clearly shown in the government of Ireland's response to the Jewish refugee situation. The Irish were well informed of what was happening to Jews in Europe, especially from late 1938 onward. Yet its response was to permit virtually no Jewish immigration. Robert Briscoe, the only Jew in the Dail, may have smuggled Jews into Ireland, but that was definitely against governmental policy; Ireland maintained a neutral stance between the perpetrators of the Holocaust and its victims. The nation's Jewish policy, as first articulated in 1938, was to admit as refugees only "Christians with Jewish blood." Later, in 1939, when Jewish professionals tried to gain asylum in southern Ireland, the minister for justice, Paddy Ruttledge, pointed out that many of these Jews were medical doctors and that the Medical Registration Council would object strongly to an admission of foreign medical practitioners. As the war continued, the reality of the Holocaust became well known, but still there was no bending. Indeed, as late as 1946, the official line, as summarized by the Department of Justice was that "our practice has been to discourage any substantial increase in the Jewish population. They do not assimilate with our people but remain a sort of colony of a world-wide Jewish community. This makes them a potential irritant in the body politic and has led to disastrous results from time to time in other countries."[9]

Once the Axis powers were close to defeat, the question became how to explain why the Irish had sat out the war. Something had to be hawked around that would play in foreign capitals, especially the United States. Early in the war, the reason most often publicly broadcast for Ireland's remaining neutral was that part of the country—the Six Counties, Ulster, Northern Ireland—was being "occupied" by a foreign power, Great Britain. The Allied response to this was for Winston Churchill, in 1940, to send a secret emissary to de Valera with a proposal for reuniting Ireland. This was that Ireland would join the Allies in return for the United Kingdom's (1) formal declaration accepting the principle of a united Ireland and (2) convening the representatives of the northern and southern governments to work out the details. De Valera viewed the offer as unacceptable, because it committed southern Ireland to a given course, supporting the war against fascism, while the United Kingdom had only to give a promise of future action. Here de Valera was very shrewdly protecting Irish self-interest. The interesting point is that he did not show an enthusiasm for continuing discussion, a clear indication that partition was not a cause of neutrality, but an excuse.[10]

By 1944, when Conor joined the Department of External Affairs, the department's primary task was to push Eire's apologia around the world. The Allies were going to win, clearly, and Ireland did not wish to be penalized for its refusal to oppose the Nazi alliance, but also wanted to get in on the spoils of victory. Most likely, these would take the form of American aid to Europe.

In this effort at international apologetics, there was not much for a third secretary to do. Conor showed up every day in a blue suit and white shirt. He was careful not to wear any of his old school ties, for they were very wrong ones indeed. He pleased his superiors by moving files quickly and being willing to produce ideas that they could label as their own. He became, in fact, a good civil servant.

His informal assignment—self-assigned to be sure—was to keep his mates entertained and, if possible, keep everyone on the top floor of Iveagh House from being bored to death. In the service of that goal, his talent at mimicry—another gift from his father—was useful. He was very good at foreign and at female voices. In that era, Irish telephones were notably erratic and their voice-reproduction was wobbly, so voices were easy to disguise. Conor, from his upstairs office, once carried on a supposedly long-distance phone conversation with a cultural affairs officer, in which he pretended to be the wife of a newly appointed ambassador from a Latin American country. He went through a complex set of queries about the woman's importing her pet parrot. How could she do it? It could not be done, the cultural officer said, there were agricultural quarantine rules. Could there not be an exception, the lady ambassadress wanted to know? No. And so on, through several calls, until finally the lady announced that she was shipping her parrot to Ireland in the diplomatic pouch. Conor also did Soviet trade officials, Vatican outriders, and officials of the Knights of Columbanus to a T.

Several of his skits still are part of the folklore of the Irish diplomatic service. There was, for example, his trick, hardly original in inspiration but with a new twist, of sending a new recruit to the department over to de Valera's office; the new entrant was to take a Bible with him and ask for the taoiseach to swear him in. Rather more nasty, and therefore sweeter in its success, was one of Conor's moves in what turned out to be a long-term war of nerves with William Fay (nephew of the famous Fays of Abbey Theatre fame). Fay was senior to Conor and a bit of a snob. He had an office facing on St. Stephen's Green and from thence he, as a man of highly refined taste, had the frequent displeasure of hearing a band concert during the summer afternoon. He loathed it. Conor took to sending a small tip and a note to the band master, with the compliments of Mr. Fay, asking for particularly boisterous tunes.[11]

• • •

One could have been forgiven for believing that Iveagh House at that time was as much an artists' colony as the nerve center of Irish international diplomacy. Two very good English-language poets, Denis Devlin and Valentine Iremonger, were in residence, Iremonger full-time, Devlin between stints at the embassy in Washington, D.C. Maire MacEntee, already a well-respected Irish-language poet and destined to become one of the major Irish-language poets of the second half of the twentieth century (and not incidentally, also destined to be Conor's second wife) joined the service in 1947. Tommy Woods, one of Conor's office mates when he first was transferred to external affairs, wrote a weekly literary column as "Thersites" in the *Irish Times*. Not surprisingly, when a new recruit was introduced, one by one, to this recondite, but productive group of writers, he or she wondered, "Does anyone do any work around here?"[12]

Conor used his slack time and his evenings in the years 1942–48 to write, and in these years he passed from a clever undergraduate to a real writer. His first important sequence of publications was in *The Bell*, at that time still under the editorship of Sean O'Faolain, and far and away the most thoughtful and original of Irish periodicals.

Conor's entry was made via an idea that O'Faolain had proposed to Vivian Mercier, a series evaluating the most vital serial publications available to the Irish public. (Mercier at this point was married and had one son. He was teaching at Rosse College and he was also on the staff of the *Church of Ireland Gazette*—which for one disastrous issue he let Conor edit—and was also doing a Ph.D. thesis on Irish realistic fiction. In other words, Vivian was living the schoolmaster's life that Conor had so dreaded, cushioned in his case, however, by the resources of his American wife.) Mercier wrote about the *Irish Press* and about *The Bell* itself. [13]

Conor's major piece, written in 1944 and published in 1945, was on the *Irish Independent*, his father's paper (and destined, in the 1990s, to be the site of his own weekly column). He shrewdly analyzed the paper as being William Martin Murphy's parallel to Alfred Harmsworth's *Daily Mail*. But it was a *Daily Mail* with a difference. Whereas the English paper catered to an irreligious market, any Irish paper had to sell to the Catholic church as well as to the populace. "From the start, every care was taken to ensure that it would succeed the *Freeman's Journal* as the favourite daily of the Catholic clergy." Like the *Daily Mail*, the *Irish Independent* became the nonparty organ of the business interests of the country. In the 1930s, this meant that it saw communism rampant everywhere there were democratic or populist tendencies. "Spanish-type journalism has been a success," Conor concluded. "We have not seen the last of it." [14]

He did an equally succinct, and very reined-in review of the Catholic press. No witticism here; Conor seemed afraid to say what he really thought. [15] And he wrote a funny and ironically appreciative commentary on *Horizon*, Cyril Connolly's epicene London production. Conor analyzed *Horizon* as if he were an anthropologist. "The English, unlike most other European nations, have retained their old upper classes, a little tattered, but still in working order." The Brahmin class that produced *Horizon* was on its way out, as much because it was tired as because of challenges from new forces. *Horizon*, Conor suggested, was slated to die, "having collected for the admiration of posterity the folklore of a society soon to be, like our ancient Gaelic aristocracy, ploughed under." [16]

These essays were written under the pseudonym of "Donat O'Donnell" and until Conor left the Irish civil service in 1961, almost everything he wrote was under that *nom de guerre*.

There is a good deal to be said for someone who plans to become a writer to start as a critic. It is a lot easier to be the hurler on the ditch than a player on the field, and, starting out as a critic gave Conor confidence. The tone of these early articles in *The Bell* is strikingly different from that of the nonfiction Conor wrote as an undergraduate. Now he says what he means. He does not meander. He has already learned a trick that was to distinguish his best short essays written in later years—he goes out on a strong exit line. The too-clever tone of his undergraduate days is almost gone, not entirely, but almost.

What was left from his undergraduate days was a strange, not entirely admirable, tense relationship with Sean O'Faolain (1900–1991). If anyone had kept the faith in literature and in the life of the mind during the Dark Ages of modern Irish cultural life—the 1930s and 1940s—it was O'Faolain. He had fought southern Ireland's slide into a gombeen republic with three novels, several distinguished collections of short stories, biographies of pivotal Irish patriots (Daniel O'Connell, the Great O'Neill, Constance Markievicz, and Eamon de Valera); and in his editorship of *The Bell* (1940–46) he brought to the public an entire new generation of Irish poets, short story tellers, and nonfiction artists. He was a meticulous editor and incurably honest. It was O'Faolain who had read Conor's undergraduate poetry and told him to get into another line of writing. Conor heeded this advice, but he never entirely forgave O'Faolain for it. Though he publicly mouthed words of gratitude, they were ashes in the mouth of a young man as yet unused to harsh criticism.

It was a sign of the integrity of O'Faolain that he let the young Mercier write a critique of *The Bell* in that very periodical, and left him alone. Mercier did a nice job, relaxed, critical, anecdotal. It was appreciative of O'Faolain as an editor without being sycophantic. Mercier was good in describing O'Faolain's excessive tinkering with other people's prose. "He kept wanting to write the darn things."[17] Fair enough. Self-criticism is a good thing for a periodical to carry. But O'Faolain went beyond licensing self-criticism and crossed to virtual masochism when he allowed Conor, in the guise of "Donat O'Donnell" to add "A Rider to the Verdict" which was a deadly accurate four-page parody of *The Bell*. Conor began with what he claimed was a "trailer" for the next issue of *The Bell*.

Contents

THE STRATEGY OF INDIRECT APPROACH	*The Editor*
WHY I AM A TANAISTE	*Seán T. O'Ceallaigh*
THE ECONOMICS OF DOG-RACING	*George O'Brien*
CRUBEENS V. BOXTY: A SYMPOSIUM	
AN OLYMPIAN AT CROKE PARK	*W.B. Stanford*
COPPERSMITHS OF CO. CARLOW	*Hubert Butler*
THE SCIENTIFIC EMBALMING OF GAELIC	*Arland Ussher*
THE THEATRE ('A ROYAL DIVORCE' AT THE GATE)	*Michael Farrell*
POEMS FROM PORTARLINGTON (REVIEW)	*Geoffrey Taylor*

PUBLIC OPINION (A LETTER ON CENSORSHIP)   *Frank O'Connor*
THE FACE AT THE WINDOW   *Gulliver*

That harpooned just about everyone of importance in Irish nonfiction writing. After doing some mock book and theater reviews, Conor concluded with a devastating burlesque of O'Faolain's style as an editorial writer.

SPEECH FROM THE DOCK. BY THE EDITOR.

Let not my epitaph be written until Ireland shall be free-lance. Comrade Mercier has spoken wisely but too well of THE BELL. There must be more wrong with it than he says: if I know anything about its contributors and would-be contributors. If you turn to his review of Joyce's *Stephen Hero* on page 172 you will find out what, and why the editor has to work like a sub-editor. It is that most Irish free-lance journalists are as lazy as sin. If most of the boys here who have ambitions to write had to live by their writing they would starve in a week; all that Patience means to them is a card-game or Gilbert and Sullivan.

Here is an example from scores of experiences. I asked a young man who had lived in Sweden to write an article on the way the small farmer lives in Sweden. I engaged the generous interest of the Swedish Consulate, procured photographs, statistics, talked it over (they always want to "talk it over"), wrote letters, waited, phoned, waited, and finally the young man wrote in that he thought it would be nicer to do an article describing a train-journey from Stockholm to Lapland (or somewhere), and sent it along. Apologies all round for time wasted. Editor, not to be defeated, asks a young man who had been to Norway to describe how the small farmer in Norway lives. Letters, "talk it over," Norwegian consulate, letters, wait, phone calls, wait, and young man writes in to say that he thought it would be nicer to do an article on a train-journey from Oslo to Trondjeim (or somewhere), and sends it along. If this were London or New York I should get my article by writing one letter to a *professional*. Comrade Mercier implies that we do too much spoonfeeding and "tinkering" with our young authors. Believe me, it would take a bull-dozer to feed some of them, and I am quite certain that some poor sap of a papa feeds the majority of them.

What you get in THE BELL is the result of a stern application of high standards. Only the tops get in. All our labour consists of patient search for the latent professionalism in Irish free-lance journalism.[18]

With that, one would have thought that honor would have been satisfied. But in Conor's March 1946 article on *Horizon*, one finds this phrase which was not really relevant to his argument. *"The Bell ...* in its caution, its realism, its profound but ambivalent nationalism, its seizures of stodginess and its bad paper, it reflects the class who write it and read it—teachers, librarians, junior civil servants, the lettered section of the Irish petty bourgeoisie."[19] A few months later, Conor and O'Faolain got into a letter-writing contest in the *Sunday Independent* over a review Conor had written of a book entitled *Art on the American Horizon*. The substance of the debate is not significant, but note the vitriol:

> Mr. O'Faolain, when he puts on his preaching clothes, is indifferent to all qualifications, reservations, and shades of meaning. Last Sunday he wanted to denounce smug young Irish intellectuals for being superior about America, and I was "it." It suited his pugnacious purpose to pretend that I believed or had implied that all American literature, including Henry James, was "coarse," and that all American writers, including "James Faulkner" (whoever he may be) should try to achieve European standards of refinement. ...
>
> Mr. O'Faolain is clearly a busy man, but I should like to ask him to read the book I was reviewing and then to do me the honour of reading my review attentively and, if possible, calmly. He might then ask himself whether what I said was really equivalent to "training Liam O'Flaherty to write like Proust," as he suggests. And if he finds that his remarks were in this case irrelevant I hope he will in future be on his guard against his tendency to play mental skittles. He might also re-read certain wise words he wrote not long ago (in *The Bell*) about the "Dublin parlour-game" of controversy. He was then, he said, "too old a controversialist not to recognise the familiar touch of the practised propagandist working himself up into a mock passion." Can he recognise it only in others?[20]

Conor and O'Faolain had another waspish exchange in the same vein in *Envoy* over a review Conor did of O'Faolain's *The Irish*.[21] All this is a good trick for a young writer who wishes to become known: paint graffiti on a national monument. Still, one has to wonder how someone who had yet to write more than a handful of publishable articles and who had not yet published anything between hard covers could be so arrogant and aggressive toward an artist of genuine achievement.

Yet, Sean O'Faolain was central to the collection of essays that Conor was putting together which eventually became the book *Maria Cross*. His essay "The Parnellism of Sean O'Faolain" was first published in *Irish Writing* in 1948. Conor posited a neologism and went dizzy dancing around it. The word is "parnellism"—no capital letter—and it has no association with political Parnellism (despite its being capitalized in the published title, which the editors of *Irish Writing* got wrong). The word "parnellism," Conor decreed, describes the triple association "between the separate ideas of national, spiritual and sexual emancipation." This kind of inclusive parnellism is said to inhere to O'Faolain's best work (such as *Bird Alone* of 1936) but not, Conor suggested, to his recent work. The assertion that there was a connection between national, spiritual, and sexual emancipation in O'Faolain's early works was tendentious: what Conor saw as sexual emancipation could just as easily have been interpreted as sexual initiation, something quite different. And, merely because a book was banned in Ireland (as was the case with *Bird Alone*) does not mean that it is about, well, you know ... *that*. But where Conor, in his personal resentment of O'Faolain is furthest off base is in his treatment of O'Faolain's biography of Daniel O'Connell (*King of the Beggars*, 1938) and, of the last great Gaelic prince (*The Great O'Neill, a Biography of Hugh O'Neill, Earl of Tyrone*, 1942). These are splendid examples of a very rare genre, lyric history. They are romantic in the same way that a Mahler symphony is romantic: sweeping, programmatic, misty, with huge variations of timbre and tempi. They work, beautifully. But Conor belittled them, the way a Trinity history undergraduate would, analyzing them as heavily tinged with German romanticism, not a nice thing to be tinged with in 1948. He saw them as bearing "the mark of heavy mental stress." [22]

Conor never got O'Faolain right but, crucially, when there was no emotional interference on his receiving set, he could catch the wave length of various modern writers with an acuteness that was remarkable. [23] During the 1940s, he completed an interrelated series of essays on several modern Catholic writers: François Mauriac, Georges Bernanos, Paul Claudel, Léon Bloy, Charles Péguy, Evelyn Waugh, Graham Greene, as well as Sean O'Faolain. These were published in various literary magazines in the years between 1946 and 1951 (see the bibliography in the Anthology for exact details). They were then drawn together and published in 1952 under the title *Maria Cross: Imaginative Patterns in a Group of Modern Catholic Writers*. Reading these essays within the context of Conor's life, one has the sense of seeing the emergence of an imago. The creature is still new, like a young butterfly, but is now adult. His writing is now so very different from the undergraduate writer who wrote political editorials for *T.C.D.* that were mannered to the point of impenetrability. There is now none of the hothouse lad who sprinkled his commonplace book with self-pity and emotional cacophemisms. Man has replaced boy.

The critical method Conor used in reading his several authors has been described as "the method of neo-new criticism as influentially practised by Cleanth Brooks and F.R. Leavis," [24] but his writing is a lot less taut than that of the well-wrought Cleanth. He writes, in fact, in a form that is distinctly Trinity of the golden age of John Pentland Mahaffy and Oscar Wilde. (One thinks of Wilde's "Lecture on Art," which went down so well in America, as a classic example of the Trinity essay.) When he is at his best (as when he is talking about Mauriac), Conor is a mixture of erudition, allusion, elusiveness, and, above all, the leaven of wit and malice. This Trinity form should not be confused with the Oxbridge tutorial essay, even at its most sophisticated. Deadly sobriety is missing; engaged reading takes its place.

When drawing the essays together into a book, Conor tried to make the resulting volumes as un-Irish as possible. The title, *Maria Cross*, refers to one of Mauriac's heroines and the reference was not at all well known in English-language circles. As Conor wrote to an editor at Alfred A. Knopf, to whom he was pitching the book, "it has the advantage of being singularly evocative, even if not self-explanatory."[25] For a time, he and his editor considered as possible titles *Children of Maria Cross* and *The Pursuit of Maria Cross*, neither of which was any less obscure. Conor also toyed with the idea of leaving out the essay on Sean O'Faolain.[26] This would have resulted in there being no Irish content whatsoever.

Paradoxically, Conor is incapable of writing a book that is not about Ireland, at least in its subtext, no matter what it ostensibly is about. He has had in his adult intellectual life two interests, religion and nationalism. No matter on what part of the world he focuses his attention, Catholicism serves as his compass and Irish Catholicism as magnetic north. He does not believe in Irish Catholicism, but he was raised to think about it constantly. Similarly, when in later life he writes about nationalism in various countries, his reference point, from which all his assessments are calibrated, is Irish nationalism. So, yes, it is true that Conor took great pleasure in being European and writing about the French intellocrats of the first half of the twentieth century. (Mauriac in particular was in the front row in the early 1950s; he won the Nobel Prize for Literature in 1952.) And, as Seamus Heaney says, Conor enjoyed reading and writing about French intellectuals who would not, certainly, be published by the Talbot Press in Dublin. These people were regarded as bannable.[27] And, yes, from the beginning of his writing career, Conor was looking for bigger terms than those that the people around him used, but nevertheless one always hears the Irish voice beneath the assumed accent (French, in the case of *Maria Cross*).

Not that the fundamental question in the centerpiece of *Maria Cross*, that on Mauriac, is parochial. Mauriac's life and work raise the question of how a novelist, who is committed to Catholicism, should use his gifts.

If one is good at portraying evil, one runs the risk of conniving at it. This uncomfortable fact leads to the question, can Catholicity and artistic integrity coexist, if each one is the real thing?

Having raised this question in the Mauriac essay, Conor does not directly pursue it when discussing the other writers. Therefore, what the people he writes about have in common is not their varied reactions to a central problem, but rather, simply, that they are writers and they are Catholics and they are interesting to Conor. As he petulantly replied to a wry, but positive, review of the 1963 reprint of *Maria Cross,* "I did not say or anywhere imply that I regard these writers as the 'best' modern writers and I do not now so regard them. They were for me interesting and important."[28]

The conclusion to *Maria Cross* was the only part of the book that had not been published previously in article form. In it, one detects the hand of an editor issuing an assignment to a first-time author: draw it all together, son, or at least try. Conor posits in that conclusion that the writers he has studied have four things in common. They share a threefold sense of exile: they are in a world that is modern but they are not; they inhabit a society that is rational and they are committed to the supernatural; and they are exiled from childhood. In addition, they all carry the "female cross." "Woman is the cross," Bloy states, and Conor finds this to be one of the common keys to their writings. This concluding essay lets Conor off the hook, for it finishes the book, but it does not explain how a Catholic writer is different, say, from a Shi'ite, who arguably would have the same threefold sense of exile and the same problem with what is female.

What Conor had done, of course, was to write about eight writers who interested him. He published essays on each and then put them together. This is a method of composing a book that is risky, but this time Conor got away with it. The *Times Literary Supplement* gave it a front-page review and very favorable it was. The book was said to be written from a "detached Catholic standpoint," and was found to be convincing because the author "has no axe to grind."[29] In sharp contrast, a more recent (1984) critic, Tom Paulin, sees the book as Conor's best because it is a passionate one, the prose "lavish, ornate, agonized and often febrile." The book is said to be admirably "instinctive and intuitive" rather than dryly rational.[30] Apparently, the volume was a projective test. One paid one's money and was permitted to see one's own reflection. The book went into a second English paperback edition in 1963.[31]

Save for the tacked-on conclusion, the pieces in *Maria Cross* were completed by the middle of 1947.[32] Even given the slack time in the Department of External Affairs, it is clear that Conor worked hard on the book, putting in lots of nights reading French and English texts, drafting and reworking the essays. One does not produce a sharp book of literary criticism in two or three years, while holding down a job, without putting in some long hours. Yet, it was no hard slog, but more in the nature of an addiction, one that was to hold him in thrall for the rest of his life. Reading, thinking, writing was the habit and, like any addict, Conor had to feed the habit, in this case with time and with energy. That had its costs. As he laconically notes today, "It wasn't terribly good for my marriage."

How good Conor and Christine's marriage was in the mid-1940s is hard to say. There are few pieces of paper remaining that throw much light on things. Conor remembers things having become by the late 1940s quite tense; Christine recalls more the good life. What is clear is that despite Conor's post in the Department of External Affairs and Christine's substitute teaching, the couple was strapped for funds. In October 1943, for instance, they were turned down for a loan by the National Bank, Ltd., as the conclusion of the first of a seemingly infinite series of correspondence with bank managers that runs through Conor's life.[33] The couple stayed through the 1940s in the same flat they had rented while Conor was doing his second moderatorship: 106 Pembroke Road, Ballsbridge, which sounds better as an address than it really was. Besides teaching, Christine acted as unpaid agent for some of Conor's writings.[34] Two more children were born: Fedelma Anne Lynd Cruise O'Brien (26 April 1945) and Katherine Alexandra Cruise O'Brien (25 June 1948), sometimes called Kathleen and, as she grew older, increasingly known as Kate. The children were baptized as Catholics, despite neither of their parents being a believer. (Kate was taught by Christine that if she had to go to a hospital, she should say she was a Protestant;[35] given the theological limits on Catholic medical practice in Ireland at the time, that was merely prudential.) Christine remembers Conor as a good father in the manner of his class and time. "He wasn't madly interested," but he had that mixture of bemusement and distance that Irish middle-class fathers were expected to show. Mostly, though, he had other things on his mind.[36]

• • •

In 1948, things suddenly changed in the Department of External Affairs and for Conor it became an exciting place to work. Eamon de Valera, whose Fianna Fail party had been in power since 1932, called an election for February 1948. No party won a majority and, surprisingly, a coalition emerged that did not include Fianna Fail. This immediately affected the department, because for the first time in the better part of two decades there was to be a minister for external affairs. Things would no longer be run out of the anteroom of the taoiseach's office.

The man chosen (it was an all-male cabinet) was Sean MacBride, and that directly affected Conor. MacBride as minister of external affairs assumed his post with a deep distrust of the senior level of the diplomatic service—understandably, as they had been under the direction of his *bête noire*, Eamon de Valera, for many years. When MacBride came into office, Conor was a second secretary in the protocol and miscellaneous section. He was doing well enough, but protocol-and-misc. was a backwater. MacBride chose as his personal private secretary Valentine Iremonger, the poet, a friend of Conor's. So, when MacBride decided to begin a major initiative on Irish unity, it was natural that he take the most able members of an existing unit and turn them into his own set of storm troopers. This he did with protocol-and-misc. Through Iremonger's good offices, Conor was promoted. He was raised to the level of counselor, thus skipping the rank of first secretary altogether. In effect, he became the chief of propaganda for the Department of External Affairs as it affected the partition of Ireland issue, the biggest single concern of the department in the MacBride years. Suddenly, instead of being an obscure second secretary in the protocol department, he was in frequent contact with the minister for foreign affairs and traveled with him internationally. The slack days in the department were over. Now he worked long hours, frequently late into the night.[37]

Sean MacBride was one of the oddest, yet most compelling, characters to pass through Irish politics in the twentieth century. Anyone who is awarded both the Nobel Peace Prize and the Lenin Peace Prize was no minor character (and this holds even though the Lenin prizes were not always awarded with scrupulous disinterestedness: witness Leonid Brezhnev's conferring the Lenin Prize for Literature on his own memoirs). But as an Irish politician, MacBride was neither very Irish nor very political, and he certainly was not lovable. He was the son of John MacBride, martyr of 1916, and of Yeats's Maude Gonne. This was the same perpetually keening, black-swathed widow who passed through Conor's teenage years in the company of Hanna Sheehy-Skeffington. Maude Gonne had separated from John MacBride in 1905 (which makes her going about in widow's weeds from 1916 onward a bit rich) and she raised Sean (born in 1904) in Paris, speaking only French to him as a child to prevent any real communication between father and son on the few occasions when they met.[38] This left Sean MacBride with a strange French accent, quite unparalleled in Irish political life.

Maude Gonne MacBride and her son Sean returned to Ireland from Paris in 1918. Sean spent some time at Mount St. Benedict's, a

Benedictine boarding school near Gorey, County Wexford, run by a priest who was a keen Sinn Fein supporter.[39] Sean's real education, however, came in serious revolutionary circles. He joined the Irish Republican Army at sixteen and did well enough to be selected one of the bodyguards who accompanied Michael Collins when he went to London to negotiate the Anglo-Irish treaty in 1921. When the Irish revolutionary movement split in 1921–22, MacBride went with the antitreaty forces—the "republicans"—and served for a time as a secretary to Eamon de Valera and then as assistant to Ernie O'Malley, the director of organization for the forces that seized the Four Courts. Thus, the first sounds that Conor remembers hearing—the bombardment of the Four Courts in 1922—were shots pouring in on, among others, Sean MacBride.

Unlike Eamon de Valera, Sean MacBride remained violently antigovernment throughout the 1920s and most of the 1930s. He did not approve of de Valera's coming above ground and forming the Fianna Fail party. Instead, MacBride stayed with the "new IRA" (so named by historians to distinguish it from the "old IRA" which won Irish independence). MacBride rose in IRA ranks and in 1936–37 served a brief tour as chief of staff. There is no doubt that, post-1921, MacBride had blood on his hands, but exactly how much no one really knows. At a meeting in the Rathmines Town Hall in January 1948, Sean MacEntee, who had unusually good information on "republicans," listed twelve serious crimes of violence—murders and attempted murders—for which he said MacBride was responsible.[40]

In any event, in 1937 MacBride quit the IRA, became a barrister, and spent a good deal of his time defending his old IRA comrades, many of whom had been locked up by the de Valera government. In July 1946, MacBride founded Clann na Poblachta, "the party of the republic" which sought by political means to achieve what MacBride had been unable to achieve by violent ones. Its program was a mixture of what today would be called social democratic ideas (which, in the context of Ireland in the 1940s were radical social reforms) and the securing of an Irish republic, one that would incorporate the entire thirty-two counties.[41]

When three by-elections were called for late October 1947, Clann na Poblachta contested all three. MacBride campaigned with the ice-cold seriousness of the born zealot. Brian Inglis who, as a journalist, followed MacBride's campaign, described him thus: "MacBride was not impressive on the platform. His face, skull-like in its contours, split rather than relaxed by his rare smile, was a little intimidating; and the foreign inflection was not as attractive on the hustings as it could be in conversation."[42] (Conor's own description of MacBride is found in the Anthology, Selection 3.) MacBride nevertheless easily won a seat for County Dublin, and when de Valera called the general election of February 1948 he not only held his seat, but Clann na Poblachta took 10 seats out of 147 in the Dail. This number was not large, but MacBride was one of the brokers of the anti-Fianna Fail coalition that took office and he skillfully leveraged the position of his own party. Noel Browne received the health portfolio and MacBride himself took external affairs.

Conor and the other young *apparatchiks* in MacBride's new satrapy were expected to devote their lives to helping MacBride break the few remaining constitutional links between the United Kingdom and Ireland and to end partition—by which was meant the replacement of the British hegemony over Northern Ireland that was so hated by the Ulster minority, with an Eire hegemony that would be hated by the Ulster majority. The necessity that Ireland be not merely a geographical entity but a single constitutional unit was taken as a matter of faith and, like most fungi and dogmas, it grew best unexamined and in the dark.

For a time, a strong geopolitical logic helped MacBride in pursuit of his goals. The partition issue had an impetus that predated MacBride. From 1922 onward it was a domestic ritual to include a reference to the separated North in almost every political speech. More compellingly, and of more impact on foreign policy, was that Ireland, having remained neutral during World War II needed both a theodicy that would explain its neutrality and, further, would help it to collect some of the spoils of victory, which came in the form of U.S. aid for the rebuilding of Europe. Therefore partition was crucial. It played, especially in North America, with its influential Irish-American political lobby. Eire was given help under the U.S. Marshall Plan, not in the form of gift aid, but in very low cost loans.[43]

Moreover, after losing the general election of 1948, Eamon de Valera took off on a world tour during which he gave a series of fierce antipartition speeches. This effectively gave a license to MacBride to whale away hard on the partition theme. His coalition partners, especially Fine Gael (the heirs of the pro-treaty party), would have preferred for him to be less vigorous on the antipartition front, but with de Valera denouncing partition in Australia, the government at home had to be at least as vocal.

Then came the strangest part of the story, which certainly was a piece of good luck for MacBride and his young men. On 7 September 1948, John Aloysius Costello, taoiseach, made a startling announcement when on a visit to Ottawa, Canada, that Eire would become a republic. This caught everyone by surprise, although Costello's cabinet colleagues pretended that they had known all along about the idea and that this was a cabinet decision.[44] For the succeeding months, Irish foreign policy was made with the same thoughtfulness exhibited by a downhill skier racing before an avalanche. Quick it was: a bill declaring Ireland to be a republic was rushed through the Oireachtas and became law on 21 December 1948, and the republic was officially proclaimed 18 April 1949.

Immediately in the new year, Sean MacBride went to the United States. Just before leaving, southern Ireland was invited by the United States to join the North Atlantic Treaty Organization. MacBride replied by delivering a memorandum to each of the twelve-member governments of NATO declaring that the Irish government was in agreement with the general aims of NATO, but begging off on the grounds that until the problem of partition was solved, his country could not join. In America, MacBride spent several weeks in a twofold mendicancy: raising antipartition consciousness among the Irish-American Catholics and dealing with the White House and the U.S. Department of State on the matter of Irish neutrality. Always, partition was the reason for not taking sides.[45]

The final stages in this skein of geopolitical events were that Ireland formally left the British Commonwealth and that in June 1949, the U.K. Parliament passed an act that promised that Northern Ireland would not cease to be part of the United Kingdom without the consent of the Northern Ireland Parliament. This was probably the minimal response London could have given; anything less would have resulted in anti-Catholic violence in the North.[46] Thus, in the years 1948–49, Conor was part of a historical cascade of events. These had a high seriousness in Irish society, but for a young diplomat, they were also exciting and, therefore, enjoyable. Conor had the pleasure of surfing in good waves. In later life, he was, if not ashamed, at least not proud of his part in MacBride's antipartition campaign, but its seductiveness for an ambitious young man was great. And—this is crucial—Conor believed in it.

The antipartition drive kicked into high gear in late January 1949, when the leaders of all of the republic's political parties met at the Mansion House, Dublin. The "Mansion House All-Party Political Committee" was to collect donations against partition. This it did by agreeing on a collection on the steps of all Catholic churches after mass the next Sunday, 30 January. That fund was augmented by monies and seconded personnel from the Department of External Affairs and from various other government departments, especially the taoiseach's office. The collection of funds from Catholics as they left mass was a time-honored mode of raising money in Ireland—Daniel O'Connell had employed it with great effect—but, although a few attempts were made at collections outside of Protestant churches,[47] this was essentially a sectarian activity, and it is hard to think of anything more symbolically repugnant to the northern Protestant population: the "chapel-gate collection" solidified in the Protestant mind (and in the minds of many English left-leaning persons who otherwise would have supported the antipartition drive) the belief that an Irish republic was automatically a Catholic republic and there was no room in it for non-Catholics.

In September 1949, Conor's section began publishing a propaganda bulletin entitled *Eire*. Conor edited it and wrote some of the articles in the MacBride years. It was not a hate-sheet, but *Eire* made no bones about what the sources of the world's evils were: successive British governments and the northern Protestants (always referred to as "unionists," not as Protestants). The bulletin was a potpourri of miscellaneous facts about Ireland, cuttings from the world's newspapers, extracts from the speeches of Irish politicians, and so on. The tone ran from pedestrian to shrill, and occasionally witty. A few examples will give the range. An early issue noted that "the Town and Country Development Committee of the Six Counties [a code phrase for Northern Ireland, the sin that dare not tell its name] Council of Social Services has suggested that the Six Counties are 'in danger because of the over-concentration of industry around Belfast.'" This was easily explained. "It is, of course obvious to any intelligent observer of demographic phenomena that a lopsided development to the detriment of the countryside is inevitable in a small area such as the Six Counties in which a large industrial city such as Belfast is situated." The answer? "… real and satisfactory balance of Belfast and countryside (including the provincial towns) could only be effected in a united Ireland. The Six Counties are lopsided because they were made that way: an artificial area designed to suit British politics rather than any real Irish needs."[48] Another issue brought good news in an article entitled "Air Freight Record": "Aer Lingus reports that the quantity of freight carried by their planes last week was an all-time record for the company. Almost 110,000 kilos of all kinds of goods, principally newspapers, plum puddings and crayfish were transported."[49] The French daily *Figaro* was chastised for the alleged solecism of publishing a map of the United Kingdom in which different regions were colored in accordance with political tendency. Northern Ireland (called in this issue of *Eire* "the North East corner of Ireland") was color-coded by the French cartographer as being "region with an

Irish majority," thus implying to the reader that being Irish was not a national quality, but a political tendency."[50] And on and on and on. These propaganda bulletins went all over the world, to embassies, trade union leaders, Irish fraternal organizations, Catholic clergy, all in the hope of macerating away the border in a rhetorical spume.

The chapel-gate collection had raised about £46,000[51] and in the late 1940s that purchased a lot of newsprint. Under the aegis of the Mansion House Conference, several pamphlets and two books were produced. One volume was the virtually unreadable (and, one suspects, virtually unread) *Finances of Partition* by Dr. Labhras O'Nuallain, senior lecturer in economics at University College, Galway. It appeared in 1952. According to Fintan O'Toole, the second book financed by the Conference was Frank Gallagher's *The Indivisible Island: The History of the Partition of Ireland*. This did not appear until 1957. Unlike O'Nuallain's book, it was a readable mixture of historical assertion and political opinion. Gallagher had been the first editor of *The Irish Press*, founded in 1931 to present the Fianna Fail viewpoint. Neither his book nor O'Nuallain's gave any indication of its origin as a governmental propaganda exercise. Gallagher's book was influential in North America, being taken as an objective account. It was, therefore, successful propaganda.[52]

The Mansion House pamphlets were published without attribution under the imprint of the All Party Anti-Partition Conference. The first appeared late in 1949, largely the work of Frank Gallagher, who held the post of research director for the conference.[53] Entitled *Ireland's Right to Unity*, the sixteen-page pamphlet (one printer's signature, a shrewd cost-cutting device) was not at all sophisticated, but it was not supposed to be. The pamphlet was striking, however, in having several maps, lots of photography, frequent typographical highlights, and several different typefaces. Today, one would deride it as looking like something done by a first-time desk-top publisher, using every trick possible, but in its time this was innovative and visually arresting. The reader was left with a simple, unambiguous message: that Ireland had for 2,000 years been a nation; that the British had partitioned the country for their own benefit; that the northern Catholics were hard done by; and that the North's problems would be solved by the inclusion of Ulster in a united Ireland. Forty years later, reflecting on the effect of *Ireland's Right to Unity*, Conor noted that although the pamphlet "didn't advocate violence of course, but by its very nature it went a long way towards *legitimising* it; if Ireland does indeed have a right to unity, and if that right is wilfully and persistently denied by the British, the Irish people are entitled to attack the British, are they not, until that right is recognised?"[54]

In 1950, 340,000 copies were distributed in Great Britain, and 160,000 in the Republic of Ireland itself. And 75,000 copies were shipped north of the border.[55] Then, early in 1953, another 50,000 copies were sent north intended for unionist (that is, Protestant) families.[56] Conor himself went north to keep his eye on the scheme. It is one of the great lost opportunities in documentary film-making that no one thought to record the way these pamphlets must have warmed the hearths and minds of Ballymacarrett and Portadown.

Equally innovative was the initiative that Conor took from within the Department of External Affairs to purchase a pamphlet entitled *John Bull's Other Ireland*, published by the farish-left Tribune Group. The author was Geoffrey Bing, an Ulster Protestant turned militant British Labour party supporter (and a man whom Conor would later encounter in Ghana in the 1960s). In 1950, Conor purchased 25,000 copies of Bing's pamphlet and began distributing them. Then, in 1951, he negotiated the purchase of another 100,000 copies. After hard bargaining he was able to get the Tribune Group to give the Irish government a one-third discount on the retail price! (Even small booksellers got that.) So, 125,000 pamphlets went to Irish embassies and antipartition societies worldwide. They had no measurable impact. Conor was able to resist the temptation to purchase quantities of the next pamphlet of Bing's that the Tribune Group published: sixteen pages entitled *Set the Pubs Free: An Inquiry into the Monopoly Power of Brewers*.[57]

Undeniably, Conor had some creative ideas to further the antipartition campaign. For instance, he wrote to a Captain Jerome of the naval service, Department of Defence, "We have been considering what steps we can take of a nature which would be likely to enhance our prestige abroad and at the same time force attention on our [partition] problem. It has occurred to me that one possible means would be to send one or more of our naval vessels on a good will cruise to American ports." He had in mind impressing the inhabitants of Baltimore, New York, Boston, and Montreal and "perhaps intermediate ports," with "say, two of our corvettes or a cruiser." The only drawback Conor could see "would be on the ground of finance."[58]

Another remarkable idea of his was that the antipartition campaigners should print up 50,000 postcards "initially, and further printing according to demand." The front of the card would feature the map of partitioned Ireland that was on the front of *Ireland's Right to Unity* and an antipartition slogan. People would be encouraged by posters and radio broadcasts to buy this—"at a price fixed to increase the revenues of the anti-partition fund"—and send them to their friends in America.[59] This was too much even for Frank Gallagher. He saw the flaw at once. "Our difficulty is to see how such postcards could be put into circulation. A postcard is, as you know, a communication between friends." Gallagher then explained something about your average Irish family. "In Ireland, if people write to their relations at all, they usually do not do so on postcards. Only the political-minded would do such a thing as send a postcard on partition and the numbers of these are very difficult to estimate." His committee's conclusion was that "if 5,000 people would send out such a postcard, it would be a miracle. Therefore, your suggestion of printing 50,000 would, I am afraid, leave you with several tens of thousands on your hands."[60]

In 1950, Conor published an article in French under his pseudonym "Donat O'Donnell" in the *Revue Général Belge* arguing the case for Irish unity.[61] In roughly this same period, he wrote what has become the Lost Book of O'Brien. This arose out of Sean MacBride's courting of the Irish-Americans, whom he saw as one of the levers for removing partition. Presumably the Americans would pressure the British to cut their ties with Northern Ireland. One of the Irish-Americans whose cooperation MacBride craved was Ed Flynn, boss of the Bronx and one of the most corrupt politicians in America. At MacBride's request, Conor ghost-wrote a history of Ireland. The idea was that it would be published under Flynn's name, and that, in turn, Flynn would do some useful arranging for the antipartition cause. The book was completed, but never published, and were it never to be found, Conor would not be displeased.[62]

One of Conor's responsibilities was to help and to keep track of antipartition societies worldwide, especially those in the United States. His activities ranged from trying to put together an all-party delegation to visit the States "for a long and widespread anti-partition rally,"[63] to encourage members of the U.S. Congress who were of Irish descent to support the position of the government of southern Ireland on partition,[64] to assaying the use of Robert Briscoe, Fianna Fail TD and the only Jew in the Dail, in mobilizing American Jewish opinion. This was of special interest to Conor: "We have, I think, never been sufficiently active in enlisting Jewish support."[65] And, inevitably, he was engaged in damage control, such as keeping everyone clear of the illegal Sweeps ticket sales conducted in the United States in aid of the Irish Republican Army.[66] In 1952 there arose the necessity of dealing with the proposal of vice-president-elect Richard Nixon, that the United States apply economic pressure on Great Britain to bring about Irish unification. Cooperating with the Republican and Protestant Nixon would have wrong-footed all the Catholic and Democratic Irish-American politicians who were the main base of the antipartition movement in the United States. Besides, being endorsed by Richard Nixon was not something either Conor or the Irish government wanted on their conscience.[67]

Where Conor showed the most sinister dexterity and, on the other hand, the most dextrous sincerity, was in the establishment and management of the Irish News Agency (INA). This was supposed to be an international news service that delivered the Irish viewpoint around the world, especially on the partition issue. A bill to create the agency was introduced in July 1949 by Sean MacBride—who had spent time as a journalist before he became a lawyer and who thought he knew how to manipulate the foreign press. Although de Valera in 1945 had mooted the idea of setting up such an agency, it was a different issue when the idea was brought forward by the coalition government and, worse, by MacBride.[68] As John Healy put it, "Mr. de Valera's Fianna Fail party opposed the legislation creating the Irish News Agency. The mood was such that the party would have opposed the Ten Commandments had they been introduced by a coalitionist Moses."[69] The INA was later to be called a red front by Fianna Fail politicians, for MacBride was perceived as being far to the left politically. The person who most detested MacBride and all things associated with him was Sean MacEntee, one of the two Irish politicians since independence to have a tongue as corrosive as that of Timothy Healy.[70] MacEntee "detested MacBride with a peculiar intensity."[71] This is worth noting here, because after Conor's divorce and remarriage, Sean MacEntee became Conor's father-in-law.

MacBride intended that the Irish News Agency be run by Noel Hartnett, a Clann na Poblachta operative. Hartnett was a Pickwickian figure, small (under five feet), round, pink-faced. "He himself frequently but tenderly ridiculed the unquestionable ugliness of his face. Its most notable features were his two small menacing flinty blue eyes, and his disproportionately large nose, which gave him a rich mellifluous speaking voice. In repose his mouth went straight across his face, like two razor blades."[72] The day before the establishment of the INA and the announcement that Hartnett would be managing director, MacBride and Hartnett had a blazing row and as a result Hartnett told MacBride to stuff his job. This left MacBride with a news conference in the offing and a big seat at the table empty. He called Conor and asked him to assume the post of managing director. Conor was to continue to keep his office in Iveagh House and do all the antipartition jobs he already was engaged in.[73]

The INA was a set of mirages and paradoxes. The most basic of these was the belief, sustained publicly, but impossible to maintain in private, that it was not a propaganda agency. Rather, the legend went, it was an international news agency, whose primary goal was to balance the incorrect report of the news about southern Ireland, and incorrect interpretations of the partition issue. In theory, the INA was not to sell domestic news within Ireland. Given that the agency's public ideology and its covert purpose were so at odds with each other, it is not surprising that the operation turned into a burlesque of a real news agency.

But—and this is a signal paradox—despite its convoluted character, the INA had associated with it some of the brightest and most able persons of their era. Take, for example, Conor's fellow directors. These were Peadar O'Curry, editor of the *Catholic Standard* and, even though he seemed to be constantly doing a Bogart impersonation, actually one of the toughest journalists in Ireland; Noel Hartnett, barrister, who had got over his pique with MacBride sufficiently to take a place on the board; Robert Brennan, just back from Washington, D.C., where he had been the Irish ambassador; and Roger Green, who served as chairman of the board. He was a solicitor and successful businessman, who had a boldness in the private sector that matched Conor's buccaneering approach to the diplomatic world.[74]

The INA worked from Domas House, 76/77 Grafton Street. Conor phoned the house once or twice a day to see how things were going, but visited it only two or three times a week. The day-to-day operations were in the hands of a very sharp set of journalists, some of whom already were newspaper legends, others who were destined to become major figures in the next quarter-century. The first editorial chief was Joseph P. Gallagher, a Fleet Street veteran of great experience and little tact. The news editor was O'Dowd Gallagher, formerly a Fleet Street foreign correspondent of almost mythic stature. He was said to be the original of Corker in Evelyn Waugh's *Scoop*.[75] It was he who taught the INA's younger correspondents the elements of a truly first-class, page-one story—"Crime, Cash, Cunt, and Cookery"—get them all into one story and you were a success.[76] That this was rather difficult when the preferred topic of the day, and of every day, was the evils of partition, was not an impediment he dwelled upon. In the early days a lead reporter was Jack Smyth, a Galway man who had been a correspondent in Japan and Berlin, and he taught the INA youngsters the other lesson of modern journalism: "Kid, tell them you're going to tell them; tell them; tell them you told them."[77] Early on, the INA picked up Brian Inglis, destined later to become one of the most influential commentators on society and social history in the British Isles. Douglas Gageby, then fresh from service as assistant editor of the *Sunday Press*, became editorial chief of the INA in November 1951, leaving it in 1954 to edit the new *Evening Press*.[78] Also on staff were John Healy and Donal Foley, pros who became the most-read newspaper commentators on Irish political and social life in the 1960s and '70s.[79]

It was an all-star cast, putting on a pantomime. In reality, the INA did not have the technology to be part of the international news game. It had one teleprinter which connected Dublin and London and that was all. Every piece of copy transmitted to London had to be transcribed by a typist, stenciled, corrected, and then taken around by courier to every English paper that might run the story. "We were just marginally faster than Reuter's original pigeon-post, one hundred years before," one participant recalls. But politically dictated restrictions were an even greater limitation. Because the INA had the reputation of being a propaganda agency, foreign newspapers, except the Irish-American press, were reluctant to buy copy. Making sales in Great Britain was especially difficult because the National Union of Journalists was against the INA. That was because virtually every heavyweight Irish correspondent for the British papers was picking up the odd fiver following Dail Eireann stories and did not want the INA cutting in on their action.[80] To make up for this crippling of their sending Irish news to Britain, the agency took to selling Irish stories inside the republic, but by a circuitous route. Because Northern Ireland was (for journalistic purposes) a foreign jurisdiction, being occupied as it were by the British, the INA was permitted to sell inside of southern Ireland stories that originated in Belfast, Derry, or elsewhere in the North. The trick developed of finding an interesting story that had occurred in the Irish Republic, having it datelined Belfast and ascribing it to the INA's northern editor, Paddy Scott. Then it could be sold to the southern newspapers as news from foreign parts. It took a while before the southern newspapers were able to put a stop to this.[81]

Occasionally, the INA was able to sell some real news from abroad to Irish newspapers, as when Irish politicians attended overseas conferences. However, the agency never came close to paying its own way from news gathering. The agency was set up with £5,000 from the government, and it never had a chance of breaking even, much less paying back this original subvention.[82]

The INA was a propaganda agency, of that there is no doubt. Its purpose was to "brandish the sore thumb" of partition whenever possible. In the autumn of 1993, Garret FitzGerald, former taoiseach of Ireland and a longtime friend and rival of Conor, wrote tartly in the *Irish Times* that

> since childhood I have consistently and unremittingly rejected the thesis that Northern Ireland should be reunited with the Irish State without the consent of its people.
> My friend Conor will, indeed, recall that when, some forty years ago, he

as a civil servant was playing a major role in the official Irish News Agency as it spewed out sterile anti-partition propaganda favouring reunification without such consent, I was countering his propaganda by arguing the contrary thesis in newspapers in Britain, New Zealand, Canada, India, Australia, South and East Africa and Hong Kong, among other places.[83]

Making due allowance for the way that memory often heightens contrast, FitzGerald is right.

• • •

As a counterflow, almost as an unconscious antidote to his careerist involvement in the antipartition business, Conor engaged in a reflective, dispassionate, almost judicial exercise in Irish history. He began a Ph.D. thesis on the man who was the fulcrum of modern Irish politics, Charles Stewart Parnell. The idea of Conor's doing a doctorate in history was Professor Theodore Moody's. He was, in the words of Patrick O'Farrell, the "god-professor" of Irish history.[84] He was a massively Teutonic figure, completely out of place in Dublin, yet totally in control of a history-molding machine at Trinity. He was forever reaching for more influence, more power, and, above all, more order. Moody came to Trinity College, Dublin, in the late 1930s by way of a Belfast working-class background, the Royal Belfast Academical Institution, the Queen's University of Belfast, and the Institute of Historical Research, London. He taught briefly at Queen's, Belfast, before being elected to a fellowship at TCD in 1939 and to a professorship a few months later. Following the completion of his doctorate in 1934 (published in 1939), Moody did some original work—he co-authored a fine history of the Queen's University of Belfast, and wrote a biography of Michael Davitt. His power, however, far outstripped his productivity. This was because he introduced into Irish scholarship the academic equivalent of the Belfast factory system. He understood how to make many hands weave his cloth. He either initiated or controlled virtually every successful collective project done by Irish historians from World War II onward. He was the moving spirit behind the Irish Committee of Historical Sciences, founded in 1939; he was the founding father and longtime joint editor of *Irish Historical Studies*; he launched in 1948 and edited the important monograph series *Studies in Irish History*; and he was the founding force behind the monumental *A New History of Ireland* which, after his death is being published by the Clarendon Press for the Royal Irish Academy in roughly a dozen projected volumes.[85]

Theo Moody had a massive, leonine head and, in person, a frequently intimidating manner. He ran the Department of Modern

History at Trinity like a battalion of the Prussian Army. However, like the Wizard of Oz, Theo occasionally was a bully, and like all bullies, had a cowardly streak. "Theo could be very timid," Conor recalls. "Also, he was afraid of Micks, and I was a Mick to him! A promising Mick, but one nonetheless!"[86] That is not as strange as it may seem on the surface. To be a northern Protestant in postwar Dublin was to be a perpetual sojourner in a land of often alien and sometimes fearsome beings. Theo either had to bellow at them or run from them: there was no middle way.

If the Ph.D. was Theo Moody's idea, the topic was all Conor's: the political machine of Charles Stewart Parnell. Anyone with an interest in the modern Irish state needed to deal with Parnell, certainly, but Conor's interest was more direct. His grandfather had been in Committee Room 15 and had walked out, rather than support the adulterer. As early as the autumn of 1945, Conor had written about Parnell in *The Bell*. On that occasion he had focused on the Parnell monument at the northern end of O'Connell Street, one of the two places (the other was Glasnevin Cemetery) where, each sixth of October, the Parnellite old guard laid its annual wreath of ivy. "With each Ivy Day that passes, the reality that the few survivors knew grows more blurred," Conor observed, "while the myth represented by the monument becomes distinct and rigid. The elements that have gone to make up that myth are past counting. There is, first, Parnell's real greatness and the manner of it, with the residue of folklore that greatness leaves in the mind of a people. Then there is the natural tendency of teachers, writers, and even parents, to simplify history by a lavish application of the *Fuhrerprinzip*."[87]

That was a strange word, usable only in the immediate postwar period. In his opposition to the *Fuhrerprinzip* as a mode of analyzing Parnell's achievement, Conor here charted out the central argument of his Ph.D. thesis, several years before he even began it. "The Fuhrer school of thought leaves the real achievement of its hero in obscurity. This is because that achievement did not belong to 'the Chief' alone or primarily but was the result of a policy framed by other men, and partly executed by them with his aid."[88] This is just the opposite viewpoint of the Nietzschean or Carlylean view of history. Conor stayed with his main contention and, when his thesis eventually was published as a book, John Kelleher remarked that it was a valuable piece of work, but misnamed. "It ought to have been called 'Parnell's Party.'"[89]

This viewpoint of Conor's, formed before the thesis was begun, was not challenged by Theo Moody. As a preparation for the research project, Theo took Conor out and sat with him on a bench in college park. There he talked, for no more than twenty minutes, about the evaluation of historical sources. Very short, very compressed, but in its economy and in its teaching of fine distinctions as between various sorts of historical sources, it was marvelous teaching. It was all Conor needed.[90] Now, in 1952–54, instead of spending long nights writing antipartition literature, he spent them at Trinity and at the National Library in historical research. Sometimes Christine helped, but there were children at home. Conor and Christine were going their separate ways and the thesis was a benign way of increasing their distance one from the other.

The thesis was accepted near the end of the year 1954, but that is rather like saying St. Brendan had a successful voyage to North America: the trip was a bit more eventful than that. Once again, Conor was caught in an academic war that was not of his own making, this time between Moody and one of his two rivals at University College, Dublin. The basic situation is well explained by Patrick O'Farrell:

> [Theo Moody] was a good man, a Quaker, kind, high principled, meticulous, and very industrious, constantly enraged by what he saw as the lazy irresponsibility and devious clowning of his UCD counterparts, Dudley Edwards and Desmond Williams, who were, in different ways, the kind of eccentrics whose antics Theo found very unamusing. Indeed part of their outrageous and obstructive behaviour was deliberately aimed at Theo, cast by them as a pompous paragon of rectitude, sobriety and good sense—in which I think they detected not only Trinity side, but repellent Belfast Protestant work ethic origins.[91]

In some ways, Theo Moody was an innocent. He could not believe that anyone would play games with something so serious as a Ph.D. thesis, and he naively chose Robin Dudley Edwards as the external examiner. Moody and Edwards were joint editors of *Irish Historical Studies* at the time, but what Moody did not know was that Edwards was in personal turmoil. A fine, creative mind, Edwards had a serious writer's block and was trying to cure himself of his inability to write by using a "work diary" as therapy.[92] Moreover, he and Desmond Williams were in the midst of a great mess: they had taken over control of a collective work on the Great Famine, which, after more than a decade of effort of the sort epitomized by the West Clare Railway, still was far from being right.

So, it seems that the combination of personal frustration, when combined with a general dislike of Theo Moody, led Edwards to toy with Conor's thesis. The details, like those of most academic fights, are not worth parsing. The one substantive criticism Edwards presented was that Conor should have made better use of the Gladstone papers in the then-British Museum; that is a solid point. The rest of his criticisms, though, were frivolous, and Theo Moody responded with a mixture of helplessness and rage. When the dust had settled, Edwards (like Walter Starkie in Conor's undergraduate days) had backed away, having tormented his rival quite successfully. Theo wrote to Conor a confidential memorandum when the thesis finally was approved. It said: "If Edwards tries to postpone publication [of the thesis in book form] by the methods by which he has delayed the award of your doctorate, I am prepared to resist by all possible means. On your part there is no longer any need to submit to any of his demands."[93]

Theo Moody was not being overly sensitive; Edwards had been way off base. Dan Davin, the New Zealand novelist and an editor at Oxford University Press, came through Dublin on a talent-scouting tour. He read the thesis and with almost no revisions the manuscript was published in 1957.[94] *Parnell and His Party, 1880–90* was immediately recognized as a major piece of scholarship. Writing in the late 1980s, Roy Foster judged it to be "the classic analysis of Parnell's system and ethos."[95] The book has lasted so long and been so influential not only because of its quality as a sustained piece of historical argument, but for two additional reasons. Conor was, as D. George Boyce notes, the first of the postwar generation of Irish historians—the first generation to be trained up to the level of documentation and argument prevailing in European and American historical scholarship—to turn attention to Parnell. Thus, Conor's volume was there at the start of a historiographic era. Second, Conor's book made sense of a set of happenings that had both puzzled and saddened Irish contemporaries of Parnell and later observers as well. In Conor's analysis, which is essentially structural rather than chronological in its logic, what happened in Committee Room 15 was no surprise. Given that the Irish parliamentary party had made an alliance with Gladstone and the English liberals, the decision to jettison someone who threatened that fundamental alliance was both logical and predictable.[96]

While writing his Ph.D. thesis, Conor perfected one of the tactics that has made him such a frightening controversialist; it is what one critic calls his "disconcerting attention to factual detail."[97] Some of this was derived from T.W. Moody who, like many scholars in the British Isles in his generation, was awed by the work of Sir Lewis Namier, author of *The Structure of Politics at the Accession of George III* (1929). Conor dutifully went through a sequence of Namierite procedures, such as tabulating the educational profiles and economic backgrounds of all of the home rule members of Parliament. Indeed, his loathing of Sir Lewis's methods stems from this era—for he agrees with A.J.P. Taylor that

Namier "took the mind out of history"[98]—but nevertheless he learned how to do the historical equivalent of pointillist painting.

In his own intellectual development, the Parnell study was analogous to his moderatorship in modern history. That is, as an undergraduate he first mastered modern languages and then did history; as a mature, but still relatively young adult, he first produced a fine book of literary criticisms, *Maria Cross*, and then crossed over into historical scholarship and wrote what was to become one of the standard volumes of modern Irish historical writing.

Books are not written in a social vacuum, and certainly not books by Conor Cruise O'Brien. *Parnell and His Party*, though written in Conor's evenings and weekends, was related to Conor's work as a government of Ireland propaganda merchant. On one level, the relationship was one of antithesis. Slowly working through the private papers of Members of Parliament, reconstructing their economic and social profiles, and discovering the physics of the Irish parliamentary party was an antidote to the speciousness, paralogic, and special pleading which were inevitably involved in earning a daily living.

Yet, Conor's work as professional propagandist was not entirely divorced from his practice as an Irish historian. As we have seen, the conclusion that Conor presented in his work on Parnell in the mid-1950s was that which he had declared in *The Bell* in 1945, long before he had done any research. That is exactly how the writing of propaganda works: the conclusions come first and the facts follow. Conor got away with this in his Parnell study, because his intuitive perception—that the mechanics of Parnell's party had been obscured by the melodrama engendered by Parnell's personality—was borne out by the facts (and this has been thoroughly confirmed by later scholars). Still, starting with one's conclusion is very risky.

And, in his historical work in the mid-1950s, Conor was not yet able to deal as dispassionately with the Ulster question as he believed he did. This is hardly surprising, considering that he was being paid at his day job to harry Northern Ireland out of existence. As a historian in the 1950s, he underestimated as a historical phenomenon the intransigence of Ulster's opposition to all forms of home rule. He believed that if Gladstone and Parnell had held strongly together, they could have forced home rule down the throats of the northern Protestants. Later, in 1981, Conor published a graceful palinode, withdrawing this opinion (see the Anthology, Selection 38).

• • •

On the surface, the years 1951–54 were good ones. *Maria Cross* received positive reviews and Conor was asked to write for *Commonweal* in America and to review for the *Spectator* in England, and all the while, his Ph.D. research and writing proceeded apace. But times were, in fact, turning sour.

Most important, Conor and Christine's marriage was disintegrating, not so much crashing as it was rusting out. Every day another tiny perforation appeared and it was only a matter of time before the whole piece of social machinery fell apart.

The family's living standards improved as a result of Conor's jump to counselor rank. In 1950, Conor purchased for £2,000 a former tea house on Howth Summit named "Bayview"; it was soon renamed "Whitewater" and renovated.[99] The residence possesses an extraordinary view—it actually looks down on Baily lighthouse, Howth, and thence commands all of Dublin Bay—and it was a splendid spot to raise children. Large chunks of the area still were rural, yet public transport tied Howth into the rest of the Dublin region.

Sometime in the later 1940s, Conor and Christine seem to have worked out an understanding that permitted each of them to be involved with other people. This was not a 1960s-style "open marriage" but more something out of Paris émigré circles of the 1920s: the couple was just too, too advanced to be held to the definition of marriage that prevailed in mid-twentieth-century Catholic Ireland. Conor slept with the occasional woman friend, but he rather preferred to give his evenings over to research and writing. Christine fell in love with George Hetherington. His family was a major influence in the Dublin printing industry and, eventually, after receiving an inheritance, he became a managing director of the *Irish Times*. A gentle, self-effacing man, Hetherington was married with two children. He fell in love with Christine and would eventually divorce his wife and marry her. That was a goodly distance in the future. What held early in the 1950s was that Conor and Christine were married to each other and did not wish to be, so they did a good job of making each other unhappy. The pain spread in all directions, but probably had most impact upon the youngest, Kate, who went through infancy and childhood with unhappy parents. Had Kate not come along when she did, Conor and Christine would have felt free to end their marriage sooner than they did. That kind of a feeling, unconsciously, but inevitably, affects the way adults treat a child.

As a backdrop to this domestic fraying, Conor, though still a young rocket in the diplomatic service, was having a bit of the shine rubbed off his brass. In May 1951, a general election was called and Eamon de Valera again became taoiseach, a post he held until June 1954 when the "second coalition government" replaced him. This time, de Valera did not keep the post of minister for external affairs for himself. To replace Sean MacBride, he appointed Frank Aiken, a fifty-three-year-old former captain in the old IRA. Aiken had strong northern roots. He had been born in Camlough, County Armagh, and educated in Newry. He had been the commandant of the northern division of the old IRA in the war of independence and then chief of staff in 1923 of the antitreaty IRA. In previous cabinets, he had served as minister for defense, minister for lands and fisheries, and minister for finance. In almost every way, he was a contrast to Sean MacBride. He had great political experience; he knew the north of Ireland; and he was a classic Fianna Fail politician, with scant knowledge of French verbs, but a complete command of the language and beliefs of rural Irish patriotism.

During Aiken's term of office, the Mansion House Conference effectively wound down. One of the reasons for this was that the world, and especially the United States, was bored with the constant brandishing-the-sore-thumb propaganda and simply switched off. The result of this was summarized by John Kelleher in *Foreign Affairs* in 1955: "If one tries to follow Irish events in the American press, one finds that the news from there is about on a par with weather reports from Kerguelen—scarce and indicating fog. The Irish Question has vanished, mined out like the Mesabi range. Where once the mountain reared its impregnable head, two small states and the partition problem are vaguely discernible amid the surrounding emptiness."[100]

Domestic politics also cut into the all-party antipartition effort. The "first coalition government" of 1948–51 had fallen as the consequence of a great fracas over mother and child health care, sometimes known as the "Browne affair." Therein, the Catholic bishops, skillfully manipulated by the Irish Medical Association, had vetoed a plan to give free medical care to mothers and to their children up to age sixteen. (In the 1950s the bishops did indeed have the power to veto any piece of governmental legislation.) The "Mother and Child" issue put the bishops off cooperating with the government, even a traditional Fianna Fail one. That meant the effective end of the Mansion House anticoalition drive, since it had depended on the Catholic clergy for help in fund raising and in the formation of local antipartition societies.

Antipartition work continued within the Department of External Affairs, but at a markedly lower level of intensity. Conor, though no longer the hand-reared *apparatchik* he had been under MacBride, got along quite well with Aiken—in fact, Conor always related well with

Group of five exhibitioners at the Dominican Convent, Eccles Street, Dublin.
Conor's mother, Kathleen Sheehy, is in the center.

University graduation. Right: Kathleen Sheehy. Flag states "Votes for Women."
Left: Conor's aunt, Hanna Sheehy.

Francis Sheehy-Skeffington

Tom Kettle

Conor at Ring, learning Irish, mid-1930s.

Conor at Sandford Park School, 1934.

Christine, holding Fedelma, 1945.

Fedelma, Donal, Kate, 1950.

Conor, center, as managing director of *Irish News Agency*, in Chicago, 1950.
On Conor's left, John Mary Conway, Irish consul in Chicago and on his right,
Joe Gallagher of the Irish News Agency. (Courtesy: Transworld Airlines)

Christine and Kate, 1954.

Christine, La Frette sur Seine, 1955.

Leo T. McCauley, Irish ambassador to Spain, presents Maire MacEntee, secretary to the Irish Embassy, to General Franco. (Courtesy: *Irish News Agency*)

United Nations, fifteenth session, September 1960. Conor, center, top row; on Conor's right is Frank Aiken. On his left is Eamonn Kennedy, then Joe Shields. The Haitian delegation below seems to be having more fun. (Courtesy: The United Nations)

Conor in Albertville, north Katanga, with the Sikh major who was in charge of the United Nations cavalry.

Conor and Maire in UN transport in the Congo. It smelled of dried fish, its previous usage being unmistakable.

Conor and Maire's wedding reception, 1962. George Ivan Smith, Maire, Conor, Ralph Bunche.

Conor and Maire with her parents, Margaret and Sean MacEntee, on the front steps at "Whitewater," spring 1962.

Conor boogies at the Vice-Chancellor's Lodge,
University of Ghana, 1962.

Conor addressing the University of Ghana, 1964. W.E.B. Du Bois is in center.
Conor conferred the university's honorary doctorate on him.

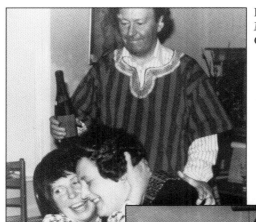

Family birthday party, 1966. Maire, her sister Barbara, and Conor, in Afro-Hibernian garb.

Maire, Conor, and Kate, departing Dublin for New York University, 1965.

Maire and Conor at wedding of Fedelma to Nicholas Simms, St. Patrick's Cathedral, Dublin.

Conor and Maire and infant Patrick, with Mr. and
Mrs. de Valera, 1969.

Conor spreading the gospel: electioneering, 1969.

Frank Cluskey and Gerry Fitt,
at annual Labour conference,
early 1970s.

Conor, Maire, and Patrick at an
anti-apartheid demonstration in the
early 1970s, Dublin.

In Chicago, 1972, anti-IRA tour.

Just back from Chicago, 1972. (Courtesy: the *Observer*)

Campaigning on Howth docks, 1973.

Coalition cabinet, 1973. Top row, from left: Thomas Fitzpatrick, Michael O'Leary, Thomas O'Donnell, Garret FitzGerald, Conor, Richard Burke, Peter Barry, Justin Keating, Patrick Cooney, Declan Costello. Front row, from left: James Tully, Paddy Dunegan, Liam Cosgrave, Mr. de Valera, Brendan Corish, Richie Ryan, Mark Clinton. (Courtesy: Department of the Taoiseach)

Conor, right, mystified by posts and telegraphs technology, mid-1970s.

men who could have been his father. Aiken was willing to continue some of the antipartition business. However, the Irish News Agency was particularly vulnerable because it was the brain child of Sean MacBride, and MacBride was a *bête noire* of Fianna Fail in general and particularly of Sean MacEntee, the minister for finance. And this did not help Conor's career at all, for MacEntee "thought I was a howling red and the fact that I was closely allied with MacBride simply confirmed his suspicion."[101] Aiken was willing to keep the INA going for a while and the Cabinet went along with him, but the handwriting was on the wall. Conor continued to oversee the INA, but now was the managerial equivalent of night watchman.[102]

In contrast to Sean MacBride, Frank Aiken believed that the policy of brandishing the sore thumb all over the world could be unproductive. Instead, he focused many of the Department of External Affairs resources on antipartitionist activities within Northern Ireland, and in so doing, he and his ministry came close to breaking the rule of international diplomacy. For instance, the department supported "The Irish Anti-Partition League" which had a network of affiliates not only in the republic, but also in Northern Ireland. The purpose of this league was the abolition of the government of Northern Ireland and its subsumption by the Irish Republic—"Unity and Independence for All Ireland" was the motto on the league's letterhead—so the department was supporting a campaign in a foreign jurisdiction whose purpose was the overthrow of that jurisdiction.[103] In a related set of activities, the department aided as much as it could those nationalist politicians in Northern Ireland who were considered trustworthy. Eddie MacAteer, head of the nationalist party, was a particularly important client. Conor was on a "Dear Eddie," and "Dear Conor" basis with him, in an era when first names were used only among close friends and family.[104]

Under Frank Aiken's direction, Conor spent a fair amount of time in the North. Some of this involved the management of foreign journalists or other visitors on visits to Ulster. For instance, on 21 and 22 July 1954, Conor was assigned to escort a young English Jesuit, a former lecturer in medieval history at Oxford, Father Wingfield-Digby, around Ulster. Father Wingfield-Digby had been charged by the English province of the Jesuits with the investigation of the condition of the Catholics in Northern Ireland. Conor in his "indoctrination of Father Wingfield-Digby" (as he called it in his department report) took the Englishman to the more unattractive sights in the North, and he had him meet trustworthy Catholic figures: Eddie MacAteer; Senator P.F. McGill, editor of the *Ulster Herald* and one of the leaders of the Irish Anti-Partition League; Dr. Pearse O'Malley, a consultant psychiatrist at the Mater Hospital in Belfast, and his wife, councillor Mary O'Malley, who was one of the most active members of the Irish Labour party; Paddy Scott, who was still working for the Irish News Agency, and J.G. Lennon, a leading member of the Ancient Order of Hibernians.[105]

In Armagh, Gerry Lennon showed them an electoral map of the city and then took them on a tour. He pointed out to Father Wingfield-Digby a classic bit of anti-Catholic gerrymandering, where a ward boundary suddenly skipped across a terrace street so as to catch three Catholic homes. The good father saw this as an example of primitive bigotry. "How perfectly stupid!" he said. Gerry Lennon, who as a northern Catholic knew that there was nothing about northern discrimination that was not calculated and efficient, looked sourly at the Jesuit. "In the name of God," he asked, "what's *stupid* about it?"[106]

Later, in Derry, they met with Eddie MacAteer and the Jesuit asked him and his friends how many Catholic unionists there were and how many Protestant nationalists. MacAteer and his associates scratched their heads and managed to think of one Catholic unionist, but he had been snubbed by the one side and boycotted by the other, so he gave it up. As for Protestant nationalists, well, there was a professor at Magee College who fit that description. "Of course, he calls himself a communist. It's safer, you see."[107]

One time Aiken directed Conor to go north to the Sperrin Mountains and there suggest to the leaders of the local Catholics that they stop abstaining from local government elections ("abstentionism" was one of the classic political acts of the northern minority) and, instead, try to gain power on the local council. One of the elders took Conor for a long walk. From the Sperrins the two men looked down on a valley. A long silence ensued until Conor, trying to make conversation, asked, "Well, how many Protestants are there around here?"

The old man pointed down the valley with his stick and replied "Just one, but with luck we'll have him out by Christmas."[108]

Much of what Conor did on his visits to Northern Ireland could be described as intelligence gathering. The southern government was interested not only in how well the northern Catholic community was doing politically, but it was also particularly concerned with the IRA, which held the government of the Irish Republic to be every bit as illegitimate as that of Northern Ireland.[109] Much of Conor's intelligence gathering was the sort of thing that officials of any embassy do for their home government: collect and evaluate basic information about what is happening in the society to which they are sent as diplomats. What was different here was that Conor was not accredited to the jurisdiction from which he was gathering intelligence and, further, his official brief was to support an organization whose goal (however nonviolent in method) was the abolition of that jurisdiction. Why did the U.K. government put up with this and with similar activities by other officials of the republic? The reason, I suspect, was simply that the easiest way for the Royal Ulster Constabulary and the U.K. military intelligence units to control this sort of activity was to let it roll. I would be very surprised if, when the full history of these years is written, it is not discovered that British and RUC counterintelligence groups did not have detailed information on such visits. Indeed, the easiest way to keep tabs on the Anti-Partition League would have been to let the government of the Irish Republic keep track of it, and then just lift (or buy from an informant) their information.[110]

Conor was both shrewd and ambitious, and he had the wit to see that the Ireland-right-to-unity campaign was not going anywhere. He needed to extricate himself from it or his career would be marked by its incipient failure. This concern for his career should not be confused with any loss in faith in the basic Irish nationalist position, that the country should be reunited irrespective of the wishes of the northern Protestant majority. People who heard him speak publicly as late as 1956 tell me that he did not in any sense take an original or non-nationalist line. He spoke as a person who was completely identified with the goals of the Irish Republic's Department of External Affairs. While he might have had increasing doubts about the methods used to reach the desired ends, he still believed in the irredentist principles which were at the heart of Irish diplomacy: the North should cease to exist as a distinct governmental entity and should be incorporated into the republic.[111]

It was important for his career that he find another string for his bow. The Irish News Agency was in perilous health (and was finally buried in 1957). Conor's preferred route out of the antipartition *cul-de-sac* was to get himself assigned to one of the European embassies. Here *Maria Cross* helped, for it paved the way for him to make cultural visits to various countries and thus to increase his European exposure. For example, in October 1953, he gave a series of cultural lectures in Sweden at venues ranging from the Anglo-Swedish Society to the Swedish-Irish Society and points in between. He gave two news conferences and lectured on "Anglo-Irish Literature" and on "The Influence of Joyce on Modern Writers." As reported in the Swedish newspapers, some of the things he said were startling enough to animate the Scandinavians, no mean feat. For instance, at Gothenburg University, he informed his audience that "many writers would be feeling better if it were not for

Joyce." The Swedish-Irish Society was told that all Ireland was producing at the moment were "prominent lyricists. W.R. Rodgers (a drinking buddy of Conor's at the time), and Patrick Kavanagh were praised. "The rest are all second-rate writers." They were also informed that the only modern Irish drama worth mention was M.J. Molloy's *The King of Friday's Men.*[112]

A year later, Conor went on a junket given by the press department of the Federal Republic of Germany. Besides being shown around (and taking in an admission hearing for persons who had bolted from East Germany), he gave a lecture to the German-Irish Society on James Joyce. "The lecture is said to have pleased the Society, which is, however, on the whole not a lively one," Conor reported, and then explained, "a natural enough circumstance considering that Bonn is really a small town and that the Society is mainly in the hands of Celtic philologists from Bonn University."[113]

Fianna Fail left office in May 1954 and was replaced by the "second coalition government" headed by John Aloysius Costello. Liam Cosgrave became minister for external affairs and he was no enthusiast of animated antipartition efforts. Cosgrave's desire to clean out the old antipartition section coincided with Conor's desire for a foreign posting. Conor was appointed a counselor at the Irish embassy in Paris, where he was also to be a representative at the Organization for Economic and Cultural Development. The year 1954, therefore, ended on a happy note, a chance to get his career on track, and an opportunity, perhaps, for Conor and Christine's marriage to knit itself back together.

CHAPTER 6

TO PARIS, AND NEW YORK, AND KATANGA, AND BACK: 1955–1961

To be a foreign diplomat in Paris sounds lovely; it turned out to be nothing of the sort. As counselor, Conor was in charge of the Paris embassy when the ambassador was not around. Otherwise, he was the number two person, a very good job on paper. The problem was that the ambassador was an old foe, William Fay, whose pompous ways Conor had bedeviled in the days when they both were in Iveagh House. Fay was not a bad man, but he was an incurable collector of titled persons, which was not at all difficult to do in postwar France. Displaced aristocrats from all over Eastern Europe, and even royalty, were always available to be wined and dined. In this regard, the Irish Republic's ambassador to France was anything but a republican. Conor, who has never suffered easily either snobbery or fools, did not get along at all well with this bunch.

But it was the political stance implicit in Fay's social preferences that put ambassador and counselor totally out of sympathy with each other. The social milieu of the Irish embassy in Paris was basically right wing. At this time, France was conducting a colonial war in Algeria. Privately, Conor abhorred it. The Irish governmental line, however, was to go along with the French, and this was a specially strong commitment of Ambassador Fay.[1] So, what should have been a good posting turned into a purgatory.

Then purgatory turned into outright hell as Conor and Christine's marriage fell totally to pieces. The foreign setting did not bring them closer together but, instead, brought them to realize how far apart they actually were. Christine was in love with George Hetherington and at war with Conor. Eventually, this set of tensions affected her health and finally became too much. She returned for a time to Dublin, leaving Conor with Kate (aged seven) and Fedelma (aged ten). Donal at this time was at Newtown School, Waterford. Later the family was reunited, first in Paris for a time and then, after the tour of duty in France was completed, at "Whitewater." There Conor and Christine lived, in Christine's words, "strictly as a game for the sake of the children." Paris, then, for all practical purposes, ended the marriage.

Kate Cruise O'Brien later wrote a fine story entitled "A Sunday Walk" (found in her collection, *A Gift Horse*, 1978) which deals with the Paris years from the viewpoint of herself as a young girl. "Her mother had departed a few days ago in a flurry of tissue paper," is the dramatic frame for the story. Kate had comforted her mother in that falsely grown-up way that children can assume in the face of trouble, and had even made her mother laugh as she prepared to leave. "But her face had looked stretched and glassy and her eyes shone as if she might cry." And then, her mother gone, a whole new set of social nuances arose in Kate's life. "And now her father wanted to go for a walk and it seemed strange to go for a walk just with her father though her father had taken her for walks during the winter when her mother was ill. She supposed it seemed strange now because her mother was away and not at home in bed."

Kate and Conor walk and he is edgy, not very good at relating to his youngest child, but in a lovely, symbolic, and appropriate gesture, he asks her if she would like to take his walking stick. "The stick was beautiful. It was a blackthorn, strong and knobbly with a surprisingly smooth warm handle. Her father used to use it at home. He used to swing it over the ruts in the lane and thrash it through the ferns on the headlands."

And, yes, "I'd love to take the stick, thank you." And now, just as she had comforted her mother, she "wished she could give him something to comfort him, and as soon as she wished that, she knew that he needed comfort and she knew that she'd known this for a long time." [2]

Kate diagnosed in Conor a sadness that was the soft side of a welter of emotions that included deep pain, anger, and a touch of self-destructiveness; not all of these stemmed from the marriage, but from a life of which the marriage was a central part. Conor in Paris in these pained days drank too much, his friends agree. He always had been a Guinness drinker, and willing to take wine, but now he lived in a place where quality claret was cheap. He was sick-drunk more often than he should have been, sometimes at diplomatic gatherings. It was almost as if he were staging a contest to see if his undoubted abilities would protect him from the consequences of his increasingly bad behavior. On some occasions he messed up completely, as the time he was left by Bill Fay to host a reception and totally forgot about it.

What saved Conor was his real addiction: he just could not stop using his mind. He decided to learn Russian and did so to a high standard; he passed the British Foreign Service entrance examination in that language. The story goes that he took the exam after a formidable night out in Soho. According to a friend, "being Conor, he not only had to speak it, he had to get drunk in it."[3]

Although Conor did not engage in any major intellectual project during the time he was in Paris, he by then was well enough known as a critic to receive regular reviewing assignments from the *Spectator*, the *New Statesman* and from *Commonweal*, the leading Catholic-left periodical in the United States. He did these assignments well and became a regular and, often, a featured reviewer. He also did reviews for both the *Spectator* and the *New Statesman* of Paris theater, and of the occasional Dublin theatrical event (which he took in while home on leave). This theatrical interest was the foundation of his later work in writing pieces of political theater. All these assignments—which continued throughout the 1950s—were done in his "Donat O'Donnell" persona. As a professional diplomat he still was denied his own voice. (For a detailed listing of the work done in this period, see the Bibliography in the Anthology.)

There was one long-term benefit of being forced to conduct his professional life within a culture that was conducting a colonial war, as the French were doing. Conor began to change his definition of colonialism, from a characteristic of the British to something inherent in Western cultures. Previously, he had known this on an abstract level (he had, after all, been an adult during the Nazi onslaught and during the postwar Soviet grab of Eastern Europe), but now he met Algerian refugees in private and French colonialists and their right-wing supporters at public functions, and the reality of what colonialism meant moved off the printed page into the world of live human beings. This was the first stage in his developing a realization that imperialism is a set of behaviors that can emerge in any country (even Ireland), and it was a piece of intellectual liberation on which his later magisterial heresies about the nature of Irish nationalism depended.

• • •

Once more, Paddy Lynch saved Conor. As well as being a scholar on the staff of University College, Dublin, he was an economic adviser to

Liam Cosgrave, minister of external affairs and also to the taoiseach, John A. Costello. His friend Conor needed a sane-making post.

The best ones opening up in external affairs were in the new UN section. In 1946 Ireland had applied for admission to the United Nations, but had been vetoed by the Soviet Union for the publicly expressed reasons that Ireland and the Soviet Union did not have normal diplomatic relations with each other. Privately, the Soviets were convinced that Ireland would be in the American bloc (hardly a naive suspicion, given that in the late 1940s Ireland was working hard at getting as much American aid as it could). Ireland kept knocking at the door and finally in 1955 a big-power trade between the United States and the Soviets allowed Ireland to join. This was formally effected on 14 December 1955.

Paddy Lynch called Conor to the attention of Cosgrave and Costello, just at the time the Department of External Affairs was creating a UN section in Iveagh House. Freddie Boland was to be in charge of the actual mission in New York City (under, of course, the supervision of the Irish minister for external affairs), and the prize post beneath Boland was head of the UN section in Dublin, which held the bonus bauble of travel to New York as a support for the heads of delegations. Conor won. He became head of the United Nations section in Dublin. The symbol of his new position was a massive office in Iveagh House, one level above the ground floor, easily forty feet long and twenty wide, fronting on St. Stephen's Green. At one time, members of the Guinness family had looked down from these same windows and scored the passing parade. Conor had arrived. His family life still was in turmoil, but his career was back on trajectory.

Among the things that escape from Paris effected was the resurrection of Conor's sense of humor. He wrote a story, "Carey Bloom," for the *Atlantic*, about his misadventures in bringing a dog back from Paris, just before Christmas 1955, in contravention of all quarantine regulations and at some risk to his career. (The story is found in the Anthology, Selection 8.) The tale is wonderfully funny, without being self-consciously humorous and is confident in the sense that Conor was willing to show himself to be as big a fool as everyone else when it came to large, lovable nonhuman mammals. Indeed, anyone who tries to smuggle a shaggy, Kerry-blue dog of significant size and aggressive temperament past the British Isles' antirabies authorities could hardly keep up the pretense of supernal wisdom and dignity. And Conor, in this story, is happy to have us join him in laughing at his own folly. The story is an indication of the way that Conor was to write when at his best—in an easy, apparently natural manner that reminds one of the only intelligent thing that John Wayne ever said: "The hardest job in acting is to act natural." Having "Carey Bloom" accepted by the *Atlantic* was the first time that Conor realized he was really a writer, not just a clever diplomat with a hobby.[4]

Conor's job in the new United Nations section was to be the link-man. There were two persons senior to him in the UN section who needed information and support: the foreign minister of Ireland (a member of Dail Eireann and of the Irish cabinet) and Freddie Boland, who was the Irish permanent representative. Boland, back from a stint (1950–56) at Ireland's most prestigious ambassadorial post—ambassador to the court of St. James—had previously been secretary of the department (1946–50) and before that (1938–46) an assistant secretary of the department. He knew Conor well and at this stage they got along well. Conor was the pivot man between the two top representatives and the department in Iveagh House. The number of people in his section varied and the personnel rotated, but the section usually had two or three third secretaries (Robert McDonagh and Noel Dorr were two of them, each of whom later became a major figure in Irish diplomacy). Then, there would be one or two somewhat more senior individuals: Paul Keating and Eamonn Kennedy (who later became Ireland's ambassador to Nigeria and later still, to Rome), were among these. Also at this level was Maire MacEntee. A prodigy at languages and already a major poet in the Irish language, MacEntee was there very much on her own abilities. That said, she was good insulation for the department, for her father, Sean MacEntee, was the Irish equivalent of the American Senator Joseph R. McCarthy, seeing and denouncing reds everywhere although, being rather brighter than McCarthy, he was not quite so good at it.[5]

Working for, or with, Conor, was either heaven or hell, nothing in between. He was the kind of boss and colleague one either loved or hated: aggressive, demanding, entertaining, iconoclastic, and wounding one minute, flattering and seductive the next. Among his fellow civil servants in external affairs he was easily the most admired officer and, equally, the least trusted. That was a portent of how he would be perceived when, later, he entered Irish political life.

Conor's section was known for having "dash," a sense of style and exuberance that went beyond the muted tones and hairline smiles of the lads who had spent most of their formative years with the Jesuits. Diplomacy, if you were working under Conor, was fun.[6] Conor himself was known for his wit. Now, it is a cruel thing to label anyone a "Dublin wit," and one would not do that to him, but one of Conor's hip-shots went around Dublin at this period, and is worth noting. The story is that he was sitting in his office in Iveagh House, overlooking St. Stephen's Green. A newspaper reporter wanted to talk to him.

"*The Irish Catholic* is on the line," his secretary said.

Conor, busy, snapped, "Offer him £5 for his horse!"

There is a shared history here. It runs from the eighteenth-century penal laws to de Valera's Ireland, and Conor's deep immersion in Irish history is the plinth from which it was launched.

The UN section was a glory section, for each September, most of the section would take off for New York for a ten– or twelve–week session of the General Assembly and its associated committees. One or two third secretaries would be left behind, but even this rotated, so that everyone had a chance to savor fall in New York. In overseas postings, Irish diplomats were treated well. They were on full expenses, of course. Through the 1957 session, the Irish delegation stayed at the Beekman Towers Hotel, but then switched to the San Carlos on 50th Street, between Third and Lexington. This was an apartment hotel. Everyone had his or her own flat and it was possible for the delegates to lead a lively private life.

New York was intoxicating: an autumn walk, across 50th Street, toward the East River, a few blocks down First Avenue and then passage through the security-controlled gate into the UN gardens (no tourists here) and finally into the diplomatic equivalent of the Temple Mount. There, if one were to believe the various mottoes inscribed on the walls and to assimilate the iconographic content of the numerous murals, the world's best hope resided. The Irish delegation could be excused if, at first, it acted awed, and, then, like a band of school prefects, strutted from issue to issue, proposing solutions for everything from nuclear proliferation to the perpetual two-Chinas problem.

Up to March 1957, Liam Cosgrave, minister for external affairs, headed the Irish UN mission. He gave a significant speech in the Dail in July 1956 (written for him by Freddie Boland) which set down Ireland's attachment to the United Nations.[7] These were (1) that Ireland would be scrupulously faithful to the UN and its obligations under the UN charter; (2) that Ireland would try to maintain an independent position, avoiding any particular bloc; but (3) that Ireland would act in the United Nations to preserve "Christian civilization of which we are a part." Ireland, as a Christian nation, recognized that it was part of the constellation made up of the United States, Canada, and Western Europe.[8] That third point obviously is in conflict with the second, but Cosgrave and Boland wanted it that way: they wanted Ireland to be nonaligned and in the American camp; a contradiction in terms.

The insistence that the Republic of Ireland was participating in the world organization as a Christian nation played well in the Dail—the Christian part was an antidote to the fear that the UN was some sort of a communist organization, for communism was the big bogey among Irish politicians in the mid-1950s. It also reflected Liam Cosgrave's personal inclination (as well as Boland's skill as a speech writer): Cosgrave had been an altar boy until he was twenty-four years of age. But for all his religiosity, Liam Cosgrave was a shrewd politician, especially as it affected his own constituency, Dun Laoghaire-Rathdown. Thus, we see the delicate cartoon of Cosgrave, Boland, and Conor, sitting in a row in the General Assembly of the UN during Ireland's first session, each wearing a dark suit, white shirt, and sober tie, the minister being scheduled to give a speech on the subject of the Middle East. The speech had been crafted by Conor along lines laid down by Freddie Boland. The minister was making last-minute changes, going over the speech, page by page. On the last page, he wrote something and passed it to Boland, who read it, twitched, and passed it on to Conor. The new draft concluded by appealing to the Jews and Muslims to settle their differences according to Christian principles.

"Have you anything to say about that?" asked Boland.

"Of course, it's the minister's speech," Conor replied, "but Jews and Muslims are not likely to settle their differences on Christian terms."

Turning to Cosgrave, Boland said, "Conor seems to think it won't go down at all well in the Middle East."

Liam Cosgrave smiled and said nothing.

Freddie Boland, however, read the minister's mind. He explained to Conor, "It may not go down well in the Middle East, but the minister seems to think it will go down well in Dun Laoghaire-Rathdown."[9]

The first session for the Irish, 1956, was an exciting one, for both the Hungarian uprising and the Suez Canal invasion were debated. Conor was stunned by what he perceived as the cynicism of the U.S. government. The United States had long encouraged the Eastern European countries to rise up against their Soviet oppressors. This finally occurred in 1956, when the Hungarians revolted and put Imre Nagy in power. Nagy appealed to the United Nations. What should be done? The answer from the U.S. delegation, headed by Henry Cabot Lodge, was "nothing, absolutely nothing." Conor was in fact lobbied by a member of the U.S. delegation in those very terms. Do nothing, the risk was not worth it. So, the Soviets rolled in and only when they were firmly in control did the United States back a draft resolution calling on the Soviet Union to withdraw from Hungary—which, of course, the Soviets vetoed. The Eisenhower administration then claimed it had tried to help and that it was the United Nations that had failed.[10] The lesson that a delegate from a small nation might reasonably draw from this incident was that the Bible was right: put not your trust in princes or powers.

Conor, for historical reasons well known to virtually every Irish person north or south, was not at all surprised by the behavior of the British on the Suez affair of the same year. Britain and France, having struck for the Suez Canal in 1956, in concert with an Israeli invasion of the Sinai, were forced to withdraw by U.S. and Soviet pressure. This left the Israelis holding the Sinai. It was, therefore, more than a trifle hypocritical when the British delegate, a Commander Noble, told the General Assembly that Britain did not condone Israel's attack on Egypt and called on Israel to withdraw. Conor took pleasure in drafting the opening words of the Irish delegation's statement on the matter to the General Assembly. "Far be it from our delegation to be any less censorious, about an attack on Egypt, than the distinguished delegate of the United Kingdom judges it appropriate to be."[11]

Cut-glass ironic as that was, it was only an occasional pleasure; being an Irish delegate became a good deal more enjoyable for Conor after the Irish general election of March 1957 which brought Fianna Fail back to power and Frank Aiken again to the office of minister of external affairs. (He was destined to hold the post for twelve years, longer than any other Irish foreign minister.) Aiken modeled himself on his chief, Eamon de Valera who, when he had served simultaneously as taoiseach and foreign minister, had been active in the League of Nations. Aiken, therefore, was in favor of a strong and independent Irish foreign policy. This meant that of the "three principles" set down by Liam Cosgrave and Freddie Boland, the third would take precedence over the second: that is, independence of action would have a stronger valence than would unity with the other Western and Christian nations.

Aiken was a naturally taciturn man, something of a walking megalith. His manner was that of the County Louth farmers whom he had faithfully represented since the 1920s. He could unbend and be amusing in private, especially when telling his war-of-independence stories but, on the other hand, he would not discuss anything but the barest outlines of Irish foreign policy in Dail Eireann.[12] This had the advantage that if one convinced Aiken of something, he was quite willing to follow it through without letting parliamentary democracy get in the way.

The Irish line at the United Nations would have become increasingly independent with Aiken in charge, but Conor pushed things further. He was very keen on what was called the "Swedish model," in sharp contrast to the Cosgrave-Boland line which involved supporting the United States on every important vote. The view of Conor and of the younger diplomats in the department at the time was that Sweden was a model in international affairs as its actions were "independent, disinterested, and honourable."[13] He hoped that Ireland would join a small group of nations, mostly Scandinavian, whose chief concern was to safeguard the "moral authority" of the United Nations in general, and to uphold the secretary general against excessive big-power pressure, in particular. This group was known (among themselves) as "the decent countries."[14] The Swedish model implied independence from all big-power blocs and—even in the event of war between the blocs—a maintenance of complete independence. There was not only a good deal of moral righteousness among "the decent countries," but also a good deal of peacock-like preening.[15]

It is quite possible to be highly skeptical of the Swedish model, while understanding why Irish diplomats might be interested in it. As a serious geopolitical strategy, the Swedish position of staying neutral as between the contestants of any conflict was similar to the impartiality articulated by the whilom vice-president of the United States, Spiro Agnew, who said that he always tried to find the Golden Mean between right and wrong (and, I cannot imagine that anyone who was in deep trouble would be heartened to hear their rescuers calling out "Send in the Swedes"; but then, they're my people and I may not quite understand fully their fearsome analgesic and eirenic qualities). However, for a small power, the Swedish model provided a license similar to that which Irish patriotism around the issue of "God Save the King" had given to Francis Cruise O'Brien: a license to maintain the moral high ground while being a royal pain in the arse.

Given that Frank Aiken wanted to take a more independent line in the UN and that Eamon de Valera was in favor of the actions of anyone who modeled himself on Himself, the question then became, on what issue would the new independence be manifest? Conor managed a long talk with Aiken in Dublin before the 1957 session of the General Assembly. When Aiken told him that he wanted to take up more of a nonaligned position, Conor said, "If you want to take up a non-aligned position, there is just one test of that—it's the vote on the question of the representation of China."

At that time, the Americans and the British were adopting a solidly united front of not talking about Chinese representation, because they did not have a solidly united position: Britain was doing business with Peking and the United States was limiting its China trade to its client state, Taiwan, so the last thing either country wanted was a real debate. "If you vote against the discussion of the representation of China,"

Conor told the Irish foreign minister, "you will be classified by all sides in the UN as essentially in the pocket of the U.S. on anything that matters." But the alternative policy had its cost. "If you shift from the previous policy of voting with the U.S., you're going to run into a lot of trouble."

According to Conor's recollection, Aiken made his decision at that point. "Right," he said. "I am going to vote in favour of the discussion." And, in Conor's words, "he hitched his shoulders in a soldierly manner which he used to do in moments of crisis."[16]

In convincing Frank Aiken to make his move toward nonalignment in the most visible way possible—the China issue—Conor permanently alienated Freddie Boland, who favored supporting the United States on the China issue, and on most others. From that moment on, the friendship of Conor and Boland turned into dislike and eventually into deep enmity.[17]

Frank Aiken was scheduled to make a speech in the General Assembly in the afternoon of Monday, 23 September 1957. This was the annual discussion of the admission of China to the UN and Aiken had de Valera's approval to change the Irish position and to vote in favor of discussing the issue—not admitting China, but *discussing* admission—and as a precaution against having the Americans vent their displeasure in public if they were totally surprised, the Irish delegation informed the U.S. delegation of the new line they would be taking. This was done about 11:00 in the morning.

By noon, Francis Cardinal Spellman, Archbishop of New York, who as a Catholic church leader was in the same league as John Charles McQuaid, no petty prince, was on the telephone wanting to know if the story was true. His Eminence had just heard of the planned Irish perfidy from Irene Dunne, a faithful Irish Catholic, who, in her twilight as a Hollywood star, had been appointed to the American delegation to the United Nations. (Her last film was in 1952. Called *It Grows on Trees*, it was about a backyard tree that started to grow money.) Spellman thundered, "Tell Aiken that if he votes for Red China, we'll raise the devil." That was not an inconsiderable threat and had it been, say 1950, when the Irish government was courting the Irish-Americans on the partition issue, it well might have been enough. But those days were over: the Fianna Fail government of the late 1950s was so solidly identified at home with church and fatherland, that a fuming American cardinal was no real danger. Aiken stood firm.[18]

That was heady stuff, and so too were the other independent positions that Ireland adopted. Aiken proposed that both Soviet and Western troops draw back on their respective sides of the East

European border.[19] And he took a strong position against apartheid. In 1957, Ireland joined twenty-nine African and Asian countries in condemning South Africa, a proposition which the United Kingdom voted against and on which the United States abstained.[20]

Thus liberated from following the Western powers, Ireland for a time became a leading anticolonialist nation. At that time, the influx of new African and Asian countries into the UN was just beginning. Ireland, by virtue of its long experience of colonialism and of opposition to it, was an older-brother figure. The *Economist* went so far in 1959 as to describe the new temper of the General Assembly as being that of the "Afro-Irish assembly."[21] As a result of this increasingly nonaligned position, in 1959 Freddie Boland was selected as president of the General Assembly for 1960–61: the independent Irish position made him acceptable to East Europeans as well as to the West. (The irony of his benefiting from Ireland's having adopted a diplomatic stance that he opposed is obvious.)

One characteristic of official Irish anticolonialism in these years bears remark: Ireland was notably silent about partition. There was no brandishing-of-the-sore-thumb. This change made good sense, for southern Ireland's forever harping on the partition issue in international forums had simply made the major players ignore Ireland whenever possible. There was more to the change than mere tactics, however. The Irish delegation recognized an important fact: an antipartition motion in the General Assembly almost certainly would attract a good deal of support and that had to be avoided! As Conor explained in 1959 to Joseph Shields, who had been a member of the first Irish delegation to the UN in 1956 and now was a counselor in the Irish embassy in Washington, D.C., "no resolution in favour of Irish unity would be likely to be carried in the United Nations without the active support of the United States: and that even if it could be carried by a small majority, such a resolution, if not supported by the United States, would remain a dead letter—it might even be actually damaging, if all the votes for the resolution proved to be anti-Western. Unfortunately, we have at present no reason to suppose that the United States would actively support us if the matter came before the United Nations."[22] Conor here was diplomatically pointing to two realities. The first was that the United States would not support an antipartition resolution because the United Kingdom was more crucial to American interests than was Ireland. And, second, the wrong sort of countries—new African and Asian nations—and worse, the communist bloc—would support an antipartition resolution. Association with these countries, and especially the communist nations, would not be well received within Ireland, and particularly not by the Irish Catholic religious leaders. Thus, as a price of playing in the world arena, partition dropped almost completely out of the Irish diplomatic portfolio.[23]

The rhythm of Conor's everyday life while at the United Nations alternated between a strut and a shuffle. It would have taken a desert ascetic not to have felt pride, and from thence to embrace hubris, when participating, even as a relatively minor figure, in a body that claimed to be the world's parliament. Whether doing research in the plush and extensive UN library, or buttonholing other delegates and talking to them in French, English, and, occasionally Russian, or having a drink in the delegates' lounge, with its discreetly separated conversational groupings of leather chairs, set in a room half the size of a football field—all this had to make one feel a very important person indeed.

The shuffle was the day-to-day committee work. Backing up Frank Aiken in the General Assembly was satisfactory, for he took well to sensible ghost-writing of his speeches. Aiken was the only foreign minister of any country actually to spend the entire session each year in New York and he was very serious about the UN. But, for Conor, the committees were mostly tedium. The UN at that time divided its workload into several committees of the full membership, and Ireland parceled out committee assignments to the various members of its delegation. With the exception of the first committee which dealt with political and security questions and was a special interest of Frank Aiken's, it was a world of professional diplomats. Assignments rotated somewhat, but Conor's usual assignment was to back up Boland on the first committee if Freddie Boland was absent, and to represent Ireland on the Special Political Committee which dealt with issues so enduringly divisive that they had to be hived off from the general debates: notably the Palestinian refugee issue and the question of apartheid in South Africa.

The quality of debate in the several UN committees was much closer to the soporific discourse of a medieval quodlibetical session than to the slash-and-burn style of Irish political debate. Andrew Boyd, a tough British journalist for the *Economist*, assigned to the United Nations in the 1959 session, sat through several committee sessions and found most of the debates "almost wholly divorced from reality." He singled out as especially impressive in this regard the Social and Cultural Committee. "This committee's chief claim to fame in 1959 was its decision that 'freedom of information' should not extend so far as to entitle journalists, those notorious nuisances, to 'seek information'; at most, they could 'gather it.'" He added, "It was left to the redoubtable Princess Ping Peang of Cambodia to strike a rare note of honesty by revealing that several of the speeches had sent her off to sleep."[24]

Even Conor's interventions were formal and sluggish. (Mind you, the UN's style of parliamentary reporting in the form of indirect discourse would bleach the life out of any exchange.) One finds him in October 1957 telling the Special Political Committee that Ireland believed there was a full agreement among all delegations represented on the committee that racial discrimination was fundamentally wrong and immoral. This fact was very encouraging, he said, because two decades earlier, several of the member states had held racialist doctrines. In that encouraging historical perspective, therefore, he hoped that the Special Political Committee would persevere in attempts at impressing the government of South Africa that its politics were condemned by the overwhelming majority of mankind and that consequently their policies ought to be changed.[25] Nor could anyone have accused Conor of being inflammatory when in 1959 he stated that he "would vote in favour of the draft resolution, A/SPC/L.38/Rev. 1. He would vote for operative paragraph four in the hope that the Palestine Conciliation Commission would be able usefully to explore the possibilities of an application, by phases, of the principle of free choice, while taking care to safeguard the national security of Israel. ... His delegation cherished the hope that some degree of progress, however limited it might be, would be achieved at the fifteenth session of the general assembly."[26]

(Actually, the prize for Irish oratory at the UN has to go to Frank Aiken who, in October 1959, in a General Assembly debate on Tibet, solemnly told the world community that the sympathy of the Irish people had long gone out to the Tibetan people. He instanced Michael Davitt, Irish patriot and social reformer, who, when lecturing in the United States in 1904 had called attention to the oppression of the Tibetan people. Aiken then read large portions of a speech he had given recently in Dundalk "the principal, largest town in county Louth," in a constituency that he had represented "without a break since 1923," and whose populace, he said, was "troubled about the news from Tibet."[27] Aiken, in his speech to his troubled constituents, was admirably anti-imperialist, and it is pleasing to contemplate the calming effect this must have had on the citizens of Dundalk.)

After listening to what must have seemed like decades of solecisms and gaffes in committee and in the General Assembly, Freddie Boland developed a phrase that became the Irish delegation's anthem. After some impressively ill-judged intervention in a discussion, they would utter Boland's theme sentence: "Il a raté un bonne occasion de se taire" (He missed a good opportunity to keep his mouth shut).[28]

Amid the day-to-day shuffling, there were diverting moments. Conor was present in the General Assembly in the autumn of 1960 when Nikita Kruschev took off his shoe and hammered on his desk in an effort to interrupt an address being given by the United Kingdom's Harold Macmillan. (In Conor's judgment this was not a political gesture. "It was partly high spirits, partly boredom, partly the desire of one ham to upstage another ham.")[29]

And he watched with sad amusement in early 1961 as Adlai Stevenson, once the conscience of a generation of liberal Americans, awkwardly trundled around the official lies of the Kennedy administration concerning its invasion of Cuba. It was early on a depressing morning when Stevenson addressed the First Committee on the subject of the Bay of Pigs invasion, an incident which, Stevenson stated, the Americans knew nothing about and had nothing to do with. Stevenson, who had too much residual conscience to be a good liar, stumbled frequently during his speech. He ended the speech by reading a peroration that said, "I have told you of Castro's crimes against *man*. But there is even worse: the record of Castro's crimes against *God*."

Even by the standards of UN debates, that sausage was a bit off; several delegates looked distinctly ill.

"Fidel Castro has ..." and here Stevenson, turning a page, lost his concentration, "... has *circumcised* the freedoms of the Catholics of Cuba. ..."

Conor was sitting next to an Israeli delegate at the time. The Israeli turned to him and said, "I always knew that *we* should be blamed for this, sooner or later."[30]

That incident highlights one of the most important long-term effects on Conor of his years at the United Nations: the reinforcement of his instinctive identification with things Jewish and, now, increasingly, with things Israeli. This early affinity with Jews came from his days at Sandford Park School and, indeed, went all the way back to his father's friendships with leading figures in the Dublin Jewish community. However, the point of confirming his attitudes was a matter of the alphabet: when Ireland joined the United Nations, it was slotted into various committees in alphabetical order. In what may have been the most efficient peace-keeping action that the Irish ever engaged in, they took their place between Iraq and Israel.

For five successive years, Conor made the same basic speech in the Special Political Committee, and balanced it was. The first time he gave it, he met in the corridor a Jewish-American newspaper woman, a close friend. She asked how the speech had gone. Conor replied that he had been thanked by both the delegates of Israel and of Iraq. "Christ!" she said, "Was it as bad as that?"[31]

Despite this governmentally dictated balancing in official postures as between the various Arab groups and the Israelis, Conor's personal po-

sition tilted strongly toward the Israelis. They were embattled, surrounded, under siege, he believed, and that was a condition with which
he could personally identify. This inclination ran counter to the general
tenor of the nonaligned bloc (which was mostly pro-Arab) and also
against the general tone of Irish popular beliefs, which were mildly anti-
Semitic—not through direct knowledge of Jews (most Irish people of
the time probably had not met more than half a dozen Jews in their life-
times), but stemming from the anti-Semitism inherent in most forms of
Christianity and, in those years, still explicitly sanctioned in Roman
Catholic dogma. This endemic, if mild, anti-Semitism among the Irish
caused Conor some professional difficulty when the great Irish actress
Siobhan McKenna arrived in Manhattan and was interviewed on television. Known in Irish cultural circles for her patriotic garrulousness,
she was a perpetual danger to the public peace.

"How is the Irish economy doing, Miss McKenna?" the interviewer
asked.

"Terrible. Awful," she replied, never one to understate a case.
"Unspeakable. Ruin."

"Really, Miss McKenna. And how do you account for that?"

"The Jews," was her straightforward reply.[32]

That took some patching over.

• • •

Two-thirds of Conor's time in the period 1956–61 was spent in Dublin,
doing the backup work at Iveagh House for the UN representation.
Conor and Christine still shared the same legal address, "Whitewater,"
but the children, for whom the fiction of marriage was being drawn,
knew that things were amiss. Christine's heart was with George
Hetherington; Conor had a string of what his second wife, Maire, called
"his golden girls," stylish single women who looked good and knew how
to carry on a conversation.

This is the appropriate point to deal with Conor's basic sexual orientation. It was nothing unusual. He liked women and he slept with them.
As far as I can determine, there were no men in his sex life and no significant sexual deviations. (All this is said with the full knowledge that
horrendous gargoyles sometimes are found under the bed, decades
later; but I am very skeptical that anything clinically unusual will turn
up.)

Late in the afternoon on a bitter cold Thursday, two days after
Christmas, 1956, Conor and a member of his section, Maire MacEntee,
were working in Iveagh House. Conor was back from the United
Nations, and Maire, relatively new to the section, had not spent the session in New York. Most of the staff of Iveagh House were away for the

Christmas holidays and everyone else had gone home. The dark afternoon turned into a beastly cold evening and the only heat was an electric fire Conor had in his office. He sat at his desk, in the faint circle of light cast by his green-shaded desk lamp. He was wearing his overcoat and trying to keep his hands from freezing. Maire joined him. They talked for a long while. Both of them were filling the holiday time by working. Conor's domestic life was uncomfortable and Maire did not wish to spend any more time than necessary with her parents. (Like every other woman of managerial rank in the diplomatic service she was unmarried, which meant that she received vast earfuls of advice from her parents.) Eventually, the two of them went out to dinner—the excuse was that Conor owed Maire a meal as payment for an election bet she had won—and then they went to Maire's flat and made love. Thus began a relationship that developed into one that is about as permanent as these things get. [33]

Maire MacEntee was an extraordinary person who came of an unusual family. Her mother and father were of the class of upstart revolutionaries who had displaced the home rule parliamentarians on whom Bessie Sheehy had planned to build the new Irish elite. Maire's mother, born Margaret Browne in Grangemockler, County Tipperary, had taken a double first at UCD. Her flat in Parnell Square, Dublin, was used by Michael Collins in the war of independence. During the civil war she took the "republican" side. She was formidable even when young and now, in the 1950s, she was a large woman, giving one pause, in the same way one would treat the phenomenon seriously if one encountered a Henry Moore sculpture that began slowly to move.

In 1921, Margaret Browne had married Sean MacEntee, a bantam cock of a Belfast man and one of the hardest men of a generation that prided itself on hardness. He had served with the old IRA from 1916 to 1921 and then had become a "republican," fighting against the new government of the Irish Free State. He had entered above-ground politics in 1927 and became one of the first cohort of Fianna Fail deputies in the Dail. He held a succession of cabinet posts from 1932 onward. In 1957–65 he was minister for health and, in 1959–65 was tanaiste, that is, deputy prime minister of Ireland. Sean MacEntee was immensely vain (he had hand-crafted wooden hangers made for his tailor-made suits), extremely caustic, and the most fanatical anticommunist among the Fianna Fail leadership. Everywhere, he saw reds. [34]

Maire MacEntee grew up in a confusing mixture of privilege and deprivation. As befitted a daughter of one of the most powerful men in Ireland (frequently reckoned to be the second most powerful man in the country in the late 1950s), she had never done housework. The family had maids for everything. The only household task Maire learned to do as a girl was to iron dresses that were too expensive to be trusted to the maids. Her father was emotionally distant; her mother frequently great fun. Her mother had three brothers who had entered the church: Monsignor Patrick Browne, president of University College, Galway; Father Maurice Browne, parish priest of Ballymore Eustace in County Kildare; and Michael Cardinal Browne, a leading Dominican.

Both of Maire's Browne grandparents spoke Irish and one of her clerical uncles built a summer house for the family at Dunquin, Dingle, County Kerry, so that Maire and her brother and sister could learn Irish in a Gaeltacht. This immersion in the Irish language and associated culture was one of the privileges of Maire's life and it provided her with her greatest passion—caring for, loving, caressing the words of the old culture and, eventually keening, as it slowly dies.

Maire, though five years younger than Conor (she was born in 1922) left university at the same time he did, 1941. She had prepared at a Dunquin national school, then Alexandra College, Dublin (a private Anglican school where her mother had taught for a time, because this was the only girls' secondary school that would employ someone—even as a part-time teacher—who would not take the oath of loyalty to the new Irish Free State), and Beaufort High School, Rathfarnham. At University College, Dublin, Maire was easily the brightest student in her year, taking a double degree in modern languages and in Celtic studies. She received first-class honors overall, as well as ranking first among the students in each of those two separate subjects. During the war, she was a scholar at the Dublin Institute for Advanced Studies, which published in 1946 her *Two Irish Arthurian Romances*. In the years 1945–47 she had a traveling studentship, spent in Paris. When she came back from Paris, at her father's direction (not suggestion, direction: this was Sean MacEntee) she studied intensely for the bar and qualified. She had no interest in practicing law, however, so Maire took the entrance examination to the Department of External Affairs (which, after World War II, held separate exams rather than rely on the common civil service entrance examination). She did well and became a third secretary. She served in France and in Spain and worked her way up the ladder and as a first secretary became part of the new United Nations section. When in New York in the years 1957–60, she served on the sixth committee (legal questions), the fourth (trusteeship), and the third (social, cultural, and humanitarian matters—usually called "the women's committee"). She was the diplomatic officer who fielded the threats from Cardinal Spellman and his henchmen concerning what would happen if the Irish did not follow the U.S. line on China. That was purely fortuitous, but Maire was the person in the Irish delegation one would have chosen to receive the call: when one's pet uncle is a cardinal, one is not impressed by bad-mannered ecclesiastical princes.

At the same time she was pursuing her diplomatic career Maire was writing and translating. A collection of her own work, *Margadh Na Saoirse* (The Hiring Fair), was published in Dublin in 1956, and a set of translations from the Irish, *A Heartful of Thought*, appeared in 1959. One of the things that made Maire attractive to Conor was her often-contradictory mixture of serious devotion to being a good civil servant and skilled diplomat and the incandescent passion she had for a culture and a system of values whose roots were premodern and, indeed, pre-Christian. One moment she argued geopolitics, the next Old Irish metrics.

Similarly, Maire was highly respectful of the structure of authority within the civil service and within the government in general (her father had raised her to a sense of hierarchy) but, if asked her opinion by a superior, she would give it with a candor that made one wonder if such queries really were good operational procedure. She was very skeptical of Conor when she arrived in his section. "At first I thought that the department was too small to hold both of us. I thought him cynical, overbearing, and time-serving."[35] And she let him know it.

Not physically prepossessing (a friend of that era remembers that Maire always looked as if she had just been pulled through a hedge), she had a quality that came from the aura of energy stored up. She seemed to be a tightly wound spring, just waiting to be set off. This was a female version of her father's mien: he always gave the impression of holding himself in check, the kind of person who, if you accidentally bumped against him, might put a fist in your face in an instant and unthinking reflex action. Maire's energy was more benign and more apt to be channeled into positive enthusiasms, especially for the Irish language and its literature, but there was always the sense of her being on a hair-trigger. That was very attractive to Conor.

When Maire and Conor's tours in New York overlapped (Conor was there for almost all of each session; Maire somewhat less), life was good indeed. They and compatible members of other delegations and members of the press contingent (notably Andrew Boyd of the *Economist*) used to drink and misbehave at the Murray Hill Bar and Grill, two blocks from the UN. There pitchers of draft were $2.50 and the fights were thrown in free. (On one occasion, Conor had Frank Aiken along with him as he went into another favorite tavern, this one on Third Avenue. As they entered, a brawl was going on. "This," Conor told the Irish foreign minister, "shows how close we are to the American public.")[36] Frank Aiken was something of an impediment to Conor's relationship with Maire. He knew about the affair but affected not to know. That was fine; what was difficult was that Aiken, being alone in New York, wanted company in the evening hours. There is, Maire and Conor discovered, a limit to the number of meals one can eat in Chinese restaurants with the Irish foreign minister, especially when one wants to be at the San Carlos Hotel, in bed. To avoid him near the end of the working day, they took to ducking into stairwells, hiding in the loo, and so on; at times they felt like they were in a Marx Brothers film being shot at the United Nations.

Late in 1960, Maire received a good posting. She was appointed a permanent representative to the European Community in Strasbourg. That meant she would be splitting her years between Strasbourg and Dublin.

As the affair between Maire and Conor went on year after year, it became recognized within a limited social circle in Dublin as a de facto marriage. Maire and Christine of course already knew each other (Dublin was a very small town in those days). The two women became friends in an uneasy sort of way. They both understood that their individual self-interest would be served if they got along. In 1960 and 1961, Maire spent a good deal of time with Christine, Fedelma, and Kate (Donal having spent 1959–60 reading economics at TCD, went to Peterhouse, Cambridge, in the autumn of 1960 to do history) and with George Hetherington.

What kept things from developing as quickly as they might was the asymmetrical nature of the relationships involved. George Hetherington was rather keener on marrying Christine than Conor was on marrying Maire. He loved her, yes, but whether or not he was ready to commit to a second marriage even before the first one was dissolved, was another matter entirely. There was, thus, always the distinct possibility that he would arrange a divorce from Christine, but not marry Maire. These pieces of social physics were not known to all the participants, but they affected the way each of them related to the others.

When, in 1960, Freddie Boland became president of the General Assembly of the United Nations for a two-year period, Conor's responsibilities increased. He was raised to an assistant secretaryship of the Department of External Affairs (equivalent in rank to an ambassadorship) and was made responsible for the political, cultural, and information activities of the department. This was in addition to his UN duties. Conor was on track to receive in the future a choice ambassadorship—London, Paris, or Washington, D.C.—and eventually to become secretary of the department. It seemed to be written in the stars.

Yet, simultaneously, Conor was gambling on a different one of fortune's wheels. In March 1961 Dag Hammarskjold asked the Irish government to release Conor so that he could be the on-ground head of the
UN mission in the Congo. This was the first of the sort of peace-keeping
missions that the UN engages in today (in contrast to the Korea-type UN
operation which had been essentially the labeling of a U.S. army as a UN
force). The Irish government turned down the secretary general's
request.

That was strange, in view of the Dail's act of 1960 which had authorized the sending of Irish troops to the Congo under UN command.
However, the Irish government and especially Fianna Fail, were jumpy
about the Congo matter. Sean MacEntee brooded that the Congo business was part of a communist conspiracy, and Frank Aiken was said to
have reservations about sending Irish troops to central Africa—on the
interesting grounds that the Irish lads could not stand the heat.[37]

Conor badly wanted the UN job, and over drinks in a bar near the UN
headquarters, he suggested to a ranking member of the UN secretariat
that they should apply for him again, and that this time they not mention the Congo.[38] It worked. At the end of May the new request was
granted. This made Conor happy and brought almost as much pleasure
to Freddie Boland who had strongly supported the application.[39]
Boland was pleased to see Conor leave in June 1961 for darkest Africa,
but he would have been equally pleased to have seen him go anyplace,
just so that it was far away.

That any sane person would wish to betake himself into the middle
of a central African war takes some explaining. That Conor, with no
military experience whatsoever, and no knowledge of riot control or
counterinsurgency methods, and who had never brokered anything
more complex than a diplomatic bridge game, would take such an assignment surpasses strange. Except ... except for two considerations.
One of these is that Conor has one of the lowest thresholds of boredom
one can encounter in a mature adult. He learns so quickly and is so in-
conveniently bright that he is like a mathematical prodigy who moves
from one difficult problem to another and simply cannot stand life when
there is not something complex to solve.

And, at that time, in his mid-forties, Conor was extremely ambitious.
I think that what he was doing in the Congo can be explained by an
analogy. There is a classic book by Norman Sykes on that most venal
of religious institutions, the Church of England in the eighteenth century. In his book, the Rev. Dr. Sykes employs a metaphor common in
the eighteenth century to explain the system of ecclesiastical careers:
namely, that it all was a system of lotteries. A poor curate would throw

in an application for a rich benefice, the same way that he would buy and deposit a lottery ticket in a lottery drum or wheel. There it might turn up a prize, and then it was possible to transfer to some better ecclesiastical wheel, where the prizes were better. If one were very lucky and won on successive lottery wheels, eventually one might become a bishop or, ultimately, an archbishop. The trick was to do well in one lottery and then take one's winnings to the next level, where the payoffs were higher.[40] That, I think, is what Conor was doing with the UN mission to the Congo. He was having a flutter on the big lottery, the upper level of the UN career service. If he did well, there was every chance that he would be offered a permanent job in the Secretariat and at a rank that would give him frequent access to the secretary general.[41] And once at that level, anything could happen.

• • •

The situation into which Conor was sent in June 1961 was not intellectually complicated, but messy, and in human terms, tragic. The Congo had been one of the oldest European colonies (from 1885 onward) and year-in, year-out, one of the harshest run. When the Belgians pulled out in June 1960, they left a people largely unprepared for self-rule. The country was well worth ruling, however. One of the largest nations in Africa—ten times the size of Great Britain; one-quarter the area of the United States—it was the world's largest producer of cobalt, and second largest producer of industrial diamonds, and a major exporter of copper. The population of roughly 35 million was split into four major tribal groups—the Ba-Kongo, the Ba-Mongo, the Ba-Luba, and the Ba-Lunda—and dozens of smaller tribes and clans. Rivalries among these groups were extremely bitter. The government of the newly independent state had not only to control tribal warfare, but to put down a break away movement in the southern province, Katanga, which was rich in copper and cobalt. This was especially difficult because agents of the former colonial power, Belgium, and also of Britain and, to a lesser extent, of France, would have liked to have seen an independent Congo. The British were crucial because, through their hegemony over Rhodesia, they had a corridor into Katanga and many right-wing politicians and businessmen saw the province as theirs for the picking.

The scale of the UN peace-keeping operation in the Congo was impressive: close to 20,000 troops, making it the biggest UN operation of its sort until the late 1980s. There is a significant literature on the Congo crisis of 1960–61, but this is not the place to engage in its exegesis, if we want to keep the focus primarily on Conor and especially on what the Congo episode did to him personally, emotionally, and domestically.[42] Thus, as a means of framing the picture around Conor, I present two schema: my own judgments about the way he handled his mission considered in administrative and personal terms, and a chronology that can be used as a backdrop for viewing the more nuanced aspects of his personal drama. First, here are my own judgments:

1. Conor did in the Congo what he was expected to do by his superiors. He was not in charge of the UN in the Congo, and was under orders. His tone may have been arrogant, but his actions were within the mandate provided by the UN resolutions, by Hammarskjold's instructions, and by the logic of the situation (see Chapter 7).
2. He made one big mistake in announcing on 13 September 1961 that the Katangese secession was over, when certainly it was not.
3. In the case of the operation that preceded that announcement, he was just plain unlucky. It should have worked.
4. His superiors, Dag Hammarskjold and, later, U Thant, sacrificed him to the big powers, especially the United Kingdom.

Now, here is a chronology of events, including the more important events that relate to Conor's personal life.[43]

30 June 1960	The Congo becomes independent.
4 July	Mutiny of Congolese soldiers and attacks on Europeans begin.
11 July	Katanga declares itself independent.
12	July Patrice Lumumba (prime minister of the national government) and Joseph Kasavubu (head of state) appeal for UN military assistance because Belgian troops are present, ostensibly to protect Europeans.
16 July	First UN troops arrive.
7 August	Moise Tshombe elected head of state of Katanga. Belgian troops leave all provinces except Katanga.
20 August	Rajeshwar Dayal appointed as Hammarskjold's special representative in the Congo.
5 September	Split between Kasavubu and Lumumba.
1 December	Lumumba captured by Katangese troops.
17 January 1961	Lumumba murdered by Katangese captors.
21 February	Security Council adopts resolution permitting all necessary steps to stop the civil war in the Congo, including "the use of force, if necessary, in the last resort."
25 May	Dayal removed as special UN representative.

29 May	Conor leaves Dublin to report for duty at UN in New York.
8 June	Conor leaves for Congo, via Brussels and Paris.
14 June	Conor arrives in Elisabethville as special UN representative of Dag Hammarskjold.
Month of July	Donal Cruise O'Brien, on summer holidays from Cambridge, visits his father in Elisabethville.
11 July	Katanga celebrates first anniversary of independence.
12 July	Hammarskjold and Belgian authorities in Geneva negotiate "final" withdrawal of Belgian troops.
28 August	Operation Rumpunch is largely successful in arresting foreign mercenaries on whom Katangese depend. At behest of Belgian consular corps, the arrests are stopped before process is complete.
12 September	Tshombe refuses Conor's demand that he repatriate the remaining mercenaries.
13 September	Operation Morthor in Elisabethville. Another attempt to arrest Katangese operatives fails and fighting ensues. Conor, however, announces that the Katanga secession is at an end.
13 September	Dag Hammarskjold arrives in Leopoldville.
13 September	British foreign office begins public campaign against UN action. Sir Roy Welensky, prime minister of Rhodesia, strongly denounces UN.
14 September	Irish troops attacked by Katangese.
14 September	Tshombe announces total war on the UN.
16 September	Tshombe and Hammarskjold agree to meet in Rhodesia.
17 September	Hammarskjold leaves for Rhodesia. His plane crashes and he dies.
15 October	Conor advised by F. Boland to request transfer back to UN in New York City, in order to please British foreign office. He refuses.
31 October	Maire arrives in Elisabethville.
16 November	Recalled to New York, Conor leaves; Maire stays.
28 November	Maire, Brian Urquhart (Conor's successor), and George Ivan Smith beaten up by Katangese para-commandos.

29–30 November	Maire returns from Elisabethville to Dublin.
30 November	U Thant demands that Ireland ask for Conor's recall. Conor and Frank Aiken agree.
1 December	Conor returns to the Irish diplomatic service.
1 December	Maire resigns from Irish diplomatic service.
2 December	Conor gives statement to *New York Times* and to the London *Observer*. He resigns from Irish diplomatic service.
3 December	Conor's statement is published.
4 December	Conor gives major press conference, breaking all the rules of UN diplomacy.
14–21 December	Permanent ceasefire arranged with Katangese. Secession virtually ended.
1965	Joseph-Désiré Mobutu becomes president (dictator) of the Congo.
1971	Congo renamed Zaire.
April 1991	Mobutu declares end to single-party rule.

Behind this sparse chronology were a number of very human faces. The first of these was Eamon de Valera. He now was president of Ireland; that is, the ceremonial head of state, and he resided in Aras an Uachtarain, that magnificent monument to colonial rule in the Phoenix Park. He summoned Conor in order to wish him luck. His eyes were failing, but aided by thick lenses, he was able to make out faces and figures. "You came to see me with Mr. MacBride," he recalled. He was right.

"I thought then," he continued, "I thought: that man is interested in politics." He smiled, the famous unnerving de Valera smile and Conor immediately thought of James Dillon's observation that "Dev has a smile like moonlight on a tombstone."

De Valera could be thoughtful and sentimental, and as a good luck piece he gave to Conor a nineteenth-century daguerreotype of Conor's great uncle, Father Eugene Sheehy, who had been de Valera's parish priest in his youth. On the picture the president wrote in Irish "He taught me patriotism." That was a lovely thing to do and the sentiment requires only a flavoring of cynicism to put it in perspective. That was provided by Conor's friend (and frequent legal counsel) Alexis FitzGerald whom Conor met on the street in central Dublin a little while later. Conor proudly showed him the daguerreotype and de Valera's inscription. FitzGerald, a Fine Gael supporter of impeccable pro-treaty lineage, looked at the inscription and then remarked, "Your great-uncle has a lot to answer for."[44]

The next figure, equal in magnitude to de Valera, was Dag Hammarskjold whom Conor met several times (but, as events later showed, not often enough) in New York in preparation for his Congo mission. Hammarskjold inspired awe, alloyed only by a solemnity that sometimes tipped over into the lugubrious. He was anything but a democrat. His family had been granted a knighthood in the seventeenth century and his own father had been Swedish prime minister during World War I and was far to the right on the political spectrum. Hammarskjold knew that he was born to rule, but unlike his father, the entire world became his kingdom. Conor was greatly drawn to Hammarskjold who, although only a dozen years older than Conor, had a weight and authority that made him less like an older brother than a patriarch, a father-figure. "Someone said of Saint-Just that he carried his head like the Holy Sacrament. I was reminded of that phrase when I first met Hammarskjold."[45] Hammarskjold also possessed an ability to form utterances, and even operational directives, whose meaning was clear to him but not to others. Conor left for the Congo thinking that he knew what was in Dag Hammarskjold's mind and, perhaps he did.

The human figures, some of them grotesques, others gargoyles, others secular saints, that populated the mephitic underworld into which Conor now descended are brilliantly described in Conor's *To Katanga and Back* (which is assayed in detail in chapter 7), and there is no profit in here repeating those verbal etchings. What that book necessarily leaves out is the fact that while Conor was trying to bring order, and if not peace at least quiet, to central Africa, he was simultaneously having to work out the most complex and wrenching details of his own emotional and personal life. Christine and George Hetherington were keen to be married and obviously that meant Conor and Christine must divorce; the children had to be told and brought through the pain; Maire was devoted to Conor and wanted to spend her life with him. All that, with a tribal war going on, plus having to deal with the inscrutable Dag Hammarskjold and the internal politics of the UN secretariat would be enough to send almost anyone over the brink.

At the end of May, Maire had written to Conor in New York that Christine was going to England and "she may speak to Donal" about the divorce between his parents. (In the actual event, she did not do so until later.) Maire added: "I will tell Christine that I do not think the little girls should be told anything until we have something pleasant to tell them"—meaning a wedding date for Conor and Maire.[46] A day later, Maire reported, "I had lunch with Christine and it went off very well. I do not think there is any fear that she will tell the little girls anything prematurely. We agreed to keep in very close touch and to take them out together when possible." Everyone was being very adult about things, but the situation inevitably held its tensions. "I am relieved to find that on the whole she is anxious for the settlement to go through speedily," Maire told Conor. "I worked very hard to overcome our mutual reserve towards each other. I cannot say with what success."[47]

What Maire and Christine were trying to do was actually something in equal parts complex and, if it worked, wonderful: to make a transition in family structure in a way that would not hurt the two girls (Donal, at university, was assumed to be able to handle things himself). After the Conor-Christine divorce and the Conor-Maire marriage and the Christine-George marriage, the girls would have to deal with two new step-parents as well as seeing in future their mother and their father in totally different domestic contexts.[48] So, Conor should have been buoyed to hear snippets of news such as, for example, that at Fedelma's suggestion, Maire and the girls went off on a long drive to Skerries "and there was no disharmony whatsoever."[49] The trouble was that there was always the stomach-knotting worry that perhaps the planned transition would not work and that the girls would be seriously traumatized.

Soon after Conor arrived in Elisabethville, he had a letter from Maire saying "Christine and I talked late and I stayed the night [at 'Whitewater']." "C. and G. plan to hurry things which is all to the good for us. I have distinct impression the children know and are not upset. They have not been told. C. would like you to tell Donal when he joins you." (Donal, on summer vacation from Peterhouse, Cambridge, was to join Conor in the Congo for the month of July. He was leaving on 20 June, Maire reported, and added "lucky little horror!")[50]

This sort of progress can only have been heartening to Conor—always assuming that he really was as keen on being married to Maire as he was on being divorced from Christine. And Maire's letters were for the most part not soppy, but loving, devoted and divertingly newsy. (One treasures the report that Douglas Gageby had refused to contemplate sending the *Irish Times* to Conor for free as part of the national effort, on the grounds that Conor would always buy it anyway, so there would be no return for the investment; that nugget indicates in an instant why Gageby was a truly great newspaper manager.)[51]

But amid the gossip and love and news items, there were things that made Conor worry. Maire was coping with a career-war within the Department of External Affairs. Her Strasbourg post normally would have involved a promotion to counselor, but the financial meanness of the Department of Finance was holding that back (eventually she won, but too late to do any good). Frequently in her letters, Maire apologizes for being down or depressed. Conor and Maire and the girls were able to meet in Europe during his three-week leave in August, and that was immensely heartening. But the girls still had not been told.

And, after that holiday, everything became exciting, both in Africa and at Howth. On 28 August, an operation called "Rumpunch" and directed by Conor rounded up most of the 500 foreign mercenaries (mostly Belgian) who held key posts in the army of the breakaway Katanga state. However, just over 100 of them escaped, because, at the request of the Belgian consul-general, the UN stopped the arrests in order to permit the Belgian government to remove the rest of the mercenaries. The Belgian government then defaulted on its part of the bargain.

It was at this point that it became clear that the old colonial powers were going to do what they could to subvert the UN peace-keeping mission. The United Kingdom joined the Belgian government in being obstructive, for the idea of the breakaway mineral-rich Katangan province joining Rhodesia was very inviting. Thus, Conor was vilified in the British right-wing press as a war-monger, a mini-Castro. Simultaneously, in Katanga, Moise Tshombe, prime minister of the new state, launched a campaign against the UN. Further victimization of the Ba-Luba tribe began, so that soon 35,000 Ba-Luba were crowded into a UN refugee camp in Elisabethville, weakly guarded from attack by a small Swedish army contingent.

While Conor was being buffeted by all these events, he had trouble getting mail to Maire, even when he had time to write. "A letter or a wire or phone call would keep me going at least a week," Maire plaintively declared.[52] "I long to see you," she wrote, and in the first hint that the two of them were planning to see each other in the Congo, she added "Second half of October would be good."[53]

That letter must have arrived in Elisabethville at about the same time Dag Hammarskjold was landing in Leopoldville; and at approximately the same time that Conor, in Elisabethville, was unsuccessfully attempting in Operation Morthor to arrest the rest of the foreign mercenaries.

In the short period between Operation Morthor and Dag Hammarskjold's fatal plane flight (events she could not have known about when writing), Maire wrote two letters, both of them distraught for lack of word from Conor. "Heart, should I come out at once and chuck the Department? By the time you get this I may have done so already—probably not, but it is what is uppermost in my mind just now."[54] A day later, Maire wrote from a train en route to Brussels where she had diplomatic duties. "I am writing this ... in the hope that [Frank Aiken who was going to the Congo to investigate reports of Irish troop deaths], whom I hope to meet this evening will carry it to you. I will also ask him to take me with him, but I know there is no chance that he will." Maire continued, "However, as soon as I can contact you and know that you agree, I will come—either for always or for fourteen days, whatever seems best."[55]

In the shocked days after Dag Hammarskjold's crashed plane was found (on 18 September), a temporary ceasefire was arranged between the UN troops and the Katangese rebels. For the time being, the Katangese were the victors. They regained control of the public buildings in Elisabethville and were allowed to set up the apparatus of an independent state.

Now Conor's stock plummeted. The British wanted him gone and so did leading members of the UN Secretariat who did not approve his brashness. And, in some unconscious way, they probably blamed him for Hammarskjold's death. The only thing that kept Conor from being cashiered immediately was the Afro-Asian block which admired the way he stood up to the imperial powers. So, isolated in Elisabethville, walking around an ill-maintained and scarred villa, eating tinned food, and clutching at straws, Conor sat out October.

In that environment, Conor received a sequence of letters from Maire that began by telling him of some unspecified "*nerventkrieg*"— "The details of which are such that I cannot commit them to paper, but it is important that you should know that you owe a great deal to the courage and devotion of all your friends and particularly to Christine and George."[56] What this was about is unclear, but certainly Christine and George had defended Conor against a good deal of local badmouthing. "You should show the maximum generosity to C. and G., not only for the children's sake, but because they most richly deserve it," Maire advised.[57]

Some of the debt owed may have had to do with Sean and Margaret MacEntee, for a few days later, Maire wrote that "I have also reestablished cordial relations with home. They were somewhat strained over the last fortnite." Maire continued: "I will give you that whole story when I meet you. I couldn't leave the poor old things facing the poll and the count unsupported."[58] That was both a metaphor and a reference to the general election of 4 October.

The real issue was how Kate and Fedelma would be told about Conor and Christine's divorce and about the two impending (or, at least, implied) marriages. News of how this had been accomplished reached Conor in mid-October. Maire reported that she had gone out to Howth on Sunday afternoon, the first of October. "It was to find that Christine had already told the girls the night before. She tells me it was heart-rending and that both wept bitterly." That Sunday afternoon and evening, the day after the girls had been told, must have been emotionally exhausting for everyone. Fedelma and Kate, Maire reported, "were a little quiet and withdrawn towards me in the early part of the evening, but allowed themselves to be coaxed into sitting on my knee and being cuddled and hugged very quickly and after that things were much better."[59] In fact, a celebration followed. George Hetherington's adult children arrived and everyone drank champagne. For a time, the girls were very worldly and grown-up. Kate, age thirteen, speculated about the propriety of ladies in Christine's and Maire's circumstances wearing veils and carrying wreaths to get married. The girls, though, had their fears, especially the dread of losing Conor. That night when Fedelma was unable to sleep, Maire spent the night in the same room with her.

Soon thereafter, Christine and the girls moved into a house that George engaged, "Rookstown," which is also on Howth summit, just over the hill from "Whitewater." From Rookstown, Kate sent Conor a gloriously reassuring letter. She began by asking him for a "photo of yourself to be (framed of course) for my new room." She told him that the news of the new domestic arrangements did not upset her very much. "Of course, I had always known so that it was not such a big fright." But it did "hurt a bit to know that you would not remain married." Very generously she added, "But *nothing* else matters so long as I know that all four of you are happy."[60]

Maire moved into "Whitewater" and worried about whether it should be sold. She advised Conor against selling, however, at least for a time, as the sale would hurt the girls too much. A tenant could be found.[61] In the meantime, Maire had to move to "Rookstown" for a while to take care of the girls while Christine went to Cambridge and to Holland.[62]

By early October, it was decided that Maire definitely would be going to the Congo. "I can hardly control my excitement at the thought of seeing you," she wrote from "Whitewater" on 5 October.[63] Her plan was to go to Strasbourg under cover of attending a diplomatic meeting and then to sneak away and fly to Leopoldville. She added: "I am wildly happy."[64]

This was cutting things a bit fine. Not only was Maire planning to absent herself without permission from her diplomatic post, but there was the danger of potential publicity. News of Conor's actions were in every British and Irish daily newspaper and there were reporters and stringers in the Congo who would have loved to turn his personal life into a sensation. Maire had expressed some worries about this: "Fleet St. is waiting to pounce and that might not suit your book at the moment."[65] And Donal, who despite his relative youth frequently acted as an adviser to Conor, worried. "Be careful," he told Maire in a very sensible letter. "I know that you will have taken all the relevant considerations and on the whole I think you would be right to go: do think over the publicity side, however." Almost paternally, he explained something about his own father. "The trouble is Conor does not quite realize the intensity of the campaign in the dirty press."[66]

Donal was right. But even if Conor had understood that every British paper to the right of the *Guardian* and the *Observer* wanted his head, I doubt if he would have been cautious. Caution has never been his way, and here, something more was also at play. Another historical analogy may help. It relates to Charles Stewart Parnell. One of the scarlet threads that runs through Parnell's life was a continuous and frequent testing of his own omnipotence. He was forever disproving his own mortality by doing things that he should never have done and was extremely lucky to get away with. Not until the very last, the O'Shea affair, did he have to pay directly for his behavior. Now, Conor at this time was very much like Parnell in that if he wished to keep his career intact, he would be well advised to act very prudently. He was already vulnerable because his gambles in Katanga had left that problem unsolved and also because he was associated, however vaguely, with the death of Dag Hammarskjold. The last thing he should have contemplated was to import an Irish woman diplomat who was AWOL from her post. To do so was to assert an independence from the probabilities that governed and limited the lives of everyday mortals.

But he did it. Thus we find his penciling "urgent" on a message that he telexed to his friend and UN colleague, Walter Fulcheri, in Leopoldville: "I have a friend and colleague Miss MacEntee of the Irish department of external affairs arriving in Leopoldville from Brussels today. Would it be too much to ask you to meet or have her met and let me know how and when she is coming to Elisabethville."[67]

Conor and Maire spent a fortnight together. It may not have been idyllic, but it certainly was diverting: they watched the central government officials take over control of Albertville and attended a mass funeral for tribesmen killed in rioting, and somehow stayed out of the viewfinders of the yellow press. On 16 November, however, Conor and the Irish commander in the Congo, General Sean McKeown, were called to New York where the Security Council was about to debate the Congo situation.

Here is the twist: Conor left Maire in Elisabethville in the company of George Ivan Smith, the principal public relations officer for the UN in the Congo. A wild and winning Irish-Australian, Smith and Conor had become good friends. Why would Conor leave Maire in the Congo? Because he believed he would be back quickly. In *To Katanga and Back*, Conor suggests that he naively believed he would receive a fair hearing at the highest level.[68]

When Conor arrived in New York, it quickly became apparent just how deeply he was in disgrace. Freddie Boland, now president of the UN General Assembly, gave a dinner party to permit informal discussion of the Congo situation. The guest list consisted of Charles Ritchie (Canada), Sir Patrick Dean (United Kingdom), Ralph Bunche (of the UN Secretariat), General McKeown, and their partners. "I hope you won't mind my not asking Conor," said Boland to McKeown, "but he's not quite the right colour."[69] Elsewhere, Mrs. Boland was reported as saying that Conor was "a fucking crook," an unusually clear indication in UN circles of where Conor stood, which was nowhere.[70]

In fact, he was expected to become a nonbeing. Without Conor's being told, Brian Urquhart, who had been dispatched to the Congo, was named his successor. Conor understood what he was expected to do under UN rules of etiquette: fall on his sword, just as his predecessor Rajeshwar Dayal had done. That is, he was expected to take the blame for the less-than-successful actions that had followed from the policies and directives of the Security Council and of the secretary general. In particular, U Thant expected Conor to take the blame for the administrative and logistical failings of his own predecessor, Dag Hammarskjold.

Conor recognized that this was not merely the end of his brief UN career, but also that pleading guilty (as it were) probably would put a ceiling to his future in the Irish diplomatic corps. He would forever be shunted from one unimportant job to another, still an assistant secretary, but in charge of nothing—save perhaps writing the history of the department—and he would be referred to as "poor O'Brien." Conor's world was collapsing and both mentally and physically he was a mess.

• • •

How Conor would have concluded his days as a UN diplomat if on, say, 26 November, he had gotten himself together, is anyone's guess. Thereafter, everything changed, because of an extraordinary set of events in the Congo, events of which Maire was (at least from Conor's point of view) the epicenter.[71]

On 27 or 28 November 1961 (Conor cannot quite remember) Ralph Bunche called Conor into his office and asked him, "Who is Miss

MacAndrew?" He was referring to Maire. Conor told him who she was and that the two of them expected to be married and that he had left her in Elisabethville, as he had expected to be back soon.

"I think that you have made a mistake," Bunche said.

Maire, in fact, almost became a casualty. On the afternoon of 28 November, she received word from Conor to return to Dublin. However, she first attended a cocktail party in Elisabethville given by some people whom she liked in honor of Senator Thomas Dodd of Connecticut and his wife. This was generous because Dodd, in addition to being notably corrupt politically, was a strong backer of Tshombe and of the Katangese secessionists. After the reception, Maire, George Ivan Smith, Brian Urquhart, and Fitzhugh Green (of the U.S. Information Service) got into a UN car driven by a courageous Irish army private, Patrick Wall. They were to be taken to a dinner party for Senator Dodd hosted by Mobil Oil. Just before they reached Mobil Oil House, they were stopped by an almost out-of-control squad of Katangese paracommandos. They managed to get into the house, however, and there just had time to get a drink and compose themselves when half a dozen or more men broke in, armed with automatic weapons and highly excited. Brian Urquhart immediately took a hit in the face with a rifle butt. Paddy Wall and Maire jumped between the paras and Urquhart, who was spurting blood, and flim-flammed them for a couple of minutes in the French creole that was the common language of the Katangese tribal groups. As she stood beside Paddy Wall, Brian Urquhart's blood spurting all over the back of her blouse, automatic rifles being shoved in her face, one of the thoughts that raced through Maire's mind was, "here goes our hope of a quiet divorce."

The delaying tactics were working until, suddenly, another bunch of paras arrived. They punched Maire in the face, threw Paddy Wall aside, and grabbed and took away George Ivan Smith, Brian Urquhart, and Fitzhugh Green.[72] As events worked out, the three hostages survived. They were lucky, for the Katangese troops were looking for blood. Maire the next morning caught a flight to Leopoldville. (The Cuban pilot came in too steeply and snapped the propeller of the plane, but there were no injuries) and thence she returned to Dublin.

The story of what had happened reached the United Nations on the evening of 29 November and was in papers all over the world the next day. The story was susceptible to all sorts of interpretations, ranging from indicating that the Katangese were not ready to be an independent state, to revealing that the former UN special representative in the Congo, a married man, had been entertaining his girlfriend at UN expense. U Thant hated bad press and immediately demanded that the

Irish government recall Conor. Frank Aiken and Conor had a discussion in Aiken's room in the San Carlos Hotel and they agreed that Aiken would ask for Conor's recall. The alternative was that U Thant would publicly fire Conor, which would have been a collective disgrace to the Irish foreign service. To let Aiken off the hook, Conor wrote out a letter asking him to petition U Thant for his return to the Irish service.

Was Conor going to fall on his sword, after all? It was still possible. He called Maire on the evening of 1 December, soon after she had arrived in Dublin and told her that he had decided to resign from the Irish diplomatic service. She replied that she already had done so that morning! (Given that she was going to be married and that at this time no married female diplomatic officers were allowed, she would have been resigning in any case, but there was great satisfaction in doing it dramatically.) The next day, Saturday, 2 December, Conor resigned from the Department of External Affairs.

But even here matters spun crazily. Conor went out to celebrate (read: get drunk) with some friends and one of them asked him how, indeed, he had handed in his resignation. Conor was stunned. Then he burst into mirthless laughter. He had forgotten actually to write the letter. So he wrote one out in the bar and had a friend take it over to the San Carlos and give the resignation to Frank Aiken.[73]

No: Conor was not going to fall on his sword. Before going drinking on Saturday, he had written a long statement explaining why he was leaving the UN and Irish service and had sent it to the *New York Times* and to the London *Observer*. It was published the next day, Sunday. From then on, everything was irrevocable.

What Conor had decided was that if he had to commit professional suicide, he would do it in his own way: an *auto-da-fé* in the biggest public square in town, and he would at least have the pleasure of lighting the first faggot. Thus, on Monday the world's press descended on a news conference where he aired the dirty linen of several countries, especially Belgium and the United Kingdom. And he slagged the British gutter press. He went easier on Dag Hammarskjold than he was to do later when he had fuller information about Hammarskjold's behavior. And he announced that he would be married to Miss Maire MacEntee.

There, if this were a film, the story would end. The couple would next be seen walking hand in hand on a sandy beach, at peace and in love.

In the real world, things were messier and crueller.

At home in Dublin, Maire was not being cosseted, or even treated very well. She arrived in Dublin exhausted from her exodus from

Katanga, her face bruised and swollen from being punched by the paracommandos, and was immediately placed under house arrest. Her father, as tanaiste, was able to command special branch officers to have her locked up on his own say-so, not in jail, but in the family home. Very medieval, very Irish. Maire's captivity came to an end after some days when her mother took her side. Margaret MacEntee told Sean that "I would have done the same for you, when I loved you, Sean" and that was as powerful as Moses hitting the rock. The next night, the guard was diverted (Sean MacEntee, even when surrendering, had to keep face) and a van driven by two men, arranged by Christine who accompanied them, pulled up to the MacEntee's house. Maire's mother helped Maire out of the window and she was free.[74] (Conor, later in the month, had the unenviable task of calling on the MacEntees and trying to explain. Of course he succeeded, for he could talk a penguin into flying; and in fact he later became quite fond of both the MacEntees and close with Sean.)

Another result was that the mess splashed onto the two O'Brien girls, Kate and Fedelma. When events in the Congo hit the newspapers, the English gutter press took the low road. Kate was followed to school by English reporters who tried to get her to denounce her father. And, inevitably, both girls were the victims of clucking tongues, something no teenage girl enjoys. The yellow press was especially keen to set up a polarity—Conor as a philandering husband, Christine as a virtuous and wronged wife. Christine was much too smart to buy that package and slammed the door on the reporters.

Conor returned home and dealt with the cold business of marriage law. Since divorce was impossible in Ireland, the process was expensive. On 1 January 1962, he and Christine signed a formal separation agreement and he immediately flew to Juarez, Chihuahua, Mexico. There on 3 January, he divorced her on grounds of "incompatibility of character." The children were placed in their mother's custody (a formality, as Conor was allowed full access) and no alimony was awarded (George Hetherington's financial resources made that unnecessary, and Conor continued to pay the girls' school fees, and the like).[75] Christine Foster married George Hetherington on 19 June 1962 on Long Island, New York, and today they remain a loyal and happy couple.

Conor and Maire were married on 9 January 1962 at the Carmelite church, Our Lady of the Scapular, in Manhattan. Normally, divorced persons are not allowed to remarry in a Catholic church, but Conor had previously been married only in a civil ceremony; according to canon law, that was no marriage. Any doubts there might have been were stilled by the celebrant's being Michael Cardinal Browne, head of the worldwide Dominican order and one of Maire's three clerical uncles. Conor, though still an unbeliever, had no objection to a church wedding: considering the hell Maire had gone through on his account, this really was not much for her to ask.

Conor and Maire went off to Trinidad for a honeymoon. Each was sufficiently bruised to be no longer naive, and sufficiently hardened to know how to protect what counted; and they were old enough and smart enough to know what, indeed, mattered.

PART 3

SURVIVING THE SIXTIES

CHAPTER 7

REFLECTIONS ON A WATERSHED

If you have ever traversed a major watershed—the genuine item, from which on one side the water runs, say, south, and on the other side, north—you probably were disappointed. "Watershed" is a dramatic word and it is indeed of real consequence that at one point a continent drains, say to Hudson's Bay, and, at another nearby point, to the Gulf of Mexico. Yet, on the face of things, the change is undramatic and apparently unimportant. Only downstream, after the watershed has been left hundreds of miles behind, does the acceleration of the current, the widening of the rivers, with the amplification of their force, ever growing, ever more powerful, make one realize that the watershed was a big deal after all.

Although Conor's (and Maire's) experiences in the Congo were anything but undramatic—the events were illuminated by rockets and flares that made them visible worldwide—the apparent changes in Conor were minimal. He did not become less witty, less acerbic, or notably more humble. He did not become craven or risk-avoiding. He stayed the same man. Yet, he did cross a personal watershed and its significance is easy to miss, precisely because his outward style changed so little. On a variety of matters, Conor quietly changed direction. As in the instance of a major watershed in the geophysical world, the import of this change of direction in Conor's emotional world was to become clear only further downstream. In particular, it was in the 1970s, when Conor began his great antiterrorism campaign, that it became clear just how momentous the Congo had been in sensitizing him to a crucial reality: that the veneer of civilization is very thin and that social anarchy, which he had experienced at first hand, was only a millimeter away.[1] Equally important, the Katanga affray permitted him to become in public what he had long been in private, a writer. Ever since "Carey Bloom" was published in the *Atlantic* in 1958, he had thought of himself as a writer, but he did not own his own name nor his own voice. "Above all, the writer in me began to take over as soon as the crisis had been reached," Conor later observed.[2] No longer a civil servant, from now on he no longer needed to be "Donat O'Donnell." Now he wrote as Conor Cruise O'Brien, and now there was no list of proscribed topics. These changes made possible what ultimately became Conor's great achievement: using the power of words to keep at bay the beast within human society.

What Conor tried to do now was to come to terms with a related series of subjects: what had happened in the Congo, what the character of the United Nations really was, and what mystery lay at the heart of the life and death of the tragically mystic Dag Hammarskjold. His concern with these matters ran through the 1960s, when Conor was vice-chancellor of the University of Ghana (1962–65) and then Schweitzer Professor at New York University (1965–69). These matters constitute a distinct and fundamental tonality in Conor's life in the sixties. Rather like the ground-bass in early polyphonic music, they were never far from his consciousness. They related to other matters basic to Conor's personality: Holy Mother Church and his own father.

The United Nations was the closest thing to a True Church that Conor ever knew. He believed in it, venerated it, and it had cast him out. Thus, he had to work out his relationship with the United Nations in much the same way that a spoiled priest has to work out his relationship to Holy Mother Church. This Conor did successfully, for he developed ways of remaining a believer.

Simultaneously Conor tried to work through his relationship with his second father, Dag Hammarskjold. Just as his first father had "failed" Conor—at the very moment he was bending life's bow for his son—so Dag had failed Conor. He too had bent the bow for Conor, had sent him forth to war in the world, and then, like Conor's real father, had disappeared abruptly from this earth. Unlike the matter of the United Nations, Conor did not quite put this question to rest during the 1960s. Today, in his later seventies, he still broods about Hammarskjold's death and still will not accept its tragic illogic.

• • •

The London *Observer* of the 1960s was the thinking family's way to get through Sunday. It had enough business and sports news to keep one on top of the barons and the Barbarians; and it published several first-rate columnists who, usually, yielded sufficient talking points to enable one to survive unscathed Sunday supper with the neighbors, who inevitably read the Sunday *Telegraph*. Editorially, the paper had a consistent record of anticolonialism and was particularly strong on African affairs. It was, therefore, the perfect place for Conor to tell his side of the story.

Conor talked to this audience with only a touch of abnegation. If he was going to be shot down for his actions in the Congo, he was going to give off a ferocious glow as he crashed. The first of two feature articles that he wrote for the *Observer* (10 December 1961) was uncharacteristic of Conor in that he used the broadsword rather than the rapier. He opened bluntly:

> My resignation from the United Nations and from the Irish Foreign Service is a result of British Government policy. That policy, as I have experienced it in practice, has been to give all aid covertly possible to the secessionist regime in Katanga while paying—in an attempt to delude the United States and the Afro-Asian commonwealth—lip-service to the unity of the Congo.

Later in the article he asserted that

> at my press conference in New York, I referred to the present British government as showing to the world at the UN on behalf of Britain, the face of Pecksniff. On reflection I think I was wrong. Pecksniff would have blushed had he been forced to make some of the recent declarations of British spokesmen about Britain's support of the UN effort in the Congo.

The entire article, his first attempt at written explanation, was like that. Although factually accurate (the U.K. government indeed had undercut the UN in the Congo), the piece was too crude, too Manichean, too self-pitying to be convincing. The only part that goes beyond self-justification and touches a human chord was Conor's obvious pain at finding that "there was some serious misunderstanding, the nature of which we could not quite grasp, between ourselves and Mr. Hammarskjold." But scant wonder, considering what Conor had just been through, that he wrote so crudely.

The real wonder is how quickly he righted himself. The next Sunday (17 December 1961), *Observer* readers were greeted with the second part of "My Case," and it was witty, pungent, controlled, and, therefore, much more likely to be politically lethal (see the Anthology, Selection 22). The piece began with a modest—indeed excessively modest, as Conor later realized—explanation of why Conor had been placed in charge of such an important UN mission. His suggestion was singular: not only did Conor come from a "reliable" country, but Hammarskjold "happened to have read a book of mine. This book, *Maria Cross*, had appeared some years earlier, not under my own name. ... Mr. Hammarskjold was one of the very few people who had read it, and he liked it. This is the reason he picked me and not some other person from a 'reliable' country to represent the U.N. in Katanga." After that bit of dissimulation (Conor was appointed for his ability and for perfectly sensible geopolitical and administrative reasons),[3] Conor got down to writing in the form that he seemed to have mastered instantly. The form was the short story. Not the short story of fiction, but a presentation of facts and characterizations—each of them capable of being documented—that worked by the kaleidoscopic presentation of images, color, personality. Occasionally, pieces of exposition provided transition, but these were minimal. So strong is the narrative and the anecdotal sequence that Conor does not have to draw a conclusion for the reader: once inside the story, the only possible conclusion the reader can have is that Conor is right.

The three main characters in this *Observer* story are Dag Hammarskjold, Mahmoud Khiary (Conor's superior on the ground in the Congo), and, of course, Conor himself. "My trouble, in my fleeting contacts with Mr. Hammarskjold, was that he seldom laughed at anything, and never at anything I considered funny." Hammarskjold "had, as a critical fellow-countryman Professor Herbert Tingsten observed, 'a humourless twinkle in his eye.'" Yet, Conor viewed him with great respect, the same kind of distant awe that Irish children of Conor's generation were taught to give to their fathers:

> As will be gathered, I was not at all close to Mr. Hammarskjold, but regarded him with immense respect, verging on awe. I saw in him absolute integrity devoted, with bravery and high intelligence, to a noble end. His aim was the creation of a centre of international moral authority, rising out of a chaos of nationalisms and clashing ideologies, to defend the common human cause of peace and justice. He himself, in the eyes of many people, and in my own eyes, incarnated this authority.

Against this incarnation stood a devil or, rather, a mischievous imp, Mr. Mahmoud Khiary, a Tunisian who in practice was the chief on-the-ground authority over Conor and who was the conduit of orders from the secretary general: "I cannot here attempt a portrait of Mahmoud Khiary, but it is necessary to say a few things about him. He is in the fullest sense of the word, a fabulous man: towering, mysterious, exotic, of vast capacities and not entirely worthy of belief."

From this fabulous imp, Conor received verbal instructions that authorized the use of force in its final and unsuccessful form. Khiary claimed to be in direct and secret communication with Dag Hammarskjold by means of ex-file telegrams. In the presence of four witnesses, Khiary gave Conor instructions to move forward militarily, with the final results that are well known. At the time of writing, in December 1961, Conor believed that although the secretary general was beginning to favor strong action in the Congo, he did not actually know of the orders that Khiary was parceling out. But whether or not he knew, Hammarskjold pulled back from the operation as soon as it failed. In an attempt to negotiate with the Katangese rebels he flew to Ndola in what was then northern Rhodesia (and today is part of Zambia). Hammarskjold's plane came down eight miles short of the airport:

> I learned of his death over the Telex in the cluttered signals room of U.N. headquarters in Elisabethville, among the stolid Canadian sergeants and their pinups from *Playboy* magazine. Outside, someone was mortaring the grounds in an inaccurate and desultory way for headline purposes (KATANGA FIGHTS ON). I cannot honestly say that I immediately felt a deep sense of loss. The recent telegrams had left me too numb for that. What I felt was something of what men have felt in all ages, hearing of the end of a great reign and knowing the succession uncertain.

End of story—and also, the kernel of a brilliant book. The main characters are there, the colossus Hammarskjold and the little boy Conor, neck cricked from looking upward so long. There too is the final, tragic separation of the two.

Also present in this extraordinarily compressed, controlled, and (within the confines of what Conor knew at the time) accurate short story, are the two central points on which one must judge Conor's actions in the Congo. Is it true that he was acting on orders? And did Dag Hammarskjold (for whatever reason) hang Conor out to dry, sublimating himself into his mist-shrouded Olympus, willfully ignoring the possibility that what had occurred was the logical working out of a paradigm he had himself created?

The writing of *To Katanga and Back: A un Case History* was amazingly quick. The book was published in London by Hutchinson on 12 November 1962. That this volume—which, with Conor's biography of

Edmund Burke are his triumphs in full-length prose writing—could be done so quickly is in part a monument to the passion that underlies it: passion about the Congo, the UN, and Dag, and also passion for Maire, who now was interwoven into the tapestry as a major figure. Conor dedicated the book to her. She helped greatly, and not solely emotionally, but in prosaic ways. Conor wrote the entire volume in his jumpy longhand (he always has had secretaries working for him, so he has never learned to type), and she translated for the typists, helped collate old letters and memoranda, recalled anecdotes, and kept the entire project rolling at speed. The O'Briens had returned from the Congo and New York with loads of information. They both had sharp memories and they both were disciplined to hard work through years spent as elite civil servants. That, however, does not explain why *To Katanga and Back* is such a marvelous book, merely how it came to be that way.

Leaving aside for the moment the aesthetic question, the book had one clear result. Conor won. He swept his opponents. True, he did this by breaking the rules, but these were rules intended to prevent the dissemination of facts. On 15 December 1961, the acting secretary general of the United Nations, U Thant, wrote to Conor reminding him of the UN staff regulation "1.5" which stated that UN employees "shall not communicate to any person any information known to them by reason of their official position which has not been made public, except in the course of their duties or by authorization of the secretary-general. Nor shall they at any time use such information to private advantage. These obligations do not cease upon separation from the Secretariat."[4] In other words, stick with the company story.

Conor had little intention of supporting the UN's agreed-lie about the Congo imbroglio, the less so because it made him the fall guy. Besides piles of UN documents, he and Maire had very acute memories for dates and places. Moreover, since Conor had written to Maire almost daily, in a mixture of Irish, English, and Russian (with the security-sensitive parts in Irish), he also had the equivalent of a daily diary of events. As I will argue in a moment, I think that Conor wrote the first successful picaresque novel of postcolonial Africa, but it is a novel that is built almost entirely of fact. Of course these facts are not arranged as if by the hand of the Almighty, or even as if done by the geopoliticians of the United Nations. This novel is an intensely personal story. It is the story of a major construction project as told from the viewpoint of one very heavily hammered nail.

Conor, as narrator, adopts the posture that makes his tale most palatable to readers who had an interest in what was at the time a set of live real-world issues: he presents his story in the guise of a historian. He explains, first, the big picture: how the UN works, how he as a young Irish diplomat came to be posted to the UN and then seconded to its full-time service, as Dag Hammarskjold's special representative in the Congo. And he details the sources for his own writing. Several times in the book, Conor tells the reader of points on which he has changed his view of events since obtaining fuller information than when he was in the UN service. The most important of these is that he comes to realize that Hammarskjold knew a lot more about how things were going than Conor originally thought. And Conor confesses several of his own gaffes and repents of one earlier set of falsehoods that he told reporters while he was on the UN payroll and expected to retail the company line.[5] The result is that one ends up trusting Conor's story. That O'Brien—he might have been a bit of a lad when in the Congo, but he's no liar.

Conor is a great storyteller. His characterizations read as if they came from the Red Hand Cycle, rewritten by Jonathan Swift: a saga, as it were, of the Sons of Usna as sonsofbitches. How can one not shudder when the malevolent Godefroid Munongo, minister of the interior of secessionist Katanga, is introduced?

> Munongo was the most impressive personality. He had features such as one sees on certain African wood-carvings, with long, almost flat cheeks and a heavy pouting under-lip. You could not tell what his eyes were like—because of the famous dark glasses which he invariably wore—and this increased the rather uncanny sculptural effect. Tall and well-built, he carried his head high, with the bearing of one who was conscious of being an aristocrat. He spoke good French in a low, deep voice which came in rapid surges and as he spoke he had the habit of turning his head slowly from side to side, making the light flash from his spectacles. When things went normally, as on this occasion, he used to sit well back in his chair, immobile save for the restlessness of his head and long, well-manicured hands. If warmed by argument, however, he was liable to violent, convulsive movements. Once, a few weeks later, I happened to mention the name of Lumumba in his presence. He raised his right arm with a jerk and then sharply slapped the back of his neck. At first I thought he had been bitten by an insect: then I realized that his instinctive reaction, which he had barely, at the last moment, brought under control, was to strike the man who mentioned Lumumba's name.[6]

That etching is a Dürer, but when appropriate Conor could do the single-brush stroke portrait too, as when he depicted the commander of the Katangese forces. "Colonel Crèvecoeur, contrary to his dramatic name and reputation, was a shy gentle-mannered, rather lymphatic officer, with a belief that he was misunderstood."[7]

The most fanatical Katangese officer was one Commandant Falques, a French-Algerian mercenary in charge of training elite combat troops. Conor pressed Moise Tshombe, president of Katanga, to send Falques packing, in the interest of peace. This was part of the dialogue:

> *Tshombe:* He does essential work. We cannot part with him.
>
> *Self:* We have been studying together the possibilities of the UN supplying replacements. Perhaps we could help you here?
>
> *Tshombe:* That's a very good idea. He is in charge of the School for paracommandos. If you can let us have a competent officer to take over from him here, we shall get rid of him.[8]

"The idea of the UN training Katangan paracommandos likely to be used to fight against the Central Government was only an extreme example of the difficulties inherent in the whole scheme," was Conor's straight-faced comment.[9]

Some of the diplomatic intersections were no less bizarre, as when Conor called on Charles Mutaka-Wa-Dilomba, cousin of Godefroid Munongo, and speaker of the self-declared Katanga National Assembly:

> M Mutaka's drawing-room was festooned with rifles and stenguns. M Mutaka's servants, who were also, it seemed, his tribal henchmen, kept going and coming in groups, into and out of the drawing-room, like a *corps de ballet*, portraying fear and resentment. M Mutaka himself was fairly drunk and a little tearful. He had, he explained, got 89 per cent in his law exams. He removed some lethal weapons from a chair and offered me a glass of beer.[10]

Not that the characters on Conor's side of the fence were much more reassuring:

> Pacification had stopped short at Kabalo, because the UN Ethiopian forces had blown up a gendarmerie steamer on the Lualaba river, and had also captured and expelled a sizeable contingent of European officers and soldiers. The commander of this Ethiopian force was Colonel Alemu, a handsome and dashing young officer who spoke excellent English, French and Spanish in addition to his native Amharic. The Colonel's authority over his men was, to say the least of it, impressive: not merely did they seem to carry out all orders at the double but while the order was actually being given, they used

to twitch or shudder in a mixture of awe and propitiation; I do not know what penalties the Ethiopian military code prescribes, but I suspect there is nothing mawkish about it. When, at a later stage, Colonel Alemu and I became friends I found his disposition was exceptionally sunny, with a slightly madcap Brigadier Gerard touch. At this point, however, his attitude was solemn, even forbidding. He informed me, not without relish, that if I were so much as to step out into the street, I would be instantly "lynched": the mere sight of my white, or pink, face would, it seemed, be enough. I could not see at the time why he took so much pleasure in conveying this rather depressing piece of information. I found out later that he had spent some time on a training course at a military base in an American southern State—North Carolina, I think—and had found his movements severely limited by his pigmentation. It was natural enough for him to enjoy letting me know that my particular type of skin was not always and everywhere a passport to universal esteem and mobility.[11]

These characterizations are worth quoting at length because they illustrate the uncanny control that Conor possessed, a mixture of a jurist's eye and a novelist's hand. Conor could also see clearly into the mirror. For example, he understood just how useless he was, once he had been recalled to UN headquarters in New York: "The body, the physical remains of the administratively defunct O'Brien, was still shuffling, zombie-like up and down the long corridor of the 38th floor, being 'consulted,' rather as the Chinese consult their deceased ancestors."[12]

Tom Jones in Postcolonial Africa well might have been the title of this extraordinary production. The book is funny, tragic, biting, sentimental, idealistic, wounded, cynical, and satirical, all within the compass of an argument about the real world and using only verifiable, factual statements that are testable by the standard of historical scholarship. (One can argue about specific details, but the point is that each one is historically based.) These uses of historical materials, however, should not obscure the fact that the creation is a work of literature and very self-consciously so. The volume begins with U Thant's letter to Conor citing, in an attempt to silence him, "staff regulation 1.5." And the book closes this way:

I shall leave the last word with Dr Luce. I had the pleasure and the privilege, shortly after the events here narrated, of sitting beside Dr Luce at a term dinner in Trinity College, Dublin. He is the great authority on Berkeley's philosophy, and a highly respected senior figure in Trinity.

"What shall we talk about," he asked me kindly, "and what shall we not talk about?"

We talked about the Venerable Bede, and then about the Albigensian Crusade. We did not talk about contemporary politics.

Dr Luce asked me whether I was writing a book.

I said I was.

What would the book be about? asked Dr Luce.

I said well, the Congo, mainly.

Dr Luce sipped his claret. I could see that he was trying to place the Congo in the perspective of the history of human thought.

He turned on me the benevolent but disconcerting scrutiny of his pale, luminous eyes.

"The Congo?" he said. "Is there a book in that, do you think?"[13]

The beginning and the end are clear sign-posts: reader, they say, this is a literary construct.

Three points are necessary if one is to appreciate where *To Katanga and Back* should fit in African literature in the English language. First, the book is clearly postcolonial. Conor's entire personal history—from his Irish nationalist childhood to his anti-Franco activism to his spear-heading Sean MacBride's antipartition campaign—made him deeply anti-imperialist in spirit. And his experience was postcolonial in practice. Second, by virtue of his Irish roots, Conor had the self-confidence to adopt a form that English-language writers of postcolonial Africa had not assayed with real success: the picaresque, with its mixture of ground-glass irony and broad burlesque, and tragedy. This is a form that requires a good deal of self-confidence (especially if one makes oneself the main character). Conor had several centuries of Irish writing—covert and subversive in the seventeenth and early eighteenth centuries, anti-imperialist in the later eighteenth and nineteenth centuries, and, after independence, thoroughly postcolonial—to build upon. That the first great picaresque novel of postcolonial Africa was written by an Irishman makes sense, actually.

That leads to a third point, one essential for understanding Conor both as a writer and as a personality. In *To Katanga and Back* one finds a great sensitivity to the nuances of tribe, but hardly any sense of race. That is just the way Conor is. He is the purest old-fashioned liberal that I have ever encountered in matters of race: that is, race in the sense of prejudice and discrimination (either negative or positive) is totally alien to him. As far as I can discover, he is emotionally unacquainted with it. Throughout his life, a friend has been a friend and an enemy an enemy, totally without regard to race. This leads him to do things that are not multiculturally correct in the present climate, such as his calling a black African dictator a crook or a despot when the evidence warrants it. This point about race is of some moment personally, given that Conor and Maire eventually adopted and raised two children of mixed race (white and African), and that Conor was the head of the Irish branch of the anti-apartheid movement. Indeed, to the extent that he has a knowledge of racial discrimination, it is the sort of knowledge that a tone-deaf person acquires from reading the biography of a composer. It has no personal resonance. This pure and amazing old-fashioned liberalism is one reason why *To Katanga and Back* works. Although set in Africa, violent, tribally nuanced, filled with a weird mixture of whites and blacks, with browns thrown in, there are no cardboard cut-outs, no stereotypes from the multicultural identikit. It is about individuals, real ones.

Against such a tour de force, the official stories, the company lies, the career-protecting press releases had little chance, although UN officials did their best. Members of the UN Secretariat obtained advance copies of the book, so that when it was published on 12 November 1962, the UN Secretariat called a news conference in New York to issue an immediate official denial. The book was an "irresponsible fabrication" and Dr. O'Brien, the officials said, had falsified the UN's intentions.[14] Simultaneously, the British government laid down its own denial campaign. The book's publication and its contents were covered in virtually every major English-language newspaper and most continental European ones. It was reviewed in several score publications.[15]

The one review that deserves particular attention was anonymous. It was published in the *Times Literary Supplement* on 16 November 1962. The author was Brian Urquhart who had been assistant to the secretary general's special representative in the Congo from July to October 1960, and who had taken over Conor's post as the UN representative in Elisabethville and served there from November 1961 to January 1962. Urquhart was a serving member of the UN Secretariat at the time he wrote the *TLS* review. Today this review would be ethically unacceptable in most high-quality publications in the form in which it appeared: anonymously, and with no statement of the personal conflict of interest as a prelude to the judgments that were presented. That, however, is not Urquhart's fault; anonymous reviewing still was practiced in England in the 1960s and the flagship *TLS* still was its bastion.

Brian Urquhart saw much of the book as "a brilliant and intuitive account of the current situation in Katanga and of the characters who act it out." Then, he added, that "Mr. O'Brien ... has done two things which are, to say the least, questionable (except in terms of circulation). One is to use private conversations, confidential information and acquaintance with persons, some now dead, ... all of which are based on knowledge resulting from his privileged position as a United Nations official." Urquhart's review also argued that Conor had "changed radically" his views on what had happened since his *Observer* articles of December 1961. There were other *ad hominem* points (such as that Conor had not taken his lumps silently like Rajeshwar Dayal of India who "was the victim of a savage and particularly discreditable smear campaign of much the same origins as that of which Mr. O'Brien complains," and, crucially, that Conor "did not like Hammarskjold," a sin in the UN Secretariat just short of favoring nuclear war).

Conor replied in a letter from Legon, Ghana, where he was now vice-chancellor of the University of Ghana. For him it was a remarkably restrained letter. Conor pointed out that on the very day that the book was published, the UN Secretariat in New York had issued its official attack and that four days later the anonymous review had appeared in the *TLS*. "Many, perhaps most, of your readers," Conor observed in his letter to the editor (22 February 1963), "will have formed the opinion that this article, issued with the authority of your respected paper, represented a corroboration, from an impartial and objective source, of the United Nation's Secretariat's original attack on my book." With those facts noted, he left the readers to make up their own minds.

But what of the two main points in Brian Urquhart's anonymous review? The first, that Conor had used privileged information, came down to the implication that Conor was not a gentleman, a murmur that may have had force in certain English social circles, but is of no use in evaluating the book's historical claims. In fact, Urquhart's charge on this issue really was a validation of the historical accuracy of Conor's story: the blighter knew too much and he had the bad taste to tell the company secrets.

The second charge, Conor's alleged radical changes in viewpoint between December 1961 and the publication of the book in November 1962, are of interest, but they are matters that Conor points out in the book, not issues that a percipient reviewer has assiduously ferreted out. In any case, Conor's main claim remained unchanged from earliest days onward: namely that he had not been fighting a lunatic little war on his own, but had been acting under orders. What had changed was that in December 1961 Conor had been inclined to believe that Mahmoud Khiary, who gave him direct orders, was acting without New York's— and especially without Hammarskjold's—really knowing what he was up to. But, given several months of research, and access to the memories and documents of several serving officers of the period, Conor came to the conclusion that Dag Hammarskjold had known more than Conor at first thought was the case. Someone who wants to defend Hammarskjold is left with only two alternatives: either Hammarskjold knew what was happening and he was a knave, or he did not, and in that case, he was an administrative fool. In either case, Conor would have been receiving orders from a superior.

Conor's basic factual argument concerning pivotal events—especially that he was working under orders, however uncertain their source—was confirmed in 1965 in Catherine Hoskyns's *The Congo Since Independence: January 1960–December 1961*, published by Oxford University Press for the Royal Institute of International Affairs. This validation is significant, because Hoskyns's book, published by a very British-establishment institute, was quite critical of some of Conor's judgment calls, and was certainly skeptical of his fitness for such a sensitive posting.

The really interesting validation came from Brian Urquhart, after he had retired from the UN. Urquhart had a very distinguished UN career, rising to the rank of undersecretary general for special political affairs, 1974–76. He received the International Peace Academy Prize in 1985 and was also knighted by Her Majesty's government. Urquhart published his autobiography in 1987. With a quarter-century to reflect on the Congo experience, he came to this conclusion: "In retrospect, it is clear that, in taking on this praiseworthy course, Hammarskjold made two mistakes. He did not give his representatives in the Congo any clear idea of his intentions. And he did not categorically tell them to abstain from action pending his arrival, sending instead complicated instructions which could be, and were, misunderstood by people under the pressure of a violent and frustrating local situation."[16] One can still argue about whether the murkiness of the instructions was intentional, and about how much Hammarskjold knew about events on the ground, but, clearly the people on the spot should not have had to carry the can for what was, at minimum, major administrative incompetence at the top.[17] Hammarskjold, once things had started to unravel, did not back his subordinates. He did not do what any good boss or commander does: assume the blame on the basic grounds that the buck stops here.

And, ironically, one of the shrewdest judgments concerning Conor in the Katanga affair comes from Brian Urquhart. "He was a brilliant and creative man, but not necessarily suited to the task of superintendent in a lunatic asylum."[18] An unlikely superintendent for an asylum, indeed, but Lord, he could write.

• • •

Conor still had a major theodicy to accomplish if he was to make sense of his UN experience. He was caught on the horns of a dilemma: he continued to believe in the value and virtue of the United Nations; yet this was the very agency that had acted incompetently and had rejected him. Two quick ways out of the dilemma were unacceptable, namely that either he could chant *mea culpa* and blame himself for everything that happened, or he could suddenly turn on the UN and denounce it as a corrupt institution. Neither was a course of integrity. What Conor needed to do, both emotionally and intellectually, was to thread the needle between these two extremes.

Unlike his defense of his own actions in *To Katanga and Back*, this explanation had to be conducted at a low temperature and at a slow pace. It needed academic, or at least scholastic, grounding. An invitation to deliver the twenty-first Montague Burton Lecture on International Relations at the University of Leeds provided the opportunity to begin this exercise. This was a prestigious endowed lectureship (previous lecturers included Gilbert Murray, Harold Nicolson, and Ralph Bunche). On 1 March 1963, Conor delivered the lecture, titled "Conflicting Concepts of the United Nations." The title is revealing, in that as much as the conflicting concepts were those of the geopolitical-academic world, they were his own as well.

Conor's primary assumption in this lecture was that it was perfectly all right to criticize constructively the United Nations. "I shall take it, then, as axiomatic that the United Nations ... is a necessary human institution and likely to survive as long as organized human society, however long that may be." (This, clearly, was a statement of faith.) "If we take that for granted, we are enabled to set aside the argument of those who would stifle criticism of the organization's imperfections and its sometimes inflated pretensions, by alleging that such criticism endangers the last, best hope of man."[19] (This was an operating principle, a license to criticize the institution, while still remaining within the Church.)

Then, like a good moral theologian, Conor introduced everyday reality. He described the assumptions that everyday workers in the UN Secretariat held: that if the United States does not want a given course of action, it would not be taken; any UN action must fit with U.S. diplomatic interests; growth in UN power would most likely be at the expense of the Soviet Union; the UN is not apt to encourage the interests of America's allies; that if anyone's interest were to be sacrificed it would not be those of the United States; and, now, in the early 1960s, the United States and the African-Asian bloc would henceforth control the UN.[20]

This was an ill-presented list, but the introduction of the United States as the flywheel of the UN's machinery gave Conor a clear opening to affirm simultaneously that the UN was indeed the last best hope of humanity and that it had flaws which were not primarily its own fault. As a particularly telling case, he showed in detail how, during the Hungarian unrest in 1956, the United States used the UN to avoid a Soviet-U.S. confrontation. The U.S. delegation, headed by Henry Cabot Lodge, worked the UN corridors, lobbying against the Nagy government by telling everyone that Nagy was just as much a communist as was Kruschev, and that the whole affair was a dispute among thieves. Only after the Hungarian uprising had been crushed (and thus there was no need for the United States to intervene), did the Americans turn and hail Nagy and his colleagues as heroes and martyrs.[21]

Conor thus was able to reach a narrow ground, permitting him to both believe in the UN and to criticize it.

> I believe that the role of the Secretariat, from the foundation of the organization up to now, has to be seen in relation, not directly to the international community in the rather mystical manner imagined by Hammarskjold, but in relation to its immediate and real environment: those buildings on the East River in which the Security Council, the General Assembly and the other organs work. In that environment, the influence of the United States was, as I have suggested, once supreme, and is now conditionally predominant.[22]

So, Conor kept his faith in his church, the UN, blemished though it might be, by U.S. hegemony. In 1981, when he was editor in chief of the *Observer*, he formulated his most succinct statement of his faith: "The United Nations is the most important international institution that has ever existed, and its survival is bound up with the survival of the human race."[23] Though flawed by U.S. domination it had real practical value. "He who takes a donkey to the top of a minaret must also know how to get it down," was an Iraqi proverb Conor had heard at the UN in 1956. "The thing the United Nations is best at is helping donkeys down from minarets, while saving some part of the faces of the gentlemen responsible for getting the donkeys there in the first place."[24] Thus, in the later 1960s, Conor came to believe that the UN offered the United States a means of saving face, of getting the donkey down from the minaret that was America's war in Vietnam.[25]

This theodicy was satisfactory intellectually, but not entirely satisfying emotionally.[26] Conor therefore cast about for a better form of understanding and developed a set of ideas that were in part liturgical in nature, in part aesthetically postmodern (well before the term was in popular use). The practical result was a spectacularly unsuccessful bit of bookmaking, entitled *The United Nations: Sacred Drama*.

Conor's main partner in this venture, Feliks Topolski, was one of England's best-known painters and illustrators. At the time, he was in his late fifties and at the top of his form. Born and educated in Poland, Topolski had settled in Great Britain before World War II. He became an official war artist and did a famous series on the Battle of Britain. He painted the mural "The Cavalcade of Commonwealth" for the Festival of Britain in 1951 and thereafter had a successful career in the border-line region between high art and celebrity illustration. He also was a West End stage designer of note. He and Conor became acquainted through the agency of Harold Harris of Hutchinson publishers in London. In the autumn of 1966, Harris wrote to Conor saying that Topolski's daughter would be studying at New York University, and would Conor help her to settle in?[27] So, when Topolski followed up with a note of his own,[28] Conor was pleased to help. At this stage Conor and Topolski had not met but Conor professed to have known and admired Topolski's art, and the eventual partnership grew from that point.[29]

The trouble with the project (eventually published by Hutchinson in London and by Simon and Schuster in New York in 1968) was neither with Topolski nor O'Brien, but rather with the project itself. It was messy from a business point of view, involving two separate publishers, two authors (and an additional consultant), and two distinct media.[30] The deeper problem was that the text and the illustrations did not marry. It turned into a visual and verbal smorgasbord with no point of control. The nature of this semi-art book was further confused by the inclusion of an article by a friend of Conor's son Donal, David Brokensha of the Department of Anthropology of the University of California, Santa Barbara, on the peace-making function of priests in certain African societies. Rather generously, the *TLS* suggested that "Topolski's drawings are not to everyone's taste. But if you like them, here are more than 100 full pages of them—to adorn and complete a cautionary tale which will one day no doubt be a collector's piece."[31] Conor himself is more realistic. Today, he sees the book as a mistake.

Conor's contribution to this mixed-media performance was a 60,000 word essay that attempted to keep aloft a single metaphor.[32] But the metaphor was just too heavy to be kept in the air with ease for that long a time. Reading *The United Nations: Sacred Drama* is like watching a variety show entertainer juggle chain-saws: the act is not a thing of beauty, but that Conor pulls it off without loss of life or limb is enough to gain our grudging admiration.

The book is based on what was taken by reviewers at the time to be a heuristic device, namely,

The United Nations is an imaginative creation, deliberately designed from its beginnings—in the Atlantic Charter, the Washington and Moscow Declarations, and the unveiling of the Charter in the San Francisco Opera House—to appeal to the imagination of mankind.[33]

Therefore:

The present essay is based on the supposition that it may be useful to approach this imaginative work as we approach others of the same kind: that is to say with the realization that its truths are not literal truths, and its power not a material power. If this be granted, it follows that style and gesture, and even decor, may be more significant than the analysis of "voting patterns," and the impact of a scene or a personage more significant than the letter of the Charter.[34]

Actually, however, this was not a heuristic construct, for what had started as metaphor became a reality in itself. *"Literal truth is irrelevant here,"* Conor asserts in describing the Preamble to the Charter of the United Nations (the italics are mine). That is a big step to take, but with only a touch of punctuation to make us pause, he steps into the world of postliteral reality. "This [the UN Charter's Preamble], is an invocation, the initiation of a series of solemn acts, designed to propitiate and purify. It is also the prelude to the creation of institutions symbolic of the prayer for peace and dedicated to the continued offering of that prayer: the Security Council, the General Assembly, the Secretariat."[35]

In other words, the UN is a drama, a sacred drama. Its role is not to do anything; its role is rôle. "A General Assembly resolution has the force of law in the same sense as has a sacred song: it provides spiritual encouragement and comfort and induces a sense of collective righteousness and of the legitimacy of a common endeavour."[36] As Conor expands on this, detail upon detail, example after example, it becomes clear that not only are we dealing with a metaphor that has turned into a belief, but a belief that could only be propounded by someone who was deeply influenced by Holy Mother Church. The UN, during much of the 1950s and 1960s, was Conor's church.

Where, in this church, does the secretary general fit? W.H. Auden was told jokingly by Dag Hammarskjold that to be secretary general of the United Nations "is like being a secular Pope and the Papal throne is a lonely eminence." Conor comments, "There is no joke at all in his [Hammarskjold's] private notations, about his conception of the divine purpose behind the United Nations, and of his own role, combining that of high-priest and victim, essentially the idea of Christ's Vicar reenacting the sacrifice of Christ."[37] Conor, in his interpretation of the UN as sacred drama, accepts Hammarskjold's view: the secretary general is a piacular thaumaturge, and in Hammarskjold's case, his life was sacrificed.

None of Conor's usual irony or wit is here present. He believed. "It is the contention of the present writer," he argued, "that it is both possible and urgently necessary to restore and safeguard the spiritual authority of the secretary general." How is this to be achieved? "This can only be ensured by taking responsibility for peace-keeping away from him." Lest one think that this is an accidental nonsequitur, Conor repeats himself a moment later, in italics. "*This necessitates the absolute avoidance of responsibility for the conduct of any military operation whatsoever*, no matter how excellent its purposes, and even if it is blessed by the Security Council and the General Assembly."[38]

Thus, the UN becomes a parallel to the Roman Catholic Church after the fall of the Holy Roman Empire, and the secretary general the pontiff, a creature with spiritual but no secular powers. Conor proposes that to avoid contamination the new Holy Father (the secretary general) should be forbidden the power to intervene in the secular world (the world of military force). Among other things, this prohibition would prevent the Holy Father from falling into conflict with his acolytes (such as occurred in the Congo). The secretary general's imperium would be in the world of the invisible, the spiritual, and the eternal; the acolytes would work in the land of the visible, the temporal, and, inevitably, the corrupt.

• • •

The extreme position that Conor took in *Sacred Drama* could not be maintained in its fullness very long and Conor quietly jettisoned the concept of the sacred drama during the 1970s. (Besides the obvious intellectual problems of the belief-system, there was the slightly comic visual problem: while one could imagine Dag Hammarskjold as a secular pontiff, the substitution of, say, U Thant, undercut the solemnity necessary to the whole concept.) Conor maintained his conception of the UN as being something like a theatrical stage, however.[39] Despite the failure of the book, the concepts in *The United Nations: Sacred Drama* are significant in Conor's artistic development, for they served as a fulcrum that permitted the writing in late 1967 of his book-drama *Murderous Angels* (1968).[40]

To appreciate the unusual, if highly imperfect, achievement that *Murderous Angels* represents, one has to break out of the industrial categories by which artistic and intellectual forms usually are evaluated—

fiction, nonfiction, novel, historical/narrative, drama, journalism, and so on. Conor has devoted much of his life to breaking down the walls between these categories and his own work makes sense only in nontraditional terms. He constantly has pushed the envelope of the possible and that, more than anything else, probably explains why he is not appreciated more widely as the major writer that he is. By refusing to fit into the usual literary categories, Conor has inadvertently ruled himself ineligible for the kudos which, like shiny statuettes at awards ceremonies, are handed out according to preconceived definitions.

Thus, in rating *Murderous Angels*, we have to follow the example of Conor, who, as writer, broke out of the mold. Just as *To Katanga and Back* was very unusual, a historical narrative that took the rhetorical form of the picaresque novel, so too is *Murderous Angels* different. This is a book of history that pretends to be the text of a stage play. Indeed, *Murderous Angels* was to the intellectual classes of New York and London of the 1960s what a hinny is to the world of biologists: a perfectly legitimate form, but so unusual as to be misidentified.

The first point, then, is that *Murderous Angels* is primarily a book and only secondarily a play for the stage. Here another analogy is helpful: during the 1980s, it became common for film scripts to be published. Increasingly, scripts that had virtually no chance of ever being filmed (and, indeed, many of them were written without the authors wanting them to be filmed) were published, read, and criticized, as a genre of their own. Thus, the film script as a genre of literature emerged. This genre has to be read differently from other forms of fiction or of narrative, for it has as its background convention certain set ways of presenting dialogue and description, and it involves the agreed assumption that certain forms of visualization are understood. (The cue "cu" for instance tells the reader that he or she should see things as if in a close-up lens.) That process parallels what Conor was doing with *Murderous Angels*. He wrote a historical story, a piece of historical speculation, which was intended to be read within the conventions and the limitation of the literary form that is the stage script.

This book-drama deals with a tragedy that was one of the background reasons for Conor's being in the Congo in 1961. Patrice Lumumba, a great pan-Africanist leader of the 1950s, became prime minister of the newly independent Congo in June 1960. This scared the U.S. government, which viewed him as another Fidel Castro, and it distinctly crimped the mining interests that previously had controlled the Belgian Congo. Hence, the mining interests fostered the breakaway state of Katanga under Moise Tshombe, and the United States sided with Lumumba's enemies in the newly created Congo government:

most especially, Joseph Kasavubu, the Congo's ceremonial president, and Colonel Mobuto, the military chief of staff. Lumumba was first put under house arrest by Mobuto and after an escape, ended up in the hands of the Katanga government, whence he was tortured and then killed.

The moment one picks up *Murderous Angels*, it is clear that this artistic construct is a book, not a straight stage play. For one thing, it has documentary endnotes: not comments on stage directions or amplification of characterization, but tightly packed, small-print notes that fully document the incidents articulated in the text. Further, a well-argued appendix, based on the then-most-recent scholarly work, documents not only the involvement of the CIA in Patrice Lumumba's death, but the failure of Dag Hammarskjold, who clearly knew of Lumumba's physical vulnerability, to prevent his capture by the Katangese and his subsequent murder.

This bounty of information follows the text of the play. Immediately before the text an extensive "author's preface" explains the historical background and tells how Conor came to write the play. He had been working on *The United Nations: Sacred Drama* and was rethinking his time in the Congo, especially in light of Catherine Hoskyns's book, *The Congo Since Independence*. "While I was preoccupied by these questions, I dreamt one night that a new notebook of Dag Hammarskjold's had been discovered which constituted a sort of political key or equivalent to the spiritual cogitations of Hammarskjold which have been published under the title *Markings*. In the dream I seemed not to have access to the new notebook, and was vaguely distressed by this."[41] Rhetorically, Conor adopted the guise of the Celtic *aisling*, the dream vision.[42] It is a well-worn mode and at least to his Irish readers, his modern usage of the form had rich, well-understood connotations.

That the *aisling* was sparked by Dag Hammarskjold's *Markings* requires comment. Published in 1964, *Markings* was a translation from the Swedish, posthumously published, of a manuscript found among Hammarskjold's belongings in his home in New York City. It was translated by Leif Sjoberg and W.H. Auden and bore a foreword by Auden. The book is a puzzling document and is not made less so by Auden's introduction. *Markings* is a psychic road map to a country that is not named, a mixture of poetry, self-minted sayings, an elegy for Hammarskjold's pet monkey, quotations from scripture, and all rewritten and edited carefully over time by Hammarskjold himself. Whatever it might be, the contents of this volume would not have reassured anyone who was counting on Hammarskjold to save humankind through clarity of vision and sureness of action.[43]

At the time of the publication of *Murderous Angels*, it would have been easy to suggest (although few did), that Conor was trying to have things two ways. He was attempting to make it clear that Dag Hammarskjold had played a part in Patrice Lumumba's downfall and that he could have saved Lumumba's life but did not do so, and that, nevertheless, this was not a "realistic play." "My Hammarskjold and My Lumumba, then, are not to be thought of as the 'real' characters of that name, but as personages shaped by the imitation of a real action associated with their names."[44] Yet, if they are not real characters, then why all the footnotes and the other documentary devices?

When Dan Sullivan, a *Guardian* journalist, taxed Conor with "doing things with history that a historian would not dare do, and presenting it to an audience as, in fact, history," Conor immodestly replied: "But there are marvellous precedents for taking liberties with history. What great dramatist has not done it? Aristotle sanctions it. Shakespeare does it in Richard III, Henry VII and the other history plays."[45] In the climate of the late 1980s and early 1990s, he would not have had to answer such a question, since critical theory has left most literary critics believing that historiography is "constructed" in no essential way differently than is pure fiction. (That this is a position that Conor himself does not share is not germane; the relevant point is that in many ways his book-drama would have been more readily received today than it was at the time of its publication.)[46]

The "murderous angels" of the title comes from a poem by Conor's friend, Denis Devlin, "The Tomb of Michael Collins," which posited:

> Better Beast and know your end, and die
> Than Man with murderous angels in his head.

(Devlin was one of the band of talented literati who flourished in the Department of External Affairs in Ireland. Nine years older than Conor, he had entered the diplomatic service in the mid-1930s; he died in 1959, aged fifty-one, Ireland's first ambassador to Italy).

The two murderous angels are Freedom (represented by Lumumba) and Peace (incarnated as Hammarskjold). But, in this morality play, the two angels are not really the protagonists, but are themselves victims of vice. Vice in two senses: their own personal vices (self-gratification on Lumumba's part and self-memorialization on Hammarskjold's), but, more important, each is caught in the vice of circumstance, the geopolitics of the Congo, the ambiguous position of the UN. Lumumba, as a father and a tribal leader, should be present at the burial of his recently-deceased daughter, dangerous as that is to his physical safety. Lumumba has to decide whether or not to do his duty, and Hammarskjold whether or not to protect him.

All that sounds very heavy, but on the printed page it works well, because Conor knows how to write dialogue and anecdotes that read well. Lumumba and his white mistress are a lively semicomic turn, and there is some amusing slagging of the secretary general by those who work with him. "He's in love with himself," an assistant to Hammarskjold says, "and it's just like any other love affair. If he becomes friendly with someone, then he immediately becomes jealous of that person, for being on too friendly terms with his beloved—to wit, himself."[47] By the middle of Act 2, however (this is a five-act tale), the fatal dice are cast. Under pressure from the United States, Hammarskjold sizes up the situation as follows: "If I am to save the United Nations, and the peace, I must help you to destroy Patrice Lumumba."[48] The U.S. ambassador presses him: "Well, what do you say? Do you accept? Do you vote for the death of Patrice Lumumba?" Hammarskjold replies, "I do. The logic of the situation you have constructed leaves me no choice."[49] Thereafter, the mills of the gods grind slowly and extremely fine: first Lumumba and then Hammarskjold are destroyed.

The subtitle of this book-drama is "a political tragedy and comedy in black and white," and there is no doubt that race has a good deal to do with it. Not race in the sense of individual prejudice, however, but race as white hegemony in the mostly black colonial and postcolonial world. The racial subtheme is stylized, like the black and white pattern on a chess board, and not really felt. Conor has always understood racialism in the same way he understands, for instance, religious fundamentalism. It is something whose characteristics he can recognize intellectually, and which he can fight (as he has) politically, but, being no part of himself, it is a distinct and alien thing. So this book-drama is really the story of two men, Lumumba and Hammarskjold, and it is from their individual characters, not their race, that the passion emerges.[50]

There is an additional, major character in this drama, one not found in the cast list: Conor Cruise O'Brien. He is there as the invisible guest at the feast. This is O'Brien's play, we all know, and all his documentation, preface, and appendix remind us that he actually was there, in the middle of the real stage in the Congo. Just at the end of Act 4, O'Brien-as-character is announced. Now, with Lumumba already dead, Hammarskjold still has problems to deal with in the Congo and he has decided to crack down: "I am going to put real pressure on Katanga to abandon secession, and if they won't, or their backers won't, then force will be used."[51] The person whom he chooses to put on the pressure is described by one of the secretary general's senior aides as follows:

> He's a trouble-maker, if that's what you want. Clever. Bumptious. Talks too much. The British say he's a Communist, but they just mean that he's Irish. He likes to hobnob with Africans and Asians, and behaves a bit like one. He would just love himself as a kind of anti-imperialist proconsul. In short, he's the very man to sent to Katanga if you want all hell to break loose.[52]

That, of course, is Conor. And Hammarskjold quickly replies to his senior aide's objections:

> Yes. I'm going to send him there because that's where all hell has to break loose at this moment. If it's not to break loose elsewhere on a much greater scale. Go send for him—and tell him to get ready to leave for Elisabethville.[53]

Thereafter, although Conor does not appear on stage, he is an explicit character. Unseen, he has the touch of Banquo's ghost, with perhaps a tithe of the force. Conor, as a character, is simultaneously an actor in the drama and a portent of tragedy.

At one point, a reporter points out to the secretary general that "your representative in Elisabethville is quoted as having declared the secession of Katanga at an end. How do you reconcile this with your own repeated statements that the United Nations does not intervene in the internal affairs of the Congo?" Hammarskjold's reply is unambiguous and totally dishonest: "My representative must have been misquoted. The United Nations does not intervene in the internal affairs of the Congo."[54] Following this lie—whether cowardly betrayal or the mendacity of necessity, is for the audience to adjudge—Hammarskjold's path to his tragic end is swift. An alliance of Katangese (led by the sanguinary Godefroid Munongo) and old-imperialist mercenaries, learning that Hammarskjold is going to Rhodesia to broker a peace that will destroy their own positions, decide either to kidnap or assassinate him (it is never clear what they actually intend). In the book-drama, as in history, Dag Hammarskjold dies before he reaches Ndola.

"Postmodern" is not a phrase that was in widespread usage when Conor wrote this book-drama, but it is postmodern with a vengeance— and, perhaps, it is vengeance via the postmodern. Conor has done here, less thoroughly and less skillfully, what Hugh Leonard has done in his beautifully crafted play *Da* (1973). He has rerun history so that he can interrogate it. (It is a felicitous parallel that the colloquial Irish term for father—"Da"—and the vernacular elisions of Hammarskjold's first name in Swedish—also "Da"—are very close.) In rerunning history, Conor has adopted the assumption shared by almost all postmodernists: that scientists and empiricists to the contrary, time's arrow does not fly in only one direction. The past actually can be rerun and when that is done, it comes out differently, through the active intervention of the artist.

Why (aside from the enviable joy that any creator has in playing with his creation) does Conor do this? My guess—and since we are dealing with the infinite complexities of the human personality, it can only be a guess—is that Conor is here dealing with the two sources of the greatest unresolved emotional turmoil in his life: the death of his father and the death of Dag Hammarskjold. These are not identical matters, but they are in many ways congruent. Conor's father died when Conor was just ten, in the act of helping Conor to learn to bend a bow. Of course the death was not Conor's fault, but there is a large literature that indicates that children often feel great guilt—and later, anger—at the death of a parent. These feelings are often repressed and kept below the verbal level. In the case of Dag Hammarskjold, there were also sources of guilt. First, it was possible for Conor to feel that if I, Conor, had done my job better, Hammarskjold would not have even considered flying to Rhodesia; and, second, I, Conor, should have been on the fatal plane with him.

Murderous Angels is a major step (but not the final one) in dealing with Dag Hammarskjold's death, and should be kept in the context of Conor's earlier work. In his early *Observer* pieces Conor could not conceive that the secretary general was implicated in the Congo mission going awry (Khiary is blamed). In *Katanga and Back*, the probability that Hammarskjold was deeply involved is clearly documented, but Conor backs away from harsh judgments. It is a strangely forgiving book (a characteristic that was missed by those in the UN Secretariat who publicly denounced it). And then, in *The United Nations: Sacred Drama*, Conor sets up the secretary general as a secular equivalent of the Holy Father and suggests ways to keep His Holiness from being sullied. All this is very peculiar, in that one defensible reading of the historical record is that in the year 1960–61, Dag Hammarskjold was a frightful administrator, a narcissist, who valued his image as a totemic figure more highly than the lives of real people, and a moral coward, who failed to back his subordinates, but instead left them twisting in the wind. If there was anyone in the world who might be expected to take this view of the secretary general, it was Conor. Yet to conceive of such gaping flaws in his hero, his father-figure, was just too much.

Until *Murderous Angels*, when Conor finally deals with Dag—his "Da"—straight on. The rerunning of history in this drama changed the structure of the past very little factually; the big change was that connections which in the welter of the real past are only latent, here are made manifest. The story becomes a moral diptych. In the first panel, the innocent Patrice Lumumba goes to his death because of the decisions (constrained by circumstances, to be sure) of Dag Hammarskjold. If Lumumba and Hammarskjold were murderous angels, Dag was much the more murderous. Therefore, a moral analogy is established. If Hammarskjold would sell out Lumumba (for whatever high principles), then he would sell out somebody else in the future. (In real life, the next person he sold out was Conor.)

So when, in the second panel of the diptych, the secretary general walks up the ramp for his fatal plane trip to Rhodesia, we are viewing a moral paradigm being played out. Hammarskjold would not have needed to board the plane had he not been the sort of person who sold out real people for cold principles, and who, in this case had failed to be loyal to his representative in Elisabethville. Without ever saying the words directly, at this moment, Conor is telling the reader (and more important, himself) that Dag—my "Da"—died because he deserved to. This anger connects back across time to his real Da, about whose death Conor could (like so many children who are bereaved) feel guilty; and also toward whom he could feel real anger, for having let him down by dying—and by dying so deeply in debt that the money-lenders and bailiffs haunted the family house, at one point even taking away young Conor's most precious books.[55]

• • •

Inside this rich and confusing book-drama was a conventional play—conventional in the sense that it could go on the boards without all the notes, appendix, and prefatory matter that were integral to the printed version.

The first interest in producing the play came early, before the book was published, at a time when the script was available only in mimeograph form.[56] In April 1968, the Nottingham Playhouse was seriously considering putting the play on in its fall season, but despite Conor's agreement, nothing came of it.[57] However, working through friends in London—especially Feliks Topolski—Conor interested Sir Laurence Oliver, who was taken with the idea of playing the character Baron

D'Auge, head of the Belgian mining syndicate and an embodiment of old-rich European capitalism and imperialism. This part would have particularly suited Olivier's talents. "I have no doubt that if he would play it he would steal the show with it," Conor told Feliks Topolski (who was himself to be the play's stage designer).[58] Kenneth Tynan liked the script a lot and recommended that the National Theatre mount a production.[59] However, the board of directors began to get cold feet when the matter of potential libel was raised.[60] This was not entirely frivolous, since English libel laws are notably restrictive. But, clearly, there were matters other than libel on the minds of the National Theatre authorities. Both Tynan and Michael Blackmore (who was to direct the production) became quite keen, and a meeting took place with Blackmore, Conor, and Olivier. The plans were for Sir John Gielgud to play Hammarskjold as overtly gay. This would have worked brilliantly, one suspects, in tension with Olivier's Baron D'Auge. However, "Oli had some complicated qualms about it, seeming mainly to turn on the wish not to have Gielgud play a homosexual Hammarskjold."[61] Thus, in early January 1969 it was decided (whether by Conor's decision or that of the National Theatre is unclear) that there would be no National Theatre production.[62] Later, after the British edition of *Murderous Angels* had been published (in the spring of 1969) and there had been no libel writs, it became clear that the legal fears were unjustified. There were hopes that the private producers, George W. George and Frank Granat, would mount the play in the West End after it was staged in North America but nothing came of this.[63]

Meanwhile, the Abbey Theatre in Dublin considered the script and rejected it. "It was not found to be suitable," Phil O'Kelly, the Abbey's general manager explained in late January 1969. "One of the reasons was it required quite a number of Negro actors." Given that there were scores of well-trained black actors just a boat-ticket away in England, this should not have been crippling, except that the Abbey was a nationalist monument and was not willing to import foreigners. "We are a repertory company and it would be difficult to meet the requirements," O'Kelly explained.[64]

Fortunately, the play was taken up in Los Angeles, at the Mark Taper Forum, in a Gordon Davidson production. It opened in early February 1970 and was very well reviewed, even among those who were critical of the play's politics. "I was fascinated by it. I admired it. I was often moved by it," said Winfred Blevens in the Los Angeles *Herald-Examiner*. Then, the reviewer put a finger on the fundamental problem of the play as a stage production. "I also found it more engrossing as an

address to the intellect than to the whole man, more intriguing as a document and a thesis than as drama."[65] The Irish playwright Tom
Murphy (who in 1972 received the Irish Academy of Letters award for
distinction and in 1973 became a board member of the Abbey) saw the
play in Los Angeles and was riveted by the first half, disappointed by the
second. Murphy's comments are the admirably direct ones of the practical playwright: the script is too long, he says, and the second half is too
intellectual.[66] Still, with a first-rate cast—Lou Gossett as Patrice
Lumumba and George Voskovec as Dag Hammarskjold—it was good-
enough theater. On the basis of a strong review from Clive Barnes, the
Gordon Davidson production went to New York. "It did not come off,"
Conor candidly admits. "The atmosphere in New York at that time was
unfavourable: white liberals disliked the Hammarskjold part and black
militants objected to Lumumba." There were demonstrations. "The
black actors became unnerved by black militant demonstrations and
their playing ... just collapsed."[67]

A Berlin production, at the Schillerteater, was a disaster. As Conor
explained, "The producer, a veteran by the name of Perayla, thought it
necessary to have all the black parts played by blacks despite the fact that
there are no black actors in West Germany and hardly any blacks who
can speak German properly." Therefore, the producer scrambled to fill
the black parts with amateurs who spoke German well, but really were
not actors. "When the white actors found that they were required to
play opposite black nonactors they threw in their parts and we ended up
with a grisly cast indeed."[68]

After that, it was a relief when, in March 1971, *Murderous Angels*
opened at the Gaiety Theatre as part of the Thirteenth Dublin Theatre
Festival. The director, Laurence Bourne, cut about half an hour out of
the published version of the play and half a dozen marginal characters.[69]
The reception was what the *Irish Times* called "a mixed bag of reviews."
Its own reviewer, David Nowlan, added, "Thanks largely to a hopelessly
inadequate period of rehearsal and a lack of technical facilities in the
theatre, [it] seemed very close to falling into that category of festival
plays which are 'very interesting' and which, without a festival, we
might not have seen."[70]

The final, almost burlesque, production, was done in France in 1974
at the TNP under the direction of Joan Littlewood. "The production was
an elaborate and absolute disaster and was quite rightly panned by the
critics," recalled Conor, with the candor that is his hallmark. "I made
the great mistake of giving Joan *carte blanche* with the production and
she turned it into excruciatingly corny revolutionary propaganda. Wole
Soyinka [a leading Nigerian—Yorubu—playwright] played Lumumba.

He substituted his own lines for mine and made Lumumba a flawless hero. The whole thing was a nightmare."[71]

The kaleidoscope of tribulations that the stage play *Murderous Angels* went through is both sad and amusing. Taken together, they confirm one simple fact: *Murderous Angels* is not a play in the conventional sense. It is a book-drama, and as such was made to be read, not played.

• • •

The watershed that was the Congo episode made Conor a very different man. He became serious; previously, he had been merely gifted.

After the Congo, Conor began to deal with the great formative experience of his youth, the death of his father. The resolution was not completed in the 1960s (indeed, it probably never will be) but the overlay of Dag Hammarskjold and Conor's own Da produced some major and very challenging artistic work. The death of the father-figure still haunts Conor, although not as ferociously as it once did. Dag Hammarskjold's demise is still a concern, and Conor still needs to see that tragedy as a complicated, but comprehensible conspiracy—and thus to fit into an understandable pattern the otherwise horribly random mystery of that death.

The big transformation in Conor, however, was successfully transacted. He became not only a writer, but a writer of a very special sort. He became, and remains, a work-artist, a term that classic Marxists frequently used, but rarely effected successfully. In 1970, reflecting on the previous decade of his life in an interview with Donald Cameron, Conor said,

> Here [in Ireland] we've had an attempt at a tradition that the writer, for example, should keep out of politics, keep out of public life. Harold Macmillan gave this advice to Frank O'Connor, the Irish short-story writer, who had been on the board of the Abbey Theatre, and Macmillan advised him that for the sake of writing he should withdraw from all this. And I think Frank O'Connor was an excellent writer, and I think it was a disaster for his writing that he should have withdrawn from the nitty-gritty. ... I think it was also a disaster for Sean O'Casey, when he went away to live in his ivory tower in Devon and never wrote anything again that was any good.

What did this have to do with Conor's own recent life? "In fact, looking back at my own life, what I'm inclined to deplore is not having been pushed in at the deep end, as it were, in the Congo, but having led a relatively isolated and also limited middle-class life up till then."[72]

CHAPTER 8

AFRICAN ACADEME: GHANA, 1962-1965

In late 1961 and early 1962, Conor set a pattern that he was to follow for the rest of his life: grabbing a handy lifeline and swinging with seeming ease from the deck of a burning boat to that of a better-class vessel that fortuitously was passing alongside. From the time of his leaving the UN and the Irish civil service, right to the 1990s, every time he has left a long-term job it has not been by calculation, but because he was fired, forced to resign, or simply not rehired; and each time, by virtue of being alert and just plain lucky, he has landed in a new and better position.

As one of his lifelong friends has said, "Ever since I've known Conor, he's had to have a catastrophe. If it didn't happen, he created one." It is also true that somehow he has escaped the worst consequences of these catastrophes.[1] He walks away whistling, the one person upon whom none of the debris of the boiler-room explosion has fallen.

The first thread of Conor's lifeline out of the Katanga imbroglio took the form of a September 1961 telegram from Dr. Kwame Nkrumah, president of Ghana. This was a message, addressed to United Nations headquarters, of concern for Conor's personal safety.[2] The telegram reflected not only a genuine concern for Conor's well-being, but also was an indication of Nkrumah's own self-definition. As head of the first African state to become fully independent, Nkrumah had considerable international prestige and immense personal vanity. He viewed himself as the leader of the pan-African movement and expected that he would be the inaugural head of any union of independent African states. Secessionist Katanga, of course, was close enough to Ghana geographically to be a worry for Nkrumah, so concern for the success of Conor's

United Nations mission was part of Ghana's foreign policy as well as an aspect of Nkrumah's pan-African sentiments.[3] In December 1961, in response to Conor's public accusations that the British government was intent on wrecking the UN effort, Nkrumah sent a long protest note to the U.K. prime minister, Harold Macmillan. It read, in part:

> Recent statements made by Dr. O'Brien and General McKeown concerning United Nations operations in Katanga have caused me some concern. I know that I can speak to you in all sincerity because you appreciate the necessity for frankness in the issues that arise between your country and mine. The statements made by these high officials of the United Nations in the Congo indicate that Great Britain and France deliberately hampered the operations in the Congo in clear contravention of the Security Council Resolutions. ...
>
> The Congo situation is becoming a running sore which must be healed quickly before it is allowed to fester and poison international relations that I am afraid it is beginning to do. I wish to appeal most earnestly to you, therefore, Mr. Prime Minister, to continue to lend your full support and influence to United Nations action in the Congo and to the steps now being taken to bring the Katanga secession to an end.[4]

Nkrumah was diplomatically active on other fronts as well, doing what he could to contain the Katanga secession.[5]

At home, Nkrumah had a smaller, but pressing, problem. A newly reconstituted institution, the University of Ghana, into which a fortune in governmental money was being poured, had a restive faculty and no one of stature to put things in order. Nkrumah, besides being head of state, was chancellor of the university (which, in the British tradition, meant that he was the titular head, an implied limitation on his power that he never fully accepted). It was his task to find a suitable vice-chancellor to do the actual administration, and here his foreign policy interests, his pan-Africanism, and his local needs coincided. The Irishman, O'Brien, who had tried to do the right thing in the Congo, would be the right person for the University of Ghana, he decided. Conor and Dr. Nkrumah had met twice previously—in Dublin in May 1960 when Nkrumah gave an anti-apartheid speech, and in New York in September 1960 when Nkrumah addressed the secretary general's advisory committee on the Congo on which Conor served.[6] There is no question that it was Conor's actions in the Congo that accounted for his selection by Nkrumah for the vice-chancellorship.[7] Nkrumah sent a telegram to Conor inviting him to take up a three-year appointment (presumably a renewable one if things went well) as vice-chancellor.[8] There were no tiresome interviews, no selection committees, simply, would Conor take the job?

Conor and Maire hesitated. They were recently married—on 9 January 1962—and had been battered by a mind-numbing sequence of events in the Congo. They were waist-deep in hostile stories in the British and American press; and both were out of work. Whereas previously they had been reasonably well paid members of the most prestigious arm of the Irish civil service, secure in their employment and starred for continuous future promotion, now they were unemployed, their money dwindling fast, and without immediate prospects. The post in Ghana meant getting out of Ireland, out of the British Isles, out of the ambit of the UN establishment. Here was a chance to start their marriage in relative peace and a new career for Conor. Why hesitate?

Mostly because they were not sure that they were wanted in Accra. The University of Ghana had recently been in mild turmoil (more of that in a moment) and the faculty was jumpy; the O'Briens would be part of a white elite in a black land; and the character of the expatriate community in Accra was of concern—would they be welcoming or put off by the O'Briens' notoriety after the Congo affray? Dr. Nkrumah shrewdly suggested that they come to Accra and have a look at the university. This they did in February 1962.

Even Nkrumah's most hostile critics agreed that he could be a person of immense charm. He had the mien of a man who genuinely liked to say nice things to people and to make them feel good. (This is why, in the long run, he turned out to be unsuccessful as a dictator; there was not enough despot in his soul.) He was self-dramatizing even in conversation. This left most observers feeling that they had just encountered a great man; later they were to wonder if they had merely met a good actor. Nkrumah could assume the *gravitas* of a Roman senator when discussing matters of importance. Indeed, when cloaked in the traditional *kente*—the multihued robe of Ashanti and Fanti of high status— his glabrous forehead crinkling under the weight of so-great wisdom, he seemed to be an African Augustus.

President Nkrumah had the O'Briens taken up to Legon Hill, eight miles north of the capital, the site of the rapidly expanding University of Ghana. From that mountain Conor and Maire were told to survey a world that could be theirs. It was a seductive sight. To the north and west, the Accra interior plains were visible, an exotic, if parched, mixture of Guinea grass and scrub, broken by ten-foot high termite mounds. The Akwapim-Togo range formed a broken horizon. Looking toward the sea, the vegetation was somewhat more lush, dotted with copses of dense bush and fan and oil palms. Herds of cattle wandered the coastal strip, sometimes attended by young boys, sometimes finding their own way, moving slowly. The main roads were paved, but dust contrails marked the passage of motor bikes and of Land Rovers as they negotiated the dry scrub. In 1962, the city of Accra was a mixture of fishing village, national capital, and a semideveloped industrial harbor. Accra and its surrounding region had a population of about 150,000. From Legon Hill one could clearly see the city of Accra's governmental buildings and modern department stores situated not far from a fishing village that had changed little in centuries. There was a residual harbor (soon to be displaced by that of Tema) where surf-boats were loaded with cocoa and taken out to ocean-going vessels that could not dock in the shallows. This part of Ghana, they were told, had only two seasons—wet and dry—and even these were not that variable: the average daily local temperature varied from 75° Fahrenheit in July to 82° in March. The relative humidity was high (an average of 81 percent in Accra), and the average annual rainfall was a bit under 29 inches a year.[9] The place was not perfect, but it was visually exciting, prosperous by African standards, and a lot more comfortable than was Ireland in that cold February of 1962.

Conor talked at length with representative staff members, spent some time with students, and visited leading members of the expatriate community. He came to the conclusion that the expatriates (especially the Americans and the British, and their associated diplomatic personnel) would not be hostile. The students seemed remarkably pleasant. Most important, the staff wanted him to take the appointment. "I rather got the feeling," he later wrote, "that their idea was that if I didn't take it, somebody worse might be found."[10] In fact, Conor was an excellent choice, a first-rate scholarly mind with broad administrative experience and a record of unimpeachable anti-imperialism. In Conor's own assessment, given in an interview for *The Listener* with his old friend Brian Inglis, "Both the expatriate Europeans and the Ghanaians were very anxious for me to come, because they felt that I could give them a kind of umbrella under which they could continue life as a university without harassment from the sensitive and touchy government of a new state."[11]

Conor was not naive about what he was getting into, although, undeniably he was a bit optimistic. At one stage in the visit, Conor was being interviewed by Nkrumah in Flagstaff House, the seat of government, and the conversation took an unexpected turn.

"Are you a socialist?" asked Nkrumah.

"Yes," Conor replied immediately. This answer was technically correct in that Conor had been a card-carrying member of the Irish Labour party and could hold forth in ideospeak as well as any party comrade. But, in fact, he was no more a committed socialist than was Nkrumah. For each of them socialism, at this stage in their careers, was a form of rhetoric, not a sharply defined ideological commitment.

"People have been telling me," the president continued, "that you are a liberal."

Conor said nothing.[12] He knew what liberalism implied in Africa in those days: a myopic tolerance of Western (and especially U.S.) impe-rialisms, in their various forms, and a quickness to criticize nations and persons who advocated basic reforms, such as land redistribution and the protection of local economies against outside exploitation. In that sense, Conor was anything but a liberal. But he was a liberal in another sense:

> As I drove home from my interview with the leader, I had to realize that a liberal, incurably, was what I was. Whatever I might argue, I was more pro-foundly attached to liberal concepts of freedom—freedom of speech and of the press, academic freedom, independent judgment and independent judges—than I was to the idea of a disciplined party mobilizing all the forces of society for the creation of a social order guaranteeing more real freedom for all instead of just for a few. The revolutionary idea both impressed me and struck me as more *immediately* relevant for most of humanity than were the liberal concepts. But it was the liberal concepts and their long-term im-portance—though not the name of liberal—that held my allegiance.[13]

That this sort of liberalism could clash with Nkrumah's form of social-ism was a possibility of which Conor was well aware. "I was not partic-ularly starry-eyed about Nkrumah," he later wrote. "I expected him to be a despot, but thought he would be a fairly enlightened one. I was skeptical about Ghanaian socialism, but I did expect Nkrumah to be se-rious about trying to make it work, for the benefit of his people." That was not written in hindsight, for Conor indeed was skeptical from the very first. But a codicil to this statement was written with the benefit of hindsight: "I did expect Nkrumah to be serious about trying to make it work, for the benefit of his people. *What I found was different.*"[14]

· · ·

Conor and Maire went home to Ireland. Maire prayed, Conor walked up and down the hill of Howth, talked to trusted friends (especially Paddy Lynch), consulted his three children, and decided to accept. Conor spent the next months writing his electric marvel, *To Katanga and Back*. Betimes he consulted experts on African universities, notably

Sir Alexander Carr-Saunders, former director of the London School of Economics and a leading authority on higher education in Africa.[15] And then, in early October 1962, Conor and Maire were in Accra, Conor giving his inaugural address as vice-chancellor of the University of Ghana.

The early 1960s were a good time to be heading a university. Most nations, Western, Eastern bloc, and Third World, were throwing large piles of money at universities, and top administrators had the pleasure of seeing their institutions grow bigger, better, prettier, wealthier each year. In fast-emerging postcolonial Africa, Ghana was the best place to be, since Ghana was relatively wealthy, the nation's politicians were committed to spending on education, and the University of Ghana was the top of the national educational scheme. In 1962, there were roughly one million students enrolled in primary and middle schools (precise numbers are not available) and there were an estimated 16,000 students in academic secondary schools which taught up to the level of English "A" levels.[16] That latter number—16,000—is important. Although not large, it meant that there was enough of an academically streamed indigenous population to fill a traditional Western university. Entrance to the University of Ghana required five subjects, two of which had to be at "A" level. Unlike most universities in newly independent African countries, the University of Ghana did not have to be a combination secondary school and university. It operated comfortably in its undergraduate curriculum at roughly the same level as British and American state-funded universities.

In the period immediately before Conor and Maire's arrival, the university had gone through some rough water. Founded in 1948 as the University College of the Gold Coast, its intellectual standards had been guaranteed by a "special relationship" with the University of London. Entrance requirements were equal to those of London. Representatives of the University of London jointly set syllabuses with members of the University College. Examinations were jointly monitored by faculty of the two institutions. This gave the Ghanaian education a par value with that of universities in Great Britain. The system worked well, in a parochial way, markedly insulated from the realities of African life. Although the University College had an Institute of African Studies, the curriculum was essentially English in its details. Even the style of management was English, for the University College's first principal, David Balme, unilaterally decided that the institution would be governed by the regulations of the University of Cambridge. When Balme retired in 1957, his successor, Dr. R.H. Stoughton, tried to introduce a governance plan based on English civic universities and this led to a two-year internal war among the faculty and administration. Out of this turmoil came a faculty demand that the University College become a university in its own right, no longer tied to London.[17]

This demand coincided with political pressures that were developing outside of the college. Ever since Ghana had obtained its political independence in 1957, an implied analogy floated over the college: namely that, if we, as Ghanaians, are able to run our own country, certainly we should be able to control our own university. Thus, in 1961, the government decided to set up two independent institutions, the Kwame Nkrumah University of Science and Technology and the University of Ghana. The former was previously the Kumasi College of Technology which had been founded in 1951, and which operated not quite at university standard, but rather at a level of what in England at that time were called colleges of advanced technology. Kumasi was something of a backwater. For example, in 1967 a commission investigating the institution found that the head of discipline at Kwame Nkrumah University had decided cases of student discipline by using an "occult pendulum" to determine their guilt or innocence.[18]

The University of Ghana (created by the University Act, 1961), gave the staff of the former University College most of what they had wanted, and indigestion besides.[19] This occurred because the government-dominated "interim council" that carried out the transition from university college to full university status temporarily sacked the entire faculty. The council decided that the existing employment contracts no longer were valid and that, therefore, everyone was terminated. New contracts had to be issued—or not issued, as the case might be. The effect on morale was dreadful. In the end, all but 6 of the faculty of roughly 170 were rehired, and those who lost their posts received financial compensation.[20] But universities are jittery places, especially if three out of four staff members are expatriates.[21] This explains why the staff was keen to have as strong a personality as possible in their vice-chancellor, and also why they hoped that Conor would act as a bulwark behind which they could shelter.

The academic world that Conor and Maire entered was something of a Wonderland, and not unworthy of Alice. It was in part wonderful, in part inane, in part vicious.

The best part was the money lavished on university education. The government had provided the university with a site of five square miles on Legon Hill. The institution was fully residential and residences for 1,000 students were nearly completed by the time the O'Briens arrived. These were part of a long-term scheme to build a university for 5,000 students.[22] The physical plant was first-class: the building for 1,000 students cost approximately 10,000 pounds sterling for each student, a very high price considering that this was 1960s currency spent in a Third World country.[23] During Conor's tenure, the university enrollment grew from 884 full-time students at Legon in 1962–63[24] to over 1,600 in 1964–65.[25] Most of the students were male—85 to 90 percent of the undergraduates in the early 1960s—and they were older than the usual undergraduate in the British Isles and North America.[26] The Ghanaian pattern was for men to delay their advanced education until after a period of employment. Nearly 80 percent of the undergraduates were twenty-two or older.[27] The undergraduates were secure in their knowledge that they constituted a tiny elite.

On paper, the teaching staff of the new university had qualifications—in terms of Ph.D.s, previous appointments, and publications— roughly equal to those of a good English provincial university or an American state university. In reality, however, the staff was a bit different than it looked on paper. The commitment to pure scholarship was generally less than would have been the case in comparable institutions in the British Isles and North America, and for good reason. The expatriate staff tended to pass through fairly quickly (three years being a typical length of service) and to view their time in Ghana more as a *practicum* than as an opportunity for pure scholarship. Several of the expatriate staff members were in Ghana out of a sense of moral or political commitment to an emerging African nation. Thus, they spent their time in practical activities. The Ghanaian scholars (whose proportion kept rising during Conor's tenure) were for the most part products of British universities. Inevitably, by virtue of their being part of a very small elite, they had distracting civic obligations.

Conor was fortunate in having two close friends on staff, persons of ability and unimpeachable integrity: Alexander A. Kwapong and William Burnett Harvey. Alex Kwapong is the kind of man who makes others feel good: energetic, humorous, ironic, slightly larger than life. In the early 1960s he was in his mid-thirties, an academic rocket. He had been educated at Ghanaian Presbyterian schools and then at Achimota College, the nation's best secondary school. Thereafter, he attended King's College, Cambridge, and received his honors B.A. and Ph.D. Alex joined the then-University College in the late 1950s and was a senior lecturer in classics at the time the University of Ghana was established. He was not one of the representative faculty whom Conor and Maire had met on their visit of February 1962, because he was on leave at Princeton University at the time. He arrived back in Ghana at about the same time that the O'Briens appeared. Kwapong had perfected a repertoire of American singing television commercials with which he could collapse any staid dinner party. He and Conor got on immediately, sharing a sense of irony, a love of anecdotes, and a taste for the local beer (about which they argued, Alex favoring Club Beer, Conor loyal to Ghana Star). Alex was appointed to a full professorship when he returned to Ghana. (This decision was made prior to Conor's arrival and was independent of his influence.) Almost immediately upon return Kwapong was elected dean of the faculty of arts and then, in January 1963, his colleagues elected him pro-vice-chancellor, the number two position in the university. Alex Kwapong, therefore, was both the youngest full professor and the most powerful.[28]

Like Kwapong, William Burnett Harvey, the dean of the law school, was appointed before Conor became head of the university. He was forty years old, an experienced lawyer, and now was professor of law at the University of Michigan from which he was on a two-year leave (1962–64). Harvey in many ways was a contrast to Alex Kwapong. A native of Greenville, South Carolina, he was one of those slow-talking Americans whom it is easy to underestimate intellectually. Calm, very serious, totally committed to the Law, he was not a man who sat around, joked, and traded stories. Consequently, he was never as close personally with Conor as was Alex Kwapong. But he shared with Conor and Alex a deep commitment to academic integrity. He was not a zealot: he was willing to compromise and he understood the need to adapt the law school to African realities. In fact, his mission was to break the stranglehold of English traditions and precedents that bound the Ghanaian legal system. But, on key matters of principle, he would not compromise and this was important in later events, because the law school of the University of Ghana became the epicenter of a whole circle of institutional convulsions, quakes that went to the very heart of the Ghanaian political system.[29]

So the university precincts, the governmental funding, the quality of the faculty, and the presence of trustworthy lieutenants—all this was to the good. Where things started to bend toward the absurd was in the fundamental nature of the university itself. In its essentials, the university was African fustian. Despite Ghana's strong anticolonialism, the government attempted to create a mini-Oxbridge, and although academic standards were certainly adequate, the social trappings hovered between burlesque and travesty. The university, being residential, housed almost all of its students on Legon Hill, away from the everyday world of Accra. The five college halls of residence (Legon Hall, Akuafo Hall, Commonwealth Hall, Volta Hall for women, and later Mensah Sarbah Hall) were built on the English system of quadrangles. With white-faced concrete and orpiment-coloured roof-tiles, they were intentionally inward-looking. Legon Hall was constructed on the floor plan of Clare College, Cambridge, of which Dr. Balme, the founding principal of the former University College, was a graduate. Each student had his or her own room, and in the case of Mensah Sarbah Hall, a small set of rooms, including a porch that opened onto the central courtyard. Over the entire complex loomed the Independence Tower, an ornament particularly dear to President Nkrumah. Like a folly constructed by an eighteenth-century gentleman, its purpose was just to stand there.

The students paid no tuition. University education was free. They were an academic elite, but most came not from rich families but from the new bourgeoisie that inevitably arose as colonialism receded. Undergraduates were treated very well indeed. They were served their meals by servants, had their beds made each day, and had only to leave their shoes outside their doors for them to be blacked and polished. In imitation of Oxbridge, the students wore gowns, but they went the original one better: each hall had its own color. Each hall had its own unique set of bylaws and officers: a master, senior tutor, chaplain. In imitation of sixteenth-century Oxford, the college servant who served as catering officer and purchasing agent was known as the "manciple." Each hall had its own social life and there was very little general college life. The dining halls were baronial and there was a sharp distinction between the high table on a six-inch platform for the staff and the low table where students ate. Students stood up when the staff, gowned of course, entered. At meals a Latin grace was said before the servants brought the first course. The fellows of each hall had their own senior common room, with a bar and a billiard room.

None of this was Conor's doing. It was all in place before he came. Ultimately, however, it was a public relations nightmare and educationally disastrous. Implicitly, it taught the undergraduates that they were special, and that they should turn away from the realities of the world outside. They looked inward, not at the city of Accra, where the problems of the future Ghana were being defined. And the university, opulent, sitting on a hill, looking downward, was easy to hate. Ordinary people, civil servants, politicians, shopkeepers, could easily learn to loathe the privileged city on the hill.

In a sense, the university was so unreal as to be a stage set, and Conor stepped onto it with all the aplomb of an experienced actor. He did so without cynicism. Conor honestly believes in the value of old forms and rituals and he performs them superbly. (As pro-chancellor of the University of Dublin from 1972 to 1992, he marched in countless processions and bestowed thousands of degrees with dignity and pleasure all around.) In the case of the University of Ghana, he had been there before—for the University of Ghana in the early 1960s was much like Trinity College, Dublin, in the 1930s. It was an intentionally cultivated set of anachronisms, a precolonial talisman in a postcolonial world. Conor had so loved Trinity, and been so successful there, that when he dealt with its analog in the Third World, he did not see anything strange about the place he headed. It just seemed natural that things were done in this fashion.

Conor and Maire were provided with a "Vice-Chancellor's Lodge" of impressive dimensions. Maire, who had grown up with servants in her family house, managed the staff with no difficulty except on one matter. The lodge had been built on the Mediterranean concept, with internal patios. That is not a bad idea in Europe, but Ghana is very close to the equator, so that for most of the day the sun bakes down like a blast bomb. Something had to be developed to make the patios habitable. The O'Briens had pergolas put up, so that trellises covered with vines would provide shade. These lovely structures attracted birds, especially hummingbirds, and that was charming. However, they also attracted snakes, some of them poisonous, and it was a constant fight for Maire to get the staff to sweep these areas or, indeed, go anywhere near them, for fear of their lives. (There was one other problem with the lodge: having been planned by an architect with a monumental-mindset, it had huge teak doors, very heavy, hand-made locally. The doors would be opened during the day and then, about six o'clock in the evening when a strong cooling breeze would blow across Legon Hill, the doors would slam. Anyone caught by one of these doors risked serious bodily injury; finally a system of shims and wedges brought the teak slabs to heel.)

The vice-chancellor and his ladywife were expected to entertain and this they did: staff, students, government officials, ambassadors, high commissioners. Among the Ghanaian governmental officials who were frequently present in the early days was Geoffrey Bing. Born in Craigavad, County Down, Bing was at one time a far-left Labour Member of Parliament in the United Kingdom. He was attorney-general of Ghana from 1957–61 and stayed on as a constitutional adviser to Nkrumah until the president was deposed in 1966. It is quite possible that it was Bing who first called Conor to Nkrumah's attention, but whatever debt that might have implied soon was wiped off the slate. Conor and Bing fell out. Conor did not like Bing's attempting to insinuate himself into the management of the university. And he was not at all keen on the heavy inroads Bing made upon the vice-chancellor's stock of Irish whiskey.[30]

More fruitful in the short run were attempts at forming a personal relationship with the president. Nkrumah dined at the lodge on several occasions. These were not large parties, because the president preferred having only one or two other guests present.[31] For a time Conor and Nkrumah got along very well, and Conor did some ghost-writing for the president on matters of foreign policy.[32] This bears notice, for one of the chief ways Nkrumah's advisers had of manipulating him was to write things for him. Conor used this tactic as part of his defense of the autonomy of the university and of academic freedom; others used it to foster attacks on the university.

Nkrumah was central to the University of Ghana not only because he ran the country but because of his position in the university's constitution. Everyday matters relating to teaching and student life were handled by an academic board that consisted of all department heads, plus two nonprofessorial members of each department, with the proviso that each department had to have at least one Ghanaian on the board. This meant that almost all African members of faculty with any seniority were involved in the administrative control of the university. However, final power lay in a university council which set policy and could overturn the academic board's decisions. This fifteen-member group included the chancellor of the university (Nkrumah), plus a Chair of Council to be appointed by him, the vice-chancellor, four other persons to be appointed by Nkrumah, and two civil servants (also to be chosen by Nkrumah). At minimum, therefore, seven of the council members (plus President Nkrumah) were state appointees and when the crunch came, they would follow the government line, not the university's best interests.[33]

The tempest that eventually split the university and government began in a nice cup of cocoa. The cocoa crop was the backbone of the Ghanaian economy. The direct tax on the crop was the single largest source of governmental revenue. More important, the Cocoa Marketing Board, being the sole buyer, grader, exporter, and merchant of the product, made huge profits. They bought at an artificially low price and sold at the world rate: in the 1950s and early 1960s Ghanaian farmers were paid less than half of the world price.[34] (The practice of this particularly ruthless form of monopoly capitalism in a socialist country was just one of the many ironies of Nkrumah's version of socialism.) In the late 1950s, the price of cocoa on the world market started to fall and in the early 1960s accelerated downward.[35] The resultant slump in the Ghanaian economy occurred just at the time a huge hydroelectric project on the Volta was soaking up most of the funds earmarked for economic development.

In 1960, 13 percent of the Ghanaian national budget was allocated to education. Roughly 40 percent of the education funds went for higher education.[36] Because the necessity of supporting education at all levels was a matter of national faith (not least, on the part of President Nkrumah), the University of Ghana's budget was not vulnerable to direct financial cuts. However, increasingly the question was raised of whether or not Ghana was getting its money's worth for all the money being poured into higher education. This was articulated in the vocabulary of political loyalty, and eventually it took the form of demands that the government control key academic appointments and that all university students undergo courses in political indoctrination.

Ghana had become independent of British rule on 6 March 1957 and on 1 July 1960 it became a republic, with an elected president.[37] The key to Ghanaian independence and its later development was the Convention People's Party (CPP) and the protean genius of its leader, Kwame Nkrumah. He was unique in Africa, a despot who shrank from violence against his own people, a dictator who wanted to be liked rather than feared.[38] Born either in 1909 or 1912 (he never knew for sure) in a small coastal village on the western Gold Coast, Kwame Nkrumah went to a local elementary school. After a year as a pupil-teacher, he entered the government's teacher training college in Accra and then attended Achimota College. In 1935 he gained admission to Lincoln University, a black college in Pennsylvania. He worked his way through, became a Freemason along the way, and graduated with a B.A. in 1939. He taught theology as an assistant lecturer at Lincoln and also took a bachelor of theology degree from Lincoln in 1942. In the same year, he received a master's degree in education from the University of Pennsylvania and began studying for a Ph.D. He completed the course work and field examinations for the doctorate, but never wrote his thesis. In 1945, Nkrumah went to London and enrolled in a Ph.D. program at London University. This he did not complete (he later received honorary doctorates), because he spent most of his time working with several African nationalist groups. In October 1945 he was one of the two organizing secretaries of the first pan-African conference, held in Manchester. He discovered that he not only had a flair for oratory (he had spent a lot of time preaching in black American churches when he was at Lincoln University), but he could also write pamphlets effectively. In November 1947, he left London to return to the Gold Coast where he became a full-time political organizer as secretary of the United Gold Coast Convention. In 1948, he broke with the convention and formed his own party, the Convention People's Party, which was the vehicle through which he became in 1952 the first elected prime minister of the Gold Coast and then in 1957 the first head of a decolonized African state and, finally in 1960, the president of Ghana.

The secret of Nkrumah's success is hard to pinpoint. He was neither ruthless nor highly skilled at intrigues, although, like any successful politician he could be cold and devious. Watching him operate in the 1950s, one has the same sensation one gets when watching a professional soccer or basketball star. He was fluid, moved efficiently, and rarely did anything startling. Yet he always seemed to be at the right place at the right time. He was famous for his weekend visits to out-country villages, seemingly arriving with telepathic accuracy just in time to turn some disgruntled tribal elder into a firm and trustworthy ally. He played the old British imperial authorities very well: he looked like the kind of democratic black African they wanted to see: sober, yet smiling, exotic in his *kente*, but equally at ease in his Savile Row bespoke suits. An elegant man of the people. A real pro.

By the early 1960s, however, Nkrumah was starting to lose his touch. The stratagem of establishing a republic in mid-1960 was the first indication of that fact. By allowing Nkrumah to receive his mandate directly from the people, rather than from members of Parliament, it permitted Nkrumah to gain short-term power, but the British-derived parliamentary system that he had played so well disappeared. Now he essentially set up a parallel government that reported directly to him and excluded the legislature from real power. "Flagstaff House," the administrative building in Accra in which the president's administrative staff worked, became the funnel through which all real power passed. It was a confused place. No one knew from day to day who was responsible for what activity, but that was the point: all power was to issue from the president.[39] The creation of the parallel government had fatal long-term effects. Ghana had been left with the legacy from the colonial years of a first-rate civil service. Now its morale and its very legitimacy were destroyed. Second, the power of the elected representative was greatly reduced, since everything important passed through the rabbit warrens of Flagstaff House. Conor's analysis of what this led to is shrewd. Nkrumah in his later years was "operating a process of counter-selection. That is to say that among active and ambitious Ghanaians, the pliable and corrupt were being favoured and rewarded; those who possessed integrity in addition to ability were being cold-shouldered."[40]

This system of personal rule was tied to a personality cult of monumental proportions. In the governmentally controlled press and in CPP political oratory the references to Nkrumah went beyond the merely laudatory: "Father of the Nation," "Fount of Honour," and "His High Messianic Dedication," were among them.[41] The *Evening News*, one of the papers of the Convention People's Party, regularly carried a picture of Nkrumah with the standing inscription "Your Messianic Dedication." This was the same paper that frequently referred to him as "The Holy One" and the "Son of God."[42] Nkrumah particularly enjoyed the title "Osagyefo," which had been used for one of the great Ashanti warrior chiefs. When Nkrumah became president in mid-1960, the king of the Ashanti people, Asantehene, is said to have declared that the new president had done so much for Ghana that he deserved this title. According to Nkrumah's private secretary, "This matter came up for the cabinet's approval and Dr. Nkrumah fought against it, but, in his own words, 'the Cabinet prevailed against me and won. I gave in reluctantly.' "[43]

The personality cult had some bizarre manifestations. Conor recalls that one day Nkrumah had made a speech and that same day a small earthquake ran through the country. The editorial in the next day's *Evening News* proclaimed the connection that obviously existed between the two events: "Oh ye of little faith," the editorial said, "Have ye not seen, have ye not heard? He spoke and the earth shook!"[44]

The dangerous effects of Nkrumah's cult of personality were blunted in two ways. One of these was that Nkrumah and his CPP were wrapped in a blanket of disabling ideospeak, a contradictory, half-mad mixture of Leninism, euthenics, and pan-Africanism. With the aid of various ghost-writers, the president produced a series of volumes that adumbrated "Nkrumahism," a special kind of socialism for Ghanaian conditions. A few of these volumes can be read with pleasure, although not of the sort that the president would have hoped. For instance, in *Consciencism* (1964), Nkrumah and his ghost-writers attempted to prove in twenty-two semimathematical propositions the necessity of the union of the independent African states.[45] As an academic burlesque, this book would rate high, but one suspects that Nkrumah believed. The only memorable slogan from all of Nkrumah's writing was the apothegm "Seek ye first the political kingdom and all others shall be added unto thee," a conflation of two biblical texts.

Perhaps the greatest limitation on the potentially malign aspects of Nkrumah's cult of personality was the sheer good temper of the Ghanaian people. The level of corruption on the part of CPP officials, union leaders, and most politicians was impressive, but it was not vindictive or bad-tempered. Conor in various places has told the story of a visit he and Alex Kwapong made to the opening of the Ghanaian legislature.

The first state occasion I attended in Ghana was the annual opening of parliament by Nkrumah. It was an imposing spectacle: the full panoply of Westminster, plus certain ceremonies associated with the formal appear-

ances of the great chiefs of the Twi-speaking peoples. The parliamentary
benches were lined with the members of Nkrumah's Convention People's
Party, fat men all wearing the *kente*.

Nkrumah read a prepared speech. Most of it was about Africa at large, but
at one point he did get down to Ghanaian specifics. Ghanaians, he said, were
not allowed to hold funds deposited in banks abroad. He said he knew that
even certain members of parliament had infringed this rule. Still, he offered
an amnesty to all who would repatriate their foreign currency holdings by a
certain date. Those who continued to hold monies to deposit abroad after
that date would be severely penalized.

Throughout this entire passage of their president's speech, his entire parliament rocked with laughter. They found the bit about the amnesty and the
bit about the penalties equally hilarious. And as the parliament laughed, the
president was smiling.[46]

The same scene—same parliament, same laughter, same smile on the
part of the homilist—was repeated at the openings of Parliament in the
two succeeding years.[47]

Conor's point was this: "There was and there remains in the
Ghanaian character an elastic, astute power of adjustment, good-
humoured in appearance and also (but in a somewhat different way)
good-humoured in substance. Influenced by this characteristic, the actual workings of the dictatorship were never as horrendous as the zeal
of its own press sought to suggest."[48] Conor was not here being romantic. Other observers confirmed these same characteristics, either anec-
dotally[49] or, in one case, through a major empirical study.[50]

• • •

To Conor fell the day-in day-out job of running a university and his
everyday duties would have been much the same, whether he was in a
democracy or, as was the case, under a fairly amiable dictatorship. He
did his daily tasks well. Conor had been a top-class civil servant and he
knew that the small things counted. He answered his mail quickly. He
made a point of consulting interested persons within the university
about decisions that might affect them. He used luncheon and drinks to
meet with his faculty and he formed close ties with the people in the expatriate community who counted—particularly William Mahoney, the
U.S. ambassador to Ghana. (Conor had a friendship with the Chinese
ambassador as well, based largely on their mutual dislike of the Soviet
ambassador.)[51] Conor and Maire visited the high tables of the various
halls frequently and they made a point of meeting the undergraduates
in the various junior common rooms. On occasion there were parties

for staff and students in the Vice-Chancellor's Lodge, where Conor demonstrated by dancing that, whatever other attributes he might have, a sense of rhythm was not among them.

In February 1962, not long before Conor took up the vice-chancellorship, Kwame Nkrumah had written to him to explain the facts of life that governed the University of Ghana.[52] The institution was expected to engage in practical research related to the problems of Ghana; to set the tone for the "general academic advancement" of the nation by showing leadership in such things as creating lower school textbooks; and to play a part in the establishment of pan-African unity through facilitating the exchange of professors with other postcolonial African nations.[53]

Conor, a committed anti-imperialist and, equally, a believer in the virtues of Western university education, felt that he could navigate between the rocks of excessive Ghanaianization on the one side, and excessive Western traditionalism on the other. The growth in enrollment, and thus in staff size, during his tenure, when combined with a fairly high turnover rate among expatriate (that is, non-African) staff, meant that by 1964 the teaching staff which had been about one-quarter African when he arrived, was now 40 percent African and the trend was projected to continue.[54]

In his first public address as vice-chancellor, on 12 October 1962, Conor gave an extended discourse to the Academic Board. He discussed two central concerns, namely what the role of a university should be in a newly independent country and what characterized the nature and condition of academic freedom. "There is a thesis," he said, "which has powerful and respectable defenders, that the role of a university is everywhere and always exactly the same and that whether the role is exercised in a newly-independent country, or in a rich and advanced one, makes absolutely no difference." He rejected this view, referring to the recent history of the University of Ghana (prior to his arrival) and to the trauma that unbending traditionalism had produced. Given that he headed a staff that still had strong traditionalist leanings, he aimed most of his comments at them. "Many, perhaps most, of you will feel that political affairs are quite peripheral to your concerns." Almost avuncularly, he added, "I have no quarrel with any of these attitudes and no wish to politicize the University: on the contrary indeed. The only attitude which I think should *not* have a place here is that of radical rejection of our environment." That was a coded message and good advice to an academic staff that too often had looked down upon the locals: do not sit on Legon Hill, Conor in effect said, and sneer at other people, the ones who are paying the bills. He continued. "The second question on which

I think it is right to state my views is that of the nature and conditions of academic freedom, in our context here and now. This is obviously something of great practical importance to us all. A lecturer cannot get on with teaching his subject, a scholar cannot get on with his research, if he feels that in these activities he is subject to some kind of extra-academic surveillance and interference. ... If academic freedom in that sense were ever to be assailed here, it should be my duty as vice-chancellor to defend it by all means in my power, and I should do so." With a bit more hope than historicity, he continued, "But I have no reason whatever to believe that this basic freedom is under attack or likely to become so." Then, in an obvious tugging of the forelock to the government, he added that he rejected the "concept of academic freedom ... which was known in mediaeval times as benefit of clergy: the concept that academic people, we as *clerks*, enjoy or should enjoy, a privileged position in relation to the general laws of the land in which we live."[55]

As a public performance this speech was shrewd indeed, for it could be read in Flagstaff House as favoring relevance and Ghanaianization, while within the university it could be heard as a defense of academic freedom.

Later, on 24 February 1963, Conor effected another tactical move relating to academic freedom, and this one was of genuine brilliance. On that day in February Nkrumah was scheduled to attend a formal dinner of recent graduates of the university and Osagyefo (as he now usually was addressed) asked Conor to prepare a speech for him to deliver. Conor put together a draft that, in his own words, "was long on academic freedom and university autonomy. Nkrumah hacked the draft around a bit, but used a surprising amount of it—probably because he wanted to make a favourable impression on the new graduates."[56] So, Osagyefo, who was chancellor of the University of Ghana as well as president of the nation, ringingly endorsed academic freedom. "We know," he found himself saying, "that the objectives of a university cannot be achieved without scrupulous respect for academic freedom, for without academic freedom there can be no university." He was unequivocal: "Teachers must be free to teach their subjects without any other concern than to convey to their students the truth as faithfully as they know it. Scholars must be free to pursue the truth and to publish the results of their research without fear, for true scholarship fears nothing."[57] There was a good deal more in that vein, as strong a defense of academic freedom as one would have heard at the time at, say, Yale or Princeton. Having ghosted this piece, Conor later obtained the president's permission to include this forceful statement on academic freedom in his own annual report as vice-chancellor.[58] Thereafter, Conor frequently quoted Nkrumah's public statement, as an antidote to Osagyefo's increasing tendency to abrogate academic freedom.

This was Conor at his smoothest—being "cute" in the Irish sense. He took great joy in little maneuvres such as this. Conor has always enjoyed the tiny by-plays of human management, in the same way that a master bridge player enjoys completing a tiny, but smooth finesse. Conor had learned the technique of writing words for other people to mouth while in the Department of External Affairs, and he long had known that being modest, staying behind the scenes on certain occasions, was sometimes the surest way to be powerful. (Mind you, this cats-paw method of operating was not always used for the highest of ends. Both Alex Kwapong and Burnett Harvey recall Conor's dumping a particularly lousy job on Alex, namely defending before the academic board a call for out-of-country compensation while on university business. Conor went missing and Alex, who was also the presiding officer of the board, had to defend a scale of allowances that gave twelve pounds a day to lecturers, twenty to senior professors, and twenty-eight pounds a day to the vice-chancellor. Things blew up, the academic board split dead evenly and Alex, with a wide smile announced, "I think I am being called upon to demonstrate my virtue." Whereupon he cast the deciding vote against the policy. But note: Conor's hands, win or lose, were clean; that's the value of the cats-paw method.)

The first academic year over, Conor and Maire were able to spend the summer of 1963 in Ireland, at Howth and in the west, a pattern that they maintained throughout the 1960s. Conor, because of the necessity of recruiting staff (both expatriates and Ghanaians educated in Britain), made several trips a year to London. Thus he was able to keep his hand in various anticolonial pressure groups, such as the 1964 conference on Sanctions Against South Africa.[59] Things were going well.

And then, slowly at first, but with increasing rapidity, everything unraveled. For the sake of exposition, it is useful to separate out the various issues that arose, but in fact they overlapped with each other and Conor was faced with a cascade of bad news that started with the confused and ended in the chaotic. Five separate matters were involved: the medical school, the law school, the Cape College of Education, demands that the university become a political indoctrination center, and, the greatest random factor: the increasingly unpredictable, often bizarre behavior of Kwame Nkrumah.

The initial focus of Conor's troubles was the law school. The legal profession in Ghana was notably venal and also extraordinarily traditionalist. Ghana might be a postcolonial nation, but the forms and practices of the English law course were a talisman clutched close to the breast of the country's lawyers. Burnett Harvey, "a slight, sandy-haired man of forty-two," was on a two-year contract, 1962–64, as professor of law and, as the university grew, as dean of the faculty of law.[60] He knew how to make haste and, more important, how to make haste slowly. Harvey was notably long-suffering. For example, the previous professor of law had resigned because President Nkrumah had appointed a CPP party *apparatchik*, one Alex Kuma, as "Presidential Professor of Law," a post created and an appointment effected without consultation with the university. The resignation of the previous professor left the faculty of law with only three lecturers, all Ghanaian, and an English research fellow.[61] In contrast to his predecessor, Harvey as professor of law simply bowed to reality and got on with his job. Shortly after arriving, Conor asked Harvey what he was going to do about Alex Kuma. "Nothing," replied Harvey, and that was shrewd. He assigned the Presidential Professor no duties and the two of them thereafter got along fine. Professor Kuma and Professor Harvey frequently would meet, usually when Kuma was bouncing along the roadway on his pony on his way back to the university after playing polo down at his club.[62] Eventually, the polo-playing socialist fell afoul of Nkrumah, but that was not of Harvey's doing.

A large part of the problems that arose at the law school centered on matters of educational technique. Burnett Harvey attempted to introduce certain aspects of American-style legal education and the instinctive traditionalism of a recently colonial context militated against this. Harvey's view (endorsed by Conor) was that instead of class sessions consisting of a professor reading off notes and students copying them down, the American system of case analysis, with rigorous daily debate, should be introduced. This was paired with the belief, dominant in American law schools of the time, that the law should be an active agent of social reform. With Conor's support, Harvey was able to recruit a very good staff. For the 1963–64 academic year, he brought on three very able Ghanaians—Joseph K. Agyemang (London University degree), George K. Ofuso-Amaah (formerly a lawyer in the general counsel's office of the United Nations), and Thomas A. Mensah (LL.M. from Yale). He also recruited four well-qualified activist lawyers from abroad: Michael Thoyer (LL.M. from Columbia), Jeremy T. Harrison (LL.M. from Harvard and a former lecturer at the Catholic University of America), Vern G. Davidson (a former associate in law at Columbia University), plus Gordon R. Woodman (who had a Cambridge law degree). This was in addition to two appointments made earlier in the previous year: Robert B. Seidman (Harvard College B.A., one-time senior editor of the *Columbia Law Review*, and a practicing attorney of fourteen years experience) and William Cornelius Ekow-Daniels (of whom more later).[63]

Paradoxically, although the American presence was potentially revolutionary as far as the study of law was concerned, it was viewed by the Ghanaian elite as being potentially politically reactionary. In this view, they were not entirely naive. One must remember that the United States at this time was waging a land war in Southeast Asia and was supporting, at least covertly, most of the remaining colonial regimes in Africa (the United States was hedging its bets by supporting simultaneously a number of the revolutionary groups). Thus, a series of letters in the government-controlled *Evening News* attacked the law school of the University of Ghana. These attacks began as early as November 1962. "Only socialist legislators can initiate socialist laws," one editorial letter argued, "But you need socialist lawyers to draft, interpret, and administer them ... above all, don't let anyone who is not a socialist teach the lawyer who will have to practice law in a socialist country" (27 Nov. 1962).

Such attacks might have been heard and then forgotten, but on 6 January 1963, Nkrumah attended a rally in Accra. He left early, just before a grenade (or two or three) was lobbed into the crowd, causing death and injuries. The president himself had been wounded earlier, in August 1962, when a grenade had been thrown into his car, and the possibility of being assassinated weighed heavily upon him. When in public he took to wearing outfits that covered his entire body up to the neck. This not only concealed his wound but permitted him to wear body armor when in dangerous proximity to his more active critics. A few days after the incident at the rally, a brief article in the *Evening News* asked what the "so-called Michigan professor at Legon" was doing in the stadium behind Osagyefo's reviewing stand. In fact, Burnett Harvey had not been anywhere near the stadium, but the implication was that he had been involved in the terrorist attack. Conor went to see President Nkrumah and Osagyefo said he knew nothing about such accusations. There things lay for a time.[64]

Then Burnett Harvey made what was perhaps the only serious mistake of his time in Ghana and it was a wholly innocent one, the sort that scholars make. In the tradition of English universities, it was customary for a professor to give a formal inaugural lecture, and this Harvey did in Commonwealth Hall on 24 May 1963. Students, senior members of the law society, politicians, and university staff were present. Harvey's lecture, "A Value Analysis of Ghanaian Legal Developments since Independence," was a sober and thoughtful discussion of the need for continuing legal change and particularly the inclusion of African customary law in the legal system. It was a long lecture, but near the start of the speech, before his audience had drifted off to sleep, daydream, or contemplate the slowly moving ceiling fans, Professor Harvey asserted that law "is value-neutral, being merely a technique of social ordering available for use in support of any value judgement that the manipulators of the technique entertain." Then he added, "I recognise the apartheid enactments of South Africa, which I abhor, as *law* in as full a sense as the prohibitions of racial discrimination in American legislation, which I strongly support."[65]

Disaster. Although W. Burnett Harvey had said that he abhorred apartheid, his suggestion that the law of apartheid was, indeed, law, was easily taken out of context—the more easily because his sentence was one of those backward-leaning monsters so beloved by academics, the ones that mean the opposite of what they would seem to mean if the listener is not paying very strict attention. Thereafter, any politician who wanted to attack the university had only to claim that the professor of law (who was already associated in print with terrorism) was in favor of apartheid.[66]

The anti-Americanism that the new personnel and new methods kindled in the law school fed into another matter, the proposed medical school for the University of Ghana. Founding a medical school was one of Conor's priorities and his main preoccupation in his first year of office. By the spring of 1963, some very complex arrangements had been knitted together between the America Aid agency, the several universities of the Philadelphia area, and the Ghana government. The arrangements promised a quick start-up, minimal cost to Ghana (a lot of U.S. money was involved), and no qualitative problems. (The Philadelphia area medical schools would see to that.) Dr. Richard Cross, formerly of the University of Pittsburgh medical school, was appointed as professor of medicine and dean of the embryonic medical faculty. He and Conor were busy in the autumn of 1963 recruiting staff, and students were to begin clinical work in October 1964. The U.S. government was slow, however, in giving final approval for the funding, and this delay allowed local opposition to arise. Conor's position as chairman of the committee on the medical school was undercut by Dr. Joseph Gillman, a South African medical doctor, who was director of the Ghana Institute of Health. He was ideologically opposed to any agreement with the government of the United States and, crucially, he had access to Dr. Nkrumah. The result was that in November 1963 the Cabinet (meaning, really, Nkrumah) decided that negotiations with the American authorities were to be terminated.[67]

A year and a half later, Conor wryly told an audience at the University of California, Berkeley,

I don't know if any of you are likely to be appointed chairmen of committees in one-party states, but if you are, I might give you some advice about them. If you are going to the leader, you do *not* say to him, if you are wise, that a strong majority of the committee favours such and such a course of action. The reason that would not be wise is that the reaction of the leader in such a state is to the following effect: "Well, if that is so, I will show that majority where it gets off."

What you should do (and, by implication, what Conor should have done) was now clear:

> The right approach, within such a framework, is to say to the leader: "The majority of the committee are obstructive and possibly they consist of sab-oteurs, some of them at least. I have been trying to do your will on the com-mittee, these people have blocked me, I want please your support, one word from you and the whole thing would be changed." That is the way to do it, but I learned it too late.[68]

Here Conor was being too hard on himself, for his own sense of integ-rity would not have let him enact the kind of cringe that was required. He was trapped in a situation where, given Dr. Gillman's access to the president and the increasing anti-American attitudes in Ghana—especially the fear of the CIA and of American subversion—he could not win. Thus, even with everything for the medical school in place, ready to be signed, things fell apart. Conor's response when he learned of the decision to kill the medical school was that "this isn't changing horses in mid-stream; it amounts to shooting your horse under you just as you reach the opposite bank."[69] Nevertheless, he remained committed to the idea of Ghana's having its own medical school, although he was skeptical of the new wisdom from Flagstaff House, that a medical school could be created with resources already in Accra and at the university. Despite the radical change in direction, Conor soon left on a recruiting trip to Europe to find teaching faculty for the new medical institution. (The timing of this trip is an important part of the later story of the uni-versity's troubles—however, here one bit of irony is worth foretasting. After all of Conor's work, in late February 1964, President Nkrumah decided that the Ghana medical school was to be established independ-ently of the University of Ghana and that it would award its own de-grees and diplomas.)[70]

Back to the law school. Throughout the autumn of 1963, problems continually mounted for Conor and Burnett Harvey. The key interme-diate figure in the game was W.C. Ekow-Daniels (the ultimate figure, of course, was Osagyefo). Ekow-Daniels was a young man in a hurry. "A young, pipe-smoking stocky man with a pudgy face," Ekow-Daniels was a Ghanaian at a time when that counted.[71] He had received a University of London LL.B. and subsequently a Ph.D. from the same university. He had been called to the English bar and then returned to Ghana, became active in the Convention People's Party and came to have direct access to Kwame Nkrumah. Ekow-Daniels was (or at least had been) a mountebank in two narrow senses of that word. As in the older, literal meaning, when someone mounted a *banco* or bench to attract attention, Ekow-Daniels gave stump speeches, both in the university precincts and elsewhere. Moreover, he had been convicted of personation—in this case for taking an examination for someone else. He had, however, received a pardon from Nkrumah's government, or he would not have been permitted to be called to the English bar. Neither the conviction nor the pardon was something that Ekow-Daniels featured on his employment applications.[72]

Whether or not Ekow-Daniels was a mountebank in a larger sense is impossible to determine. He was indeed very critical of the way the law faculty of the University of Ghana was run, but this could have stemmed from an honest desire to serve the Ghanaian national interest; on the other hand, careerism is also a possibility. Virtually from the day of his arrival at Legon Hill, Ekow-Daniels made it clear that he was hostile to Burnett Harvey. Harvey tended to give him the benefit of the doubt, largely because he was young. Originally, Harvey had been skeptical of the wisdom of appointing Ekow-Daniels as a lecturer in law because he had a poor degree (a lower second) in law from London. However, Harvey was convinced by his Ghanaian colleagues that Ekow-Daniels was indeed a mature scholar.[73] In fact, Ekow-Daniels did publish fairly widely: four articles and one paper in 1962–63. Equally important, the government during the year 1962–63 paid for him to take trips to political conferences in London, Addis Ababa, and Dar-es-Salaam, a sure sign that he stood well with Osagyefo.[74]

The *apparent* influence of Ekow-Daniels became notable on 26 October 1963. President Nkrumah was visiting the university to give a speech at the official opening of the Institute of African Studies. The speech was ghost-written for him by the director of the institute, Thomas Hodgkin.[75] Everything went well until, in the middle of the speech, appeared two paragraphs that had nothing to do with the words the president had uttered up until that point. They dealt with the law school. Osagyefo declared:

> Our students in the Faculty of Law must be taught to appreciate the very intimate link that exists between law and social values. It is therefore important that the Law Faculty should be staffed by Africans.

There is no dearth of men and women among us qualified to teach in the Law Faculty.[76]

Now, it is immaterial whether these words were written by Ekow-Daniels (as was widely believed at the time, but which he subsequently denied), nor is it crucial whether or not he boasted at the time that he had written them (this too was widely believed, although, again, later denied by Ekow-Daniels). The key point is that Osagyefo, president of Ghana, chancellor of the University of Ghana, had called publicly for an all-African law staff.[77]

Conor, already deep in the mire of the medical school negotiations (and still involved in day-to-day administrative tasks) now had to protect the law school. Victimization of the expatriate teaching staff loomed; major violations of academic freedom were possible, and, worse, racialist criteria for academic appointments were conceivable. Conor immediately made an appointment to see Nkrumah. They met the next day, 27 October, at Flagstaff House. And here the maddening niceness of Nkrumah came into play. When Conor pointed out that the law syllabus had been revised in a progressive and revolutionary manner, from the Anglophilic traditional bias to one that was based on African circumstances, the president was impressed and asked how long Professor Harvey would be with the university. "One more year," Conor replied and then Osagyefo asked if Harvey could not be prevailed upon to stay a year longer! "No," said Conor, but perhaps his chief deputy, Robert Seidman, could be prevailed upon to stay indefinitely. The meeting ended happily. The president said that he would be happy to talk with Professor Harvey.[78]

The calm was deceptive.

President Nkrumah dined with Conor and Maire at the Vice-Chancellor's Lodge on Friday, 1 November. Something must have gone terribly wrong, for the next day Nkrumah sent Conor a letter advising that the appointment of all heads of departments and faculties, "such as Political Science, Law, and other departments could be made after you have discussed such appointments with me as Chancellor of the University."[79] This meant that the president desired, but would not quite demand in writing, a veto over appointments to law, political science, and other politically sensitive faculties.[80]

And now, Nkrumah refused to see Professor Harvey. On the Monday after the weekend he had the secretary to the Cabinet write to Conor saying that "Osagyefo does not consider that such a meeting with Professor Harvey is necessary now, in view of the full discussion he had with you at your earlier meeting, and I believe also at the dinner in your house last Friday." And, ominously, "Osagyefo has asked me to reiterate the view he expressed at the opening of the Institute of African Studies that steps should be taken to insure that the staff of the Law Faculty is Africanized completely as soon as possible."[81] Conor later heard from a member of the university in whom he had confidence that the wording of the letter that shut the door on Professor Harvey's meeting the president was the result of the intervention of W.C. Ekow-Daniels.[82]

A few days later, Conor received a verbal message from Nkrumah demanding that he sack all expatriate (read: white) members of the law faculty. Conor refused.[83] He believed he could sit out the president.[84] There matters rested until December, when Conor had to go away to recruit faculty for the ill-starred medical school.

Enough problems? There were more. During the autumn of 1963, the university came under pressure to indoctrinate the undergraduates in the tenets of Ghanaian socialism, or Nkrumahism or Consciencism, whichever label was favored that week. *The Spark*, the government's ideological organ, frequently attacked the university, as did other Accra papers, also under government control. The gravamen of these attacks was that the young members of the elite were not growing up good socialists. The minister of the interior (and acting minister of education) Kwaku Boateng was given responsibility for introducing a "citizenship training programme" into the university. Conor knew what this meant: a course in political indoctrination. He tried to head it off by employing the old civil service expedient, "yessing it to death." Rather than fight directly, he proceeded obliquely. He proposed that the university organize a series of lectures under the general title "The Future Graduate as Citizen," which would have two lectures on Ghana's seven-year plan, one dealing with agriculture and another with industry, three lectures on pan-African union, and others on Ghanaian culture and government.[85] When Conor met Kwaku Boateng on 3 October, the discussion was friendly enough, but they fundamentally disagreed. Conor said that it was not the university's role to further any single political viewpoint. Boateng agreed in theory, but since he was himself convinced that socialism was the only valid political viewpoint, he wanted an opportunity to put this position to the students. Boateng wanted to start the course of lectures immediately, but Conor put them off until January and held firmly to the position that attendance at the lectures should be voluntary and that the students would not be examined on their content.[86]

Conor was doing everything he could to avoid a direct conflict between the university and the government, while at the same time preserving the fundamentals of university independence. Unlike the matters of the medical school and the law school, the political indoctrination issue involved the spine of the university, the departments in the arts and sciences. Here Conor was strongly backed by Alex Kwapong, the pro-vice-chancellor; by Ado Boahen, a Ghanaian in his early thirties and the senior scholar in the Department of History, which at that time had no full professor; by Professor Christian Baeta of the Department of Religion; and by E.A. Kofi Edzii, the registrar (who, in the British tradition, was much more than a pecksniffian record keeper, but instead was the head of the central administrative offices of the university).

On the other side, however, was one of the most remarkable personalities on the staff, William Emmanuel Abraham. Known as "Willy" by friend and foe alike, he was not yet thirty years of age in the autumn of 1963. Willy Abraham possessed one of the nimblest minds among his generation of African academics. He had taken a degree at London University, then an honors B.A. and a B.Phil. at Oxford. From 1959–62, he was a Fellow of All Soul's College, Oxford, the first African to be elected. This gave him a great glory back in Ghana when he explained what this meant, something he was quite willing to do. Although he was trained as a technical philosopher, his claim to prominence in pan-African circles arose from a volume that he published in 1962 entitled *The Mind of Africa*. Written in the midst of the decolonization of Africa, the book strikes the present-day reader not only as admirable in its clarity of argument, but refreshing in its optimism. Abraham's argument, and clearly his temperament, differed sharply from those murky theorists of decolonization (especially the French theorists) whose gloom and bitterness is matched only by the opaqueness of their prose. Abraham believed in an upbeat form of pan-Africanism, one that would not only cleanse Africa of colonialism, but would also be a prophylaxis against the dangers of tribalism. (Had he only been right!) Willy Abraham was appointed associate professor of philosophy and head of that department before Conor arrived. The appointment was well merited. That said, it did not hurt Abraham's case that he had made himself known to President Nkrumah and that he had sent the manuscript of his book to Osagyefo before publication: "Above all, I am deeply grateful to Osagyefo Dr. Kwame Nkrumah who bestowed on this book the honor of reading it in typescript form," was the conclusion of his work's preface.[87]

It was generally believed in academic circles that Willy Abraham was the chief ghost-writer of Osagyefo's gnomic *Consciencism*, although there was a supplementary view in some circles that the book had mostly been lifted by Nkrumah from French sources.[88]

Abraham—"a bantam cock of a man"—was often seen surrounded by students, instructing them in proper politics.[89] In this he worked in tandem with Ekow-Daniels. Didacticism was not always enough to kindle enthusiasm for the CPP among the elite young of Ghana, so on one occasion, at least, it became known that Ekow-Daniels and Abraham had distributed money to their student cadre in one of the residence halls. Presumably this was to impress upon the students the direct benefits that might accrue through party membership.[90]

As compared to Ekow-Daniels, Willy Abraham was less naked in his ambition (although ambitious he certainly was) and less implacable in his maneuverings. "In fairness to Professor Abraham," a contemporary expert on Ghanaian politics observed, "it should be recorded that he never gave me the impression that he really believed in the nonsense he propounded."[91] That seems a bit harsh and, I think, misses the more likely interpretation that Abraham indeed believed in his own philosophical conceits, but that he was willing to push them only so far and then, in that peculiarly Ghanaian way, to back off with a smile.

That this is probably the case is indicated by a series of events that happened somewhat later, in November 1964. Abraham at that time accepted the chairmanship of a committee established by the government with the power to inspect the publications in all bookshops, libraries, schools, colleges, and universities, and to remove those that did not reflect Convention People's Party ideology. Conor managed to have the University of Ghana library exempted from the edict, but the campus bookshop came under its purview. One day, Willy Abraham came into the bookshop and asked if the shop sold a new history of Ghana, one written by Dennis Austin.[92]

"Yes, I have it," replied the bookshop manager, Mrs. Marguerite Harris. "There it is."

Abraham quickly gave judgment. "Oh, I see that you have five copies of it on display. I think it would be enough to display two." He repeated: "Don't have more than two copies on display at any one time."[93]

Here Willy Abraham's rhetoric and behavior could be taken as an example of what Conor has called "the Ghanaian gap between frightening theory and sometimes rather endearing practice."[94] This does not mean that Abraham was much fun for the university leaders to have around, or that he was much of a democrat. In one speech during this period, Abraham advocated using the university to teach socialism.

"How will that be done?" he was asked from the audience.

"By indoctrination," he said. When queried further, he explained that indoctrination meant compulsion and that he favored having university students repeat by rote the formulas that were given to them in indoctrination lectures. In the audience at the time of this speech was the wife of the cabinet minister who was charged by Nkrumah with effecting the political indoctrination program. She stood up and said that as a devoted socialist she resented the tying together of socialism and compulsion. "It was not a comfortable evening," one observer wryly noted.[95]

(In this same period, Abraham gave a talk about the position of the university in a revolutionary society. He developed the theory that in the future university there should be no status differences between individuals, especially faculty and students. He wanted the elimination of high and low tables. Then, after developing to this point, to everyone's amazement he added, "After high table is eliminated, don't expect me to eat the same food as the students! Because I pay more and therefore I ought to eat better!"[96] Thus the human face of Ghanaian socialism.)[97]

So, as the month of December 1963 opened, Conor was being pressed hard to allow compulsory political indoctrination in the university, was having to resist the removal of all expatriate staff from the law school, and was trying to stitch up the arrangements for a medical school, which were a mess. None of these things was his fault. Early in December, Conor went off to Europe to recruit medical staff, leaving Alex Kwapong in charge of daily university affairs. In mid-December, Burnett Harvey went to lecture and do research elsewhere in Africa, leaving Robert Seidman as his deputy in charge of the law faculty. And just then the politics of Ghana went mad.

• • •

Like everything else in Ghanaian politics of the time, the crisis that began in December 1963 pivoted around the person of Kwame Nkrumah. Recall that in January 1963 there had been an unsuccessful grenade attack on Osagyefo. Arrests were made and a set of trials was held before a special court consisting of the chief justice of Ghana, Sir Arku Korsah, and two other justices. In the first of two trials, seven persons were sentenced to death for various forms of treason. Another set of arrests was made and a second trial began in the autumn and its results were announced on 9 December 1963. Two men were sentenced to death for treason, but the court declared three others not guilty. These were three significant political figures—the former minister for foreign affairs, the former minister for information and broadcasting, and the former general secretary of the CPP—and the charges against them can only have been politically motivated. There was virtually no evidence linking them to the assassination attempt.[98] Nevertheless, Osagyefo immediately sacked the chief justice of Ghana. The government-controlled press bayed for blood.

At this point Conor either made a major tactical error or took a heroic stand for human rights (or, perhaps, both). He was in Geneva when all this broke and he was in contact with his old boss and sometime

Siren, Sean MacBride. Since abandoning his earlier incarnation as commandant of the Irish Republican Army and, subsequently as a hate-merchant in the campaign against the Northern Protestants, MacBride had been on a march toward secular sainthood. He had been chairman of Amnesty International since 1961 and he was for a long time chairman of the Irish section of the International Commission of Jurists. In 1963, he had become secretary general of that international body. Conor gave testimony before the jurists and issued a statement to the press condemning the dismissal of Sir Arku Korsah. He demanded the reinstatement of the chief justice. At the time, Conor explained that he was not in the habit of saying one thing in front of Nkrumah and another behind his back, and that his statements were made in his capacity as head of a university that had a faculty of law.[99]

When Conor returned to Ghana on 20 December, he immediately tried to obtain an interview with Nkrumah, but Osagyefo, furious, refused. Thereupon, Conor wrote a letter to the president in which he repeated the assertion that he had followed the treason trial carefully, that the evidence would not support a conviction, and that he was giving his opinion not in his personal capacity, but as vice-chancellor of the university, and that respect for fact was central to the entire role of the university in Ghanaian society.[100] The net result of these actions was that from 20 December 1963 until 24 January 1964, Conor, and most others who shared Conor's viewpoint on university matters, were unable to get to the one man in the country whose opinion on such things mattered most, President Nkrumah.[101]

The law school, the medical school, and the issue of political indoctrination all were on the line. And then, incredibly, the stakes doubled, and doubled again.

Late in December, Nkrumah called a referendum for 24 January 1964. In fact, however, this was not so much a referendum as a national vote of confidence. Four questions were posed, but they were to be answered with only a single "yes" or "no." The two queries that counted most asked, in effect, should Osagyefo be able to fire at will any judge of the high court or supreme court? And should, henceforth, there be only a single legal party, the Convention People's Party? As Henry Bretton explains, this second question really asked whether or not Nkrumah's personal political machine should be the only legitimate form of political power in Ghana[102] Eventually, the referendum passed with approximately 99 percent of those casting votes choosing "yes."[103]

The results of that referendum, however, were in the future. What made the referendum campaign such a disturbing reality for the university was that on 2 January 1964, as the president was leaving Flagstaff

House for lunch, a police constable on guard, one Seth Ametewee, fired five shots at him at close range. The shots missed Nkrumah completely, but killed a security guard. The attacker then chased the president into Flagstaff House and momentarily cornered him in the kitchen where he bit Osagyefo on the face. (Later, when asked by foreign journalists how he had responded to being chased by a rabid member of his own police force, Nkrumah summoned his dignity and replied that "I endeavoured to place distance between myself and the constable.")[104] The immediate result was that Nkrumah went into the bunker, both literally and metaphorically. He took to doing most of his work in Christiansborg Castle, his chief residence. This seventeenth-century fortress built by the Danes to help them control the slave trade sits right on the Atlantic behind massive stone walls. Nkrumah had it surrounded by a perimeter fence and patrolled by a large staff of guards.[105] Nkrumah's behavior at this time makes it clear that he saw the world as being against him; and part of that enemy world was the University of Ghana and its vice-chancellor.

On 17 January, a Friday in the first week of Lent term, the government suddenly announced a seventeen-day recess in all university-level institutions in Ghana. Ostensibly this was so the students could go home and vote in the referendum, but since most students were not registered as voters, this rang hollow.

Just as the news of the forced recess spread across the university, a squad of security police arrived to arrest two staff: Dr. J.C. de Graft-Johnson and D.G. Osborne. The latter was a British physicist, a devout evangelical with no political leanings. Dr. de Graft-Johnson, a Ghanaian, was master of Commonwealth Hall and director of the university's Institute of Public Education. He had been an active supporter of the old United opposition to Nkrumah, but of recent years was a strong supporter of the CPP and in favor of the political indoctrination program. Presumably de Graft-Johnson had run afoul of political intrigue within the Nkrumah government. Why Osborne was arrested no one ever discovered.

As the security police fanned out through Commonwealth Hall, students gathered. Already upset about the closing of the university, they now started to heckle the police. Willy Abraham arrived and chatted away to the deputy police commissioner, who was in charge of the operation, and then started to leave. The students circled him and began shouting "Stooge! Stooge!" Trapped in a circle fifteen or twenty feet in diameter, he darted about, trying to escape. The students stood firm, not using force, but standing shoulder to shoulder, arms folded, chanting. Finally he broke through and ran away.[106]

Conor, still locked out of Osagyefo's presence, managed to obtain an interview next morning with Kofi Baako, the minister of defense, who had succeeded Kwaku Boateng as overseer of the "citizenship training programme." Baako told him that if the students did not disperse to their homes, the government would send in troops. The students, for their part, made it clear that they intended to stay. So Conor had to make one of the most important speeches of his life; the danger of bloodshed was real. He convened a meeting in the open-air amphitheatre of Commonwealth Hall. About 1,500 students were present. It was a muggy day and the noon-time sun blasted down. His speech was brief: the university was fragile and easily destroyed; they must leave, for the good of the institution they loved. There are no transcripts of this speech, but one witness recalled the almost physical way that Conor controlled the crowd. At the start of his talk he motioned the students toward him and they came in like a tide; he held up his hand and they stopped in place; he gestured for silence and they instantly obeyed.[107] Whatever magic Conor had that day, it was prepotent. The students left quietly and by Monday morning the university was deserted, save for staff.

At the end of the first week of enforced recess, on Friday, 24 January, Conor finally was permitted to speak personally with President Nkrumah. Conor pleaded the case for the release from detention of the British physicist, Dr. Osborne. This, combined with the efforts of Professor Alan Nunn May, Presidential Professor of physics and head of the Physics Department, resulted in Osborne's being paroled on the condition that he not leave Ghana without permission and that he not carry on discussions with any Ghanaian.[108] Nothing Conor and Professor May could do was any help to the other detainee, Dr. de Graft-Johnson.

(Here, lest the contradictory nature of Nkrumah's dictatorship be forgotten and the singular amiability of many Ghanaians lost, the details of Dr. Osborne's detention in the days before his parole must be noted. Detention it was and, technically, Dr. Osborne was incommunicado. But Osborne was kept at a local police station, not at a prison, and he was not required to stay in his cell. He sat out on the station's verandah when he pleased, and although the acting British high commissioner was not permitted to see him—hence, he was incommunicado—his friends could drop by for a chat any time. He wrote letters and his friends posted them. The sergeant in charge of the jail, when notified that a higher-up would be coming by, politely asked, "Dr. Osborne, would you mind going back to your cell? It will only be for a few minutes." When Conor came to pick up Osborne after parole was granted, the policemen of the station carried his bags to the car and then, obviously pleased that he was released, lined up on the verandah to wave him goodbye.)[109]

On 27 January, Dr. Nkrumah sent a letter to Conor making six demands concerning university administration. Conor replied two days later, attempting to calm the agitated president, by agreeing to everything, but in such a way as to minimize the actual interference in university life. Nkrumah's six requests and Conor's answers were as follows. Demand One: all tutors in the halls of residence should be Ghanaian. Answer: this presents no difficulty; twenty of the thirty-two tutors already are Ghanaian; the only problem might be Volta Hall, the female residence, since there is a shortage of Ghanaian women university teachers. Demand Two: the appointment of heads of departments and faculties must receive the approval of Osagyefo in his capacity as chancellor of the university. Answer: "I shall seek your approval as chancellor on any future appointments. Such approval will be sought after the appointment committee of the Academic Board has made its decision." Demand Three: all academic appointments should carry adequate teaching obligations. Answer: virtually all do so already, but Conor will inform the board of the chancellor's demand and will ask it to establish norms. Demand Four: the chancellor must be informed of all academic staff who are not being paid by the university. Answer: such a staff list will be drawn up. Demand Five: all university scholarships must be subject to annual review on the basis of "satisfactory performance and good conduct," by each student. Answer: the university, under a process to be established by the academic and tutorial boards will institute such an annual review. Demand Six: all scholarships tenable by Ghanaians in the various universities of Ghana should be channeled through a to-be-created "Scholarship Secretariat," a committee which will include representatives of the universities. Answer: the University of Ghana is willing to participate in this procedure.[110]

Since throughout his adult life, Conor has been characterized often as being unnecessarily combative and often egregiously arrogant, it is well to note here how he was operating. He was doing everything possible to avoid setting off Nkrumah, who was at this time a bomb, primed to go off. The items that the president demanded were distasteful, certainly, but they did not violate any fundamental criterion of academic freedom. Conor, thereafter, acted with exigent and expedient humility in putting up with a little governmental meddling, in the hope that Nkrumah would calm down and leave the university alone.[111]

This did not work. Much more worrisome anti-university action already was in train. On the morning of 30 January, two men appeared in Conor's office. They were heavies: Mr. Otoo, head of Ghanaian security, and Mr. Mfodwa, of the Special Branch. They told Conor that they had reliable evidence that four senior members of the university were engaged in activities prejudicial to the security of the state. Therefore, they asked Conor to require these four persons to resign. Who were they? Predictably, Burnett Harvey headed the list. (Poor Harvey: he had returned from his lecture tour on 27 January and by the morning of the twenty-ninth he was flat on his back with a medley of tropical and non-tropical diseases—pleurisy, typhoid, malaria, and hepatitis among them.) Robert Seidman, the second-ranking person in the law school, was also to resign. Conor argued with the security men: these two were well known to him, they were totally dedicated to their teaching and to scholarship and he could not believe that either of them was connected with subversion. The third person on the list was a "Mr. Chester."

"Who?" asked Conor.

"Mr. Chester," was the reply. The security men did not have any details concerning this person and Conor had never heard of him. The fourth person on the list was Gaston Greco, a West Indian married to a metropolitan French woman. Conor refused to vouch for Greco because, as he told the security men, Greco had been reprimanded by the head of his department for failure to give adequate attention to his educational duties. His departmental head reported that "he appeared to give most of his time to outside activities." (This was a fact that had to be known already by the security men, since Greco acted as Nkrumah's French interpreter; presumably he was caught up in some intradepartmental squabble, for he was on the governmental payroll, as well as the university's.) During the conversation with the security men, which rambled over various matters of general university policy and of student behavior, two salient details emerged. One of these was that when Conor suggested that Harvey and Seidman well might be the object of malicious denunciation by interested parties from within the university, an individual or individuals who might gain by the departure of the two ranking persons in the faculty of law, Mr. Mfodwa gestured in what Conor took to be agreement. The second point is that when the two security men were asked if the president were aware of their visit to the university and of the demands that they were making, the two security men answered "no."[112]

Conor took the statement of Osagyefo's noninvolvement at face value and that afternoon fired off a memorandum to the president summarizing what had happened. Two days later, on Friday, 31 January, Conor was walking across the campus when he was stopped by yet another security man who attempted to serve him with a deportation order in the name of "Professor Chester"! This was how Conor learned that deportations were in effect. Harvey, Seidman, "Chester," and Greco were to be deported and two new names had been added to the list: the chaplain of Legon Hall, the Rev. Mr. Stewart, and an American lecturer in African studies, Dr. Jean-Pierre.[113]

As always under Nkrumah, farce and tragedy were closely inter-mingled. Conor still had no idea who Professor Chester might be. Not until a day later did it became clear that the security men were looking for Professor Schuster. He had been in Ghana only two months. Still, it reflects badly, albeit accurately, on the quality of the Ghanaian intelligence service that they confused Conor with Professor Schuster—especially given that Schuster was an African-American.

Conor tried to see Nkrumah, but the president's door was once again barred to him. He had to be satisfied with dashing off a letter of protest whose language was much less diplomatic than he usually employed. Two sections are salient:

> I have not been informed of the charges made against Professor Harvey and Dr. Seidman. I am aware, however, that a Lecturer in the Faculty of Law—who has applied for the posts of Professor and Senior Lecturer—has persistently, over several months, sought in various ways to bring about departures by which he stands to gain, financially and in status. I believe therefore that these gentlemen—scholars of high attainment and repute who have given most valuable service to the University—are the victims of malicious and self-interested delation.[114]

Conor continued,

> In view of my last conversation with you on 24 January, I find it hard to believe that this police action can have been taken with your knowledge or that you have seen my letter of Thursday [29 Jan.]. If I am wrong in this, if the police action has been taken with your approval, ignoring my letter and request for an interview, then it is evident that my opinion carries no weight with you and consequently that my continued tenure as Vice-Chancellor would serve no useful purpose.[115]

Osagyefo still refused to see Conor, but at least the deportations were postponed until Saturday, 8 February 1964. This apparent boon was potentially a bomb, however, since it gave time for public passions to flame. On Tuesday, the fourth, the students began to return from their forced recess, and they came back agitated. In the city of Accra itself, a crowd of CPP activists demonstrated outside the American embassy, rather like a warm-up drill before a sports event. What the big event would be was clear, for a campaign against the university was run in all the newspapers. In relation to the scheduled deportations, the *Ghanaian Times* thundered, "Today the Yankee gun-running act has come to Ghana. The dopes and drunks who run the murder incorporation known as CIA are after the blood of Kwame Nkrumah because he is the biggest thorn in their neo-colonialist ambitions." The next day, the same paper asserted that "it is imperative that our universities be brought to heel. ... It is our determination that our universities must turn out only men and women who will serve the Party and the nation with loyalty and dedication and contribute actively towards Nkrumahist socialism in Ghana and Africa."

Within the university, things were tense, understandably. The students scheduled a big demonstration for Saturday morning, the day of the scheduled deportations.

Conor knew that he had to keep the staff behind him—or at least quiet. On Monday the third, he had convened a meeting of the academic board and there he received unanimous backing for the representations he was making on behalf of those under deportation orders.[116] According to one eyewitness, a strange by-play occurred during that meeting. Professor Posner, head of the French Department, announced that Gaston Greco's deportation order had been cancelled. Thereupon W.C. Ekow-Daniels jumped up and heatedly denounced "vicious rumours" that were circulating about him.

"What rumours?" asked an unidentified voice.

"The rumours that I procured the cancellation of Mr. Greco's deportation."

Professor Posner arose. "That is exactly what Mr. Greco told me." She had a very demure manner and was all the more cutting for having it. She added "... in the presence of other members of the staff."[117]

Next day the animus among staff members against Ekow-Daniels increased, when faculty became aware that Jean-Pierre and Greco—both named on the original deportation orders—were next-door neighbors to Ekow-Daniels in Achimota.[118]

During the next week, the government sent small groups of demonstrators up to the universities—sorties, rather than serious attacks. Conor was talking to a roomful of students during one of these orchestrated events, when he heard the demonstration change from rhythmic clapping and chanting to sounds of violence. He went outside to find the man who had organized the demonstration being beaten on his napiform head with staves that a minute before had held his own placards.

He had not shown up with the promised money to pay the demonstrators. Conor can be forgiven for finding this development "satisfactory."[119]

A student strike was called for Thursday the sixth, but the hall tutors managed to convince the Students Representative Council that a strike, and its inevitable accompanying demonstration, should be postponed until the vice-chancellor could see Osagyefo. The next day Conor finally got to see Nkrumah, but only by virtual subterfuge. The distinguished English academic, John Fulton, vice-chancellor of the University of Sussex, was an external member of the University of Ghana's governing council. He was in Accra as part of his official duties and Nkrumah granted him an interview. Conor went along and, when Fulton was called in to see the president, Conor barged in and pleaded the case of the faculty about to be deported. Nkrumah, always polite, was angrier than ever Conor had seen him. He coldly told Conor that he had enough evidence to convict Harvey and Seidman in court, although he did not say on what crime the conviction would come. Conor responded, if that were the case, then the two law teachers should be tried in court and if convicted, they should be punished. The president said that deportation was his decision, and there the discussion ended.[120]

Robert Seidman, who because of Burnett Harvey's serious illness was effectively head of the law school, convened a meeting of all law students and staff at 3:00 on Friday afternoon. The theme of his remarks and of almost all members of the staff who commented after he had addressed the students, was that the big demonstration called for Saturday could destroy the university. The one staff member who was notably silent was W.C. Ekow-Daniels. Finally a fourth-year student asked him directly to state his opinion.

Ekow-Daniels stood up.

"Gee ... Gee!" echoed through the room. That is the Ghanaian form of booing. Only with difficulty could Ekow-Daniels make himself heard. He again denounced vicious rumors and especially one that he had personally served the deportation orders (which certainly he had not done). Then one of the students asked, "What steps have you taken to have them revoked?" Ekow-Daniels did not reply. He hastily excused himself and left.[121]

(Remember that this was Ghana: the poison in the air could be mitigated by Ghanaian charm. After chairing this meeting Seidman had to go down to the Criminal Investigation headquarters to sort out details of his own deportation, scheduled for the next day. At headquarters, the chief came up to him. The man had been studying law at the university in his spare time. He shook Seidman's hand. "I am very sorry you are leaving. I hope that the order will some day be reversed and that you will come back to teach.")[122]

That Friday evening, Conor addressed Convocation, which included all of the senior teaching and administrative staff. He gave a long narrative of the events of the past weeks and then asked for questions and discussion. Ekow-Daniels took the floor and gave his by-now familiar complaint about vicious rumours. He sat down to silence and Conor coldly remarked that it might be better to pay attention to the serious matters at hand. The Convocation passed unanimously a resolution supporting the vice-chancellor's actions.[123] Everyone went away apprehensive about what the next day would bring: the deportations. But before that the students planned a major demonstration and the government was known to be planning an even bigger counterdemonstration. A serious riot was possible, indeed probable.

The next morning, Saturday, at 8:00, Conor addressed the assembled students. He warned them that extremists in the ranks of the CPP wanted to goad them into doing something stupid. The best way for them to protect the university and to protect academic freedom was to exercise rigid self-control. He had just finished his speech when word came that a mass demonstration was on its way up to the university. Between 9:30 and 10:00, some 2,000 to 3,000 demonstrators arrived. Some of them, workers for the Ghana National Construction Company, arrived in company trucks. Other workers arrived stripped to the waist and carrying clubs. Party women of the CPP, in traditional costumes, danced along to drumming; schoolchildren came along for the excitement and riot police flanked the marchers, blue-helmeted, arms swinging. They made it clear whose side they were on.[124]

The university students stayed amazingly calm. The demonstrators, their signs reading "No More Intellectuals!" and "Down With Students!" pushed into Commonwealth Hall. The demonstrators went from hall to hall, doing minor vandalism along the way. (Conor later sent the CPP a bill for £120.14s.6d, which, not surprisingly, went unpaid.) The students did not strike back. In Volta Hall, the women's residence, the students stood on the balcony, icily disdainful of the demonstrators, who shouted obscenities at them.[125]

(The ironic, amiable counterpoint was not missing here. As this minor vandalism of the halls was taking place, a young expatriate lecturer, just arrived from England, was walking around the university precincts. A demonstrator shoved into his face a placard stating "Colonialist Snakes Go Home!"

"Can't you read that?" demanded the demonstrator.

The young lecturer mildly replied, "Well, I can, but it would be a little early for me to go home. I only came here last Tuesday."

At this the demonstrator took his placard away, shook the new lecturer warmly by the hand and said, "Welcome to Ghana. I hope you will have a very pleasant visit.")[126]

Conor tried to argue with the leader of the demonstrators, Nathaniel Welbeck, organizing secretary of the CPP, but he got nowhere. So he hurried off to Flagstaff House where he saw the secretary of the Cabinet, Enoch Okoh, who was surprised and distressed at the events. Okoh left immediately to talk to President Nkrumah, who was holed up in Christiansborg Castle, and asked him to have the demonstration called off.[127]

While Conor was gone, Alex Kwapong, as pro-vice-chancellor and Kofi Edzii, as registrar, acted brilliantly. They detached Nathaniel Welbeck and the other leaders from their followers by inviting the leaders into the university's council chambers to discuss matters. There Kwapong and Edzii held firm, and, equally important, they held the leaders' attention while outside, the directionless demonstration gradually lost momentum. As Alex Kwapong said later, laughing, "if you remove the head of a snake, the rest is just a piece of rope."[128] So, by noon, the demonstration was fizzling out and the students, by not being provoked, had essentially won the day. Still, the next Monday the government press declared the demonstration to have been a great victory: "BARE-CHESTED GHANAIAN WORKERS BREAK THROUGH VARSITY ARROGANCE. STUDENTS JUMP THROUGH WINDOWS AS WORKERS AND FARMERS WARN THEM OF CONSEQUENCES OF CONTINUED SUBVERSION!" shouted one extended headline.[129]

After all this, Conor debated with himself about whether he should go to the airport for the deportations.[130] He did well to quell his doubts, because the afternoon of Saturday, 8 February, saw one of those rare occasions where courage and dignity are united in a living ceremony. The leave-taking of the deportees was as stately and as sure as those incised on ancient petroglyphs. The five deportees (minus now Mr. Greco who had been reprieved), were to leave soon after sunset. Conor, Maire, Alex Kwapong, Kofi Edzii, Adu Boahen, Christian Baeta, perhaps half the senior staff of the university, all of the members of the law faculty (save one), servants, secretaries, administrative functionaries, people with a lot to lose, they all showed up. They said goodbye to the deportees with a mixture of gravity and amiability that had everyone in tears. Darkness fell. At 6:30 P.M. the deportees walked up the ramp. Burnett Harvey was carried up on a stretcher, as he was too ill to walk. Then the plane was gone.[131]

Should Conor have gone back to the lodge, taken out a sheet of paper and written his resignation? He decided to stay on. Two months later he wrote to Burnett Harvey, saying: "I do not think that I would be discharging my responsibilities to the students and staff properly by bailing out, unless, of course on some good and sufficient issue. The nearest thing to such an issue has been the deportations and I am myself not sure whether I did the right thing on that occasion."[132]

The deportations would have been a logical point of closure: Conor would have been leaving on moral high ground. The government's violation of academic freedom was unambiguous and was visible from afar. It would have been understood in the British Isles and North America. Against leaving was Conor's devotion to the university, his need of employment (the vice-chancellorship was, after all, a job), and his not wanting to make a career of resigning posts.

One malicious conjecture that must be scotched as totally inaccurate is that by staying on Conor was endorsing the government's actions against the University of Ghana. This opinion was noised about in English intellectual circles in the spring of 1964.[133] Nor can one accept the idea that, as Stephanie Harrington wrote in the *Village Voice* of 24 November 1966, Conor had confined himself to "private protestations" and that he had publicly acquiesced to Nkrumah's attacks on the university. The correspondence and oral testimony relating to the period make it clear that Conor fought Nkrumah constantly. Like the great Roman general, Fabius, he used the limited resources he had. He fought well; not omnisciently, but occasionally brilliantly, and always with courage. Soon after the *Village Voice* slur appeared, it was answered by Burnett Harvey who recounted talking to Conor immediately after the deportation orders were served. "I told him that I thought a protest resignation was the safe course for him. It would protect him from the kind of charges Mrs. Harrington [Stephanie Harrington was the wife of the social activist Michael Harrington] has made. At the same time it would have been disastrous for the university. ... Many of us had fought hard for the integrity of the university, but O'Brien had an irreplaceable combination of assets for continuing the fight."[134] The other deportee from the law faculty, Robert Seidman, writing not long after his own deportation, summarized the situation as it existed after 8 February: "In Ghana today, he is the only official who will disagree with Nkrumah to his face, although no doubt O'Brien does that, as he does most things, most tactfully."[135]

· · ·

Conor desperately needed a break from the unremitting aggravation. In fact, he got none, only more troubles. But that provides an opportunity to ask a question one poses of anybody who is under constant pressure—how does he or she stay sane? Conor's answers at that time were ones that worked for him for almost his entire adult life. He drank quite a bit—at this time, mostly beer and wine—and, more to the point, he read voraciously, thought skeptically, and wrote wonderfully. Conor is a true intellectual in the sense that using his mind, far from tiring him, refreshes him and provides energy for the daily grind.

The amount of high-quality intellectual work he accomplished during his off-hours while vice-chancellor is remarkable. He published roughly twenty articles in journals such as the *New Statesman*, the *New York Review of Books*, and *Studies on the Left*. For the most part these were reviews, albeit of a characteristically free-ranging sort. One of his essays from this period, on Yeats and fascism (which will be discussed in chapter 9), remains one of the single most important essays on Yeats and still has an unsettling effect on the field of Yeats criticism. Conor also published a book, *Writers and Politics*, which was a compendium of essays, most of which had been previously published.

For the first time, Conor had the liberty of using his own name and the corresponding responsibility. No more "Donat O'Donnell." The voice now is unswervingly that of Conor Cruise O'Brien. It is already a mature voice. There is no fumbling, no rhetorical adolescence. "Conor Cruise O'Brien" as a literary voice hit the public as a full-blown talent. He was fortunate in having been forced to write as "Donat O'Donnell" during his chrysalis years.

The vices of his writing in these years are easily stated, but the flaws are epidermal, not fundamental. Much of the writing has a distracted quality. The man had a lot on his mind and sometimes he let a sentence get out of control, allowed a nonsequitur to lurch down a paragraph. At times, one feels that he is writing with the thought of a brick coming through the window on his mind. And who can blame him?

Also, *Writers and Politics* (1965) introduces a form of publication that was admirably honest on Conor's part, but fundamentally lazy. Unfortunately, the book sold well, so the habit stuck until very late in life, the habit of selecting and reprinting essays from various sources without tailoring them into a cohesive book. In this case, the pieces go back to his "Donat O'Donnell" days and include two speeches Conor made while under great pressure as vice-chancellor of the University of Ghana. The historian can only be grateful that Conor set a policy of not tinkering with previously published pieces (this with very minor exceptions, which he sign-posts): Conor's own training as a historian inhibited him from messing about with what were now, in a sense, archival documents. But the reader encountering *Writers and Politics* for the first time will be aware that it does not work as a book.

But in some of the shorter pieces written during the Ghana years, he was brilliant. We see a marvelous mixture of integrity, anecdote, and scimitar-sharp irony. The integrity comes through in almost everything, but is especially notable in two pieces. One, published in 1963 in the *New Statesman* was a review of *The Irish Comic Tradition* by Conor's old "wife"—that is, his Trinity roommate—Vivian Mercier. The book already had taken a slating in Ireland. Conor neither springs unthinkingly to the volume's defense—which he well might have done, not only because Mercier was an old and valued friend, but also because Mercier, now an American academic, could be of use to Conor when the time came for him to get out of Ghana—nor does he make a big thing about a potential conflict of interest. He just reviews the book and explains that Mercier has gone astray because he is beguiled with the idea that there is such a thing as an "Irish mind" that has "its own peculiar quirks, not shared even by other Europeans." Conor suggests that instead of there being a distinct "Irish mind," there has been at least since the seventeenth century an Irish predicament and that has produced the distinctive character not only of Irish humor, but also of the best of Irish literature. The vein common to Swift, Wilde, Shaw, and Joyce, Conor suggests, is the ironical mode, the weapon of the disadvantaged. "You have your bayonets," the rasp-tongued nationalist Tim Healy said. "Do not begrudge us our Billingsgate."[136]

Conor's integrity—the keel that balanced the sail of his new-found liberty, the right to speak in his own persona—also came through when he took on the impossible task of reviewing a history of the *New Statesman*, in the *New Statesman*. In this review, he agreed with Edward Hyams, the author of the history, that the *New Statesman* in its early years had been a mixture of hard-edged Marxist assumptions about how society worked and the conflicting belief that "most people are pretty decent chaps, really." Conor also agreed that "many of the rest of us inside and outside the British Left" shared with the *New Statesman* "the capacity to be surprised and angry when the man whom he expected to punch him on the nose, punched him on the nose." Conor refused to accept the position put forward by Hyams, however, that in its editorial policy on Hitler's crackdown on Czechoslovakia that the journal was not a sell-out. On the Munich issue, Conor said, the *New Statesman* "preferred settling down among the hopeful illusions of its readers— including you and me—to losing popularity and 'influence' by rasping those illusions."[137] That is Conor at his most balefully honest: nothing of the mystagogue about him, merely an unflinching witness to a truth from which others would prefer to avert their eyes.

Conor's reviews could be stinging, as when he took apart a book on Albert Schweitzer (about whom Conor himself had severe reservations, but reasoned ones), a slash-job written by one Gerald McKnight. "Mr. McKnight's writing has the worst features of the kind of British mass-circulation journalism which formed it; cockiness, ignorance, carelessness, prurience, innuendo and lip-service to the highest moral standards."[138] The sting there is in the tail: high moral standards, indeed.

When Conor reviewed the first volume of Jean-Paul Sartre's autobiography, a curious volume that is nothing if not articulate about the self-conscious intellectuality of Sartre as a child, Conor suggested: "Sartre, in short, like the good novelist he is, is lying: brilliantly and to our great entertainment and instruction, and with many touches of truth, but lying. Among all those intricately placed, pivoting mirrors which the novelist turns so dexterously for our amusement, the bloody business of childhood has managed to get itself left out."[139]

Now that he could use his own name and his own voice, Conor increasingly employed anecdotes. He does this with an apparent casualness that masks the art involved, and always with irony. Here is the way he concluded a review of a biography of Hugh Gaitskell. No ponderous paragraph of summing up for him:

> I remember, in a pub in Ireland, seeing Gaitskell on television at the time of Suez. A crowd accustomed to be cynical both about politicians and about Englishmen, was deeply moved by Gaitskell's controlled and genuine passion and by his power of argument. Most understood the political and moral courage which it took to make such a speech at such a time. A tram-driver lowered his pint. "You can't beat an Englishman," he said, "when he's straight."[140]

Conor knew exactly what he was doing and this was a technique that he later perfected in his columns in the *Observer* and the *Irish Times*. What appeared to be an intellectual essay (and indeed was) transformed itself into a tiny short story, and the reader was left with an image and a question—straight? sure, but how many Englishmen are straight?

In the essays written during his Ghana years, Conor's work is dominated by two and a half themes. One theme concerned the political responsibilities of the literary critic which were, first, to care a bit about the real world and, second, to get it right when one does care. In a discussion of Dwight Macdonald's critical work for the *New Yorker* and of his book *Against the American Grain*, Conor noted the falseness of Macdonald's self-proclaimed radicalism. "You could say *almost* anything about Mark Twain, James Joyce, James Agee, Ernest Hemingway, James Cozzens, Colin Wilson, the English of revised Bibles, or Webster's International Dictionary—to list most of Mr. Macdonald's subjects—without causing a *New Yorker* reader to wince." "If, however," said Conor, twisting the knife, "your favourite authors happened to be Mao Tse-Tung and Fidel Castro and you tried to say so in the *New Yorker* then you *would* be going 'against the American grain' and you would not be likely to go very far." In sum: "There was a time when Dwight Macdonald in his prickly and indignant independence, might have been thought of as an American Orwell. ... Mr. Macdonald has not quite fallen for the kind of nonsense symbolized by 'Eustace Tilley,' but his choice of 'classes' against 'masses' makes the monocle—emblem of pretentious myopia—a disturbingly appropriate symbol to appear above his recent writing."[141]

But caring about the masses, as well as the classes, was not enough. When dealing with the real world, a literary critic had to acquire a facility with facts, and learn to respect, not dice, them. Thus, when Conor reviewed Edmund Wilson's pamphlet *The Cold War and the Income Tax: A Protest*, he admired the politics but was too gimlet-eyed to let Wilson get away with special pleading. Wilson's pamphlet was basically a discussion of a small Road-to-Damascus conversion; in this case, the chronicle of how dealing with his income tax problems had led him to study, and then reject, the intellectual premises of the then-raging cold war. Trouble was, "as far as one can make out from Mr. Wilson's confused account of his tax situation, he does not seem to have been treated unjustly, and his own suggestion that he may have been in some way penalised for having four wives, or having been a leftist in the distant past, seems to lack foundation. His tax offense [not filing for several years] is adequate, by itself, to explain what happened to him." As for the substance of Wilson's argument on the nature of the American cold war mentality, "the critic in Mr. Wilson has been struck dumb and blind by the prophet. The confusion which marks the opening pages on personal finance and taxation lifts somewhat, but never altogether clears, in the rest of the book." Wilson, Conor pointed out, had swallowed whole the bogus story of Major Claude Eatherly, the Hiroshima pilot whose later-life behaviorial problems were supposed to have been caused by guilt over dropping the bomb. Wilson had bought this story despite plenty of evidence pointing in the opposite direction. Presciently (like Burke foretelling the rancid side of the French Revolution long before anyone else did), Conor warned: "It is not true, as Mr. Wilson seems to imagine, that if America reduces her military expenditure and tax levels, the cold war will be at an end. The real cold war—that between the underdeveloped and developed countries—has still a long course to run."[142]

The Wilson piece relates to Conor's second major intellectual con-

cern in the essays he wrote during his Ghana years: the nature of the
neo-colonialist world in the era of American hegemony. In a major
essay, "Contemporary Forms of Imperialism," published in *Studies on
the Left*, Conor began with the assumption that imperialism in the 1960s
was something sharply different from that of the 1890s. The earlier
form involved capitalist countries bilking noncapitalist ones; whereas
modern imperialism had no "economic taproot," in the classic phrase.
It was therefore something entirely different. Given his opening assumption (a questionable one, certainly, but worth granting for the moment) Conor suggested that there had to be a distinct, new driving force
behind the new (neo-colonial) imperialism. Neo-colonialism, in his
view, was characterized by a single characteristic that ran through all of
its forms: the high degree of success with which Western whites controlled nonwhite peoples. Because of this racist element, "it is meaningful to speak of Western imperialism, in this sense, as one of the greatest
and most dangerous forces in the world today."[143] Paradoxically, the
Western world, and especially the linchpin of Western imperialism,
American society, did not advocate such racism or even publicly approve of it. How, then, did the Western democracies justify their imperialism, even while refusing to admit that they had empires? They
did it by adhering to the declared goal of the United States, which was
not just to prevent Soviet and Chinese territorial expansion, but to stop
the spread of a specific political doctrine—namely, communism.
"Containing communism," in Conor's view, was one of the greatest
dangers to world peace. This was a theme that he was to develop much
more strongly in his years at New York University in the second half of
the 1960s. His apperception, though, came much earlier. "An 'anti-
communist' foreign policy involves an indefinite number of such un-
controllable and therefore potentially explosive commitments."[144]
Conor's views on imperialism were not congenial either to serious
Marxists (the idea that neo-colonialism was more racial than economic
was noncanonical) nor to standard-issue liberals (to whom anticommunism was something to be deplored for domestic civil-liberties reasons, but not as a primary danger to world peace).

If two big issues were on Conor's mind during the Ghana years—the
political responsibility of the literary critic and the nature of neo-
colonialism in the American Age—a half-theme niggled at him and it
is very revealing. This is his fascination with conspiracies. Conor was
not—nor did he ever become—a conspiracy nut, but his concern with
such things is only partially intellectual, and it was not a passing phase.
As a very good historian, Conor loved teasing out patterns that others
had missed. Looking beneath the surface was an intellectual joy for him,

like solving difficult puzzles is for some people. But I think there was more to his interest in conspiracies than that, and this becomes clearer as he becomes older.

One of the conspiracies that he sniffed out in these years involved *Encounter* magazine. This was an establishment-liberal publication, edited in London, which in the 1950s and 1960s published the most fashionable of American and English political liberals. It was mildly left, often iconoclastic, trendy, highly readable, but in some hard-to-define way, inhibited. The inhibitions, it later became clear, arose from its being funded by the Central Intelligence Agency through a front, the Congress of Cultural Freedom. In December 1963, Conor sounded the first alarm about the nature of *Encounter*.

> Almost every issue has contained some cleverly written material favourable to the United States and hostile to the Soviet Union. ... Reading through the files of *Encounter* I found little evidence of vigilance against non-Soviet intellectual dishonesty. ... Great vigilance is shown about oppression in the communist world; apathy and inconsequence largely prevail where the oppression is non-communist or anti-communist. ... Silence about oppression has been, if possible, total where the oppressors were believed to be identified with the interests of the United States. [145]

Later, in 1966, Conor developed further this textually based commentary and it led to a famous lawsuit in which he was victorious, in part because the fact of CIA funding eventually leaked out. Here, the point is that long before investigative reporters (in particular, those for *Ramparts*) found the subterranean financial conduits between the CIA and *Encounter*, Conor recognized from textual evidence that the magazine was bent. That he had himself set up a propaganda agency for the Irish government at the behest of Sean MacBride—the Irish News Agency—and that therefore he recognized bent journalism when he saw it, in no way detracts from Conor's percipience; it merely helps to explain it.

Conor's second bout with conspiracy as an intellectual matter during these years was less convincing and, in retrospect, somewhat embarrassing. He took up the case of Alger Hiss in a review in the *New York Review of Books* of Whittaker Chambers's posthumous volume *Cold Friday*. (Chambers had named Hiss as a communist, in the days when that was as damning as uttering a blood libel.) Conor in the first paragraph of his review dismisses any alleged revelations found in the Chambers volume and goes quickly for the kill. "What the book does, however, is to raise again the interesting question of the liar as saint: the question of why this veteran liar should have become a saint in the eyes of so many intelligent people who dislike lies, or say they do." No punches pulled there. The trouble is that Conor's argument thereafter hinges on Chambers's having stated, wrongly, that there are nine inflections of the Russian noun. Conor details an imaginary interrogation of Whittaker Chambers by Richard Nixon and then gives his own cool explication:

> The "nine inflections of the Russian noun" are of course a mistake, not a lie, but the mistake is, I think, a revealing one because...there was a "need," a motive for it. In this case—and I suspect, often though not always elsewhere in Chambers's writings and testimony—the pressure to distort is a rhetorical pressure. "All nine of the inflections of the Russian noun" gives just the reverberation Chambers needed at this point in his boomy incantation. "Nine" is good, both as sound and number. As sound it gives a solemn chime, sonorous corroboration of all those domes and minarets. As number it is mystic and appropriately large: ordinary languages do not have as many inflections of the noun; the number, in its solemn excess, corresponds to the vastness of the Russian land, the ceremonious endurance of the Russian soul.[146]

That is Conor at his worst. He is reminding us that he knows Russian (and to British Foreign Service standard, he might add) and that he can play word games at Olympic level. He is showing off. There is nothing of substance in the rest of the essay and one is left feeling rather more sorry for Chambers than for Hiss. That Conor took a terrible thumping for this review from William Buckley, himself moving across the cusp from being a prodigy to becoming prematurely venerable, was only justice.[147]

Nevertheless, we should not turn away from Conor's instinctive fascination with conspiracies, for it goes to something central in his personality. I think it is this: ever since his father's death, when he was only ten, parts, very important parts, of the world did not make sense to Conor. What was seen could not be all that there was: there *had* to be more. So, for example, there had to be a reason why Dag Hammarskjold's plane went down, some reason beyond the obvious. Conor acquired the mental habit of looking for extraordinary explanations to what were, alas, ordinary tragedies. He did not exhibit this habit constantly, nor regularly, but the propensity to see conspiracies was always to hand. It was an intellectual prism that he picked up often, sometimes with great effect, other times with embarrassing results.

Whatever the academic qualities of this habit of thought, it was an attempt to slake an inner thirst whose origins were not merely intellectual.

$$\bullet \quad \bullet \quad \bullet$$

Return now to the land of the magenta crest: that was the color of the presidential emblem and of the embossed letterhead that Dr. Nkrumah used when he was very serious about something. Conor in the spring of 1964 received lots of magenta-embossed letters, none of them pleasant.

One of these arrived from the castle, dated 20 February 1964, less than a fortnight after the deportations. Osagyefo made three demands (in addition to conveying his decision that the proposed new medical school would be independent of the university). These were that Willy Abraham be appointed head of the Department of Philosophy (a strange request, given that he already was head; what Nkrumah presumably wanted was for Abraham to be made a full professor), that W.C. Ekow-Daniels be named head of the faculty of law, and that a Dr. Yaw Manu (who, unlike the other two, had not been a major player in university politics, merely a faithful CPP follower) be made head of the Department of Political Studies.[148] Even granting Dr. Nkrumah's status as chancellor of the university—a position not unlike that of the viceroy in the self-governing countries of the British Commonwealth—this was a major attack on academic freedom. Nkrumah responded to Conor's attempts at befogging the issue by pointedly telling him that he, as chancellor, had the power to appoint all heads of departments.[149] "I must respectfully, but firmly, state that I cannot acquiesce in any such procedure," was Conor's reply, no longer pulling his punches. "The principle that teaching appointments are made by the academic body on academic grounds is, I believe, essential to the intellectual and moral health of a university and, even taking due account of the respect which I owe to you as chancellor and head of state, I feel I cannot give way on this vital matter of principle."[150]

Two statements in this letter were tactically important. "If you insist that these appointments must be made," Conor told Nkrumah, "it will be necessary for you to replace me as vice-chancellor." Somewhat more diplomatically, but equally firmly: "I fully realize that it is for Ghana, and not for me to decide what kind of university Ghana needs. Having felt, to my grief, over the past six months that my own recommendations have been uniformly disregarded or set aside, I am beginning to be forced to the conclusion—as it would appear you also must be—that I am not in tune with your present conception of what the future of the university should be. If this is the case, the remedy is in your hands."[151]

Osagyefo replied from his castle, demanding that the three appointments be effected. "If, as I understand it, you find it difficult or impossible to accept the position that the vice-chancellor of the university must work in the closest co-operation with the chancellor in all matters affecting the university, including the nomination and appointment of staff, then, as far as I am concerned, I fail to see how the university can continue to function satisfactorily in such a situation. It seems to me that the decision rests entirely with you as to whether or not you are prepared to co-operate with the chancellor or to leave the university."[152]

Conor wants Nkrumah to fire him; Nkrumah wants Conor to resign. Each challenges the other to take the fatal step. Why are they playing this game? In Osagyefo's case, it is because he would suffer a black eye internationally if he fired someone as prominent as O'Brien, who was popular and respected in anticolonial circles and particularly in Africa. Conor was too big to fire easily, so making him resign was preferable. On Conor's part, being fired was much more desirable than resigning. His being turfed out while fighting to protect academic appointments against political interference would have gained for him the moral high ground, while merely resigning could easily be interpreted as petulance or, at best, battle fatigue. In the actual event, the two men, evenly matched, kept up this game until Conor's three-year term as vice-chancellor was completed. The game ended in a draw.

The presidential pressure to make the three appointments, and Conor's resistance, is the background to what several observers feel was his best speech to the university, an address given to the university Congregation on Saturday, 14 March 1964. This was the first occasion on which the University of Ghana had conferred its own degrees. Conor's speech on paper is a low-temperature document, but in person it was electric. A U.S. State Department official, relying on local observations (which, presumably, were those of the ambassador William Mahoney and his wife) reported: "The vice-chancellor spoke in the courtyard of the Great Hall at Legon ... on the occasion of the awarding of degrees before an audience of some 1,000 faculty, students, members of the diplomatic corps, paramount chiefs, politicians and Ghanaian friends. ... He spoke with relaxed confidence, wit and eloquence."[153] And, he spoke with quiet, piercing anger. Not only was President Nkrumah carrying on an attack on the university, but, in a tiny, diagnostic recent event, Conor had seen an aspect of Osagyefo that he had not known previously, a shabby callousness. On Wednesday morning, 11 March, while Conor was in his office working on the Congregation address, the floor started to heave. An earthquake. Almost immediately afterward, Nkrumah telephoned Conor and asked whether any of the buildings, and particularly the Independence Tower, of which he was extremely proud, had been damaged. Conor said "No, no damage," and the president hung up. Shortly thereafter, Alex Kwapong walked in to talk and found Conor furious that Nkrumah had not bothered to ask if any students or staff were hurt.[154]

That explains why in his address to Congregation, Conor began by talking about the earthquake. He used the quake as a rhetorical fulcrum to lever an attack on Nkrumah's policies on university education, without doing so directly. "The vibration which shook our campus was a reminder—a kind of which it is said academics need from time-to-time—that we stand on the same soil as the rest of the community." He developed this apparently unexceptional idea for a time and then turned his metaphor into a stiletto. "The slight seismic shock which interrupted our trains of thought on Wednesday morning was not the first shock our peaceful community has experienced this term." His audience well knew to what he was referring. Will we find, he asked "in our time of trial that the moral and intellectual fabric of the university is such that it too will stand against shock, so that those values which are more important to us even than the University organization, or its physical fabric, will be handed down to future generations in all essentials intact?" But was not the university a perpetuation of colonialist and neo-colonialist values? No. "Respect of truth; intellectual courage in the pursuit of truth; moral courage in the telling of truth: these are the qualities essential to the life of learning and teaching; these are the qualities of a real, of a living university. ... These are not European values; they are universal values." Then, devastatingly, Conor quoted what he called an "important passage from a speech made by our chancellor a little more than a year ago. ..." It was the defense of academic freedom that Conor had ghosted for Nkrumah![155]

The Spark ("A Socialist Weekly of the African Revolution" its masthead declared) devoted most of an entire issue to "Our critical analysis" of the speech, and critical it was. WE DISAGREE was the headline and Conor was criticized for devoting less than 3 percent of his speech to a discussion of Ghana's most recent Seven Year Plan. He was described as a racialist ("O'Brien's Racialist Doctrine," one subhead read) apparently on the basis that Professor Harvey, "deported American professor," had supported obedience to apartheid laws.[156] Raw polemic this was, but serviceable. At least that was what the CPP stalwarts within the university thought: a mimeographed sheet went around the campus stating that the relevant issue of *The Spark* was available at the department of philosophy.[157]

Thereafter, Conor decided to retreat on the matter of the appointments that Nkrumah wanted, but not to give up on the fundamental principle that the academic authorities made academic appointments. In conducting his retreat he used the entire bag of tricks he had acquired through years of international diplomacy: memos, citations of statutes, recitations of precedents, obfuscation wrapped in protestations of respect. These ploys do not require chronicling in detail, but here is one example of how he conducted the retreat. On 17 March, Conor wrote to Osagyefo about the three appointments. First, he said "Professor Abraham is head of the department of philosophy." Conor told the president, however, that Abraham's promotion to full professor had been considered inappropriate by the appointments board because of a negative assessment by one of the external assessors. The matter could be reopened if Abraham had additional information to submit. Second, Conor told the president that Dr. Yaw Manu had not applied for the headship of political science because the post was not vacant. Manu had applied to be a senior lecturer and that application would be considered by the appointments board in due course. And, third, he explained, Dr. Ekow-Daniels had made two applications, one for the chair and professorship of law, the other for a senior lectureship. Those applications would be considered in due course. "Anxious though I am to give you the fullest co-operation I properly can, I cannot conscientiously alter or disguise the firm opinion I have formed and conveyed to you regarding the merits of Dr. Daniels."[158]

At this time, supporters of Nkrumah (not, it must be emphasized, Nkrumah himself) began to play rough, trying to make Conor's life hell. For instance, someone in the government began putting out the story that Conor was resigning as vice-chancellor. The item was posted on the government's foreign news service and came back to Conor after it was announced as a fact on Radio Monrovia.[159] In another instance, in early April 1964, the CPP students union organized a lecture in Commonwealth Hall on the state of the university. Conor, never afraid of public debate, agreed to be present and to participate. In the actual event, the meeting turned into a lecture by a visiting CPP figure who spoke on the theme that the real quarrel was not with the university but with the vice-chancellor. Conor was given only two minutes to reply. So, instead of replying he asked a single question—how did the speaker reconcile the CPP position that there was no right of dissent with the requirements of the University of Ghana Act that students be taught the methods of critical and independent thought? The speaker did not respond well, and the audience became restless. Maire O'Brien asked for the floor on a point of order and she was refused. Alex Kwapong, who was sitting with the O'Briens, rose and said that anyone who asked to be heard on a point of order had to be. Thereupon, the speaker, ignoring this point, went back to talking. The audience started shuffling their feet and making noise and finally the speaker lost the thread of his thought and fell silent. At that point, one of the platform party started shouting insulting remarks at Maire: nothing obscene or racist, but stupid sexist remarks, "silly cow," and the like. Conor and Maire rose and left the meeting.[160]

The rawness of the situation made Conor's Fabian retreat all the more necessary. He let the Abraham appointment to full professor go through. It was a borderline matter, he believed, and although unjustified at present, Abraham would have been promoted in any event in the course of time. Yaw Manu was appointed senior lecturer and was offered the post of acting head (not head, but with real power) of the Department of Political Science.[161] But on Ekow-Daniels's proposed headship of the law faculty, Conor held firm and won, in a way that was either extraordinarily cunning or highly fortuitous. Conor convened a meeting of the appointments board of which Willy Abraham was a member and which, now that his own case was settled, Abraham could attend without conflict of interest. The board interviewed Ekow-Daniels, which was unfortunate for his candidacy. He claimed to have been teaching school in the years in the 1950s when he was in fact in prison for personation. The impression this made was so bad that the entire appointments board—including Willy Abraham—voted against the appointment.[162]

Conor informed Nkrumah of this, and the president was left grasping a very difficult nettle: if Willy Abraham, a key intellectual in the CPP, found Ekow-Daniel unsuitable as head of the law faculty, either Abraham indeed was a sage (and therefore Ekow-Daniels was unworthy to head the law faculty) or Ekow-Daniels was a worthy candidate—and therefore Abraham did not have the wisdom that he was supposed to have. Faced with this Hobson's choice, Osagyefo saved face by appointing Ekow-Daniels director of legal education of the General Legal Council of Ghana and director of the Ghana Law School. This second appointment entailed resuscitating the corpse of a small law school in Ghana consisting of part-time students and part-time staff that had operated since its founding in 1958 under the auspices of the General Legal Council. Actually, it had not as yet produced its first graduates and was scheduled to be closed in July 1964.[163] President Nkrumah now announced its "re-opening." Ekow-Daniels was to head this institution while at the same time continuing as a lecturer at the University of Ghana. Aside from some unedifying, niggling infighting about details, there the Ekow-Daniels debacle ended.[164]

Conor and Maire went home to Dublin and to Dunquin for a rest. In mid-August, Conor received a letter from Burnett Harvey, now back in the United States. "The decision you are called on to make with respect to your own tenure is a difficult and delicate one. ... I fully appreciate the stakes, and would never attempt to second guess the judgement you may form there as to when decent education in Ghana will be better served by your departure than by your staying. Certainly continuing in the circumstances does involve some risk of personal damage."[165]

Once out of the country, even for a summer holiday, Conor was vulnerable, and Nkrumah moved with great skill. He sent down a presidential order on 31 August that the Institute of Education of the University of Ghana be transferred to the University College of Science Education, Cape Coast. At this time, the head of the University Council (essentially appointed by Nkrumah) was Kwaku Boateng who had been the originator of the political indoctrination program and who now was minister for education. Kwaku Boateng was typical of some of the most vocal Ghanaian nationalist politicians, in that he believed that political interference in the university by the head of state was perfectly all right, but at the same time he was a staunch supporter of all of the old colonial-era educational magic: academic gowns, high table, Latin graces.[166] While Conor was out of the country, the acting vice-chancellor was Earnest A. Boateng, the professor of geography. Professor Boateng knew that Conor was completely opposed to the stripping of the Institute of Education from the university, but, having sought Conor's approval, did not give him time to reply. By the time Conor could say "no," the presidential command was issued. Conor fought the proposed change, but by March 1965, the cause was lost.[167]

On 11 November, Conor wrote to Osagyefo, informing him that when his term as vice-chancellor ended (at the end of August 1965), he did not wish to be reappointed. The president did not deign to reply.[168]

Shortly thereafter, one more nasty piece of skullduggery occurred. *The Spark* published on its front page a facsimile of the title page of a document taken from the university library, a German-language orientation manual for the Nazi party. "What the University of Ghana is teaching your children" was the message. This treachery particularly angered Conor, because he believed that the article was produced by members of his own staff. There were two or three expatriates who were members of the British Communist party and who wished to influence events in Ghana—"to take over Nkrumahism, in the interests of their own particular form of neo-colonialism."[169] Later, his anger long past, he reflected that "I seem to be doomed to spend my life combatting the anti-communist strategies of Western governments, while being sniped at by the British and American communist parties."[170]

Somehow, Conor kept his head up. Virtually everyone on the university staff and in Flagstaff House knew that he would be leaving when his term as vice-chancellor was done, so he was an easy target. Anyone who wished could shy stones at him. His good friends, Alex Kwapong, Adu Boahen, Christian Baeta, and Kofi Edzii stayed loyal, but any staff member with a grain of concern for his own future had to worry about what would happen to his or her job after Conor's tenure was completed.

In March 1965, when it became clear that the battle to save the Institute of Education (and, more important, the integrity of the University of Ghana Act) was irrevocably lost, Conor decided to resign. He already was in negotiation for a big-time American professorship (more of that in chapter 9), but that was not why he decided to pack it in. He wanted to go out on a matter of principle. So he decided to use the late-March 1965 meeting of the university Congregation and Convocation as the time to exit. He decided that when Congregation (composed of staff, graduates, and students) met on Saturday, 27 March 1965, he would give a formal address that outlined the nature of the university's problems; then, on the following Monday, when the Convocation (made up of the teaching and upper administrative staff) moved into an in-camera session, he would spell out the grittier details and then announce that he was resigning. Thereafter, he would submit his resignation to Osagyefo, as chancellor of the university, and then make a public announcement. "My problem in drafting the public announcement is to make it clear that the reasons for my resigning are adequate while at the same time doing no more damage to the university than is absolutely necessary," Conor wrote to Burnett Harvey. "I would have preferred, as you know, to sweat it out until the end of my tenure, but the present issues are so clear that I feel I could not stay on without having compromised on essential principles and collaborated in the establishment of vicious precedents for the future."[171]

Events changed things. Conor did indeed give his public talk on the general nature of the university problem to Congregation on Saturday[172] but by Monday he was back, determined to fight. He decided that on Monday he would indeed air all the dirty linen at Convocation, but he would let his colleagues decide if he should resign or not. What made Conor change his plan is unclear, but one thing is certain: he was thoroughly enraged by being made the victim of one more dirty trick. This was the report that was broadcast by the BBC that he had resigned. (This follows the pattern set by earlier false stories about his resignation planted by the governmental officials, so he was fully justified in viewing the story as more than a simple journalistic accident.) The story infuriated him and I think it was this that stiffened his resolve. He issued a correction on Sunday which denied that he had resigned and, crucially, "Dr. O'Brien indicated that before taking any decisions he would consult the convocation of the University of Ghana, the assembly of the entire teaching body."[173]

The in-camera session of Convocation heard not only Conor, but also Kwaku Boateng who, as minister of education and as chairman of the University Council, had no small degree of influence over the future employment of the staff. It is therefore impressive that by a vote of 131 to 4, the teaching body of the university voted that Conor should not resign, but should stay until the end of his term.[174] This vote of confidence meant a lot to Conor who fully understood the risk the staff were taking in voicing their support for him.

The end of his years in African academe was now in sight and, buoyed by the vote of confidence, he and Maire enjoyed their last few months. They went to Northwestern University, Evanston, Illinois, in the late spring for a major Yeats conference and it was there that Conor delivered the paper on Yeats and fascism that still boggles Yeats scholarship. And after that, they flew to Berkeley, California, bringing Kate and Fedelma with them. Donal, now a graduate student at Berkeley, was marrying Rita Abel, "a very attractive and intelligent American girl who is also just finishing post graduate studies at Berkeley." As for Donal's marrying an American, Conor wrote to a friend, "He was born on the fourth of July, so I suppose his doom was sealed by the stars!"[175]

• • •

Frequently in later years, Conor emphasized that he had fulfilled his term at the university and that meant something to him. The tone of voice, part pride, part incomprehension that he had decided to stick it through all the troubles, resembled that of someone who says he made it through Special Forces training.

That points to the push-and-pull that characterized almost his entire time in Ghana. He genuinely loved the university and his balancing of the costs that his resignation would do to the university against the dangerous personal implications if he was perceived as staying on and being complicitous in governmental actions was for him a matter of real moral calculus. A deeper, structural tug of war lay behind that, however, and he hinted at this when he observed on 30 March 1965, after being strongly endorsed by Convocation, that "there was too much discretion among all concerned to be altogether healthy and among many, though not all of the expatriates, an attitude of detachment as if controversy about university autonomy and academic freedom in an African country were somewhat unreal, and, in any case, no affair of theirs."[176] That is a big question: to what extent do outside whites have a right to be involved in the affairs of black nations to which they have access as professionals, but not as citizens? And, most important, to what extent are Western European concepts such as university autonomy and academic freedom applicable in the Third World?

After all the ugliness, everyone tried to end the dance with a bit of grace. On 5 July, Conor wrote to Nkrumah—as "dear Chancellor"—"I think you know that my tenure will terminate at the end of August? [think! Nkrumah was counting the days] I am accordingly now preparing to leave Ghana. I shall travel to Europe on 14 July." After that Conor and Maire could complete some final recruiting duties for the university in London. They would spend most of their leave time in Ireland and then on to New York to Conor's new appointment at New York University. Conor concluded the letter to Nkrumah diplomatically, with a touch of salt. "I would like to thank you on behalf of my wife and myself for the opportunity to come to Ghana and work here for the last three years."[177]

What results these three years of work had yielded depend upon one's viewpoint. The university's Academic Board at its final meeting for 1964–65 recorded its appreciation of the "outstanding service" rendered to the university by Conor and especially "the integrity with which he endeavoured at all times to uphold the interests of the university as an academic community."[178] Sir Eric Ashby, who knew more about African university education than did any other person of the time, summarized Conor's work: "For three years with masterly skill and extraordinary patience, O'Brien worked to preserve autonomy in the university and to ensure that it served Ghana's needs."[179]

Kwame Nkrumah saw things differently, as he made clear in the last interview that he granted Conor. This took place in the Christiansborg Castle, in the formal room, about the size of a tennis court, in which Osagyefo gave audiences. The president's desk was at one end of the room and in the middle was a little round table with two chairs. If you were in the good graces of Dr. Nkrumah, he would greet you in the center of the room and converse with you there at the table. Otherwise, one made the long walk all the way down to his desk, to Canossa, as it were.

On the day of the final interview, Conor was shown in by Nkrumah's private secretary. Osagyefo was at the far end of the room and did not look up. Conor trekked slowly the length of the room and stood before the dictator's desk. Finally, Nkrumah raised his eyes.

"Dr. O'Brien, I would like to thank you for what you did for the University of Ghana."

Silence. Conor blinked, Osagyefo meditated, and then concluded his thank you.

"Whatever it was."

To his credit, Conor continues to tell this story. And each time, he ends with a great, deep laugh, in equal parts ironic and admiring.[180]

CHAPTER 9

IN THE KINGDOM OF THE NEW YORK INTELLECTUALS: 1965–1969

Conor and Maire now moved from the dominion of a condescending, albeit sometimes charming despot, to a land where many of Conor's colleagues and acquaintances thought of themselves as philosopher kings. It was not a huge transition, really, from a land of sorcery and witchcraft to one in which veneficial words did the dirty work.

As it became increasingly clear that Conor's term as vice-chancellor of the University of Ghana would not be renewed, even had he wished it to be, he looked around for employment. One opportunity was the University of East Africa. This was supposed to be an analogue to the merger of Kenya, Tanzania, and Uganda into the Federation of East Africa, and itself a step toward the holy grail of African unity. In fact, the political federation of three African nations never came about, but for a brief time—1963–70—there was a University of East Africa. This was based on the University College, Nairobi, Kenya; on the University College, Dar-es-Salaam, Tanzania; and the Makerere University College, Kampala, Uganda.

Conor, as representative of the University of Ghana, had been present in Nairobi at the official opening of the University of East Africa in 1963 and had met most of the academic leaders and some important politicians, notably Julius Nyerere, president of Tanzania. (Nyerere he found a "refreshing" change from Kwame Nkrumah, "down-to-earth and unassuming, talking like one human being to another.")[1] So, as things started to come apart in Ghana, Conor opened talks about the possibility of becoming vice-chancellor of the new three-campus, three-nation institution. This new university would have been an administrative nightmare even if one did not have to take into account the political instability of the Ugandan part of the triangle, and Conor's even considering the job is an indication of how bleak he felt his employment prospects were. It was his good fortune that the future of the new university was so clouded that the three countries involved would not promise to keep the university in operation beyond 1967. And by the time they finally committed themselves to keeping the institution alive at least until 1970, Conor was able to respond to a query from Kampala ("Grateful to know if you are still available for office of vice-chancellor") with a laconic cable: "Regret now unavailable."[2]

That was in December 1965, and he had no real regrets about being "now unavailable," for instead of having to serve in an academic *ultima thule*, he was in New York as an academic superstar. How did that come about? No one knows entirely, but Conor believes that his old TCD "wife," Vivian Mercier, teaching in New York City, started the dominoes falling in the right direction. Mercier had co-edited an anthology of Irish prose, published in 1952, with David H. Greene and they remained good friends.[3] David Greene in 1964 became head of the university-wide Department of English at New York University, a post of considerable influence. Hence, the likelihood of Mercier's mentioning that his old roommate O'Brien needing work was high.[4]

The moment was especially good, because the United States, still in the bloom of postwar prosperity, now was throwing money at all levels of the educational system, in an attempt to catch up with the Russians. As part of this almost magical belief in education as national armament, the New York State legislature in 1964 created five Albert Einstein Chairs in the sciences and five Albert Schweitzer Chairs in the humanities and social sciences. The goal was to attract top-grade talent— "superstars" in the unabashed vocabulary of the sponsors—to the various universities in New York State. One of the rules was that the person appointed had to be from outside New York State. The chairs in the humanities and social sciences provided (in the usual case) $30,000 a year for the salary of the professor and an additional $70,000 to be under the professor's control for setting up whatever academic program he or she desired. This was a lot of money in the mid-1960s.

David H. Greene saw the possibility of grabbing a superstar for NYU, and in April 1965 he wrote to Conor, with whom he already was acquainted, telling him of the Schweitzer Chair and asking if he would be interested. Answer: yes indeed! Thereafter life moved very quickly. Conor and Maire came to the United States for the major Yeats Centenary conference, and for the wedding of Donal and Rita Abel, and, not incidentally, for interviews in New York City. By 2 June, NYU was able to issue a news release that Conor had been appointed "Regents Professor and holder of the Albert Schweitzer Chair in the Humanities at New York University." The post came with permanent tenure.[5]

The only thing that marred the O'Briens' relief and pleasure at this turn of events is that upon returning to Africa to tidy up affairs, Conor contracted malaria. Having escaped the illness throughout all his time in Africa, he had to suffer from it at home in Ireland. There, he had the first hint of what awaited him in the New York intellectual community. "I believe John Chamberlain [former book editor of *Harper's* and now a King Features daily columnist] has been knocking my appointment in his syndicated column, for which I am sorry," Conor wrote to David Greene. "And also that Sidney Hook was moaning at a recent *Partisan Review* seance at Rutgers that he had not been consulted about my appointment. This does not worry me either ... ; it could, perhaps, have been divined by *a priori* reasoning."[6] To keep things in perspective, he added a postscript. "You will be amused at the end of a letter which I received from my Aunt Cathleen, who, as you possibly know, is the widow of the novelist Eimar O'Duffy. Cathleen must, I think, be going on 90 by now ... and she is entirely fixed in the world of her youth and in the prejudices of what she has always assumed to be her class (why I don't know). She was distressed by my going to Africa, but is relatively pleased by the new appointment and writes the following: 'America is young, but fairly civilized, and I know your influence will be an entirely good one.' "[7]

Certainly the legislators of the State of New York expected the influence of the Schweitzer superstars to be an entirely good one, but what the individual universities wanted the new professors to do was very fuzzy. "To add prestige" was a common answer. Scholarly prestige? Not really. An editorial in the *New York Times* early in 1968 listed the humanists and social scientists holding the endowed chairs and noted, "It is doubtful that all the members would be included in any list of the world's outstanding scholars drawn up, say, by a poll of American professors. However, at least some of the five would rank high in any list of persons with academic connections who have been able to win considerable fame for themselves and their ideas." Publicity, the editorial concluded, should not be the standard of any university.[8] This scolding was not entirely unwarranted when we consider the appointees: Barbara Ward, the best-selling advocate of feel-good developmental economics, who did not measure up to the standards of Columbia's economics department; media guru Marshall McLuhan who arrived from Canada and from outer space amid a furore at Fordham; Arthur Schlesinger, Jr., who once had been a major scholar of the Jacksonian era and of the New Deal, but who in the 1960s had become best known as a Kennedy hanger-on and a movie reviewer. (One observer wryly noted that Schlesinger was said to have accepted the Schweitzer post at City University of New York in order to be close to his reviewing post at *Vogue* magazine.)[9] Only Dwight Waldo, a scholar of public administration, whom Syracuse University appointed, would have made the list solely on scholarly merit. And Conor? Although he had published loads of articles, a nice set of critical essays, and a workmanlike study of Parnell, he was not yet a world-class scholar or close to it. He was known mostly for the Congo episode and as a very attractive, sharp-witted person, anti-establishment, and yet with the knowledge of how to knot a tie properly and wear an evening suit with grace.

One of the measures of Conor's fiber is that in what was a very morally seductive environment—lots of money, no job description, and with only the obligation of bringing NYU as much good publicity as possible—he worked very hard and with great success. He established, from scratch, an academic program that drew together a network of otherwise distant scholars; organized major conferences; wrote books, plays, and scholarly articles; and was very active politically. He had the great good luck to be handed the NYU post; and NYU had the great good fortune that he gave back to them more than measure for measure.

• • •

Conor and Maire arrived in New York in mid-September 1965 and were immediately given a large subsidized apartment in one of the many buildings that New York University owned near its Washington Square campus. In a situation unusual for a professor and his wife in an urban university in the United States, they virtually lived on campus, in Washington Square Village. This was not only immensely convenient, but it placed them in one of the most charming areas of Manhattan. New York University, a private institution with about 42,000 students in 1965, was centered right at the foot of Fifth Avenue in the heart of Greenwich Village. Conor, in an early letter to his aunt Mary Kettle (Tom Kettle's widow), reported, "We have a nice apartment in Washington Square Village which in no way resembles any village known to man." The area around Washington Square, he told her, was comparable to Paris's Left Bank.[10] Later, writing in the *Irish Times* in 1969, he was somewhat less romantic. "To the south of us," he told his Irish readers, "beyond Houston Street, the Village's southern boundary—is a vague territory of nineteenth century red-brick warehouses and shabby shops and offices, bristling with fire-escapes. ... To the southeast of us is Mott Street, New York's small rather smug China-town. To the north of that, quite near, the Bowery, that sad quiet street with its low, seedy buildings, and its slow-moving population ... whom life in this city has utterly crushed." On the east was the old Lower East Side, now called the East Village, and filled, Conor noted, with two kinds of poverty, "Ukrainian, Polish and Puerto Rican blue collar work-ers, and drop-outs of the White Anglo-Saxon Protestant middle class. ... The East Village is hippy territory and anti-hippy territory."[11] It was also dangerous. "The East Village, an area the size of Rathmines, had an annual homicide rate in those years much greater than that of the whole of the United Kingdom, let alone Ireland."[12]

If dangerous after dark, Washington Square was an elegant quadran-gle by day. When, a year later, the university authorities allocated the O'Briens a Washington Mews house, they were able to live in one of New York's most prized areas: a private street composed of two long rows of town houses, an ambiance that had changed little since Henry James published *Washington Square* in 1880.

Under James Hester, one of the 1960s go-getter university presi-dents, NYU was on its way up. Hester and the central power figures in the humanities—notably Dean William Buckler and Professor David Greene—backed Conor strongly. When Conor arrived, he had no sec-retary and only a makeshift office on the second floor of 19 University Place. However, the university helped him to recruit and to obtain an American green card for Eileen Sheerin, an Irish civil servant of consid-erable ability, to be his administrative assistant. Reading through the correspondence of Conor's NYU years (some seven linear feet of it in the NYU Archives), it becomes clear that Eileen Sheerin was something of an administrative genius. Conor had the good sense to delegate much to her. (Conor would not have been so insensitive as to draw the par-allel, but one is reminded of Archbishop Richard Whately, who, when chafed about his delegating everyday matters to his chaplains, replied, "I keep a dog. Why should I take the bother of barking myself?")[13] In fact, Conor has always been good at choosing subordinates to whom he can grant real powers.

So, when, in the autumn of his second year, 1966, the university al-located prime offices to Conor and to the program that he was devel-oping, it was Eileen Sheerin who negotiated the details. What NYU gave Conor was a large suite of offices at about as good an address as one could find—1 Fifth Avenue, just around the corner from Washington Mews and half a block from Washington Square. It was a converted graystone hotel in which the university rented space for several of its programs. They renovated the suites, so he and Eileen each had an office, besides a library and a seminar room, and three offices of varying sizes for his teaching colleagues.[14]

The program that Conor devised, "Literature and Society," represented "an effort to restore the writer's activity to its historical, social, and political contexts, instead of studying it in isolation."[15] Conor had created the ideal job-description for himself. It encompassed his main intellectual preoccupations, but without limiting his focus to a specific nation or history period.

The only problem was that NYU, like any university, was a dovecote, filled with the perpetually jealous and territorial, and occasionally things were very frustrating. When balked, either intellectually or personally, Conor in his adult life has gone to one of two extremes: he has been extremely diplomatic (his usual response) or he has endeavored verbally to gralloch his opponent in the way a highland gillie disembowels a stag: nothing in between. In his dealings with his colleagues and with the administration at NYU, he worked almost entirely in the diplomatic mode. This was important, because the Schweitzer Chair was not a department—it did not provide a degree program—and to some extent it depended on the good will of traditional departments. Thus, Conor gently negotiated arrangements so that the courses in literature and society received credit in various departments. (The requests could be sticky: at one point, the Philosophy Department refused to give credit for a graduate seminar taught by George Steiner.)[16] When he recruited staff, Conor often was able to convince department heads to share the expense of his staff, all of whom were temporary visitors and most of whom were of international stature.[17] The chief exception to this diplomatic mien was a fight Conor conducted with the university's legal counsel about whether or not two of Conor's staff had to take the New York State loyalty oath—a leftover from the McCarthy era. Even on this issue, when he saw that he would lose, he concluded surrender terms with reasonable grace.[18]

On paper, the growth of the Literature and Society program looks like the expansion of any conventional bureaucracy.[19]

1965–66
One undergraduate course
  Literature and Society

1966–67
Three and a half undergraduate courses
  Literature and Society
  Literary Appreciation: Currents of Change

Marxism and the Writer
Politics and the Contemporary Theatre (one semester)
Two graduate seminars
Conservative-Authoritative Ideas in Pre-World War II European Literature
Form and Content: Writers on the Left

1967–68
One and a half undergraduate courses
Literature and Society
Intellectual Leadership in Developing Countries (one semester)
Two graduate seminars
Romanticism and Revolution
Commitment: Theory and Practice (one semester)
The United States and the U.N. (one semester)

1968–69
Four and a half undergraduate courses
Literature and Society
The Black Writer in America
Contemporary Writing in Africa
Revolution and Literature
Art and Politics (one semester)

With enrollment in each of the undergraduate courses running from fifty to ninety students, and in the graduate seminars from eight to twenty-two students, this appears to be an interesting but not extraordinary program. But when the student government of NYU evaluated the curriculum in 1966–67 (an exercise conducted independently of the administration), the Schweitzer program received the highest ratings given to any single department.[20] In fact, something special was going on.[21]

Conor himself was teaching brilliantly and the people he recruited for the most part were stellar. The appointments were for a term, one year, or at most two years, and most were part-time. This placed a great weight on his ability at persuasion. In the program's second year (Conor was the only faculty member the first year, 1965–66), he succeeded in recruiting George Steiner, David Caute, and John Arden, an amazing set.[22]

John Arden, who taught a one-term course on politics and the contemporary theater, was then in his mid-thirties. He lived on an island near Oughterard, County Galway. In 1959 he had shared (with Arnold

Wesker) the *Evening Standard* award for the most promising playwright of the year. He was recruited to teach a course at NYU and to give one public lecture—"The Playwright as Nuisance." He and Conor became fairly close friends and Arden acted as a consultant for Conor's *Murderous Angels.*[23]

More conventionally academic, but no less outstanding, was David Caute. In 1966, he was barely thirty, but already had spent six years as a fellow of All Souls. (This was a post he was soon to resign as a protest against the college's refusal to expand on a broader basis into graduate studies.) One of England's young academic stars, Caute already had published a major book on communism and the French intellectuals in the twentieth century and he had in press a study of the European left since 1789. This was in addition to three novels, one of which had won the Rhys Prize.

How does one recruit someone of that caliber for a one-year post? Even given that New York City well might be attractive to a young academic, something extra was needed. In the usual case, the promise of intellectual excitement was the chief bait that Conor presented to prospective staff. But, in Caute's case, one sees Conor at his cutest (again, in the Irish sense). Conor had been mugged, on 12 September 1965, soon after his arrival in New York, when he was attending a socialist scholars' conference at Columbia University.

> It was an odd little scene. It was lunchtime and I went for a walk in Morningside Park. I was going along reading Ivan Illich or something of the kind and two young blacks grabbed me from behind and two from in front and made gestures as of using a knife. I put up no resistance—they took my watch and my wallet and disappeared.

The mugging done, Conor called the police from a phone booth.

> A squad car came up and I told them my misadventure; they told me to get in the car and we'd take a look, which surprised me. I soon found out what it meant. We drove along through the streets of Harlem: "Is it that one, is it that one?"—anybody I picked would have been charged and convicted on my word. The police officer wanted the book to be cleared. And as I said, "No, no, no," he got nastier and nastier, with sarcastic implications of one kind or another. I was very glad to be out of that car.[24]

Conor put the story to good use in trying to recruit David Caute, who had a competing offer from Columbia. "In order to help him make up his mind" (as Conor explained to Dean William Buckler), he wrote the details to Caute, with an admonition concerning Columbia.[25] "The fringes of occupied territory—Harlem—are not, I think, the most attractive area in which to set up house. Down here at this end of the island, on the other hand, we enjoy the blessings of a zany kind of peace. However, suit yourself; and if you want to keep in touch by personal experience with one of the most pressing social problems of our time, by all means go to Columbia."[26] As Conor airily told Dean Buckler, "If this doesn't weigh directly with him, it may with his wife. We shall see."[27] Caute made the decision Conor desired. He taught a one-year course for undergraduates on Marxism and the writer, and he shared a graduate seminar with Conor on writers on the left. The year in New York did neither his body nor his career any harm: Caute returned to England to a new post as Reader in Social and Political Theory at Brunel University.

The real supernova of that first year of a full program, 1966–67, however, was George Steiner. As early as mid-June 1965, while the ink on his own letter of appointment was hardly dry, Conor thought of Steiner as a potential colleague in the Schweitzer program. When Karl Miller, literary editor of the *New Statesman*, suggested that this might not be such a good idea, Conor responded, "I am sorry that you disapprove of Steiner. I met him and his wife once and liked him. And I also like with some reservation his two critical books. I don't like his short stories very much."[28]

At this time Steiner was a fellow of Churchill College, Cambridge, which, as a means of identification, is as adequate as describing Abraham Lincoln as a late Illinois politician. One cannot do a thumbnail sketch of Steiner any more than one can do a quick word picture of the aurora borealis, for, not only was he a kaleidoscopic talent, but like the aurora, he sometimes is less than he seems, sometimes more. Born in 1929, to a European Jewish family, he was educated at a French lycée and in New York City to which his family fled in 1940; then he took a first degree in Paris, and an A.B. (*summa cum laude*) at the University of Chicago, took an M.A. at Harvard, and did a D.Phil. at Oxford. Along the way, he was on the editorial staff of the London *Economist*, a fellow of the Institute for Advanced Study at Princeton, the author of several short stories (the winner of the O. Henry Short Story Award for 1958), author of two major critical studies, a fellow of the Royal Society of Literature—a genuine polymath.

A short, intense man, given to three-piece suits, Steiner was all the more a compelling figure by virtue of his possessing a withered arm, which, instead of disguising, he used as a social weapon. In these years he was undergoing radiation treatment and frequently looked weary beyond words. He took teaching very seriously. Later, in his sixties, Steiner reflected:

> All my writing, my whole life, everything I do—and this is radically Jewish—grows out of teaching. And what does a teacher do? He crams down the throats of other people things they don't want to swallow. That's the very definition of a teacher. If he's successful, a tiny number of them, instead of spitting it out as soon as they get out of the room, will swallow it and it'll start growing inside them, and they say "it doesn't taste awfully good, and it was very hard to get down, but I'm beginning to grow." That's the miracle, and it doesn't happen very often.[29]

Conor and Steiner corresponded seriously in the autumn of 1965 about teaching a course together and they held a planning session in the spring of 1966. Eventually they shared a graduate seminar on conservative and authoritarian ideas in European literature before World War II. It was an eclectic circus, Conor playing the left-radical, Steiner the right-establishment. In a sense, Steiner had been brought by Conor to NYU to teach the right-wing viewpoint (albeit a very moderate culturally conservative one, in something like the Burkean sense), and David Caute to teach the left-wing outlook. In each case, Conor was to be the foil. The tension between O'Brien and Steiner was not merely theatrical, however. Both are immensely vain men, but Conor has always applied the Irish sense of irony to himself, as well as to others. There is no parallel characteristic in Steiner's makeup, and because he knows so much, he frequently assumes an air of omniscience. So in their shared graduate seminar, Steiner would launch into great rhetorical arabesques, untinged by humor or irony, sentences that seemed as if they would never come to an end, and then Conor would puncture them with a jibe. To be a graduate student in that seminar and to see those two giants thus at play must have been a joy.[30]

But to see them at war was not pleasant, although it certainly was diverting. One former NYU faculty member of the time remembers Conor and George Steiner having a terrible row. They differed sharply on the Vietnam War (Conor strongly opposed it; Steiner believed that the regime in South Vietnam, corrupt though it was, was preferable to the terror that would come from the North). Equally, they had opposite views on the student protest movement (Conor was quite strongly supportive; Steiner, when it came time to face the destruction of library card files and similar sabotage, said loudly, "No, enough"). One evening at the O'Briens' house, they were arguing these matters and words became heated. Maire, who always was as supportive of her husband in any public fracas as if she were at a faction fight in Mullingar in 1867, weighed in and called Steiner an *agent provocateur*.

The next morning, George Steiner appeared at 1 Fifth Avenue.

"When do you want me to resign?" he asked Conor.

"Oh, George, forget it," replied Conor. "We were all drunk."

That would be enough of an explanation in Dublin, but it did not suit George Steiner in Manhattan. "He stood straight and raised his withered arm. 'If I forget thee, O Jerusalem,' he quoted (Psalm 137:5), 'let my right hand forget her cunning.' He lowered his arm, which *had* forgot its cunning, as he well knew, turned, and was gone."[31]

That was George Steiner at his most devastating, a walking, corporeal, self-carved archetype. The ruckus with Steiner probably occurred sometime in late April or May 1967. In August, Steiner, wishing to bridge the gap, wrote to Conor: "I do not know where you are just now or have your Irish address (which small fact seems almost to express the silence and sadness that has come between us)." He referred to the death of their mutual friend, the great historian of Russia, Isaac Deutscher, and added, "Our own last good occasion together was that dinner with him at One Fifth, on 18 April."[32] The two men managed a distant acquaintanceship from then on, and the relationship was somewhat repaired when, in the mid-1980s, Steiner handsomely reviewed Conor's history of Israel, *The Siege*.[33]

Keeping things up to the level of 1966–67 probably was impossible. Conor worked hard at recruiting, however, and a few of his failures are worth note. He tried to tempt the novelist and critic Iris Murdoch with an offer of $15,000, plus plane fare for herself and her husband, if she would teach two courses.[34] She was flattered, but had pressing obligations in Oxford: moreover, she feared that her membership in the Communist party twenty-five years previously would make it difficult for her to obtain an American visa ("The proceedings make one so angry, it is a real deterrent.")[35] Later, Conor tried unsuccessfully to interest the English social historian Eric Hobsbawm.[36] The West Indian novelist, essayist, and social observer V.S. Naipaul also declined.[37]

Still, for the academic year 1967–68, Conor again did well. After a good deal of difficult negotiating, he arranged that Edward Thompson—the English historian whose *The Making of the English Working Class* (1963) was arguably the most important work of English historical writing of the 1960s—teach a spring-term graduate seminar in romanticism and revolution.[38] He was to share it with Conor's old teacher from TCD, R.B. McDowell, who in his own eccentric way had become a world authority on the eighteenth century, and with David V.

Erdman, who was a specialist in the study of William Blake and the holder of the John Adams Chair at Hofstra University. The bulk of that year's program, however, was taught by Conor, by Jonathan Mirsky (a very bright young China specialist with political views on Vietnam that coincided with Conor's), Thompson Bradley (a recent Ph.D. in Russian language and literature), and by Peter Nettl. The latter, Nettl, was a former reader in political history at Leeds University and had been called to Conor's attention by George Steiner, who strongly argued for his appointment. Of a Czech-born immigrant family in England, Nettl had undergone a perfectly proper English public school education, and he did not learn until he was twenty-six years of age that he was Jewish. Fluent in French, German, Italian, Russian, and English, he wrote a major two-volume life of Rosa Luxemburg. He also wrote three novels, under the name of Paul Norwood. Now, at forty, he held an appointment at the Institute for Advanced Studies at Princeton. He taught twice a week in New York. Tragically, he died in an air accident before completing his time in the United States.

One cannot disguise the fact that even when guest lectures by Alger Hiss, Gabriel Kolko, and Leonard Boudin were added to the program, things had declined somewhat from the Steiner-Caute years. And that leads us to the peculiar design of Conor's last year at NYU, 1968–69. As early as May 1967, Conor had begun to develop a project, "a sort of continuing colloquium here on literature and revolution in the under-developed world."[39] He had hoped to have Michael Crowder, a leading historian of Nigeria, on staff for 1968–69, but Crowder backed away from his commitment to teach at NYU on the basis of Conor's support for Biafra.[40] So, instead of an all-star, or at least a major-league program, the 1968–69 year had a group of decent, hard-working second-line performers, and Conor was absent on fall-term sabbatical. The curriculum that year focused on African and on African-American literature. The lead teacher was Julian Mayfield, a Ghanaian novelist of real but not major talent, who was a former aide to Kwame Nkrumah. Neither Mayfield nor the two other persons who taught courses on contemporary writing in Africa—Sylvia Boone and Peter Molotsi—had doctoral degrees or impressive publication records, and there is no way of avoiding the judgment that in pedagogical and scholarly terms, the program took a quantum drop downward in 1968–69. The graduate seminar disappeared, and the only immediate positive result was that 40 or 50 of the roughly 345 students who took courses in the program that year were African-Americans.[41] When one reads the day-to-day administrative files, it becomes clear that Conor was letting things go.

From the late spring of 1968 onward, Conor was not doing his job very well. File that for the minute: the story of his time in New York will lead us eventually to understand it.

• • •

Isolate, therefore, the years 1965–68, as a period in which Conor lived, with some success, in the land of the New York intellectuals. Today, that term is one of abuse—like calling someone a big-butter-and-eggs-man—but from the 1930s through the 1960s it was a real phenomenon, the New York intellectual, and it is not one to treat derisively.[42] Like any generalization, however, it is only that: a label that covers a wide body of disparate phenomena. "The New York intellectuals are perhaps the only group America has ever had that could be described as an *intelligentsia*," one of the group's core members, Irving Howe, wrote in a classic reflection.[43] America, Howe said,

> is a culture in which people rattle around.
>
> A seeming exception is the group of writers who have come to be known, these past few decades, as the New York intellectuals. They appear to have a common history, prolonged now for more than thirty years; a common political outlook, even if marked by ceaseless internecine quarrels; a common style of thought and perhaps composition; a common focus of intellectual interests; and once you get past politeness—which becomes, these days, easier and easier—a common ethnic origin. They are, or until recently have been, anti-Communist; they are, or until some time ago were, radicals; they have a fondness for ideological speculation; they write literary criticism with a strong social emphasis; they revel in polemic; they strive self-consciously to be "brilliant"; and by birth or osmosis, they are Jews.[44]

Actually, the shop was open to non-Jews. As the historian John Patrick Diggins has noted,

> There were also eminent non-Jews (Edmund Wilson, Dwight Macdonald, Arthur M. Schlesinger, Jr.), sin-struck Christians (W.H. Auden, R.P. Blackmur), Catholics both loyal (James Agee) and lapsed (William Barrett, James T. Farrell, Michael Harrington, Mary McCarthy), blacks (James Baldwin, Ralph Ellison, the early Richard Wright), classical liberals (Jacques Barzun), and even conservatives (Wallace Stevens), especially southern (John Crowe Ransom, Allen Tate, Robert Penn Warren). Yet the real inner circle consisted of those who had gone to the City College of New York, who engaged in fierce debates about Trotsky in the college alcoves, and who in the post-Second World War years hung out in Greenwich Village bars and engaged in equally fierce discussions about the art of abstract expressionism.[45]

The front row of names—Sidney Hook, Norman Podhoretz, Harold Rosenberg, Hannah Arendt, Daniel Bell, Irving Kristol, Irving Howe, Leslie Fiedler, Paul Goodman, Saul Bellow—is a *Who's Who* of mid-twentieth-century American intellectuals. As well, there was a strong second row, mostly in New York, consisting of tenured academics and leaders of faculty unions, all forming, by the mid-1960s, an *haute bourgeois* intellectual caste, with turf to defend. Although by the mid-1960s, most of the group had moved uptown (Upper East Side addresses were especially favored), the spiritual home of the New York intellectuals still was Greenwich Village and its epicenter, Washington Square.[46] Symbolically at least, a strange foreigner, Conor Cruise O'Brien, was taking over their turf.

What Conor shared with the *echten* New York intellectuals was a deep concern with the relationship of political action and the life of the mind. For them all, this was in part moralistic, in equal part narcissistic, and in each case led to a great deal of reflection on the position of the intellectual in society. The Literature and Society program that Conor created at New York University was devoted to that very issue and it was tightly focused, because Conor effectively defined society as meaning political life rather than social structure. This commonality of concern meant that a genuine rapport was possible between Conor and some of the leading New York intellectuals. Equally, however, it provided an opportunity for rivalry: the new kid on the block not only had a lot of money at his disposal, but he was playing in *our* park, Washington Square, as if he owned it.

To return our focus to how Conor did his job as a professor at the Washington Square campus: his success in creating *ex nihilo* an academic program has been noted, as has the *éclat* of the program in the great Steiner-Caute years. Second, it is clear that Conor did his own teaching on writers and politics very well.[47] Third, he and Maire ran a salon (although they would not have used that word). During term time, they invited Conor's best students, their friends, visiting intellectuals, and politicians (almost always of the then-left) to the house to which they moved at 3 Washington Mews. A house is nothing extraordinary for most people in Western society, but in Manhattan no one lives in a house unless they are famous or old rich. This was a former carriage house just off Washington Square. One could imagine Henry James walking in the mews, as he once had, and viewing severely the ever lowering standards (as they always were to Mr. James) of the inhabitants. In the 1960s this was one of the few surviving private streets in New York City. It was one block long, with hand-wrought iron gates at both ends, so that vehicle traffic was restricted to residents and to those called upon to repair their ever-failing plumbing and damp ceilings. At each end was a serious sign: "Private Street. Curb your dog in the Mews." The house had a ground floor, an upper story, two bedrooms, a full kitchen, and a decent-sized sitting room which the O'Briens filled with African art, simple furnishings, and books—books everywhere. In this environment Maire was a brilliant hostess, mostly because she refused to be one. She would put the wine and beer (still Conor's favorite drinks in those days) on the sideboard, set out soda and spirits for the ardent, arrange the small eats (sometimes catered, frequently not), and then pitch into the discussions herself. Conor would introduce to his students the stars of the week—Melina Mercouri, André Schiffrin, whomever—and things rolled, social life and intellectual life being of a single piece.[48] Conor and Maire were doing for Conor's students what Conor's grandmother had done in her salon for Irish students of an earlier age, such as young Jimmy Joyce.

During the period 1965–68, Conor perfected the art of being in more than one place at once. He gave a surprising number of public speeches, all the while keeping the Schweitzer program in operation (and, one should add, spending two or three months each summer in Ireland). Even a simple list (and an incomplete one at that) for the spring term of 1966 makes clear how keen he was on showing the flag, advertising NYU and his Schweitzer program.

25 January	Foreign Affairs Round Table, Lotus Club, New York City.
17 February	Kirkland House, Harvard University.
23 March	Adelphi College, Garden City, New York. Grouts Lecture, "Burke, Yeats and the Conservative Imagination."
26 March	Degree-granting ceremony, University of Ghana.
7 April	Center for International Studies, NYU. "Britain's Role as a Non-imperial Power."
21 April	Princeton University. Lecture, "Literary Imagination and Political Power."
— April	Public lecture at NYU, "Burke and Marx."
1 May	Featured guest at Second Annual Irish Arts Festival, John Hancock Hall, Boston.
12 May	African Studies Club, Columbia University.[49]

This list omits political meetings and, in the era of the anti-Vietnam War movement, there were one or two antiwar appearances a month, sometimes more. For his nonpolitical appearances, Conor received $200 to $300 from those who had money, sometimes more. In the case of other groups, such as the Wesleyan students who were considering doing social service in Africa, he received nothing and paid his expenses from university funds.[50]

The great magnifying effect—the "multiplier" in economic terms—came from a further activity, namely Conor's using the scholars in his program as a base for a series of annual Schweitzer Lectures. The first series of these, in the spring of 1967, focused on "Literature and Society": David Caute on "Sartre and Communism," John Arden on "The Playwright as Nuisance," Conor on "Burke and Marx," and the headliner, George Steiner, on "Trotsky and the Tragic Imagination."[51] This series was expanded in 1967–68 to eight lectures on "Power and Consciousness," a perpetual worry of the self-conscious intellectual, and the participants were all stars. Besides Peter Nettl, David Erdman, E.P. Thompson and Conor—all from the Schweitzer program—featured lectures were given by Gabriel Kolko (then one of the coming young-left historians of America), Eric Bentley (one of the two or three most powerful drama critics in America, and professor of drama at Columbia University); Noam Chomsky (at that time America's leading linguistic theoretician and a major antiwar crusader); and Stuart Hampshire (formerly of All Souls, chairman of the Department of Philosophy at Princeton).[52] In the third year of the series, 1968–69, the focus was on "The Prince," the occasion being the 500th anniversary of Machiavelli's birth and the underlying question being how power is wielded in modern societies. That year the participants were Jonathan Mirsky, Thompson Bradley, Julian Mayfield, and, of course, Conor, plus I.F. Stone (editor and publisher of *I.F. Stone's Weekly*, lodestone for every right-thinking, and indeed, every left-thinking New York intellectual), Grattan Freyer (an eccentric choice, an Irish author of evanescent reputation), William Barrett (professor of philosophy at NYU and one of the world's leading authorities on existentialism), and Leonard Boudin (a good friend of Conor's and the legal counsel for Benjamin Spock in his anti-Vietnam difficulties.)[53] In the case of each of these lectures, a heavyweight local person introduced the speakers. Conor's personal invitation lists—to take the 1967 series as an example—included almost everyone of intellectual chic in New York—Irving Howe, Jack Newfield, Alfred Kazin, Ved Mehta, André Schiffrin, Dwight Macdonald, Hannah Arendt, Henry Steele Commager, Leslie Fiedler, and so on.[54] Then, as a final touch, most of the lectures were published. The best such production was *Power and Consciousness* which Conor edited jointly with his graduate assistant William Dean Vanech, published in 1969 by the New York University Press and in England by the University of London Press.

• • •

Conor became an intellectual figure in North America not just for his frequent public appearances, but for his ideas. The basis of his North American reputation was established by a famous lecture, "Passion and Cunning," on William Butler Yeats which he delivered at Northwestern University on 29 April 1965. The occasion was the Yeats Centenary conference held in Evanston, Illinois, under the baton of the great Yeats and Joyce scholar Richard Ellman. Conor's talk was written before he left Ghana, and, indeed, was delivered while he still was in the employ of the University of Ghana. Nevertheless, it is central to his American years and it also is part of his reexamination and redefinition of the nature of Irish nationalism which he undertook in the mid-1960s and thereafter.

In the 1960s, the poetry of William Butler Yeats was at once the subject of an academic industry, a cultural icon of immense stature, and a talisman for many persons of Irish ancestry. (The same characteristics hold today, but with much less robustness.) Yeats was viewed both as a miracle and a piece of architecture, Lourdes and a great cathedral all in one. The centenary conference, therefore, was not the place to utter impieties about the man with the bow tie.

That hardly weighed with Conor. He had a score to settle with Yeats just as he had a bone to pick with James Joyce (see the Anthology, Selection 42). Conor, in any case, was not very much impressed with the average academic literary specialist. (He had an immense respect for his friend Richard Ellman, and for Ellman's scholarly guide, John V. Kelleher, but these were giants among midgets.) This was a long-standing judgment. In the mid-fifties, for example, Conor (as "Donat O'Donnell") had reviewed in the *Spectator* a set of essays by R.P. Blackmur and found them to be in crucial passages extremely obscure. He came to the conclusion that "the critic who teaches in a university and writes in the academic quarterlies is like a prison chaplain." How so? "He has a captive audience to which he commends a discipline, but his audience has no means of commending discipline to him."[55]

Conor intended to commend some discipline to the Yeatsians, and it would have to do with politics. One of his long-standing beliefs (as he suggested in his review of R.W.B. Lewis's influential *The Picaresque Saint* in 1960) was that it was unfortunately common for an intelligent critic to be explicitly conscious of the importance of politics in the work of a writer, and yet to turn aside from the implications of those politics. "This kind of criticism—acute on small matters and absent-minded on very large ones, inventive of diversions, cosmically concerned and terrestrially calm—is important not in itself, but as marking a dangerously close intellectual atmosphere. The canary in the mine shaft is important when its song hesitates and stops."[56]

Yeats and fascism was one of those large matters on which literary critics and Yeats enthusiasts alike had been absent-minded. Granted, Louis MacNeice had discussed the topic, but he had not really made up his mind what it all meant. At one point, he wrote of Yeats's "own elegant brand of fascism," and of "the later Yeats, the man who nearly became a fascist."[57] And Frank O'Connor in conversation had talked directly about Yeats's fascist beliefs. But no one had directly faced the issue. To break the Yeats industry out of its absent-mindedness on this large issue, Conor adopted an epistemology that was largely historical. This allowed him to swing around the flank of the bulk of the Yeats people, who were closely textually orientated, or fixated on tiny points of personal detail of the poet's life, and who had surprisingly little knowledge of (or concern with) the Irish and European political contexts in which Yeats had operated.

Employing both passion and cunning, Conor wrapped this historical epistemology in the one rhetorical mode that would give it the most force: the anecdotal and the personal. He began with the story of lunching with his aunt, Hanna Sheehy-Skeffington, widow of the martyred pacifist of 1916, and of hearing of Yeats's death. The year was 1939. Conor expressed pain at Yeats's death.

His aunt spoke. " 'Yes,' she said, 'he was a Link with the Past.' "[58]

Aunt Hanna was thinking of the political past, and Conor forced his listeners to think of Yeats the politician. Several times in his discussion he invoked personal memories or anecdotes—his father at the Arts Club doing a parody of Yeats's "fascism," and various stories about the great poet's proto-fascist stance in Irish society in the 1920s and 1930s. The stories are apposite, always, but they carry a coded message that required no great act of subaudition for his listeners (and, later, his readers) to understand. It was "Don't mess with me, for unlike you academics, I've been there; my family and their friends knew the real Yeats, the man whom you know only from texts as through a streaked and dirty glass."

Presented in that way, Conor's historical argument was devastating. Indeed, it would have been hard for him to lose this argument, given that Yeats wrote to Olivia Shakespear in July 1933: "... How can we not feel emulous when we see Hitler juggling with his sausage of stocking. Our chosen colour is blue, and blue shirts are marching about all over the country and their organizer tells me that it was my suggestion—suggestion that I have entirely forgotten—that made them select for their flag red St. Patrick's cross on a blue ground."[59] Or, when one finds Yeats writing in *On the Boiler* (1938) that "The Fascist countries know that civilization has reached a crisis, and found their eloquence upon that knowledge."[60] Yeats apparently expected that the fascists would win in Europe and probably deserved to. There is more, much more, historical documentation, but as impressive as is Conor's use of evidence, even more so is his refusal to be simplistic. His exposition is nuanced and it shows that Yeats was both an Irish nationalist and a fascist, that both his nationalism and his fascism flooded, ebbed, flooded again, and that both of these ideological commitments had roots that went back at least as far as 1903. They were integral to his entire mature career, not cosmetic. One, therefore, could not properly accept Yeats the Irish nationalist and refuse to reckon with Yeats the fascist; one could not have Yeats the poet without accepting Yeats the politician; and Yeats the gyring metaphysician had to be tempered with Yeats the ugly pragmatist.

Nearly a quarter of a century later, Geoffrey Wheatcroft in the *New Republic* called "Passion and Cunning" "one of the best short pieces written about politics and culture in early twentieth-century Ireland."[61] That was after the dust had settled. The immediate reaction, however, was one of horror. (An accurate measure of the dismay with which the essay was greeted is that Conor later observed that the only thing he had ever written that annoyed more people was his *States of Ireland*, 1972, which almost ended his political career.)[62] Leland Lyons, soon to become one of the skein of official biographers of Yeats, took up Conor on some of his more charged judgments.[63] Patrick Cosgrave ("later to distinguish himself as Margaret Thatcher's mid-term biographer," in one observer's tart characterization),[64] produced a shrill attack on Conor's historical knowledge, on his use of poetry to make "a cheap and partial political comment," and, centrally, upon Conor's motives: "his actions on this occasion remain inexplicable."[65] A considered counterattack did not come until 1981, and this was not by a historical scholar, but by Elizabeth Cullingford, a graduate student in English literature whom Richard Ellman "assigned" (in Conor's perception at least) to do a Ph.D. on Yeats and fascism. The resulting book was deeply knowledgeable about Yeats's poetry, but its historical segments (which were the centerpiece of Conor's original argument) were based entirely upon secondary sources, upon a very superficial knowledge of Irish politics and upon an almost total innocence of European politics in the 1920s and 1930s.[66] Conor published a generous review of Cullingford's book in the *Observer*.[67] (This review is printed in the Anthology, Selection 39.)[68] In 1986, the gimlet-eyed Irish critic W.J. McCormack summarized the matter, and by implication explained why Conor's essay was so hard for Yeatsians, especially Americans, to assimilate: "O'Brien brought to Ireland a kind of analysis which was virtually unknown previously, an analysis which assumed a European context while yet reading the poetry with a discerning eye, an analysis which set out from no *a priori* separation of politics and poetics."[69]

What problems there are with "Passion and Cunning" seem to me not to be in its historical explication or in its reading of texts, but in matters related to Conor as a person. There were intellectual issues that he was not at the time willing to tackle, and for perfectly understandable reasons. One of these is that, although he established that one could be both an Irish nationalist and fascistically Irish (as Yeats clearly was), Conor did not at this stage wish to examine directly the possibility that a worm was entwined around the heart of Irish nationalism—and that creature was fascism. Or, to put it another way, that Irish nationalism was inherently fascistic. In the mid-1960s, Conor was feeling his way toward a definition of his view on several matters, among them Irish nationalism, and he was proceeding slowly. It was as late as 1981 that he clearly articulated a final position about one sector of the Irish nationalist movement, namely, that "those who want to oppose fascism in Ireland will start opposing it where it is really to be found: at the heart of the Republican Movement."[70]

The other matter that Conor dances away from is one of the biggest of ethical questions for an intellectual. As George Steiner recently phrased it, "Does aesthetic creativity, even of the first order, ever justify the favourable presentation of, let alone systematic incitement to, inhumanity?"[71] For Conor, the great problem was that Yeats was a fascist, or very near to being one, at the very time he was writing his greatest poetry.[72] So, "how can those of us who loathe such politics continue not merely to admire but to love the poetry, and perhaps, most of all the poems with a political bearing?"[73] Conor's answer is that the process of poetic transformation cleansed everything. "The purity and integrity—including the truth about politics as Yeats apprehended it—are in the poetry concentrated in metaphors of such power that they thrust aside all calculated intent."[74] There he leaves it. For once, Conor has not said clearly what his own text implies: the poetry is so good that the fascism is forgivable.

After "Passion and Cunning," Conor returned to make one further major comment on Yeats. As he continued to teach the Literature and Society courses at NYU, he became aware that he had missed something important in Yeats and he had an opportunity to repair this omission in November 1969 in the prestigious T.S. Eliot Memorial Lectures, given at the invitation of his old friend and frequent critic, Leland Lyons, the master of Eliot College in the University of Kent. The lectures, presented after he left NYU, actually were the result of his reflections in 1967–68. What Conor had missed earlier, he confessed, was that

Richard Ellman was wrong in his view that although Yeats had read Nietzsche, he had discarded the implications of Nietzsche's ethics. Conor argued, first, that the so-called "gentle-Nietzsche" was a major misinterpretation of who the philosopher really was.[75] Moreover, the "fierce-Nietzsche" had made a great impact on Yeats in 1902. Finally, that impact had a continuing influence on Yeats. In Yeats's later poems and dramas, the fierce-Nietzsche is increasingly heard, "linking the themes of violence and joy." [76] This line of thought buttressed Conor's argument that Yeats, indeed, was seriously fascistic, but it simultaneously gave him room to breathe on the question of how inherently fascistic Irish nationalism was. Nietzsche may have been part of William Butler Yeats's cultural programming, but the philosopher's writings certainly were not of the marrow of Irish nationalism.

• • •

Besides being a step in working out his own understanding of Irish nationalism, Conor's work on Yeats was implicitly an attack on a segment of the American academic establishment. This was not a direct assault on the New York intellectuals, but Conor's next public discourse was. In October 1966, the heavily endowed Society for the Humanities at Cornell University was inaugurated with a set of lectures that was published under the title *The Morality of Scholarship*.[77] Organized and chaired by Max Black (Russian-born professor of philosophy at Cornell, and expert on linguistic philosophy), the theme of the lectures had evolved from an article published in *Encounter*, that most New York intellectual of periodicals, in July 1965. In that essay, Lionel Trilling had asked if the study of literature still could be justified, as it had been in Victorian times, as having a "unique effectiveness in opening the mind and illuminating it, in purging the mind of prejudices and received ideas, in making the mind free and active."[78] Interestingly, three *auslander* were brought in to answer these queries: Northrop Frye from the University of Toronto, Canada's most distinguished literary critic and an ordained minister of the United Church of Canada; Stuart Hampshire, English-born and educated, professor of philosophy at Princeton since 1963; and Conor, who had arrived only in 1965. Foreigners, non-New Yorkers, were being asked to assay one of the fundamental doubts that was bedeviling the New York intellectuals.

They asked for faith, but Conor gave them hell, elegantly. He began by pointing to the phenomenon of "revolutionary subordination," the imperative which operated under Mao and Trotsky and Stalin, requiring that just as every writer must be a propagandist, so every literary critic must be a critic of propaganda and, if possible, an improver of the product. This of course was repulsive to all good liberals. But Conor asked, would we never praise a bad book for political reasons? What if by praising a bad novel we could save the lives of some children? Would we "remain morally obliged to knock the novel and let the children die?" "If we turn professional ethics into an absolute, which cannot in any circumstance be subordinated to any other values, we are forced, I think, to approve the incorruptible, infanticidal book reviewer."[79] To an audience that prided itself on professionalism, this was unsettling.

No more palatable to a readership that was strongly anticommunist, if "liberal" in some sense, was Conor's argument that "the freedoms that writers and scholars possess in the capitalist world are on a much narrower basis than many Western writers like to suggest. They are in fact an appanage of the rich and moderately rich strata in that world."[80] The societies that produce this wealth—and thus permit the existence of intellectual ornaments—spend a great deal of time and money in the protection of their interests, especially against communism. Conor believed that Western governments' "real objection to communism is not to its repressive practices but on the contrary to its positive social content, and to the fact that its extension would make the relation of the principal capitalist centres to the resources of the underdeveloped world less profitable and more onerous."[81]

Crucially, the American academic and intellectual elite were implicitly engaged in supporting the principle of *counterrevolutionary subordination* (the italics are his).[82] That is, they were in essence no different from the allegedly sold-out intellectuals under Mao, Trotsky, or Stalin.

Conor from a great height (the opening of the Society for the Humanities at Cornell was the most prestigious event in the humanities in 1966) was referring, without saying so directly, to the great disgrace of the New York intellectuals: the discovery that their flagship organization, the American Conference for Cultural Freedom and one of their most prestigious periodicals, the transatlantic *Encounter*, were benefiting from financial support by the Central Intelligence Agency.[83] Recall here that while still in Ghana, Conor had written an article in the *New Statesman* (December 1963) in which he argued, solely through an analysis of the content of the magazine itself, that *Encounter* was suspect. It was, in the vocabulary of his Cornell lecture, an example of counterrevolutionary subordination.

This particular case—and actually it was not a case but an entire syndrome—involved an international body, the Congress for Cultural Freedom, its American affiliate, the American Congress for Cultural Freedom, and the London-based *Encounter*, most of whose high offices were filled by New York intellectuals (in the sense that historians of the

1950s and 1960s use the term). The Congress for Cultural Freedom was founded in Berlin in 1950 (its headquarters later moved to Paris). It was an attempt to merge the viewpoint of American and European noncommunist intellectuals into a single anticommunist voice. The Americans among the founders included Melvin J. Lasky (of whom more in a moment), Sidney Hook, Arthur Schlesinger, Jr., and a host of others from what Irving Howe denominated as America's only self-conscious intelligentsia. The American Congress for Cultural Freedom was even more under their influence. In 1963, *Encounter* magazine was founded, a blend of slightly left English intellectuals (Hugh Trevor-Roper is a good example) and New York-oriented Americans. Among the editors over the years were Irving Kristol, Stephen Spender, and Melvin Lasky. Dwight Macdonald assisted editorially for a time as well.

Here Conor was placing pressure on a hidden fault-line among the New York intellectuals. Although as a group they were generally anticommunist, many of them not only opposed communism but also opposed *Encounter* and the Congress for Cultural Freedom. Irving Howe and the group centered around *Dissent* were nearly as critical of the CCF as was Conor. However, the CCF group, as organized by Melvin Lasky, had more resources.

Melvin Lasky had been involved with the Congress for Cultural Freedom from the beginning. He was a former employee of the American Information Service and had been editor of *Der Monat*, a propaganda magazine sponsored by the United States High Commission in Germany. Lasky himself had been a pre-World War II Trotskyite, and now claimed to have no part in politics. Among the contributors to *Encounter*: Leslie Fiedler, Nathan Glazer, Arthur Schlesinger, Jr., John Kenneth Galbraith, Bertrand Russell, Irving Kristol, Frank Kermode (who served as an editor in the 1960s), Diana Trilling, and Sidney Hook. The Congress for Cultural Freedom and, indirectly, *Encounter*, were on the CIA payroll from 1953 until 1966 (accounts vary as to the termination date). According to the CIA officer who was in charge of the operation, at least one of the *Encounter* editors was knowingly part of the conspiracy. (Suspicion fell on Lasky, but he strenuously denied being aware of the funding.) It matters not, in fact, who the agent was, for most of the individuals who wrote for *Encounter* had no idea of its CIA funding. What is clear, however, is that as a group, the contributors to *Encounter* gave the CIA very good value for its money. They presented the U.S. government's view that communism was a great moral evil, and that it was a force so strong that the "free world" was within an ace of losing to that force.[84]

Interestingly, despite his 1963 piece on *Encounter* (which was reprinted in Conor's *Writers and Politics* in 1965), Conor in the spring of

1966 had consented to review a book for *Encounter*. Normally, that would not be unusual, for Conor has been willing to write for just about anyone whose check is good and who does not censor what he says. But *Encounter* was a special case and, therefore, he reconsidered his agreement to review. In April 1966, the English writer Claude Cockburn was considering whether or not to contribute to a special *Encounter* supplement on Ireland, and Conor advised him as follows:

> As regards *Encounter* the enclosed copy of a letter I have just sent to [Frank] Kermode returning the book they had sent me for review is, I think, the best answer I can give. Melvin [Lasky] I regard as a sort of cultural Cold War conman. Kermode on the other hand is a man whom I respect, but he is in danger of being used as a front by Lasky which is, I think, what happened to Spender. As you will see from the fact that I originally accepted the book for review from them, I vacillated on this question myself, but I finally came down on the side that even apparently quite innocent anti-Cold War contributions to *Encounter* will be used as bait or camouflage: "Cold War? Who, us? Why we printed Conor Cruise O'Brien and Claude Cockburn!" Their main strength, as a cultural Cold War operation, has been their facade of impartiality and I rather reluctantly reached the conclusion that I ought not to help them maintain the facade.[85]

That was before the big story broke. On 27 April 1966, the *New York Times* reported that the Central Intelligence Agency had supported the Congress for Cultural Freedom and that *Encounter* had been one of the financial beneficiaries of funds that had been channeled to the Congress for Cultural Freedom through various conduits.

The collective reaction of the New York intellectuals who had been associated with the Congress for Cultural Freedom and with *Encounter* ran roughly as follows: (1) it isn't true; (2) I, at least, did not know about any of this, although I cannot speak for my colleagues; (3) besides, the CIA money did not at all affect either my own contribution or the collective tone of the journal; and (4) in any case, we were in a battle against totalitarian communism, so whatever we have done, it was in a good cause.[86]

The immediate reaction of those most intimately concerned, however, was to try frantically to squirt ink in the water, like a cornered squid. Stephen Spender, Melvin Lasky, and Irving Kristol, all of whom had been editors at one time, wrote a letter to the *New York Times* (10 May 1966) which stated that all of *Encounter*'s funds came from recognized foundations, listed in official directories. True enough, but the official directories included various CIA fronts set up specially to channel funds. On the same day, another letter appeared in the *New York Times*, this one signed by Arthur Schlesinger, Jr., John Kenneth Galbraith, Robert Oppenheimer, and George Kennan, arguing that since *Encounter* had complete editorial freedom, it could not have been a tool of the CIA.[87]

That was the situation when Conor gave a major endowed lecture, the Homer Watt Lecture at NYU on 19 May 1966. In that public forum, in vivid detail, he detailed the "treason of the clerks" and not only tied *Encounter* to the New York intellectuals, but did so in a way that tied their treason to intellectual integrity to their intellectual mediocrity. "In a skillfully executed political operation of the *Encounter* type, the writing specifically required by the power structure was done by people who, as writers, were of the third or fourth rank, but who were, as the Belgians used to say about Moise Tshombe, *compréhensifs*, that is, they could take a hint." (The entire speech is found in the Anthology, Selection 19.)

Conor heightened the impact of his opinions by having a slightly abridged version printed as "Politics and the Writer" in *Book Week* (12 June 1966) and also having it distributed gratis to the delegates at the International P.E.N. Congress which convened in New York in July. Thus, many of the hosts of the congress, figures whom Third World writers held up as heroes, were suddenly made to look ridiculous, and in public.

Conor made lots of enemies by doing this, many more than he realized, but there were two with whom he locked on, in mutual hatred. One of these was Arthur Schlesinger, Jr., who was Schweitzer professor at City University of New York. The two were an unequal match. Conor, who had been forced to make his living by his wits ever since his entry into Trinity College, Dublin (where he made his way through winning prizes), parentless from late adolescence onward, was a verbal in-fighter in the classic Swiftian tradition, elegant, ironic, needling, erudite by turn. He was overtrained and undermatched. Schlesinger in contrast had grown up soft and intellectually cosseted: the offspring of one of America's truly distinguished historians, he had a Harvard A.B., had been a junior fellow at Harvard, had served in the OSS (the World War II predecessor of the CIA), then went back to Harvard and climbed the professorial ladder virtually by hereditary right. In the years 1961–64 he was a special assistant (read: courtier) to President John F. Kennedy. Whereas Conor could be elegant in person, especially in debate, Schlesinger resembled a small bullfrog with a bow tie, an impression that was unfortunately enhanced by a slight speech impediment. He could be convincing in writing, but was inept at impromptu debate. When, on 30 May 1966, an O'Brien-Schlesinger debate was carried on Metromedia Television in New York, Conor used Schlesinger like soap. The defining moment in the debate was when Conor asked Schlesinger, "Did you not *know*, when you signed that letter [of 10 May 1966] that the CIA paid for the Congress [for Cultural Freedom]?" Schlesinger replied after a pause. "I *did* know about it while I was in government." The effect was devastating, for it was an admission of duplicity. He had known while in government, but, somehow, later, when out of government, Schlesinger had not known.[88]

Conor and Schlesinger fought a further round in *Book Week* in mid-September. They conducted a letter exchange, two letters for each writer. The key part was Schlesinger's second letter, in which he asserted that "so long as I have been a member of the *Encounter* trust, *Encounter* has not been the beneficiary, direct or indirect of CIA funds." Conor, the historian with a stiletto, replied, "It is satisfactory to learn that as long as Professor Schlesinger has been a member of the *Encounter* trust—how long is that?—*Encounter* has not been the beneficiary, directly or indirectly, of CIA funds."[89] Game over.

Shortly after that, Conor tried to make peace with Schlesinger, but it was too late: they remained virtually lifelong enemies, although this diminished on Conor's part to mere contempt and then, in later years, to something approaching toleration.[90]

The enmity with Melvin Lasky was nastier. Conor had unmasked Lasky and *Encounter* in the cruelest way: by simply reading what *Encounter* printed. The empire had to strike back, and it did so through the pen of Goronwy Rees, a regular contributor to the magazine. In an editorial column signed only "R," Rees very skillfully slagged Conor's attacks on *Encounter*. "It is as if J.Edgar Hoover had taken to what Mr. O'Brien calls 'political-cultural criticism,'" wrote Rees, and he compared Conor to Senator Joseph McCarthy. Rees talked of "the transformation of the Machiavelli of Peace into the Joe McCarthy of political-cultural criticism, hunting for CIA agents beneath the beds of Stephen Spender, Irving Kristol, Melvin Lasky, and Frank Kermode, and from his one-man radar station, relentlessly tracking the fate of the Q-ship *Encounter* as it sets course for the Bay of Pigs."[91] The skillful part of the piece was that, although there was no direct denial of CIA funding of *Encounter*, the overall impression was that such an idea was patent nonsense, the product of a sick imagination and flawed character.

Conor's published view is that this editorial was planned as a trap. "The editors of *Encounter* and other senior people connected with the magazine sat round a table and considered the wording of the article very carefully, fully conscious that I might seek to come back at them in some way. They were actually hoping that I would sue them. If I did so, I would be falling into a trap."[92] In a private letter to Owen Sheehy-

Skeffington, Conor identified those whom he believed were involved in the planning: the joint editors Melvin Lasky and Frank Kermode (who had at that time taken up appointment as Winterstoke Professor of English in the University of Bristol), Robert Conquest (a freelance, somewhat right-wing commentator whose most recent book at that time was *The Egyptologists*, written with Kingsley Amis), and of course Goronwy Rees.[93] Rees, a sometime fellow of All Souls and principal of University College Aberystwyth from 1953–57, novelist and translator, was described as follows in a letter Conor wrote to his friend and legal counsel, Alexis FitzGerald: "Rees is a person that would be unlikely to make a very favourable impression in court. Specifically, he is in a very poor position to compare others to Senator [Joe] McCarthy. He had been a friend of Guy Burgess's and after Burgess's defection, published in the *People* a strange series of articles to the general effect that the Foreign Office was full of communism, etc. Aberystwyth University ... set up a special academic committee to consider whether the publication of these articles was consistent with his academic role. On consideration that it wasn't, he was removed from office (an unusual set of events at a British University)."[94]

It is impossible to say what trap, if any, the *Encounter* people were preparing to spring, but Conor began to hear from people with whom he was on friendly terms—Desmond Williams, a historian at University College, Dublin; Paul Keating, then a counselor officer in the Irish Ministry of External Affairs; Donald Gordon, professor of English in the University of Reading; and the several editors of the *New Left Review*—that *Encounter* had a "thick dossier" on him which contained details of his financial transactions in Africa and New York and on his past political associations.[95] In reality, the "thick dossiers" melted away. Conor may not have led a pristine life, but certainly there was nothing that would be mortally wounding if read into the public record.[96]

In point of fact, Conor was not inclined to sue. His view then—and now—is that good ideas drive out bad, and that if he can receive a fair hearing, that is enough. So, he was satisfied when Karl Miller of the *New Statesman* offered him space to reply to the Rees column. He drafted a reply and it was set in type, ready to print. (The full text is found in the Anthology, Selection 20.) Its publication would have been enough. Honor would have been satisfied. However (according to Conor's information), Frank Kermode rang Karl Miller and said that if the *New Statesman* printed anything in which Conor quoted references to *Encounter* found in the *New York Times*, they would sue.[97] Conor's draft reply did indeed quote from the *New York Times* (not exactly a source of left-wing polemic), so to avoid a libel suit, or even the aggravation of having to face down a threatened suit, the *New Statesman* pulled Conor's reply.

This left a libel suit as the only way to make his case. Conor went through the appropriate procedures, first demanding an apology, and then, when it was refused, he took an action which was set for hearing in Dublin in February 1967. As the court date approached, several intermediaries tried to act as eirenic go-betweens, among them Robert Silvers of the *New York Review of Books*. The *Encounter* group suggested various forms of apology, but each one involved Conor's having to back away in some degree from his basic, long-held position that *Encounter* was bent, and badly at that. So, the February high court date in Dublin on 14 February came. And went: the directors of *Encounter* did not send a lawyer to defend themselves, on the grounds that they did not feel themselves bound to defend any case taken outside of Great Britain. Jury hearing was set for 3 May in Dublin to determine damages.[98]

Apparently *Encounter* was planning on ignoring the Irish verdict. However, Conor had a bit of good fortune. In March 1967, *Ramparts* magazine published a now-classic exposé of the CIA penetration and subsidization of a whole variety of domestic American groups, including the Congress of Cultural Freedom, and its beneficiary, *Encounter*. Immediately, the legal counsel for *Encounter* realized that the magazine would be well advised to settle with Conor, for not only was the periodical's relationship to the CIA no longer deniable, but Conor now had heavily publicized corroboration of his earlier literary deduction. If Conor wished, he could bring an action in a British court and almost certainly he would be awarded large damages. Hence, when the Dublin court convened on 3 May, an agreed apology was read out in court. It withdrew all imputations against the character of Conor Cruise O'Brien. "We further acknowledge that Dr. O'Brien as a writer and critic and whilst serving the United Nations, has always maintained the highest standards of personal integrity and we regret that the article we published should have made charges against his integrity which were without justification.[99] Conor specified that this apology, which was to be printed in *Encounter*'s next issue, be published adjacent to Goronwy Rees's column. *Encounter* paid all of Conor's legal costs and, as symbolic guilt-money, paid a sum to a charity.[100]

• • •

Seven years later, Melvin Lasky wrote to the *Irish Times* arguing that *Encounter* had not been found guilty of libel (it had not, for it grovelingly had apologized) and that the magazine's lawyers had persuaded the editors that a number of their "literary references to Dr. O'Brien's political and intellectual style could be taken as reflecting on his integrity as a scholar and a public person. We apologized and Dr. O'Brien accepted it." Sure, and they all had a nice cup of tea afterward. This was dishonesty of the same sort that had made the magazine such a meretricious bit of colportage, but, like the periodical itself, Lasky's letter had a bit of truth wrapped in the mendacity: "Our old differences with Dr. O'Brien—which date back to his time in the UN, the Congo, his career in Nkrumah's Ghana and his political line as a New York professor—had generally to do with our attitudes, far less radical than his, on matters of revolution and reform, violence or peaceful change, militant dictatorship or democratic compromise."[101]

Scrubbed of the self-righteous rhetoric, Lasky's letter accurately pointed to one of the reasons that Conor did not fit in with what was generally described as the New York intellectuals. He was more radical, rather more to the left in conventional terms, than were the bulk of them. In large part this was because the encounter with communism which those with East European or Russian roots had experienced (either directly or via family members) left them much more afraid of the Soviet empire than was Conor. On two matters of central importance, he differed strongly from them: he was deeply "anti-American" in the sense of seeing U.S. foreign policy (and its home-front apologists) as being the greatest danger to world peace, and, further, he was much more in sync with the New Left, the radical students and the cultural revolutionaries, than were most of the New York intellectuals, whose heritage was that of the Old Left—a cultural program that determined many of their attitudes, even while most of them had migrated to being mildly liberal or embryonic neo-conservatives. (This is not to deny that a significant minority—including such figures as Paul Goodman, Norman Mailer, and Dwight Macdonald—were receptive to the ideas of the New Left.)

In 1967, the *Partisan Review* sent around a question to leading New York intellectuals (and a few others) asking them to comment on "What's happening to America." Conor's response focused chiefly on foreign policy and made two central arguments. The first of these is that there was no need to be afraid of indigenous revolutions, even if led by communists. "In fact, except partly in the somewhat farcical case of Albania's devotion to China, there is no example of a country in which *indigenous* communist forces won power, and then put their country under the control of another communist country."[102] Hence, in predicating its foreign policy on preventing the spread of communism, the United States was likely to be forced into policing ever-larger portions of the Third World, and there to spend its time preventing indigenous revolutions, since such revolutions often took the label of communist. Therefore, America was locked into a fierce imperialism of its own. The doctrine of anticommunism "is a logic of imperialism" and, "if America is to avoid an imperialist destiny, it must avoid anti-communist interventions in other people's countries."[103] In a speech given at an anti-Vietnam War rally, 5 November 1966, Conor summarized the situation:

> The idea of containment—which I think the people of this country originally accepted as the doctrine that the Soviet Union and China would not be allowed to expand the area of their power by armed force—is now interpreted to mean that any country in the world which is not now communist must be saved from communism, if necessary by the armed force of this country. ... There has been a logical progression from the theory of containment to the practice of *imperialism*.[104]

Anticommunism was a creed; it implied an entire world view, a mode of apprehending issues, a method of presenting them to the public, and a way of formulating action.[105]

In a widely quoted and reprinted essay, "The Counterrevolutionary Reflex," Conor went to the heart of the issue, arguing that anticommunism was no longer in the self-interest of the United States:

> I challenge the assumption that it is necessary for the U.S. to stop the spread of communism. I do so on the following grounds:
> • The old assumption on which anti-Communist policy was devised no longer holds. There is no longer a monolithic Communist empire whose power can be thought of as increased by every new country that "goes Communist."
> • Active hostility to the U.S. is not a necessary permanent attribute of every Communist country. The richest and most powerful country in the world must expect to attract considerable ill-feeling in Capitalist as well as Communist countries. Policy shall seek, however, to prevent ill-feeling from passing over into active hostility. Active hostility is fanned by U.S. anti-Communist actions such as Vietnam. If Asian communism is today bitterly anti-American—as it is—this is a resultant of American anti-Communist activity in Asia.
> • Where it may be thought U.S. interests are menaced by the spread of communism there are nonideological means of defending those interests. The Truman Doctrine, to the extent that it provided against the territorial expansion of Russian military power, was nonideological. The principle expressed in Eisenhower's formula of

"checking indirect aggression" is ideological, involving an indefinitely extended series of political judgments, and of actions based on
such judgments, about the internal affairs of other countries. Once
it is the business of the United States to prevent Communists from
coming to power in a given country, then everything in that country
comes under permanent U.S. surveillance, which may, in certain circumstances turn into U.S. tutelage. The result is an incalculable extension of this country's commitments. A doctrine against offensive
weapons or bases, or soldiers, in this hemisphere would make more
sense and involve fewer risks than the present policy against future
Castros. Similarly, economic measures damaging to U.S. interests
could be met by appropriate economic countermeasures. The doctrine of containment could be interpreted to mean that the extension
of Russian or Chinese power *by force* would be damaging to U.S. interests and would involve risks of retaliation.[106]

Conor frequently was taxed about being too anti-American and
being blind to Soviet repression. His answer, in metaphor, was that we,
as writers, have to keep "chipping away" at the misleading lies and dis-
tortive mind-sets that make our world dangerous and that we each have
to work on our own side of the wall. "My own guess is that the liberation of the communist world, and of the poor world, from their crude
forms of mendacity, will have to proceed from within and that the liberation of the Western world from its subtler and perhaps deadlier
forms of mendacity will also have to proceed from within," he wrote just
before coming to New York. "From the other side we can hear a few
writers, Poles, Russians, Hungarians and others, busily chipping away.
Our applause can neither encourage nor help them. What might help
would be that, from our own side also, should be heard the sound of
chipping."[107] Prescient indeed: the Eastern bloc's chipping from within
was to have its effect a quarter of a century later.[108]
    If Conor's anti-Americanism, as defined earlier, was tarter than was
the criticism of U.S. foreign policy expressed by the bulk of the New
York intellectuals, his fuzzy, semisocialist vocabulary pushed him closer
to the younger academics of the New Left and to the more politicized
students of the late 1960s than it did to the old guard. The following exchange with Brian Inglis, which took place in 1973, is revealing in this
regard.

    Inglis: While you were in America, you got the reputation of being a
Marxist?
    Conor: I was never a Marxist, and the more I studied Marx, the less of a

Marxist I became. The nearest I ever was to being a Marxist was as a very young undergraduate when I had read absolutely no Marx at all.[109]

Both halves of that exchange are based on factual premises: that Conor was perceived during his NYU years as being a Marxist, or socialist, and that, in fact he was not Marxist or socialist. The labeling occurred because Conor was at times quite willing to attach to himself the term "socialist" (a term that has a wide variety of meanings). His real introduction to New York City, the mugging at Morningside Heights in 1965, occurred when he was attending a socialist congress at Columbia University.[110] He registered for, but was unable to attend, a socialist cultural congress in Cuba in 1968.[111] And, as late as 1972, he was a speaker at the Twelfth Congress of the Socialist International held in Vienna.[112] A significant portion of Conor's publishing in these years was in periodicals whose titles were clear labels: *Studies on the Left*, *New Left Review*, and the *Socialist Register*. And Conor frequently talked in the language of the socialists of that era. For example, when he was unable to attend the socialist cultural congress in Havana in 1969, he nevertheless filled in a questionnaire about his beliefs:

> *Query:* How would you appraise the importance of the cultural congress which is going to take place at Havana?
> *Answer:* The fact that this congress is taking place in Havana, attended by so many of the world's leading intellectuals, is in itself of high significance. It symbolizes the failure, on the spiritual and intellectual plane, of the strenuous efforts made by imperialist forces to isolate Cuba.
> *Query:* Is the main problem of the intellectual to find solutions or merely present facts or situations …?
> *Answer:* He [the intellectual] must present and interpret facts and situations and the relationship between facts and situations, and in doing so he must help towards the finding of solutions, mainly by elimination through the rejection of false solutions.[113]

This sort of mind-numbing incantation (even the metrics are thudding, the trudge of heavy boots earnestly progressing) was limited, mercifully. Indeed, on occasion, Conor's socialist fascia and his much-deeper literary preoccupations could intersect productively. Contrast the preceding excerpt with the way he started a speech to the Modern Humanities Research Association in August 1968:

> My theme this morning will be what is in common between the process of imaginative creation, as described by Yeats in *The Circus Animal's Desertion*,

and the process by which political concepts and systems emerge, which is, I think, basically though not necessarily in details, the process discerned by Marx.

To bring Yeats and Marx together in this way is a procedure which both men would, of course, have strongly resented. It may also well seem to many of you eccentrically eclectic. There are, I agree, significant differences between what Yeats is saying about the creation of poetry and what Marx is saying about the creation of political and other systems. Yet these differences are less than one might imagine. It is true that Marx seems to concentrate on a single factor—economic interest—whereas Yeats's rag-and-bone shop is a notably miscellaneous emporium of which, as you will remember, he details the contents. Yet among the old bones, the old bottles and the sweepings and other sordid items in this basic layer, or lair, there is a single human figure. Marx knew her well. She is:

That raving slut who keeps the till.

Nor is Marx's own thought quite so narrowly concentrated on the economic factor as is sometimes suggested. It is not true to say that he sees a simple kind of greed as the engine of human conduct and thought. Very early on, in his magnificent commentary on a passage in *Timon of Athens*, Marx makes it clear that his conception of "economic interest" is not a matter of mere greed or avarice, but a sort of funnel—the sort of funnel one sees in the paintings of Hieronymus Bosch—through which crawl for satisfaction, through the transmuting power of money, not only gluttony and avarice but also pride, lust, envy, rage; even sloth, though it will not make money, is best fulfilled by its unearned possession.

Yeats's rag-and-bone shop contains a till; Marx's till is situated in a rag-and-bone shop.[114]

The contrast between the diligent socialist of the Havana questionnaire and the incisive critic at the Humanities Research Association could scarcely be sharper. The contrast indicates, among other things, that although in his NYU years Conor employed the socialist tag freely, he was not in fact very comfortable with it.

Nor should he have been, because, in fact, he never really was a socialist. The basis of Conor's cosmology, from his earliest days in the fading light of Joyceland to the present day, has been founded on the belief that, more than anything else, ideas count. This belief—so central to his outlook as to be unstated – is fundamentally at odds with classic Marxism and its modern derivatives. Far from accepting the idea that economic substructure determines cultural superstructure, Conor believed (and believes) the opposite: culture and cultures count more than do economic substrata.

If Conor was a socialist at all, he was a socialist in the sense that George Orwell had been. Orwell's socialism was that of the "decent Englishman" and Conor's was that of the decent Irishman: against bullying, whether by imperialists, or civil servants, or factory managers, or secretaries of state.[115]

For a brief moment in American history the sort of rhetoric that Conor employed meshed with the tone of a student protest movement and with an amorphous New Left. Conor fitted in, or seemed to. These phenomena, the student protest movement and the New Left in the 1960s, have generated a massive literature, but they remain a mystery, a maze of galvanic connections that produced heat and energy and then, suddenly, were twisted wires on the junk pile of history. Both of these phenomena were geographically located outside the traditional East Coast (especially New York City) radical centers. Madison, Wisconsin; Ann Arbor, Michigan; and Berkeley, California; these were the flash points. When the NYU students picked up on these flashes, they were not buying into the Old Left but were rejecting it. Further, they radically refused to accept the old orthodoxies of structural Marxism and for the most part rejected rigorous theorizing. They saw music as being as important as materialistic causation, dancing more consequential than dialectic, social sharing more important than socialistic redistribution. Conor's eclectic, socialist-sounding vocabulary of these years, when combined with his vigorous anti-imperialism and anticolonialism, aligned him with the various groups, especially the young, who frightened the more traditional of the New York intellectuals.[116]

New York University was not the center of student radicalism in New York City, but it was one of the metropoles. Immediately upon arriving at NYU, Conor started to support anti-Vietnam War activities. In mid-October 1965, he agreed to serve as faculty adviser to the NYU Committee to End the War in Vietnam.[117] At the same time, he became a backer, although not an official sponsor, of the Students for Democratic Reform, which was the NYU chapter of the Students for a Democratic Society. (The chapter really was reform-Democrat rather than fully radical and it was eventually read out of the national SDS.) When, in an effort at political censorship, the administration of NYU tried to charge the students $88.00 for the use of a room for a mid-November 1965 Teach-In on Vietnam, Conor backed their protests and the fee was dropped.[118] And, when, in April 1968, a national convulsion followed the assassination of Martin Luther King, NYU held a Day of Mourning that spread to a full week and included discussions of the larger issue of racism in the United States, Conor's view was that something good was happening. "Students and faculty worked out a series of demands which the administration has accepted, in principle of course."[119] As the fringe of the student movement became increasingly given to disruption of university life through the use of physical force, Conor backed away a bit. However, as late as the spring of 1969, he was one of a group of NYU professors who were demonstrating for open (as distinct from in-camera) hearings for students who had shut down a meeting in a university building because of a speaker of whom they did not approve: in this instance, the distinguished journalist James Reston (see the Anthology, Selection 25, for Conor's description of this event).[120]

Conor's honeymoon with student radicals ran roughly from his arrival in mid-1965 to the late spring of 1968, and he was sufficiently in their thrall to write a one-act play glorifying them, *Salome and the Wild Man*. This play, as far as I can discover, was never performed (it was given a public reading at the University of Kent, Canterbury, in 1972), but was printed in a later collection of Conor's essays. Of it he says: "*Salome and the Wild Man* represents the high water mark of the [he means "my"] tendency to idealize the student revolution. And the moral purity—if not the intelligence of the revolutionary."[121] The play was Rousseauian (to use a term that Conor would shudder to acknowledge), at least if one can conceive of Jean Jacques Rousseau as writing about virtuous mid-1960s radical students whose physical setting is the school of Philo of Alexandria. The main characters are a professorial figure, who learns more from his students than they from him, namely Philo the Sophist of Alexandria; a Wild Man, who is a Jewish revolutionary who has a great deal of energy but cannot explain exactly what his movement is about; a Roman security officer; and Salome, a princess who is young, dark, beautiful and who, for the love of life, dances naked (this is the 1960s, after all). The one revealing moment is when Philo the Skeptic (read: Conor the Schweitzer professor), appears on stage bloody and bedraggled, having been dealt with by the security forces. "Well, Sophist," Salome exclaims, "so you've found the answer to your question! What is Freedom? Freedom is what you have when the police let you go."[122]

The reference is to one of Conor's most painful moments in America: his being beaten up by the decent Irish police of New York City. The trail that leads to the policeman's boot is worth tracing. Conor and Maire both were active in peace demonstrations from their earliest days in New York City. Conor was always able to leaven his passion with a bit of skepticism: concerning the November 1965 teach-in, he told Irving Howe that "there is of course the ever-present danger of exercising our right of free speech when one has nothing particular to say."[123] In November 1965 he took part in the march on Washington.[124] A year later (he still had been a legal resident of the

United States for only fourteen months), Conor was a featured speaker at an anti-Vietnam War rally in Times Square. There he had the good sense to emphasize that this was an American problem. "Only the American people can correct the errors of the American government," he told the crowd. "Quite literally, your country's foreign policy is the most important thing in the world today. It is time you took a hand in it."[125] Conor became a significant figure in the antiwar movement, not a leader but someone who could be counted on to show up when he said he would and to give a speech in equal parts intelligent and passionate. He and Maire participated in the Peace Secretaries Roundtable of the American Friends Service Committee in the winter of 1967.[126] And Conor was one of the lead speakers at the University of Toronto International Teach-In (chaired by Jeffrey Rose and Michael Ignatieff) in the autumn of 1967.[127]

In the autumn of 1966, Conor was asked by Peader MacSwiney to become one of the letterhead-leaders of the Irish Council on the War in Vietnam, and he agreed.[128] This led to one of the most interesting speeches he gave to an American audience in that year. He told them a parable, the story of Terence MacSwiney, Lord Mayor of Cork, who was arrested in August 1920 for being "a Sinn Feiner, equivalent in the eyes of the British Government of those days to being what American officials and some journalists call 'Viet Cong' today." Arrested by the "agents of counter-terror," MacSwiney went on a hunger strike. "His death, after seventy-four days in hunger strike, aroused strong protests in the country and in Britain itself and elsewhere in the world. It was among the reasons why the British government of the day—which had said it would never shake hands with murder—came to the conference to be with representatives of the rebellion." Conor switched to a more conversational tone. "About two months ago, I received a letter from Terence MacSwiney's widow who now lives in Paris. She was obviously distressed by the news from Vietnam and wanted to hear to what extent the people in America were concerned about it and exactly what they were doing." So Conor corresponded with her and in her most recent letter, the widow MacSwiney wrote: "When one thinks of the noble and generous way America helped Ireland in a similar predicament, one is appalled that the United States is now taking the place of Britain (with more perfected means of torture and destruction) as a world imperialist power." She concluded with "heartfelt thanks to all Americans fighting this situation and especially to the lads who burn or tear up their draught cards in public."[129]

During the late 1980s, the memories of the Vietnam years were sanitized (by television, by veteran's groups, by old radicals), their harsh edges minced down, and it is easy to forget how deep the division concerning the war ran in American society. Brothers literally were set against brothers, fathers against sons. The divisions were especially deep within the group called the Irish-Americans—a code name for Catholics of Irish extraction. Irish-Americans were the second-most privileged ethnic group in America, as measured by educational level, income, and prestige of the jobs they held (the only group that was more privileged were the members of the American Jewish community and, given that the memory of the Holocaust in Europe still burned, they were probably less psychologically secure in America in the 1960s than were the Irish-Americans).[130] In New York City, a large number of Irish-Americans had not quite made it up to the plateau of privilege, but held solid jobs as senior administrators in civic administration and the police force. They had little tolerance for demonstrators who combined anti-Americanism (as they saw it) with public obstruction and with disrespect for authority.[131]

Conor's intersection with an Irish-American cop's boot took place early in December in front of the Armed Forces Induction Center in Manhattan. There he and Maire joined Dr. Benjamin Spock, Allen Ginsberg, and a number of other demonstrators—estimates ran up to 2,500—in an attempt to block entry to the center. New York's mayor, John Lindsay, ordered full police protection for the center and thus about 3,000 police were in the immediate vicinity. So tightly were they packed around the building that Dr. Spock had to plead for an opening in their ranks so that he could sit on the entrance steps and be arrested. "Don't go! Don't go!" the demonstrators chanted, but none of the inducted turned away from the door. In response to the police orders to disperse, the demonstrators went limp and waited to be arrested. The police were not in a mood to be gentle. The mounted police drove their horses into the sitting group. Maire, who knew a great deal more about such things than did city-bred Conor, told him to lie still, because a horse has to be abused before it will step on a human being. She was right. The horses picked their way through. Soon, however, the foot policemen moved in. One of them—"no prizes for guessing his ethnicity," Conor would say later—a big middle-aged old pro, very skillfully kicked Conor in the hip, not enough to fracture his pelvis, but enough to keep him in pain for several months. Then Maire, Conor and 262 others were arrested.[132]

Maire was given bail quickly enough, but not Conor. A former student of his, Claudia Dreifus, discovered him in Bellevue Hospital (where she was a trade union organizer). She found him bloody, handcuffed, surrounded by police. She called Eileen Sheerin, Conor's administrative assistant, and Maire, but did not let Conor out of her sight until he was in safe hands.[133]

It took several months for Conor to recover fully, after a week in bed. He suffered no permanent damage. He and Maire continued to be seriously involved in anti-Vietnam War work, but they became slightly less keen. Increasingly, the radical wing of the antiwar movement was crossing the line between protest and violence. In 1968, students in dozens of universities used force, and not merely symbolically. Biker helmets became standard gear for the really committed, for confrontation now led to serious head-bashing by the police. The O'Briens, still active in the movement, were coming to the conclusion that America's problems ran much deeper than the Vietnam War and that these deeper problems could be dealt with only by Americans.[134]

• • •

Conor's energetic anti-imperialism had other facets than the anti-Vietnam War movement. In May 1966, he became chairman of the Irish Anti-Apartheid Movement. Most of the work was done by Kader Asmal, the vice-chairman, but Conor was more than a mere figurehead. During his summer holidays in Ireland, he worked for the group. In July 1966, he gave a lecture for the Irish Anti-Apartheid Movement that was subsequently published as *Ireland, the United Nations and Southern Africa*.[135] In New York, he was one of the sponsors of the Alexandra Defence Committee, an organization aiding victims of apartheid in South Africa. He helped the committee to draft their fund appeal and let his name be used on their letterhead.[136] Conor's opposition to apartheid was not limited to South Africa; it included the cognate forms of racial manipulation practiced in Rhodesia. He was particularly outspoken against the American government's implicit policy of hands-off South Africa and Rhodesia, based on the fear that to intervene in their racial arrangements would be to send them into the communist camp. To a fellow professor at NYU, who presented this argument to him, Conor replied, "I must make clear my own position: that if ending the caste system of white supremacy in South Africa and Rhodesia means 'loss to the West' of these areas, then I am in favour of their loss to the West."[137]

Conor's new major commitment in Africa in these years was Nigeria, specifically the part of eastern Nigeria that became known as Biafra. Nigeria had emerged from what was once British West Africa (Gambia, Sierra Leone, and Nigeria) with a strong economy, large oil reserves, and a tribal (or ethnic) split that had three major fractures: Ibo, Yoruba, and Hausa. The eastern region was mostly (but by no means entirely) Ibo and was also the region where most of the oil was found. As a state created by colonial rulers, rather than by natural unity, Nigeria was vulnerable to any political upset. Such upsets occurred in the federal election of 1964–65 when the Ibo-based parapolitical party refused to participate, believing that the federal government would be dominated by the largely Muslim and Hausa northern region. Talk of Ibo secession began. A military coup occurred in January 1966, the leader of which was an army major-general, an Ibo. He ruled Nigeria for only six months, and in July 1966, a countercoup took place. That was the beginning of the Nigerian civil war. Ibos living in the northern parts of Nigeria were killed—probably as many as 30,000 were massacred in northern Muslim towns. There was counterviolence by the Ibos, but they were the main victims of the civil unrest. Two million Ibos (of a Nigeria-wide tribal total of eight million) fled southward. In May 1967, Colonel Chukwuemeka Ojukwu, formerly governor of the eastern region of Nigeria, declared that area to be an independent nation, the Republic of Biafra.

Conor went to Biafra in mid-September 1967, to examine a land in the throes of civil war. His primary brief was to write pieces for the *Observer* and for the *New York Review of Books*. His main partner on this trip (and on a second journey to Biafra which he made in the spring of 1969) was Stanley Diamond. A poet, left-wing anthropologist, professor at the New School, Diamond was an expert on Africa and his views shaped Conor's outlook. Well before they left for Biafra, Diamond, Conor, and Audrey Chapman of Barnard College (who also made the 1967 journey) had set up a committee for the relief of Biafran refugees.[138] Conor was not going as an objective observer; as always, he was engaged, fully.

The journey itself was a courageous one. Trigger-happy sentries frequently blocked their way and the visitors easily could have become casualties. The *New York Review of Books* article was entitled "A Condemned People," and indicted the federal government of Nigeria for genocide and the West for its failure to report accurately what had occurred.[139] As Conor later summarized things in the *Listener*, "Whatever the official international observers say, I am convinced that genocide has taken place: that is, the deliberate and systematic massacre of persons belonging to a particular ethnic group, in conditions where the mere fact of belonging to that group carries the death sentence with it."[140]

Conor served as one of the trustees of the American Biafra Relief Services Foundation and as a patron of the American Committee to Keep Biafra Alive. He lobbied the State Department and politicians (Eugene McCarthy and Gerald Ford among them) and wrote to U Thant presenting the Biafran case.[141] When Conor went back to Biafra with Stanley Diamond in early April 1969, he found the genocide somewhat abated, the starvation horrendous. (Two of his articles on

Biafra, from 1967 and from 1969, are reprinted in the Anthology, Selections 24 and 26.) His *New York Review of Books* article on the second journey was one of the longest (and probably *the* longest) the periodical ever published.[142] In all of his writings, and in his private correspondence about Biafra, Conor continually argued that any analogy between Katanga and Biafra was misdrawn. Granted, each region was mineral-rich and part of a larger federal unity, but unlike the case of Katanga, Biafra was an instance of a genuine indigenously based independence movement. Conor was willing to point out one salient similarity, however: namely, that the imperial powers had weighed in on the wrong side. As Conor told the Irish Parliament in July 1969, "Great Britain ... shares with the Soviet Union the responsibility for what is being done to Biafra and Biafrans by the Nigerian government which is armed to the teeth by Britain and the Soviet Union."[143]

Instinctive and deep as was Conor's identification with the Ibo, the encounter with the Biafran problem was part of a longer-term rethinking of the character of Ireland. Eventually this rethinking changed the way many (perhaps most) Irish people today regard their history. Here is one of the clues to that reevaluation of Ireland: in a mid-term test that Conor gave to his undergraduate Literature and Society class at the beginning of November 1967—just at the time he was writing the first set of articles on Biafra—he placed at the top of the examination sheet the following quotation from Edmund Burke: "To love the little platoon we belong to in society is the first (the germ as it were) of public affections." An essay was to be written on that quotation, using it to reflect on contemporary realities. "Some relevant categories and concepts are: nation, tribe, Zionism, Black Power, chauvinism and fascism, assimilation, detribalization and the ideal of planetary man."[144]

To define "the little platoon" was to ask which groups are legitimate, which congeries of people deserve our loyalty and our love. That, for Conor, was an inevitably Irish question, as was almost everything else he thought about. As Christopher Hitchens perceptively wrote: "He has taken the subject of colonialism and anticolonialism for his own and, as was once famously said in *The Eighteenth Brumaire*, has translated each new language back into the language of his birth."[145] Conor at this point was in the early stages of a revolution in Irish historiography, one which would eventually lead him to the conclusion that modern Irish nationalism, in its insistence on forcing national unity upon the Ulster Protestants, was (like the Nigerian federal authorities in spirit, if not in action) ineluctably and rebarbatively imperialistic.

Conor had already taken the first steps down this radical road when he accepted an invitation of the energetic and creative Owen Dudley Edwards to participate in a special supplement of the *Irish Times* planned for the fiftieth anniversary of the Easter Rising of 1916. (This piece is reproduced in full in the Anthology, Selection 18.) The fulcrum of the essay, "The Embers of Easter," was a terribly unsettling question. "If Pearse and Connolly could have had a foresight of the Ireland of 1966 would they have gone with that high courage to certain death?"[146] More baldly: was it all worth it? The answer was not at all easy to give, Conor explained. Certainly James Connolly "who knew his Belfast" would not have been surprised that the country still was partitioned. What would come as a surprise to him was that when Ireland became a member of the United Nations, successive governments did not raise the matter of partition in the General Assembly. The Catholic Church (which did not want to be associated with communist countries who certainly would support any antipartition resolution) was nothing if not vague; and the British and the Americans would have been seriously annoyed. So, upon entry into the United Nations, the Irish government tacitly dropped the old antipartition campaign and thus implicitly accepted the permanence (albeit not the legitimacy) of Northern Ireland. This, Conor argued, had a terrible psychological impact on his own generation, for it had grown up believing in the national creed of one Ireland, but had been forced to accept a divided Ireland as a reality. Thus, the generation was defined by the value system in which they had been indoctrinated, as failures. Similarly, the idea of a Gaelic Ireland, culturally and linguistically, had been abandoned in practice while still honored in rhetoric. "We were bred to be patriotic, only to find that there was nothing to be patriotic about; we were republicans of a republic that wasn't there." For Conor's generation "a desperate game of let's pretend" was played, a game unsettling and dispiriting.

So, for Conor, the fiftieth anniversary of the Easter Rising was a time of commemoration but not a time of celebration. "The national objective of Pearse and Connolly is now finally and necessarily buried."

This strong (and in the context of Ireland of the mid-1960s), heretical essay revealed that Conor had come a long way since his days working for Sean MacBride. ("The present writer blushes to recall that at one time he devoted a considerable part of his professional activity as a member of the Department of External Affairs, to what was known as 'anti-partition.' The only positive result of this activity as far as I was concerned, was that it led me to discover the cavernous inanities of 'anti-partition' and of government propaganda generally.")[147] In May 1966, Conor was asked to become a patron of the National Democratic Group, a mildly nationalist, nonsectarian student organization at the Queen's University of Belfast. In reply to the invitation, he spelled out what were then his views on the matter of Irish unity:

First of all, I believe that the roots of Irish disunity go very deep indeed.

Second, I believe that Ireland is unlikely to be reunited without major changes inside both parts of the country and probably in Britain as well.

Thirdly, I believe that pressure from the Twenty-Six Counties on the Six—whether it be military, diplomatic or propagandist—has negative effects only.

Fourthly, I believe in the promotion of contacts between people in the North and South and in the cultivation of common interests, economic, social and cultural. ...[148]

Conor, who already had more experience in the North than did most southern Irish writers and politicians, kept in touch with northern development. In July 1966, he, Maire, Conor's daughter Kate, and Deirdre Levinson, a colleague at NYU, went to Belfast for the Twelfth celebrations of the Orange Order, commemorating the victory of William of Orange over the Catholic absolutist James II in 1690. They stayed with Conor's former father-in-law, Alec Foster, and went to the Field at Finaghy. "Come along and see a tribal ritual enacted," was the way Conor had phrased the invitation to Deirdre, but that was misleadingly blithe. She recalled that he was thoroughly depressed by the Orange performance. Only when the party crossed the border back into the south did Conor change. He was not a happy man in the North, but in an unpublished essay that he wrote describing the Twelfth he got one main point dead right (and another one dead wrong). The correct observation, one that had major implications for the future, was that the Protestant youth seemed to be becoming more politicized, or at least more Orange. There were more "younger brethren" than usual, and also more young girls. "They were dressed like teenagers in any big city on a summer outing, except that their straw hats carried slogans like 'No surrender' and 'Paisley.' Their songs were also regional. One sweet young thing, with a Botticelli face and vacant eyes, was inviting Fenians to kiss her Orange arse."[149] What Conor missed (as did virtually every other commentator of the time) was the vulnerability of northern unionism. At the time, Protestant supremacy appeared unshakable.

That soon changed in the late 1960s, with the advent of the Northern Ireland civil rights movement. Conor immediately aligned himself with it. He and Paul O'Dwyer, a longtime nationalist activist in the United States, became co-presidents in late 1969 of the Northern Ireland Civil Rights Association in America.[150] In January 1969, in the *Irish Times*, he wrote an optimistic endorsement of the future in the North, and gave two pieces of unsolicited advice to southern governmental authorities and to young idealists: that the republic's governmental authorities should work only in private in pressing London and the Northern Ireland government to act. To young student idealists, those who were themselves fed up with sectarian divisions in Ulster, he suggested that they should nevertheless understand that religion in Northern Ireland was more important than they reckoned and that it could be ignored only at peril.[151]

The mixture of passion, cold-eyed analysis, insight, and self-contradictory attitudes on Northern Ireland that Conor evinced in this period is hardly a failing. The Northern Ireland situation was developing more quickly and in more dimensions than anyone predicted. Thus, it is not surprising to find Conor mixing together his support for the Northern Ireland civil rights movement and his opposition to the war in Vietnam. For instance, when he and the nationalist MP and civil rights leader Austin Currie spoke at a rally at the University of Pennsylvania in mid-March 1968, Conor melded everything into a sincere, but unreflective, mass. "Any Irishman who supports the Vietnam War is in my opinion denying the struggle for freedom of the Irish people."[152] At that point a "red-headed Irishman" stood up and said that he would not stand for that sort of talk and then walked out, followed by two others. In a later part of this same speech, Conor defined Ulster unionism as demeaning and as opposed to human dignity. "The Civil Rights movement is part of the great world struggle for social reform and change. Anyone who denies civil rights for negroes [in the United States] also denies civil rights for the Irish [in Ulster]."[153]

A lot was going on here, and it was not well controlled. In early 1969, we are seeing, under the pressure of the civil rights campaign, Conor wrestling with the same question that he had begun to work with in the less-fraught mid-1960s: what, after all, is Ireland?

• • •

From mid-1965 to mid-1968, Conor's life encompassed an immense amount of work, a staggering amount of travel, a good deal of political activity, pedagogic brilliance, and some very important writing. The projects that were completed were impressive indeed.

Yet, there is in these years a hint of malaise, of dreams touched but not realized. The number of projects Conor planned but did not complete is revealing. In 1961, soon after completing *To Katanga and Back*, he had accepted a commission to produce a study of Anglo-Irish literature. ("I shall begin with Ossian," he told a reporter, "who was neither Anglo, nor Irish, nor literature.")[154] Nothing came of this. Early in 1966, he proposed to his old editor and friend, Dan Davin, now secretary to the Syndics of Oxford University Press, a book of 200–250 pages on the relationship of Burke and Marx. "Burke is always casting veils over things," he told Davin, "while Marx is always ripping veils off."[155] Yes, we are interested, was Davin's immediate reply.[156] But again, no book appeared, although Conor did some interesting shorter pieces concerning Burke and Marx (see the Anthology, Selection 21). Later in the same year, Conor was confessing to his agent Elaine Greene that, "The Africa book, I have done nothing about."[157] This referred to a contract he had entered into in late 1965 and eventually failed to fulfill.[158] In July 1967, Conor signed with Aldous Books to write a 10,000 word essay on antiromanticism and reaction.[159] But this did not see the light either.

Another symptom that, even while being lionized in New York, Conor was not at ease, is that almost from his day of arrival, he was potentially on the move. Before his years at NYU, he and Maire had talked about going to work in Poland or some Eastern bloc country.[160] Now they considered more up-market possibilities. In late 1965, as Noel Annan's provostship of King's College, Cambridge, was drawing to a close, some of the fellows asked Conor to permit his name to be put forward. He agreed, surmising, correctly, that the chances of his election were slim.[161] Closer to home, in the spring of 1967, he and Maire went to see friends at the State University of New York at Stony Brook. At the time this was designated as the flagship of the New York State public university system, and for a time it bid fair to become a major institution. There Conor had some serious discussions of the possibility of an appointment. His terms for such a move included taking some of his teaching staff and his administrative assistant, Eileen Sheerin, with him. This move did not work out, but it was discussed seriously for the 1967–68 academic year.[162] In the late summer of 1967, George Steiner asked him if it were true, as the rumor had it, that he had applied for the chair of English at Trinity College, Dublin.[163] Conor replied that it was not true, "though, as you know, I would like to go back to Dublin some time, but am in no hurry."[164] Soon after that, he was writing to Asa Briggs, vice-chancellor of the University of Sussex, to say that he was interested in a post he had seen advertised, namely, the directorship of Sussex's new Institute for the Study of International Relationships.[165]

All high-profile academics are courted, and in the great educational boom of the 1960s, a star always was in demand. Conor, like most human beings (and especially academics and intellectuals), loves to be petted, flattered, praised. Fair enough. This desire to be sought after by academic institutions was also a continuation of a pattern that went back to his undergraduate days. Conor had worked his way through university by taking examinations and winning prizes. He believed (and still believes today) that university examination systems are fairly accurate assessments of intellectual worth.

But behind all that was the fact that he and Maire did not fit in to New York City. The two of them remember, with the same delight that a once-parched person remembers a glass of ice water, escaping whenever possible to Canada. They took short trips north whenever they could and Conor accepted almost any Canadian invitation he received. Canada felt more like home. In Montreal they could enjoy French language and culture, and also deal with the old Anglo set; in English Canada, a place that in the mid-1960s had not yet lost its ties with the Old World, they found people who acted like the friends at home with whom they had grown up.

New York City—and, actually, America—just was not home. Doctor Johnson once said that when a man was tired of London he was tired of life. Conor increasingly came to the view that when a man tired of New York City, he was ready for civilization. "I lived in New York for some years," he told Dail Eireann in 1971, "and it has the sad distinction of being one of the most polluted cities in the world both in regard to water and air. The air pollution was such that the act of breathing during certain days of the summer months was accompanied by a positive sensation of disgust and discomfort." This was an indication not of a technical problem, but of a cultural one. "In New York, as distinct from London, there is a strong tradition of unrestricted free enterprise. One does not interfere with business if it can be avoided. ... In London and Paris, as in most European cities, there is a tradition of public responsibility and control and the public interest coming first and of the right to control anti-social activities by business enterprises being firmly asserted." His fear was that Ireland would "drift more in the New York direction, that is to say to let business rip."[166]

Yet, it was the provincialism of America, the unconscious, but almost all-pervasive belief that America was the hub of the universe, that most vexed Conor and made him realize he could never fit. For someone who knew European literature, who was fluent in French and Russian and could read several other languages, and who was conversant with geopolitics on a world scale, the naive Americocentric view of life—which, if anything, was more pronounced among the intellectual *haute bourgeois* of Manhattan than in the cornfields of southern Iowa—was almost pitiable.

In December 1969, shortly after Conor had left New York to move home to Ireland, he returned to New York to give a delightfully off-beat talk to the annual banquet of the National Emergency Civil Liberties

Committee. Entitled "America First, or Varieties of Americocentrism," it is vintage O'Brien in its mixture of the personal and the general. As in all of Conor's best rhetoric, he used anecdote to get his audience off guard. He began with a simple *mise en scène*:

> I was a resident in the United States from 1965 to the early summer of this year, when I returned to Ireland to live, and I still hold—though not for much longer—the little green card of the resident alien.
>
> Coming back here to speak at this gathering, I was told at the American Embassy in Dublin that I did not require a visa; I could come in on my little green card. When I presented myself at Immigration at Kennedy airport, I had to explain why, though technically a resident alien, I had become, as it were, more alien than resident. The officers who questioned me were gentle and polite with, in their manner, an indefinable compound of the baffled, the compassionate and the faintly alarmed. It reminded me of something which I could not for the moment place. Then I got it—I came from a Catholic country, and the manner of these Immigration officers reminded me, in its full range, of a sympathetic Catholic priest trying to find out why someone has stopped going to mass.

Then, having induced his audience to smile, to lower its guard, he moved quickly:

> It also reminded me, this manner, of something else of the demeanour of some of my American left-wing friends—of whom I love, I am glad to say, a great many—when I told them this Spring that I was resigning from New York University and going back to Ireland to run in politics. Now the Immigration officers and these friends were very unlike in other ways. The Immigration officers were, I believe, patriotic Americans in a traditional and unquestioning way. My friends were all, in different ways, in revolt against the forces that dominate America today. The first group would sincerely regard the second as anti-American. Yet the two groups have more in common than they know. They are both in the grip of an Americocentrism of which they are not fully conscious. All members of the first group approve of foreigners loving America; the members of the second approve of foreigners hating America. The concept that there are many millions of foreigners who never think of America at all—and many who never even heard of it—would strike most members of both groups as unlikely, suspect and generally unsatisfactory.[167]

There was more, a good deal more. It was not the language of one who wanted a noyade, for Conor liked many individual Americans very much. But he could not live in a culture that was the equivalent of the Flat Earth Society.

There was one nigglingly pragmatic aspect of Conor's increasing discomfort in the United States. For a time, he refused to file his income taxes, as a protest against the Vietnam War. That did not have much financial impact, because almost all of the tax that he owed was automatically taken out of his university pay check, but it gave the U.S. government a handle against him if they wished. As a foreign national, he was particularly vulnerable. There was always the possibility that after one of his foreign trips he would be denied readmission to the United States. That is one of the reasons, as he explained to Asa Briggs, that he was considering academic posts in other countries.[168]

• • •

Recall that from the late spring of 1968 onward, Conor let the administrative and teaching side of his Literature and Society program slide. That is a diagnostic item, and we do not need to understand fully its causes to accept it as a warning flag that something was going on. Also, recall that (as discussed in chapter 7) in 1967 and 1968, while producing *The United Nations: Sacred Drama* and *Murderous Angels*, Conor was indirectly, but vigorously, trying to resolve his relationship to his Holy Mother Church, the United Nations, and to the father-figures of his life, his own Da, and Dag Hammarskjold. Further, he was wrestling in several ways with his own identity as an Irishman (in the Yeats essays and especially in the "Embers of Easter" piece), all the while being more and more repelled by U.S. governmental imperialism and by America's cultural parochialism. Thus, a wide range of powerful forces was whirling through Conor's life, which had the potential to come together to form a cyclone that could destroy him psychologically, or, alternately deposit him safely in some far and distant place.

One final force came into play and this completed the whirlwind: Conor and Maire's marriage came under a great deal of stress. William Trevor recently has written with great wisdom of the difficulties of trying to understand the marriage of his own father and mother. "What children of a marriage rarely witness is the nature of the love that brought the whole thing—themselves included—into being in the first place. The marriage of parents is almost always mysterious; the sensual elements scarcely bear thinking about, the romantic past is only to be guessed at, and all such curiosity invariably comes too late."[169] Even less can a biographer reconstruct the everyday quality, much less the mysterious, sensual, painful, and destructive aspects of any marriage. But, that admitted, during the 1960s, especially in the NYU years, I think that the marriage was troubled.

Conor and Maire still were very much in love, however. In bad moods, Maire would tell Conor that he never really loved her, only her father's exalted position in the Irish government, but that was not true. He had loved her, still did, and if passion had changed to partnership (with Conor always the senior partner), that was not a failing, merely an evolution. If they fought viciously verbally when having taken too much drink, it was a mixture of Billingsgate and high-culture insult that they half-enjoyed as well-matched fighters. The fights, like their marriage, made sense. The great balance wheel of the relationship was that Maire expressed both the romantic in Conor and a sort of mad Irishness, right back to the sagas, that he was attracted to, but had a hard time expressing for himself.

Was there violence? As far as I can tell—and I have talked to a lot of their intimates—Conor never used physical force, no matter how nasty the verbal duels became. Maire occasionally beat on Conor (and once in a while on any of his friends who were caught, literally, in the middle) with her fists or with a tin tray, but it was in a ritual way, not doing any real damage. Conor took this with the same head-bowed, mildly amused smile that he would have worn if he were being buffeted by a weak girl with a large pillow.

And between these moments of aggravation, they worked well together. They went on peace marches and entertained students and NYU staff and visitors to Conor's program. Maire frequently helped with Conor's writing, as in the case of his edition of Burke's *Reflections on the Revolution in France*, for which she prepared the annotations. The marriage was a traditional Irish patriarchal arrangement, and that, for a woman of Maire's great talent, sometimes was hard to bear. But I don't think that was the problem, since they both had been raised in Irish culture in a time when such things were not questioned.

Nor were Conor and Maire doing any 1960s silliness with chemicals. The two of them must be the only two Manhattan intellectuals to go through the 1960s and never use any drugs other than Valium (which Conor has not used for decades now). Alcohol was another matter. "They drank too much," was the almost universal judgment of those around them at the time, but this is the opinion of Americans who do not understand Irish drinking standards. Wine and beer were Conor's choice in the period and wine was Maire's. Later, in the 1980s, Conor turned into a whiskey drinker. In the 1960s, Conor probably was a borderline alcoholic and later he became a real one, but one of a special type, and this needs sorting out here. If, before his marriage to Maire, he was occasionally an idiotic drinker—getting sick at the table at diplomatic functions—after the marriage his drinking was almost entirely a managed affair, a ritual part of his day. Only rarely did it interfere with his work, because work—not alcohol—has always been his real addiction. Even in the 1980s, when he became a serious spirits drinker, his intake was controlled, if high. His working day—even in his late seventies—is as follows: at his desk writing, between 6 and 8 A.M.; write continuously, with a lunch break and a walk, until 5:00 P.M.; then two pints at the local, half a bottle of claret at dinner, several post prandial whiskeys, and then, with slurred speech, slightly whirling vision, and a wobbly walk, off to bed, to sleep soundly and wake and work early the next morning. This seven days a week. The point is that what Conor's New York friends perceived as too much drinking may have been so from a textbook point of view, but it was part of a pattern that allowed him to work more intensively, and for longer periods of time, than all but a few writers. Alcohol has served the same purpose for him that going to the squash court or doing gardening has served for others, and though the medical profession might shudder, it has been a winning formula. Conor has stayed in good health and performed at a high level of intellectual productivity for longer than all the medical doctors who told him to shape up.

I think that the reason the marriage was troubled was family. Conor and Maire desperately wanted to have biological children of their own. Conor was forty-five and Maire forty when they were married, and they began at once to try to have children, but without success. Eventually they went through the battery of tests and examinations associated with infertility, tests that are supposed to be clinically neutral but inevitably are an invasive indignity and raise anxieties and tensions.

By the time they arrived at New York University, Conor and Maire were keen on adopting children. Their earliest inquiries were made in December 1965, when Conor told Jonathan Mirsky, then a new friend and a prospective colleague, that "Maire and I have decided that we want to adopt a Vietnamese war orphan. We think that the best way of doing this would be through the Friends or through some group or organization recommended by them."[170] Did Mirsky know of any person or group with whom they could communicate on this matter? He replied by giving them the name and address of Pearl Buck, the Nobel Prize-winning novelist, who had a longtime interest in the welfare of Asian children.[171]

At the same time adoption inquiries were being made, another set of family matters intensified the stress on the O'Briens' marriage. Conor had stayed in close touch with each of his three children (the files for the 1960s are full of chatty, charming letters back and forth to the kids). He paid school fees and supported the children financially. Now, in the 1960s, Donal was married and on his way to being a first-rank

Africanist. He and his wife Rita went from Berkeley to London where he worked on his Ph.D. (As a father, Conor had given Donal some pungent advice about the London School of Economics: Michael Oakeshott "is a fraud and is apt to attract other frauds," and Ernest Gellner "strikes some faintly suspicious chord, but I can't say what.")[172] Donal and Rita did field research in Senegal in 1966–67, and Donal received his Ph.D. in 1969.[173] The second of the children of Conor's first marriage, Fedelma, was a student at Trinity College, Dublin, reading modern history. She received her undergraduate degree at about the same time Donal received his doctorate and in fact did some key research for Conor concerning the family origins of Edmund Burke. After university she married Nicholas Simms, son of the beloved Protestant archbishop of Dublin, George Otto Simms. Both Fedelma and Donal had been old enough during the divorce between Conor and Christine to be able to take matters in stride.

Not Kate, the youngest. She had been only thirteen and highly vulnerable. Kate has become a distinguished short story writer (winner of the Rooney Prize and the Hennessy Award) and one hopes that someday she will do a memoir of these painful, but pivotal, years in her own life. It is clear that she was hurt by her parent's divorce and was working out how she should feel toward each of them, and toward Maire. Her work at secondary schools was uneven, and she was not putting together a good enough academic record to gain admission to an Irish or British university. For Conor, the idea that one of his offspring might not take a university degree was unthinkable: academic accolades, if possible, but academic certification at minimum are the prerequisites to the entry to civilized society. New York University seemed a perfect opportunity to repair Kate's deficits. As the daughter of a NYU professor, she was eligible for free tuition. So, for 1965–66, Kate, aged seventeen and admitted as a part-time student to NYU, was to live with Conor and Maire in New York City.

It did not work out well. Kate, who was not a keen student, was homesick for Ireland and very unhappy. Also she thought she was overweight. Kate recalls, "I was barred from class because I refused to have my weight checked and my photograph taken. I was very fat at the time and didn't want anyone to notice."[174] She then developed an eating disorder and became anorexic. Kate spent most of the year living not with Conor and Maire, but with Deirdre Levinson, who was at that time on the staff of the NYU English Department.

All this put increased strain on the marriage and, in Maire's view, it was on the verge of coming apart. Conor and Maire continued to try to adopt a Vietnamese child, but by the spring of 1967 they had made no headway and had given up. "We are now considering adopting an American child," Conor wrote to an acquaintance, "probably a coloured one, as these have the greatest difficulties in getting adopted."[175] Conor and Maire began dealing with the Catholic Home Bureau for Dependent Children in New York City. Maire, as a declared Catholic, had to have her parish priest fill out and directly mail in to the adoption worker a questionnaire about her religious suitability.[176] Conor, being an agnostic, was spared this particular inquisition. One of the workers they encountered at the agency put this question to them. "Do you insist on white children?" (Most white adoptive parents in America at that time did.) Their answer was no, we have lived in Africa and have no racial prejudice.

Later in the process, a different adoption worker rephrased the question. "Why do you want to adopt colored children?"

A short pause—and then, before either of the O'Briens could answer, she added, "Why don't you get an ocelot instead?"[177]

The process dragged on, and it became clear that nothing was going to happen. Conor and Maire were not quite the sort of people whom the adoption service approved of; and in their turn, the O'Briens could not tolerate the mixture of righteousness and racism among the adoption workers.

Nevertheless, the ill-intended question of the adoption worker bears consideration. Any white couple that adopts a black child is making some kind of a statement, however unconscious. I think, however, that Maire and Conor each were making different statements. Conor would have been equally happy with a baby of any race, for he is color blind. But Maire had a very strong positive valence toward African-ancestry children. She had fallen in love with the children of Ghana, not in any patronizing way, but rather in the way an innocent to the world's great art may by chance enter an art gallery and be bowled over by a world of beautiful things she had never known existed. One needs to read her magnificent anthem in Irish to the African-ancestry son they eventually adopted to realize how strong the valence was: "Little clustered head sweet as the blackberry," it began. (The entire poem is found in chapter 11.)

When the O'Briens returned home to Ireland for the summer of 1968, they were dispirited about the adoption matter and distracted by all the swirl that was taking place in Conor's life. Fortunately, they talked to one of Maire's uncles, the Right Rev. Monsignor Maurice Browne, parish priest of Ballymore Eustace, County Kildare, a man unbesmirched by unctuous holiness. He had been a great breeder of racing greyhounds, and when that cheerless episcopal monolith, John Charles McQuaid, had told him to get rid of the dogs, he had done so, but had replaced them with a large painting of the finish of a greyhound race in which one of the dominant spectators at the finish line was His Grace, John Charles. Father Browne, then in his mid-seventies, was the picture-perfect wise priest, white-haired, kindly, a bit worldly, and he made a practical suggestion. Why not adopt a child in Ireland? And if they wanted a child of mixed race, so much the better. In Ireland, these children were especially difficult adoption placements. He would make inquiries.

The result was that in the middle of the summer, 1969, Conor and Maire became the adoptive parents of a boy, half-Ghanaian, half-Irish: Sean Patrick (known as Patrick from earliest days), born 18 May 1968. The adoption process was very stressful, in large part because of the O'Briens' special situation under Irish law. The big problem was that they were not legally married in Ireland, despite the fact that their union had been celebrated in a Catholic ceremony. In this instance, Irish law literally was more popish than the pope, for the Republic of Ireland did not recognize any form of dissolution of marriage—even a papal dissolution was not acceptable! So they were in the midst of the following conundrum: (1) Conor still was legally married to Christine under Irish civil law; (2) Conor, in Catholic canon law, never had been validly married to Christine, as they had been joined in a non-Catholic ceremony and therefore his marriage to Maire in canon law was valid; (3) Maire was validly married to Conor in Catholic canon law, but (4) she was not validly married to Conor in Irish civil law, since his wife of the first marriage still was alive, and marriages are indissoluble. That was the situation if anybody, a civil servant or adoption worker, had wanted to press hard. But Ireland is a small country and Maire's having one uncle who had been a beloved parish priest, another a priest and a university president, another a cardinal, and a father who was a long-serving Fianna Fail front bencher and former deputy prime minister, and still a sitting member of the Dail—well, no one was going to press too hard.

Nevertheless, the O'Briens protected themselves by having a lawyer act as an intermediary with the biological mother of Patrick and contractual arrangements made their irregular marital status irrelevant as far as the validity of the adoption was concerned. (They followed the same precaution when they adopted Margaret, also half-African, half-Irish, in 1971). The national adoption review panel approved the adoption and, finally, the pieces of their life were coming together. They would have a child of their own and Conor, who was just then working out his own relationship to male authority, was himself once again a father, once again bending the bow of a young son's life.

Then they hit a vexing legal snag. Under Irish law, adoptions did not become final until a child was six months old, and until that age the law said that the child could not be issued a passport or taken from the country. It was Conor and Maire's belief that these regulations were not usually enforced, but that they were in this case through a direct order of the minister of external affairs and tanaiste, Frank Aiken.[178] That meant that Patrick could not be taken out of Ireland until mid-November at the earliest. Conor, on very short notice, told the authorities of New York University of his problem and requested a half-year's sabbatical. With immense generosity they immediately agreed.

Out of this legal snag came one nice side event, besides the sabbatical at home in Ireland. Maire, through her family political contacts, talked to Miss Marie O'Kelly, private secretary to the aged Eamon de Valera, who was at that time the president of Ireland (a ceremonial post, as distinct from the taoiseach, the prime minister). De Valera called the foreign minister on the O'Briens' behalf, but could not get him to budge. However, President de Valera rang the O'Briens at their home in Howth and asked them to come up to Aras an Uachtarain in the Phoenix Park and to bring infant Patrick with them. Maire, who took the call, asked, "And when should we come?"

"At our age," replied President de Valera, who was in his mid-eighties, "it doesn't do to put off a pleasure." He concluded: "Come tomorrow."

The meeting was charming, with President and Mrs. de Valera saying all the right things about the infant and serving champagne in honor of the occasion. De Valera, a deeply metaphysical intellect, had not paid all that much attention in life to things such as children, and he had little experience with adopted children. He had, however, read some place that mothers should not drink, because brain damage or alcohol dependency could result from the infant's taking too much alcohol in his mother's milk. Proceeding syllogistically, as he often did, he applied the general law to the particular case. "I suppose under present conditions you must not want this," he said to Maire, while filling everyone else's champagne glass.[179]

Several pictures were taken on this occasion and here is Conor's later description of one of them: "I am talking to de Valera, and he is listening intently, with an expression on his face of something resembling horror. I'm not quite sure why this should be, but I think I was talking about his native city of New York; in many ways an alarming subject, especially at that time."[180]

That was not a throwaway line, and in substance it accurately reflects something that was haunting Conor in the autumn of 1968. He walked on the hill of Howth and looked down on Dublin Bay, and he realized that he was within a half-hour of one of the British Isles' better research libraries at TCD, and that in Dublin he was able (in those, alas, departed days) to go any place, at any time of day or night without fear of mugging. And he had to ask himself, is not the old civilization preferable to the new barbarism? Do we really wish to raise our son in New York City?

This question had a sharp edge because of Patrick's mixed heritage. In America, he would be perceived as black, and only as black, Conor knew. And Conor knew full well the long history of serious racial violence and of systemic discrimination in the United States. The year 1968 was a particularly tense time in American racial relations. Martin Luther King had been assassinated in early April. There were major riots in Detroit in August, and New York, Los Angeles, and Chicago faced serious trouble. Blacks and whites were becoming increasingly polarized. Julian Mayfield, the Ghanaian novelist and one of the people whom Conor brought to teach in the Literature and Society program in 1968–69, publicly expressed the fear that an impending white backlash would reach such a pitch that the blacks of America would be extirpated just as were the European Jews.[181]

That this was a near-paranoid vision is beside the point: Conor and Maire, who were plugged into the intellectual elite of the New York black community, picked up on both the fear running through the general black community, and the reactive racism that increasingly was emanating from African-American groups. A decade later, Conor phrased the situation this way:

Ten years ago, in New York, Los Angeles, and elsewhere, there was an atmosphere of civil war between black and white. My wife and I and our adopted son—then only a few months old—were involved in that war. Patrick is of mixed race: half African, half Irish. By American terminology, though not by African, he is black. We feared for him, and for ourselves, if we went on living in New York. We were afraid not so much of the whites, whom we could handle, as of the blacks, whom we could not. We were afraid that black militants would teach Patrick that he ought to hate us, his white parents, and so destroy us all. There were many reasons why we decided to leave New York, but that was the deepest of them.[182]

Almost certainly Conor and Maire decided to leave New York City not after the spring of 1969, but before they went back to New York after adopting Patrick. I suspect that the decision effectively was made while they still were in Ireland in the autumn and early winter of 1968. This is implied by the announcement just before Christmas, 1968, in the *Observer* and several Irish newspapers that Conor's career was to take another turn. He had joined the Irish Labour party and would be returning from New York to fight for a Labour seat in the next Dail election. If he won, he would come back permanently to Ireland. ("If all this comes off, he could make a future Irish Prime Minister," the *Observer* noted, and quickly added, "which would probably be the most dramatic thing to have happened in Ireland since St. Patrick."[183] The details of the political negotiations that led to this decision to run for office are discussed in chapter 10, but the obvious point is that they took a while. Conor had to have been working them out since the early autumn 1968.

He wrote to his administrative assistant Eileen Sheerin (who virtually single-handedly was administering the Literature and Society program in Conor's extended absence), "I think I should probably tell Bill Buckler [formerly dean of NYU's Washington Square College and now vice-chancellor for academic planning] what is afoot and what it may imply as far as NYU is concerned."[184] That was after Christmas, when his plans had been in the Irish and British newspapers. Revealingly, in his original dictation, Conor had said "I think I shall probably tell Bill Buckler," implying mere calculation. In hand, he corrected the draft to read, "I think I should tell" implying a certain sense of probity. The first draft was closer to the mark. Conor told Buckler about his arrangements in Irish politics and that NYU might be deprived of his services. Hence "irrespective of the outcome of this political interest, the university might wish to appoint a successor for 1970–71," and therefore he would resign if that were desirable from the university's point of view. All this was honorable, if a bit late in coming, but the disingenuous point about Conor's communication was a statement that if he did not win a parliamentary seat in Ireland he would like to continue at NYU.[185]

This implied a commitment to NYU that really was not there. Conor and Maire took advantage of the university's generosity by not returning to New York until the end of January 1969, even though Patrick's adoption was final and his passport all arranged before Christmas, 1968. When the three of them came to New York ("we are just about settling in with the new baby, who doesn't yet seem quite sure that Columbus had the right idea"), Conor was charm itself.[186] He visited the various powers, gave them books, kept everyone happy. It is a measure of his charisma that when he resigned the Schweitzer Chair, the university authorities, far from jumping on him for the cavalier way he had let his program slide in his last year, celebrated him. Conor gave a valedictory lecture on 23 April 1969 at which the university's president, James M. Hester, presided and praised Conor's achievements. Conor gave a splendid lecture, a mixture of a discussion of Machiavelli's *The Prince*, with a personal apologia, a denunciation of American imperialism, and, as always, a good exit line. A fine mimic, Conor ended this way: "I thank you all and it is not without a real pang of regret that I must use [here he began to flounce just a touch] the once-famous words [and here his voice became whiskey-dark] of Greta Garbo: ay tank ay go home."[187]

They loved it, and he left the great majority of his students and associates at NYU with fond, if not serene, memories. But was Conor really so sure of his election to Dail Eireann that he would resign his star professorship? Public resignation means no return. Was he really running for the Dail without a safety net?

That is what he told the newspapers, but I think he had an insurance policy, and it does not require any great feat of archaeological detection to uncover it.[188] Conor, who had visited Montreal several times during his NYU years, was negotiating for the position of principal and vice-chancellor of Sir George Williams University in that city. This was an English-language institution, formerly a night- and continuing-education school, which was moving quickly toward becoming a full-line university. It was overshadowed by the major Anglo institution, McGill University, but its niche in Montreal was expanding. There were plans (realized in 1974) to merge with another English-language institution, Loyola College of Montreal, to form the second largest Anglo university in the province of Quebec. This was a good situation professionally and, equally important, it was in Montreal, the most European and cosmopolitan city in North America, a place that Conor and Maire appreciated. Each of them was fluently bilingual in French and English. They loved the architecture of the Old City of Montreal which recalled European styles before the era of industrialization, and they were able to relax and dander about, in the knowledge that they could go most places in Montreal in complete safety. There was at that time virtually no black-white problem in Montreal, certainly nothing to approach the tensions of New York. In other words, it would be a very good place to raise young Patrick.

The board of governors of Sir George Williams offered Conor the top post, with an annual salary of $35,000 (Canadian) per year, plus an expense account limited only by the requirement that he obtain board approval for any single expense item in excess of $1,000. The board understood Conor's situation in Ireland and (although they put it more delicately), if he lost the election they would be happy to have him as principal and vice-chancellor.[189] In the actual event, when on 18 June 1969, the dice were cast, he was successful: so Conor became not the head of a Canadian university, but an Irish parliamentarian.

Conor's years in New York City in many ways were very successful, and in even more ways, highly eventful. But he would have been out of New York by the autumn of 1969 in any case. He and New York never really suited each other. He was too worldly wise to be overawed, too courageous to be quiet. Still, he had some good days in the New York sun, particulate polluted though they were. In 1973, a bit more than four years after Conor had returned to Ireland, the *New York Review of Books*, the one product of the New York intellectuals that had moved out of the 1960s and into the 1970s with style, substance, intellectual integrity, and a cosmopolitan outlook (which is to say that its editors recognized that European and African culture existed), published its tenth anniversary issue. This special edition's cover listed all of the heavyweights—a virtual transatlantic all-star team—who contributed to the issue.

Edmund Wilson
I.F. Stone • Isaiah Berlin
Stuart Hampshire
Gore Vidal • Conor O'Brien
Elizabeth Hardwick
Susan Sontag • Robert Craft
V.S. Pritchett
Henry Steele Commager
H.R. Trevor-Roper
Ada Louise Huxtable
Christopher Lasch
W.H. Auden • David Levine [190]

Thus, Conor left behind at least one monument in the kingdom of the New York intellectuals.

PART 4

AN IRISH PATRIOT

CHAPTER 10

"HAD LIFE BEEN NORMAL": 1969–1972

In April 1969, a young lad at Summerhill College in Sligo wrote to Conor in New York. He had been assigned to write on behalf of his class in connection with a civics project. "I wish to know, with your kind co-operation, if you smoke a pipe, cigarettes or cigars, and if so, what quantity do you consume on a daily average? Hopefully, awaiting your reply."[1] Conor already was back in Ireland and his administrative assistant, Eileen Sheerin, replied: "Dr. O'Brien has gone back to Dublin where he will stand for election as a Labour candidate on June 18 next. I can tell you, however, that not only does Dr. O'Brien not smoke a pipe, cigars, or cigarettes, but he has never done so in his life. He thinks it is healthier not to smoke at all."[2]

Ms. Sheerin did not add, nor, indeed, could she have known, that being an Irish politician in 1969 and in the years immediately thereafter was to become a considerably greater risk to one's health than burning tobacco leaves. Not that Conor would have paid any attention to a health warning even if it had been attached to his nomination papers. As Brendan Halligan, general secretary of the Irish Labour party at the time noted, "had life been normal, Conor would have gotten bored."[3]

In these years, Conor increasingly relied on his son Donal—now an experienced anthropologist and a very steady person—as a sounding board and as a source of advice. When Conor decided to run for office, Donal asked him why he was doing this. Conor replied, "Well, the experience will be interesting."

Donal's judgment was phrased in the form of a query. "Haven't you had enough experience already?"[4]

Conor entered Irish politics as an overnight sensation, a very skillfully managed one. In 1967, Brendan Corish, leader of the Irish Labour
party, had assigned the then-new political director (and, as of January
1968, general secretary) of the party, Brendan Halligan, the task of recruiting four well-known personages to the party. On Corish's list were
Justin Keating, Garret FitzGerald, Declan Costello, and Conor Cruise
O'Brien. Halligan was the right man for the task. He was an extraordinarily shrewd political tactician and in many ways the perfect back-
room boy, because he did not look like one. Tall and slim, he had the
carriage of a first-class cricketer. A convinced socialist, Halligan saw
nothing wrong with using guile in a good cause. By Irish standards of
the time, he was very young—just in his thirties—and not yet hobbled
by a sense of the limitations of politics.

When Conor was at home in Ireland in the summer and autumn of
1968, Halligan made his move. As an entry wedge, he used Michael
McInerney, a good friend of Conor's. McInerney was the senior political journalist in Ireland and, as political correspondent for the *Irish
Times*, the most influential. He was an amazing man, just the mixture of
good storyteller, political idealist, and serious drinker that Conor loved.
Eleven years older than Conor, he had done it all: been a ship's carpen-
ter, a railroad worker, a serious communist, and an Irish republican. He
was proud of two instances of personal good judgment. One involved
losing his virginity when he came to Dublin from Limerick for the
World Eucharistic Congress in 1932. The other happened when he was
living in London in 1939 at the time the infamous Coventry bicycle
bomb went off; he decided to flush down the toilet the parcel that the
lads who had set the bomb had left with him. From then on, McInerney
eschewed all forms of political violence. During and after the war he
spent eighteen years as an industrial correspondent for the *Irish Times*
before taking over the political beat. He was the lead hand in the crew
that Douglas Gageby was using to turn the paper from an old unionist
sheet into the voice of the new Ireland.[5]

When Halligan asked, McInerney said, "I'll arrange for you to meet
Conor." This took place on a Sunday afternoon in the autumn of 1968
in McInerney's Dublin flat. Halligan, with the brashness of youth,
preached evangelically to Conor, McInerney, and his wife Nancy, about
the direction the Irish Labour party was taking. The party, he said, was
in the midst of an escape from its rural (and thus inevitably conservative)
roots and was turning into a modern urban-based social democratic
party. It was nearly two hours before Conor got to open his mouth, but
he bought the package. Something was happening, clearly. Conor was
invited to rejoin the party (he had been a member as an undergraduate)

and he accepted on the spot.[6] (In December 1968 Conor formally became a party member and also a comrade of the Clerical and Miscellaneous Section of the Irish Transport and General Workers' Union.)[7]

Immediately after leaving Conor and the McInerneys, Brendan Halligan got on the phone to Dan Brown, who was the vice-chairman of the Labour party and head of the Dublin regional council. He was the archetypal trade union man, very conservative, a good bureaucrat, tough as nails, and shrewd enough to recognize that catching Conor for the party opened the door to a good deal of valuable publicity. He and Halligan arranged for a special meeting of the Dublin regional council in mid-January at Liberty Hall to welcome Conor.

The meeting was a brilliant success. Six hundred people packed the auditorium. Both Dan Brown and Brendan Corish welcomed Conor and lavished praise upon him. When Conor rose to speak, before uttering a word, he received a standing ovation. His speech—which, not surprisingly, given McInerney's involvement, was printed in detail in the *Irish Times* the next day—was interrupted several times by prolonged applause. Conor began by defining three historical shifts in Irish politics: from the old Irish party of the 1860s to the party of Parnell; from that party to Sinn Fein in 1918; from Cumann na nGaedheal to Fianna Fail in 1932. And now, a fourth historical shift was in train, he declared, the rise of the Labour party. He went on to praise the civil rights movement in Northern Ireland, pointing out the parallel between it and the civil rights movement in the American South. He sat down to a long standing ovation. According to veteran political observers, the mood of the party faithful was one of euphoria.[8]

The Liberty Hall triumph completed, Dan Brown and Brendan Halligan took Conor down to Finnegan's in the Liberties. Now demolished, Finnegan's was a workers' pub with old-fashioned draught pulls and a decent pint. "Look, Conor," said Dan Brown when they were on their second pint, "you want to be a candidate, right?"

Conor said yes.

"You go back to New York. Don't worry about this. We"—he nodded toward Brendan Halligan—"we'll get you a nomination. OK? That's our job."[9]

And Conor, knowing professionals when he saw them, agreed. However, before he went back to New York, Conor made two significant public appearances. One of these was at the annual conference of the entire Labour party in January 1969, when, in an off-hand moment in a long speech, he suggested that the Irish diplomatic mission in Catholic, but fascist, Portugal should be closed and one in communist

Cuba be opened instead.[10] This opened a flank for later red-baiting by his enemies. He also spoke to the Limerick branch of the Labour party where, at Connolly Hall, he drew a crowd of more than 300, "including four young priests." He predicted a Labour victory whenever a general election was called and, more important, called for the abolition of the special position of the Roman Catholic Church as defined in Article 44 of the constitution of the Irish Republic.[11]

The political situation that Conor was entering was built on a long-quiescent fault line. Along this line, there were signs of great tectonic stress, but not many people were paying attention. On the surface everything was stable. Basically, Irish politics from the 1920s through the early 1970s were based on two sets of arrangements, each of which had produced in its own sphere a seemingly permanent equilibrium. The first of these, in the Twenty-Six Counties, was that politics was dominated by two parties, Fine Gael and Fianna Fail, whose origins went back, respectively, to those who in the 1920s had favored acceptance of the Anglo-Irish treaty and those who had opposed it. Between these two parties were only very slight ideological differences. In terms of contemporary European politics, both were far to the right; indeed, both would have been to the right of the center of the U.S. Republican party of the period. The constituency of each was historically determined, and each was strongly clientelist. Thus the parties were not distinguished so much by their platforms or policies, as by the benefits of their patronage. Seemingly, Fine Gael and Fianna Fail had a lock on Irish political life, even though the Irish system of proportional representation permitted smaller parties to operate.

In Northern Ireland, a parallel state of equilibrium seemed to have been reached between the Protestant majority (the "unionists" in political parlance) and the Catholic minority (the "nationalists"). The Protestant majority discriminated significantly against the Catholics, but the standard of living and of all governmental social benefits was much higher in Northern Ireland than in the republic and this was the relevant reference point for most northerners. That, and the fact that the standard of living had risen markedly and continually since the end of World War II, helps to explain why the northern Catholics, while restive, were not revolutionary. The demography of Northern Ireland was stable because although Catholics had a higher birth rate than did Protestants, they emigrated at a correspondingly higher rate, in considerable degree due to the diminishment of economic opportunity through discrimination. Gradually, during the 1960s, civil discrimination against Catholics was being reduced. In the mid-1960s, Ulster seemed to be stable, and slowly improving. In fact, it was in a state of unstable equilibrium, and only needed a mild force in the right direction to send everything crashing.

What virtually no one recognized, even in the late 1960s, was that these two sets of frozen politics, north and south, were interrelated and that anything which upset the equilibrium in Northern Ireland would cause disequilibrium in the republic as well. If politics in the Six Counties went wild, so would those of the Twenty-Six.

On the eve of the political earthquake of the early 1970s, the Irish Labour party was planning very rationally, very tactically, to reshape southern Irish politics along the left-right spectrum that prevailed elsewhere in Europe. The party planners' basic goal was to force a realignment of Irish politics, so that Fianna Fail and Fine Gael would be pressed, at minimum, into a coalition with each other, and, ultimately it was hoped, into union. Since they both were right-of-center parties, this would produce a binary system, with Labour being the natural alternative to the combined Fianna Fail-Fine Gael entity. Thus, Labour was committing itself to refusing to be involved in any coalition. In fact, the party strategists had decided that if Labour held the balance of power between Fine Gael and Fianna Fail, it would ally with neither. Instead, it would nominate Brendan Corish as taoiseach, and continue to do so until this forced the other two parties either to coalesce or to call another general election.[12] That plan sounds a trifle bizarre, and indeed it was, but it was a good indication of the mood of the Labour party as it entered the year 1969, certain that an election would be called before year's end, and equally certain that the 1970s belonged to Labour.

This was far out of touch with reality. In the late 1960s, Labour resembled a bunch of Winnebago owners driving down the highway convinced that their motorized bathtubs are macho Harley Davidson motorcycles. That was Labour, a flotilla of Winnebagos. The party had almost no maneuverability in actuality. Its control was split between the annual conference (which, like its British counterpart, had bloc votes allocated to the major trade unions and other special interest groups, and which, when it met, inevitably produced a series of screaming matches that would have done credit to a primal therapy group); the parliamentary Labour party (PLP), comprising the sitting members of the Dail and Seanad; and an administrative council which was supposed to control the everyday affairs of the party.[13] Steering this machine was difficult in the best of times, yet the Labour party in 1969 was in high gear. It again declared itself to be a socialist party ("I am a socialist" had been the concluding words of speaker after speaker at the 1966 annual conference). The 1970s were declared to be the Decade of Labour. The party put out a 150-page policy statement that promised everything from more worker democracy to the nationalization of the land of incompetent and idle farmers, a complete revision of the educational system, the nationalization of all building land, and a massive housing program. It was a good policy booklet from the political viewpoint, but it was somewhat limited by the necessity, as one later analyst noted, "of a fifteen-year spell in government with unlimited funds at the party's disposal."[14]

In that heady atmosphere there were scores of individuals who suddenly wished to be adopted as Labour candidates, and Brendan Halligan and Dan Brown had no real idea of where to find a constituency for Conor. Most of the constituencies were big "five-seaters," which, under proportional representation, protected minority parties, but made it hard for Labour to elect more than one member per constituency. The selection process for Labour candidates was democratic, in that there were several branches of the party within each constituency and each branch had an equal number of votes in the selection of candidates. There really was no place for Conor. Then, Denis Larkin, Labour member for Dublin North-East, decided not to stand. His brother, James Larkin, had been general secretary of the Workers' Union of Ireland, a union that was virtually a family fiefdom, having been founded by James Larkin, Sr. When James Jr. died, Denis Larkin, out of filial piety, decided to take the union secretaryship. Fortunately for Conor's candidacy, Denis Larkin told the Labour party insiders of his intentions privately, and Brendan Halligan and his outriders rushed to fill the gap. This was the perfect place for Conor: his home in Howth was in the constituency. He was quickly signed up as a member of the Howth branch of the party. Before Conor went back to New York in late January 1969, he was taken around by members of the party executive to meet the local members. Mostly, the branch was working class (Howth at that time had a considerable fishing industry) and there was a good deal of subsidized housing, as well as up-market homes toward Howth summit. Conor went down well with the average voter. It sounds a small thing, but the locals liked the fact that he drank pints. He went off to the pub with the local committee members and they expected him to take brandy or shorts, but he sat there and drank pints as good as they did. He could be one of the boys and not be a fake.[15]

Even before the general election was called, Conor's selection was taken care of: a selection conference for Dublin North-East was held in mid-March and Conor, still in New York, was adopted as a Labour candidate. In a phone interview from New York, he promised that if he was elected he would quit his job at New York University and return to

Ireland. He also referred to his immediate travel plans: to Biafra at the end of March, then to Nigeria, then London, then Dublin on 12 April and finally back to New York.[16] (When Conor once declared in *Who's Who* that travel was his hobby, he understated the case.) The Dail was dissolved on 22 May, and Michael McInerney sent a two-word telegram: DUBLINWARDS SOONEST. Conor immediately returned home. There was never any doubt that he would keep his word.[17]

One of the changes in Irish political life that occurred when the 1969 general election was called was that Sean MacEntee, Conor's father-in-law, announced his retirement.[18] This was fortunate for Conor, because the actual election campaign turned out to be one of the nastiest in decades and much of it was fought, on the part of Fianna Fail, by the red-scare methods that MacEntee had used so effectively for years. Conor and MacEntee had come to terms with each other in the 1960s and there was an affection between them; this friendship, however, would have been severely strained if MacEntee still had been deeply involved in politics. As it was, he publicly stated that Labour stood for Lenin, Stalin, and "the red flames of burning homesteads in Meath."[19]

In the general election of 1969, most of the attacks on Labour came from Fianna Fail, headed by Jack Lynch. He was often underrated by contemporaries as a political tactician; he was in fact very shrewd. Lynch understood the central strategic fact of this election: that the real danger to Fianna Fail in 1969 came not from its traditional rival, Fine Gael, but from Labour. He took seriously the possibility of Labour's forcing Fianna Fail and Fine Gael together to the rightward end of the political spectrum, and he believed that Labour had to be crushed, quickly, before it upset the traditional equilibrium of Irish politics.

Lynch ran an election campaign that came to be known among political journalists as "the convent circuit election." He literally went from one convent to another, had tea with the mother superior and the nuns, and explained why he and his party of good Catholics were so concerned: it's that the country is threatened, Reverend Mother, by godless socialists; they even admit it, some of them; and, Reverend Mother, some of them are even agnostics. One of them is even divorced; and they want to take our embassy out of good Catholic Portugal and put one up in godless, atheistic, socialistic, communistic Cuba; that's what they want. Lynch's campaign was skillful and very nasty. His colleagues weighed in, on other fronts, and the election was judged by political commentators to be the dirtiest in decades. Yet, that sort of thing should not have surprised anyone who had studied Jack Lynch's form: no one wins six all-Ireland medals for playing in the middle of the pitch with a hurley stick without blood on his elbows. Lynch had been known on the playing field as a very rough character who was rarely found out by the referee. Labour tacticians forgot that.[20]

Given that a good deal of the good-Catholic versus red-agent attention was focused on Conor, this is an appropriate point to return to the question that had popped up in the 1960s. How much of a socialist was he? There is no question that the Irish Labour party was enthusiastic in pinning the socialist label to its own lapels, and that Conor loyally kept to the party line on major social issues. And there is no question that he tried to explain to Irish audiences that socialism, despite being an international doctrine, was fit for the Irish domestic mind. "The socialism of the Irish Labour Party is in no way un-Christian," he told one audience. "On the contrary, it is far more consistent with Christianity than is the *laissez-faire* devil-take-the-hindmost ideology of capitalism as practised in this country and elsewhere." Nor was socialism un-Irish. "It is the direct continuation in terms of the present day of the thought of Fintan Lalor, Michael Davitt, James Connolly, and James Larkin."[21]

But when he was in an international context, Conor invoked the international socialist saints, whose names dared not be mentioned in Ireland: Leon Trotsky and his associates. And, he could drop into a "brother comrades" mode of address when required, as at the Twelfth Congress of the Socialist International held in Vienna in June 1972.[22] Conor represented the Irish Labour party at a meeting of socialist parties of the European Community (and of prospective members) in May 1972.[23] In the mid-1970s, he went to Chequers, where the U.K. prime minister, Harold Wilson, was hosting a conference of Europe's socialist leaders: Willy Brandt, Bruno Kreisky, Olaf Palme, François Mitterand, and the like. (This occasion is worth noting chiefly because Sir Harold, anything but an instinctive democrat, was searching for a biographer and trolled Conor as a possibility. "As an historian, Conor, do you think ..." he began, and paused to puff on his pipe, "... do you think that one who owes as much to History as I do, owes something to History in return?")[24]

Despite these socialist affiliations, I agree with Conor's former colleague in the Labour party, the distinguished journalist and university lecturer John Horgan, when he suggests that Conor never was a socialist. (This opinion implies no moral judgment whatsoever, though serious socialists will condemn Conor for lack of the true faith, and neo-conservatives will see his distance from real socialism as an indication of some virtue, however pale.) For one thing, Conor is a stranger to economics, the very basis of most forms of socialism. More than that, I think that Conor was happy to call himself a socialist because the agenda of the socialists in Ireland in the late 1960s and early 1970s overlapped with his own: anticolonialism (especially concerning South Africa), greater freedom for women, a reduction in the Catholic Church's control of most aspects of social life in Ireland and its veto over public policy matters, and the protection of small ethnic minorities (such as the Biafrans) from the form of imperialism that disguises itself as federalism. As these items became part of the program of Irish liberals in general (as was to occur in the 1980s) Conor stayed with them, but he was no longer required to be a socialist to forward them.[25]

In the campaign of 1969, Conor's declared socialism may have scared some electors, but in person he was very reassuring. He turned out to be very skilled in meeting people. "O'Brien's Surprise Value," was the headline of the *Irish Times*' Election Notebook column by Mary Maher (2 June 1969). The surprise she referred to was a double one, that of professional politicians who were surprised that Conor campaigned so well, just like an old pro, and that of locals in the constituency who found him on their doorstep while they were in the middle of watching "The Avengers."

> Standing rather stiffly, soberly dressed in grey tweeds, he smiles with an uneasy shyness while the accompanying branch member performs the canvassing rite:
> "Good evening. We're from the Labour Party. This is Dr. Conor Cruise O'Brien who is a candidate in this area."
> Realisation dawns; the bored patient face turns quickly amazed, curious and polite:
> "Oh yes, of course, I recognize your face." Dr. O'Brien's extended hand is grasped.
> "I live at the top of the hill," he tells the Howth residents. ...[26]

Up and down the council estates in Howth Conor went, and then to the privately owned semidetached homes of Raheny and the up-market homes of Sutton, and on to the still-rural parts of the constituency. He needed the advantage of his celebrity status (based on his time in the Congo), and his way with voters because, in addition to the red-scare smear, he had another liability. Conor missed the mark on an important local issue: land speculation by Charles J. Haughey, minister for finance and Fianna Fail candidate in Dublin North-East.

This issue would not merit attention except that the hatred for each other that Conor and Haughey came to share became one of the staples of Irish politics, lasting through Conor's career as a minister, Haughey's as prime minister, and outlasting the political career of each. And, Conor's misreading of the local electorate on this issue served as a predictor of how he would do in future. This is the background: born in Castlebar, County Mayo (in 1925), Haughey had entered the Dail in 1957, after marrying, in 1951, the daughter of Sean Lemass who became de Valera's successor. Haughey won a seat in Dublin North-East and held it thereafter, so that he was thought of as something of a local boy. An accountant and property trader, he amassed a large personal fortune by methods that have never been explained and probably are beyond historical documentation. In the late 1960s, he was minister for finance. What greatly vexed Conor was that at a time when land prices were rising rapidly, making it very difficult for the average family to find housing, Haughey flipped a piece of real estate, his house and attached farm lands in Raheny, for £205,500 and immediately bought "Abbeyville," an eighteenth-century Gandon mansion on twenty-six acres in Kinsealy. Given that planning permission was necessary for his farm to be turned into development land, this was, in Conor's view, a *prima facie* case of conflict of interest, and Conor went after it hard.[27]

The electorate did not understand what Conor was on about. He had been away from Ireland too long and was applying outside standards. Unlike the United States, Canada, and most European countries, the Republic of Ireland had no law requiring politicians to disclose their personal assets or to put their investments in a blind trust while in high office. The concept of conflict of interest, as something to be avoided, was virtually unknown in southern Ireland: indeed, traditionally, one went into Irish politics so that one could straddle the private and the public sectors and thus do well for oneself, friends, and family. It would have taken a long period of voter education before the bulk of the electorate saw anything wrong with the minister for finance turning a profit on a big private land sale, especially if the deal was economically contingent upon either local or central government planning approval.[28]

Nevertheless, when the poll came, on 18 June 1969, Conor was elected on the first count. Charles Haughey led the poll, however, receiving 4,000 first preference votes more than did Conor.[29]

What about the rest of the Irish Labour party, those lads (it was an overwhelmingly male party) in the Winnebagos who fantasized that they were riding Harleys? They hit reality. In a Dail in which Fianna Fail's seats had risen from 72 (at dissolution) to 75, and Fine Gael's from 47 to 50, Labour had dropped from 22 TDs to 18. The 1970s, clearly, would not be the decade of socialism, after all.

Admittedly, the parliamentary Labour party was transformed from being predominantly rural to urban (which the party strategists had wanted), and was fairly stuffed with intellectuals (as will be discussed in a moment). But the loss in the number of seats sent the party into deep despondency. At a caucus of the PLP soon after the election, Stevie Coughlan, who had held his seat for East Limerick, tried to explain what had gone wrong. Coughlan had earned his living as a bookie, and thought mathematically.

"Euclid," was his explanation.

Conor asked him to explain more fully.

"Euclid," was all he could say.[30]

Perhaps he meant that the Labour party had gotten its political geometry all wrong. It had forgotten reality: Euclid.

• • •

Yet, although the Labour party's bid to shove southern Irish politics out of the old ruts that ran back to the Irish civil war of 1922–23 failed, politics soon were transformed anyway. This occurred because of events in Northern Ireland. The course of the Northern Ireland civil rights movement is too well known to require recitation. In reality, of course, it was not a fight for civil rights, which the northern Catholics already had, but against discrimination, which they also had, in plenty.[31] The movement reached Gael-force in 1968. It was something entirely new in Ulster politics, namely, a decision on the part of the Catholics to increase their participation in Northern Ireland politics. Previously, almost all of their political activities had been focused on getting out of Northern Ireland; that is, on the traditional goal of reuniting Ireland, and of employing as a major tactic, noncooperation with the Six Counties government, frequently in the form of "abstentionism" from government at all levels. Further, the civil rights movement was unique in being entirely lay-led and secular in spirit. Previously, the northern nationalists' political activities had invoked faith-and-fatherland and had granted a good deal of authority to clerics.

Conor directly entered the Irish picture in the summer of 1969. (He and Paul O'Dwyer had, as mentioned in chapter 9, headed a support group in New York for Northern Ireland civil rights, but that was peripheral to events at home.) On 1 May 1969, Northern Ireland's mildly reformist prime minister, Terence O'Neill, was dumped by hard-liners and replaced by Major James Chichester-Clark, a member of an old Ulster family whose lineage ran back to the first governor of colonial Ulster. He was a man with a fine military bearing, a strong jawline, and not much cerebral power. This new prime minister of Northern Ireland hardly brought peace. The beginning of a summer of turmoil was sig-

naled by the Twelfth of July parades of the Orange Order. These traditional parades were highly insulting to the Catholic population.
Usually the Catholics had the good judgment to stay home, but in
Derry the Orange parade was followed by street fighting and by looting
and arson by Catholic hooligans. On subsequent days pitched battles
between the police and Catholics took place, and fighting also erupted
between the police and Protestant mobs which were trying to attack the
Catholic sector of Derry. Similar flare-ups occurred in several smaller
towns in Ulster. But the real trouble was not unleashed until the second
of August when Protestant and Catholic mobs clashed in Belfast. These
clashes recurred night after night, while barricades were thrown up for
protection by each side. The police were unable to control the rioting
and arson and appeared to have been anything but impartial in their efforts to restore order. Sectarian violence, which had dwindled momentarily in Derry, was rekindled on 12 August when the Apprentice Boys
of Derry, a Protestant fraternal order, held their annual parade. Finally,
the U.K. government, realizing that the "Stormont government" (that
is, the government of Northern Ireland) had lost control of the situation, sent in troops. The troops arrived on 14–15 August and were concentrated chiefly in Belfast and Londonderry. The very day the troops
arrived the rioting claimed its first fatality.

Significantly, the arrival of British troops was considered a victory by
the Catholics, for the British were believed to be more impartial in protecting lives and property than were the Protestant-dominated Royal
Ulster Constabulary and the "B Specials," a part-time police force, entirely Protestant. Moreover, the necessity of British intervention was a
judgment of incompetence against the Northern Ireland government,
so in this instance pragmatic considerations overcame the traditional
nationalist opposition to having British troops on Irish soil; the soldiers were hailed as allies by the Catholics. The British, however, were
not immediately able to restore order. Severe rioting continued in
Londonderry and Belfast.

On 14 August, the parliamentary Labour party met to decide what
its response should be. The signal characteristic of this new caucus was
that although its numbers had been diminished by the recent general
election, it had a number of strong personalities, several of whom could
justifiably be labeled "intellectuals." Indeed, during the election, one of
this set, Dr. David Thornley, had redefined the classic four pillars of
British socialism to mean the three pillars of Irish socialism: "the
unions, the party, and the intellectuals."[32] This intellectual richness in
the Parliamentary Labour party was splendid during debates in the
Dail—Brendan Halligan estimated that Labour could go down to its
number seven or eight batsman and still be better than the number one

of the other parties and, except for Garret FitzGerald of Fine Gael, he probably was right—but when closeted together in caucus, with no external enemy to claw at, the Labour TDs were very good at attacking each other; and, in the way of academics, arguing around all sides of an issue as a way of avoiding making a decision.

Thus, the debate on what to do about the North asked, Should we delegate an investigative commission? On one side—in this case on the side of perpetual indecision—was David Thornley. He was English-born, educated at St. Paul's School, London, and had taken a history and political science degree at Trinity. He stayed on in Ireland and became a fellow of TCD in 1964. In his mid-thirties, ruggedly handsome—he was very proud of having been a university middleweight boxer and also of having won the Royal Irish Academy of Music's Ludwig Cup for singing. In 1970, he was Ireland's premier telly don, serving as a fixture on "Seven Days," and "Division," two highly rated programs. Thornley alternated between elation and expressions of self-doubt and failure. Eventually, in the 1970s, he drank himself into a bloated parody of his once-handsome self, just before his death.[33] At the 14 August caucus meeting, Thornley havered and dithered. As the debate developed, it appeared that the party would indeed send an investigatory group to the North, but Thornley could not decide whether or not to go.

Facing him across the table was Frank Cluskey, the one real working man in the Labour caucus. Born just off Dorset Street in Dublin in 1930, he had left school after his thirteenth year and, after doing odd jobs, became an apprentice butcher at age sixteen. Cluskey was only barely functionally literate—a deficiency which he skillfully hid—but he was extraordinarily bright and his tongue was fearsome. He had been elected a Labour member of the Dublin corporation in 1960, a TD in 1965 and was Dublin's Lord Mayor in 1968. Cluskey peered at the world through dark-framed glasses (the classic National Health Special) and usually had a full day's stubble on his face.[34]

So, Frank Cluskey, who could not tolerate preciousness, listened with growing irritation to David Thornley agonizing about whether or not to risk the trip north. Finally, Thornley, referring to the negotiation of the Anglo-Irish treaty, said, "I think I know how Michael Collins felt in 1921."

Cluskey looked up. "Yes, and if you fucking keep going on like this, you'll fucking know how Michael Collins felt in 1922."[35]

The next day the Labour caucus's delegation went to the North (David Thornley decided to stay at home). In addition to Conor and Frank Cluskey, the delegation included Justin Keating, Noel Browne, and Stephen (always Stevie) Coughlan. Coughlan was very nationalistic and on the far right of the party. (In 1972, he was to narrowly avoid expulsion from the Labour party for having uttered anti-Semitic remarks: being anti-Semitic in Limerick takes some imagination as well as very strange political convictions.) Dr. Justin Keating was another TCD don, a veterinarian, a former communist of republican background. He probably understood Marxist dialectic better than anyone in caucus, a useful skill which he conjoined to considerable ability in property speculation. Dr. Noel Browne was a physician who had been at the center of the Mother and Child health controversy in 1951. Depending on one's viewpoint, he was either the conscience of the Irish nation or the loosest cannon on the political deck. Browne was a dandy, both sartorially and morally. In this era he favored leather jackets, striped shirts, wildly figured ties, and an absolute commitment to his own private brand of socialism.[36]

This band of TDs, accompanied by party functionaries, headed north. It temporarily divided into two sets, one going directly to Belfast, the other, Conor's group, going to Derry by way of Armagh. In Armagh, the customary courtesy call was paid on the Primate of All Ireland, William Cardinal Conway. Conor's band, headed as it was by a person both avowedly agnostic and legally divorced, received a very frosty reception, indeed.[37] Next in Derry, Conor's group met with the leaders of the Bogside, an intensely local group. (When one member of Conor's party asked to speak to Bernadette Devlin, who had been seen the day before on world wide television, he was told that she was in her room, crying.[38] Bernadette was not a Derry person and the locals were not pleased with her having upstaged them.) From the Bogside defense committee came the reply to the question "What should we tell London?" The reply was simple: "Tell them to send in more troops."

Only later did it occur to Conor how unnatural was something that everyone in the republic's Labour party took as natural: in their formal meetings they spoke only to Catholics. In the case of Derry, this was particularly striking, as it was a Catholic attack on a Protestant parade that had started the local confrontation. "I think we were all in the grip of a visceral tribal Irish Catholic reflex without realising what was happening to us. Several of us were intellectuals who thought of ourselves as tremendously non-sectarian and secular, even agnostic. But whatever we thought we were, our gut reactions were Irish Catholic when the crunch came in August 1969."[39]

Conor's group joined up with the other half of the Labour delegation in Belfast a day later. There, although officially the group met only Catholics, it encountered a few Protestants. (One cannot infer the religious adhesion of the taxi driver in Belfast who provided Conor with a balanced, indeed, ecumenical view of the problem. When asked what should be done, he turned round to look at his passenger and said, "Burn Bernadette and the effin' Bible.")[40] In addition to a meeting with the Central Defence Committee in the Falls Road, Conor met informally in the house of his former father-in-law, Alec Foster, in the Ravenhill Road, with Catholics and a few liberal Protestants. Nevertheless, it was very much a tribal congress. Gerry Fitt, Paddy Devlin, and others sat and drank, talked of the problem, and sang songs of the Dubliners and the Clanceys and not a bar, certainly, of "Dolly's Brae," or "The Southdown Militia."[41] Now, the mention of Devlin and Fitt, both Westminster MPs, is important. Neither of them at this time got along very well with Conor (Devlin was keen on arming the northern Catholics and Fitt was not pleased with southern politicians complicating matters in the North), but they are crucial figures because they represented the northern version of Frank Cluskey: honest-to-God working-class leaders, not intellectual blow-ins. Despite major disagreements (Devlin began a lawsuit against Conor over the use of the word "nutcase" to describe IRA hardliners, but dropped it before the case came to court, a pity in its way, as Sean MacBride was briefed to act as lead barrister against Conor),[42] during the mid-1970s the three came closer and closer together and eventually reached by the late 1970s not only a position of mutual respect, but a common rejection of the violent strand in Irish nationalism.

For the moment, however, the relationship was uneasy. Conor and northern Catholic leaders (Devlin, Fitt and company) went to London where they met with Harold Wilson's government. Conor was the spokesman for the group. In London he told the governing Labour party what the northern Catholics wanted him to say: that they needed more British troops and, simultaneously, the disbandment of the hated B Specials; those twinned moves would save lives.[43]

• • •

If those were Conor's immediate and instinctively tribal responses to an unprecedented set of events, there was a deeper stream of thought developing. Conor has always been an idea-processing entity, a man addicted to serious scholarship and learning. Thus, his actions in 1969 and thereafter should be seen through a specific lens: his mind was developing in the late 1960s and early 1970s independently of the flares ignited by the northern situation.

One crucial sector of his thought in the mid and late 1960s was his fascination with Edmund Burke, a fascination that grew in importance into the 1990s when he published his monumental biography of Burke.

Conor spent most of the summer of 1967 writing a 30,000-word introduction to Burke's *Reflections on the Revolution in France* for Pelican and
Penguin Books for a series of republications of works by great Western
thinkers.[44] In this essay, Conor presented in germ the ideas that were
to be the heart of his magisterial *The Great Melody* (1992). He saw Burke
as a writer of deep inner consistency, not always of language or opinion,
but of feeling.[45] Conor maintained that far from being an English
writer, Burke was "in fact, Irish to the marrow of his bones."[46] But not
just Irish: Irish Catholic. In his introduction to the *Reflections*, Conor
floats the idea, which he was to develop later, that Burke's own father
had apostatized from the Catholic church under the pressure of the
penal laws.[47] And, further, Conor argues that despite being very successfully anglicized, Burke had maintained a close touch with Celtic culture: "In fact, Burke was as 'Gaelic' as any modern [Irish] nationalist
and more Gaelic than some."[48]

Edmund Burke, thus described, comes to resemble Conor Cruise
O'Brien. This identification with Burke means that in this introduction
to the *Reflections* one is reading the results of an internal dialogue Conor
has had with himself. He insists that Burke was a liberal, and that
Burke's career was about the preservation of liberty. This insistence is
germane to Conor's own political career. "He [Burke] defines that freedom which he loves: 'The Liberty I mean is *social* freedom [wrote
Burke]. It is the state of things in which Liberty is secured by the equality of Restraint.'"[49] Those words, "equality of Restraint," are noteworthy, for they relate to Conor's developing position on political violence
in general and on that of the IRA in particular.

In his Burke piece, Conor worked hard to dissociate Burke from
right-wing ideologues propounding the most un-Burkean ideas: extreme, even anarchic, libertarianism, or, the other far-right nostrum,
virtual fascism. In attempting to extract Burke from the oleaginous pool
of right-wing associations, Conor is not quite successful. That is because of his own presentism, which is the downside of his admirable
ability to keep old ideas alive. Writing in *Power and Consciousness* in the
same period, Conor suggested that "there is a real sense in which the
cold war can be said to have begun in November 1790 with the publication of Edmund Burke's *Reflections on the Revolution in France*."[50] That
means that if, in the context of the 1960s and 1970s, one identified with
Burke, one was almost automatically opposed to his opposite, to Karl
Marx.

That is a hard position for a self-declared socialist to maintain, and
it is reflected in Conor's inability to produce successfully a book that he
had proposed to Dan Davin, one on the relationship of Burke and Marx.

The closest he came to dealing with the relationship was in a lecture he gave at the University of Chicago in December 1966. (It is reprinted in the Anthology, Selection 21.) This was not a finished statement, but in the T.S. Eliot Memorial Lectures delivered at the University of Kent in November 1969, Conor made it clear which side he came down on. He closed the series of lectures by pointing out that "traditional left-wing thought has not concerned itself enough with what man is actually like. It has made wildly optimistic assumptions about transforming man through education, or through revolution." And, "in fact, its taste for dialectical polemics and high abstraction has failed to compensate for its poverty in psychology and for its concomitant lack of interest in that depth of human understanding which exists in the work of the great imaginative writers." He concluded thus: "I would ask you to turn over in your minds the possible meanings of one pregnant phrase of Edmund Burke's: Art is man's nature."[51]

When transferred to the context of Irish life, this meant that Conor had decided that, should they clash, he was committed to Irish patriotism (his version, to be sure) over internationalism, to human psychology over Marxist theory, and to the belief that Irish liberty and the "equality of Restraint," were not only compatible, but that the former well might depend upon the latter.

A second intellectual path in the 1960s also affected Conor's political outlook. During 1969–70, he fashioned an essay, "The Gentle Nietzscheans," that flustered mainline intellectual historians of Europe. (The essay is reprinted in the Anthology, Selection 30.) At the time the piece appeared, the dominant view of Nietzsche, especially in America, was that of Walter Kaufmann, the Princeton professor who had edited and commented on most of the German philosopher's writings. Kaufmann's viewpoint was descended from that of Thomas Mann: Nietzsche did not invent fascism; fascism invented Nietzsche. That vantage point permitted an erasure of the caricature of Nietzsche as the mad philosopher who created Hitler; a subtler picture emerged, but in its very gentleness, it was misleading. The dominant reading of Nietzsche came to emphasize his spiritual aspects and to read the nastier parts of his writing as metaphors. "When Nietzsche praises, as he often does, war and cruelty, we are told we must understand him as calling for spiritual struggle and a stern mastery over the self," Conor commented. Also, he pointed out, Nietzsche's jagged edges were worn smooth by the academic trick of compartmentalization: various works, being labeled as important pieces of psychological insight, or as contributions to German prosody, could then be ignored in their political content. In describing these two tricks, metaphorization and compartmentalization, which make Nietzsche into a gentle old German with smoke curling from his meerschaum pipe, Conor effectively destroys them. The essay itself is remarkably gentle in tone, and in its argumentation is a tiny masterpiece. The strength of character and intellect required to deal with Germany's national philosopher could also be used to deal with Ireland's philosophy of nationalism.[52]

Given that Conor was reflecting upon the nature of nationalism, it was virtually inevitable that he would also focus on the nature of colonialism and imperialism. He was particularly sensitized to those issues in the 1960s by writing a volume on Albert Camus for the Fontana "Modern Masters" series. Like the essay on Nietzsche, the work was a wonder of compression: fewer than 100 pages, but rich, not a word wasted. The Camus book was old-fashioned literary and intellectual criticism in that one knows more after reading it than one does before starting. Conor faced a difficult audience problem: his readers ranged from senior undergraduates who would have read a bit of Camus, to senior scholars who knew the canon well. He managed to provide compressed, but engaged, retelling of the plots of *The Plague*, *The Stranger*, and *The Fall*, without distracting from his major point that Camus, in his depiction of a pan-Mediterranean culture, which seemed admirably noncolonial, actually served to legitimize French imperialism in North Africa.[53] Conor had been interested in the North African situation ever since his posting to the Paris embassy in 1956, and he happened to have been in Paris in 1958, when an attempted military coup by Algerian colonists was averted by Charles de Gaulle's abolishing the fourth republic.[54] Although not precisely parallel to the Irish situation, the whole question of a large colonial power and weaker, but geographically close, neighbor, had a set of intellectual sparks relating to Ireland. Camus was particularly instructive in his illustration of the possibility that someone who seemed to be actively anticolonialist might actually be unintentionally imperialist. Tom Paulin, who is certainly not an uncritical admirer of Conor, uses the term "sweet rigour" to describe the system of arguments in *Camus* and "lucid and brilliant" to summarize the book's character.[55]

In October 1969, a play of Conor's, *King Herod Explains*, was produced at the Gate Theatre in Dublin as part of a double bill with Michael MacLiammoir's vignette *The Liar*. The play was a brilliant meteorite, frightfully dated now, but absolutely riveting at the time. Roughly an hour in length, the piece was made to be performed, not read, quite unlike *Murderous Angels*, Conor's book-drama. The drama focuses on King Herod the Great (played with great success by Hilton Edwards) who, in ornate robes, sits enthroned and cigar smoking. He complains loudly that he was not really responsible for the Slaughter of the Innocents and he is particularly vexed that he has received inaccurate media coverage—from St. Matthew in particular. The issues that Conor uses Herod to deal with are central to any civilized society. Who is really responsible for violence? And on whose hands is there not blood? The combination of Conor's writing and Hilton Edwards's considerable genius kept this from being yet another of those two-dimensional Sunday School lessons that were so popular on stage in the 1960s.[56]

In the late 1960s, and early 1970s, Conor worked on the question of the justification of violence within a specifically Irish historical context: the life and death of the Irish patriot Michael Collins. This came through association with a motion picture production company that had bought the rights to various essays and biographic treatments of Collins and planned a major film on his life. Conor's immediate motivation to get involved was economic—upon resignation from NYU and his taking a seat in the Dail, his base income dropped from about $35,000 annually to £2,500—but the Collins project was also intrinsically interesting to him. However, the production company was not willing to give Conor, as scriptwriter, sufficient leeway. They wanted a patriotic monument, with blood all over the floor and symphonic music while it was spilled. The author of *King Herod Explains* was not willing to glorify violence, especially not patriotic gore. The film was never made.[57]

Each of these various projects of the late 1960s and early 1970s—Burke's *Reflections*, the "Gentle Nietzscheans," *Camus*, *King Herod Explains*, and the Michael Collins film project—are of interest on their own accounts. However, their great value is in helping one to understand Conor's unique trajectory among Irish politicians during the North-dominated 1970s. They indicate that he already was deeply concerned with the very issues that Northern Ireland raised, well before the Ulster situation turned crazy: the morality of violence and the locus of responsibility for it; the relationship between apparent anti-imperialism and latent colonialism; the propensity of intellectuals to hide from unpleasant realities; and, of course, the nature of Irish nationalism itself. No other politician active in the Republic of Ireland in the 1960s had thought deeply about all these issues. It is hardly surprising, therefore, that Conor's path veered so very far from that of the pack.

• • •

Nevertheless, Conor was a politician himself, and there were parts of that job at which he was very good indeed. One of these was being the Opposition Critic from Hell. Having had decades of practice as a debater, and having played in grander theaters than Leinster House (the United Nations, for example), Conor was neither intimidated by the atmosphere of Dail Eireann nor unprepared for its rough ways. Persons accustomed to the decorous debates of the American legislative system (especially the polished orations in the U.S. Senate) are usually surprised when they see how politicians behave in legislative assemblies that are based on the London model (and that includes Westminster itself). Dail Eireann was no exception. Its debates fluctuated from barequorum affairs with TDs sleeping their way through debates on sewerage acts and the like, to scenes of near violence, the air alive with invective and name calling. It was the perfect arena for Conor, for he knew how to frame tough questions for a minister and then how to interrupt and needle him. He was cleverer by far in free-form debate than anyone on the government front benches, and he could send Fianna Fail into apoplexy almost anytime he wished.

On his very first day in the Dail, 2 July 1969, he went after Charles Haughey's land dealing ("in most other democratic countries in Western Europe, a minister who had been seen to act in this way would not be renominated ...").[58] Then Conor decried the abandonment of "any attempt to sustain independence in foreign policy."[59] He did so with such verve that Kevin Boland, minister for local government, totally lost the thread of his own contribution and wandered into a bizarre denunciation, calling Conor "Deputy Conor Cuba O'Brien" and claiming that the "delegate to the Rumanian Party" (whatever that was) would agree with Conor's ideas.[60] Conor could elicit that kind of fractured, out of control response almost at will, and that was damaging to a governing party. It showed the government to be volatile, and not quite in control.

For the most part, Conor kept his parliamentary tactics within the lines of permissible behavior. He had, however, little respect for the Ceann Comhairle (the speaker of the Dail), Cormac Breslin, a Donegal man who had sat as a Fianna Fail TD since 1937. Conor came to believe that the speaker favored Fianna Fail and that appears to be an accurate judgment. The trouble is, Conor said as much in public. One of the points of Dail procedure, inherited from seventeenth-century English practice, is that no Member of Parliament may publicly criticize the speaker. In an interview published on 12 December 1969 in *This Week in Ireland*, Conor said, "I feel the Ceann Comhairle is subconsciously biased in favour of his own party." That was all. However, the speaker had Conor called up for a breach of privilege. A Dail committee, chaired by the Fianna Fail chief whip, and having a Fianna Fail majority, investigated the allegations. Conor responded by agreeing that the

Ceann Comhairle had to be above everyday political barracking, but argued that the rule that a Dail deputy could not make *any* criticism in any public forum of the Ceann Comhairle, and that the press could not publish any such criticism if it were made, was dangerous to democracy. On a split vote, Conor was judged to have been in breach of privilege, but the committee accepted his explanation that he had meant no offense to the speaker and therefore took no legal action against him or the magazine that had published his remarks.[61]

Conor's official role within the parliamentary Labour party was that of spokesman on foreign affairs and on Northern Ireland. Frank Aiken, elected yet again as a TD for Louth, chose to resign his long-time ministership for foreign affairs in favor of Dr. Patrick Hillery, and thus truly venomous question-time exchanges were avoided. As it was, Conor kept Hillery honest, but did not go at him with great zeal. On most issues relating to international affairs, Conor's own personal system of values and that of the Labour party coincided, and therefore he was able to press for the positions he favored in concert with other Labour TDs. Increased aid for Biafra was one such concern.[62] In 1971, having gone to Calcutta and northern Pakistan to investigate famine, he pressed hard for more aid to refugees.[63] Both of these matters, Biafra and the Indian subcontinent, were humanitarian matters, but there was also a diplomatic subtext. Conor was pointing out the need for Ireland once again to become active in cooperative international activities and to identify with the small independent states of the world, not with the American power bloc.

One small, but revealing, matter that Conor raised was related to the International Development Association Bill of 1971. In the debate on the bill, he suggested that excessive population growth in underdeveloped countries was a major cause of impending disaster. "In the light of the population problem, the urgency of curing population growth through family planning becomes very real indeed," he postulated. "I would hope that Ireland will not now, as she has done in the past, stand in the way of international planning efforts. Ireland was among the countries which on what I described as ecclesiastical, rather than religious grounds, did in the past hinder the making available in the poorer countries of methods of family planning." Even in a sleepy Dail, everyone paid attention. "I would regard that as an extremely immoral and wrong thing to do," Conor added.[64] Conor was here playing with dynamite and he knew it. Only a few weeks earlier, in July 1971, a bill proposed in the senate by Mary Robinson to decriminalize the distribution of contraception devices and information on birth control under certain restricted circumstances was refused a first reading, something that vir-

tually never occurred in everyday Irish politics: birth control was politically dangerous.

Conor had the good sense not to push the population limitation idea
too hard and, in fact, he knew that one could only go so far in antag-
onizing the church. When, at a public meeting of the Labour party in
Tramore in late April 1971, Noel Browne compared the Catholic
Church in the south to the Orange Order in the North and set forth an
array of policies for the party that included virtual secularization of Irish
society, Conor strongly opposed him. Conor may have agreed with
most of Browne's ideas in his heart, but he understood Irish political reality. "You can't afford to fight the church."[65]

How far would Conor go in stifling his own beliefs, and on what issues? There were two test cases. The first of these was the proposed
Irish entry into the European Community. The annual conference of
the Irish Labour party had adopted a formal policy of opposition to
Irish entry and the parliamentary Labour party was required to defend
that decision publicly. Conor, although never very keen on Ireland's
joining Europe, was not in principle opposed to it. However, he recognized that if he did not push this foreign policy position, he would be
removed from his foreign affairs spokesmanship and, more important,
from the associated spokesmanship on Northern Ireland. Therefore,
"to be able to go on telling the truth [about Northern Ireland], I told
a whopping great lie."[66] He argued elegantly against entry into
Europe[67] and then was greatly relieved when, in May 1972, Irish entry
was approved by the electorate by a landslide five-to-one margin.
(Ironically, in January 1973, Conor was chosen by the Dail as one of the
Labour Members of the European Parliament. There was no salary at
that time for being an MEP, but the travel allowance was good and
watching yet-another parliament was entertaining. Conor remained an
MEP only until the spring of 1973, when he became a cabinet minister
in the Dail and found he had no time for extra-Irish duties.[68]

In trimming his political beliefs, Conor was doing what any politician has to do, but it bothered him. He reflected on Edmund Burke's
words, "We must practice an economy of truth that we may live to tell
it longer," but he later admitted that having to do so was a "deplorable
experience."[69] More distasteful than peddling the anti-Europe line was
his having to oppose in late 1972 an Offences Against the State Bill
which made it possible to convict terrorists solely on the evidence of a
senior garda (police) officer. Conor, though he did not like the bill very
much, thought it might be useful in reducing the killing in Northern
Ireland. At first, he refused to fight the bill. However, as Labour's
northern spokesman, he was expected to lead an attack on it and to do

so on the grounds that it diminished civil liberties in the republic and would not do any good in the North. The matter came to a head when Frank Cluskey (who was Conor's backer on most issues relating to Northern Ireland) told him that if he did not oppose the bill, he would cease to be Northern Ireland spokesman. Conor opposed the bill.[70]

. . .

Northern Ireland, then, was the issue that counted and for which he was willing to compromise in other spheres. Why Northern Ireland? That is akin to asking Saul of Tarsus, "Why Christianity?" One can describe the events that led to Conor's conversion on the issue of Northern Ireland, one can define his former beliefs and his later ones, but the central question of why and, especially, why did he come to care so much are really beyond answer. At some point all explanations of human behavior become tautological: Conor adopted certain beliefs and engaged in certain actions because they fit his personality and, of course, a person's beliefs and actions are the only definition that we can have of a person's personality.

The reference to Saul of Tarsus is not *outré*, but is, in fact, productive and this for three reasons. First, Saul's transformation from an orthodox person who persecuted the heterodox minority, to an advocate of that minority, is the archetypal conversion experience. So radical is it that Saul's alter ego, Paul, has to explain it to his later readers by referring to a physical experience on the road to Damascus of seeing a great light and hearing the voice of Yahweh. Paul's metaphor offers a brilliant encapsulation of what conversion does to a person, but it should not be taken as meaning that the conversion actually occurred instantly. Nor did Conor's, which was equally radical. His path had altered several times since the days he was a keen participant in Sean MacBride's antiunionist (and covertly anti-Protestant) hate campaign of the late 1940s and early 1950s; but by the mid-1970s he was facing in exactly the opposite direction he had taken in 1949. When Saul changed direction, moreover, he liberated immense energy into his new persona as Paul. The same thing occurred in Conor's case. He became a man on a mission, charged with energy. The most important thing in his life became (and remains) the prevention of civil war in Northern Ireland.

And, as is the case with the Saul-Paul conversion, how one judges the results depends entirely on one's own ideology and moral values. The apostle Paul is adjudged either to have been the greatest missionary in Christian history or the church's greatest disaster, as the weaver of anti-Semitism, patriarchy, and sexual paranoia into the fabric of Christianity. Similarly, in his crusade on Northern Ireland, Conor becomes either the greatest living Irishman or Irish nationalism's most treacherous and dangerous foe.

In late June 1970, Conor was once again in Belfast. This was because on 26 June Bernadette Devlin had been arrested for her part in the Derry riots of the previous year and new riots had begun in Derry and especially in Belfast. Conor went north with his friend Jack Dowling, a former Irish army officer who knew Northern Ireland well and had family in Newry. They visited Gerry Fitt, his house now bearing a big iron grid on the basement windows to protect against Protestant attack (and, later, the whole front of the house was to be heavily reinforced against Catholic attack, such being the complex ways of northern politics). Conor talked with Paddy Devlin, who still wanted guns for Catholic defense. Conor and Jack Dowling were at St. Matthew's Church, part of a small Catholic enclave in the Newtonards Road, surrounded by Protestant housing, when the church was attacked. This was, in fact, the second night of attack; the previous evening, two Protestants had been shot. This evening, about midnight, in the eerie glow of mercury lights, a Protestant mob again was on the attack. A fog of tear gas came from the canisters shot into the crowd by the British soldiers who were defending the church. The crowd retreated; there were no deaths this time.[71]

At this stage, Conor still was identifying solely with the Catholics, but not with great emotional heat. Soon after his Belfast visit, he met in Dublin with Rory O'Brady, the then-leader of the newly formed Provisional IRA. He found O'Brady charming in a peculiar way, and Conor was willing to contemplate working out a common Catholic front that would include Sinn Fein as well as the regular southern Irish political parties.[72]

On 5 July, Conor returned to Northern Ireland, accompanied by Michael O'Leary, a mercurial, brilliant young colleague who in subsequent months came to share most of Conor's opinions on the North (and who briefly in 1981–82 himself became leader of the Labour party). They spent the day on the Falls Road and then went back to Dublin. Conor was back in Belfast on the thirteenth (the Twelfth fell on Sunday that year) for the big display at the Field, Finaghy. "If ye hate Gerry Fitt, clap yer hands" was the chant for the year, and a lot did.[73]

Conor was picking up a data bank on the North, which, based as it was on his earlier intelligence work for the southern government during the 1950s, and upon his having spent a fair amount of time in the North by virtue of his first wife's having been from Northern Ireland, was quite extensive. It did not rival the data banks of northern politicians, but was far more extensive than that of almost any other politician in the

Irish Republic. Although Conor's initial instinct was to identify solely with the northern Catholics, rather than with both sides in Northern Ireland, his overall coolness was notable, almost unnerving.

For instance, Conor went to Derry in the company of his brother-in-law Seamus MacEntee, for the August 1970 parade of the Apprentice Boys (a slightly up-market affiliate of the Orange Order). Conor's face was well-enough known that he had to be careful. (In Belfast, in June, Jack Dowling had replaced Conor's duncher with his own trilby, saying, "For God's sake, hide your face, man.") So, attending a march-past and speech-session of irritable Protestants was either an act of considerable courage or pure folly. Early in the day, an Apprentice Boy, in bowler and sash, brushed against Conor and asked, "Were ye ever in the Congo?" Conor said yes and the man gave him what was intended as a friendly warning. "I wanted ye to know ye've been spotted. It will be safer for you to leave town." Conor did not take this advice and he and Seamus attended the afternoon meeting. As it was drawing to a close, a group of young toughs, noting that Conor and Seamus were not ap- plauding the anti-Catholic rhetoric, started elbowing and kicking them from behind. These were hangers-on, not Apprentice Boys. When Conor and Seamus made to leave, the thugs thumped them and punched them about. They were saved by three Apprentice Boys, but when Conor and Seamus had gone on farther down the street, they were spotted again and this time Conor was punched to the ground and kicked about. He was rescued by a big sergeant-major of a man, an Apprentice Boy, who appeared, shouted, "Is it murder ye want?" and warned off the thugs.

From a historian's point of view, the striking thing about this event is the absolutely calm, nonjudgmental manner in which Conor recorded it in his diary.[74] I do not think the *sang froid* was faked. Conor was pick- ing up information on the northern situation and being there is how one did it.

(As a parenthesis, Conor's physical courage is something that one is apt to take for granted, because he does. He has been beaten up by New York cops, Protestant thugs, and attacked by South African black mil- itants. He has traveled through some of the nastier combat zones of our times—the Congo, Biafra, Nicaragua—yet, he just keeps going places that he should not. Whether or not one respects physical courage is a matter of personal taste, but certainly one must recognize its existence, for that courage was one of the things that made his eventual stance on Northern Ireland possible, in the face of threats to his life.)

What finally tipped Conor out of his cool, information-gathering mode concerning Northern Ireland was a set of events that actually had as much to do with the republic as with the North. This was the sequence of events that evolved into the "arms trial," and which, subsequently, wraps itself around and around Irish politics in this period like a parasitic vine. To understand where this came from, one must realize how much the arrival of British troops in Northern Ireland in August 1969 had confused the government of Jack Lynch. The government had nothing resembling a policy in place, and it merely reacted in a contradictory, near-chaotic fashion. One of these reactions was to order a mobilization of 2,000 reservists and to send a small proportion of the Irish Republic's regular army of 8,500 troops to border areas. There was no possible functional reason for this move. An invasion of the North would have been an insanity, and in all probability the troops from southern Ireland would have been unable to overcome the Royal Ulster Constabulary and its auxiliaries and even less the British army. (Insane as it now seems, the republic's army did have a contingency plan for invading the North, and certain cabinet members actually desired to put it into operation.) In any case, the arrival of British troops was considered by the Ulster Catholics to be a victory over the Stormont government. Rather lamely, Dr. Hillery tried at first to explain that the troops had been sent to the border on the assumption that the United Kingdom would agree to a joint Anglo-Irish peace-keeping force, a possibility only slightly less remote than the republic's army being able to conquer the North. Then, beginning to realize its mistake, the Lynch government explained that the troops had been sent to the border to protect the recently established field hospitals and refugee centers, although precisely from whom never was made clear. Actually, there was no rational reason for calling up the troops, and from a diplomatic point of view the mobilization was dysfunctional, for it cast the Dublin government in the role of an aggressive trouble-making meddler.

Just how impassioned the southern government could become was indicated by a massive propaganda campaign initiated by the taoiseach. On Lynch's orders fifteen public relations experts from various governmental agencies and state corporations were seconded to prepare a propaganda drive. By 30 August, 20,000 copies of a booklet entitled "The Story in Pictures of the North's Distress" were printed and were being shipped to Irish embassies for distribution throughout the world. The booklet was visual propaganda at its worst. Ten of the twenty photographs were of British troops. The clear implication was that the British troops were in some way responsible for the afflictions of the Ulster nationalists when the truth was that at that time the troops were protecting the Catholics. Lynch's propaganda was so shoddy that it was not even acceptable for consumption within Ireland. The *Irish Times* denounced the pamphlet as did the liberal periodicals. Clearly counterproductive as a diplomatic move, the Lynch administration's propaganda campaign may best be described as emotional therapy and left at that.

During most of the crisis period Lynch was content to allow day-to-day policy to be set by a four-man "Northern Sub-Committee," the two functioning members of which were Charles Haughey and Neil Blaney, both of whom were senior cabinet ministers. To what extent these men acted with Lynch's approval probably never will be known for sure. What is morally (as distinct from legally) certain is, first, that Haughey and Blaney were involved in an effort to smuggle arms to northern guerilla leaders; second, a subsequent Dail investigation revealed that at least £30,000 of £100,000 voted by the Dail for relief of the distress of the northern Catholics did not go for the purposes for which it was intended and in all probability was subverted to buy arms; third, it appears that a band of Fianna Fail politicians promised large sums of money for arms to one branch of the then-splitting IRA—the Provisionals—if they would cease political activities in the south of Ireland and concentrate on military action in Ulster. The other branch—the "Officials"—was a Marxist group with a fairly broad social agenda and they already had refused to limit their activities to the North. With their traditional republican rhetoric and their progressive social agenda, they were a potential threat to Fianna Fail's traditional nationalist political base in the south. The Provisional IRA—the "Provos" as they became known—were much less menacing, it was thought, since they were straight old-fashioned sectarian republicans. Once armed, however, they quickly outpaced the Officials, who stood down in mid-1972 and disappeared into ideological fragmentation and, finally, dust. The Provos, once helped to emerge from the bottle, were dangerous as any necromancer's genie.[75]

That Charles Haughey, minister for finance and Neil Blaney, minister for agriculture, had gone very far out of bounds emerged during the sensational arms trial. On 6 May 1970, Jack Lynch announced that Haughey and Blaney had been dismissed. (Kevin Boland, minister for local government, resigned of his own volition at the same time, but this was a side issue.) This became Ireland's biggest political sensation since the Mother and Child health affray of 1951. The Dail debate on the dismissals ranged from Billingsgate to oratory of classical nobility, and back to Billingsgate, like a great rhetorical rollercoaster. In the Billingsgate sections were remarks such as those of Joseph Lenehan, TD for West Mayo, who interrupted the soft-voiced comments of Liam Cosgrave of Fine Gael with "Ah, shut up! Your father sold the north and damn well you know it."[76] Brendan Corish, leader of the Labour party, was calmly devastating. "Over the last eighteen months, Fianna Fail have spoken with two voices on this matter of national unity. We had the Taoiseach, the Fianna Fail party spokesman condemning violence...and we had the other voice through the now-Deputy Blaney and others, who intend that the use of force is legitimate and practicable."[77] The most effective attack came on the third day of the four-day debate on the dismissals, and was by Fine Gael's Garret FitzGerald. Proceeding as if he were teaching accounting to first-year undergraduates, he made it clear that a large pile of cash had disappeared and that the Dail accounts would not make it past the eye of any competent auditor.[78]

Conor's own response was in its surface content too partisan to be very effective. Referring to Fianna Fail, he said that "the party is sick with a dangerous and infectious sickness. It is incubating the germs of a possible future civil war."[79] Yet, his intense attacks on Fianna Fail had behind them a serious long-term worry. Conor was beginning to be concerned about the possible existence in Ireland of what the ancient Greeks called kakistocracy, that is, government by the worst citizens. Thus, he referred to Jack Lynch's having pointed to the long tradition of family service of the two cashiered cabinet members (and of Kevin Boland as well). Then, he introduced a most unusual analogy: "In the animal kingdom there are devices for ending a quarrel. There is a technique called 'presentation'; this is analogous to the presenting of arms in the military code. In the animal world if a pair of dogs or wolves are on the verge of a fight one will expose his jugular to the other animal. Then, the fight is over, one has submitted, a hierarchy is established between them and they proceed as a united pack."[80] What did this have to do with recent events?

> [I was] interested in this matter because it seemed to me that what was happening here when the Taoiseach made this reference to his family not having had the same traditions of service as did the families of Deputies Boland, Haughey, Blaney and, perhaps, O'Morain that he was "presenting," he was appeasing. This is very odd because formally what he was doing was humiliating them, pushing them out. They should have been presenting their jugular vein or the backs of their heads or any appropriate part of their anatomy. But no, it was the other way round. I hope Deputies will not think I have dealt with this facetiously, but I think these comparisons are valid. The real point is that he was acknowledging their continuing authority within the Fianna Fail Party, and they do have such authority, and, considering the views they have, such authority is extremely dangerous.[81]

Jack Lynch survived the arms debacle by playing quite brilliantly the fool's defense: he had not, he claimed, known anything about what his rogue cabinet ministers were doing. And, given that Fianna Fail had a safe majority in the Dail, a vote of nonconfidence had no chance of success. Then, in late May, Charles Haughey and Neil Blaney were arrested and charged with conspiring to import arms and ammunition. Note that the attorney general defined the charge against the men not as having stolen public funds or as having smuggled arms to Northern Ireland, but as having illegally *imported* them into the republic! The charge against Blaney was dropped early in July and Haughey was acquitted late in October. No one was ever tried on the real charge, of gun-running to the North. Next, when the Public Accounts Committee of the Dail looked into how the Northern Ireland Distress money had disappeared when Charles Haughey was minister for finance, it discovered that most of the Relief Fund had been misapplied; yet no prosecutions were engaged.[82]

When he applied his historian's perspective to the situation, what Conor saw as happening was the replacement of the de Valera generation of Fianna Fail politicians who, whatever else they may have been, had been men of great principle, with what Conor later called "the new men, cocksure and ignorant children of the great de Valera success story, the avid heirs to the hottest political property in the country."[83] As the events of 1969–70 showed, these individuals—of whom Charles Haughey was the archetype—were soaked in nationalist rhetoric, but were unable to control what happened when those vapors mixed with the oxygen of the real world. This was explosive, a danger to democracy, because "to them the Nation—embodying the sacred claim to the whole island—is on a higher plane than the State."[84] In 1986, Conor summarized how his judgments had firmed: "I felt from the Arms Trial period on, that Fianna Fail with Haughey in it was very dangerous to the whole country and eventually to democracy itself, and I have not changed that view since."[85]

A Newtonian moral equation therefore was coming into operation. If the Irish nationalist tradition was not all-virtuous, then, probably, the Ulster unionist position was not all-vice. Conor, in 1969 and 1970 was not merely instinctively identifying with the northern Catholics, but was engaged simultaneously in the very difficult task of thinking about the northern Protestants, reflecting on, among other things, why a bunch of them would want to thump him, nonviolent southern nationalist that he was. He came to the conclusion, bemusedly at first, and then with increasing assertiveness, that, indeed, the Protestants were

human beings and had a right to exist, even if the Prods collectively refused to join up with the republic to the south.

As early as 1963, Conor had given his opinion at a St. Patrick's Day
interview to the London *People* that "to accept partition as a fact is the
best way of beginning the process of ending it." The first step must be
"a public declaration that the Irish government will not attempt in any
way—either by force or propaganda—to change the situation of the Six
Counties without the agreement of a majority of the people in the
area."[86] Further, in 1970, Conor was in the midst of a restudy of the
issue of minority rights as a general matter and obviously this affected
both groups in Northern Ireland (the Catholics who were a minority
within the Six Counties and the Protestants who were a minority within
the Thirty-Two Counties). One philosophical position that Conor
adopted at this time implied that the partition of Ireland perhaps had
been a historical necessity. In a lecture on the rights of minorities, he
said, "I believe that secession is an evil, or rather the recognition of an
evil, a breakdown in human relations. I also believe that no minority is
likely to have recourse to it, with all its dangers, unless the pressures on
the minority are felt to be intolerable, and unless there are other sufficient conditions to make it possible—I have in mind such factors as nu-
merical strength, terrain, diplomatic conjuncture, and so on."[87] If one
fed certain historical data into that equation, one could possibly (not
necessarily, but possibly) come to the conclusion that the secession of
the northern Protestant minority from the rest of Ireland in the period
1912–14 (which was ratified in 1920) was historically justified.

Conor in 1969 and in the early 1970s also was becoming acquainted
with more and more northern Protestants. With the exception of
Garret FitzGerald, it is hard to think of any southern Catholic politician
of note who had more than a handful of northern Protestant friends,
and most had fewer, if any. Conor's daughter Fedelma had recently
married Nicholas Simms, son of the Protestant archbishop of Armagh
(and formerly archbishop of Dublin) and this gave Conor entry to a circle of liberal Protestants. Through northern Labour circles, Conor
came to know some of the shop stewards, all of them Protestants, in the
Belfast shipyards and for a time was taken with their particular brand of
peace making.[88] He liked their trick of colluding with management
when they sensed that sectarian problems were about to erupt on the
shop floor. They would get management to introduce some new regulation or work practice that was obnoxious to the workers. The workers
would join together, management would resist, and class conflict would,
therefore, be artificially created to distract workers from the real conflict, which was sectarian.[89]

Increasingly, Conor was acquiring an attitude of understanding and of tolerance of the bulk of northern Protestants (not the thugs, mind you), and this was about as incorrect as one could get. He was reproved, on the highest of intellectual planes, for this in 1977 by Seamus Deane, who, in the first issue of the *Crane Bag*, rendered this judgment:

> The kind of humanism which Conor Cruise O'Brien sponsors is precisely that kind of humanism, totally detached from its atavisms, which, though welcome from a rational point of view, renders much of what he says either irrelevant or simply wrong, particularly in relation to the North where bigotry is so much part of the psyche. ... The very clarity of O'Brien's position is just what is most objectionable. It serves to give a rational clarity to the Northern situation which is untrue to the reality. In other words, is not his humanism here being used as an excuse to rid Ireland of the atavisms which give it life even though the life may be in some ways brutal?[90]

• • •

From mid-1971 onward, events in Northern Ireland occurred so quickly and with such vividness that one seems to be watching an action-painting by an artist with a very broad palette knife and heavy oils; layer upon layer of paint piled onto the canvas, each covering the layer beneath and, in turn, obscured by a subsequent layer. The June 1970 U.K. election replaced the Labour government in London with Edward Heath's Tories. In March 1971, James Chichester-Clark resigned as Northern Ireland's prime minister and was succeeded by Brian Faulkner. Crucially, as background fluorescence to this scene, violence of all sorts increased. The number of violent deaths in the Six Counties was on a sharp upcurve: 225 in 1970, 174 in 1971, 467 in 1972.[91] The lead group in this toll was the rapidly expanding Provisional IRA which was shouldering aside the Officials, and was conducting a terror campaign in the North that mostly killed civilians.

Conor's response was missionary, almost Pauline. As his friend Brian Garrett, formerly chairman of the Northern Ireland Labour party, observes, at first Conor was most afraid that the Provo offensive would result in a sectarian backlash that would literally set the Catholic neighborhoods on fire and would produce horrendous Catholic casualties. Soon, however, he came to perceive the Provos' campaign as a major problem, whether or not it produced a Protestant backlash. In those days, the Provos concentrated on "soft" targets such as department stores, public lavatories, libraries and other public buildings and the people they most terrorized were women, children, and old-age pensioners.[92]

In response, Conor began a series of visits in the Twenty-Six
Counties to any place that would have him: mostly constituency
branches of the Labour party, but anything from a library study group
to a writers' workshop would do. He preached a very simple gospel: that
violence as a means to any obtainable or desirable political end in
Northern Ireland was wrong; the IRA was not forwarding classical Irish
nationalism, but, rather, atavistic sectarianism and tribalism; that supporting violence in the North would have long-term costs in the south.
His visitations were particularly effective within the Labour party.
When someone from down-the-country would call the Dublin headquarters and complain that that man O'Brien was being unpatriotic and
not supporting our people in the North and should be got rid of, party
headquarters would say, "Well, we'll send him down and you can tell
him yourself where he is wrong." Conor would go down to the local
branch and, in the usual case, the local Sinn Fein enthusiasts would not
show up or would arrive and be gloomily silent. This he did week after
week and by mid-1971 he probably had talked to more local constituency groups than any other member of the parliamentary Labour party
save the leader, Brendan Corish, and he had twenty-five years' head
start as a Labour member of the Dail.[93]

A very sharp bend in Conor's road occurred in June 1971. The Irish
Transport and General Workers' Union held its annual conference in
Galway that year. Most of the members came with instructions from
their union locals on how to vote on each issue. The agenda being well
known in advance, the voting on major motions was tightly choreographed. An annual ritual was to pass a motion about republican prisoners. The form it was to take in 1971 was "that this conference calls
for the immediate release of Irish political prisoners presently held in
England and Northern Ireland."[94] There was no doubt that this would
pass, given union bloc voting, but the motion rankled Conor. He recognized that its subtext was an affirmation, however oblique, of a sectarian war being carried on in the North in the name of Irish
nationalism.

Brendan Corish was sitting next to Conor, but Conor gave him no
warning. He stood up and asked, "What does the term 'political prisoner' mean?" That stunned the conference. "Is a man convicted in
court and jailed for inciting and leading a sectarian mob a political prisoner? or a man who booby-traps a car? or plants a bomb, injuring children and innocent people? or a man who guns down another man?"[95]
He was heard in complete silence. No one had ever dared to raise such
issues. When he sat down, he was applauded by most delegates. Then,
however, he was denounced by a series of five republican speakers,

mostly former prisoners or detainees themselves, and in the style of the Citizen in Joyce's *Ulysses*. Conor's suggestion that the Irish trade union movement, being nonsectarian, should avoid all resolutions that might estrange the Protestant workers of the North from the movement, was ignored.[96]

As Conor was being successively denounced, Brendan Corish prepared himself to intervene. Corish bears note, for he moves through the early 1970s rather like a silver-screen idol of the silent picture era, often on screen, but historically voiceless. He is easily underestimated. In part this is because he was an immensely handsome man, along the lines of John Barrymore, and, indeed, he would have preferred to have been an actor. He was among the least likely of political leaders, for although he had virtually inherited his seat for Wexford (his father had been a founding figure in the Irish labor movement, very much involved with James Larkin and James Connolly), he was that rare animal, a genuinely reluctant leader. Yet, he was a good political tactician, a terrific annual-conference orator, and he was the perfect party leader for a caucus full of intellectuals, because he had no intellectual pretensions himself.

Corish, after hearing his parliamentary party member being slagged, stood up and did what a good leader has to do: back his man. He told the delegates that Dr. O'Brien deserved to be heard. He was, Corish reminded them, foremost among the Labour party people who had gone to the North when the Troubles broke, and he was a key member of the delegation that convinced the British government to abandon the B Specials.[97] Corish's action essentially fireproofed Conor with the general membership of the Labour party and when the original motion was passed by the Irish Transport and General Workers' Union conference, it was no wound to Conor's political position.

This event received a good deal of national publicity and made obvious nationally what had not been clear while Conor was going from constituency to constituency, preaching. The one politician in the republic who most stood in the way of traditional republicanism and of terrorism (not the same thing, but too often related) was Conor Cruise O'Brien. Thus, his removal from the position of Labour spokesman on Northern Ireland became a prime goal of the sympathizers with traditional republicanism in the Twenty-Six Counties. And he was hated even more by the terrorists.

That raises a question. Why, in the span from 1971 to 1977 (when he left the Dail), was Conor not killed? Part of the answer lies in the Provos' general order number eight, which forbade the shooting of southern politicians as long as they remained in the Twenty-Six Counties. Another reason lies in the way Conor tailored his crusade.

Although he directly and unambiguously opposed terrorism, he heeded some very shrewd advice from his son Donal. "If you are attacking them, never do it in a personal way; don't single out individuals; and, above all, never laugh at any individual, or hold him up to ridicule." As an afterthought, Donal added, "and if you are attacking them in print, do it in journals that they don't read. The *Observer* for example."[98] And when Conor was in office, he had a bodyguard, as did most members of the republic's cabinet from 1973 onward (and minders to protect against the kidnapping of family members as well). Still, I suspect that he also was just plain lucky. I would not be at all surprised if, as once-young terrorists become garrulous old men, we do not hear of more than one of them having been assigned to do O'Brien, but, for one reason or another, not getting the job done.

From the middle of 1971 onward, Conor was on a mission. He veered occasionally from this path, but always returned. "I only became a serious person in 1971," he says. "Before that I was an *homme sen-suel*."[99] If there has to be a moment of epiphany, a date the blinding light shone, it was 11 June 1971 and the moment was the meeting of the Irish Transport and General Workers' Union.

In late July 1971, a fund to commemorate Erskine Childers was scheduled to be launched at the St. Lawrence Hotel, Howth. Childers, who had been executed in 1923 by the new government of the Irish Free State for his "republican" activities had, in 1914, been captain of the *Asgard* which had run guns into Howth. Conor refused to attend. "The reason is simply this," he wrote to the head of the commemoration committee, "that in the recent time, with its steadily increasing tempo of political violence, commemorations of this kind are liable to be exploited for purposes disruptive of peace in this country."[100] There was more: but what counted was that in a political culture that sacralized patriotic martyrs, Conor was taking a virtually revolutionary position.

"Conor, you're going too fast," Brendan Halligan told him soon thereafter.

He replied, "I intend to administer an electric shock to the Irish psyche."[101] He did so not just by continuing to preach against all forms of violence in the North, but to assert, in a series of speeches that ran parallel to his message against violence, that Articles 2 and 3 of the constitution of the Republic of Ireland—which declare, in essence, that the republic has the right to rule the North—should be abandoned. The interweaving of these two themes not only gained a great deal of public attention, but began to disturb in a serious way people inside the Labour party. Conor was challenging beliefs that they had been taught, literally, since they entered elementary school.

The fault lines in the Labour party became clear after the introduction in Northern Ireland of internment without trial on 9 August 1971. The arrest of 342 persons, almost all of them Catholics, resulted in rioting that killed nearly a score of people and led to the burning of at least 150 houses in Belfast. Fortunately for the political fortune of the Labour party, the Dail had adjourned three days earlier and was not scheduled to be recalled until 20 October. Conor did not at that time favor internment (he was soon to start pressing the British government to release the detainees), but anything that raised the temperature in Northern Ireland automatically heightened differences on the northern issue.

On 7 October 1971, Conor abruptly resigned as the Labour party spokesman on foreign affairs and on Northern Ireland. He did this because he believed that Brendan Halligan and Justin Keating (the party's EC spokesman) had cut him out of a meeting in England with British Labour party officials. Brendan Halligan tried to explain that there had been no formal delegation.[102] But Conor, vanity wounded (and beginning to distrust Halligan and Keating's long-term intentions), reaffirmed his resignation in a remarkably petulant letter. Its conclusion, however, cut surgically to the point about the party's Northern Ireland policy:

> I am not prepared either (a) to equivocate about the North, (b) to say things about it which I do not believe, (c) to refrain from saying things which I do believe and which I believe it important to say, or (d) to act as spokesman for a party which wants to have it both ways: "We are all for peace, but we understand the need for violence; we condemn the IRA but only the Provisionals. We want good relations with England and a boycott of British goods. We do not want to coerce the Protestants of Northern Ireland (sorry, the 6 counties), but we demand a United Socialist Ireland in which they must be included, whether they like it or not."
> No one can be spokesman for a medley like that.[103]

Brendan Corish did not accept Conor's resignation, but that does not obscure the fact that Labour was badly split. When the Dail resumed sitting, the Labour TDs showed divisions among themselves in debates on the North held on 20 and 21 October.[104]

Conor continued his shocks to the national psyche. On 23 October, at Newman House, Dublin, he debated Tomas Mac Giolla, president of Official Sinn Fein. Conor decried all forms of IRA violence, both branches, and repeated the question that had been posed recently by the northern Catholic bishops: "Who in their sane senses wants to bomb a million Protestants into a united Ireland?"[105] That was not upsetting to his Labour colleagues, but what was deeply troubling was Conor's clear articulation in an article in Dublin's *Irish Independent* (7 December 1971) of the case against Article 3 of the constitution of the republic. "The right to exercise jurisdiction [in the North] is bound to be seen as the right of the Twenty-Six Counties government to exercise jurisdiction over the Six Counties—*essentially a colonial claim*" (emphasis mine). That idea, corrosive of the heart-metal of southern Irish nationalism, brilliant and difficult to refute, was something the average Labour politician, let alone the average Irish citizen, could assimilate only with a lot of preparation, and none had been provided. This was just another shock to the psyche.

In return for this, Conor almost was handed his head. A motion to remove Conor as northern spokesman was put forward at the meeting of the parliamentary Labour party on Friday, 10 December 1971. This turned out to be a moment of truth for what political scientists of the day labeled "the 1969 generation."[106] The form the challenge took was a motion by David Thornley to reject Conor's idea that Article 3 of the Irish Republic's constitution, which claimed a "right" of rule over the entire Thirty-Two Counties, be changed to an "aspiration." Supporting Thornley were Stevie Coughlan and Sean Treacy. Treacy was only six years older than Conor but he was an honorable embodiment of an earlier generation's nationalism. He was one of the Dail's last practitioners of nineteenth-century oratory and he was not at all uncomfortable using orotund phrases, such as his reference to "the great truth that God fixed the boundary for the Irish nation when he fixed as its frontier the encircling sea."[107] The spine of Conor's support came from Frank Cluskey and from Michael O'Leary. O'Leary was in his mid-thirties, impatient with the old ways.[108] But absent from Conor's side of the fight was Conor himself. He was in New York for the opening of *Murderous Angels.*

The question was, how would the floaters—the middle ground—react? Although an intellectually gifted group, the Labour party was extremely cranky. Noel Browne, known to be strongly opposed to the old verities, nevertheless was always willing to put the needle into Conor. Justin Keating, though nominally a friend of Conor, had ambitions of his own, and Conor was a competitor for any future cabinet plums if Labour came to power, either on its own or, as was more likely, in a coalition government. Totally unpredictable was Dr. John O'Donovan, educated at UCD, Oxford, and Harvard, longtime Department of Finance civil servant and now professor of political economy at University College, Dublin. The oldest of Labour's 1969 generation—

born in 1908—he was both brilliant and given to doing someone down every time he opened his mouth. He had once awakened from sleep during a parliamentary Labour party caucus, shaken himself and begun to denounce Conor. Only after he had gone on for a while did it become clear to everyone that he had mistaken Conor for Noel Browne. He was known as "Mad John" to his colleagues.[109]

The meeting convened in the parliamentary Labour party caucus room in the 1932 Annexe in Leinster House.[110] Much of the decision hung on how well Brendan Corish would run the meeting. Effective as he was both at public oratory and in one-to-one meetings, Corish was weak in the middle ground, such as caucus meetings. He was not an effective chair of a meeting, for he was much too tolerant of diversions. A revealing indication of this was the way he had dealt with one of Noel Browne's more gothic outbursts in a caucus meeting in 1970. Browne arrived late to caucus, did not apologize, but instead moved a chair right up to Corish's left side, sat down, and, paying no heed to the agenda, began addressing his party leader in a penetrating whisper, his face about nine inches from Corish. For three or four minutes, he reminded Corish of one thing: that he had once said that he was a Catholic first and an Irishman second, a sin that Noel Browne would not permit to lie still on anyone's conscience. Would Corish call Browne out of order? He sat calmly and before he had to make a decision, Browne abruptly stopped, stood up, and disappeared from the room, an apparition come and gone in a handful of minutes.[111] Later, in 1973 and thereafter, Corish wisely let his deputy leader run the actual meetings. Now, in December 1971, he still was in the chair, if not completely in control.

As the meeting ran its course, it became clear that the caucus was evenly split over Conor's statements and therefore Brendan Corish would have to make the decision himself. He had not foreseen this eventuality, and he briefly adjourned the meeting to consider his own position. The room that he left was a miasma of cigarette smoke and ill will. Frank Cluskey, whose views on human nature were ever-realistic, remarked loudly that if Brendan Corish came back into the room and resigned (a real possibility, since he clearly had lost control of caucus), he reckoned everyone in the room would consider himself as a candidate for the party leadership. "Except," he added, "that not one of y' bastards could find a seconder." Corish returned. He was not going to dump Conor. The meeting was over.[112]

Conor was frequently criticized for his habit of announcing his personal views as Labour party policy and thus forcing the party either to fire him or adopt this viewpoint.[113] However, in the six weeks after the caucus decision, he worked constructively as a member of a committee that drew up a Labour policy on the North for presentation to the annual conference of the Labour party scheduled for the end of February 1972. That document was a set of compromises, on which neither side could feel entirely comfortable. It was signed by Conor, Barry Desmond, and Michael O'Leary on the one side, and David Thornley and Sean Treacy on the other. This policy document unequivocally repudiated the use of force to unite Ireland, but then added that this should not be taken as acquiescence in the political division of the country. The document called for the end of the "sectarian unionist regime in the Six Counties" and the withdrawal of British troops as soon as a political solution permitted. The document added that the Troubles were caused by the deliberate worsening of Catholic and Protestant relations by "landowners and capitalists."[114]

This was a long way from Conor's recently enunciated view that the irredentist claim of the Twenty-Six Counties to Northern Ireland was itself a form of colonialism, and one wonders how long he would have worn the chafing collar of compromise. However, on 30 January 1972, there occurred a set of events that were as emotionally wrenching to the republic polity as had been those of mid-summer 1969: Bloody Sunday in Derry. Thirteen unarmed demonstrators, acting illegally to be sure; taunting troops, undeniably; attacking them with nonlethal force, certainly; were shot dead, unjustifiably. The paroxysms of rage that ran through the republic were palpable and the traditional nationalist reactions, the same ones that had been raised in mid-1969, reappeared.

Conor himself was deeply affected and seemed to repudiate his entire previous position. By Monday, he was on the RTE program, "The News at One-Thirty," saying that he hoped, as the first item, British paratroops would be withdrawn from Northern Ireland and that an international inquiry into the shootings would take place. "That has happened before. I think if the people who did this are identified, they should be put on trial for murder, as happened with American officers and men responsible for similar actions—at My Lai in Vietnam." He continued, "The problem of withdrawing all the British troops is more complicated because it is difficult to see what force could replace them that would not be resisted by the majority in the area."[115]

He then flew off, as Labour party spokesman on Northern Ireland, to London and spent three days there. He talked with the leaders of the two British opposition parties, Harold Wilson, Labour, and Jeremy Thorpe, Liberal, and to the home secretary, Reginald Maudling, under whose authority Northern Ireland lay.[116] By the time that he saw Maudling, a flu that Conor had been fighting had caught up with him, and he was running a high fever. He was not, he later reflected, making a great deal of sense. "It is possible that this was fortunate; I may have made more impact than if I had made more sense."[117] Conor meant that he was himself an excellent example of the fevered condition of the people of the Irish Republic. He told Reginald Maudling that the intensity of feeling in the republic could only be compared to the revulsion that had occurred after the executions of 1916. Further, although he previously had been warning about the dangers of civil war in Northern Ireland if the British army was withdrawn, he now told the U.K. home secretary that the army was so unacceptable to the minority in the North and to the majority in the south, that the troops had to go, completely. Not immediately, but a date had to be set.[118]

This was as radical a reversal of viewpoint as one could imagine. Had Saul recanted and become again an orthodox Pharisee? Only momentarily, but this emotional swing was real and, if temporary, deep.

Conor repeated his demand for full British troop withdrawal in an article that he wrote for the London *Observer*, published on 6 February,[119] and, later, in the Dail he expanded on his fear of imminent civil war. And he went so far as to argue that the economic effects of the Troubles, unless soon stopped, would cause "a disaster comparable even to the Great Famine of the last century."[120]

Conor did not stay enswooned very long. On 2 February, while he was in London, a national day of mourning was declared in the Twenty-Six Counties, and a Dublin crowd burned the British embassy. Maire telephoned him with the news. She, of impeccably republican roots, told him that this was not 1916; the British embassy was burning, but there was no terrible beauty being born. Maire said that in the cold and gray dawn of another day, the bulk of the Irish people would not be for a war against England, but would grieve for lost jobs, lost trade, lost tourists. The message did not immediately take hold, but in the weeks thereafter, Conor mulled it over and realized that Maire was right.[121]

Further, a group of individuals whom he greatly respected landed on him hard: leaders of the Northern Ireland Labour party, the only genuinely nonsectarian political group in Northern Ireland at that time. The party leader, Erskine Holmes (a Protestant), and its leading tactician, Brian Garrett (of a Catholic-Protestant marriage), called on Conor and taxed him, in Holmes's words, for surrendering "to the politics of the last atrocity." This was an economical and elegant summary of much that was debilitating in relation to the Ulster situation: that people of good will often reacted through a series of revulsions, and their viewpoint depended on which side had been injured most recently, rather than on their keeping the whole picture in view. They told Conor that, in responding in resonance with the Catholic community,

he was losing sight of the reactions in the Protestant culture. Holmes
and Garrett were especially worried that if it were announced that the
British troops were to be pulled out as of a certain date, the Protestants'
reactions might be just as dire as those engendered among the Catholics
by having the troops stay in the North. Things were not as simple, they
reminded him, as emotions of the moment made them appear.[122]

Conor was pushed further away from the instinctive tribalism of his
response to Bloody Sunday by events within the Labour party. The annual conference of the party was scheduled for 25, 26, and 27 February.
This was an annual circus, in which roughly 900 delegates flooded into
some provincial town, and it combined for many of them elements of
a prayer meeting and a drunken spree. That this year's conference, to
be held in Wexford, would be no treat for Conor became clear early on:
he was rejected as constituency delegate by the Dublin North-East constituency association and had to attend solely as a member of the parliamentary Labour party.[123]

The annual conference promised to be unusually divisive in any case:
the left wing, believing that the party was drifting rightward, wanted a
reaffirmation of socialism; three TDs (Stevie Coughlan, Dan Spring, and
Michael Pat Murphy) were facing expulsion from the party because of
various indisciplines; the new agreed statement on Northern Ireland
was up for confirmation; and more than a few delegates wanted Conor
to be dropped as Northern Ireland spokesman.

The tone of the conference was affected by two events which took
the edge off the public reaction to Bloody Sunday, and further cooled
Conor's rapidly diminishing ardor on the subject. On 22 February, a
bomb planted by the Official IRA killed six civilians and an army chaplain at Aldershot in England. And on 25 February, John Taylor,
Northern Ireland's minister of home affairs, was shot several times, although not fatally. This was the first time that politicians had been put
on the front line and it had sobering analogies for all Irish politicians,
north and south.

On the twenty-fifth, the delegates crowded into Wexford, filling
every hotel and guest house. The site of the actual conference, St.
Mary's Hall, on the main street in Wexford, was too small to hold all
the delegates and therefore, when the big issues arose—particularly
Northern Ireland—the place was packed, stifling hot, and blue with
smoke.[124] The conference was chaired by Roddy Connolly, son of
James Connolly. He was an old-fashioned pulpit orator in the pure socialist and republican tradition. His opening speech to conference used
vintage terms such as "British army of occupation," and he ascribed
Bloody Sunday to the "violent occupation of part of our country by

troops of a foreign power."[125] This did not bode well for Conor. Nor did the words of Brendan Corish, who in his own speech as leader of the Labour party was much more nationalistic than usual. He proposed the withdrawal of all troops from Catholic areas in the North, an end to internment without trial, the abolition of the Stormont parliament and its replacement by a representative commission, and the announcement of a specific date for complete British troop withdrawal from Northern Ireland.[126]

Northern Ireland was what this conference was all about (the issue of left-wing dissatisfaction, meantime, was easily deflected by the device of reactivating the committee that had drawn up the much admired "socialist" party policy platform of 1969; and the threatened expulsion of the three contumacious TDs never was formally moved). The spotlight narrowed in on Northern Ireland on Saturday afternoon, 26 February. Despite the best efforts of Roddy Connolly, the agenda soon was in shreds; the topic was too emotive to keep within the bounds of the usual rules of order. The debate was supposed to focus on whether or not to accept the document on Northern Ireland policy, the compromise between Conor's wing of the party and the traditionalists. However, things began to go awry when the chair accepted an amendment, expressing no-confidence in Conor and calling for his removal as party spokesman on northern affairs. Under most systems of debate this would not have been permitted, as the amendment was substantively distant from the main motion. Thus, the delegates at the same time were debating both the compromise policy on Northern Ireland and Conor's spokesmanship, very different issues indeed.

The man behind the no-confidence motion was Sean Treacy. Conor had sought, he said, to make a mockery of all who sought to fight for Irish freedom, and he had denigrated the founder of the Irish Labour party, James Connolly. He accused Conor of "spineless, supine, unprincipled shoneenism." Treacy had a lot more to say along that line and he concluded by asking the conference to take control of the parliamentary Labour party and to fulfill the dream of republican socialism which their commander in chief James Connolly had handed down to them from the General Post Office in 1916. During this speech there were cries of agreement from around the hall and the odd obscene epithet directed at Conor.

While this was going on, Conor's friends had been out rounding up support. They had realized early in the afternoon that things would get rough and, more than anyone else, they needed Frank Cluskey to stand up and back Conor. Cluskey had more credibility with the rank and file than did anybody else in the parliamentary Labour party. Cluskey had been up all night drinking and still was drinking the next afternoon and was a mess. The whippers-in from Conor's side found him and started pouring coffee into him. By the time Treacy's speech was winding up, Cluskey was on the platform, very drunk still, blinking into the arc of the bright lights, but able to walk and to talk. He stood up immediately after Treacy spoke and, clutching the podium to steady himself, made a brilliant three-minute address in the gutteral accent of the Dublin working man. The goal of a socialist party, he said, was to bring about the unity of all, north and south, Catholic, Anglican, and Presbyterian. Now the bomb and the bullet were being used by at least two organizations. To great applause, he rasped out, "I not only resent those people and their killing people. *I resent them doing it in my name.*" He staggered away from the rostrum, having turned the meeting.

Thereafter, Barry Desmond spoke briefly and then Conor stood up. He rose to an ovation and this indicated that his side was in the majority (later, he guessed that the ratio of supporters to opponents was five to one).[127] His speech touched all the right buttons—mentions of Connolly, references to socialist unity, the incompatibility of terrorism with a socialist movement and with true socialism and honest nationalism. He directly attacked those who, under the guise of patriotism, were taking Ireland along the road to national suicide.

> It is right that action should be taken to insure that the territory of this state should not be used as a base for terrorist attacks either in Northern Ireland or in Britain. Such action should be taken fearlessly and even-handedly. I am not satisfied that what the government is now doing is evenhanded. They are arresting people whose connections with violence are fairly remote—people in the open political official Sinn Fein movement—while leaving untouched notorious military leaders of the Provisional IRA. This is playing party politics with the lives of our people and the security of the state.
>
> I believe the left-wing people who became involved with the official IRA are tragically mistaken, sincerely and from high motives. Some of them have acknowledged their error. ... Some others surely must have realized it as they heard the Official IRA claim what it regards as credit for Aldershot and the attempted murder of John Taylor. I would rather see these people given time to think that over than see them jailed, while reputed killers on the right wing of the IRA remain at large.
>
> The fantastic thing is that those who support these campaigns of violence actually accuse us who oppose them of callousness, of cold indifference, to the suffering of the Catholics of the North. ... The Catholics of the North are suffering as no section of the Irish people have suffered for fifty years. They want to see the last of the British Army. They also want to see the end

of the activities of their so-called defenders, the green militarists who have no objection to what they call the inevitable urban casualties of an urban guerrilla war. [128]

In full form, Conor became overconfident and very nearly blew himself out of the water with a swipe at Sean Treacy, an understandable, but unnecessary act. Conor mentioned that Treacy had been one of three Labour TDs to vote with the clerically sycophantic Fianna Fail party in a debate on a bill that would have legalized the prescription and sale of contraceptive devices in certain circumstances. This debate had been held in the Dail in the previous week, but Conor's memory here failed him. Immediately he made this accusation Treacy was on his feet, screaming that this was a "libel." Brendan Corish and Roddy Connolly urgently tried to signal to Conor. Finally they caught his attention. "You've made a mistake," they told him. By this time, the conference was in an uproar and Treacy, taking the platform, milked the incident for a full five minutes. Not only had he supported Labour's position in favor of "legalizing contraception," he said, "but I was the first in behind my leader, Brendan Corish, to do so." Conor could only stand helplessly off to the side, deep red with embarrassment.

When Sean Treacy paused, Conor came forward and apologized. Treacy accepted this with a cold demeanor and went back to his seat with the hauteur of a matron who has detected the hotel management's using skim milk in the scones. Conor took up the threads of his speech, but it took him a long time to recover himself. Two more times in the course of the talk, he apologized to Treacy. One shrewd observer, Donal Foley, suggested later that the evidence of Conor as a mere mortal, no longer arrogant, and manifestly just as capable of error as the next delegate, helped his cause. [129]

When Conor was done, Matt Merrigan, general secretary of the Irish Transport and General Workers' Union, briefly patronized both Conor and Sean Treacy. They should not be blamed for their scrapping, he said, because the Irish Labour party had picked up the petty bourgeois idea of unity in place of the real thing, socialist unity. Fortunately, Paddy Devlin, who was present as a fraternal delegate, brought everyone together by slagging the Fianna Fail government in serious Belfast terms, and then appealed for the withdrawal of the censure on Conor.

While Devlin was making his speech, Brendan Halligan was going back and forth from faction to faction, working out a deal: if the Treacy people would withdraw the motion of no-confidence in Conor, the other side would withdraw the motion endorsing the new composite Northern Ireland policy. So, after Paddy Devlin was done, Sean Treacy returned to the rostrum and made a very dignified, old-fashioned speech about fears and doubts and ambiguities, and these having been clarified by the debate, they could now all stand together as a united party. The motions were withdrawn. Conor came forward. "Hold Treacy's hand up," Halligan hissed to him and the two men stood behind the rostrum, arms raised in unity. It was a moment of great catharsis. The hall erupted; people stood on chairs, and cheered. Bang! went the chairman's gavel and the meeting was adjourned.

What few delegates noticed in their euphoria was that in fact nothing had been decided. No decision was taken on northern policy, although Conor's position as spokesman was safe for the moment.

When on 24 March 1972, the Northern Ireland Parliament was suspended, Conor was pleased. Although this was in theory a temporary move, everyone knew it was the end for Stormont. Conor had argued in the London *Observer* four months earlier that the answer to the question "What can England do?" was to "ensure that the same equality of opportunity that obtains elsewhere in the United Kingdom prevails also in Northern Ireland. That means a practical application of direct rule."[130] Direct rule marked a major change in the United Kingdom's policy. It had moved from attempting to effect policies approved by the Protestants in Northern Ireland, to policies designed to attract Catholic support.[131]

• • •

Earlier I suggested that a transformation in Irish politics, north and south, was begun in the late 1960s. It broke each part of the country out of nearly half a century of ideological and social homeostasis. The instrumentalities were three. First, as we have seen, the Catholic civil rights movement of the later 1960s was crucial, because northern Catholics stopped opting out of northern political structures and, instead, demanded in. Next, the creation of a terrorist movement, dating from mid-1969, went beyond anything the security forces of the Irish Republic and of Northern Ireland were accustomed to dealing with. In the North, sectarian rioting was something the culture could deal with: a map of rioting in Belfast in the mid-nineteenth-century was not much different from a map of riot spots in the late 1960s. What was new was the creation of terrorist movements that targeted civilian populations, using the technology of explosives that became widespread after World War II. From mid-1969 until the end of May 1972, both the Provos and the Officials were active. On 29 May of that year, the Officials suspended their Northern Ireland activities, and thereafter the Provos made the running.

The third major instrument of change was the Social Democratic and Labour Party (SDLP) which reoriented the politics of the bulk of the Ulster Catholics. Until 1970, the Catholic vote in Northern Ireland had been split into several rival factions, of which the Nationalist Party and the Republican Labour Party were the most important. These several nationalist groups had not worked at all well together and some of them gained elective positions on an "abstentionist" platform, which meant that their leaders were elected on the promise that they would not take the office for which they were elected. In August 1970, six nationalist Stormont MPs came together as the SDLP. This party differed from earlier Catholic efforts at forming a single nonviolent political front in the North in its being much more middle class in leadership and orientation than were previous Catholic parties and in having a much stronger Derry orientation. This latter characteristic over the long run was crucial. Traditional Catholic parties in Ulster, being Belfast-based, were essentially defensive, being those of a people surrounded on all sides by the Protestant majority. Derry, on the other hand, was the locus of the West-of-the-Bann Catholic quadrant which was contiguous with the Irish Republic. As the SDLP developed, its Derry attitude, its sense of assurance, made it much more effective than its predecessors.

There are many stories of how the SDLP came into being—success indeed does have a hundred fathers—and two of these are here germane, somewhat mythological though each may be. One is the legend adopted by the leadership of the Irish Labour party of the period. According to the origin myth they endorsed, the SDLP was conceived in England, and Dublin was its midwife. This story credits Maurice Foley as the key. Foley, the English-born child of Irish parents (his mother's maiden name was O'Riordan) had been an electric fitter, an official of the Irish Transport and General Workers' Union, Labour MP for West Bromwich from 1963 onward, and undersecretary of the home office and later a junior minister for defense. He was very well informed on Irish affairs—better than most Irish politicians in the judgment of those who dealt with him—and at a British party congress he mooted with Michael McInerney and Brendan Halligan the possibility of creating a party in Northern Ireland that would swing Catholic politics out of its old ghetto mentality. This played well, and other southern leaders, Fine Gael's Declan Costello and Garret FitzGerald, helped Labour to pull the strings: they encouraged Gerry Fitt, Paddy Devlin, and Ivan Cooper, as well as the then-new politician John Hume.[132]

The chief alternative origin myth is that John Hume, elected as a Stormont MP for Foyle in 1969, was largely responsible. This Derry origin myth has Hume stretching forth his hand and the party coming full into being.[133] Whatever the real details, the main point is that a symbiotic set of conditions existed. There were indigenous pressures within the Northern Ireland Catholic community for an effective pan-Catholic constitutionalist party, and there were equally strong pressures within the Irish Republic that welcomed this development and were willing to help the SDLP emerge quickly.

From early days, the SDLP was John Hume's property, although it took the other founders of the party a few years to understand that fact. Gerry Fitt at first was titular chairman of the party, with Hume as deputy chairman, but it was Hume who set the agenda. Paddy Devlin was active in early days, but became disillusioned by what he saw as the SDLP's truckling to the Catholic Church and its not working very hard for Irish unity—in other words, acting like the old nationalist party. Eventually, in 1977, Devlin was expelled for voicing these views. A year after that, Gerry Fitt and Ivan Cooper officially left the SDLP, having been marginalized years earlier.

Therefore, to talk about the SDLP is to talk about John Hume. Arguably, he has been far and away the most skillful person in Irish politics, north and south, in the last quarter century. In his mid-thirties in the early 1970s (b. 1937), Hume was schooled at St. Columb's College and then entered Maynooth Seminary, intent on becoming a priest. He dropped out, however, before completing the ordination course. He became a secondary school teacher and helped to found a credit union in Derry. Hume came to the fore during the civil rights movement and was elected to the Northern Ireland Parliament in 1969.

The impressive thing about John Hume is how he parlayed a tiny stake into the best-controlled fiefdom in Irish politics, either side of the border. He was (and is) a master of the small move and, occasionally, the big bluff. Watching his development over the years is like seeing some young lad with a few pence in his pocket enter a big-time poker game. After a while one realizes that he has quietly been winning more than his share and then, suddenly, one recognizes that he is the biggest winner at the table and that all the older players who thought they were going to teach him how the big boys play, have themselves been taken to school. Thus, he moved from being deputy leader of the SDLP to being its chief policy maker during the 1970s, to becoming leader in 1979. Since 1979 he has been a member of the European Parliament and since 1983 an MP in the United Kingdom's Parliament. For the Westminster seat, in 1993, he received a salary of £30,854, plus over £40,000 in office expenses, and almost £11,000 for staying overnight in London; for the MEP position, he received £10,284, in addition to an allowance of up to £32,000 for office and research expenditures.[134]

More important, Hume acquired in the 1970s a license granted him willingly by all the major political parties in the republic: the franchise to speak for Northern Ireland's Catholics. If John Hume does not approve of something, no southern government will touch it. And, equally important, the Provisional IRA have granted him recognition as the constitutionally elected leader in the Catholic community with whom they will speak with any degree of seriousness. Thus, he has been able to serve as the sole conduit between the northern Catholics and southern politicians, and as the primary conduit to both London and Dublin governments on what the Provos might be willing to accept in any peace negotiations.

Hume and Conor would have been at each other's throats in the best of times and the early 1970s certainly were not that. Each man is immensely vain and they could not have sat at the same table for very long, even if they had agreed on everything. But their differences were fundamental, not personal. Conor, once he had recovered from the emotional swerve caused by Bloody Sunday, went back to preaching that the Ulster Protestants had to be considered in any successful solution to the northern Troubles, and not just in a cursory way. Hume, in contrast, operated as an unabashedly Catholic and devil-take-the-Prods politician. Furthermore, Conor was deeply opposed to anything that even implicitly gave legitimacy to any branch of the IRA. He perceived Hume's propensity for negotiating with terrorists, even while publicly deploring their violence, as hypocritical and in the long run helpful to the IRA. In the year 1972, Hume was just coming into his own as the de facto power in the SDLP, and he could not help but recognize that Conor stood between him and real power. Conor had a broad variety of contacts in the Catholic community in the North, going all the way back to his days in the antipartition campaign, and that fact alone was an impediment to Hume's becoming the sole conduit between the northern Catholics and the major political parties in the south. And Conor's own views about the North had to be discredited if John Hume was to parlay his small stake in Derry into ownership of his own casino. [135]

At first the brushes between Conor and John Hume were minor. For instance, in early August 1972, the Fianna Fail government helicoptered a northern Catholic delegation to Dublin for political conversations it saw as urgent. (It is not irrelevant that a by-election was being conducted in mid-Cork at the time.) The interesting point is that Gerry Fitt, head of the SDLP, was not part of the delegation and that it was headed by John Hume. Fitt, in London when the meeting was called, somehow was not contacted. Conor made a small fuss about this, nothing major, but it put him squarely in the way of John Hume's career trajectory, which involved elbowing aside Gerry Fitt.[136] Then, more important, on 20 September, the SDLP released a policy document, *Towards a New Ireland*, which argued that the U.K. government should declare itself in favor of the eventual unity of Ireland, that London and Dublin should have joint sovereignty over Northern Ireland, that there should be a Northern Ireland "assembly," a mini-parliament with real power, and that there should be an all-Ireland senate. Fianna Fail came out very strongly in favor of these proposals, but Labour was divided. Conor's opinion, argued with considerable force at Blackpool, where the British Labour party conference was debating Northern Ireland, was that the first items on the agenda should not be those in the SDLP package, but should be "to get rid of sectarian discrimination in the north, providing full equality of opportunity in jobs, housing, and political influence and *at the same time*, in the south, to get rid of the Republic's more subtle forms of sectarian discrimination—and *even more important* to eliminate the factor of territorial irredentism which served as a standing justification for bigotry in the north" (emphasis added).[137] Thus, there was no way Conor could approve of the SDLP document, since it implied a bullying of the Protestants in a manner that precluded reconciliation, and, therefore, actually impeded national unity. Conor led a fight within the Labour caucus against endorsing the SDLP position.

The inevitable fight between Conor and John Hume occurred in early October 1972, and in a way that showed Hume's brilliance as a tactician, for he managed the event so that he could not get hurt, only Conor. He used members of the republic's Labour party as his cat's paw; and, in a touch of sheer political genius, he made it appear that his differences with Conor were simply literary—he used a book review in the *Irish Times* as his mode of attack.

This was possible because at the beginning of October 1972, Conor's *States of Ireland* was published. In the long term, this has proved to be the most influential book about Irish nationalism and Irish politics written in the second half of the twentieth century. Unlike most works of history, it was intended to influence the real world.[138]

Today, *States of Ireland* is generally viewed as a piece of "revisionist" writing on Irish history. This is accurate, as long as one realizes that "revisionist" is a term that has different meanings in different countries. For instance, "revisionism" in North America and England today refers chiefly to the lunatic efforts to deny that the Holocaust ever occurred. "Revisionism" in Irish history, in the context of the last one-third of the twentieth century, refers to the rethinking of the history of Irish nationalism, based on the research of the last two generations of professional historians' work. The overall result of Irish revisionism has been to call into question the cult of blood sacrifice and of patriotic tribalism, the tenets of which have been drummed into Irish children in the national schools year after year, generation after generation. The foundation of revisionism was the development of a genuinely professional historical guild in Ireland in the late 1930s when the Irish Committee of Historical Sciences was formed and the journal *Irish Historical Studies* was founded. Although by 1972 the new ideas had replaced a lot of the old blood and gore and damn-the-English passages in school and university texts, the striking thing was how little this affected the version of Irish history held in the public mind in the republic.[139]

States of Ireland changed all that. It affected the viewpoint of the educated, politically conscious middle class like nothing before it or since. People read it and, suddenly, they rearranged in their minds, all the history of their nation that they thought they had known. It would be impossible for any book to have the same impact in North America or in Great Britain, because these countries are not a single homogeneous culture and, further, the various nations' children are not educated in a single national school system. In the Irish Republic, which is overwhelmingly ethnically homogeneous, and in which the great bulk of the people have gone through nearly identical schooling, the resonance of this work was both possible and amazing. And for every person who actually read the text, scores became familiar with its ideas through television, radio, and everyday conversation.

What Conor told his reader was this: the history you were taught as a child was wrong. You were taught to glorify violence and to denigrate constitutional change; you learned a history that was supposed to be truly national, but was actually sectarian; you learned that you, an Irish person, were automatically an anti-imperialist, and yet you became unconsciously colonialist.

The people of Ireland were willing to think about such issues in mid-1972, because the products of their history were erupting on the streets of Northern Ireland and, sometimes, exploding in buildings in Dublin. But not just any book would gain public attention. Conor's book worked because it was an intriguing mixture of history and personal reminiscence; shards of autobiography were used to illustrate larger national issues. The book's shape and its complexity were part of its merit—it worked like a fish hook. The first half of the book was based on a series of radio lectures Conor had given on RTE in 1966. They were an elegant mixture of reminiscence and of rethinking of Irish history, but at a very cool emotional level. Then, the tone became warmer, as the topic curved toward recent days: the civil rights movement and the beginning of the Troubles. Then, the rhetorical line bent sharply, forming the barb of the hook. Now if one had followed Conor thus far, his last four anguished chapters, ill-shaped and out of control as they were, focused on the crazing of 1970–71, held one hooked, even against one's will. The *Times Literary Supplement* was right when it said "the book seems a bit of a mess," but that was not to imply disapproval. "The mess, so to speak, is the message." [140]

To show, as Conor had done, that Irish history was a mess; to suggest that violence had never gotten Irish patriots anything more than they could have obtained peacefully; to dare imply that the Protestants had a right to exist as a culture and, perhaps, as some kind of political entity; to make it clear that the Northern Irish problem was an *Irish* problem, one that had to be dealt with by Irish people, without the usual blaming of the old enemy; all this was heresy, and for each convert (and there were, probably, hundreds of thousands eventually) there was a corresponding hard-edged enemy. "The response to his action is a perfect case of peace-making perceived as treachery," one shrewd reviewer noted. [141] In a significant understatement, another reviewer noted, concerning Conor's ideas, that "at this moment he carries his political life in his hands for saying them." [142] This was an understatement, because, in fact, his physical life was not beyond danger. It was reported early in 1972—before the book came out—that a Sinn Fein conference had agreed to have Conor tried at some future date by Sinn Fein courts. "Shoot him! Shoot him!" delegates were reported as shouting during the discussion. [143]

In fact, the immediate danger was far subtler. In the *Irish Times* of Monday, 9 October 1972, John Hume published a review that ostensibly was about *States of Ireland*, but, equally, was about getting rid of Conor politically. This was the perfect moment to move because on Wednesday of the same week, two matters were coming before the parliamentary Labour party. One of these was whether or not to endorse the SDLP document *Towards a New Ireland*, and also David Thornley, who was at that time on a republican jag, had put down a motion for the removal of Conor as spokesman on foreign affairs and on Northern Ireland. These matters would be debated before anyone had read Conor's book, but after everyone would have read Hume's review. Moreover, it was a realistic possibility that a double victory could be effected: Conor could be dumped and the SDLP policy adopted, all in one afternoon. And this well might be done without John Hume getting blood on his hands at all (the decisions, after all, were internal to the republic's parliamentary Labour party).

Hume's politically brilliant review was an early and classic example of what, among connoisseurs of Irish politics, has become known as Humespeak, an uncanny ability to speak on two levels at once, a form so effective and so instinctive that it can only be characterized as a form of genius. Humespeak, whatever the topic, works by sending a muffled, slightly ambiguous message which to a general audience, or to an audience of non-Irish persons, seems innocuous enough, but within that surface message is encoded a set of words and rhythms that carry an unmistakable meaning to whatever small group within Irish society Hume wishes to reach. It is magic, of a sort, and on 9 October, the Northern Magus spoke publicly to the general middle-class readership of the *Irish Times* and in code to the members of the Irish parliamentary Labour party.

Hume began his review with a half a dozen paragraphs of dullish reviewing, composed of the sort of phrases one gets in undergraduate essays—O'Brien's book was made up of linked essays whose theme was hard to determine; the book would usefully promote public debate, and so on. But John Hume was being dull on purpose, for he was setting up the following paragraphs:

> [Conor] is particularly severe on Connolly, the founder of his own party, a fact which may well have serious repercussions within that party. The nub of his devaluation of Connolly is that he was nothing more than an Irish Catholic nationalist in his thinking. [here Hume quotes Conor] "When Connolly uses the term 'the Irish race'—as he does quite often—it always seems to be the Catholics he has in mind ... Irish history—Connolly's— seems to mean for Connolly what it has meant to most Irish Catholics: the history of the Irish nationalist (alias national) movement ... It is hard to resist the conclusion that the Protestant workers of Belfast, *as they actually were and with the feelings and loyalties they actually had*, were not consistently felt by Connolly to be part of Irish history or of the record of labour, of the working classes or of the masses."[144]

Conor's words within the context of the Irish Labour party and quoted by Hume in this review were akin to accusing someone of committing the equivalent of Christianity's Unforgivable Sin. And in case one had any doubts about the results of such a sin, Hume adjudged that "Conor Cruise O'Brien's case is a more subtle and effective defence of Unionism than any that has come from any Unionist quarter."[145]

Brilliant. Conor went into Wednesday's caucus meeting in very deep trouble. He was in double jeopardy, because even if David Thornley's motion to remove his spokesmanship was defeated, the second motion, moved by Dr. John O'Connell (later destined to be a Fianna Fail cabinet member), approving SDLP policy would, if passed, force his resignation.

The meeting was extremely tense; Conor was controlled, but coiled taut, like a tight watch spring. He has an unconscious habit, when thinking or when nervous, of placing a ballpoint pen in his hands, a cheap biro with a hexagonal barrel, and twirling the implement with his right hand while letting it resonate through the fingers of his left. The sound is remarkably irritating. Conor did this throughout the meeting.

The surprise enemy came at Conor from behind. Usually, the leading figures in the parliamentary Labour party sat around the table, but this time Justin Keating sat behind Conor in a second, outer circle. Conor was amazed to hear Justin suddenly change direction and call for him to resign his spokesmanship for the good of the party.

The vote was close (exactly how close is not recorded), but with Frank Cluskey and Brendan Corish on his side, Conor was not removed from his shadow office.[146]

The second motion, approving SDLP policy, was closer. Only by a clever ploy on Corish's part—he put an amendment that provided for the Labour TDs to meet the SDLP for discussion—was the SDLP's *Towards a New Ireland* sidestepped. And even then, Corish had to use his own casting vote.[147]

• • •

Although this was the last formal challenge to Conor's spokesmanship on northern affairs for the Labour party, his road continued to be rough, and, certainly, controversial. John Horgan, surveying Conor's Pauline mission from the vantage point of the mid-1980s, wrote:

> Nor is it possible to underestimate the effectiveness of the crusade—for it was little short of that—waged against the IRA by Conor Cruise O'Brien. Armed with quite extraordinary verbal dexterity, and an appeal to reason which was none the less effective because it was advanced in circumstances of high emotion, O'Brien could turn heckles, jeers, and the passionate outbursts of Republican party members [of the Labour party] back at them in such a way that opposition was all but silenced. In this way he could, for example, when invited to condemn illegal violence by the security forces in Northern Ireland, declare in ringing tones that he denounced all violence—but more especially the violence that was committed in our name.[148]

This crusade, though it had its focal point within the Labour party, was literally worldwide. Conor preached in Blackpool and Boston, as well as in Belfast and Blackrock.

As IRA violence escalated in late 1972, 1973, and 1974, Conor came to adopt a single, dominant criterion of judgment. Given that the terrorists and those who favored violence were the chief impediment to peace and thus to eventual reconciliation in the North, either you were for them or against them. Everything one did, he came to believe, should be judged chiefly on that criterion. Ask if what one is doing is going to help or hurt them, and if it is going to help them, then do not do it.[149]

This simple, but far from simple-minded, approach was hard won, after an interrogation of Irish history quite beyond the sophistication of all but a few Irish politicians of the day, and it put Conor immediately at odds with any group or individual who was willing to deal with the IRA. This included, in 1972 for example, Harold Wilson, leader of the British Labour party; William Whitelaw, secretary of state for Northern Ireland; and almost the entire Fianna Fail and SDLP parties. Conor's view, simply, was that one did not talk to the IRA, for that gave them credibility. When they renounce terrorism, and practice peace for a reasonable period of time, then, and only then, should one treat with them. In America, Conor told Irish-American audiences that they should not send money to the IRA, or its fronts. Giving dollars to Sinn Fein or to Noraid, he told them, was simply to pay for one segment of the Irish working class to blow up another.

Reconciliation was the ultimate goal, the only way for there to be real peace in the North, he believed. And reconciliation could be effected, Conor believed, only by dealing with the northern Protestants. But relations with them were not possible unless one recognized that they had a right to exist: what political form that might take was a matter of legitimate discussion, but no one had the right simply to assume the Protestants out of existence.

This meant that Conor was preaching (and trying to teach) a form of geopolitical geometry that was radically different from that of any other major southern politician. The conventional geometry was triangular: the northern Ireland problem would be solved by Dublin, London, and the northern Catholic minority (as represented by the SDLP). Conor's position was that all talking, thinking, and negotiating had to be based on a quadrangle: London, Dublin, the northern Catholic minority, and the northern Protestant majority.

In his attempt to expand the conceptual framework of southern Irish politics as it concerned the North, I think that Conor was ultimately right, but in many ways naive, especially within the context of southern society in 1972. He presented his ideas with the confidence of an Enlightenment man dealing with pre-Enlightenment passions. He really thought that good ideas simply drive out bad ones by virtue of their being intellectually and morally better. This Enlightenment na- iveté is well caught in a brief coda to the story of John Hume's almost scuttling Conor through his *Irish Times* review of *States of Ireland*. Before the fateful meeting, Conor learned that a telegram in support of his retaining the northern spokesmanship had arrived from Belfast. It came from Billy Blease, chairman of the Northern Ireland Committee of the Irish Congress of Trades Unions.

The telegram was not read out during the caucus debate. After cau- cus adjourned, Conor asked Brendan Halligan why.

"It wouldn't have done you any good," Halligan replied. Then, in the flat tones of a real political professional, he added, "Billy Blease is a Protestant."[150]

CHAPTER 11

THE CHAINS OF OFFICE: 1973–1977

I once knew a publican, a hard, shrewd, sometimes charming, always private man, as one had to be given his background and vocation. A County Donegal Catholic, he had made his living serving drinks, lending money, listening to the confidences of Carrickfergus, Whitehead, and Islandmagee Protestants. He had learned a few things in life and one of these was "never shut a door all the way: you may have to go back through."

That was the sort of advice that Conor and a few other leaders of the Irish Labour party started to give to their colleagues even before the year 1969 was out. It was all very enjoyable to fantasize about forcing Fine Gael and Fianna Fail into a merger on the right end of the Irish political spectrum, thereupon leaving Labour in possession of the other half of the spectrum. But the 1970s turned out to be less the decade of socialism than even the 1870s had been.

After the disappointing results of the 1969 election, and after listening to the party's shrewder tacticians, the administrative council of the party succeeded in 1970 in having the no-coalition policy reversed.[1] So, from the middle of 1970 onward, Labour was seeking a partner for a temporary marriage. Fine Gael was the only possibility. Fine Gael was no more left of center than was Fianna Fail as far as social issues were concerned, but it was much less hard-line nationalist and, further, Fine Gael had not resorted to red-scare techniques in the 1969 election.

By the late autumn of 1972, the outlines of a coalition had been worked out privately by Labour and Fine Gael, although in public the required behavior was to speak tentatively of coalition, as if it still were only a possibility. For instance, in mid-November, Conor gave a talk to one of the local branches of the party within his constituency—the Raheny branch—and he spoke of what would be required were any coalition to have his sanction: broad social programs (of an unspecified nature) had to be forwarded, and speculation in land development (his *bête noire*) had to be controlled.[2] On 5 February 1973, Jack Lynch dissolved the Dail and the next day Brendan Corish (Labour), and Liam Cosgrave (Fine Gael) announced a fourteen-point joint program.

Within a system of proportional representation such as operates in Ireland, wherein each party puts up several candidates in each constituency, the biggest demand of a pre-election coalition agreement is to convince one's own party voters to put down as second preference the candidate of the other party in the coalition. If a two-party coalition is envisaged, the transfer of votes on the second round of the count cannot be allowed to go to a third party, in this case, Fianna Fail. This requires both a good deal of trust between the two parties and strong discipline of the voters.

Dublin North-East had been reduced from a five-seat to a four-seat constituency. Both Charles Haughey and Conor were safe, having been elected on the first count in 1969, and Conor, now getting Fine Gael second preference votes, was doubly safe. Nevertheless, he ran hard, especially against Haughey, a man whom he believed to be deeply evil. Conor called particular attention to reports of Haughey's "assuring IRA sympathizers in Dublin North-East of his sympathy with them, using the words, 'deep down I feel exactly as you do, and if I am returned to office, I will see things are done our way.'"[3]

When the votes were counted on 14 March 1973, Conor won easily and the coalition as a whole held. Hence, although Labour's share of the first-place votes fell from 17.0 percent to 13.7 percent, its seats went up from 18 to 19. Fianna Fail, now with 69 seats, was out.[4] Labour was the junior partner in the "national coalition," but in practice both parties were remarkably respectful of each other, especially so considering the pressures that came to bear on them from events in Northern Ireland and from the world oil crisis.

Liam Cosgrave, the head of Fine Gael and the new taoiseach, had been Conor's boss in 1954–57, when he was minister for external affairs, and it was he who had led the first Irish delegation to the United Nations. Cosgrave was probably the least charismatic person ever to be prime minister of Ireland, but he had an astute tactical sense. He had virtually inherited his position in Fine Gael, as he was the son of William T. Cosgrave, the first prime minister of independent Ireland. He was repelled by the ugliness of what was happening in Northern

Ireland and wanted as little to do with northern affairs as possible. On the other hand, he was deeply concerned with anything that involved the security of the Twenty-Six Counties. And he was deeply committed to preserving Catholic moral standards in everyday life and quite willing to use the power of the state to do so.

Given that Conor gained a reputation as a firebrand, it is well to emphasize that in relation to Cosgrave as taoiseach, to Brendan Corish, as head of Labour, and to the national coalition in general, Conor was notable for his loyalty. He did not intrigue politically, in part, doubtlessly, because he had no ambition to become party leader or head of government himself. There was more to this loyalty, however: Conor, for all his hell-raising, has always simultaneously believed in hierarchy and in the robes that often cloak hierarchy, ritual.

In the national coalition of 1973–77, Fine Gael held ten cabinet seats and five parliamentary secretaryships. Labour's share was five cabinet seats (Brendan Corish, tanaiste and health and social welfare; James Tully, local government; Michael O'Leary, labor; Justin Keating, industry and commerce; and Conor, posts and telegraphs) and two parliamentary secretaryships (Michael P. Murphy, agriculture and fisheries, and Frank Cluskey, social welfare). Notice who was missing: David Thornley, who had lost his seat in Cabra, and Noel Browne who had taken a senate seat for Trinity College. Browne, although he kept up his affiliation with the Labour party, did not join the parliamentary caucus.[5] The tone of the parliamentary Labour party was further improved (at least from Conor's viewpoint) by Sean Treacy's being appointed speaker of the Dail. Party business was conducted more efficiently than in the past because Brendan Corish, though still head of the party, allowed other TDs to serve terms as chair of the PLP. Labour party discipline also improved in part because each TD was required to sign a pledge obliging him to resign his seat if asked to do so by the administrative council. This pledge was modeled on that signed by members of the old Irish parliamentary party in the days of Charles Stewart Parnell and of John Redmond, and in large part was crafted by Conor.[6]

The star of the coalition was Garret FitzGerald, who to everyone's surprise, including his own, was named foreign minister. This portfolio included responsibility for Northern Ireland. He had been expected to be minister of finance, the post that had been his shadow responsibility and for which he was strongly qualified. FitzGerald, like Cosgrave, had a virtually hereditary right to be in a Fine Gael cabinet: his father had been minister for external affairs of the Irish Free State from 1922–27, and minister for defense from 1927–32. In his forties, FitzGerald was the Fine Gael version of Conor, his party's leading intellectual. Less clever with words than was Conor, he understood things Conor did not: numbers, quantitative thinking, and economics. FitzGerald was the Irish director of the *Economist* intelligence unit, and he was also a lecturer in economics at University College, Dublin. Unlike Conor, FitzGerald was politically ambitious. He was keen on becoming the leader of Fine Gael and he did what he could quietly to unsettle Liam Cosgrave, often through leaks to the press. Nevertheless, there was something fundamentally trustworthy about FitzGerald, even if he tended to be garrulous and therefore not good at keeping confidences. Here is how Conor later described him:

> Garret ... is more of a Gladstone type. He is full of genuine concern for the public good and full also of information, much of it statistical, which he burns to impart, in a breathless rush of words and figures. He knows that other people don't know as much as he does. And he wants to help them with their education, urgently. He would not address Mrs. Thatcher like a public meeting as Gladstone did the Queen, but he might give her a tutorial.[7]

FitzGerald was one of those souls who was born optimistic and older voters viewed him as one would an energetic and promising nephew; younger people saw him as a kindly, if fluttery, uncle.[8]

The actual division of offices within the coalition was done by Liam Cosgrave and Brendan Corish with little consultation with the other deputies. According to FitzGerald, he was told less than half an hour before the composition of the new government was formally announced that he would not have the finance portfolio. He and the others who could expect office were told to assemble at the taoiseach's office at 5:30 on 14 March, just before the new Dail met. He was called into Cosgrave's office, the new taoiseach stepped forward, shook his hand and said, "Foreign affairs. Is that all right?" FitzGerald agreed and that was all there was to it.[9] Finance went to Richard (always "Richie") Ryan of Fine Gael who had the misfortune to take on the job just as the oil shortage was looming. "Richie is a fierce choleric little man," Conor once said. "If you took something off Richie that he thought was his, he wouldn't be content with tending to censure. He would yell bloody murder and come after you with the poker."[10] A good choice, actually, for hard times.

Where did this leave Conor? In two areas he had both experience and an interest: education and foreign affairs. The first, however, was out, as he would have been unacceptable to the educational establishment. Education in the Republic of Ireland in this period, although funded largely by the state, was largely under the control of the Catholic

Church.[11] Even if Conor had never said a word publicly about education, as an avowed agnostic he would have been unacceptable. However, in the Dail in February 1972 he had criticized the entire structure. "The education of more than ninety-five percent of the children is in the hands, broadly speaking, under the general control of the Catholic ecclesiastical authorities. This poses a problem which I think may be unique in the world. It is a sort of double helix arrangement. You have on one side a structure of democratic responsibility for education. ... And you have parallel with that a hierarchical system in which educational responsibility comes from the top down."[12] Further, the Department of Education was one of the fountainheads of the hate-the-English school of Irish nationalism. Conor had asked in the Dail after the Aldershot murders, "Were the seeds of Aldershot sown in an Irish classroom?"[13] No, Conor would not do as minister of education.

Undoubtedly, Conor would have been the most knowledgeable and best-prepared minister for foreign affairs in the history of independent Ireland; and he desperately wanted the job. Yet, on Sunday morning, 11 March, he was having a preluncheon drink with some friends at the Sheaf of Wheat in Coolock, when Brendan Corish rang him. "Would you take posts and telegraphs, Conor?" Not pleased, but realizing that the number of Labour seats in the new Cabinet was tightly limited, he said "yes." Better to have a ministry of one's own than to be a parliamentary secretary.[14]

Having been denied the post of minister for foreign affairs probably rankles Conor more than any single occurrence in his entire political life. He believed, and still believes, that, even though the Labour party was to have only five seats, he nevertheless could have had foreign affairs. Conor believes that Brendan Halligan, secretary of the Labour party, allied himself with Justin Keating so that Keating would gain the industry and commerce portfolio. For that, they traded away foreign affairs.[15]

Perhaps. But whether or not there was internal Labour party intrigue that worked against Conor's appointment, it nevertheless is true that appointing Conor to foreign affairs would have required more courage than a coalition could reasonably have been expected to exhibit. The problem was not the foreign affairs portion of the portfolio: indeed, many of his colleagues would have found it congenial for him to be frequently in foreign places. The problem was that the portfolio included Northern Ireland, and Conor would not have accepted the foreign ministry if the Northern Ireland section had been broken off from it. Conor's views on Northern Ireland were so strong, and his behavior so unpredictable on that topic, that a prudent government could not give him that role. In fact, there was only one other person who could fill the foreign affairs post and not be dwarfed by it: Garret FitzGerald. In essence, the Cabinet was built around his appointment.

In terms of the Northern Ireland segment of the portfolio, FitzGerald had an unusually useful background. His mother was a McConville, an Ulster Protestant distilling family, and his father, a Catholic, had been born and brought up in London. Unlike virtually every Irish politician of his generation (including Conor), FitzGerald had been opposed from early days to the antipartition line of the 1940s and 1950s. He had consistently been for conciliation with the Protestants. Later, Conor came around to FitzGerald's basic viewpoint, and the two had picketed together against the IRA front, Provisional Sinn Fein, in the early 1970s.[16]

Liam Cosgrave hated to think about the Six Counties and, though he delegated most northern responsibilities to FitzGerald, he did not fully trust him. So, he used Conor as a choke-chain on FitzGerald. Cosgrave did this by not raising any objections to Conor's continuing to be Labour party (not government, Labour party) spokesman on Northern Ireland. Further, Cosgrave approved the development of a government information office, for which Conor was the vicar and Dail spokesman, even though, technically, the Information Office was run by the office of the taoiseach. Everyone, including Garret FitzGerald, was supposed to go through the Government Information Office before making public pronouncements. The most important of these were apt to be on Northern Ireland. Thus, without quite saying so publicly, Liam Cosgrave permitted Conor to be more than just another cabinet member as far as Northern Ireland was concerned.

Naturally, there was tension between FitzGerald and Conor. FitzGerald was essentially an optimist about Northern Ireland. He believed that peace and eventual unity could be worked out. Conor, like Liam Cosgrave, was a pessimist, and saw the possibility of civil war in the North as being as great as that of peace. Further, FitzGerald was almost entirely dependent on John Hume for policy guidance, whereas Conor was deeply suspicious of Hume. Given these differences, it is amazing that Conor and Garret got along as well as they did. (When Irish governmental files for the period are opened, they will reveal a diverting cache of letters from Conor to Garret FitzGerald and also to Frank Cluskey. Conor liked to start his morning as a cabinet minister by firing off a blistering rocket to either FitzGerald or Cluskey. He once taxed Cluskey with never replying to his letters. Cluskey rasped, "Ye've heard of all those letters from Paul haven't you? Ever wonder why there's no fecking letter *from* the Ephesians?"[17]

Overall, the national coalition that was elected in 1973 worked as well together, and perhaps better, than a single-party government. Some of the credit for this has to go to the aging Eamon de Valera, who, in one of his last official acts as president of Ireland (Erskine Childers, elected in late May 1973, assumed the presidency late in June) presided over a dinner for the new coalition. Mr. de Valera was in failing health and was dispirited by the fact that a coalition, something he always abhorred, had come to power. The dinner he presided over was black-tie, somber, with coalition TDs and party functionaries present, all unnaturally grave as if taking their cues from the president. No speech was planned, so it was a surprise when Mr. de Valera stood up, clutched the back of his chair for support, and very slowly pronounced a homily.

"I have long had reservations about the system of vote ..." He paused, frequently, weak. "... the system of voting called proportional representation ..." Another pause. "... because I forewarned that if persisted in, this system was bound to lead eventually to ..."

A very long pause. The new coalition members leaned forward to catch the old chief's words.

"... lead eventually to coalition government."

The infelicity of this remark was so great that several TDs, led by the whooping great laugh of Liam Cosgrave, broke into merriment.

Mr. de Valera, as ever in his political life, went on his own way as if nothing had happened. Since the electorate had regrettably refused to abandon proportional representation, there was only one thing to do. "You *must* make it work." He swiveled slowly, as if to look at everyone present, a superogatory gesture as he was now almost totally blind. "The only way it will work is for all of you to put loyalty to the taoiseach before every consideration of party advantage."[18]

That was the best—and perhaps the only—gift the old patriot could have given to this new government.

• • •

The members of the government were further brought together by the fact that each of their lives was in danger, and those of their families as well. Although the Provisional IRA had ruled that cabinet members of the Irish Republic's government were out of bounds as targets (so long as they stayed within the Twenty-Six Counties), there were several splinter groups with no such inhibitions, plus "independents" who were interested in kidnapping for ransom. In March 1974, Bill Fox, a Protestant member of the republic's Senate, was murdered. Cabinet members all had bodyguards, something that previously had been necessary in Irish politics only during the civil war of 1922–23. When it was discovered that freelance kidnappers were planning to grab children of cabinet members, minders had to be provided for family. James Tully was particularly graphic in denouncing the way his family had to put up with telephoned descriptions of what would happen to them if Tully voted the wrong way on a state security bill.[19]

In the O'Brien household, Maire and the children became accustomed to having a special branch man in the garden and an attendant for the children on their way to school. When asked on BBC television in October 1975 by Ludovic Kennedy if the IRA had threatened his life, Conor replied yes.

"Did it frighten you?"

"It didn't please me much, but these things happen."[20]

This period—known as the "Great Siege" in family tradition[21]—was a time of great unity and of equally great worry. As Donal Cruise O'Brien recalls, "Everyone was—and still is—afraid that some IRA killer is going to get him."[22]

Young Patrick continued to be a heart's joy. Maire wrote the following poem for him. (The original is in Irish; the translation is Maire's):

THE HERO'S SLEEP

Little clustered head sweet as the blackberry,
Little foreign son, my part of this world,
Welcome and nest in my heart,
Welcome under the rafters of this house,
Little morning star come from a long way off.

Blood from without is good;
Look at my little bull calf of a man;
Head him off from the doorway
Or wedge him in a tub:
As healthy as a trout, I swear it!
And every limb prospering:
Beauty a crown for strength—

You took your colour from the autumn
And from the dun rose;
Every yellow is beautiful from its relationship with you.
See Conor our son
Not as was planned, but as
The higher powers willed his coming

Come to my arms, little barley hen,
The lamp is lighting and the night is threatening;
The fox is walking the road;
May no cat from the sea lead him snapping in your direction,
Since you are the candle of the household on a little golden
    candlestick.

When you are asleep under my breast
My love is a wall about you—
But when you set out on your kingly progress
It is in vain for me to spy on you:
What defence will you bring with you?
A charm? A talisman? Or a taboo?
'Never trust the white',
Is the proper prayer for your race.

Like every mother at times
I turn over thoughts in my mind,
And while I dwell on them,
Suddenly you have caught up a wooden spoon!
On the instant as in a dream I see
The hero's light over your countenance,
As though coming towards me there were
The little boy from Eamhain, the Hound of Feats![23]

Patrick was a delightful child. The only worry was that he frequently had severe stomach pains, probably because of a genetically based inability to digest easily certain Western foods. By age six he had been in hospital twice for this condition.[24]

So happy were they with Patrick, that Conor and Maire adopted a second child, half Zambian, half Irish. This was Margaret—so named in honor of Maire's mother—born 16 January 1971 and placed in the O'Brien home in September of that year.[25] As they had done with Patrick, the O'Briens were especially careful in making legal arrangements for Margaret's adoption for, in at least one interpretation of Irish family law, Maire and Conor were not legally married. This second adoption was as successful as the first; Margaret grew up less outgoing than Patrick, but gifted, on the borderline of genius with languages.

The problem common to both children was to find a balance between the cultural heritage of Irish society—Maire was especially keen on having them learn Irish while young—and the fact that they were

black and obviously in some sense had an African heritage. Conor and
Maire took Patrick to Ghana in the mid-1970s when Conor received an
honorary doctorate at the University of Ghana.[26] For Patrick's first
communion, a special Ghanaian communion garb was bespoke.[27] This
respect for the dual cultural heritage of the children is something that
answers to no formula and has no objective measure of its success. My
own opinion is that what the O'Briens did worked: both children grew
up knowing who they are, that they are loved, and that they are Irish,
and more.

Meanwhile, the children of Conor's first marriage flourished.
Donal's major monograph, *The Mourides of Senegal*, was published by
Oxford in 1971 and he was well launched in his academic career in the
University of London. Fedelma continued to help Conor with the research for his historical writings. Her husband, Nicholas Simms, was a
research officer at RTE (and was soon to join Conor's own staff). Kate,
after the rough years of adolescence, returned to Dublin and entered
Trinity College. She married Joseph Kearney, a talented linguist, in
1971, finished her English degree, took a Higher Diploma in Education
and, along the way, became a very gifted writer. There were grandchil-
dren from each of the three marriages.

In 1972, Conor and Maire put £10,000 into renovating and expanding their house on Howth summit.[28] In summer, they spent as much
time as possible down-the-country, in the Dunquin cottage that had
been built by Maire's family so that she and her brother and sister could
be in touch with a real Gaeltacht.

Kate, in a story written in the mid-1970s and published in her collection *A Gift Horse*, captured the complex way that Conor related to his
now-adult daughter. "When she had told her father that their dear
friend was going to die, she had been nervous. He might expose himself,
expose an unbearable feeling which she knew she couldn't deal with.
Expose the lack in their relationship. The lack of simplicity on which it
was founded. Complex mutual respect the substitute."[29] That, I suspect,
is an x-ray summary of the relationship Conor had with the three children of his first marriage: complex mutual respect.

The little bungalow in Dunquin helped Patrick and Margaret to
learn real, not Dublin, Irish, but they were also sent as youngsters to
Scoil Neasain in Harmonstown where they were taught through the
medium of Irish.[30] Maire and Conor helped the locals in 1970–71 to
fight the closing of their tiny national school at Dunquin, but to no
avail.[31] Not only did the local people and the O'Briens have the educational bureaucracy against them, but they took a good deal of ridicule
from John Healy, the "Backbencher" columnist of the *Irish Times*. "I

have some sympathy for Maire MacEntee. I dislike seeing the paternal sins of neglect [a reference to Maire's father, Sean MacEntee] visited upon the head of a charming daughter: she doesn't deserve it as Mrs. Conor Cruise O'Brien. It was, as I say, a great place for the family. And maybe there's another book in the place: 'Twenty Years a-Dying.'"[32]

Dunquin, however, was Maire and Conor's only significant domestic defeat during Conor's Dail years. They wrote together a book, *A Concise History of Ireland* (1972), commissioned by Thames and Hudson. It was well received and was into a third revised edition in 1985. Maire's own book of poems, *Coldladh an Ghaiscigh*, appeared in 1973, and she was recognized as one of the most important Irish language poets of her time.

Although the O'Brien family did not exactly form itself into a laager, there is no question that during Conor's cabinet years, 1973–77, the family was under a great deal of external pressure and that brought everyone closer together. Maire in these years was especially important because of something she seems to have inherited directly from her Belfast-hardened, old IRA gunman father: intense loyalty to "her own" and a readiness to attack those who attacked her own. When riled, she rivaled the Furies in their ferocity and the Strategic Air Command in speed of response. Nobody, but nobody, messed with her family.

• • •

As a politician, Conor had a handful of jobs: he still was a Labour member of the European Parliament, a post he soon relinquished under the pressure of other tasks.[33] He was in charge of the Government Information Office; Labour spokesman on foreign affairs and on Northern Ireland, and he was minister for posts and telegraphs, which was in reality two ministries: postal and telephone services, and broadcasting. And the amount of traveling that he did was considerable.[34]

The cabinet assignment, posts and telegraphs, would have been enough to send most mortals into despair. Before taking the appointment, Conor had to pay several months' worth of overdue phone bills of his own and had to borrow from his father-in-law, Sean MacEntee, to clear the bill.[35] Thereafter, he had to deal every day with the old post office (renamed "posts and telegraphs" under an act of 1924), which was the biggest employer among Irish government agencies. It had about 23,000 persons on its payroll and a history of labor unrest. Although the post was quite efficient, the phone service in the Twenty-Six Counties was terrible, and that on a good day. In the spring of 1975, for example, there were 42,000 persons on the waiting list for phones to be installed. The department's claim was that this backlog represented one year, but cases kept coming to light of families being kept two and three years awaiting a phone to be installed.[36] After the phone was on line, the public received the worst telephone service in Europe save, possibly, Italy.

Whether or not Conor was a good cabinet minister will not be known until the departmental records are open to the public. I suspect that he will be found to have been a better manager than he was thought to be at the time. Basically, he divided his department into two compartments: that which bored him and that which interested him. The interesting part to him was television and radio broadcasting (more of that in a minute); the tiresome part was the postal and phone service. Of course he left the day-to-day administration of these boring areas in the hands of professional civil servants. He had been a civil servant himself, so he trusted the service, if not everyone in it. When he arrived at posts and telegraphs, the secretary of the department (that is, the head civil servant) was Proinnsais O'Colmain (var: Frank Colman) who seemed to Conor to be obstructive. Further, Colman had written speeches for Conor's predecessor in office, Gerry Collins, which were not merely technical in nature, but enthusiastically political. Colman went. He was replaced by the assistant secretary, Liam O'Reagain. This was an interesting appointment, as O'Reagain had been a close mutual friend of Conor and his first wife, Christine, in their undergraduate days.[37]

Conor's ministerial office was in the General Post Office, Dublin, so it was inevitable that he became known to his higher civil service staff as "Con the Post," after the character in the Dion Boucicault melodrama, *The Shaughraun*. For Conor, a typical day was to arrive at the office at 9:30, work until noon and either have a working lunch, a cabinet meeting, or a caucus session with the parliamentary Labour party, then spend the afternoon and evening in the Dail and be at home by midnight. Always, he was accompanied by a driver-bodyguard.[38]

Conor never learned even the most elementary details of how the postal and telephone systems worked, but then, anything mechanical or electrical has always been wholly mysterious to him. Nor did he understand the economic concepts behind the phone and postal services. Garret FitzGerald recalls that at one time the phone section had a problem with overcapacity on some lines and undercapacity on others. In order to even out the overload, Garret suggested that differential prices be used. Conor could not get his mind around this idea and finally had to have FitzGerald come in to explain the idea to his higher civil servants.[39]

What Conor did understand fully was how to fight his corner in the annual budget carve-up. Even in the days of the oil crisis, his department received more than its fair share and that is why his department was relatively peaceful.[40] In fact, if one does not discount for inflation, the amount of money invested in capital equipment in the phone system in the years 1973–77—£350 million—was greater than the sum total of capital investment in the system from the day it had been founded until 1973.[41] Further, Conor was the first minister to put forward seriously the idea that an efficient semistate corporation would do the job better than keeping postal and telephone services as part of the civil service.[42] However, Conor received little credit for the work he did on these fronts, largely because he was notably naive about the long-term improvements he was effecting. He should have been shouting from the housetops, but instead, he mentioned these things only modestly and at intervals. His successor, Albert Reynolds, cashed in on them and eventually became taoiseach.

Instead of receiving credit for working out the long-term solution to the country's telephone problems—the solution, invest money in modern equipment—Conor was subjected daily in the Dail to a list of complaints. The phones, and to a lesser extent, the post, were matters on which a TD could prove to his constituents that he was looking after their interests. So there were scores of questions, inevitably, but beyond that, Fianna Fail very cleverly made sure that there was a barrage of orchestrated complaints, day after day in question time. In turn, Conor had to spend his energy explaining why his department was not responding to the urgent need for the erection of telephone kiosks at Burncourt, Cahir, County Tipperary; why the phone service in Bracknagh was unsatisfactory; why there was no post office at Mount Melleray, and on and on, even to Charlie Haughey's demand that Conor arrange to have a public telephone kiosk provided on the pier at Howth in the vicinity of the yacht club for the use of fishermen.[43] This harassment went on in question periods for four years and it was an extremely shrewd political tactic. It resulted in Conor being associated in the public mind with something that did not work. Indeed, it made him look a bit of a clown, or at least incompetent, and this undercut his credibility on other, much more important issues.

The Government Information Office gave Conor a great deal of influence about what was said about Northern Ireland. And also, to control somewhat the effusions of Garret FitzGerald: this control, even FitzGerald admits, was not entirely effective. The person who headed the Government Information Office was Muiris MacConghail, an excellent choice, made at the suggestion of FitzGerald's wife, Joan.[44] An accomplished Irish-language scholar, and a prize-winning television producer ("John Hume's Derry" was one of his early works), MacConghail had been the producer of "Seven Days," an investigative television weekly that had looked into some things that the Fianna Fail government of the time did not want investigated, so he had been dropped. Still only thirty, he had become head of radio features and current affairs at RTE, before Conor offered him the government job. At first he was reluctant to leave RTE, but Conor picked up the phone, called Liam Cosgrave, and the next day MacConghail found himself as a member of the Irish public service as an assistant secretary in the taoiseach's office. His conditions on taking the job were that he be permitted to attend cabinet meetings and that he not be required to lie at press briefings. Thus, he sometimes went silent at press briefings, but better stumm than deceitful, he believed.[45] His relationship with Conor was very close. In mid-1975, he went back to a plum producing job at RTE and his post was filled by Ted Nealon, a very bright young psephologist, who eventually became a Fine Gael TD, but with whom Conor never became close.[46]

· · ·

In office, Conor did not abandon his mission of delivering electric shocks to the Irish psyche, but he proceeded differently, now that he was part of a coalition government that actually could make laws. Concerning the north of Ireland, his view continued to be that if one wanted national unity, one first needed peace and reconciliation. Further: peace and reconciliation were worth having on their own even if national unity did not follow. The immediate impediment to peace was terrorist violence, but behind that was a more fundamental cause. In his view, this was the toxic way in which religion and nationalism had mixed together within the Republic of Ireland to produce a state that was deeply sectarian, but largely unconscious of that fact.

In December 1972, a majority of voters who participated in a referendum had decided to remove from Eamon de Valera's 1937 constitution the subsections of Article 44 that recognized the "special position" of the Roman Catholic Church and also specified as recognized denominations certain other faiths. This was a start and there was some hope that, if one walked gently, it would be possible to abolish some of the sectarian laws that operated in the republic. For example, there was some hope that in a limited context the distribution of literature on birth control and the importation and sale of contraceptive devices would no longer be subject to criminal prosecution. Senator Mary Robinson and two other senators had tried to introduce such a bill in July 1971, but had been refused a first reading. In December 1973, how ever, the act of 1935 that made the importation of contraceptives illegal was declared unconstitutional.[47] It still was illegal to distribute them, however. Senator Mary Robinson tried to introduce a bill liberalizing import and sale but the Catholic Church killed it. ("Cardinal says contraception would affect quality of life," one headline explained, and on this both sides would have agreed.)[48]

The coalition government itself introduced a bill that would have permitted the importation and sale of contraceptives—but only by holders of a license granted by the government. These persons (mostly pharmacists) would be able to sell only to a restricted class of people: married persons. Convictions under various clauses of the bill ran up to a fine of £1,000 and two years imprisonment.

What one must understand about this bill is that it was a major piece of liberalization—pharmacists who sold to married people condoms or the pill were not to be adjudged criminals. And, from a parliamentary viewpoint, the interesting thing is that this was not a government bill. It was, indeed, drawn up by the minister for justice, Patrick (Paddy) Cooney, but it was not a government measure. During the second stage of debate, in July 1974, it was clearly announced that from the government side this would be a free vote. No whip would be applied.[49] Fianna Fail, on the other hand, was keen on keeping the faith-and-fatherland vote: it would vote *en bloc* against liberalization.

Conor did everything he could to get Liam Cosgrave to commit himself one way or the other. Three times in one cabinet meeting, Conor asked Cosgrave whether he would vote for the bill and all Cosgrave would do was mutter "free vote" through his mustache.[50] Cosgrave, it must be emphasized, was not intentionally deceiving anyone. He simply refused to say how he would vote. Both parties in the coalition convinced themselves that the taoiseach would be voting for the bill, and John Kelly, Fine Gael chief whip, and Tom Kyne, chair of the parliamentary Labour party, put heavy pressure on their respective TDs. Most members of the coalition government were convinced that the bill would pass.[51]

Even so, Conor worked hard behind the scenes. Just before the Dail debate began, he had a member of his staff (Nicholas Simms) collect relevant research studies, and these he had distributed. The studies showed, first, that 54 percent of all Irish adults over age sixteen (and over two-thirds of those between sixteen and forty-four) favored the sale of contraceptives through pharmacists, both to married and to unmarried persons. And, second, data from the Economic and Social Research Institute of Ireland indicated that because of the large size of families among married people in the Irish Republic and because of the high proportion of persons who never married, Ireland bore heavy economic and psychological costs.[52]

Although Conor made no secret in debate that he thought the bill inadequate—for heaven's sake, why not let unmarried as well as married persons buy condoms?—he supported its passage. One of his arguments for passage sounds almost contrived, until one recalls that this was the Ireland of the 1970s. He pointed out that all the major Protestant denominations believed that contraception was necessary for normal family life: birth limitation was part of responsible family behavior. In Conor's view, if the Dail defeated a bill that would allow married couples in the republic to practice conveniently legal birth control, it would be a clear violation of the civil liberties of the religious minority, and, clearly sectarian. It would be exactly the kind of thing that would confirm northern Protestant fears of what would happen in a united Ireland: even their family practices would be made illegal.[53]

Had anyone else played that card, it would have been merely clever politics, but with Conor the argument was deeply felt. Indeed, a bit later, in mid-1976, Conor was to get into a major public argument with the Most Rev. Dr. Newman, bishop of Limerick, over the church's alleged right to dictate sectarian morality, and over the effect this had on prolonging the Northern Ireland conflict.[54]

Still, in July 1974, it seemed as if one tiny crack was being made in the sectarian wall. It seemed so right up to the moment the final vote on the contraceptive bill was taken. The TDs were already passing into the division lobbies when the Fine Gael whip, John Kelly, learned that Liam Cosgrave actually was going to vote against the bill. The taoiseach's intention was to wait to the very end, so as to permit a truly free vote and then to join Fianna Fail in the negative ranks. That was bad enough in itself, but John Kelly quickly realized that it was doubly bad: it would leave some Fine Gael TDs from rural areas totally exposed. They would have voted against the church and done so in a free vote, when even the taoiseach had not done so. They would be politically dead from that moment on. So Kelly urged Cosgrave to vote immediately and then those Fine Gael TDs who wanted to stay on the church's good books, could still do so, by following Cosgrave's lead. Cosgrave did vote immediately and the bill was narrowly defeated.[55]

The reaction of most members of the coalition Cabinet was first, absolute astonishment, and then, as what had happened sank in, dispiritedness. Some, like Conor, took themselves home to mourn in the company of wife and glass. Others, like Michael O'Leary, were angry and killed their despondency by going back to their offices until the early morning hours, turning their inner turmoil into work.

O'Leary later told Conor that as he was leaving Leinster House, just about sunrise, the cleaning women were in the midst of scrubbing the floor. They understood what had happened a lot more realistically than did the nation's elected representatives. One of them chatted with O'Leary for a bit. At the mention of Liam Cosgrave, the cleaning woman reared back on her haunches and exclaimed, "God's name! What'd you expect him to do? Sure, wasn't he an altar boy until he was twenty-four?"[56]

• • •

The Irish language was a cultural area in which Conor wished to deliver another of his electric shocks to the national psyche. Not that he did not love the language in his own way, as a literary medium, but he disliked the way it had become a political talisman. The belief that the Irish language had virtually magical qualities went very deep in the history of the Twenty-Six Counties. For example, the first head of the Irish Free State, W.T. Cosgrave, asserted: "The possession of a cultivated national language is known by every people who have it to be a secure guarantee of the national future."[57] Eamon de Valera told the Gaelic League, "It is my opinion that Ireland with its language and without freedom is preferable to Ireland with freedom and without its language."[58] Eoin MacNeill, first minister for education of the Irish Free State, declared that for the members of the government to abandon the attempt to revive Irish would be to abandon their own nation.[59] Among politically influential persons, the belief that the nation's identity hinges on the Irish language persisted. "The Irish language is the most distinctive sign of our nationality," was categorically stated in a 1965 government white paper on the restoration of the language.[60] Such quotations could be multiplied almost endlessly, each one having the ring of a sincere evangelical faith.

The politicization of the language was reinforced by a very clever twist in terminology (whether consciously calculated or unconsciously motivated is unclear) whereby in the twentieth century the language revivalists stopped talking about the Gaelic language and began pressing for the revival of the *Irish* language. This simple maneuver won for them the field because one now had a set of natural opposites: the English and the Irish languages which, by false but convincing analogy, were depicted as being as antagonistic as English soldiers and Irish heroes. The emotion attached to these linguistic antitheses precluded rational debate, for how could a patriotic Irishman be anti-Irish? That the native language of most Irishmen was English and thus part of the Irish nation's culture was a fact that was almost totally obfuscated by the English-Irish antithesis. The political fantasy about the language was encapsulated in Article 8 of the 1937 constitution which defined Irish as "the first official language." English was recognized as "a second official language."

Early in 1974, Conor gave a speech at Waterford that set nerves jangling for months. In a metaphor that was too accurate to be forgivable, he referred to this institutionalization and politicization of the language as being the creation of a "bog oak monolith." "I have great respect for the Irish language," he said, "but I have very little respect for what is called 'the first official language,' and I believe 'the first official language' and the narrow concept of the national culture go hand in dreary hand."[61]

Hearing this, the Gaelic industry went mad. That night Maire had to spend three hours on the phone calming down Donall O'Morain, head of Gael-Linn and, not incidentally, the head of the RTE Broadcasting Authority.[62] The Government Information Office was swamped with irate calls, most of which Muiris MacConghail was able to abbreviate by dealing with them in the first official language.[63]

Conor modulated his voice on this issue, but he did not change his position. In the Dail and elsewhere, he ceased inserting the ritual beginning in Irish and using isolated Irish phrases when English was the language being spoken. If someone wanted to question him in the Dail in the Irish language, he was happy to reply in it, but he would no longer deal with the language as a sort of venerable relic—one that one did not much use, but kept in the back room for use on ceremonial occasions. English was the language he was best at and from now on he proposed to speak it without apology.[64]

What was especially repugnant to Conor was the sectarian aspect that the privileging of Irish language culture implied. No matter how hard one tried to hide from the fact, the Irish language was associated solely with Catholicism and with Irish nationalism. (The odd early twentieth-century Protestant Irish enthusiast could be trotted out as an exception, but Douglas Hyde really did not count as Protestant north of Newry.) Conor pointed to the statement made in the Dail by one deputy who explained that what *he* meant by Irish national culture was a thirty-two-county Gaelic-speaking Ireland![65] This was an extreme case, but in fact the enthronement of a language, toward which very few Protestants, either north or south, had an ancestral cultural attachment—like the enthronement of Catholic family law in the statutes of the republic—was an impediment to reconciliation between Protestants and Catholics and to eventual Irish unity. And the language matter had a curious dysfunctional backspin in the republic. "The threat of the territorial claim was being compounded by the thought of linguistic domination. Since only very small minorities paid more than lip-service to these aims in the Republic, Unionist fears [in the Six Counties] were correspondingly seen there as artificial, a cheap election-winning gimmick to solidify the Unionist party's vote. This was a considerable underestimation."[66]

Conor was on a winning wicket on the legal side of the language issue, because the fourteen-point concordat on which the national co-alition government was based had included an end to the require-ment—introduced in the late 1920s—that entry into the Twenty-Six Counties civil service be reserved for those who had a high degree of proficiency in Irish; and also the limitation of the school-leaving certifi-cate—required for entry into university and into all the higher profes-sions—to those who passed an Irish examination at a modest level of proficiency. Here Garret FitzGerald was central, for in 1967, he had succeeded in having Fine Gael commit itself to the abolition of compul-sory Irish[67] and in November 1974, it was abolished in these two areas. An immediate result was that it became possible for the first time for the government of the Irish Republic to begin acting as if it took seriously the idea of national unity: a significant intake of new civil servants whose homes were in Northern Ireland became possible, and they no longer had to be Catholics as previously had been the case (since Protestant schools in the north did not teach Irish). This was a small, but real step toward unity.[68]

In his own sphere of responsibility, Conor won a victory for which the Irish language lobby still has not forgiven him. This was part of a major reform in the legislation covering broadcasting that he intro-duced in 1975 and which was passed in 1976. (The other important seg-ment of that broadcasting measure will be discussed later, but here the point is that he successfully took the hate-edge off the language issue.) When Conor came to office, the existing legislation required that the Broadcasting Authority "shall bear constantly in mind the national aims of restoring the Irish language and preserving and developing the na-tional culture and shall endeavour to promote the attainment of these aims."[69] That was code: it meant, shall promote Gaelic-Catholic-nationalist culture as the righteous culture of the Irish state. In Waterford in February 1974, Conor announced his intention of requir-ing the Broadcasting Authority in his new legislation to "bear in mind the need to promote peace, reconciliation and better understanding be-tween Irish people of different traditions."[70] In his Broadcasting Act, as finally signed into law, the Broadcasting Authority had the following duties that related to the Irish language:

[to] be responsive to the interests and concerns of the whole community, be mindful of the need for understanding and peace within the whole island of Ireland, ensure that the programmes reflect the varied elements which make

up the culture of the people of the whole island of Ireland, and have special regard for the elements which distinguish that culture, and in particular for the Irish language.[71]

That was not a revolution, but it was a fair step forward. Here was a legislative change that replaced exclusivism with pluralism, and sectarianism with respect for other traditions than that which had formerly been the official culture of the Twenty-Six County state.

If Conor's galvanic stirring of the Irish psyche—in his opposition to church-dictated morality, such as on the matter of contraception, and in his opposition to the country's having a single governmentally approved national culture—made people twitch violently, his announcement, in late June 1974, that he was no longer actively working for national unity virtually produced a seizure. His announcement was made on RTE radio's "This Week," and its shock value was equal to the head of the Paulists announcing that he no longer thought converting unbelievers was a sensible way to spend time. As always, Conor here garnered attention by presenting his point in an outrageous form, and then qualifying it in subsequent statements so that it no longer was outrageous, but, by this time, everyone was talking about what he had said. So, why had he announced that he was not working for the reunification of Ireland? Because he did not regard it as a practical goal. "I would be absolutely overjoyed if Ireland were to become united peacefully and by consent. There is no political outcome that could bring me greater and more lasting joy than that." In a looping nonsequitur, he continued: "But the fact that I would like to see it happen does not justify me [sic] claiming that it is likely or in pretending that it is likely when I know it is not. I know it is not and I regard it as my duty to honestly say so."[72]

Conor had a large problem of logic here. One could, after all, be working hard for the reunification of Ireland even if one believed it was a long way off. However, his real message had nothing to do with logic in any case, but with a formulation of an approach to Irish unity that was almost Zen-like in its construction. He went on to say that peace and reconciliation (and, therefore, that unspoken word, unity) would be hastened if everyone would stop chanting unity-is-our-goal, something that made Northern Protestants very nervous indeed. This point was aimed particularly at the SDLP, the northern Catholic political party, and in the south at Fianna Fail. Conor believed that were an honest attempt at reconciliation made, one that was not manipulative and not irredentist—getting rid of Articles 2 and 3 in the republic's constitution would be an important step, he suggested—then, paradoxically, the chances of unity actually would increase. Very Zen: the only way to obtain Irish unity was to stop working for it.

• • •

In 1973, Conor had a very funny, very biting one-act play produced at the Peacock Theatre, the experimental venue of the Abbey.[73] This was *King Herod Advises*, the third of the trilogy that comprises the Herod sequence. In this incarnation, King Herod is a sinister psychiatrist— "something between Herman Kahn, and Wandering Jew, and Satan," Conor told Brian Inglis[74]—whose speciality is curing people who have blockages of their aggressive impulses. Herod first cures a Dublin Marxist politician who is having trouble in starting real aggression in the North. Herod helps him to get rid of all that working-class-unity verbiage and to get down to real tribal hatred. "Nationalism, *plus* Catholicism, *plus* money, *plus* arms, *minus* Marxism" is the prescription that Herod gives—a "provisional one," in a dreadful pun.[75]

Next Herod, great psychiatrist that he is, cures a unionist politician whose loyalty to Britain keeps him from being truly violently sectarian. Here the aggression-freeing prescription is "Ulster Protestantism, *plus* Ulster Nationalism, *minus* British loyalism, *plus* money, *plus* arms."[76] And, finally, Herod has a go at curing a wishy-washy Catholic priest who, as a left-wing, proto-liberation-theologian, sympathizes with the IRA, but has reservations about violence. This one gets away: he is not quite ready to repeat the mantra "institutional violence" during his prayers, that phrase being guaranteed to excuse all political terrorism. But King Herod is not dismayed. "That priest got away—somewhat to my surprise. But I could easily have shown you priests who did not get away. Priests hooked forever on drugged words, incurable addicts in the cells of sophistry, with their genuine compassion turned inside out and converted into callousness."[77]

The real-life play of 1973 was the Sunningdale circus, a promising set of negotiations on Northern Ireland that turned into a brutal disappointment. The term "Sunningdale" serves as shorthand for a conference held at a civil service college in Sunningdale, Berkshire, from 6 to 9 December 1973. In attendance were representatives of the Irish Republic, of the United Kingdom, of the Northern Catholic SDLP, and of some of the northern Protestant political groups; "Sunningdale" also refers to the arrangements made before and after the conference and to the ensuing collapse of those arrangements. The Sunningdale period can be taken as running from April 1973, when Garret FitzGerald paid his first visit as foreign minister to Northern Ireland, until things came unstuck in May 1975.

The late John Whyte, who knew more about the literature on Northern Ireland than did anyone, used to say that for its size, Northern Ireland had more written about it than any other area on earth. Still, not until the archives of the various governments and political parties that were engaged with Sunningdale are opened, will what happened in Berkshire be fully known. Even then it will be tricky: more than 120 persons were involved and, many of the decisions were made in satellite meetings; and, by unanimous agreement of those present, full and open bars dotted the building, so that many of the memories of the participants are more hazy than usually would be the case.

The outline of events, however, is simple. In 1973, direct rule of Northern Ireland from London still seemed unnatural (today it is the norm). The Tory government of Edward Heath proposed a unicameral assembly for Northern Ireland that would have some of the powers that the old Stormont government had had. It would include a "power-sharing executive," meaning that representatives of both the Catholic and Protestant communities would sit on it. This structure was brought into being by a statute of 1973. The scheme for the seventy-eight-member assembly that was to semigovern Northern Ireland was fairly canny. Activities that throughout modern Irish history have been religiously divisive—police, courts, security—were to be left in the hands of London for the time being, but most other governmental matters were to be transferred to Ulster politicians if—and this was a very big "if"—a Protestant-Catholic coalition were prepared to take the reins of power. This was a very shrewd idea, for it played upon the desire of politicians everywhere to have power. Why else, after all, be a politician? An election was held for Northern Ireland assembly seats in June 1973 and in late November that year one Protestant party (the Official Unionist party), one Catholic party (the SDLP), and one ecumenical party (Alliance) tentatively agreed to form a power-sharing coalition.

The actual Sunningdale Agreement, of December 1973, had all sorts of complex filigree, but its central machinery comprised two very simple moving parts. First, increased powers would be transferred from London to the "Northern Ireland assembly" and to its power-sharing executive. These would inevitably (given Ulster demography) be going to an assembly and executive that had a Protestant majority, although Catholics would be in the power-sharing executive. Second, an "all-Ireland council" would be formed. This device, which harked back to the provisions of the Government of Ireland Act of 1920 (the Partition Act) was to be a consultative body made up of representatives of both parts of Ireland (but to have no British participants). In the immediate short term, it was to have only consultative powers; in the long term, it had the potential, its backers believed, of evolving into a constituent assembly or even into a parliament for a United Ireland.

The southern Irish negotiating team consisted of Liam Cosgrave, Brendan Corish, Garret FitzGerald, and Conor; FitzGerald was the lead figure. In the chair of the meeting was Edward Heath of the United Kingdom. The British negotiating team was headed by Sir Alec Douglas-Hume, and with him were Francis Pym, Peter Rawlinson, and David Howell. The SDLP was led by John Hume. Gerry Fitt was present, although he was not very active. Rather more active was Paddy Devlin. Oliver Napier and Robert Cooper represented Alliance. The chief Ulster Unionist negotiator was Brian Faulkner.

Anyone with any real knowledge of the social physics of Ulster at the time could have told these assembled politicians that the machine they were constructing, simple though it might be, would not work. This was because the Northern Protestants, though they could be made to swallow the bitter pill of sharing the government of their statelet with Catholics, would not at the same time accept a council of Ireland whose latent message was this: you are not merely sharing power with Catholics, but some day you will inevitably be swallowed up in an Irish Catholic thirty-two-county republic. It was just too much humiliation to put on them at one time.

Paddy Devlin understood this. Conor understood it. Garret FitzGerald, however, and the other members of the southern Irish delegation did not. Twenty years later, FitzGerald quite handsomely admitted that "any objective historian of the period will be forced to conclude that he [Conor] was more nearly right than I and the rest of us were in the run-up to Sunningdale and in his judgement of the conference itself."[78] Seemingly alone among the SDLP, John Hume pushed hard for the council of Ireland and not just for a hole-in-the-wall bit of construction that would be a codicil to the main agreement on power sharing, but a high-profile, gin palace of a structure. Garret FitzGerald in this period was entirely under the sway of Hume. During the August break in 1973, he and his wife Joan had spent much of their holiday with John and Pat Hume in Donegal.[79] Brian Faulkner, the chief Official Unionist party representative, was so desperate to have a devolved government returned to Northern Ireland, that he accepted things at Sunningdale that he had no chance of selling to the Ulster Protestants. At one point, Paddy Devlin, who had about as hard-edged an awareness of the realities of the Protestant community in the north as anyone could have, told his fellow SDLP negotiators, "Look, we've got to catch ourself on here. Brian Faulkner is being nailed to a cross. There is no way Faulkner can sell this."[80] This was exactly what Conor had been saying.

Nevertheless, Faulkner signed the agreement.

For the SDLP, Gerry Fitt signed and also did some radio interviews. But John Hume did the television interviews.[81] It was from television that most of the Protestants of Northern Ireland learned the details of power sharing and also of the council of Ireland. And, they heard from John Hume exactly what it all meant. Hume did this with the concerned smile that he usually reserves for talk about intercommunal relations, but he could not conceal his sense of triumph. What Protestants saw was the triumphant look of a seventeenth-century Irish chief holding aloft the severed head of an enemy. From that moment onward, Sunningdale was dead.

In fact, John Hume understood exactly the physics of Northern Ireland, as had Paddy Devlin and Conor: he just had different uses for that knowledge. Although his pressure for a high-profile all-Ireland council almost certainly foredoomed the power-sharing experiment, it quite brilliantly had placed his party in a win-win position. In the unlikely event that the Ulster Protestants accepted both power sharing and the council of Ireland, this would be an unparalleled victory for Hume and his northern Catholic constituents. And if—as was much more likely—the Protestant population repudiated the deal, they would look very bad on the international stage and especially bad in Great Britain, which desperately wanted to get out of Northern Ireland as quickly as it could.

A power-sharing executive did indeed come into office in Northern Ireland on 1 January 1974, and it immediately started to shred. Amid the general public, an "Ulster Workers' Council" was formed and it threatened direct action. Conor, though pessimistic about the future, put his energies into making Sunningdale a success, but he was limited to cheerleading. In mid-April 1974, as things came apart, he wrote: "The Sunningdale arrangements are in danger. It remains true—in spite of the immediate level of violence—that the substance of the Sunningdale arrangements is the best, and perhaps the only, hope in the middle and long term for peace in Northern Ireland."[82] On the streets, however, things became very rough. In mid-May, the Ulster Workers' Council declared a general strike. This was the real thing, the sort of general strike that revolutionaries talk about but almost never actually achieve. The entire province was closed down. All public transport was shut down and driving a motor vehicle was possible only with the benefit of a pass from the Uster Workers' Council. A state of emergency was declared. Harold Wilson, prime minister of the United Kingdom by virtue of a general election victory in February, promised on 25 May that his government would be constant in its support of the power-sharing executive. Four days later, he surrendered: direct rule from London was reimposed. Both power sharing and the council of Ireland were erased. Conor in the Dail said that the greatest hope for peace in Northern Ireland went with the fall of the power-sharing executive.[83]

In the wake of the northern Protestant workers' victory, Conor drafted for private circulation to the administrative council of the Labour party a document that someone (certainly not Conor) leaked to the press, where it became known as the "Doomsday Paper." This was an attempt to deal with a question that no one wanted to face: what would happen if the northern Protestants, who recently had shown both muscle and organizational ability, seized control of Northern Ireland and issued a unilateral declaration of independence? Conor's answer was that *if* the British army withdrew there would be a civil war and the casualties in the North would be heavy, and not negligible in the republic. Conor's estimate was that the Irish army was capable of capturing and holding only one border town (Newry) and that the northern Catholics would therefore be on their own and would lose heavily.[84]

Although Conor was virtually alone in daring to articulate the consequences of a Protestant seizure of power in the North, he was not alone in realizing that if the British troops pulled out, all hell would ensue. This probability, however, was repugnant to the canons of Irish nationalism, both in its northern and southern branches, so to point out what a great many people knew—that the British troops had to stay—was a sure road to political unpopularity. Conor, in those days, liked to repeat as a parable of nationalist double-think on this matter a story concerning Kevin McNamara, the British Labour party's spokesman on Northern Ireland:

> He had been publicly calling for "troops out" and then I noticed that he suddenly seemed to have dropped this demand. When I asked him why, he told me of an experience he had had in Belfast.
>
> He was an associate of a committee which supplied comforts to the internees [1971 and thereafter]. Most of the members, he told me, were mothers, wives or girlfriends of IRA men. At the close of one meeting, he asked those present whether they favoured pulling out the troops. They replied with a chorus of "No!" When he asked why, the answer was: "Sure, we'd all be murdered."[85]

That, at least, was realism.

• • •

As a day-to-day cabinet minister Conor focused most of his energies on broadcasting policy, but even there things curled into the great snakes of Irish national identity, self-image, cultural preservation, and attitudes toward violence. Conor could concentrate on broadcasting because Liam O'Reagain, first, as assistant secretary and then, as a secretary of the department, was highly efficient and trustworthy. He understood how the massive phone and postal bureaucracies worked. (This did not, however, prevent Conor as minister from being praised for coming close to achieving Wolfe Tone's ideal of breaking the connection with England; fair comment on the phone service, actually.)[86]

Conor ran into management problems with the posts and telegraphs sections only when he tried to break down the rigid class distinctions within the Irish civil service. He attempted to promote from the professional to the administrative class (that is, from technical to top management jobs) qualified engineers and technicians. He got only a few across and then the civil servants in the administrative class closed ranks and fought the changes all the way.[87] As far as one can tell (again, the files are not yet open), Conor did not use the massive public payroll of his department for party or clientelist purposes. (There was the story in the Dublin papers of his vetting a very thick promotion file, full of favorable letters of recommendation, and asking "Who is this guy anyway? He must be a member of the Fine Gael wing of the Official IRA." But that was a good political joke.)[88] The only appointment he made that could be construed as jobbery (and even this caused only minimal hostile comment) was the appointment of his son-in-law, Nicholas Simms, as "assistant on broadcasting to the minister of posts and telegraphs," and this was a post for which Simms was well qualified: he had a good economics degree from TCD, several years experience as a research officer in broadcasting, first at RTE and then with the Irish Marketing Survey. He knew the field well and could be trusted.

Conor and a few others in the national coalition set what has since become a pattern in Irish ministerial arrangements of bringing in their own secretaries and assistants, instead of relying solely on civil servants. In this case, the imports were concerned only with broadcasting. In addition to Nicholas Simms, Conor had a wonderful administrative assistant, Mary O'Hanlon (who later married Tony Brown, Labour party economics expert), plus a temporary secretary to take care of specifically political matters and three clerical officers: not a large personal staff by the standards of most parliamentary democracies.[89]

Some of the improvements that Conor wanted in Irish broadcasting were effected fairly smoothly: cable was expanded in Dublin, Cork and, subsequently, other major cities; the restriction that RTE broadcast in color only a few hours a week was removed. (This had been put in place to keep the importation of color sets from burgeoning and thus hurting the Irish economy!); broadcasting hours for RTE television were expanded; the license fees, which provided most of RTE's revenue, were indexed to inflation so that both radio and television were less dependent on the political pressures that could be exercised through the purse strings; and a complaints section with teeth in it was established, composed of distinguished members of the general public, not politicians.

The basic points to be remembered about radio and television broadcasting in Ireland in this period are that broadcasting was a governmental monopoly and that both radio and television were consciously employed as a form of state control of culture and of social control.[90] This second function was rarely articulated—"preserving national culture" was the circumlocution most commonly employed. Eamon de Valera had put clearly the fear the Irish government and the cultural establishment held of television in his address on the opening of the republic's channel Telefis Eireann on 31 December 1961. "Never before was there in the hands of men an instrument so powerful to influence the thoughts and actions of the multitude. The persistent policy pursued over radio and television, apart from imparting knowledge, can build up the character of the whole people, including sturdiness and vigour and confidence. On the other hand, it can lead through demoralization to decadence and disillusion."[91] In practice, radio was not a concern, but television, believed to be more influential, more seductive, was one of those things that those concerned with cultural probity and social control wanted in hands that were neither foreign nor under private control.

In the 1970s, there was only one channel broadcasting in the Republic of Ireland, that of Telefis Eireann. However, in the Dublin region, those on community antennas ("piped TV," in the language of the time) received four channels in addition to RTE: BBC-1, BBC-2, Ulster TV and Harlech TV. Also, about 60 percent of the television sets in the republic (roughly, those along the east coast and along the Northern Ireland border) could pick up some British television on their individual antennae, usually BBC-1. The people in the south and west of Ireland paid the same license fees as those who received "multi-channel" television, but were stuck with RTE and only RTE. So there was an equity question behind what came to be called "open broadcasting."

Conor proposed a simple solution. Give everyone more than one channel. Put British public television on the Irish transmitters as a second service and make it available all around the country. BBC-1 (Northern Ireland) was a high-quality, noncommercial service, unfailingly up-market and improving in its programming. How could anyone object? Moreover, how could anyone object who had an interest in national reconciliation and national unity? Conor's goal was to work out a trade with BBC-1 (Northern Ireland). Then RTE television would be broadcast in the North and BBC-1 (Northern Ireland) in the south. In effect, the country would have two all-Ireland networks, and at a bargain price.[92]

The sky almost fell. The Republic of Ireland was not yet ready for cultural pluralism and, additionally, a variety of vested interest groups fought open broadcasting. Understandably, RTE did not want a rival channel telecast nationally, and lobbied hard for the establishment of a second channel—RTE-2—that it would control. The Irish Actors Equity wanted any extra money put into TV broadcasting to be used for the production of Irish programs, employing Irish actors. They linked up with the Irish Transport and General Workers' Union and through them with British trade unions to produce an effective lobby on both sides of the Irish Sea. The Association of Advertisers in Ireland, a lobby group, also opposed open broadcasting: if viewers in single-channel areas suddenly had a choice of channels, they might well switch off RTE and then advertising revenues would drop.[93]

Conor had perhaps a fifty-fifty chance of beating these forces, since he had the Cabinet behind him at this point. But there was another, ill-defined, but pervasive force that, ultimately, he could not overcome. This was a mixture of Anglophobia (the idea of helping the culture of the Old Enemy to spread in Ireland stuck in the craw of many), romantic ideas about the purity of Irish back-country life, cultural isolationism and, especially, the Irish language lobby. The latter was concerned not only with language preservation, but with the maintenance of what it believed was Irish culture in as pure a form as possible. The Anglophobia was rarely articulated as such, but when it was, the vocabulary was strangely eloquent. For example, P.L. Henry, the professor of Old and Medieval English at University College, Galway, at a meeting of Conradh na Gaeilge in Galway denounced open broadcasting as being part of the "continuing and accelerating assimilation of the Irish people into British mass culture." He continued: "To give BBC free run of Ireland, as suggested by the minister of posts and telegraphs, is tantamount to reconquest. The same minister is involved in the distortion of Irish history and the movement to displace the Irish language." Professor Henry's conclusion turned the concept of cultural pluralism on its head. "This kind of activity is known the world over as treacherous or treasonable. When you combine the three things: displacement of the language, distortion of our history, and ramming the BBC down our throats, you have a definition of tyranny."[94]

Conor could shrug off such views, defamatory as they were, but what got under his skin was the idea that the country people of Ireland, who would under his plan have more than one channel to watch, were frail museum pieces who had to be kept under glass. As he told a group in Clonmel, some commentators, like Deputy Robert Molloy of Fianna Fail, appeared to believe that viewers in the country and towns were more likely to be culturally corrupted than viewers in the cities. "The fact is that Irish people can no more be turned into 'little English' by exposure to British television than they can be turned into medieval Gaels by denying them such exposure." He added, "It is an odd idea that we can demonstrate our Irishness by denying to Irish people in the south and west what is freely available and eagerly accepted in the north and east."[95]

The Gaelic lobby wanted to keep the far west and south as culturally pure as possible: meaning nonpluralistic, non-European, but very Catholic, very nationalistic, and, whenever possible, Irish-speaking. Conor particularly raised their ire in a speech he made at Oxford in July 1974 on the subject of the media in Ireland, for in it he rejected one of the Gaelic lobby's chief items of faith. "I have argued that we must not regard the Irish and English languages as hostile to one another, but rather as complementary for Irish people."[96] This is exactly what one would believe and say if one were seriously interested in reconciling the basic cultural conflicts in Ireland and in eventual national unity. However, Conradh na Gaeilge were enraged. In reply, an organizational release stated the correct dogmatics: "The two languages are in conflict simply because English seeks to push Irish out of existence."[97]

Probably the most impressive of the Gaelgeori who fought Conor was Donall O'Morain whom Conor had appointed in May 1973 as head of the RTE Authority.[98] A tall, balding, well-built man, O'Morain resembled a retired but still fit rugby forward (although, of course, he would have played only Gaelic games) and he had great presence. He had been sacked, along with all of his colleagues, from the RTE Authority in November 1972 in a Fianna Fail purge of the authority. Conor's reappointment of him was both a vindication of his character and a chance for Conor to put a thumb in the eye of Fianna Fail.

As head of the Broadcasting Authority (in everyday speech "RTE Authority" and "Broadcasting Authority" were used as interchangeable terms), O'Morain met Conor weekly. O'Morain viewed his task as keeping the minister for posts and telegraphs on the rails, for, in his view, Conor was very excitable in this period and was apt to make snap judgments without hearing both sides of the story. O'Morain was capable of presenting his own position with all the *gravitas* of a master talking to a delinquent pupil. He quite vigorously argued with Conor against open broadcasting and, behind the scenes, he let the top people at the BBC know that there were problems with their selling BBC signals to the republic.[99]

By the spring of 1975, Conor realized that he had to find a way to beat a victorious retreat on his open broadcasting plan: British trade unions were threatening to stuff up everything on their side of the Irish Sea; BBC authorities were becoming difficult to deal with; and most important, Conor, who had envisioned open broadcasting as a minor side-bar to the big broadcasting amendment bill he was trying to have passed, recognized that this relatively minor issue was apt to snarl up major reforms. So, he announced an unusual sort of a referendum. A marketing firm would conduct a random survey of about 2,000 respondents who would be asked whether they preferred as a second channel BBC-1 or the channel that RTE wished to create, RTE-2. Conor announced in late October that RTE-2 had won: 62 to 35 percent, and thus the public having spoken, the problem was solved.[100]

What is unclear is whether or not Conor took a dive. He was reported in August 1975 to be stumping the country, telling people in single-channel areas that they must have what they wanted and "that they should want BBC."[101] But even a boxer taking a dive goes through the motions. The interesting point about the mini-referendum on open broadcasting was how little effort was taken to keep it unbiased. The sampling procedure was set up jointly by Conor and RTE officials. Conor agreed that RTE should have an opportunity to explain their position before the survey took place. So RTE did this by putting out a twenty-page pamphlet entitled *The Second Channel* and they also used the *RTE Guide* to extol the virtues of RTE-2.[102] There was no counterinformation from BBC advocates (the BBC itself was not about to become involved and the people who wanted BBC were individual consumers rather than producer lobby groups). Then, in the actual interviews, the respondents were shown two case cards: one showed the positive case for RTE-2 and attacked BBC-1; the other, favoring BBC-1, according to one observer "was weak, indirect, rather negative," and had not been prepared by the people who had been part of the open broadcasting campaign.[103]

Rigged or not, this survey let Conor off the hook. He announced that the creation of RTE-2 was national policy and let RTE worry about getting the job done. Although their officials promised to have the second channel on air by the end of 1977, RTE-2 did not in fact become fully operational until 1980. In that year it broadcast for an average of six hours a day, and 72 percent of its hours consisted of imported programming.[104]

The only joy that Conor may have had out of this business was that when Donall O'Morain's three-year term as chair of the Broadcasting Authority came to an end in June 1976, he did not renew it, but replaced him with Sheila Conroy.[105] "There was no bust-up or public acrimony," O'Morain recalls. He noticed that his term was coming to an end and then "the next thing I knew I had a letter from the government saying what a good fellow I had been."[106]

• • •

Conor's unsuccessful attempt at employing television broadcasting as a means to broaden the nature of Irish popular culture is the backdrop for the political action for which he is most remembered: his successful attempt to restrict what could be shown on television.

In March 1975, Conor introduced a broadcasting amendment bill which eventually was passed as the Broadcasting Act 1976, a complex piece of legislation which had three major goals. The first of these was to introduce open broadcasting, a subject on which, as we have seen, he was willing to concede defeat. Second, and more important to him, was the redefinition of the watchdog agency that oversaw RTE, so that it would be free of political interference (not free of state interference, but from meddling by any one political party). And, third, and most important to Conor, was a more precise definition of what sorts of political (read: terrorist) messages and information were to be prohibited. The last matter is usually referred to as "Section 31," that being the section of the 1960 Broadcasting Act under which antiterrorist gags were issued.

Now the second matter—the watchdog authority—was fairly simple legislatively, but involved a complex matter of political philosophy: how much control should the state have over state-financed broadcasting, and in what form should that control be exercised? The most restrictive view of the issue had been articulated in 1966 by Fianna Fail's Sean Lemass, then taoiseach. "The government reject the view that Radio Telefis Eireann should be, either generally or in regard to its current affairs and news programmes, completely independent of government supervision. It has the duty, while maintaining impartiality between political parties ... to sustain public respect for the institutions of government and, where appropriate, to assist public understanding of the policies enshrined in legislation enacted by the Oireachtas. The government will take such action ... as may be necessary to ensure that Radio Telefis Eireann does not deviate from the due performance of this duty."[107] Note that the term "government" here does not mean the state or government in a generic sense: it means government-of-the-

day, that is, the political party that has a preponderance of power in the
Dail.

In November 1969, the Fianna Fail government had been distressed
by a "Seven Days" feature on unlicensed money lending, an investigative segment that reflected badly on the government. On this and on
subsequent matters, Fianna Fail would have liked the RTE Authority to
intervene, but the authority, collectively, was of too high a quality to do
so. It consisted of individuals, high-ranking in their own professions,
who could not be bullied: Donall O'Morain, who has already been
mentioned; T.W. Moody, professor of modern history at Trinity
College; Phyllis O'Kelly, widow of the late president of Ireland;
Stephen Barrett, barrister and former TD; Liam Hyland, a County Cork
farmer and county councillor; Noel Mulcahy, head of the business management division of the Irish Management Institute; James Fanning,
editor of the *Midland Tribune*; Sean O'Murchu, industrial secretary of
the Irish Transport and General Workers' Union; and Michael
O'Callaghan, editor of the *Roscommon Herald*. The government in early
October 1971 told this group that they were to enforce a government
directive under Section 31, namely that RTE was not to broadcast anything that might aid any organization whose goal was to attain "any particular objective." When, on 16 November 1972, RTE broadcast a
summary of an interview with a spokesman for the Provisional IRA, the
government told the authority to crack down. When it refused, the entire authority was sacked.

This was done in an amazingly precipitous fashion. At 9:00 on Friday
night, 24 November, a platoon of motorcycle despatch riders was sent
out, each bearing an envelope informing a member of the authority that
he or she was cashiered. And, by 9:30, the government had announced
that for the remainder of the board's term, nine new members were appointed: several of whom had yet to be told that they had been appointed.[108]

Conor's amended broadcasting act precluded this happening again.
Under his legislation, no longer could a single party dump the media
watchdogs. If the RTE Authority, or a member of the authority, were to
be removed, henceforth it could be only by resolutions to that effect
being passed by both houses of the Oireachtas. That meant that the RTE
Authority became responsible to the entire Irish legislature, not just to
the governing party.[109]

The contentious issue was what would Conor do about Section 31.
This item has become virtually an appendage to Conor's name, but it
in fact has a very long history that has nothing to do with him. It was
put forward by Erskine Childers as Section 31 of the Broadcasting Act

of 1960, a Fianna Fail measure. In a sensible world, Section 31 would have said "spokesmen for terrorist organizations are not allowed access to broadcasting media," and one might have agreed or disagreed with it, but at least the meaning would have been clear. However, this was Ireland, and in 1960, Fianna Fail was still self-consciously the heir to the antitreaty party, the "republicans." Section 31, though directed against present-day republicans, remained very obscure. "The minister may direct the Authority in writing to refrain from broadcasting any particular matter or matter of any particular class, and the Authority shall comply with that direction."[110] That was a classic piece of Irish prose. It was based on an earlier Offences Against the State Act (meaning, an act to ban the IRA) crafted by Eamon de Valera. The circumlocutions were necessary because Fianna Fail could not very well say that it was banning the public expression of organizations, "whose aim is the re-uniting of Ireland." Two other points were salient. The 1960 act did not provide a time limit on ministerial banning; there was no sunset clause and the ban could be perpetual. Also, note that despite the intention of the 1960 act, to keep terrorist groups off the airwaves, the statute did not limit ministerial power to such political matters. At some future date, a minister could interpret his power very broadly.

When Conor came to posts and telegraphs in March 1973, it was generally expected that he would either abolish, or at least diminish, the power of Section 31. One political correspondent reported in June 1973 that Conor had promised to abolish Section 31 in the succeeding year.[111] That report may have been inaccurate, but certainly it was not an unreasonable inference, given Conor's track record when he was in opposition: in June 1971 in the Dail he had described the Prohibition of Forcible Entry Bill as "a clear incursion into freedom of speech, freedom of the Press, and freedom of association."[112] In the autumn of 1971, he had denounced the use of Section 31 against the IRA by the then-minister of posts and telegraphs. Conor objected to "people who are not charged with an offence," being "blacklisted on this particular medium [television]."[113] In mid-December 1972, he told a dinner meeting of the National Union of Journalists that Fianna Fail was trying to gain control of RTE by using the curbing of the men of violence as a pretext.[114] Thus, even if Conor did not actually promise to abolish Section 31 (he may have; he may not have), his staunch defense of civil liberties in the past had led most observers to think he might do so, and almost no one expected him to tighten security.

Then Conor came to office and his tone changed. He gave an interview in mid-May to RTE radio's "Media Brief," in which he acknowledged that there were some flaws in Section 31, but indicated that it would continue on the books. He did not foresee "at any early stage," a situation in which leaders of the IRA could be interviewed on the Irish state broadcasting system, although he said he was willing to meet with representatives of the Official IRA from the North if they wished to see him. He said his real objection to Section 31 was not that it limited certain activities but that it did not say clearly what the activities and limitations were.[115]

When it became clear that Conor did not intend to abolish Section 31 or even to withdraw the earlier orders under Section 31 made by Fianna Fail, this confused many of his old friends and backers. They could not help but contrast his longtime opposition to censorship in general to his new behavior, now that he was the censor.[116] In 1974, Conor replaced the obscure banning order that Fianna Fail had formulated under Section 31, with a very precise order that was drafted for him by his son-in-law Nicholas Simms. The vague wording was gone: now the Provos, Officials, Provisional Sinn Fein (but not Official Sinn Fein) were unambiguously banned from the airwaves, as were their advocates.[117]

Obviously both the world and Conor had changed since the days in which he was an outspoken civil rights advocate. It is fair to note that one big difference between Conor's fight (for example) against the Catholic Church's sponsoring censorship of birth control information, and the minister of posts and telegraph's censorship of terrorist advocacy, was that Conor approved of the latter and not of the former; moreover, in the latter case, he got to be the censor.

That is true enough, but if one looks at the general trend in Conor's political thinking from mid-1971 onward, the development is fairly consistent: namely that (excepting the swerve over Bloody Sunday), he became more and more convinced that the real enemies were the men of violence. After the collapse of Sunningdale in mid-1975, which he saw despite all its flaws as the best hope for peace, Conor's political logic became increasingly ruthless, and at the same time his behavior became increasingly frantic.

One finds him, for instance, rebuking Sir Charles Curran, director general of the BBC, for broadcasting an interview with Daithi O'Conaill (var: David O'Connell), one of the Provo leaders. "People who want to listen to the Irish would do better to listen to the elected representatives of the Irish, rather than the people whose claim to speak for anyone rests on nothing more than their capacity to kill."[118] That was in July 1974. In October, Conor responded to a segment of "Seven Days" that involved a discussion of internment in Northern Ireland against a backdrop of clips that made it seem as if the British troops were the aggressors in the rioting. The program indeed was loaded and the producer-director was taken off the current affairs beat and two high-management producers were reprimanded, but the interesting point here is that Conor went into his combat-mode before he even saw the actual tapes of the program.[119] He had denounced the show upon word-of-mouth evidence. When Donall O'Morain forced him to sit down and actually look at the tapes, he calmed down a bit.[120] In October 1974, he gave a speech to the St. Andrew's College annual dinner in which he claimed that certain liberals were "dancing to the tune of the IRA." He specifically denounced Senator Mary Robinson for having sat on the platform at a Mansion House meeting convened by *Hibernia* magazine at which IRA sympathizers were prominent. He said:

> I think this was a great pity. Senator Mary Robinson (for it was she) is a lady of considerable ability and style who has fought with courage and effect in the Senate for at least one important and genuinely liberal cause [contraception]. The Mansion House proceedings were so profoundly illiberal as actually to cast scorn, not only on any given political party, not on the Government, but on the central institution of democracy, parliament itself.
>
> Nor is that all. The senator, who is also a professor of law, ably attacked the practice of internment without trial, and made the case for reliance on the ordinary courts. But she is not recorded, in any reports I have seen, as referring at all to the difficulties which can be experienced under certain conditions by the courts in dealing with armed conspiracies.
>
> She is not reported as referring to the murder of two judges in Belfast last month by that same armed conspiracy whose admirers were so vocal in that room that they were only quelled by the denunciation of the democracy in which we live. The only comment she is reported as having made on judges in Northern Ireland was an aspersion on their integrity.[121]

Soon thereafter, Conor got into a slagging match in the *New Statesman* with the journalist Mary Holland and this was the start of a permanent antagonism, one that ran through his later tenure as editor in chief of the *Observer*. In a reply to Holland's charge that he was a repressive force, he stated that "ever since the Provisional IRA campaign in Northern Ireland began, I have consistently warned that the campaign, if persisted in, would lead to civil war."[122]

That was why he was so desperate in the post-Sunningdale period; Ireland, he believed, was on the verge of civil war. To prevent it, one had to eliminate from the pile of explosive chemicals the catalyst that could set everything off. That meant suppressing the Provos, and therefore, manically, assertively, using every opportunity that came to hand,

Conor fought them. He was not in this period a balanced person, or anything close. He was in the grip of a passion, a passion for his country. One might disagree with the diagnosis, but one cannot question his sincerity.

And, indeed, before assuming that he was sincere but wrong—before just assuming that he was "crying wolf," that there was no chance of civil war—one should reflect for a moment. Conor came to his judgment, and to the fear that stalked his passion for the Irish people, after having seen what very few people in Ireland at the time had witnessed: what happens when the veneer of social control breaks down. He had seen it in the Congo. In the mid-1970s, most politicians (not just in Ireland, but worldwide) still believed that anarchy and civil war were conditions that occurred only in "underdeveloped" countries (that is, black or brown countries in the Third World). Conor intuited what the rest of the Western world did not pick up until the Yugoslavian horrors of the 1990s: that white countries could descend into the chaos of religious, ethnic, and tribal warfare. He also understood that as a result of their efficient organization and their success in destroying the Sunningdale Agreement, the Protestants of the North in late 1974 and early 1975 were on a hair-trigger, ready and able to respond to Provo violence. That response would not be surgical, but crudely and massively anti-Catholic.

Hence, when one observes Conor act in a manner that seems frantic, manic, and somewhat crazed, one should not jump to the conclusion that he was crazy. Parts of his world, his beloved Ireland, were on the edge of madness. Anyone who remained calm, inert, and inactive would have been truly crazy.

In March 1975, while completing the draft of his broadcasting bill, Conor wrote to Andrée Sheehy-Skeffington, the widow of his cousin Owen, who had died in 1970:

> I was reading over the Senate debate on the original [1960] Bill to which of course Owen contributed. I found he objected to an amendment which in part closely resembled the most controversial section of my Bill (restrictions on incitement to violence of this order). However I also took the view that in an emergency the Government did of course give itself all the powers necessary. I don't know whether he would have agreed, in 1975, that one can have a sort of creeping or potential emergency in relation to which the Government needs to retain fairly drastic reserve powers to cope with various eventualities, without having recourse to new legislation during the crisis itself. For example, if the Northern situation seriously deteriorated, with streams of Catholic refugees coming south and calls for intervention by the Dublin government I would not like under those conditions, (with a majority

of three) to try to push a Bill through the Dail giving the Government emergency powers over RTE. Yet it would be precisely at such a moment that hysterical broadcasting would be most dangerous.[123]

As an exercise in legislation, two parts of Conor's broadcasting bill were unusual. One was that it required twenty-one months—from March 1975 to December 1976—to pass the bill, so crowded was the legislative calendar and so distracting were other events relating to the economy and to national security. And, second, Conor chose to introduce the bill in the Seanad, rather than in the Dail. This is permitted, although rarely done, under Irish legislative rules, and in this case it was a good idea. The more cerebral, less highly politicized character of the Seanad not only permitted Conor to present his arguments in a fuller and more intellectual arena than would have been possible in the lower house, but the quality of the criticism was high and several amendments were suggested that Conor was able to accept. Conor's speech introducing the bill was beautifully constructed and he knew it: he had the Government Information Office publish 2,000 copies of the speech in the form of a thirty-six-page booklet.[124]

Despite Conor's eloquence, senators, especially his new-found opponent, Mary Robinson, were worried about Section 31. Still, when the debates in the senate were over, he had accepted no fundamental changes. The new version of Section 31 (1) limited the matters on which the minister for posts and telegraphs could ban broadcasting access to those "likely to promote, or incite to, crime or would tend to undermine the authority of the State"; (2) limited such orders to twelve months duration, after which they could be extended for up to an additional twelve months either by another ministerial order or by a resolution of both houses of the Oireachtas; and Section 31 (3) provided that the Oireachtas could, within twenty-one days of the minister's issuing such a ban, set it aside. In sum, Conor made Section 31 much narrower than it previously had been and the orders under it of shorter duration (previously they had had no time limit) and more open to modification or cancelation by the legislature.[125]

Conor's bill soon was in the Dail, but then it was shunted aside because bigger issues intervened. These, it turns out, become part of the story of Conor and of his views on censorship, and eventually they weave back into the story of Section 31.

• • •

Early in 1976, Conor spoke to his local Howth branch of the Labour party and he told them that the year would be a tough one, both from the point of view of the economy and of security. Given the "naked horror of the sectarian guerrilla war" in Northern Ireland, "we can have no doubt any longer that civil war is not an alarmist fantasy, but a real danger against which we have to prepare."[126] By the middle of 1976, deaths in Ulster were occurring at the rate of nearly one a day. In Easter Week in Dublin, 10,000 persons attended a rally at the General Post Office, called by the Provisional IRA, and this despite the meeting's being banned by the government. In July, the United Kingdom's ambassador to the republic, Christopher Ewart-Biggs, was assassinated; in the North, Gerry Fitt, still titular leader of the SDLP, had to fight off with a gun attacks on his home by Provo supporters; and in Dublin enough explosives were found to level the entire center of the city.

Liam Cosgrave, taoiseach, became convinced that it was necessary to declare a state of national emergency and the coalition Cabinet agreed. A bill declaring this emergency was introduced into the Dail on 1 September and was quickly passed. Conor was the spokesman in the Dail for the measure. Clearly, Conor was the hard man in the coalition Cabinet, the one who most wanted an all-out war against the Provos and their front organizations: thus he was chosen as spokesman.

Attention-getting as the state of emergency was, it was not the centerpiece of the security crackdown. During August, the minister for justice, Paddy Cooney, drafted, with the help of Conor and others, a sixteen-section bill that would amend the criminal code. This bill closed down almost all the loopholes in anti-IRA legislation and made conviction of terrorists and their fronts much easier to obtain. Now, the section that concerns Conor was Section 3, and it was purposefully ambiguous. In draft, it read:

> Any person who expressly or by implication, directly or through another person or persons, or by advertisement, propaganda, or any other means, incites or invites another person (or persons generally) to join an unlawful organisation or take part in, support, or assist its activities, shall be guilty of an offence and shall be liable on conviction on indictment to imprisonment for a term not exceeding ten years.

What did this mean? The prudent political answer would be that the courts would decide. As with any piece of criminal legislation, the director of public prosecutions would, in his independent capacity, examine the alleged crime and decide if prosecution should take place. And if it did, a judge would decide the truth of the allegation.

On Section 3, Conor put on one of the least prudent performances of his political career and almost blew apart the entire piece of legislation. This occurred because he was under immense stress: he was the point man in the war against the Provos, he was working incredibly long hours to prevent what he saw as an imminent Irish civil war, and just then Maire's mother, Margaret Browne MacEntee, died.[127] So, one understands how he could lose his political judgment. It happened just when one would expect—when, for just a minute, he relaxed emotionally.

On Friday, 3 September, an old acquaintance, Bernard (Bud) Nossiter, interviewed Conor in his office in the General Post Office for the *Washington Post*. The interview was informal and, given a chance to talk to someone who was not *parti pris*, Conor talked too much. What did the proposed act mean concerning newspapers? Nossiter asked—especially that Section 3? Certainly the normal activities of a newspaper would not come under the heel of Section 3, would they? Conor responded by reaching down to a lower drawer in his desk and pulling out a file consisting of cuttings of letters to the editor of the *Irish Press*, the Fianna Fail paper owned by the de Valera family. Many of these were strongly pro-republican, indeed pro-Provo in sympathy. But Nossiter, an American liberal, was taken aback. Surely, one is not going to prosecute people who write letters to the editor? No, said Conor, it was the editors who might be prosecuted.[128]

Nossiter filed this in a *Washington Post* story,[129] but before doing so, he went to the *Irish Press* and told the story to Tim Pat Coogan, its editor.[130] By Monday morning, Conor, as a threat to freedom of the press, was a feature of every major Irish newspaper. In the Dail, on Tuesday, Conor tried to give the answer that he should have given to Nossiter, if his intentions were to cloak the real implications of Section 3: "This does not introduce censorship. It does not give special powers to the Government in relation to the press. It increases the scope of limitation on propaganda in favor of armed conspiracies ... but these limitations, the judgment and interpretation of these, are entrusted to the courts. The question of whether to bring charges before the courts is a matter for an independent official, the director of public prosecutions."[131]

It did not work. Conor has never been good at dissemblance and his old enemy Charlie Haughey nearly took him apart. That he was not being truthful is indicated not only by what he had told Bud Nossiter, but by an interview he gave not long afterward to Geoffrey Wheatcroft. "In fact," Conor told Wheatcroft, "the *Irish Press* has a very good news coverage. For all that, *I still feel that any coverage of Sinn Fein activity is too much* (emphasis added)."[132]

The coalition very nearly came a cropper. Garret FitzGerald and Declan Costello (the attorney general), each of whom had designs on the leadership of Fine Gael, attempted a revolt within their party, using

Section 3 as a pretext; the National Union of Journalists and several members of the executive council of the Irish Congress of Trade Unions demanded that the controversial section of the bill be abandoned. At least four members of the parliamentary Labour party agreed with them, so Labour was as shaky as was Fine Gael. Instead of seeing the whole bill, or indeed, the national coalition, explode, it was agreed that Paddy Cooney would remove the offending phrase concerning newspapers from Section 3, and on 14 September, this was formally agreed to. "I was left in the Indian rope trick position," is Conor's fully accurate summary of the conclusion of the episode.[133]

How did this imbroglio relate to Conor's broadcasting bill as it was slowly dragging through its remaining stages in the Dail (finally passed in December 1976)? It erased any ambiguities about how Conor intended the revised Section 31 of the broadcasting statute to be used: hard, like a blunt stone hatchet. In mid-October 1976, while the broadcasting measure was in its late stages, Conor issued a directive under the unrevised Section 31 that banned from the airwaves "spokesmen" for both branches of the IRA, for Provisional Sinn Fein, and also for any organization classified as illegal in Northern Ireland.[134]

Conor's broadcasting bill became law and he has never backed away from it.[135] Nor did succeeding Irish governments during the 1980s and early 1990s, no matter what their political stripe.[136] Only in January 1994 was it finally allowed to lapse.

• • •

What did it avail—Conor's ceaseless war *against* the romanticization of violence, *against* the sectarian assumption that Northern Ireland belonged to the Irish Republic and that the Protestants had neither rights nor weight; *against* cultural intolerance, both sectarian and linguistic— and *for* pluralism, *for* an easing of the church's grip on private morality (as in the birth control matter), and *for* acceptance that as far as the North was concerned, reconciliation must precede reunification? That question, like so many important historical questions, demands a measurable answer when the issue, of course, is immeasurable. By the very nature of the arrow of human history—always shooting forward, and never permitting us to rerun events, to discover what the effect would have been if some causal agent had been just a bit different—we cannot know what recent Irish history would have been like if Conor had not been a political and cultural missionary of always amazing, sometimes appalling, Pauline zeal.

Nobel prizes are given for stopping wars that have started, not for stopping them before they start. But if one accepts that Conor was right, that in the middle of the 1970s, the North was close to conflagration, because the Protestants were organized (more so than they have been since), and very edgy, and the Provos were trying to bait them into attacking the northern Catholics and therefore drawing the Irish Republic into what Provo strategists believed would be a war of liberation, then one has to see Conor, the stormy petrel, as, paradoxically, a crucial peace keeper.

That, of course, rests on one's historical knowledge and presuppositions. The assertion about the Provos' strategy at the time is certainly accurate. We can be less sure as to whether or not the northern Protestants were at flash point, although I believe that Conor's judgment was right on this. The view from Dublin (whose populace generally has less acquaintance with Northern Ireland than it has of London) was that Conor was skywriting; those of us who were in the North for any length of time in the mid 1970s, and paid attention to Protestant sensibilities, realize that he was either quite right, or, if wrong, not by much. It was a very close thing.

Of course a lot of people were actively seeking peace at the same time, and if not peace, at least quiet. Still, that the mid-1970s, the most volatile period we have seen in the modern Troubles, did not see Ireland slide into a Hibernian version of Bosnia has to be in part credited to those very few who had the ability to see what could happen; to those who had the courage to say so and thus to prevent the possibility of ethnic-tribal-religious warfare becoming a reality.

One small reflection of something else Conor may have accomplished is found in a revealing statistic: in 1968, approximately 80 percent of the electorate of the Twenty-Six Counties believed that the reunification of Ireland should occur whether or not the majority of people in Northern Ireland wanted it to occur. In 1978, over 60 percent said that reunification should not occur until the majority in the Six Counties wanted it.[137]

That is a litmus item. The right to impose reunification—and the absolute wrongness of anyone who opposed it—was part of the spine of beliefs that comprised the traditional Irish nationalist faith. Conor's missionary work was chiefly responsible for this change, for only he had the zeal, the crazed, but not crazy, faith that one could change the minds of the members of his beloved little platoon.

If, in the 1990s, there is some chance that agreements toward solution of the Northern Ireland problem might be made (not a solution, but steps toward a solution), it is because successive Irish governments finally have come to accept Conor's point: the northern Protestants have a right to exist, as a cultural and political group, and they are always to be invited, never forced.

PART 5

PARTICIPANT OBSERVER

CHAPTER 12

KILDARE STREET TO FLEET STREET: 1977–1981

Late in May 1977, the *Irish Times* conducted an opinion poll to determine which person the people in the Irish Republic would *least* like to see run the country. Conor led with 27 percent of the poll, but Charles Haughey was close behind him, at 25 percent.[1] Conor shrugged off these results, but knowledge of how he was viewed by his countrymen had a revealing side effect—not on what he did politically, but on the company he kept.

Despite all the pressure on Conor, as always, he somehow found time for reading and reflection. He found solace in Edmund Burke (as one would expect) and, surprisingly, in the writing of that angular French woman, Simone Weil. One does not wish here to assume a simple algorithm, that in time of heavy political combat, Conor identified with two very solitary, heroic figures, although that is part of the story. Equally important, both Burke and Weil were concerned with the hardest of political tasks: establishing simultaneously the existence of order and of freedom.[2]

The Edmund Burke to whom Conor turned during the hard years of 1976–77 was not the Burke of "equality of restraint," but the Burke who worried about the American revolution; not the philosopher Burke, but the pragmatic politician. In a lecture given in Edinburgh in July 1976, in celebration of the American Bicentenary, Conor argued that Burke's concern about British relations with America "was not that these policies were oppressive or unconstitutional, but that they were dangerously foolish."[3] This was the "commonsense, down-to-earth Burke, concerned with practical interests and assessment of forces."[4] Conor credited Burke with the repeal of the Stamp Act, this being "the most important achievement of Burke's policy of practical conciliation."[5]

The relationship to the second figure with whom Conor communed in this period, Simone Weil, is more abstruse, for Conor does not make Weil a hologram of himself. Simone Weil (1909–43) was one of the most difficult of French intellectuals, in an era when few of them could be petted without having one's hand bitten. She was Marxist, anti-Marxist, Catholic, anti-Catholic, a pure intellectual who proved this by taking labouring jobs and failing at them. Her *L'Enracinement* of 1949 (published in English in 1952 as *The Need for Roots*) is a difficult book, and Conor in writing and lecturing on it made no claim to have mastered it. Weil is immensely hard to grasp as a person, much less as an intellect. Thus, Mark Hederman's reaction to a lecture on Weil that Conor gave on 21 January 1977 is interesting, although, I think, fundamentally wrong:

> I was so intrigued to know how and why he could be devoting his attention to this French mystic, at a moment when so many practical and political issues must have been pressing urgently upon him, that I made it my business to attend his lecture. While he was talking it became apparent to me that, although his subject was Simone Weil, he was really using her as a paradigm to describe his own isolated position in Irish politics. Her unusual and high personal philosophy which led to her political martyrdom was almost like a mirror image of his own.[6]

Conor's political position at the time he gave the lecture was isolated, but hardly a martyrdom: he was a cabinet minister and the odds were strong that he would retain his seat when a general election occurred, for Irish cabinet ministers are rarely turned out of their seats, even when their party loses. Conor was not using Weil as a surrogate for his own identity, but as a corrective to Edmund Burke, with whom he did have an emotional identification. Weil trusted intelligence and distrusted friendship; Burke, in contrast, was suspicious of intelligence but not of friendship. And, to Burke, "to love the little platoon to which we belong in society, is the first, the germ as it were, of public affection"; Simone Weil saw a countertruth, that one could love the little platoon too much.[7] Weil functions as the equivalent of the loyal opposition. Conor views Weil as a "true prophet"—not a perfect one, but one who saw what appalling results could come from tendencies latent in the theories of her time.

• • •

By the beginning of 1977, it was clear that an election would be called within the next six months. Conor would have preferred its being put off longer (the coalition could have waited as late as early 1978), but that was only a preference. The coalition was divided on the issue, the rurally based TDs wanting to hit the hustings soon, the urban-based ones wishing to hold off as long as possible. More than anything Conor was concerned that the coalition "come down in one piece, so that coalition would remain a viable option."[8] And, given that in the Cabinet only Conor, Garret FitzGerald, and Richie Ryan were in favor of putting off the election, the decision was to go for a mid-summer contest and to run again as a Fine Gael-Labour coalition against Fianna Fail.[9]

As preparation for the election, Jimmy Tully, minister for local government, recarved constituency boundaries so as to improve the coalition's chances of success. An Irish extension of a democratic tradition going back to Governor Eldridge Gerry who creatively rearranged Massachusetts in 1812, the manipulation in this instance was called a "Tullymander." Tully substituted three-seaters for four-seaters in Dublin (where Fianna Fail was weakest), and replaced four-seaters with five-seaters in the countryside (where Fianna Fail was strong). These tricks would increase the Fine Gael-Labour results in the case of minor electoral swings (precluding in Dublin three-seaters, for instance, Fianna Fail picking up the fourth—and now nonexistent—seat). But what the Tullymander did not envisage was what would happen if there were a fairly large swing, say a seven or eight point improvement in Fianna Fail's standing. In that case, the Tullymander would actually magnify Fianna Fail's gains, because they would win the third seat in urban areas and the fourth and, additionally, a fifth one, in rural ones.[10]

That, in fact, is what happened. In the election of mid-June 1977, Fianna Fail received just over half the popular vote and won 84 seats in a Dail of 148. Fine Gael won 43, Labour 17, and independents 4. Justin Keating (industry and commerce), Paddy Cooney (justice), and Conor all went down to defeat.

Conor ran in a revamped constituency—called Dublin-Clontarf—and he should have had an easy win even though this was a three-seater. Charles Haughey was gone, to Dublin-Artane, and when the election was called, the only question that pundits had was whether Conor would come out on top of the poll, ahead of George Colley, a Fianna Fail veteran who was tipped as the next leader, when Jack Lynch retired. A Fine Gael legacy, Michael Joe Cosgrave, was favored to come third. Even taking into account that some of the working-class sections of the constituency had been cut off, the *Irish Times* said it was a certainty that Conor and George Colley would be elected.[11]

Where did Conor's campaign go wrong? One problem was that, although his old foe, Charles Haughey, was now running in a different constituency, Conor kept his campaign aimed at Haughey. He genuinely loathed Haughey and his ethics (as in his land dealings) and saw him as a danger to the public peace (as in his activities during the arms-trial period). Conor also foresaw (rightly) that Haughey was on the road back from ignominy to the leadership of Fianna Fail and eventually to being taoiseach. The campaign against Haughey had a certain logic: an RTE survey of December 1976 had revealed that Conor was the second most-recognized (that is, well-known) figure in the coalition government, and that Haughey was the second most well-known opposition figure.[12] And, as mentioned earlier, a survey conducted in late May 1977 showed that to the electorate in general, Conor was the most objectionable candidate in the Fine Gael-Labour coalition, and that Haughey was the most objectionable in Fianna Fail.[13]

Haughey had a completely safe seat. Conor, by continually focusing on Haughey, wrapped his own campaign in negativism. Labour party professionals and members of his personal staff tried to get him to shut up about Haughey, to talk instead about the improvements he was planning in the telephone service, to talk about anything else, but he persisted.[14] One party insider had the distinct impression that every time Conor made a speech, the Fianna Fail vote went up by 0.1 percent.[15]

The other negative aura that enshrouded Conor's campaign was his association with Northern Ireland. He later understood and articulated the fact that it was not what he said about Northern Ireland that got on most people's nerves, but that he said so much. Four years after the election, he reflected,

> When I was defeated in Dublin-Clontarf ... the Republicans interpreted that as a repudiation of my "anti-national views. ..." I think myself what an adequate number of voters on that occasion didn't like was not so much the substance of what I was saying on the north, but the fact, *that I was saying so much* [emphasis in original]. For a good many people, the north is inherently a distasteful subject, with subliminal associations of violence and fear of invasion. If a politician reminds people too much of the north, he risks being contaminated by those associations. You can have an "aspiration to unity"—by all means—but mind you, don't inhale![16]

And during the first half of 1977, Conor was making everyone inhale. In January, for instance, he said that if the coalition were reelected, he would urge a referendum on the removal from the constitution of

Irish Labourites at Cork, 1977. Conor, center, with Senator Fintan Kennedy on his right.

At Butlin's holiday camp. Patrick, age seven, with his friend Hugh Murphy.

Conor and Maire, with Patrick and Margaret, mid-1970s, hill of Howth.

Newcastle, County Down, where Conor addressed the Humanities Association, late 1970s.

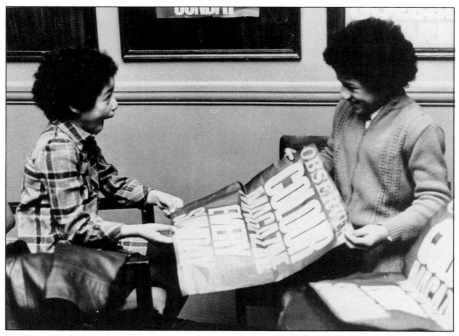

Patrick and Margaret, soon after Conor joined the *Observer*.

Conor and Patrick.

As seen by others. Conor, as commissioned for E.P. Thompson's *Writing by Candlelight*, 1980. (Courtesy: Dorothy Thompson)

Conor, early 1980s, in study at home.

Two lions. Conor and Teddy Kollek, Jerusalem, 1982.

Heavy hitters on the trail of Mrs. Thatcher. Norman Mailer and Conor, each doing a piece on Thatcher, meet in Scotland during the general election campaign, 1983.

"What's more, Dr O'Brien, he's threatening to knock the door down and break up the meeting because you referred to the academic boycott as Mickey Mouse stuff."

South African comment on Conor's 1986 visit. (Courtesy: *Cape Times*)

Remembering a good friend. Memorial service for Michael McInerney.

Articles 2 and 3 (which stated the republic's claim to incorporate Northern Ireland into the Dublin-based state). Predictably, this was ill-received by Fianna Fail. More important, it was rejected by John Hume who, as head of the sdlp had effective veto power over the northern policy of any southern government, and who, since the Sunningdale power-sharing executive had come down in 1974, had lost any interest he had in reconciling the northern Protestants. Conor, therefore, had to back off.[17] (The only immediate consequence of Conor's pushing for a referendum was that the Government Publications Office sold out its entire supply of the constitution. One lady who bought a hard-cover copy was heard to inquire, "If my husband doesn't like it, can I bring it back?")[18]

At the end of February, Conor gave a lecture to the Irish Association for Civil Liberties at the Mansion House, Dublin. There he stated that pluralism was a goal that should be sought for its own sake. "I am all too likely to find myself accused of making the history of ideas a general-election issue," he said. "I might even be accused of introducing ideas themselves into an election year—a serious matter indeed."[19] The trouble was that he *was* talking about serious matters and that was not what people wanted to hear. And especially not when he told them such as the following:

> There is thus a painful symmetry between the Orangeman's version of "civil and religious liberty" and the Republican version of "non-sectarian." Both are in fact fiercely intolerant, along tribal-national lines, and slogans derived from the Enlightenment do no more in practice than help the intolerant to feel good about their intolerance.[20]

True, but did the electorate really want to know?

What the electorate actually wanted to hear from Conor was simple: that the phone service was improving and would be getting a lot better fast. But with a few exceptions, Conor avoided the topic altogether.[21] However, during the campaign, the local Dublin-Clontarf Fianna Fail party workers operated with a certain burlesque genius on the telephone issue. The routine—so practiced that it deserves to be called a schtick—opened with a canvasser knocking on a door in Conor's constituency.

"I represent Fianna Fail." The canvasser would take out a notebook. "Ever had any trouble with your phone?"

Inevitably the answer was affirmative. "God! The phone's terrible. Chronic. It's nivver right!"

"I see." The canvasser would look deeply concerned. "Should Dr. O'Brien be interested in this? I mean, you'd think he would come around to see and try to help, wouldn't you?"

"Well ... yes. Yes indeed!"

The canvasser would look the householder in the eye. "Of course, I suppose he's too busy talking about the north."[22]

And so, another vote went to Fianna Fail.

Conor still would have survived if he had not made one absent-minded, but costly, tactical mistake almost on the eve of the election. One group of his constituents had been promised several months previously that they would be eligible for low-interest housing loans, but when the time came, there was no money in the treasury. Conor fought this hard in Cabinet and finally won: his people would have their mortgages reduced. Conor realized that they would be very happy about this and thus inclined to vote for their benefactor, so on the way home, he stopped off to give the news to the secretary of the local residents' association. The trouble is, the head of the association was one Dr. Michael Woods who was one of the twelve candidates running for the three seats in Dublin-Clontarf. He and his family were up half the night printing and distributing a newsletter on Fianna Fail letterhead announcing the great benefaction—and, implicitly, taking credit for it.[23]

When the election count was conducted on 18 June, a strange pattern emerged. George Colley of Fianna Fail easily came home, far beyond the quota. After that, however, nobody made the quota. Matters were settled only on the thirteenth count. Michael Cosgrave (Fine Gael) came second, and Dr. Michael Woods of Fianna Fail was third.[24]

Conor was out, by just over 700 votes. Nationally, Fianna Fail had a massive majority; Jack Lynch again was taoiseach, and Charles Haughey once again was on the rise.

• • •

Conor rarely uses Gaelicisms, since they usually are embarrassingly fake-Irish, but eight years after his defeat, in a panel discussion at Skidmore College on the intellectual and politics, he said that the electorate had thrown him out on his head "and I was very sore in my head for about six months, and then I was very glad."[25] The phrase "sore in my head," is right out of Maurice O'Sullivan and though used ironically, it is exactly what happened: Conor went through denial, despondency, a loss of his sense of personal compass, mourning, and, eventually, healing. Being rejected by the electorate hurt a lot.

Conor conceded defeat in public gracefully enough, but for a time he practiced a form of denial. This was effected through Seanad Eireann. Elections for the Senate followed upon the Dail elections and at the end of June 1977, Conor declared that he would be a candidate for the Dublin University (that is, TCD) panel.[26] He was elected for Trinity College along with Trevor West and Mary Robinson, a very distinguished panel indeed. Conor's senate career, however, was inglorious to the point of nonexistence. He spoke only twice and that was on a single day in November 1977, when a Telephone Capital Bill was going through the Senate and then he rose mostly to state his own record as minister for posts and telegraphs.[27]

The Senate, being a good deal more of a deliberative body than was the bear-pit Dail, could have been the perfect venue for Conor, except for two things. The first of these was that immediately after the general election defeat of the Labour-Fine Gael coalition, Brendan Corish had resigned as head of the Labour party. The parliamentary Labour party split sharply on who his successor should be. Michael O'Leary (Conor's preference) was beaten by one vote by Frank Cluskey.[28] That should have been no problem for Conor, for he and Cluskey enjoyed each other's company in a rough sort of way, and respected each other. However, Cluskey was determined to be a much tighter manager of the PLP than Corish had been, and that included clamping down on what was said about the North. "His first act as Leader after the 1977 election was to make himself spokesman on Northern Ireland," Conor wrote in 1981. "His next act was to require me to submit to him, in advance, any statements I thought of making on Northern Ireland. The consequence, as intended, was my resignation from the Parliamentary Labour Party."[29] That seems hard on Cluskey. It is difficult to see how any leader—and especially a new party leader who had assumed office in the wake of an electoral debacle—could allow any member of his party to make statements on the most potentially divisive aspect of party policy, without first having them vetted. Cluskey was asking Conor to do the same thing that Conor had demanded of Garret FitzGerald, in the days when Conor controlled the Government Information Office.

Conor sat in the Senate as an independent. Even without Frank Cluskey's gag-order, he would have found it hard to remain in the parliamentary Labour party, for his old nemesis, Justin Keating, having garnered a Senate seat on the agricultural panel, was chosen head of the Labour party in the upper house. Conor kept his seat in the Seanad until June 1979, when he resigned.[30]

Conor's alienation from the Irish Labour party was signaled in two stages. First, he resigned from the PLP in mid-September 1979, as preparation for his mute career in the Senate. Then, in the mid-1980s, he resigned from the general party over Labour's support of the Anglo-Irish agreement. The impact of this second resignation was somewhat lessened by the fact that he had not paid his dues for several years and his membership already had lapsed.[31]

These were not good times. The O'Brien family needed money and Conor needed a job. The first problem was temporarily taken care of by a legacy of £5,200 from Maire's late mother, Margaret MacEntee.[32]

As a means of making money, Conor attempted to expand for film or television a treatment called "The Uncrowned King," which he had roughed out in the 1960s. It was a life of Parnell from 1885 to Glasnevin cemetery.[33] Nothing came of this effort, nor should it have. It was written like a stage play and there was little cinematic about it.[34]

In the autumn of 1977, Conor briefly became theater critic for *Magill*, the then-new (and now unfortunately defunct) Dublin outlet for serious feature-length journalism.[35] He was good at this, being admirably unpretentious and, perhaps because he was a playwright himself, not given to scoring cheap points.[36]

Still, the career balance sheet was not nice to read: Conor, nearly sixty years old, had only a small Dail pension to look forward to and he was going to be flat broke soon. Living by his wits had always been his habit, so he was able to have a few freelance pieces published in the London *Observer*. The editor, Donald Trelford, then signed Conor on for an African sequence. Rhodesia at that time was a potential international trouble spot, and Conor was to visit the countries that bordered on Rhodesia, consult their leaders, and put together a set of essays. This was piece work, but it might well turn into something more permanent.

This assignment was set up in complete causal isolation from a set of events that were to find Conor, a few weeks later, as editor in chief of the newspaper that was sending him to Africa. That extraordinary skein of events had nothing to do with Africa, but with Ireland, and occurred as follows.

Conor was a participant over several years in a set of meetings convened by a group called the British-Irish Association. It had been founded by David Astor, at that time editor of the *Observer*, and Astor served as the association's president. The idea was to bring leading Irish politicians and British influentials together on the British mainland. The inaugural conference had been held at Magdalen College, Cambridge, in 1973, and thereafter a large annual meeting, as well as more frequent informal gatherings, was held. John Hume, Austin Currie, Garret FitzGerald, and a few unionist leaders participated. The group was decidedly up-market: the Guinness family connection became prominent and the association came to be referred to as "Toffs against Terrorism."[37]

A meeting of the association was held at Oxford on the weekend of 16–18 September 1977. Conor was in particularly good form at the dinner held at St. Edmund's Hall. There David Astor was careful to place Conor next to himself and Arnold Goodman (created Lord Goodman of the City of Westminster, 1965), a powerful, largely benevolent fixer and, not incidentally, a senior director of the *Observer*.[38] Goodman and Conor had not met before and David Astor wanted them to get to know each other.

Much of their conversation was about a speech, a public address, that Conor had given in the afternoon to the 150 or so delegates. In it, Conor had trumped even his previous heresies. Having already argued that Articles 2 and 3 of the Irish constitution were imperialistic, and announced that he was no longer working for Irish unity, what more could he do? He could put forward the teeth-rattling proposition that although the majority of people in Great Britain approved of Irish reunification, in fact, the majority of people in the island of Ireland—north and south combined—did not want Irish unity! This speech and the proposition that was its heart was vintage Conor: in its elegance of formulation, in its ability to rile opponents, and, unhappily, also in its elementary misreading of quantitative data. He committed many of the errors of method that first-year political science students are warned about.[39] What he would have been justified in saying was that the majority of people in Great Britain would approve of Irish reunification if the price (in terms of civil disorder) were not too great; and that the majority of people in Northern Ireland did not want reunification under any circumstances; and that the majority in the Irish Republic did not want reunification if the price were very high (in terms of economic and social costs).

No matter, it was the Wildean epigram—the averred paradox, that the Brits wanted Irish unity and the Irish did not—that hit the newspapers. And with it came Conor's infuriating advice to the new Fianna Fail government: "To advocate unity as the solution to the problems of Northern Ireland is unrealistic, unfruitful, and even mischievous, through the encouragement it gives to those who use force to achieve that undemocratic objective."[40] Even his own party wanted his head and this became the occasion (though not, as we have seen, the root cause) of his resigning from the parliamentary Labour party on 20 September.[41]

After the Oxford meeting closed, David Astor had given Conor a lift to London. They talked and Astor, seeing that Conor was at loose ends, said that maybe some work could be arranged. Conor was pleased, reckoning that after he completed his upcoming trip to Africa for the *Observer*, there would be more work for the paper.[42]

So, in November, Conor took off on his African assignment with a reasonable expectation that in future there would be decent writing assignments from the *Observer*. And this particular African visit was attractive, for it fit very much with his long-term opposition to colonialism and his own personal interest in Africa. His brief was to visit the states that border on what at that time was Rhodesia, which was lurching along its crisis-ridden transmutation into what eventually became Zimbabwe. Conor first went to Zambia, where he saw President Kenneth Kaunda and Joshua Nkomo, who was president of the Zimbabwe African Peoples Union and was also a major figure in the African National Congress. Next he went to Dar-es-Salaam, Tanzania, where he was fobbed off onto second-level officials (Julius Nyerere was traveling at the time) and thence to Maputo, Mozambique. There, after a lot of aggravation, he had an interview with Robert Mugabe, who, with Nkomo, was the co-leader of the patriotic front for the liberation of Zimbabwe. Then Conor went to South Africa and, finally, home.

The trip had its interesting moments from a journalistic viewpoint, but the revealing items were not the published material, but two letters that Conor sent home to Maire and Patrick and Margaret, one from Dar-es-Salaam, the other from Maputo. These are the domestic correspondences of a man who is healed. The letters are charming, attentive of the children, loving towards Maire, full of sharp anecdotes: Conor has gotten over his soreness in the head from losing the election. He meets President Kenneth Kaunda of Zambia and has him sign a copy of his book, asking him to inscribe it to Margaret because of her Zambian heritage. "He carefully wrote out on the fly leaf a little homily for her; he is a preacher's son. It will be a nice thing for her to have."[43] The appointment with Kaunda prevents him from following up an intriguing sign he has seen along the road, "Gaelic Football: Lusaka v. Ndola." He tells the family of minor local comedies: Tanzanian Airlines, he reports, flies under the livery of Air Madagascar and its boarding passes read "Botswana Airlines." "African Unity Now!" Conor suggests.[44]

From Maputo, where Conor spends day after frustrating day before getting to see Mugabe, he writes a letter home that makes the wait seem amusing. Though there are no picture cards for the kids. "The children are out of luck. This is a socialist and, at the moment, very puritanical country, and there are no postcards. (Also, no tourists.)" However, he cheers up young Patrick with the sort of news a boy would like. "Tell

Patrick that there was a hail storm here last week with hail-stones bigger than cricket balls. Five people were killed by hail-stones. The hotel awning looks as if it had been machine-gunned, but it was just hail."[45] Conor tells the family that he is trying to figure out how to get into South Africa. He has with him a card that identifies him as pro-chancellor of Trinity College, Dublin, which he uses while at home to check out books from the Trinity Library. Now he is contemplating trying to pass himself off as an academic so as to get into security-conscious South Africa.

Perhaps travel did something wonderful for Conor's soul, virtually wiping it clean of the rancidness of his electoral loss, or perhaps he had gotten himself back together before he left. In any event, by early November 1977, he was again functioning at the top of his game. How good that game was in journalistic terms at that moment, we cannot know, however, because what he feels is the best column that he filed, about the death of the saintly Steve Biko in South African police custody in September, was never printed: one of the *Observer*'s endemic mini-strikes occurred that week, the piece never appeared and is now lost.[46] However, Conor fielded an essay on the front-line leaders (which was published in January, after he had joined the paper full-time) and it begins with a revealing conversation in Maputo with Robert Mugabe.

> Mr. Mugabe asked me a question.
> "Do you support the freedom fighters in your own country?"
> I said that if, by freedom fighters, he meant the Provisional IRA, I did not support them but favoured their suppression by all lawful means. For four years I had been a member of a Government which had consistently and rigorously pursued that course.
> "Then you are a traitor?" said Mugabe. The intonation was interrogative. Mr. Mugabe smiled as he spoke.[47]

Conor's reporting this incident enraged Robert Mugabe, who did not wish to be identified as a terrorist-supporter. Later, when Mugabe was on a publicity visit to England, he learned that Conor was to be on the same BBC television program as himself, and he walked out of the studio and could not be induced to participate.[48]

One thing that Conor learned during this trip was that the *Observer* was not doing what he believed was a professional job in Africa, and this despite having on site David Martin, who worked out of Lusaka and was very close with several of the politicians of the front-line states. From Dar-es-Salaam, Conor reported to Maire that "I had a frustrating start as my expert friends on the *Observer* had made absolutely no advance contacts for me."[49] Worse was Maputo: "David Martin of the *Observer* is also here," he told Maire, "giving me every assistance short of actually helping me."[50] Conor reported that Martin had told the Mozambiquan ministry of information that Conor was not a journalist and therefore they did not need to look after him; it was for the foreign affairs department to do that. That is understandable: Martin wanted to protect his own turf, and he could hardly have foreseen that Conor soon would be his boss. Later, senior journalists on the *Observer* suggested that the coolness between Conor and David Martin was ideological. No, it was just that Conor remembered spending day after day without transport in taxiless Maputo, walking the dust-filled streets in painful black business shoes, seeking out contacts for himself.

• • •

In this era, the *Observer* must be considered as having a personality, just as much as any individual. The world's oldest Sunday newspaper—it had begun in December 1791—it was as much a cultural institution as a periodical. The modern history of the *Observer* dates from 1908 when William Waldorf (first Viscount) Astor bought the paper. In 1912 he gave it to his son. The great J.L. Garvin edited the paper from 1908 to 1942. In 1948, the Honorable David Astor (a younger son of the second Viscount Astor) took over the editorship. He was thirty-six years old, energetic, risk-taking, and in the 1950s he made the *Observer* easily the best paper in England. George Orwell, Kenneth Tynan, Vita Sackville-West regularly wrote for the paper. In the 1950s and 1960s, regular critics and reviewers included Arthur Koestler, A.J.P. Taylor, and Harold Nicolson. Under David Astor, the paper developed an unusually collegial style of management. If one can imagine a university college, where nobody has lifetime tenure, and where something actually gets done once a week, that was the *Observer*.

David Astor is the sort of figure that English intellectuals, especially academics, airily dismiss. He was just too perfectly upper-upper to be taken seriously: Eton, Balliol, Royal Marines, breath-catchingly handsome, possessed of a country estate in Berkshire and a London house on Cavendish Avenue, just a convenient stroll away from Lord's. In fact, he became a very important cultural curator. Under his editorship the *Observer* was slightly left of center. It maintained a strong anticolonialist line long before that became the acceptable thing. Arnold Goodman referred to "Astor's talented, if not wholly business-like administration,"[51] and that is fair: the paper continually lost money and was, in effect, a family charity, the equivalent of, say, an art gallery or a museum. Part of Astor's gift as editor was that, though capable of great resolution (for example, the paper had opposed Britain's Suez adventure, at considerable cost in circulation), he was remarkably gentle, a characteristic based on great innate self-confidence. Brian Inglis recalled having a job interview with Astor: "He left me with the curious impression that I had been interviewing him, to find whether he would be a suitable employer."[52] In Conor's case, Astor reckoned that he could do both the paper and Conor good, by bringing them together.

The trouble was that in 1977, David Astor no longer had a paper to call his own. Granted, he had a seat on the board, as did his friend Arnold Goodman, who had been chairman of the board since 1967. But although Astor still was godfather to the paper, he now was neither editor nor, indeed, owner. This was the case because in 1974 the *Sunday Times*, which had shared a printing plant with the *Observer*, transferred all its printing from the New Printing House Square site to a modern facility in Gray's Inn Road. The *Observer* bought the previously shared printing plant. This turned out to be a very astute real estate investment, but it left the paper saddled with 600 of the most highly paid artisans in England, and only a single-day's paper to put out. The print union was not only strong, but corrupt. It was known as the "Mickey Mouse Union" because some of its members put through fictitious time cards and received double salaries as Mickey Mouse.[53]

Just at the time these labor costs were piling up, the *Sunday Times* and the *Sunday Telegraph* were cutting into sales, so that advertising revenues were hurt. Under these circumstances, David Astor for the first time became wobbly as an editor. (One inscription in the men's lavatory of the time read: "The Editor's indecision is final.")[54] In order to sort things out, he assigned himself two tasks. The first of these was to appoint someone who would take over from him as editor and, second, he had to find someone to buy the paper.

The first task was relatively easy and it was accomplished in late 1976. Astor's choice of a new editor was Donald Trelford, who had been deputy editor since 1969. The interesting twist was that instead of making the appointment in the usual hierarchical manner, Astor held a poll (not quite an election, but close) of each member of the National Union of Journalists on the staff about who should be the new editor. Trelford was the clear winner.[55] In fact, this consultative procedure not only reinforced the paper's collegial tradition, it meant that Trelford had the staff's support.

Because Donald Trelford plays a significant part in Conor's story, he bears particular notice. Trelford, a consummate professional journalist, was a noted survivor. "Donald Trelford is the vicar of Bray," Arnold Goodman suggests. "He has a remarkable facility for staying upright in a shipwreck."[56] Educated as an exhibitioner at Selwyn College, Cambridge, he did his national service as an RAF pilot in the mid-1950s. Trelford was not yet forty when he assumed the editorship and was very distinguished looking—the sort of man who wears handmade shirts well. People who worked with him at the time remember that he had two mottoes. One was "Let's play this one into the long grass." The other was "We'll 'yes' it to death." He could, however, be very tough when necessary. When the tabloid baron Rupert Murdoch attempted to buy the *Observer*, Trelford organized the staff journalists into a virtual peasants' rebellion. Murdoch backed off.[57]

It was a sign of just how bad the financial situation was that David Astor had contemplated selling to Murdoch, for he would have treated the traditions of the *Observer* with the same respect the Visigoths expressed for classical Roman frescoes. Everyone was immensely relieved, therefore, when Robert Anderson, the head of Atlantic-Richfield, a large American oil company, became interested. Anderson struck them as the sort of businessman who knows that culture is a good thing, but is not quite sure why. He had founded the Aspen Institute for Humanistic Studies in the Colorado ski town (and later opened a German branch). At Aspen, heavyweight intellectuals met with dumb-founded business leaders and talked about Great Ideas. Because of his apparent reverence for cultural icons, Anderson seemed a potentially congenial owner. The Observer Trust sold him 90 percent of the paper in November 1976 for one pound. Anderson was to keep the *Observer* running in its accustomed form and to invest £3 million in it over a three-year period (thereafter, it was expected that the paper would become profitable). Donald Trelford and staff were to be kept on and David Astor and Arnold Goodman were to remain on the board of directors. It looked ideal.[58]

Soon, however, there was trouble. Robert Anderson wanted his cultural objects to be large and shiny, and he began to be unhappy with the merely very-competent Trelford. For his money, Anderson wanted a Great Personality, and if he could not have that, then he wanted to replace Trelford with a trustworthy sycophant, of which genre there was the odd ambitious specimen hidden in the crevices of the *Observer*. David Astor, intent on saving both Donald Trelford's editorship and the tone of the paper, came up with the idea of having someone do for the *Observer* what Helmut Schmidt, chancellor of West Germany, later was to do for *Die Zeit* after his retirement from politics: serve as an ideological figurehead, something like a viceroy in a parliamentary democracy.[59] That is what Astor had in mind that Sunday afternoon in September when he gave Conor a ride from Oxford to London, but he needed to put the pieces together before making a precise proposal.

Arnold Goodman was easy enough to interest in the idea; the problem was the Americans and the man they were appointing as chairman of the board, William Barnetson (created Baron Barnetson
of Crowborough, 1975). He was the chairman of United Newspapers,
a chain formerly known as Yorkshire Conservative Newspapers.
However, when sounded out by Astor, Barnetson liked the idea.

The next step was for Arnold Goodman to invite Robert Anderson
and Conor to meet with himself and Astor at Goodman's flat at 79
Portland Place, London. Lord Barnetson and Thornton Bradshaw, a director of the Observer Trust and, at that time, head of the NBC network
in the United States, were also invited to the meeting. Anderson had
never heard of Conor Cruise O'Brien. The first thing he wanted to
know before consenting to the meeting was if Conor was anticommunist. Astor assured him that he was.[60] He did not bother to add that
not only was Conor anticommunist, but that he was also very much
anti-anticommunist.

Conor, who had never been to Lord Goodman's residence, got off
the elevator a floor early and was greeted by a very aristocratic lady who
viewed him with experienced disapproval. She was accustomed to encountering Goodman's associates, since as head of the Arts Council and
of the Newspapers Publishers Council, he associated with obvious low-
lifes. "I think you *must* be someone for Lord Goodman," she adjudged
and pointed Conor back to the lift.[61]

The heavily masculine atmosphere of Goodman's bachelor flat, with
its dark walls and leather chairs, suited the taste of Anderson, the
American cattle rancher and oil man. Conor was at his best. After the
interview had gone on for half an hour (for it was an interview, even if
it was not clear exactly what job was involved), Anderson took
Goodman aside and said, "I'm going to have him, come what may!"[62]

That was in early December.[63] Conor left Goodman's flat with an
offer to become editor in chief of the *Observer* and a great number of
details to be worked out. Not least of these stemmed from the awkward
fact that the job did not exist. The paper already had a competent editor
and there was no suggestion that he was to leave. Indeed, from David
Astor's perspective, one of the points of the entire exercise was to protect Trelford's job.

The formula that evolved was that Conor would chair editorial conferences and be in charge of "policy," especially on political matters,
and that Donald Trelford would do the day-to-day management. That
sounded good, but like the Geneva Convention on the Conduct of War,
how it actually worked depended upon the participants.

Conor invited Donald Trelford over to Dublin the next week. The
two men had a good dinner and came to an accommodation. Conor said

that he would not take the post if Trelford objected (the parallel to Conor's being sure he was acceptable to the locals before he took the vice-chancellorship of the University of Ghana is obvious). Trelford, for his part, said that he would find Conor a useful protection against the storms that he saw gathering on the horizon. Trelford realized that Conor's presence was preferable either to being fired or to being kept on but having someone put over him who was ideologically subservient to the American oil interests.[64] Those realities recognized, Trelford can scarcely have been overjoyed. In a draft publicity release headlined "Conor Cruise O'Brien Joins the Observer as Editor in Chief," he permitted himself some irony. "Mr. Trelford commented: 'I have known Conor for many years and welcome him aboard the Observer. He's exactly our sort of man and will be a powerful inspiration to us all.'"[65] Before the story was printed on 18 December, the statement was made much less arch. "He is exactly our sort of man and the nearest thing to a modern George Orwell."[66]

Financially, Conor had hit the jackpot. He was paid £37,000 salary for the *Observer* post, and there was no objection to his continuing to write books and the occasional piece for journals such as the *Spectator*, the *New Statesman*, and the *Listener*. (His royalties and freelance fees ran roughly to £2,000 a year for these and related activities.) In addition, he was permitted to keep his Irish senate seat, if he wished. The *Observer* provided him with a £3,000 annual expense allowance for "general expenses" not taken care of by his main expense allowance, so in fact his real annual base salary was £40,000.[67] Further, because he kept his main residence in Ireland, the firm provided him with a London flat in Prince's Square.[68] Then in the spring of 1978, Conor decided to move. This caused considerable anxiety among the *Observer*'s accountants, for he chose to move to a Thames houseboat, moored beside the exclusive Cheyne Walk, Chelsea. "Well," said a friend, "he's a middle-aged hippy."[69] That might have rated a smile in Dublin, but the U.K. Inland Revenue people wondered if the purpose of the boat was residential or recreational.[70]

That Conor had scooped the pools caused immense jealousy in Ireland, especially among media people, who, because of Section 31, virtually used his name as a curse ("How is the most hated man in Ireland?" was the characteristic query of one journalist to another who had just interviewed Conor.)[71] The *Irish Times* permitted itself a sour and begrudging editorial, "Observer's New Man." It stated: "It is a nice point that he might never have gone into politics if he had been successful in an earlier bid to get into the news media full-time; he applied many years ago for the post of Director-General of RTE. He was not interviewed."[72] On the count of sourness, the *Irish Times* was easily topped, however, by Conor's hypernationalist opponents who started a rumor that he got the *Observer* post because of an alleged connection with one of the British intelligence services. (This fiction was still in circulation as late as 1992.)[73]

Actually, Conor worked hard for his money. His week might have been fun for a forty-year-old, but for someone in his sixties it was brutal, split between being a husband and father in Ireland and a bachelor newspaperman in London. Most weeks he took an early Tuesday morning flight from Dublin to London, thanking his agnostic God as he did so that the Dublin airport was on his side of the city. He worked in London through Saturday and normally caught an evening flight back home, although sometimes, if a business dinner required, he did not get home to "Whitewater" until late Sunday morning. By his own reckoning, he was not a great father to Patrick and Margaret during his *Observer* years. The responsibility on Maire was very heavy indeed, especially with Patrick becoming a teenager. A father around more would have helped.[74]

Further, Conor did a staggering amount of traveling. In 1978, for example, while still settling into his new post as editor in chief, he made trips to Germany, Africa, Canada, the United States (four times), Japan, and Holland. Also, he gave lectures—to groups ranging from the Warwick University Students Union to the Conservative Party's Northern Ireland Committee—at the rate of at least one a fortnight. And his luncheon and dinner socializing was constant and constantly chic: Rex Harrison, Lord Weidenfeld, Antonia Fraser, Edward Heath, Isaiah Berlin, and so on. He worked the territory.[75]

The work week at the *Observer* ran as follows: Tuesday was given over to answering letters, dealing with complaints, sorting out staff problems, and playing host to visitors. On Wednesday the real work began when the senior editorial staff met for long-range planning. Thursday's editorial meeting was for hard decisions on what would be in next Sunday's paper. The meetings were democratic in the sense that everyone had his or her say. Then, on Friday, they all worked like demons to finish stories and have them ready to feed into the printers on Saturday.[76]

What, besides chair editorial meetings, was an editor in chief expected to do? This question was all the more difficult because Conor was parked on the fourth floor of the *Observer* building at St. Andrew's Hill, in a corner office, with plush chairs and a sofa, and a view of the dome of St. Paul's Cathedral. Donald Trelford and all the working journalists were in the spartan confines of the second floor. "Raise the tone" was one answer to the query of what Conor was expected to do and there is no doubt that among the senior staff he did so. "He loved challenging them and inspiring them and sitting in a pub arguing," Donald Trelford recalls.[77] Conor got on especially well with the two men who were closest to his intellectual equals on the paper, Terence Kilmartin, the paper's brilliant literary editor and biographer of Proust, and John Cole, deputy editor, a tough Ulsterman on his way to becoming the leading British political journalist of the 1980s. Conor was approachable by junior staff. He was willing to sit around with the chaps at The Rising Sun pub and the sessions with him are recalled today by men who were young reporters, as a kind of journalistic equivalent of Bloomsbury. When Kilmartin, Cole, and Conor were in form, the level of the conversation was raised, the quality of the English usage, the crispness of the dialogue increased; and the young thought, yes, we're in a civilized profession after all. These sessions—which usually began about 5:00 in the afternoon and ended near 1:00 A.M., were only slightly clouded by the fear that the editor in chief might not make it up the gangway of his houseboat, when either he or the Thames were at full tide.[78]

Conor could, however, be ruthless to the intellectually flaccid. He had a word for a quality that he hated—mussification—and he would go through the copy of junior writers and hammer the young into saying what they meant to say. He could be patronizing. John Naughton, the paper's TV critic, remembered almost fifteen years after the event hearing one of the paper's copytakers being instructed by Conor. "'The atmosphere,'" intoned the Cruiser, "'was reminiscent of *fin de siècle* Vienna—that's italics f-i-n space d-e. ...' At this point the copytaker said, with infinite tact: 'I think you may take it, Dr. O'Brien, that copytakers at the *Observer* know that French is spoken in every language.'"[79]

"It did not work to have two editors," Lord Goodman says. "It was a ruse for us to give an editor's title to Conor. We should have had him as high profile leader writer instead."[80] That may be right, but the *Observer* was lumbered with two reigning editors, and they had to coexist. Indeed, the signal point is that Donald Trelford and Conor managed to live together, two male bears stuck in the same cave. Some moments must have been extremely trying for Trelford, however.

For example, during the 1979 general election in the United Kingdom, it was assumed that the *Observer* would do what it always did, which was to write a on-the-one-hand, and on-the-other-hand editorial; everyone on the senior staff would throw in his or her opinion, or at least a sentence or two, and these would all be pressed together; the editorial would be declared balanced and the readers left to make up their minds on how to vote. Conor, however, was keen on Labour, especially on James Callaghan, with whom he had a distant friendship, and he was not at all keen on the Conservatives. So, to the traditional balanced editorial he added an extra paragraph, saying, therefore we advise our readers to vote Labour! This sent the American owners into orbit, believing as they did that the British Labour party was a branch of the Red Brigades, and it certainly surprised Donald Trelford. When the Americans called to berate Conor, he reminded them that he had been promised editorial freedom and that was what he was now using. That was not what they wanted to hear.[81]

As might be expected, the issue on which Conor exercised his authority was on matters relating to Northern Ireland. Donald Trelford later reflected on the difficulties this caused. "He was over sixty years old and had never worked in a newspaper office. It was an unusual and uncomfortable relationship to have two editors effectively running Mary Holland."[82] Key name: Mary Holland was an Irish journalist who for a decade had been on the *Observer*'s staff. She was a very good senior journalist of the sort who came to the fore in the 1960s: a writer with a talent for turning the unexpected and emotionally wringing phrase. In the 1970s, she was an example of the "Derry Syndrome"—that is, she had a proclivity for a cocky glorification of Irish nationalism and identity, in contrast to the more clench-lipped Belfast branch of nationalism. This Conor did not like, any more than he liked the political incarnation of the Derry Syndrome, John Hume.

In October 1978, to mark the tenth anniversary of the start of the Troubles in Northern Ireland, the *Observer* planned a special feature about a republican family in Derry, one that had seven sons who had grown up during the Troubles; two of the lads were now in prison as terrorists and were part of the "dirty protest," that is, a refusal to wear prison clothes or to carry out routine hygienic practices. To Conor, the coded message in Mary Holland's tear-jerking depiction of this family was that these people were oppressed, and therefore that their terrorism was implicitly justified. He had a number of qualifiers inserted in the article and fired off a blistering memo to Donald Trelford and an even more sulphurous one to Mary Holland. To her he said:

> I therefore deeply regret and feel personally shamed that this piece should be published in the *Observer*. I know your own motives in writing this piece, as in all you have written, were honourable, professional and free from all propagandist intent. I also think, however, that it is a serious weakness in your coverage of Irish affairs that you are a very poor judge of Irish Catholics.

That gifted and talkative community includes some of the most expert con-
men and conwomen in the world and in this case I believe you have been
conned.[83]

He also told her of a "killing strain" of republicanism that ran in certain
families and told her that the mother usually was the carrier.[84] The
short-run result of this incident was that henceforth no major features
went forward without Conor's seeing the text in advance.[85]

• • •

The managerial difficulties at the *Observer* that beclouded Conor's first
year suddenly became a lot less important to him.

On 18 November 1978, Conor was scheduled to speak at the United
Nations University in Tokyo.[86] This had been arranged by his old
friend James Hester, formerly president of New York University and
now rector of the UN institution, and by another, older friend, Alex
Kwapong, who had left his position as vice-chancellor of the University
of Ghana in 1975 to become vice-rector for institutional planning at the
UN University. It was not a heavy engagement: Conor was to give one
of his journeyman talks on The Intellectual and Something, and see the
sights. He arrived and went off to Kyoto to look around.[87]

On 14 November, on the opposite side of the world, Maire was driving the children to school. She came over the top of a hill, the sun momentarily blinded her and there was a nasty collision. Maire was badly
injured. Her leg was broken in thirty-three places and at first it was not
clear if there were not also internal injuries as well. The children were
thrown about, but were not hurt.[88]

The bad news first went to James Hester, who called Conor and also
rang up Alex Kwapong. Hester and Kwapong went to Conor in Kyoto,
packed his things for him (Conor was almost in shock) and took him on
the bullet train to Tokyo. There they had a university car waiting to
take him to the airport. They used the weight of the UN to get him an
immediate seat to London and thence home.[89]

He found Maire in Jervis Street Hospital, surrounded by nuns and by
a please-God piety—as in "She'll be all right, please God." Conor had
always abhorred this sort of thing. Now he found himself wavering.
Maire was in serious condition and remained so for several weeks.
Later, Conor recalled that time. "I wanted to say a prayer. I stifled the
temptation."

However, "things began to move from please-God to thank-God just
before Christmas. On Christmas Day we knew for sure that she was

going to be all right. I brought the children. We shared champagne and Coke with the nurses. Thank-God sprang out on all sides. I joined in recklessly, not out of civility, but out of sheer joy. She was going to be all right. Thank God."

"It didn't matter a damn whether I believed in God or not, or even whether I *wanted* to thank Him. I was just thanking Him anyway."[90]

Only six weeks after uttering that prayer, Conor focused in on it. For a man so private with his personal emotions (as distinct from his intellectual and political passions), that was a major unlocking. And it coincided with a major change in his art.

This was fortuitous. Before Maire's accident, David Astor had suggested to Conor that he should write a weekly essay. Astor's idea was that this would play to Conor's strength (writing, not management) and would keep him off everyone's nerves, including the paper's owners whom he was beginning seriously to annoy. Conor already was writing a piece most weeks, but the form was irregular. Would it be proper, he wondered, for the editor in chief to take for himself the space for a substantial weekly essay? Yes, it would, Astor replied, and it would be well received by the staff.[91] So, in late January 1979, Conor began doing a set-format essay, and it quickly became a benchmark in British journalism.

This was a classic case of horses-for-courses. The length—roughly 2,000 words—was just right for Conor: a 500-word column was too short for the subjects he wished to raise and compression almost inevitably forces the writer into stridency. But going much longer than 2,000 words would have entered the problematic length of feature stories. Conor developed a written equivalent of the bar conversations that he engaged in with Kilmartin, Cole, and the younger *Observer* staff. The columns were argumentative, usually; anecdotal always; elegant, inevitably. Conor was not embarrassed by the word "I," but was not self-absorbed: the personal stories he introduced always had a point and were there to serve his argument, not the other way around. Conor did just the opposite of pandering to his audience. He assumed that they were well read, conversant with the world of politics and of international relations, and that they had a shared cultural vocabulary. He brought the reader up to his level, but without in any way being pedantic. Conor's weekly essays were natural, something very very hard to achieve. They had a complete self-confidence, a rhythm that was entirely their own, like a good conversation.

Just how good the essays were is indicated by Conor's receiving in 1980, Granada TV's British Columnist of the Year Award, at a time when the competition consisted of such talents as Paul Johnson,

Christopher Booker, Bernard Levin, and Anthony Howard. The citation read: "Dr. O'Brien has done as much as anyone to restore wit and elegance—yes, and irreverence too—to the British press."[92] That was true enough, and no one complained of Irish imperialism.

So, with Maire healing, and Conor himself settling into a literary form of which he became absolute master, there were some enjoyable times, and Conor had not had many of those during the preceding decade. Now, the occasional threat of death or dismemberment sent by Irish republicans or their sympathizers, as often as not landed on the desk of Donald Trelford, since the average anonymous-letter writer was no more able to distinguish between the posts of editor and editor in chief than was the average staff journalist.

Conor had taken his kicks as an Irish politician, and now as an English journalist, he received his kudos. He received an honorary D.Litt. from Nice in 1978 and from Coleraine in 1981. St. Catherine's College, Oxford, elected him a fellow for the period 1978–81. He was chosen to give a number of endowed lectureships: the Ewart-Biggs Memorial Lectures in 1978–79 (published as *Neighbours* in 1980);[93] the Independent Broadcasting Authority's Lectureship, 1979;[94] the Churchill Lecture of the English-Speaking Union, 1979;[95] the Haldane Lecture, 1980;[96] the Gilbert Murray Memorial Lecture at Oxford, 1980;[97] and the Martin Luther King Memorial Lecture at Newcastle-on-Tyne, 1980.[98]

The perks—especially the travel, which Conor loved—were good. As well, some of the trips now could be taken with Maire and the children. In March and early April 1980, Conor and Maire visited the Soviet Union, jointly on behalf of the *Observer* and the incidental hospitality of the Soviet government.[99] Conor had a number of trips to the Aspen Institute in Colorado and on one of these he was able to take Maire and the children. This expedition was especially illuminating for Patrick and Margaret, because they were traveling on a private jet owned by Atlantic-Richfield, a plane tricked out to entertain American oil men. Conor and Maire talked and drank in the forward compartment and at one point went back to check on the youngsters, who were unusually quiet. The reason was that the in-seat video included hardcore porn, which the kids were watching with unalloyed fascination.

In 1981, Conor began an essay-based book concerning Eamon de Valera and the heritage of 1916. (It had the egregious provisional title of "Eamon de Valera and the Hatching of an Easter Egg.")[100] This project seems to have grown out of a lecture he gave to his old society, the Hist—the College Historical Society of Trinity College, Dublin—in mid-November 1979. This was on the subject of the cult of Patrick Pearse, a faith that Conor believed led toward disaster. The speech was fully reported, and once again the Dublin papers were filled in equal part with O'Brien and with indignation. [101] The projected book joined the list of Conor's abandoned projects.

The chief developments in Conor's attitudes in these years concerned, first, Marxism, and second, Israel. The first issue turned into a game that he played with his friend and former colleague, Edward Thompson. Conor was irritated by a winter of strikes and repulsed by the pietisms of Tony Benn—who was forever suggesting that the Labour party was based equally on Methodism and Marxism. Conor suggested instead that there were simply two forms of Marxism—Vulgar and Refined. By "Vulgar Marxism" Conor meant the aggressive, potentially violent prescriptions that led the workers toward head-bashing, the sort of thing that was a license for social aggression and irresponsibility. [102] This earned a reply from E.P. Thompson, and Conor in a subsequent column admitted that he might have gone a bit far. [103] But he reiterated what really bothered him about Vulgar Marxism. Whereas "Refined Marxism somehow assumes the lineaments of Virginia Woolf ... Vulgar Marxism is the spitting image of Bernadette Devlin." [104]

Conor and Edward Thompson played a second match in 1980, on the subject of unilateral nuclear disarmament. Both men knew that they were involved in a game that required cooperation, even if they were competitors. Watching them is like observing a pair of squash masters, Thompson with the clear, efficient, reason-based strokes, Conor with the more elegant shots which either score beautifully from an improbable angle or fall short like a ridiculous two-wall boast. Conor's position on unilateral nuclear disarmament was encapsulated in his reflections on the death of the great Russian poet Mikhail Yurevic Lermontov, who was challenged to a duel by a man named Martynov, a man he despised as a dolt. "The duel was not really expected to be lethal; most duels were not. Lermontov did not take it seriously, and Martynov was not habitually ferocious, but it seems, rather decent. When the moment came, however, Lermontov pointed his own pistol into the air."

"I am not going to shoot at the fool," he announced.

"Maddened by this crowning insult, Martynov then shot Lermontov dead."

From this incident Conor drew the following lesson: "The fate of Lermontov shows that in certain circumstances it may be impossible to reconcile freedom of speech with survival, if you abjure the means of your defence." [105]

In drawing this interpretation, Conor was not becoming a neo-conservative—he could not, for neo-conservatism, like socialism, is based on economic theories, and such constructs are not within his ken—but was just being Conor. If the conventional wisdom among the British intellectual elite was in favor of unilateral disarmament, then he, virtually automatically, would be marching in the opposite direction.[106]

The other issue wherein the left-chic of England and Conor parted company was on the question of Israel. He would not accept the idea that Israel was a colonialist oppressor and that the Palestinians were the oppressed. Conor's instinctive attachment to Israel went back to his youth, to his having been at school with Jewish lads, to his time at the United Nations, and to his understanding of (but not exactly sympathy with) the Ulster Protestants, besieged as they believed themselves to be.[107] Conor had also developed a strong dislike for the social and political implications of certain forms of Islam. He had seen the genocide the Muslim population inflicted in Nigeria in the late 1960s. And he was willing to say in print that "I read with disgust the copious reports of barbaric punishments—such as stoning of adulterers—inflicted by fanatics in Iran."[108] The combined effect of his longtime pro-Jewish sympathies and his distaste for Islamic zealotry was such that by the end of 1980 he was on the verge of expressing some kind of personal commitment to the state of Israel.

• • •

He was also on the verge of being let go from what he later called "that agreeable but rather hazy eminence."[109] Although the *Observer*'s circulation had risen somewhat during Conor's watch, it was stuck in the 750,000 to 1,000,000 range and was constantly being pushed by the *Sunday Times* to add expensive features and to cut its advertising rates. The result was that during the Atlantic-Richfield period of ownership, cumulative losses came to about £8 million.[110] This was not a lot of red ink for American oil magnates to accept, but it was an irritant. More to the point, ever since Conor had the paper endorse Labour in the 1979 general election, the American interests had wanted him out.

Enter at this point Kenneth Harris, an associate editor of the *Observer*, who specialized in features, especially biographical articles, and who, curiously, had a seat on the board of directors. That Conor and Donald Trelford had board seats was not unusual—they were both major management players—but Harris was there for another reason: he had attached himself to Robert Anderson like a pilot fish to a shark. It was Harris who, through a mutual friend, had first raised with Anderson the idea of his purchasing the paper and it was Harris who had set up Arnold Goodman's first meeting with the oil baron.[111] Harris, therefore, was owed some gratitude and the board seat was appropriate.

He wanted more, however. In 1979, he had breakfasted with Goodman and, in Goodman's words, "ruined my meal with an intimation that he had been having conversations with Anderson—with whom he had obviously established a considerable degree of authority—and that Anderson had suggested to him, although it might have been vice versa, that he should become either the managing director or, more horrific from my point of view, the editor-in-chief."[112] Goodman told Harris in very short, sharp words that he would have no credibility in the position and, besides, Conor was still there.[113]

Harris's ambition had a certain dramatic rightness about it: a playwright would have put him on stage in these events as a dark counterfoil to Donald Trelford. Although older than Trelford (Harris was in his early sixties), he was similar in many ways. Harris had a presence that made him good on radio and television; he had come up through state schools and Wadham College, Oxford, and had had a good service record in World War II. But whereas Trelford was very much a team player, Harris insisted on being captain of the side.

When ill health forced Lord Barnetson to step down as chairman of the board in September 1980, there was no head to the *Observer* board, although Lord Goodman, as senior director, kept a watching brief and Barnetson stayed on as a regular board member. Robert Anderson announced that he was going to dump Conor and appoint Kenneth Harris as editor in chief. Upon hearing this news, Goodman flew to New York and met with Anderson and with fellow director Thornton Bradshaw at the Park Lane Hotel (owned by Atlantic-Richfield). He told them that Harris's proposal (for such it was; Anderson was endorsing it) to become editor in chief would be unacceptable. His credentials were in doubt and his appointment would meet with the disfavor of the journalists on the paper, a fatal disadvantage to a collegial paper. Anderson relented.[114]

For the moment, Conor's job had been saved, but he was not naive. He understood what was going on and knew that eventually the Americans would win. In January 1981, therefore, he was satisfied when he and Lord Barnetson and Thornton Bradshaw worked out a parachute: Conor was to resign as editor in chief and become a regular columnist. He was to be paid about as much as when he was editor in chief, to make forty contributions a year and was to be given liberal travel opportunity. He could return to Ireland and work from home. No more weekly commuting.[115]

Thus, on 25 January, a small item appeared in the paper: "For family reasons Dr. Conor Cruise O'Brien has asked to be relieved of his duties as editor-in-chief of the *Observer* from 31 March." He would, the story noted, continue to write for the paper from his home in Dublin and would also have the title of Consultant Editor. It was in fact true that Conor was needed at home—Patrick, now in adolescence, was starting to treat school like a day at the beach[116]—but the reason that Conor left was because he was shrewd enough to know that in a boardroom war with the overseas owners, he could not win.

• • •

At that point, Conor could have decamped, but that would not have been honorable. He believed in the paper—the old *Observer* of David Astor—and he was loyal to Lord Goodman and he owed Donald Trelford his support. Through some very awkward moments, Conor and Trelford had acted decently to each other and had become, in the heel of the hunt, allies.

Thus, Conor, Trelford, Goodman, and Astor were on the same side at a board confrontation that took place in mid-February 1981. It was right out of the more vulgar TV episodes of "Dallas." A couple of days before the meeting, Robert Anderson had breakfasted at Claridges with Arnold Goodman, who listened unhappily to Anderson's new plan: Anderson himself would become chairman of the board and the vice-chairman would be Kenneth Harris! Goodman told the oil man that there would be no objection to his becoming chairman, but that Harris was totally unacceptable: with Anderson spending most of his life in the United States, Harris would effectively be left as officer in charge. Hearing this, Anderson promised not to put forward the intended resolution concerning Harris's vice-chairmanship.[117]

Yet, when the board met, not only did Anderson first propose his own chairmanship—which was accepted unanimously—but, surprisingly, that Kenneth Harris should be vice-chairman. Immediately both Lord Goodman and David Astor said that they would resign if Harris became vice-chairman. The resignations would become public and embarrassingly so. Conor and Donald Trelford argued strongly against Harris, and in the face of the combined objections, Anderson took Harris out of the room and made some sort of an arrangement with him. The two men returned and Anderson withdrew his nomination of Harris.[118]

Not a great victory for Anderson. Although he had become chairman of the *Observer*, the big-time cattle and oil man had been humiliated by the Brits. He was not a man who had become immensely wealthy by permitting himself to be browbeaten. David Astor on his way from the meeting said it was likely that Anderson would now seek to sell the paper.[119] He was dead right.

Indeed, Anderson had bought the final 10 percent of the shares held by the Astor Trust during 1980 and he was ready to move quickly. Over the Christmas holidays that same year he had talked with the African-based financier, Tiny Rowland, about selling him the paper. This was a purchase Rowland long had been keen on.[120] Although at a breakfast meeting held the day after the unpleasant board meeting, Anderson assured David Astor that he had no intention of selling the paper, he proceeded to do so. He sold two-thirds of the stock to Tiny Rowland for $6 million—not a bad return on a one-pound investment.[121] Goodman, Astor, and the other members of the board learned on 25 February that all Anderson's promises of keeping the *Observer* intact as a cultural institution were gone. Goodman later reflected on Anderson: "He was not a man of great spiritual qualities."[122] But neither was he the bumpkin they had taken him to be.

· · ·

There is a coda. Conor, Donald Trelford, Lord Goodman, and David Astor fought Tiny Rowland's acquisition of the paper. Rowland—India-born, English citizen, army reject, Rhodesian farmer, African colossus—had somehow managed to combine huge Rhodesian interests and sanctions-breaking with serving as an unpaid economic adviser to the Organization of African Unity and had freer access to frontline leaders, Kaunda, Banda, and Nkomo than did the *Observer*'s own African experts.[123] *Observer* loyalists fought Rowland, using the Monopolies Commission. They testified that, for a spectrum of reasons, the purchase should not be permitted. The commission, however, approved the purchase, subject to their being six "independent" directors on the *Observer*'s board.[124] Neither David Astor nor Arnold Goodman accepted invitations to continue on the board—Rowland was just too fatally the wrong sort—and Conor was told tactfully by Robert Anderson that, in view of his comments at recent board meetings, he was assumed to wish to be relieved of his directorial responsibilities.[125]

So, by mid-July 1981, Conor no longer was a director of the *Observer*, but just a regular columnist.

Kenneth Harris became chairman of the Observer International (the foreign syndication service of the *Observer*), a post he held into the 1990s. Protected in part by the six independent directors required by the Monopolies Commission, but mostly by his own catlike grace, Donald Trelford survived as editor into the 1990s, and it was in that position that he finally had to sack Conor. Tiny Rowland was Mr. Africa and Conor's continuing to write on the subject of Africa meant that he had to go. The parachute that had been worked out for Conor, however, worked well; the landing was soft. Conor still wrote for the *Observer*, but he began in 1982 making weekly contributions to the *Irish Times* and his most robust material went there. For the year 1984–85, Conor was at Dartmouth College in New Hampshire as a Montgomery Fellow. The last payment from the *Observer* was made in January 1985, and by that time Conor had made a safe financial transition.[126]

In 1986, Conor happened to meet Donald Trelford at a convention of the International Press Institute, held in Istanbul. On the last day of the conference, Trelford took Conor out for dinner with some amiable American friends of his. They had a splendid dinner, lots of wine, good stories, and one of the Americans wanted to know why Conor was *formerly* of the *Observer*.

Conor nodded across the table at Trelford and said, "There's the guy that fired me."

Shock and horror among the decent Americans: "How on earth could you ever fire Conor?" they wanted to know.

"I fired Conor because I realized that if I fired him, Conor would survive ..." Trelford took a drink from his wine glass and continued: "... and that if I didn't fire Conor, then I would not survive."[127]

Thus spake the loss and the profits.

CHAPTER 13

AN ENVIABLE FREEDOM: 1982–1992

While he was still at the *Observer* full-time, Conor attended a conference on the subject of communication. Of course the meeting was flooded with the articulate and the persuasive.

> There was, however, one participant, a wise and distinguished Indian whose contribution to the total proceedings consisted of total silence.
>
> As I found this silence at least as interesting as many of the things that were being said, I ventured to ask my Indian friend why he chose not to speak.
>
> His answer was: "I am surprised, Dr. O'Brien, that at your age and with your experience, you have not yet realised that *communication is impossible.*"[1]

Nevertheless, like other artists, prophets, and scholars, Conor kept doing the impossible.

After he left the editorship in chief of the *Observer*, Conor did what he had done while an undergraduate at Trinity College Dublin: he lived by his wits. This was in part a matter of necessity, for he had never stayed in one post long enough to acquire a pension of any significant size; but also it was a matter of inclination. Conor was instinctively a freelance and could never serve one lord for long. His mode of making a living during the 1980s and thereafter seems on the surface to be a bit skimble-skamble and much more chaotic than most sixty-year-olds or seventy-year-olds would want, but it possessed one beneficial characteristic: in addition to keeping the roof over his family's heads, it kept Conor from being bored. It allowed him to take a series of diverting short-term assignments and it gave him time for the one long-term project that did not bore him: the life of Edmund Burke, a distant ancestor and, to Conor, a forever-alive and lively Irishman.

The tactics Conor employed for making a living are simple enough to understand; it is only the workload that is difficult to comprehend. First, he made his basic income by writing a weekly column for at least one newspaper—and these were essays, not jab-and-run columns—but often for two, and sometimes three papers. He wrote primarily for the *Irish Times* from 1982 to the spring of 1986 (while putting in about forty columns a year for the *Observer* until 1984). Then, when he and Douglas Gageby got on each other's nerves, he became the weekly essayist of the *Irish Independent*, thus completing a nice circle in the family sense: the "Indo" had been his father's paper, the one he was writing for when he died. Conor continues today writing for the Indo each Saturday, and from the summer of 1986 to the spring of 1992, he also did an essay most weeks for the *Times* of London. In addition, at least once a month he wrote an occasional piece for the *Guardian*, the *Independent* (London), the *Daily Telegraph*, or for an American or German paper.

Second, he simultaneously did a lot of freelance feature-length writing for high-quality American publications, such as *Atlantic*, *Harper's*, and the *New Republic*. They paid a lot more than did the comparable quality publications in England and they ran feature articles of considerably greater length. (For details of his writing in this period, see the Bibliography in the Anthology volume.) The sheer amount of hard work involved in this feature writing is daunting, but considering its quality—when Conor was in form he was among the best nonfiction English-language prose writers in the world—the output was astounding. That he repeated himself on occasion is hardly surprising. This was perfectly kosher as far as the newspapers were concerned: the readership of the *Times* and that of the *Irish Independent* did not overlap very much and the occasional paragraph from one paper frequently found itself in the other, with no loss to either party. On the other hand, Jack Beatty of the *Atlantic* had a right to complain when the senior editor of *Harper's*, Lewis Lapham, needled him that a piece of Conor's that the *Atlantic* ran in its October 1985 issue had included some of the same words that had appeared in *Harper's* the previous December.[2]

The immediate rewards of Conor's constant work—and of the brilliant negotiation on his behalf by his agent Elaine Greene—were that Conor in the 1980s and early 1990s was among the highest-paid periodical writers in the British Isles and almost certainly was the highest-earning writer of any sort who lived in Ireland.[3]

Conor's writing, remunerative as it may be, is founded in scholarship. It works because it has a base in an erudition which, if lightly worn, is nonetheless substantial. Therefore, as much for intellectual as for financial reasons, Conor undertook several extended tours as distinguished visiting professor or as an endowed lecturer at various American universities. (British universities in the 1980s were too bowed under Thatcherism to afford such luxuries.) These included Dartmouth, as a Montgomery Fellow for the academic year 1984–85; Williams College, 1987; the University of Pennsylvania, 1988–89; the Wilson Center, Washington, D.C., autumn 1991; the National Humanities Center, North Carolina, 1993–94. These were good visits in every sense, since they were remunerative and allowed access to good libraries and to some learned colleagues; Maire, and sometimes Patrick and Margaret, could come along (as in the Dartmouth visit).

At the universities, Conor usually taught one or two courses, gave several public lectures, and made himself available to faculty and students.[4] On both the longer and the shorter stints (the one-week distinguished lectureships) he gave good value. A fairly frequent feature of such lectureships is a required panel discussion, a frequently deadly form of exchange. But here is a transcript of a portion of a panel discussion that took place at Skidmore College in April 1985. It involves part of an exchange between Conor, George Steiner, and Leszek Kolakowski:

> *George Steiner* (concluding a paragraph that has mentioned Mozart, Salieri, Wittgenstein, Russell, Hegel, Kant, Herder, Schelling, Schopenhauer and Nietzsche): ... I don't know who would be at this table as a thinking being without what Kant and Hegel brought about in the history of the mind and consciousness.
>
> *Conor:* I'm not sure I want to be included in this company.
>
> *George:* I have tried to pay you a great compliment, Conor. Accept it, for once.
>
> *Conor:* You know, George, I fear you most when you are offering me enormous compliments.
>
> *Leszek:* I would subscribe to everything George has said, with perhaps the exception of the statement that Hegel was a master of prose. But my German might not be good enough to appreciate his literary merit. Anyway, I would certainly always prefer Lessing.
>
> *George:* I love Lessing, too, but wouldn't you like to write the *Phenomenology?*
>
> *Leszek:* No, I would not like to write it.
>
> *Conor:* I think, George, it's already been done.[5]

The honors received in the 1980s and early 1990s were pleasant: D.Litt. degrees at the Queen's University of Belfast (1984); Glasgow

(1990); Queen's University, Ontario (1991); and the National University of Ireland, awarded at University College, Dublin, in 1993. The latter degree Conor particularly prized, coming as it did from the institutional descendant of his father's university, the old Royal. So too, he was especially pleased to be elected a vice-president (that is, a patron) of the Literary and Historical Society of UCD in the early 1980s, for this was another link with his father, Francis Cruise O'Brien having been auditor of that society. (Conor had been named a vice-president of the College Historical Society at TCD in 1965, which he also prized, in this case because of the tie to Edmund Burke.)

When, in 1986, Gerry Gregg, the prize-winning Dublin independent feature producer, did an hour-long television documentary on Conor, he cooperated, but with the rueful knowledge of what his celebrity was worth in parts of his home island. At one point, he and Gregg decided to film a segment in Andersontown, West Belfast, not the safest place for Conor to be. The plan was to do one shot and then to leave. No retakes. The segment consisted of Conor standing against a Provo mural and talking about the difficulties engendered by the Provos' slogan, "Our Nation. Others Out!"

A bunch of street children heard Conor speak those closing words and came up to him, yelling "Right, Mister!" They circled this obvious celebrity and Gerry Gregg. Gregg took a few shots of them—Belfast kids being more accustomed to being filmed than any group of youngsters outside of Beverly Hills—then, as Conor and Gregg turned to leave, one of them called out, "Who's are y', Mister?"

Conor replied slowly. "Go home and tell your fathers that you've just met Conor Cruise O'Brien."

And under his breath he added, "... and they'll probably beat the life out of you."[6]

• • •

If Conor in these years was lionized, he never stopped being a lion. His work continued to have hard, raspish edges and to provoke more response, both positive and negative, than most writers enjoy. The work of his later years that is most puzzling to his friends and colleagues is *The Siege*, a history of Israel that was published in 1986.

Actually, Conor was predisposed to write such a book by his early education (Sandford Park being the preferred school of the Dublin Jewish community) and by his experience in the UN, where he got on very well with the Israeli delegates. That said, there was a sense in which Israel seemed to reflect Conor's own situation. Israelis were surrounded by enemies, threatened by terrorists (the parallel between the PLO and the

Provos was obvious to him), under siege, and thus had abandoned conventional liberalism and endorsed the use of state force against the state's enemies.

But many chemical bonds require a catalyst and for Conor it was the Jerusalem International Book Fair of April 1981. This was the scene of one of his most memorable performances. The book fair, which takes place in every odd-numbered year, is a Middle Eastern version of the Frankfurt Book Fair. About a thousand publishers exhibit or come to bargain for book rights and the highlight of the fair is the presentation of the Jerusalem Prize. This is for a corpus of work on the theme of the freedom of the individual in society. In previous years, it had gone to Jorge Luis Borges, and to Bertrand Russell. Obviously, this was a major award, to be bestowed decorously. In 1981 it was to go to Graham Greene, and Conor, who was doing work in Jerusalem for an *Observer* piece, was asked to take part in the presentation. He was to make a speech that praised Graham Greene's many virtues and explained why he was receiving this recognition.

Poor Greene. He had to sit quietly at the award presentation in front of an invited audience of distinguished writers, publishers, and government officials, while Conor, with considerable elegance, like a watch repairman in black tie, took him apart. "I must confess that it would not have occurred to me," Conor said, and then held a long dramatic pause, "... unaided—that the freedom of the individual in society is what the writing of Graham Greene is about."

Members of the audience looked at each other, wondering what was coming next, and then at Greene who, to his credit, showed neither surprise nor anger.

"*If* he is expressing it, he is expressing it in a dark, complex, paradoxical way of his own." Conor went on to criticize Greene's "heavily Catholic period" that ran from *Brighton Rock* to *The End of the Affair*. With considerable grace, Greene, in his reply, ignored Conor's comments entirely, and instead, praised Teddy Kollek.[7]

In almost any other place in the world this kind of commentary would have been considered unforgivable. In Jerusalem, it made Conor a player. Teddy Kollek, mayor of Jerusalem and a man who himself had never backed off from a confrontation, loved it. There had been comments in the corridors before the award ceremony about anti-Semitism in Greene's early work, so Kollek did not mind seeing Greene trashed.

The immediate result was that Conor was asked to join the "Jerusalem Committee," a worldwide group of notables and experts—especially in the fields of city planning, archaeology, and historic-site preservation—that Kollek had formed in 1969. (It was funded by an agency called the Jerusalem Foundation which itself had come into existence in 1966.) The key date, however, was neither 1966 or 1969, but 1967. That was the year when, as a result of the "Six Day War," Jerusalem, which previously had been partitioned and largely under Jordanian control, came fully under Israeli hegemony. Teddy Kollek, who had been the mayor of a part (and not the most prepossessing part) of the city now suddenly was in charge of the ancient capital of Israel. There were great opportunities, but also great chances of making mistakes, particularly in the form of construction that ruined historical sites. The Jerusalem Committee, though it had no actual power, had considerable influence, consisting as it did largely of international experts, and the committee prevented some major planning errors. It helped the municipality to thread the needle between protection of historical sites and the necessity of economic development. By the early 1980s, the committee had extended its purview to take in cultural matters, such as the arrangements for Arab education.[8]

The committee was supposedly nonpolitical but to serve on it, one had to accept that Jerusalem (in contravention of United Nations resolutions) was permanently reunited, that it was unalterably under Israeli rule, and that Jerusalem was the capital of Israel. Conor enthusiastically bought in, and he became an important member from the 1982 plenary meeting onward. He drafted resolutions,[9] wrote articles that Kollek approvingly distributed,[10] and spoke for the group when, in 1982, he presented an address to the president of Israel on behalf of the Jerusalem Committee.[11]

So, long before he drafted a single word of what turned into a history of Israel and of Zionism, Conor strongly identified with many of the ideological and emotional premises upon which the state of Israel was based. He seriously committed himself to the research for the project early in 1982. In mid-March he wrote to his friend Robert Silvers, editor of the *New York Review of Books*:

> A terrible thing has happened to me in my old age: I have got bitten by the Middle East bug, even to the point of setting out to write a book. The attached copy of a draft outline and a letter to Teddy Kollek will give you an idea of the state of affairs.
>
> The genesis of the thing is that after spending a while in Lebanon, Syria and Israel last autumn, I became convinced that the prevailing wisdom (in Europe) about a peace settlement embracing both the PLO and Israel is nonsense, since no basis for such a compromise exists: if a peace is to be built, compatible with the survival of Israel, it would have to be a peace between Israel and the neighbouring Arab states to the exclusion of the Palestinian emigrés. The thrust of the book will be an exploration of this line of ideas.[12]

Notice that Conor mentions Teddy Kollek in this letter. Conor has always been responsive to father-figures and Kollek, though only six years older than Conor, was a great gruff bear of a man, seemingly out of another time. An aura of hard-earned experience enveloped Kollek, the chevrons earned in prewar Austria, the kibbutz, and the Haganah.

Kollek provided Conor with introductions to large numbers of influential Israelis, whom Conor interviewed, as well as to the occasional Israeli figure overseas.[13] He also provided Conor with accommodations for a time at Miskenot Sha'ananim, a splendid row of guest houses, owned by the Jerusalem Foundation and set aside for visiting artists and scholars.[14] Built by Sir Moses Montefiore in the mid-nineteenth century as artisans' housing, the buildings had been entirely refurbished. There, a visitor could sit at his desk, and look out past his verandah, through leaded windows, and view the ancient city.

The only drawback to Conor's relationship with Teddy Kollek and to his enthusiastic participation in the work of the Jerusalem Committee was that it gave rise to the rumor (at least in British journalistic circles and probably beyond) that *The Siege* was financed by the Israeli government.[15] These rumors were almost certainly without foundation, but Conor's behavior did nothing to dispel them.[16] (One does not count as contributory the lecture that he gave at Ben-Gurion University, situated in the Negev desert, on the subject of Eamon de Valera, a feat for which he claimed admission to the Guinness Book of Records.)[17]

It is notable, however, how little contact Conor had with Palestinians of any sort. One can understand why he would be repelled by what was to him an IRA simulacrum, the PLO. He had had some unsatisfactory contacts with the PLO in Tyre in September 1981, a heavily controlled affair wherein one spokesman answered his questions, while several others in the room kept their eye on the spokesman.[18] But, in surveying the final product, *The Siege*, Christopher Hitchens, who is sometimes unfair to Conor, quite fairly notes: "The acknowledgements of the book, which run to four pages, do not include a single Arab name. ... The bibliography, which lists two hundred and ninety-six entries, features twenty books or articles written by Arabs and four written by people who might be described as their sympathizers."[19] One also notes that when, early in the research, David Astor suggested to Conor that he see Yasser Arafat, whom Astor had found both accessible and worth hearing, Conor surprisingly said, "No. I don't want to."[20]

Conor's publisher, however, was not perturbed. The original publisher was George Weidenfeld (life peer, 1976), with whom Conor first had discussed the idea when they both were in Jerusalem.[21] Weidenfeld sold a co-edition to Simon and Shuster in the United States.[22] When

464 CONOR CRUISE O'BRIEN

pressed in late 1983 by the American publisher to indicate what the conclusion of his book would be (the American market for a book of Jewish interest is a very touchy one), Conor summarized as follows: "The siege is not lifted, nor is it likely to be lifted, for generations." Therefore, Israel's trading territory for peace would not work.[23]

A tiny hiccup in developing *The Siege* was not concept, but title: for a time he called the book "The Boot and the Longing," which neither George Weidenfeld nor anyone else could understand.[24] A bigger hiccup occurred in June 1982, when Israel invaded Lebanon. This was before Conor had completed his research or done much more than outline the book, but it was after he had made the emotional and ideological commitment to his set of conclusions. The Israeli invasion, which ran all the way to Beirut, was costly in terms of Lebanese civilian casualties, but what was harder for most observers to take was the slaughter of Islamic refugees at two camps, Shatilla and Sabra, in mid-September. This was done by Christian Arabs of the Falangist faction, but (according to a commission presided over by the head of the supreme court of Israel) had been tacitly sanctioned by the Israeli minister of defence, Ariel Sharon, and his chief of staff. Conor was in Jerusalem and in southern Lebanon in the summer of 1982 and he was well informed about what was going on and, later, when he went home, about what was happening back in the Middle East.[25] The investigation, and especially the Israeli-permitted massacres in the refugee camps, bothered him greatly. "He had one terrible period when he was working on *The Siege*," his friend Brian Garrett recalls, "when the Israelis reached Beirut. And when the camps were invaded by Lebanese Christians, at least with the acquiescence of the Israeli army. It was very hard on him. Here he is watching a racist genocidal massacre. I remember attacking him in Belfast on that. I couldn't get any answer on that." Garrett concludes, "This is the only time I ever saw him come face to face with a tremendous problem of belief versus experience."[26]

This became, secondarily, a literary problem, for Conor was taking his history of Zionism and of Israel right up to the present: the invasion of Lebanon would be the last big tale in the book. But a volume of nearly 800 pages, tracing the previous century of Zionism, could not end on such a note, at least not if one expected to sell the book to the public.

Conor adjusted. How he would do so was indicated by a harsh review he published, simultaneously in *Encounter* and in the *New Republic*, of the English-language edition of Jacobo Timerman's *The Longest War: Israel in Lebanon*. Timerman, an Argentinian Jew, author of the modern classic, *Prisoner Without a Name*, found absolutely no justification for

If it is true that Israel: Ulster = PLO: IRA
And, inferentially, that Israel: Ulster = Zionism: Ulster Unionism,
Then, Israel: Ulster = Palestinians: Ulster Catholics
And therefore, Israel: Ulster = treatment of Arabs: treatment of Ulster Catholics.

But there is the problem. Whereas Conor was on record from the mid-1960s onward as a backer of the civil rights campaign of the Ulster Catholics and as a thorough-going opponent of anti-Catholic discrimination, he had no such feelings about the Palestinians. *The Siege* is very *sotto voce* about anti-Palestinian discrimination within Israel, which considerably exceeded that which the Catholics of Ulster experienced.[35]

Conor came close to grasping this issue in an essay in 1984 which concluded with the words "Israel is a democracy of Jews. I don't think it is any more capable of ceasing to be democratic in its internal arrangements than it is of ceasing to be Jewish."[36] But, he quickly shrank back, because he was too expert an Irish historian not to pick up the resonance in his own phrase, "Israel is a democracy of Jews." The parallel phrase in Irish history was "a Protestant parliament for a Protestant people," a description of the old Northern Ireland legislature, a democracy of sorts. Rather than complete the uncomfortable analogy between Israel and Ulster, Conor let it lie, fractured and frightening.

• • •

In relation to Northern Ireland itself, from 1982 onward, Conor's writing consisted of general philosophical discussions of the nature of terrorism and of the legitimate response to it. And he wrote a good deal in his newspaper essays on political issues relating to Ulster.

In May 1977, Conor had given the Cyril Foster Lecture at Oxford University on "Liberty and Terror," and the essay had become something of a modern classic. In it, he introduced a useful distinction between two types of terrorist, millenarian (for example, the Baader-Meinhof group in Germany) and secessionist-irredentist groups that wanted to control specific local pieces of land (for example, the PLO and the Provisional IRA). He suggested that although there was no certain way for a liberal democratic state to end terrorism, there were some hopeful ways of seeking to end it. These included convincing the terrorists that they are not going to get their own way (rule: don't negotiate with them); depriving them as far as possible of publicity (rule: don't let them on the air and try to keep them out of the newspapers); ignore their propaganda (see previous rule); and keep up the pressure on the terrorists by the security forces. Conor counseled against letting the concept of "institutional violence" lead one to become ineffective. "Those who use that term seldom pause to consider that it may be much better to institutionalise violence, within a democratic system, than to allow it [violence] to shape institutions of its own, which it entirely dominates—as in the case of private armies."[37] This was a very tough lecture, strong in argument, subtle in many of its interpretations.

Now, in 1986 in an *Atlantic* article, "Thinking about Terrorism," the frame of reference was pared down to only two groups, "the members of the most durable terrorist organisations of the twentieth century: the IRA (including its splinter groups) and the PLO (including its splinter groups)."[38] And the level of analysis is correspondingly reduced. Terrorists are not to be understood, Conor says, as idealists, nuts, or dupes, but as people who, while genuinely motivated by some perceived religious or national grievance, behave rationally—in the sense that the capacity to kill provides them with authority and glamor in whatever world they inhabit. Terrorism, therefore, procures immediate rewards for the terrorists, and hence terrorists are not apt to be at all keen about putting themselves out of business. "So, the prospects for ending terrorism through a negotiated settlement are not bright, whether or not the terrorists are involved in the negotiations. But the insistence that a negotiated settlement *can* end terrorism actually helps the terrorists. It does so because it places the responsibility for continuing terrorism equally on the terrorists and those they seek to terrorize."[39]

In this article Conor referred disapprovingly to the Hillsborough Agreement (alternatively called the Anglo-Irish Agreement, or, usually, the AIA)—negotiated in November 1985 by Garret FitzGerald and Margaret Thatcher. This was hailed as the beginning of a new generation of peace in Northern Ireland, and it may yet prove to have been the case; sometimes trees take a long time to bloom. However, the immediate results were baleful.

Conor's view of the AIA was that (although he did not use these words) it was a case of antinomic principles being brought together to produce antimonial toxins. The AIA contained a dozen major articles, but they boiled down to two provisions. One was that the governments of the United Kingdom and of the Republic of Ireland agreed that any change in the constitutional status of Northern Ireland would occur only with the consent of the majority of the Northern Ireland electorate; in other words, no change. But, a second principle recognized by both governments was that the southern government had an interest (purposely undefined) in the Six Counties; in other words, change. The earnest of the second principle was that a "joint ministerial conference" of British and Irish ministers would meet regularly to deal with issues concerning the Catholic minority in Northern Ireland. Technically, the

U.K. government did not cede any sovereignty; but, in everyday matters, Dublin now had the right to be consulted about such volatile issues as security policy and electoral arrangements.

From the vantage point of, say, Washington, D.C., this looked very nice—everyone is learning to get along with each other, aren't they? And it did not look bad in London or Dublin—we're doing something, aren't we? But within Northern Ireland, both Catholic and Protestant communities saw it the same way, namely that the Micks had put another one over on the Prods, another tiny step toward forcing the Protestants into a united Ireland.[40] So, in his newspaper essays written during the period, Conor was furiously opposed to the AIA, but he was very much in a minority in the Irish Republic.

In the short run, at least, Conor was right about the AIA (the long run results are not yet known). The immediate consequence of the AIA was that Protestant resistance was galvanized: in November 1985, 200,000 very upset men and women rallied outside Belfast city hall under a huge banner, "Ulster Says No." All of the fifteen Ulster unionist MPs in the Westminster Parliament resigned, thus forcing a mini-referendum on the AIA (the Tory government had refused to permit a real referendum for fear of what it would reveal). The poll showed 78 percent of the electorate was against the AIA.[41] And, so disturbed by the unionist reaction to the AIA was the Northern Ireland assembly, that this tiny vestige of representative government had to be dissolved in June 1986.

From that point onward, Conor's actions and views on Northern Ireland can be summarized under five heads. First, he greatly reduced the missionary work he did in the United States. Whereas he previously had tried to influence U.S. politicians—in practice, liberal democrats, the bloc that traditionally was most interested in the Irish situation—he now dealt mostly with scholarly and academic groups in the United States. In part this was because he was husbanding his own time and energy. But, in part, he became convinced of the invincible ignorance—to use a good Catholic theological concept—of these American politicians. He kept hearing echoes of the forthright statement of Bella Abzug, liberal democratic congresswoman for the twentieth New York district, who, at the height of the Troubles, demanded that British troops cease their occupation of Dublin. And he remembered the difficulty of dealing with Edward Kennedy, senator for Massachusetts, who, when Conor talked to him about Northern Ireland, had to be reminded by his aides what the geographic relationship of Derry and Belfast was; beyond that, he could not even frame his own questions.[42]

Second, Conor remained firmly against negotiations of any sort with the Provos, on the simple grounds that talk of such "political" solutions enhances the terrorist powers.

Third, he came to believe in the later 1980s and the early 1990s that internment without trial should again be introduced in Ulster. But this time, it should be done right: arrest the IRA godfathers and the leading Protestant thugs and put them all to making mail bags or whatever the latest prison rehabilitation technique might be.

Fourth, Conor became convinced that direct rule from London, while far from desirable in theory, was the most expedient form of government for Northern Ireland. Ideally, he would have liked a power-sharing legislature, where the Catholics and Protestants of Northern Ireland split the main jobs, but the continuing—indeed, increasing—feeling of siege on the part of the Protestants precluded this. Therefore, direct rule from London was necessary and one might as well recognize the fact.

And, finally, Conor became a unionist. As was usually the case, he used the word with his own special twist, but unionist is what he became. His own words are important here. They come from the Ian Gow Memorial Lecture which Conor gave in July 1992. Ian Gow had been a minister of state at the treasury in Margaret Thatcher's government; he was the only minister to resign in protest against the Anglo-Irish Agreement. Conor's explanation of how he became a unionist—in the sense of defending the existence of the union of Great Britain and Northern Ireland as long as the majority in Northern Ireland wanted it—was a syllogism, whose major premise was his own real and well-documented anticolonialism. Given that as a premise, he said that within the Irish context, "there is a simple empirical test, by which the sheep can be separated from the goats: Find out how a given person stands on Articles 2 and 3 of the Irish Constitution. Those Articles are a naked claim to territory, irrespective of the wishes of the inhabitants. ... The whole thing is in the style of the period in which that constitution was written: the Europe of the 1930s."[43]

But do not all the major parties in the south, and the SDLP in the north, accept the general principle that Ireland should be united only with unionist consent?

Conor replies with a counter-question:

But how is Unionist consent expected, by these politicians, to be elicited? Not by reasoned persuasion, certainly. None of them has ever seriously sought to persuade Unionists. They don't talk *to* Unionists: they talk *at* them, constantly, in the manner calculated to deepen the ancient antagonism, not to reduce it. But if not through persuasion, then how is Unionist consent to be obtained? These politicians never tell us that. We have to deduce their expectation from the pattern of their political behaviour, within the particular context in which that behaviour is situated. As I interpret that pattern, in that context the expectation is as follows. That Unionists, sooner or later will crack under the combined pressure of the new constitutional nationalist politicians and of the IRA murder campaign, with the IRA as the cutting edge of the combination. What these politicians are saying to Unionists, subliminally, is this: "If you won't listen to us, you're going to get more of the same from those fellows out there. Very sad, but that's how it is." It is a variant of the nice cop, tough cop routine. Fianna Fail and the SDLP—and other nationalists in a lesser degree—are the nice cop. The IRA is the tough one.[44]

Ultimately, this makes demands of a person, and its impact on Conor himself was as follows:

To move from being a nationalist to being a Unionist—or the reverse indeed—is not just an altered political option. It is more like an existential metamorphosis. Yet I could see that I had to accept that. It was not enough to stop playing nice cop. You had to be prepared to defend publicly the Union that was being subjected to that perfidious and murderous combined attack. I have never regretted that decision.[45]

That is the end of a long road indeed; one that started when, as Sean MacBride's fair-haired boy, Conor had been an enthusiastic participant in the campaign to force northern Protestants into a united Ireland.

• • •

One must ask the same question of Conor's actions and motives in the 1980s and 1990s as one did in the 1970s. The central question is, was his anticolonialism feigned? And, again, I can only come to the conclusion that it was not a rhetorical trick, not a *post hoc* rationalization for changes made for other reasons. It was genuine. Whether or not Conor's reasoning was right is something that everyone must judge for themselves.

A good test of this anticolonialism came in the mid 1980s: Nicaragua. There the government of Ronald Reagan was financing a gang of right-wing terrorists—the "Contras"—against a markedly incompetent, but popularly approved Sandinista government. The Sandinistas had come to power in an insurrection in 1979 against the dictatorship of Anastasio Somoza Debayle. The Sandinistas (named after Augusto Sandino, who successfully fought off the U.S. Marine invasion of Nicaragua in the years 1927–32), took to breaking up large landholdings and redistributing wealth, activities not in accord with the "trickle-down" theory of proper economic behavior adopted by the Reagan administration. In his essay "Thinking about Terrorism," Conor had suggested that the United States could not maintain international credibility and do what it was doing: it could not decry terrorism while backing it, in the form of the Contras.[46]

Conor was especially sensitive to U.S. support of terrorism because it fit into an old and abhorred mold: American anticommunism of the cold-war vintage. His attention had been focused on Nicaragua by a 1984 statement of Henry Kissinger who, as president of the Commission on Central America, told the U.S. Senate Foreign Relations Committee that Nicaragua possessed a "menacing military machine" and that "the Soviet-Cuban connection and active Sandinista support for insurgency and subversion in neighbouring countries create a fear in the region and threaten it with arms races and general militarization."[47] That was the same kind of rhetoric that the U.S. government (and, indeed, the same Dr. Kissinger) had used to justify U.S. involvement in Vietnam, and Conor, like an old war horse, answered the bugle. If the U.S. government saw the Sandinistas as worth overthrowing, then, in Conor's view, they deserved defending.

Conor did not however do the obvious thing—which would have been to point out the fact, obvious even then, that far from being a military menace, the only way the Sandinistas could export their revolution would have been if they all bought tickets on a Greyhound bus. Conor let others make that point. Instead, in an essay in the *Atlantic* entitled "God and Man in Nicaragua," he challenged the entire Reagan-Kissinger-U.S. premise, that the Nicaraguans were yet another communist threat. He argued that they were something new, a new kind of faith. This was a mixture of new-style Catholicism (the old style was on the wane in Nicaragua despite a visit by John Paul II in 1983, and despite his raising Obando y Bravo, one of the most right-wing of the bishops, to a red hat) with an almost-spiritualist veneration for Sandino (who had been assassinated in 1934). It was a mixture of faith and fatherland, and its alchemy was unique to Nicaragua, Conor argued, and no danger whatsoever to the nations in the region.[48]

This was a lively essay, compelling and readable, but that is not the point: what is here germane is that in this test case Conor was showing the same consistent opposition to imperialism that he had shown in the 1960s. His intellectual and moral base had not shifted.

• • •

That point is important not only for judging the integrity of his views about southern Irish irredentism (meaning colonialism), but also in providing perspective on his greatest frazzle during the 1980s, his trip to South Africa in 1986.

Conor's record on southern Africa was absolutely clear, although not simple-mindedly so. He knew Africa, and he knew South Africa, if not intimately, quite well. In 1965, he had attended in Natal province a conference of Umkonto we Sizwe, the armed wing of the African National Congress.[49] In 1966, he had become chair of the Irish Anti-Apartheid Movement and had given a lecture for them that was published as an anti-apartheid pamphlet. In 1970, he had joined his former father-in-law, Alec Foster, in the protests at the Lansdowne Road grounds, Dublin, against the Springboks' rugby tour. Indeed, for a time in the early 1970s he went off the deep end, at least by his own reckoning. In 1978, he told an interviewer for *Macleans*,

> I think I wanted to be the most anti-apartheid thing in sight. A certain professor asked me, deadpan, the question: "Do you think that the use of thermonuclear weapons would be justified as a last resort to end apartheid?" And I heard myself saying "Yes!" And then I sort of caught myself. End apartheid by ending everybody who lives under or over apartheid? I find a fair amount of people on the left who are still thinking that. They don't care a damn about the rest of the people—it's the principle.[50]

Conor did not soften on the subject, he just became smarter. He was in court in Pretoria, South Africa, the day in 1978 the thirteen-day-long inquest into the death of Steve Biko was handed down and he wrote about it with controlled rage. (The death was ruled not to have been the result of Biko's having been beaten severely on the head, thrown into a truck, and then driven 750 miles.)[51] A little after that, in mid-1979, Conor got slightly off track with the anti-apartheid movement in that he backed recognition of the regime of Bishop Muzorewa as the government of Rhodesia-cum-Zimbabwe (but this only if he dropped Ian Smith from the government).[52] The correct person to name was Robert Mugabe. In most eyes, however, that was less a lapse of faith on Conor's part than a case of his having backed the wrong horse.

Where Conor began to get into serious trouble with the anti-apartheid movement (Irish and British branches) was that he figured something out way ahead of most commentators. This occurred in mid-1979, when he spent quite a bit of time in South Africa attending conferences and visiting universities. Out of that visit came an extraordinarily prescient essay called "The Guilt of Afrikanerdom" in which he argued that there was "an unexpected force at work among the political class which rules South Africa." That force, "is, I believe, *guilt*."[53] He observed that Afrikaners were increasingly uncertain and were looking for answers concerning their race problem. He carried away the impression from a visit at the University of Potchefstroom (an Afrikaans-speaking institution) "of good men who had inherited certainties, which no longer convinced them, and who were now groping their way, in considerable intellectual, and some moral discomfort."[54]

Conor here was picking up what few outsiders, and, indeed, few non-Afrikaans speakers, apprehended, a fact that is absolutely requisite to an understanding of the fall of apartheid—namely, that the Afrikaners in the 1970s and 1980s were abandoning their belief in the morality of apartheid. Since their moral justification of apartheid had stemmed from religious ideology, they not only had to admit that they had been wrong, but by the very nature of their religious outlook, had to accept guilt. This massive ideological shift, of which guilt is the marker, was as much a cause of the abandonment of apartheid as was the Afrikaners' economic self-interests, which were affected by external sanctions and boycotts.[55]

The trouble is, Conor's insight into what was happening to the Afrikaner community leaders humanized them. They stopped being caricatures and became human beings. When, in 1985, Conor wrote the following, concerning the Afrikaners, he made enemies within the anti-apartheid movement: "It probably doesn't help to treat them as morally inferior to ourselves. We are morally superior to them only if we can be certain that we, *if placed in their predicament* [emphasis in the original] would act better than they do. How many of us can be certain of that?"[56]

That there is a difference between righteousness and self-righteousness is not something the self-righteous wish to hear and in their wrath they frequently shower stones on the prophet who brings them such a message. In March 1986, Conor published the long essay "What Can Become of South Africa?" which dealt with the Afrikaner *mentalité*, and suggested that the "Afrikaners are neither the uniquely virtuous *volk* of their own rhetoric ... nor yet the moral monsters depicted by outside rhetoric."[57] He was in deep trouble, not only with the Irish anti-apartheid movement, but also with its American allies, because of the following words: "I suspect that some of the righteous who denounce them from afar might behave quite like them if they were caught in a similar predicament—if, for example, there had been a black majority in America in the 1950s."[58]

Yet note: this call for a little less self-righteousness, especially within the anti-apartheid movement, was made within the context (indeed, within the same article) of Conor's declaring himself in favor of a full-scale blockade of South Africa by the major powers. The Soviet Union and the United States should act in concert to force Pretoria to turn its guilt into active dismantlement of apartheid. He wanted a real boycott, with no cracks in it.

The one kind of boycott that Conor would not accept, however, was one on ideas, and this led to his great clash with his former allies in the anti-apartheid movement. Major segments of the academic establishment in the English-speaking world, as expressed in several learned societies, had come by the mid-1980s to favor an "academic boycott" of South Africa. This had three aspects. The first was that academics employed in South African universities were not to be invited to conferences or otherwise made part of collective intellectual exchanges. This ban, where enforced, had the greatest impact on black and "coloured" lecturers and professors in South Africa, most of whom taught in the underfunded segregated universities, and had fewer resources to help them get around the ban than did teachers in the white universities. Second, several intellectual organizations and publishers refused to accept subscriptions for journals or orders for books and microfilm from South African universities or professors. The purpose was to cut off South Africa from ideas and techniques that were developing elsewhere. And, third, no one from outside was supposed to go to a conference or to accept a university engagement in South Africa, without the permission of the African National Congress. This part of the boycott was a filter that inhibited those foreign visitors who were opposed to apartheid (and therefore tended to respect the ban), while simultaneously having no influence on those who did not. In other words, it strengthened the proponents of apartheid, while weakening the opponents, a perfect example of that great ability of human beings to create systems that do exactly the opposite of what they are intended to do.

Nevertheless, the African National Congress favored the academic boycott. However, longtime white opponents of apartheid did not. The South African novelist Alan Paton told the Irish journalist Dennis Kennedy (who was covering Africa at the time) that "of all the crazy things, to impose an academic boycott is the craziest."[59] Helen Suzman, a leading white opponent of apartheid, was a bit more forgiving. "If these boycotts do you good, then use them," she said, directing her comments to foreign anti-apartheid campaigners, "but they don't do us any good."[60]

Much of the material for Conor's essay "What Can Become of South Africa?" had been collected in October and November 1985 and at that time he had broken the academic boycott. He was denounced by his old colleague, the head of the Irish movement, Kadar Asmal, who said that the people of South Africa had asked people like Conor to stay away.[61] Conor never responds well to pressure and when he found that one of the Irish groups backing the academic boycott was a set of lawyers headed by Sean MacBride, it only served to push him strongly in the other direction. So, when Conor received an invitation to return to the University of Cape Town, where he had lectured previously, he accepted. Cape Town along with the University of Witswatersrand in Johannesburg at the time were the two most racially integrated universities in South Africa and he planned to speak at Wits as well as Cape Town.

Patrick, Conor and Maire's black son (technically, in the world of apartheid he would enter, "coloured") wanted to make the trip and Conor agreed. Patrick was rising nineteen, a good athlete who knew how to take care of himself. Conor proposed to Leon Wieseltier of the *New Republic* that he and Patrick together write some articles that would show their individual responses to South Africa.[62] To this Wieseltier agreed, and the articles were written and published.[63] Like knights in an Arthurian romance, Conor and Patrick had some adventures along the road.[64]

Conor was to spend five weeks teaching, most of it in the Department of Political Studies at the University of Cape Town (UCT). He was also to give a couple of lectures at Wits. His primary host at Cape Town was Professor David Welsh, head of political studies, and at Wits the host was Professor A.W. Stadler, head of the Politics Department. The main lectures at Cape Town were to be part of a sequence titled "The Politics of Siege Societies," a jointly taught course with Heribert Adam, a professor of sociology and anthropology at Simon Fraser University, Vancouver.[65] Adam was a frequent visitor to South Africa, a strong opponent of apartheid and among his recent publications was a volume, co-written with Kogila Moodly, entitled *South Africa without Apartheid: Dismantling Racial Domination*. Adam taught the first part of the course and his lectures did not engender any student protest.

Because of the furore that occurred, one can miss that Conor was on the edge of working out what Max Beloff had rightly pointed out in his review of *The Siege*, namely, that there is a difference between those nationalisms which have been concerned with overthrowing foreign domination (Czech and Polish, for example) and those concerned with the preservation "of an area of settlement whose very title is in question ... Ulstermen, Israelis, Boers."[66] Each of these three, Afrikaners, Israelis, and Ulster Protestants, was under siege, surrounded by a hostile majority. To recognize these similarities, while working out the moral differences among the three societies, was a subtle task, and I suspect that if Conor had not been bashed about so badly in Cape Town, he would have essayed it. (As it is, he settled for a polished set of lectures, *God Land: Reflections on Religion and Nationalism*, the Massey Lectures at Harvard, 1987, which only dealt allusively with the relationship of these three cases.)[67]

Before leaving for South Africa, Conor wrote a piece for the London *Times* that turned him from just another breaker of the academic boycott into the Cape Crusader. On 6 September, 1986, a column ran over his name, with the title "Apartheid is wrong, but the rot starts here." The subheading read: "Conor Cruise O'Brien on the sinister implications of a British ban on visiting South African archaeologists." The reference was to the conference of the International Union of Pre-Historical and Proto-Historical Sciences, due to be held that month in England. The British organizers had banned all South African scholars from participating (including, ironically, one whose work solidly disproved the Afrikaner myth that there had been no indigenous settlement in most areas of pre-white South Africa). Conor denounced this as mind-control and then ended his article as follows. "Personally, I am off to Cape Town accompanied by my black son. ... I should be glad to have my visit taken as a demonstration of solidarity with the staff and students of the University of Cape Town. Also as a gesture of defiance against an intellectually disreputable attempt to isolate what I know to be an honest, open, and creative intellectual community."

Undeniably, Conor was going to South Africa with an attitude. One can only guess why, but I think that it had something to do with Patrick and something to do with Conor's abhorrence of racialism, and that these two matters were tied together by Conor's feelings as a father. Earlier, in the 1960s, when he was vice-chancellor of the University of Ghana, Conor had been forced to deal with the difficult question of the extent to which Western education, ideals, and standards should bend before African realities. He had been willing to be flexible on this, while sticking to certain basic minimal protections of academic freedom. Now, he was facing a more difficult version of the same problem. A common (but far from universal) view among anti-apartheid campaigners was that the ideas of free speech and inquiry, and academic freedom were an irrelevance at best, an impediment and an obscenity at worst, in the fight for South African racial liberation. Conor believed that one could have the best of Western culture and also have African democracy. What he distrusted was the implicit racism, deeply buried, of those white radicals who believed that the blacks and "coloureds" could not take in Plato and Nelson Mandela at the same time. And he was equally unimpressed with the racism of those nonwhites who refused to consider whole sets of ideas simply because of the skin color of their originator. These racisms Conor would not wear quietly at any time, but now, with his son along, the stakes were higher. In fighting these two forms of racism that were so deeply wound into the Cape Town "progressive" community, he was implicitly trying to carve out a position in the larger world, a zone of Enlightenment, in which his own son could live.

Conor began teaching his classes on 15 September and for two weeks there were no protests or attempts to disrupt the lectures.[68] Conor agreed, in addition to his regular teaching duties, to take part in a lunch-hour debate to be held under the auspices of the Social Sciences Students Council on Thursday, 2 October. The topic was to be the merits of the academic boycott.

He was set up.[69]

Instead of taking part in a debate, he was permitted to speak for about five minutes and then was subjected to serial questioning, mostly by white radical students. Blacks were present, but did not participate, although "coloured" and Indian students did. He was cross-examined and yelled at for about two hours. Now, the interesting point in this encounter—aside from watching a man nearly seventy years old holding his own against 250 heckling youths—is not that Conor lost his temper (he called the academic boycott Mickey Mouse, for he wanted the real thing, a superpower blockade). It is *when* he lost it: the videotapes of the confrontation show that the point at which he became really vexed, and therefore verbally aggressive, was just after he had made reference to being at the university with his black son. Immediately, the audience hooted and started hissing. "What is the ideological signification of that?" he asked, and from then on Conor was anything but conciliatory.[70]

Conor continued to teach his usual classes, but there was trouble the next Tuesday, 7 October. This was at another speaking invitation which he had accepted—over and above his required teaching—this one to the Jewish Students Association. At midday, a procession of students, led by the members of Azaso (the Azanian Students Organization, one of whose more vivid mottoes at the time was "One Settler, One Bullet"), had marched on the vice-chancellor's office, demanding that he cancel the remainder of Conor's lectures. (They carried a large sign, one side of which read VIVA UDF [United Democratic Front], and on the flip side, to taunt Conor, was VIVA IRA.)[71] The vice-chancellor said no, he would not cancel Dr. O'Brien's lectures, but that any other talks Conor gave would be held under the university's "Special Rules." This meant that only persons with university registration or staff cards would be permitted to attend.[72]

The lecture Conor was to deliver to the Jewish Students Association was on the history of modern Israel and this lecture was the commitment that Conor was most predisposed to honor. His emotional identification with the state of Israel was great and, further, he was convinced that the group most apt to be victimized in any widespread turmoil in South Africa would be the Jews: nonwhites would target them and the other white groups would give them up. So, this lecture on Israel was an act of solidarity with the Jews.

The lecture was scheduled for 8:00 in the evening and well before time about 100 protestors arrived. They refused to show their registration cards and enter the lecture hall, but stayed outside, and when the proceeding started, tried to make so much noise that the lecture could not be heard. After about half an hour, they broke down the doors. It was a very messy scene. Dr. Stuart Saunders, vice-chancellor, was in the chair, and he declared the meeting over. Conor, convoyed by some of the Jewish students, managed to get out a side door.[73]

Conor had a regular class scheduled for the next morning, and he was resolved to teach it. This time twelve campus security men controlled the entrance. Only class members were let in and when the number of protestors grew to about 150, the security men barricaded the door with two tables. Outside the door, they linked arms and tried to keep the demonstrators out. There was a general fracas, and one demonstrator used his belt buckle to slash at a security man. The protestors broke in and Conor, protected by some of the seventy-odd students in his class, fought his way out, through students who were trying to punch him.[74]

Conor and Patrick flew the next day to Johannesburg, where Conor was to deliver a lunch-time lecture at Wits. He still had three more classes to teach at the University of Cape Town. "I will certainly return," he said. "I will be teaching my classes if I can." He added, "Obviously, if some students try to knock down doors this makes teaching difficult because it disrupts concentration."[75]

Meanwhile the Cape Town vice-chancellor, Stuart Saunders, was taking his stand. "All these events are being gone into very thoroughly and the university will take the appropriate action when all the facts are known."[76] One did not have to be a soothsayer to know what that meant.

So, on Friday, while Conor and Patrick were at Wits, the vice-chancellor telephoned. He asked Conor a hypothetical question: would Conor be willing to cancel his remaining lectures if the consequences of those lectures would be violent? Yes, Conor agreed. The vice-chancellor rang off and two hours later, after talking to his advisers, he called back. There was danger of violence, he said. Conor, therefore, agreed to cancel.[77]

One should be neither surprised nor angered by the vice-chancellor's reaction. He was simply following what was standard operating procedure for university heads throughout the English-speaking world. One would be hard pressed to draw up a list of even a dozen instances where, during the 1980s, the heads of major universities in the English-speaking world acted decisively to protect the freedom of academic debate from those within their own institutions who used force to suppress it. Vice-Chancellor Saunders said to a reporter that he had told Conor: "I cannot tell you how pleased I am that you have withdrawn as I would hate to tell anyone that they could not speak at UCT."[78] That was heartfelt relief.

Conor and Patrick returned from Wits and, as a courtesy to his friends in the Political Studies Department, Conor gave a final lecture at an off-campus venue. This was virtually a secret lecture, attended by about forty persons, two-thirds undergraduates and the rest staff.[79] Conor discussed, among other things, "the enemies of human reason stalking the campus."[80]

Then he and Patrick headed home to Dublin. The very day that Conor gave his underground lecture, Vice-Chancellor Saunders announced that the university council was appointing a three-man commission to investigate what had happened. Not surprisingly, in the final report of 18 December 1986, the vice-chancellor came out fine, as did campus security and, indeed, as did the protesting students. The real problem was Conor and the Political Studies Department for having invited him. The events were presented as fundamentally political, and seen as "learning experiences in the future progress of non-racial education at UCT. The O'Brien episode was a contrived event which resulted in a hiccup in the process of integration and may one day be seen in retrospect as a lesson and not a disaster. It should not be allowed to divert UCT from its primary task."[81] As, manifestly, it had not.

But if that primary task was political, as the university's report tacitly affirmed, namely, to lead South Africa into a nonracialist future, its creators might have done well to monitor its language. The *Report*'s chronology of occurrences was concluded this way: "Shortly after that Dr. O'Brien and his adopted son left South Africa."[82] Within the racially sensitized mind-set of South Africa, that was a coded insult and, although it was probably unconscious in origin, both Conor and Patrick knew full well what it meant. It meant that Conor and Patrick could not, by virtue of their being of different races, really be father and son.

It is against such beliefs that all cultural institutions, even universities, require the unsettling leaven of human reason.

• • •

If Conor as a father was idealistic, eccentric, risk-taking—not many middle-class parents take their sons to serious academic punch-ups—he was withal successful. A good, if unusual father.

In matters of family, what Conor had never been, or had, in his life, was a brother. His cousin Owen Sheehy-Skeffington was the closest thing to a brother that he experienced and their ages were just far enough apart to keep them from the daily push-and-shove that good brothers, as alter-egos, provide for each other.

In his later years what Conor had instead of a brother was Edmund Burke, a distant ancestor. Conor's biography of Burke, *The Great Melody*, published in 1992, was both the summit of Conor's intellectual career and, indirectly, a summation of himself.[83] The book is monumental in the traditional sense—it is big, nearly 700 pages, and dense with scholarship—but also big in the sense that it is intended to be a monument to the person Conor believes encapsulated the best in Irish civilization, Edmund Burke. And this despite Burke's having had to overcome much of the worst that was Irish, especially deep religious prejudice.

The "Great Melody" of the title is a phrase of William Butler Yeats that refers to the inner harmony of Burke's variegated writings, as found in the four great causes of his life—Ireland, the American colonies, India, and France, and his "great melody" against "it"—"it" being the abuse of power in each case. As Conor says, acknowledging his own debt to Yeats's reading of Burke, "The poet's eye detected that point of vantage from which we can descry, rising high above the confusion of woods and rocks in the valley, the central commanding range of Burke's political thought and action: a range of four majestic peaks, three of them shining clear, and one always partly shrouded in its native mists."[84]

Yeats's musical image is appropriate not only to Burke but also to the way that Conor writes about Burke. I believe that *The Great Melody* will be ranked among the great biographies of the twentieth century, but its character can be appreciated only if one realizes that Conor, like one of the great innovative Renaissance composers, refused to accept the musical forms as they existed. *The Great Melody* breaks out of standard forms. Its subtitle, *A Thematic Biography and Commented Anthology of Edmund Burke*, tells us that we will be hearing something new, not just in substance but in form. Burke in this study is allowed for long passages to speak for himself, and then, at points Conor interprets him, and at still other points Conor argues—with himself, with Burke scholars and with Burke himself—about what this all means and where it is leading. It sounds disorganized, but it is not, for the Great Melody—both Burke's and now Conor's—holds everything together, with passion, respect, and love for perhaps one of the greatest of Irishmen, ever.

But Conor not only introduces a new musical form for this great melody, he also has his own unique performance mode. He does not hide anything. No artifice for its own sake. Thus, *The Great Melody* starts with the equivalent of a prolonged orchestra tune-up: twenty-five pages on previous Burke scholars, rehearsal matters that could have been condensed into one or two longish footnotes. In this tune-up, a heavy staccato is tapped on the head of the late Sir Lewis Namier, whose gnawing on history's pages had blighted British historiography from the late 1920s well into the 1960s. J.H. Plumb, reviewing *The Great Melody*, said, "This important book should have been written and published twenty years ago when it would have blown sky-high what still remained of the Namierite attitude to Edmund Burke—that he was a man of no significance, full of claptrap, hypocritical ideas and corrupt instincts. The scholarly sheep whom Namier employed followed faithfully in their master's footsteps. Such views were a disgrace to scholarship."[85] By the 1990s, however, the Namierite tunes were old, listened to, like Ediphone recordings, only for their archival value.[86]

When he stops tuning the orchestra, the Burke that Conor presents is a man rescued both from being English and from being conservative. He is Irish, and in his rage against power's abuses, a liberal. Emotionally, Burke was formed during the eighteenth-century penal era, when Catholics in Ireland were severely disadvantaged. "Given the tremendous tensions of his upbringing, in the Ireland of the Penal Laws, if you can't understand Burke's relation to the land of his upbringing, you can't understand Burke."[87]

The centrality of Burke's emotional base in Ireland to his entire Great Melody is demonstrated compellingly in Conor's textual analysis of Burke's writings. This demonstration is entirely based on sources that are convenient to public access. This point must be emphasized because there is a second set of assertions about Burke's relationship to Ireland, assertions that are biographical, probabilistic, inferential, and, in places, speculative. These concern Burke's early life, a period for which there is limited documentation. Particularly important is the position of his father, whom Conor argues probably had converted to Protestantism. These details about Burke's early life aid the larger discussion of Burke's text, for they fill in motive, but even if these biographical points prove to be less probable than Conor suggests, that would not affect his fundamental argument. (In history, as in empirical medicine, one can frequently identify the nature of a phenomenon long before one works out the interior details of how it operates.)

What Conor suggests concerning Burke's family background and his childhood is an expansion of ideas that he first published in 1968 in an introduction to the Pelican-Penguin edition of Burke's *Reflections on the Revolution in France*. This was the idea, based on research in the Conformity Rolls done by Conor's daughter Fedelma, that Edmund Burke's father *"may"* have been brought up a Catholic and had conformed to the Established (that is, Anglican) Church in order to facilitate his advancement in the practice of law during the penal times. Also, since Burke's mother was born a Catholic, Burke for a time was educated among her people—the Nagles—in a hedge school by a *"presumably"* Catholic teacher named O'Halloran in a ruined castle at Ballyduff, County Cork.[88] Later, Fedelma did more research on these matters, and Conor also dealt with scholars of the area and local antiquaries. The "may" and "presumably" were virtually erased. In the case of O'Halloran, he is described as a Catholic hedge schoolmaster, no doubts.[89] And in the case of Burke's father, the new evidence "comes close to demonstration"[90] that not only was he a convert to the Established Church in 1722, but one whose early career is established. This evidence arose from the elder Burke's apparent involvement in a case that led to an execution in 1720, when he was practicing law as a Catholic, in the penumbra of the penal laws, which winked at such transgressions by Catholics, as long as they did not rise too high (which explains his conversion in 1722). (The specific case involved one James Cotter, a relative by marriage of Edmund Burke's mother; he was executed on the charge of raping a Quaker woman, a charge that was considered to be political-judicial murder by his relatives and fellow County Cork Catholics.)

The effect of this "demonstration" of the identity and conversion of Burke's father is that Conor is able to explain graphically the nature of life in the Burke-Nagle alliance. "They permanently inhabited a zone of insecurity, in which habitual reticence was the norm, and dissimulation an occasional resource."[91] Conor is thus able to delineate a crucial cleavage in eighteenth-century Irish history, involving the relationship of families such as the Burkes and the vaunted patriots of the alleged golden era of Irish parliamentary independence, symbolized by Henry Grattan. "In reality the 'people of Burke' and the 'people of Grattan' were two distinct peoples, then in an adversarial relation to one another. Grattan's people were the Anglo-Irish, Protestant by religion, and of

English origin. Burke's people were Irish Catholic gentry of Hiberno-Norman stock long merged with Gaelic gentry. Conversions were important legally but, partly for that reason, did not bridge that gap, socially."[92]

If one grants Conor's argument that it is highly probable (not as high as Conor thinks, but high) that his identification of Edmund Burke's father is correct, then his reconstruction of Edmund Burke's formative years is compelling. It provides Burke's biographer with the most effective kind of unity, emotional. There is a strong emotional unity in Burke's family having been strongly Catholic, the only recent convert being his father. Burke's mother, Mary Nagle, had conformed briefly at the time of her marriage, but had remained a practicing Catholic all of her life. Edmund, from age six to twelve, was sent to live with a maternal uncle in Ballyduff, and there attended a Catholic hedge school. Only at age twelve, in 1741, did young Edmund leave this Catholic environment to attend a boarding school. Then he went on to Trinity College, Dublin, and to a career in a world in which adherence to the Established Church was axiomatic.

The basic outline of events is convincing. The interesting points come at the moments when Conor has to convince himself. For example, he puts forward the idea that although there is no record of the marriage of Burke's father and mother in the Anglican church records for the diocese of Cloyne, and "there is no record of a Catholic marriage, but there *must* have been one [emphasis added]. Mary Burke is known to have been a believing Catholic and could not have been content with the Anglican ceremony alone."[93] As for Edmund Burke's religious upbringing, Conor says, "there never was any danger that a party of red-coats would be sent down to Ballyduff to stop little Edmund from attending Mass with his uncle. *I feel sure* [emphasis added] that he did attend Mass regularly. Patrick Nagle would have assumed, if he was not directly told, that his sister Mary would want her son to get as much as possible of a Catholic upbringing, which could be achieved with much more security in Ballyduff than in Dublin."[94] And, in a footnote that refers to "local tradition," Conor states: "*It is virtually certain* [emphasis added] that the Nagles, like other Catholic families who managed to hold on to some land, would have had a clandestine priest, either a secular or a regular, living under their protection."[95]

None of these statements is improbable, but none of them is well documented. If, say, each has a two-to-one chance of being correct, the odds are that at least one of them is not correct. Of course historians have to make guesses frequently (call them informed speculations, call them intuitive interactions with the evidence; they are still guesses).

The salient point is that in each of these revealing instances, Conor makes all of his guesses fall on one side of the probability tree. And this is done in the particularly problematic area of Burke's early family life.

Conor's family life and Burke's were intersecting: this intersection first occurred when Fedelma sussed out Burke's father's conversion. That related to Burke's paternal side, seemingly, but what it really did was open the way to a recognition of the importance of his maternal ancestry, the Nagle side. "The mid-Blackwater Valley in which Burke was brought up from his sixth to his eleventh year was different, in the early eighteenth century, from the anglicised East Coast, not only in religion, but in language. The vernacular of the Nagle country was Irish Gaelic. Edmund's Nagle relatives spoke Irish, although they also spoke English, and probably some French as well. In the hedge school, which prepared children for the real world, English would have been the medium of instruction, but at times of recreation the language would have been Irish."[96]

Although the discovery that Edmund Burke's father probably was a Catholic who conformed to Anglicanism for careerist reasons permits Conor's emphasis upon the Catholic-Gaelic culture of the Blackwater Valley, it does not suggest it. Where do the guesses (good ones, but guesses) about the multilingual culture and upon the importance of the Irish language in Burke's background come from? Answer: from Conor's own family. While writing early versions of Burke's childhood, Conor did not pay much attention to the possibility of Burke having a Gaelic-Catholic cultural heritage. But Maire, with her own intense devotion to Gaelic Ireland, virtually forced Conor to deal with this issue— one that because of the association of Gaelicism with some aspects of the northern Troubles, he was not predisposed to consider. According to Conor, Maire did not speak to him for three weeks at one stage, because of his then-refusal to investigate the Gaelic-Catholic stratum of Burke's personality; according to Maire, the marriage almost ended on this fulcrum point.[97]

This recognition of family as the organizing construct, as the clearest path to an understanding of the interaction of the minds of Conor and of Edmund Burke is not difficult. The road is clearly sign-posted. Not only does Conor in his acknowledgment thank each of his children, but he does so in more than the usual ritualistic manner by which authors try to gain forgiveness for having been impossible human beings around the house while writing a book. Crucially, Conor invokes his own father, Francis Cruise O'Brien, whose predicament as an agnostic (in the days when the Roman Catholic Church in Ireland had, if anything, more power than did the Established Church in penal times), was not

unlike the predicament of Richard Burke, Edmund Burke's father. Each
had to ask, Does one conform? And if so, how does one keep alive and
pure some secret part of one's own identity, and how does one pass that
on to the next generation?

The intermingling of families, Burke's and Conor's, is pivotal because, in *The Great Melody*, Conor is writing about his own "brother";
and no one can write about his own brother without writing about himself. Therefore, the book is a formal biography of Edmund Burke and
an encoded and reflexive autobiography of Conor Cruise O'Brien.

Conor *knew* Burke. Not merely his writings—he could quote by
memory or paraphrase virtually every word Burke ever published—but
he occasionally spoke of him in a way that unnerved his friends. Brian
Garrett remembers a time that Conor was visiting him in Belfast. They
talked about how the biography was going and after a time, Brian said,
"Conor, I don't like what you are doing. For this reason: it sounds to
me that you're doing what you've always said you should never do.
Lionize and worship." He added, "Why, it's as if Burke is in this room."

Conor replied, "He is in the room. He is here. Now."[98]

That was not drink speaking, or flippancy, or hubris. Conor felt the
presence of his brother.[99]

One can easily compose a list of nearly three dozen parallels between
Edmund Burke and Conor Cruise O'Brien, none forced. The signal
ones are that each was an Irish patriot, raised with a mixed cultural heritage, each made a reputation in the great world, and was reviled in his
own home country. Does that mean that *The Great Melody* was merely
Conor's projecting his life into that of Edmund Burke? No. One can
check his textual references, his reading of Burke's speeches and letters,
and his statements of fact. They are accurate. His guesses and speculations are for the most part clearly labeled. This is very good history
from the technical standpoint.

What Conor achieved in *The Great Melody* is something that happens
very rarely in historical writing. It occurs when a hand, active in our
own time, picks up a glove, old, with a few threads missing, from a long-
gone time; and by a benison of time that will not be repeated, the glove
fits the hand perfectly.

That fit was what Paul Johnson was recognizing when he said, concerning *The Great Melody*, that it is "a book by the greatest living
Irishman on the greatest Irishman who ever lived."[100]

EPILOGUE

Remember the bow.

Conor's biography of Edmund Burke was not only the summit of Conor's life's work, it was also a summary, in coded form, of his own life.

The bow. . .

Conor will continue to write political essays, certainly; books, probably; acerbic letters to the editor, inevitably. Time may not be on his side, but he will use it well.

The bow is that of the Homeric archer, Philoctetes. Here is Conor's explanation of where the bow fits into the life of Edmund Burke:

> The story of Philoctetes, whose bow could never miss and whose putrid wound would never heal, is relevant here. The wound came early. I believe that it came with the humiliating discovery of his father's having conformed, out of fear, and, together with that discovery, the realisation that his own achievement would be based on the consequences of that act of conforming. The metaphorical "bow," which the wounded Burke would use to deadly effect, as the wounded Philoctetes wielded his material one against the Trojans, took the form of a tremendous concentration of mental and spiritual energies in a life-long struggle, not merely against the particular form of oppression which had wounded him in Ireland, but also against abuse of power in America, in India, and at the end, above all, in France.[1]

Conor also was given a bow and with it an equally painful, and permanent wound. The bow had been bent for him by Francis Cruise

O'Brien, but life's arrow had never been sent into flight; Francis died a moment too soon. The suppurating wound Conor experienced because of his father's death never healed, but like Philoctetes and like Edmund Burke, each forever wounded, his bow was deadly. Like Burke, Conor directed volley after volley of arrows at what he believed was oppression, dishonesty, and inhumanity. His beliefs were not always consistent intellectually, but his motives, in his struggle against establishments overweening, were.

Although the wound left by the sudden death of Conor's father cannot be healed, he of course has searched for the balm that explanation would provide. This search has centered not on Francis Cruise O'Brien, but on Conor's second father, Dag Hammarskjold. He had failed Conor, just as Francis Cruise O'Brien had done, by bending the bow, sending Conor forth to do battle, and then, with tragic illogic, disappearing from this earth.

For years, Conor has believed that Dag died as the result of a conspiracy and that is an analgesic: such a belief implies that there is a reason for Dag's death beyond the mere intersection of the laws of conservation of matter and energy, with the harsh realities of central African topography. Discovery of a hidden causality (in this case, a conspiracy) would at least make sense of the otherwise senseless and help to heal by intellectual volition a wound that is emotional in origin.

This reaching for a rational explanation for the rationally inexplicable began almost immediately after the event. As Conor said in *To Katanga and Back*, "In Elisabethville, I do not think there was anyone who believed his death was an accident."[2] Certainly not Conor.

The investigation of the crash (officially conducted by the government of Rhodesia, but with the technical forensics done by a team from the International Civil Aviation Organization, and with very strong involvement by individuals appointed by the Swedish government), concluded that pilot error was most likely the cause of Hammarskjold's death, and that no other explanation had any degree of evidentiary probability.[3] Soon after that, the United Nations conducted its own "investigation" which consisted of studying the evidence of the previous inquiry and talking to a few more witnesses. Then, in quintessential UN fashion, the conclusion was reached that no conclusion could be reached.[4] Considering that there was no "black box" on the plane, this was a safe form of indecision and had the virtue of giving the Swedish government what it most wanted at the time: the opportunity to deny that three of the most experienced pilots in that country's service had been responsible for the death of that country's most distinguished citizen.

Conor, during the 1960s, propagated the idea that there was a "seventeenth man" on Hammarskjold's plane, a Belgian mercenary who slipped aboard, attempted to hijack the plane, caused it to crash, and whose body was subsequently spirited away so that only sixteen corpses were found. The idea is presented as being worth serious investigation in the copious footnotes to *Murderous Angels*.[5] This notion originated (as far as I can discover) in a virtually lunatic collection of tales by right-wing soldiers of fortune.[6] No serious evidence in its favor has ever turned up.

Dag's death remained always on the periphery of Conor's mind, never disappearing, always worrisome. In 1992, Conor and his old friend from the Congo days, George Ivan Smith, wrote a letter to the *Guardian* that introduced another version of the death-by-conspiracy theory. This version could be taken either as an alternative to the seventeenth-man idea, or as an addition to it. (The latter is Conor's view.) Their letter to the *Guardian* reported that George Ivan Smith had collected evidence showing that "European industrialists who controlled Katanga" had sent two aircraft to intercept Hammarskjold's plane. They wanted to talk to him before he met Tshombe "so that they could persuade him to cooperate. They never meant to kill him." The Smith-O'Brien letter states that "Ivan Smith has gathered startling evidence that the industrialists gave their two rogue pilots permission to send a warning shot across the UN plane if it refused to divert to Kamina for consultations. The warning shot must have hit a wire and caused the plane to veer out of control, so that it could not complete landing. On record [note that phrase] is the second man in the rogue plane shouting 'Christ, you have hit it.' It looked like a flying accident. Two official inquiries were complete and found no evidence to the contrary. Why should they if only a wire was hit?"[7]

In an interview given to the *Guardian* at the same time, Smith explained what was meant by "on record." He stated that he had twenty taped interviews, which he had possessed for about five years. These were "originally collected by a friend who was a former senior French diplomat." The diplomat was a very well-known figure in France. "Sometime in the 1970s," Smith explained, "he was approached by some of the mercenaries involved, including the Belgian pilot of the plane that fired the shot. He [the pilot] had ended up being an alcoholic. It seemed he wanted to get it off his chest."[8]

So struck was the Swedish government by the assertion that there were taped interviews of persons who claimed to have direct knowledge of Dag Hammarskjold's death, that in late 1992 they appointed a senior foreign service officer, Bengt Rosio, to check on this item and, further, to sift once again through all the evidence concerning the crash to see if anything else new had turned up. Rosio's conclusion was that there was nothing new. Most interesting, on the matter of the alleged tapes of the Belgian pilot, and others allegedly involved, he found they did not exist. What there was instead, was the reading aloud in September 1981 to George Ivan Smith by former Ambassador de Kemoularia (the man to whom the Belgian pilot made his alleged confession) from his own notes. Further, de Kemoularia was translating into English as he read from the notes.[9] Thus, the tapes as a real source of evidence evaporated.

One might wish away Conor's faith in there being a Hammarskjold conspiracy.[10] Throughout his life, he has had a most unnerving respect for facts: yet, the very reason we should pay attention to his ideas on the circumstances of Dag's death is that they are so out of character and thus revealing. For more than three decades—half his adult life—he has held a theory that has no verifiable factual evidence behind it, and has the heavy weight of probability against it.

I think we are here witnessing something analogous to what would happen if we could bore a hole through the earth's mantle so deep that the upwelling of lava would be vented, hot, alien, and out of control. I believe the matter of Dag's death touches the same inchoate emotional lava that was plumbed that Christmas Day when Conor's Da died. The residual terror of that moment, and of its later analogue, Dag's death, is something Conor can deny, can attempt to understand, but cannot control.

Conor is a big man, a hero. But like most of us, he has needed (but rarely has had) someone to do for him what his cousin Owen did after his father died: turn on the light to protect him in life's dark room.

NOTES

PROLOGUE

1 Throughout the notes, CCOB stands for Conor Cruise O'Brien. Sources: O'Brien interviews and CCOB, "Long Day's Journey into Prayer," *Observer*, 4 Feb. 1979; CCOB, "Thank God," *Listener* 105 (18 June 1981), p. 772; Fintan O'Toole, "The Life and Times of Conor Cruise O'Brien, Part 1" *Magill* 9 (April 1986), p. 22; *Irish Times*, 27 Dec. 1927 (obituary notice). Other circumstantial details from *Irish Times*, 27 Dec. 1927–2 Jan. 1928.

CHAPTER I

1 CCOB, "The Parnellism of Sean O'Faolain," *Irish Writing*, 5 (July 1948), p. 59.
2 The classic account of Father Sheehy is found in W.E.H. Lecky, *A History of Ireland in the Eighteenth Century*, 5 vols. (Longmans, Green and Co., 1913), 2:41–44. This is fleshed out in Philip O'Connell, "The Plot against Father Nicholas Sheehy: The Historical Background," *Irish Ecclesiastical Record* 5th ser., 108 (1967), pp. 372–84. The matter is placed in modern historiographic perspective in S.J. Connolly, *Religion, Law, and Power: The Making of Protestant Ireland, 1660–1760* (Oxford: Clarendon Press, 1992), pp. 228–29.
3 CCOB, *The Great Melody: A Thematic Biography and Commented Anthology of Edmund Burke* (London: Sinclair-Stevenson, Ltd.; Chicago: University of Chicago Press, 1992), p. 54n1, citing the work of Basil O'Connell.
4 Paul Johnson, in *Independent on Sunday: Review* (4 Oct. 1992), p. 33.
5 L.J. Kettle, ed., *The Material for Victory, being the Memoirs of Andrew J. Kettle* (Dublin: C.J. Fallon, 1958), p. 49. A son of Andrew Kettle, Tom Kettle, was later to marry one of Father Sheehy's nieces. For Conor's review of this memoir, see *Spectator* (17 June 1958), p. 847.
6 J.B. Lyons, *The Enigma of Tom Kettle: Irish Patriot, Essayist, Poet, British Soldier, 1880–1916* (Dublin: Glendale Press, 1983), p. 325n3; Andrée Sheehy-Skeffington,

Skeff: The Life of Owen Sheehy-Skeffington, 1909–1970 (Dublin: Lilliput Press, 1991), p. 7. (Note: although the name Sheehy-Skeffington was hyphenated in the first generation, later usage dropped the hyphen.)

7 Kettle, p. 50.

8 See Leah Levenson and Jerry H. Natterstad, *Hanna Sheehy-Skeffington: Irish Feminist* (Syracuse: Syracuse University Press, 1986), p. 4. See also James Meenan, ed., *Centenary History of the Literary and Historical Society of University College, Dublin, 1855–1955* (Tralee: Kerrman, [1955]), p. 355.

9 William O'Brien, *Recollections* (London: Macmillan, 1905), p. 123.

10 Sheehy-Skeffington, p. 7.

11 A photograph of David Sheehy as an MP is found in Levenson and Natterstad, p. 64.

12 One treats this variable Sheehy legend with a bit of skepticism. CCOB, in *States of Ireland* (London: Hutchinson, 1972), p. 20, dates the event to sometime after Queen Victoria's Jubilee (1897) and attributes Father Sheehy's spitefulness to a reprisal for the papal indulgence that permitted Catholics to eat meat on a Friday in Her Majesty's jubilee year. In another version, CCOB, "I became an anti-Imperialist" [forthcoming, *Atlantic*, June 1994], Conor has the sermon being preached in 1887. The texts Conor gives of the sermon are incompatible.

13 William Butler Yeats, *The Autobiography of William Butler Yeats* (New York: Collier Books, 1965), p. 37.

14 For a new assessment, see Frank Callanan, *The Parnell Split, 1890–91* (Cork: Cork University Press, 1992).

15 CCOB, *States of Ireland*, pp. 31–32.

16 See, for example, "An Interview with Conor Cruise O'Brien," *James Joyce Quarterly* 11 (Spring 1974), pp. 201–3.

17 Lyons, p. 325n4.

18 Levenson and Natterstad, p. 4; Sheehy-Skeffington, p. 6.

19 One should correct Richard Ellman's belief that Mary Sheehy was the youngest in the family (*James Joyce* [New York: Oxford University Press, 1965], p. 52). This point would not be worth mentioning, save that birth-order in the Sheehy family directly affected Conor's own life.

20 Sheehy-Skeffington, p. 7.

21 CCOB, *States of Ireland*, pp. 62–63.

22 As is pointed out by Levenson and Natterstad, p. 4.

23 Sheehy-Skeffington, p. 6; CCOB, *States of Ireland*, p. 62.

24 Ellman (p. 52) has the soirées occurring every Sunday night. As the phrase "Second Sundays" implies, two-week intervals were the usual case.

25 Conor has himself made that point about the affectionate toleration with which his contemporaries in Dublin treated Joyce. He has added that Joyce was himself much more fun than his writing would make him appear. In life he was "a figure quite unlike the aloof and superior Dedalus, with whom he is often identified." "Donat O'Donnell," "Joyce at School," *Nation* 187 (6 Dec. 1958), p. 432.

26 James Joyce to Grant Richards, 5 May 1906, quoted in Ellsworth Mason and Richard Ellman, eds., *The Critical Writings of James Joyce* (Ithaca: Cornell University Press, 1959), p. 86n.

27 For a contemporary photo of the house, see Lyons, p. 103. David Norris, *Joyce's Dublin* (Dublin: Eason and Son, 1992), has a more recent view.

28 Ellman, p. 52.

29 See Stanislaus Joyce, *James Joyce's Early Years* (New York: Viking Press, 1958), p. 72.

30 For photographs of Bessie Sheehy in this era, see Levenson and Natterstad, pp. 64–65.

31 Peter Costello, *James Joyce: The Years of Growth, 1882–1915* (London: Kyle Cathie, 1992), p. 140.

32 S. Joyce, p. 72.

33 For a concise history of the institution, see Sean O'Reilly and Alistair Rowan, *University College, Dublin* (Dublin: Eason and Sons, 1990).

34 Thomas F. Bacon wrote in Meenan, p. 67: "I became a member of the College Sodality of the B.V.M., and I still possess a print of the membership roll for 1900, tastefully produced in blue and gold, in which appears the names of nearly all those who were then Members of the Literary and Historical, including James A. Joyce."

35 Costello, p. 142.

36 Eugene Sheehy, *May It Please the Court* (Dublin: C.J. Fallon, 1951), p. 34.

37 Felix E. Hackett, in Meenan, pp. 52–53. See also p. 327.

38 E. Sheehy, p. 35.

39 Ellman, p. 63.

40 Meenan, p. 327.

41 In addition to Lyons's biography of Tom Kettle (cited in note 6), see L.J. Kettle (cited in note 5).

42 The reaction is succinctly analyzed in CCOB, *States of Ireland*, pp. 59–61.

43 Costello, p. 161.

44 How the belief that Joyce was the sole holdout against philistinism became entrenched is interesting, given the fact that (as Costello notes), "he merely seems to have stood among the multitude that did not care one way or another what Yeats thought" (p. 161). The college magazine *St. Stephen's* later accused him of being the sole holdout (Costello, p. 161); his brother Stanislaus retailed the view that James stood out alone (S. Joyce, p. 94). And an earlier biographer, Herbert Gorman (*James Joyce* [London: Bodley Head, 1941], p. 60), states that all the students were coerced to sign, and did so, except Joyce. As Felix E. Hackett notes (in Meenan, p. 57), there is no evidentiary support for this. And the statistics are crushing. However, it is the Joyce of the *Portrait*, the sensitive soul, who has won the popular memory: it is a good story, after all.

45 CCOB, *States of Ireland*, p. 83.

46 Ellman, p. 97; Eugene Sheehy, in Ulick O'Connor, ed., *The Joyce We Knew* (Cork: Mercier Press, 1967), p. 23.

47 At Christmastime, either in 1900 or 1901, Margaret Sheehy produced at 2 Belvedere Place *Caste*, a popular melodrama of the time, with herself and Joyce in the leads (Ellman, p. 97; S. Joyce, p. 111). On 7 February 1905, from Austria, Joyce wrote a long letter to his brother Stanislaus (reproduced in Ellman, pp. 197–99). The letter was mostly literary, but he asked about the people in Dublin about whom he most cared. "Is Skeffington still registrar? Is Maggie [Margaret] Sheehy married? I wrote a postcard once in May—why did she never answer me?" The next sentence shifts tone sharply: "Are the [Sheehy] girls 'snotty' about Nora?" That fairly well sums it up: attachment to Margaret and a fear of the female Sheehys as a group, formed when facing their phalanx at 2 Belvedere Place. Nora was Joyce's de facto wife, Nora Barnacle. For a brilliant study, see Brenda Maddox, *Nora: A Biography of Nora Joyce* (London: Hamish Hamilton, 1988).

48 S. Joyce, p. 151.

49 Ellman, p. 52.

50 Costello, pp. 185–93. Mary Elizabeth Cleary attended the Royal with Joyce and eventually married James N. Meehan, a distinguished physician. One of their sons became professor of economics at University College, Dublin. Mrs. Meehan recalled Joyce as a common, vulgar person who told dirty stories and picked his nose. Aside from the

evidence Costello presents (which is convincing in itself), I find reinforcement in interviews with Dr. Patrick Lynch, who knew the Meehan family well because of his own long association with the Economics Department at University College, Dublin. Quite independently of Costello, he had the same (although not as extensive) information on Joyce and the eventual Mrs. Meehan.

51 CCOB, "Not So Much a City ... More a State of Mind," *Irish Independent*, 1 and 2 Jan. 1988.
52 "An Interview with Conor Cruise O'Brien," p. 203.
53 Costello, pp. 189–92.
54 "An Interview with Conor Cruise O'Brien," p. 203.
55 *St. Stephen's* 2, no. 5 (Nov. 1904).
56 *St. Stephen's* 2, no. 8 (Nov. 1905).
57 Announcement of inaugural address as auditor of Richard J. Sheehy (National Library of Ireland, Dublin, LO P115).
58 Patrick Little, in Meenan, p. 91.
59 Ibid.
60 O'Reilly and Rowan, pp. 1–6.
61 Thomas F. Bacon, in Meenan, pp. 68–69.
62 *St. Stephen's* 2, no. 1 (Dec. 1903). The editor of *St. Stephen's* at this time was Tom Kettle. For a sympathetic biography of William Delany SJ, and a view of the conflict between him and Francis Cruise O'Brien, see Thomas J. Morrissey, *Towards a National University. William Delany SJ (1835–1924). An Era of Initiative in Irish Education* (Dublin: Wolfhound Press, 1983), esp. pp. 244–74.
63 See *A Page of Irish History: The Story of University College, Dublin, 1883–1909, compiled by the Fathers of the Society of Jesus* (Dublin: Talbot Press, 1930), pp. 537–39.
64 *St. Stephen's* 2, no. 5 (Nov. 1904), pp. 112–13.
65 On the 1905 affray, see Thomas F. Bacon, in Meenan, pp. 72–75; *A Page of Irish History*, pp. 539–41; *St. Stephen's* 2, no. 8 (Nov. 1905), pp. 175–76; Sheehy, pp. 19–20. Two notes on sources. The *St. Stephen's* article was produced during the period in which Richard Sheehy was arts sub-editor. Meenan (p. 357) suggests that the material on the fracas (which was part of a larger discussion of the L. & H. by the same author) was written by R. Dudley Edwards, who later became professor of history at University College, Dublin.
66 CCOB, *Great Melody*, p. ix.
67 "I am afraid I don't know much about my Ennistymon connection. My father talked about it to me but he died when I was quite young and I have no data." CCOB to Ivar O'Brien, 5 April 1984, O'Brien papers, Howth, County Dublin—hereafter cited as Howth. This was a reply to a letter of March 1984 which suggested that Conor might be entitled to the honorific of "The O'Brien of Thomand," an honor he was quick to label "highly improbable." Dr. David Fitzpatrick informs me that the O'Briens had lost possession of Ennistymon House (now the Falls Hotel) by 1851. Thus, the gentry background was quite distant.
68 CCOB, "On Being a Jewish Wild Goose," *Observer*, 3 June 1979. Other plausible, but very vague indications of eighteenth-century gentility are found in —— to Cathleen O'Duffy, April 1973 (Howth). On Miss Cruise, see CCOB to Ann McCutcheon [n.d.], O'Brien papers, University College, Dublin.
69 Thus, in Francis Cruise O'Brien's obituary (*Irish Times*, 27 Dec. 1927), Francis's father's occupation is reported as "solicitor." In August 1920 Cathleen Cruise O'Brien married the Irish novelist and satirist Eimar O'Duffy (1893–1935). The O'Duffys had

two children, Brian and Rosalind. They permanently left Ireland in 1925. On O'Duffy, see Robert Hogan, *Eimar O'Duffy* (Lewisburg: Bucknell University Press, 1972).

70 ccob, *States of Ireland*, p. 82; O'Brien interviews.

71 Patrick Little, in Meenan, p. 91 and Appendix, "Biographical Notes," p. 351.

72 For a very useful study, see Barry M. Coldrey, *Faith and Fatherland: The Christian Brothers and the Development of Irish Nationalism, 1838–1921* (Dublin: Gill and Macmillan, 1988).

73 Ibid., pp. 118–21.

74 The Sheehy-Skeffingtons have been well served by biographers: Hanna by Levenson and Natterstad, Frank by Leah Levenson, *With Wooden Sword: A Portrait of Francis Sheehy-Skeffington, Militant Pacifist* (Dublin: Gill and Macmillan, 1983). See also Francis Sheehy-Skeffington, *Michael Davitt: Revolutionary, Agitator and Labour Leader* (London: T. Fisher Unwin, 1908), and Francis Sheehy-Skeffington, *In Dark and Evil Days* (Dublin: James Duffy, 1919). The latter includes a biographical sketch of Francis written by Hanna.

75 Costello, p. 181.

76 Ellman, pp. 162–63.

77 Levenson and Natterstad, pp. 27–28, 76.

78 Roger McHugh, "Thomas Kettle and Francis Sheehy-Skeffington," in ccob, ed., *The Shaping of Modern Ireland* (London: Routledge and Kegan Paul, 1960), p. 125.

79 Lyons, pp. 67–68; *A Page of Irish History*, pp. 489–93.

80 Lyons, p. 83.

81 Levenson and Natterstad, p. 27.

82 Shane Leslie, *The Irish Issue in Its American Aspect* (London: 1918), p. 97, quoted in Trevor West, *Horace Plunkett: Co-operation and Politics, an Irish Biography* (Gerrards Cross: Colin Smythe, 1986), p. 87.

83 Robert Lynd, *Old and New Masters* (London: T. Fisher Unwin, 1919), pp. 200–205. Robert Lynd deserves notice. Now almost entirely forgotten, he was one of the supplest Irish essayists of the first half of the twentieth century. And he weaves his way back into Conor's biography because he was a relation of Conor's first wife.

84 Lyons, pp. 38–41.

85 Meenan, pp. 77, 328; *St. Stephen's* 2, no. 10 (Feb. 1906).

86 Lyons, p. 316n2; Father Delany's portrait is reproduced in *The National University Handbook, 1908–1932* (Dublin: Senate of the National University of Ireland, 1932).

87 *A Page of Irish History*, p. 549.

88 Thomas F. Bacon, in Meenan, pp. 76–77; *A Page of Irish History*, pp. 544–45.

89 Bacon, in Meenan, pp. 77–78; Eugene Sheehy, ibid., p. 83; *A Page of Irish History*, pp. 545–48. *A Page of Irish History*, pp. 547–48, quotes a written version of events set down by Francis Cruise O'Brien. I have not been able to gain access to the full account. Probably it was in the hands of R. Dudley Edwards (see note 65).

90 James Joyce to Stanislaus Joyce, 6 Nov. 1906, quoted in Levenson and Natterstad, p. 21.

91 Eugene Sheehy, in Meenan, p. 82.

92 Lyons, p. 118.

93 "Appendix II" in O. Dudley Edwards and Fergus Pyle, eds., *1916: The Easter Rising* (London: MacGibbon and Kee, 1968), p. 260. The appendix is anonymous. Conor, who has an essay in the volume, believes that the appendix is by Owen Dudley Edwards.

94 This is thoroughly established in the monumental institutional history by T.W.

Moody and J.C. Beckett, *Queen's Belfast, 1845–1949: The History of a University*, 2 vols. (London: Faber and Faber, 1959), especially 1:381–92.

95 W.G. Fallon, in Meenan, p. 98.

96 Brian Inglis, "Moran of the *Leader* and Ryan of the *Irish Peasant*," in CCOB, *The Shaping of Modern Ireland*, p. 111. For technical details of the *Leader*, see Stephen J.M. Brown, *The Press in Ireland: A Survey and Guide* (originally published 1937; facsimile edition, New York: Lemma, 1971), pp. 42–43, 183. "A free-lance periodical independent of party, and freely criticising all parties. Quite sound from a Catholic point of view. In its early days it accomplished remarkable work in favour of the language revival" (p. 183).

97 Conor, in conversation, admits to being puzzled by his father's association with Moran. Certainly Conor had no time for Moran or what he stood for. See "Moranism and Two Nations," *Irish Times*, 13 July 1982.

98 *Freeman's Journal*, 5 Feb. 1907, cited in Levenson, pp. 69–70.

99 Lyons, p. 126.

100 *Freeman's Journal*, 5 Feb. 1907, cited in Levenson, p. 70.

101 For a penetrating analysis of the political context, see Paul Bew, *Conflict and Conciliation in Ireland, 1890–1910: Parnellites and Radical Agrarians* (Oxford: Clarendon Press, 1987).

102 F.S.L. Lyons, *The Irish Parliamentary Party, 1890–1910* (London: Faber and Faber, 1951), p. 196.

103 *Freeman's Journal*, 15 Dec. 1905, cited in Lyons, p. 75.

104 W.G. Fallon, in Meenan, p. 100; *Irish Times*, 29 Dec. 1927 and 31 Dec. 1927; *A Page of Irish History*, pp. 490–91.

105 Levenson, p. 47.

106 *A Page of Irish History*, p. 491.

107 Patrick Little, in Meenan, p. 93; *A Page of Irish History*, p. 491.

108 *Freeman's Journal*, 21 Nov. 1907, quoted in Lyons, p. 130.

109 Ibid.

110 *Freeman's Journal*, 6 May 1908; Lyons, p. 139.

111 W.G. Fallon, in Meenan, p. 101.

112 Lyons, p. 149.

113 Levenson, p. 87.

114 More than three years later, Sheehy-Skeffington was still sufficiently enraged by Kettle's breach of faith to denounce it publicly. See Levenson, pp. 87 and 100*n*32 and *n*33.

115 Levenson, pp. 86–87.

116 *Irish Times*, 29 Dec. 1927; *A Page of Irish History*, p. 492.

117 CCOB, *States of Ireland*, p. 82.

118 Ibid., pp. 81–82.

119 Memorandum, "The French Connection," enclosed in Andrée Sheehy-Skeffington to CCOB, 30 Oct. 1981 (Howth).

120 Hanna Sheehy-Skeffington to Francis Sheehy-Skeffington, 17 June 1908, quoted in Levenson and Natterstad, p. 23.

121 Levenson and Natterstad, p. 24; Cliona Murphy, *The Women's Suffrage Movement and Irish Society in the Early Twentieth Century* (New York: Harvester Wheatsheaf, 1989), p. 28.

122 Levenson, p. 109.

123 Levenson and Natterstad, p. 28; CCOB, *States of Ireland*, p. 82.

124 Francis Sheehy-Skeffington to Kathleen Sheehy, 16 March 1909, quoted in Levenson, p. 80.
125 Francis Sheehy-Skeffington to Kathleen Sheehy, 27 March 1909, ibid., p. 81.
126 Lyons, p. 157.
127 Conor tells this story in several places, with slight variations, but with the substance unchanged. See, for example, *States of Ireland*, pp. 82–83.
128 See Levenson, p. 71.
129 Lyons, p. 203.
130 CCOB, *States of Ireland*, p. 83.

CHAPTER 2

1   O'Brien interviews.
2   The standard, and very readable biography is Trevor West, *Horace Plunkett: Co-operation and Politics, an Irish Biography* (Gerrards Cross: Colin Smythe, 1986).
3   Ibid., pp. 101–2.
4   *Irish Times*, 27 Dec. 1927; Conor's birth certificate (O'Brien papers, Howth).
5   See, for example, West, pp. 87–97.
6   A sound biography of Russell is by Henry Summerfield, *That Myriad-Minded Man: A Biography of George William Russell, "A.E." (1867–1935)* (Totowa, N.J.: Rowman and Littlefield, 1975).
7   Lionel Smith-Gordon's novel of Ireland in 1918–21, *That Basilisk* (London: Thornton Butterworth, 1931) is a straightforward romance, mostly notable for the absence of working-class Dubliners.
8   Lionel Smith-Gordon and [Francis] Cruise O'Brien, *Ireland's Food in War-Time* (Dublin: Co-operative Reference Library, 1914).
9   Lionel Smith-Gordon and [Francis] Cruise O'Brien, *Starvation in Dublin* (Dublin: Wood Printing Works, 1917), p. 6.
10 CCOB, *States of Ireland* (London: Hutchinson, 1972), p. 84, identifies the volume. In no major catalogue is there a version of Lecky's *Rationalism* that is ascribed to Francis Cruise O'Brien and Guy Lloyd, but almost certainly the edition they prepared was that issued for the Rationalist Press Association Limited, and published in 1910 in London by Watts and Company.
11 W.E.G. Lloyd and F. Cruise O'Brien, *Clerical Influences: An Essay on Irish Sectarianism and English Government. By W.E.H. Lecky* (Dublin: Published for the Irish Self-Government Alliance by Maunsel, 1911), p. 29.
12 "Introduction," ibid., p. 1.
13 Ibid., p. 13.
14 Ibid.
15 Ibid.
16 For two of several references to this belief, see CCOB, *The Siege: The Saga of Israel and Zionism* (London: Weidenfeld and Nicolson, 1986), p. 19; Irish Television documentary, "Conor Cruise O'Brien: Making a Stand, Taking a Side," directed by Gerry Gregg, 1986.
17 Thomas A. Boylan and Timothy P. Foley, *Political Economy and Colonial Ireland: The Propagation and Ideological Function of Economic Discourse in the Nineteenth Century* (London: Routledge and Kegan Paul, 1992), p. 160; J.B. Lyons, *The Enigma of Tom Kettle: Irish Patriot, Essayist, Poet, British Soldier, 1880–1916)* (Dublin: Glendale Press, 1983), p. 160.

18   Lyons, p. 176.
19   Thomas Kettle to Alice Stopford-Green, 28 Dec. 1909, reproduced in Lyons, pp. 171–73.
20   Thomas Kettle to John Redmond, printed in *Freeman's Journal*, 29 Nov. 1910, quoted in Lyons, p. 185.
21   Lyons, p. 185.
22   Ibid., pp. 228–44.
23   Thomas Kettle to Alice Stopford-Green, n.d. [late 1909], quoted in Lyons, pp. 155–56.
24   Lyons, p. 199.
25   Thomas Kettle, *Home Rule Finance: An Experiment in Justice* (Dublin: Maunsel, 1911).
26   *The Life of Friedrich Nietzsche*, by Daniel Halévy. With an introduction by T.M. Kettle ([n.p.] 1911).
27   *Christianity and the Leaders of Modern Science ... by C.A. Kneller. Translated from the second German edition by T.M. Kettle* ([n.p.] 1910); *The Day's Burden: Studies, Literary and Political* (Dublin: Maunsel, 1910); *Irish Orators and Oratory,* [edited] *with an introduction by Professor T.M. Kettle* (London: Everyman's Library, 1916); *Poems and Parodies* (London: Duckworth, 1916).
28   Lyons, pp. 157, 159.
29   Richard Ellman, *James Joyce* (New York: Oxford University Press, 1965), pp. 339–40; Lyons, p. 215.
30   *Freeman's Journal*, 23 Sept. 1913, quoted in Lyons, p. 226.
31   *Freeman's Journal*, 6 Oct. 1913, quoted in Lyons, p. 228.
32   Lyons, p. 233.
33   Leah Levenson, *With Wooden Sword: A Portrait of Francis Sheehy-Skeffington, Militant Pacifist* (Dublin: Gill and Macmillan, 1983), pp. 142–47.
34   Summerfield, pp. 161–65.
35   Lyons, pp. 247–51.
36   West, pp. 101, 128, 213–14, 254.
37   Lyons, pp. 251–67.
38   See Thomas Kettle, *The Ways of War* (edited, with a memoir, by Mary S. Kettle) (New York: Charles Scribner's Sons, 1918).
39   Levenson, pp. 175–205.
40   CCOB, "Ireland's Fissures, and My Family's," *Atlantic*, 273 (Jan. 1994), p. 54.
41   This is documented in several places. One of the more interesting is Garret FitzGerald's "Our Republicanism Is More Recent Than We Realise," (*Irish Times*, 29 May 1993), in which the specific German prince is named: Joachim, sixth son of the Kaiser and the only one who, the Irish rebellion leaders thought, had not married a Protestant. In fact, a few weeks before the Rising, he had married: a Protestant.
42   The story of Sheehy-Skeffington's death has often been told. If one makes certain corrections for historical inaccuracies and for her fierce anti-British partisanship, the most moving version, to my mind, is that of his wife. See Hanna Sheehy-Skeffington, *British Imperialism in Ireland being a digest of a lecture delivered in U.S.A. in 1916* (Dublin: Clo na Saoirse, [1918]). Bowen-Colthurst was later adjudged to have been unbalanced at the time and after time as a patient in an asylum was released on half pay. He emigrated to Canada. The son of Hanna and Frank in 1966 recorded that Bowen-Colthurst had died in Canada in 1965 (Owen Sheehy-Skeffington, "Francis Sheehy-Skeffington, Portrait of a Born Rebel," *Irish Times*, 7 April 1966). Family tradition is that Bowen-Colthurst spent his life as a British Columbia bank manager, which, given the nature of Canadian bank officials, is not implausible.

43 David Krause, quoting O'Casey, in "The Conscience of Ireland: Labor, Davitt, and Sheehy-Skeffington," *Eire-Ireland* 28 (Spring 1993), pp. 29–30. This conventional view contrasts with Conor's own interpretation, that both Hanna and Frank were much closer to Connolly's revolutionary socialism than is usually believed. See ссов, "Ireland's Fissures, and My Family's," p. 70.

44 West, p. 149. Extensive excerpts from Sir Horace's diaries for Easter Week are found on pp. 147–56.

45 See the anonymous "Appendix II: Press Reaction to the Rising in General," in O. Dudley Edwards and Fergus Pyle, eds., *1916: The Easter Rising* (London: MacGibbon and Kee, 1968), pp. 251–71.

46 Mary S. Kettle, "Memoir," in *The Ways of War*, p. 32.

47 Robert Lynd, "The Work of T.M. Kettle," in *Old and New Masters* (London: T. Fisher Unwin, 1919), p. 205.

48 Mary S. Kettle, p. 32.

49 Lyons, p. 294.

50 Lynd, pp. 202, 203.

51 West, p. 85.

52 Richard Ellman (p. 412) reproduces a letter "earnest in its sympathy but oddly formal" from James Joyce to Mrs. Mary Kettle, 25 Sept. 1916. Its formality seems odd to Ellman, because of Ellman's misidentification of the former Mary Sheehy with Emma Clery and his overestimation of the degree of former intimacy between Joyce and Mary Sheehy Kettle.

53 Mick Lowe, *One Woman Army: The Life of Claire Culhane* (Toronto: Macmillan, 1992), pp. 47–50.

54 Leah Levenson and Jerry H. Natterstad, *Hanna Sheehy-Skeffington: Irish Feminist* (Syracuse: Syracuse University Press, 1986), p. 108.

55 O'Brien interviews. The official distancing from Kettle on the part of the Irish Free State was much greater. Money for a bust of Kettle to be placed in St. Stephen's Green was raised in 1917. The bust was not ready until 1927, and then, just before the planned unveiling, the commissioners of public works of the Irish Free State insisted on censoring the inscription. They eventually withdrew these objections and finally, in 1937, it was unveiled. In January 1960 the bust was thrown into the pond on St. Stephen's Green (Lyons, pp. 305–6), perhaps as political comment, perhaps as vandalism.

56 ссов, "Questions from History," *Irish Times*, 31 Oct. 1983. For a somewhat less mordant view, see ссов, "The Crime of Captain Colthurst," *Observer*, 3 May 1981.

57 The standard history of the Irish convention is R.B. McDowell, *The Irish Convention, 1917–18* (London: Routledge and Kegan Paul, 1970). See also West, pp. 157–76.

58 West, p. 251*n*25. This relates to our earlier question: Were the people who imported arms in 1914 really committed to violent revolution? In Coffey's case, obviously not.

59 McDowell, pp. 107–10; "Two Irishmen," *Proposals for an Irish Settlement, being a Draft Bill for the Government of Ireland* (Dublin: Maunsel, 1917). The one really off-beat proposal was that in the senate of the new Ireland there would be not only heads of professional associations and universities, but representative peers, plus all the Roman Catholic and Anglican bishops, and the moderator of the Presbyterian Church in Ireland. For that show, they could have charged admission.

CHAPTER 3

1 A sanitized version of the story is found in ссов, "On Being a Jewish Wild Goose," *Observer*, 3 June 1979.

2 Ibid.

3 Leah Levenson and Jerry H. Natterstad, *Hanna Sheehy-Skeffington: Irish Feminist* (Syracuse: Syracuse University Press, 1986), pp. 26–27.

4 Conor O'Brien, *Across Three Oceans: A Colonial Voyage in the Yacht "Saoirse"* (London: Edward Arnold, 1926).

5 O'Brien interviews; birth certificate in O'Brien papers (Howth). The name of "Francis" Sheehy was later corrected to Frances; later in life she became well known as Pam Collins on RTE's "Late, Late Show." In the next generation, Owen Sheehy-Skeffington sorted out the historical debt, and with a new twist. He and his wife named their first-born male child "Francis Eugène." Eugène, in this case, referred in the first instance to the French grandfather of the child, but the name permits the satisfaction of memorializing both Father Eugene Sheehy and Owen's Uncle Eugene which, presumably, had been Richard's intention.

6 O'Brien interviews; Fintan O'Toole, "The Life and Times of Conor Cruise O'Brien, Part I," *Magill* 9 (April 1986), p. 22.

7 O'Brien interviews.

8 Lionel Smith-Gordon and [Francis] Cruise O'Brien: *Co-operation in Ireland* (Manchester: Co-operative Union, Ltd., 1919) and *Co-operation in Denmark* (Manchester: Co-operative Union, Ltd., 1919).

9 Trevor West, *Horace Plunkett: Co-operation and Politics, an Irish Biography* (Gerrards Cross: Colin Smythe, 1986), pp. 182–84.

10 Ibid., p. 187. The first *Irish Statesman* of June 1919-June 1920 is often confused with the second *Irish Statesman* of 1923–30. The latter was edited by George Russell and incorporated within it the *Irish Homestead*.

11 Most recently in CCOB, "Ireland's Fissures, and My Family's," p. 50.

12 Levenson and Natterstad, pp. 164–65; Mick Lowe, *One Woman Army: The Life of Claire Culhane* (Toronto: Macmillan, 1992), pp. 47–50. Young Gary was sent to join the Montreal family after he dropped, with precise calculation, a Thom's directory from the top story of the Culhane family house onto the head of his grandfather Culhane as he approached the front door. The gentleman's life probably was saved by his top hat (O'Brien interviews). Gary Culhane became head of the British Columbia dock workers. Ronan Casey became a successful Hollywood actor.

13 CCOB, *States of Ireland* (London: Hutchinson, 1972), p. 107.

14 West, pp. 202–13.

15 Ibid., pp. 213–14.

16 Joseph J. Lee, *Ireland 1912–1985: Politics and Society* (Cambridge: Cambridge University Press, 1989), p. 57.

17 On the political and religious stance of the Irish newspapers (calibrated from a conservative Catholic viewpoint) and circulation figures, see Stephen J.M. Brown, *The Press in Ireland: A Survey and Guide* (originally published 1937; facsimile edition, New York: Lemma, 1971). For a nicely acerbic survey of the history of the *Irish Independent* by Conor, then a recent Trinity College, Dublin, graduate, see "Donat O'Donnell," "The Fourth Estate: The Irish Independent: A Business Idea," *The Bell* (Feb. 1945), pp. 386–94.

18 First published in 1916 by Henry Holt, New York. The British Isles edition was published in 1920, in London, by George Harrap. The illustrations were by Willy Pogany.

19 Mrs. Cruise O'Brien, *A First Irish Book* (London: J.M. Dent and Sons, 1924).

20 Elisabeth Young-Bruehl and Robert Hogan, *Conor Cruise O'Brien: An Appraisal* (Newark, Del.: Proscenium Press, 1974), p. 6.

21 Roman Catholic Church in Ireland, *Acta et Decreta Concillii Plenarii Episcoporum Hiberniae ... 1927* (Dublin: Brown & Nolan, 1929), pp. 155–56.

22 *Irish Catholic Directory 1945*, entry for 20 February 1944, p. 674.

23 *Divini Illius Magistri*, quoted in John Mescal, *Religion in the Irish System of Education* (Dublin: Clonmore & Reynolds, 1957), p. 23.

24 John Charles McQuaid, *Catholic Education: Its Function and Scope* (Dublin: Catholic Truth Society of Ireland, [1942]), p. 18.

25 On Sandford Park School, see Andrée Sheehy-Skeffington, *The Life of Owen Sheehy-Skeffington, 1909–1970* (Dublin: Lilliput Press, 1991), pp. 27–28.

26 O'Brien interviews.

27 O'Toole, p. 22; O'Brien interviews.

28 W.T. Cosgrave to Richard Mulcahy, 4 March 1925, reproduced in Coimisiun na Gaeltachta, *Report* (Dublin: Stationery Office, 1926), p. 3.

29 *Times Educational Supplement*, 13 Aug. 1921.

30 Ibid., 30 Oct. 1925.

31 D.H. Akenson, *The United States and Ireland* (Cambridge: Harvard University Press, 1973), pp. 158–59.

32 Denis Fahey, "The Introduction of Scholastic Philosophy into Irish Secondary Education," *Irish Ecclesiastical Record*, 5th ser., 23 (Aug. 1923), p. 177.

33 "An Irish Times Profile: Conor Cruise O'Brien," *Irish Times*, 12 June 1969; O'Toole, p. 22; ccob, *States of Ireland*, pp. 107–8.

34 *Boston Herald*, 28 April 1966.

35 ccob, "Long Day's Journey into Prayer," *Observer*, 4 Feb. 1979.

36 "The Oldie Interview: Conor Cruise O'Brien," *The Oldie* (7 Aug. 1992), p. 20. See also ccob, "Thank God," *Listener* 105 (18 June 1981), p. 772.

37 "The Oldie Interview," p. 20.

38 ccob, *States of Ireland*, pp. 109–10.

39 "The Oldie Interview," p. 20.

40 ccob, "I became an anti-Imperialist," [forthcoming, *Atlantic*, June 1994.] The off-spring of David and Bessie Sheehy, it will be noted, managed to avoid being on the side of the angels on each of the three art versus nationalism controversies of their age. They protested Yeats's *Countess Cathleen*, Synge's *The Playboy of the Western World*, and O'Casey's *The Plough and the Stars*.

41 Sheehy-Skeffington, p. 27.

42 Kathleen Cruise O'Brien to James Joyce, 28 October 1928, copy in O'Brien papers (Howth). The original of the letter is in the Poetry Collection, Lockwood Memorial Library, State University of New York, Buffalo. Richard Ellman sent it to Conor as a sidebar to a suggestion that Conor should let Yeats off the hook on his fascism, since "he wasn't a political thinker, his heart had to be touched" (Richard Ellman to ccob, 8 August 1981, O'Brien papers, Howth). Conor replied puckishly and concluded, "I shall not at all attempt to set you right as you would certainly make me very uncomfortable if I tried anything of the kind. I prefer to leave you as you are: that is to say, wrong. I know you like it better that way" (ccob to Richard Ellman, 22 Aug. 1981, O'Brien papers, Howth).

43 O'Brien interviews.

44 On the Monteagle genealogy, see *The Complete Peerage*,—vols. (9:117–19). It was the childlessness of Tom Spring-Rice, and his apparent aversion, for whatever reason, to marriage, that makes it probable that the plan was not some kind of fosterage, but adoption in the full legal sense.

45 O'Brien interviews.

46 *Complete Peerage*, 9:119.
47 CCOB to Rex Cathcart, 14 Oct. 1965 (O'Brien Papers, University College, Dublin).
48 John Silverlight, "Conor Cruise O'Brien: Irishman Extraordinary," *Observer Magazine* (2 Sept. 1973), p. 43.
49 O'Brien interviews.
50 CCOB, *The Siege: The Saga of Israel and Zionism* (London: Weidenfeld and Nicolson, 1986), p. 19.
51 Eugene Sheehy, circuit court judge, died in 1958.
52 Levenson and Natterstad, pp. 152–53.
53 A. Sheehy-Skeffington, p. 48.
54 CCOB, *States of Ireland*, pp. 117–18.
55 CCOB, "The Talk of Dublin," *Atlantic* 271 (Jan. 1993), pp. 117–18.
56 On Owen's influence, see Conor's "Foreword" to A. Sheehy-Skeffington's biography of Owen, pp. vii-xii.

CHAPTER 4

1   R.B. McDowell and D.A. Webb, *Trinity College, Dublin, 1592–1952: An Academic History* (Cambridge: Cambridge University Press, 1982), pp. 423–67.
2   The dates are taken from the *Dublin University Calendar for the Year 1939–40*. The dates did not vary more than a day or two year by year.
3   CCOB, "I Like the Pope—But Not This Visit," *Observer*, 4 April 1982.
4   Andrée Sheehy-Skeffington, *Skeff: The Life of Owen Sheehy-Skeffington, 1909–1970* (Dublin: Lilliput Press, 1991), p. 69.
5   McDowell and Webb, pp. 469–70.
6   Ibid., p. 470. The ban lasted until 1970 when, suddenly, it was no longer a mortal sin to attend Trinity College without the permission of the archbishop of Dublin. Conor, in *States of Ireland* (London: Hutchinson, 1972), p. 124, remarked, "It is not known how this decision will affect the eschatological status of Catholics who attended Trinity while the ban was in force."
7   Kenneth C. Bailey, *A History of Trinity College, Dublin, 1892–1945* (Dublin: Dublin University Press, 1947), p. 78. The entrance examination of the era give a good idea of the level required, which was not high. The TCD English exam asked for an essay on one of several topics (unemployment, the modern novel, school life); the mathematics exam involved only algebra; the history exam asked for a map of Northern Ireland's six counties, with the chief towns, rivers and mountains to be marked. The scholarship examinations were harder, but even so, hardly sophisticated. "Write about one poem in the *Golden Treasury of Longer Poems* which has given you pleasure," was the chief English literature question in 1940 (entrance examination for 1940, Trinity College Library, Dublin).
8   Bailey, pp. 80–83; McDowell and Webb, pp. 445–48.
9   Transcript of CCOB's academic record (Trinity College, Dublin—hereafter TCD).
10 See *Dublin University Calendar for the Year 1938–39*, pp. 22–36.
11 For a list of the fellows in Conor's era, see ibid., pp. 18–19.
12 McDowell and Webb, pp. 436–37.
13 For a list of publications by the TCD staff, see the *Dublin University Calendar for the Year 1938–39*, pp. 69–74. Items range from scientific research to Walter Starkie's "contributions to the Gypsy Lore Society."
14 *Dublin University Calendar for the Year 1938–39*, p. 26.

15 McDowell and Webb, p. 457.
16 Ibid., p. 458.
17 Ibid.
18 Sheehy-Skeffington, p. 37.
19 McDowell and Webb, p. 438.
20 Hilary Term 1940 examinations, in library, TCD.
21 *Dublin University Calendar for the Year 1939–40*, pp. 128–29.
22 Sheehy-Skeffington, p. 37.
23 Ibid., pp. 87–89.
24 *Dublin University Calendar for the Year 1938–39*, p. 26; McDowell and Webb, p. 458. With considerable generosity, McDowell and Webb conclude concerning Starkie, "He was the sort of professor of which every university should have one, but not more than one" (p. 458).
25 O'Brien interviews.
26 For the sizarship benefits, see *Dublin University Calendar for the Year 1939–40*, pp. 22–23.
27 Ibid., pp. 241–42, and transcript of CCOB's academic record.
28 *Dublin University Calendar for the Year 1938–39* and transcript of CCOB's academic record.
29 For the rules on waiterships, see *Dublin University Calendar for the Year 1938–39*, p. 193.
30 The raw data are in Bailey, p. 178.
31 McDowell and Webb, p. 445.
32 For a description of the accommodations as of the mid-1940s, see Bailey, pp. 159–61.
33 In later years, Conor was to summarize Mercier's intellectual career as follows: "I have known Dr. Mercier for many years. We were in the same year at Trinity College and shared rooms. He has an original mind and was acknowledged as one of the best students at Trinity in his day. For some years after graduation he was rather less productive than his friends expected. This was due to certain difficulties in his life and partly I think too that he came into full intellectual maturity rather late." CCOB to Guggenheim Foundation, 14 Dec. 1967, O'Brien papers, University College, Dublin—hereafter UCD.
34 CCOB, Commonplace Book, entry for 12 Feb. 1940, O'Brien papers, UCD. See also Sheehy-Skeffington, pp. 88–89.
35 CCOB, Commonplace Book, entry for 12 Feb. 1940.
36 Ibid., entry for—Feb. 1939.
37 Ibid.
38 O'Brien interviews; the terms of the competition are found in *Dublin University Calendar for the Year 1939–40*, p. 243. On Conor's winning and Mercier's second see *Dublin University Calendar for the Year 1940–41*, p. 421.
39 *Dublin University Calendar for the Year 1940–41*, p. 423.
40 On Gageby's importance, see Gene Kerrigan, "The Life and Irish Times of Douglas Gageby," *Magill* 3 (December 1979), pp. 14–32.
41 For a later-life view of Conor, see Roy Bradford, "Unionism's Eire Ally," *Ulster News-Letter* (8 June 1992), pp. 14–15.
42 Sheehy-Skeffington, p. 69.
43 The *Irish Times* in this era has been very well served by Tony Gray, *Mr. Smyllie, Sir* (Dublin: Gill and Macmillan, 1991), and Brian Inglis, *West Briton* (London: Faber and Faber, 1962), pp. 39–58.

44 Irish Labour Party, *Seventh Annual Report being the report of the Administrative Council for the year 1937 and the Report of the Proceedings of the Annual Conference held on the 4th, 5th and 6th April 1938* (Dublin: Labour Party, 1938), p. 192.

45 Ibid.

46 *Irish Weekly Independent*, 9 April 1938.

47 Sheehy-Skeffington, p. 90.

48 CCOB, Commonplace Book, entry for 24 May 1940. Owen remained a lifelong radical and voice in the wilderness. His subsequent history with the Irish left, however, was not happy. He was thrown out of the Irish Labour party in 1943 for being too radical and deposed in 1950 from chairmanship of the Fabian Society for not being far enough left.

49 Conor, in his later life said that he enjoyed the controversy of his Franco speech, "but I wasn't very serious and I'm not very proud of it." Fintan O'Toole, "The Life and Times of Conor Cruise O'Brien, Part 1," *Magill* 9 (April 1986), p. 24.

50 Owen Sheehy-Skeffington wrote a perceptive memoir of the Hist in the 1930s as a feature article in the *Irish Times*, 5 March 1970.

51 *Dublin University Calendar for the Year 1938–39*, p. 44.

52 *Dublin University Calendar for the Year 1939–40*, p. 45.

53 Ibid., p. 56. On 8 November 1938 Conor read a paper to the society titled "Après Port-de-Piles Quoi?" *T.C.D.: A College Miscellany* (3 Nov. 1938), p. 230.

54 The story has passed into Trinity College folklore. This, the most parsimonious version, is based on an entry in Conor's Commonplace Book for 25 April 1939.

55 Kenneth Bailey to CCOB and Mercier, n.d. 1938 (UCD). The lady in question almost certainly was Christine Foster. On 2 December 1938, the junior dean wrote to Conor stating that "you may entertain Miss Foster in your rooms *one* afternoon a week without asking my permission. If you want to entertain more frequently, you must ask." Kenneth Bailey to CCOB, 2 Dec. 1938, (UCD).

56 Garry Wills, "The Words that Remade America: Lincoln at Gettysburg," *Atlantic* 269 (June 1992), p. 71.

57 O'Toole, p. 24.

58 Mercier's poetry is found in *T.C.D.: A College Miscellany* under the pseudonyms of "Mezz." and "Cal. Feutre."

59 O'Toole, p. 24.

60 *T.C.D.: A College Miscellany* (3 Nov. 1938), p. 234.

61 Ibid., p. 229. Conor's pseudonym here was "Shrdlu," which has no meaning; it was a sequence of letters that frequently came up in the then-prevailing technology, when a line of print broke.

62 *T.C.D.: A College Miscellany* (12 June 1940), pp. 200–201.

63 CCOB, Commonplace Book, entry for 7 Jan. 1940.

64 Ibid., entry for 5 Jan. 1940.

65 O'Toole, p. 27.

66 Published in *T.C.D.: A College Miscellany* (26 May 1939), p. 173. The Somerville and Ross story is found in *Experiences of an Irish R.M.* (London: J.M. Dent, 1944), pp. 205–15.

67 McDowell and Webb, p. 463.

68 *T.C.D.: A College Miscellany* (26 Oct. 1939), p. 1.

69 Ibid., p. 2.

70 The phrase raised hackles. See letter to editor by R.D. French, ibid. (16 Nov. 1939), pp. 42–43.

71 Christine Foster Hetherington interview.
72 CCOB, Commonplace Book, entry for 24 May 1940.
73 Ibid., entry for 18 June 1940.
74 See transcript of CCOB's academic record; "An Irish Times Profile: Conor Cruise O'Brien," *Irish Times*, 12 June 1969; *Dublin University Calendar for the Year 1939–40*, academic calendar on unnumbered preliminary pages.
75 The description of a typical degree conferral of the period is from Bailey, p. 170. Incidentally, it was this same Bailey who, as junior dean, disciplined O'Brien and Mercier for improperly entertaining a lady in their rooms.
76 O'Brien interviews. Again, this is a story one hears in several versions from Trinity graduates of that era.
77 CCOB, Commonplace Book, entry for 3 June 1939.
78 Garret Fitzgerald, *All in a Life: An Autobiography* (Dublin: Gill and Macmillan, 1991), p. 3. The Lynd girls were close friends of Fitzgerald's mother. Other sources: CCOB, *States of Ireland*, pp. 140–41; and interview with Christine Foster Hetherington.
79 *Irish Times*, 26 Aug. 1972 (obituary).
80 The exact dates are not clear. Conor is listed on the Belfast Road Academy (BRA) staff list for 1938–39 as "substitute" (BRA Archives, Belfast, "School Register"). In his Commonplace Book, an entry for 25 April 1939 refers to his being in Belfast.
81 For the early history of the BRA, see A.T.Q. Stewart, *Belfast Royal Academy: The First Century, 1785–1885* (Belfast: BRA, 1985). The BRA, like the other leading Belfast Protestant schools—the Methodist College and the Royal Belfast Academical Institution—drew from a catchment area that ran well into Counties Antrim and Down, areas that were well served by a rail network.
82 John M. Cole interview. A variant version is that Conor said, "Hands up, all those who would be prepared to die for their religion!" Interview with Edward McCamley, archivist of BRA.
83 Conor tells this story without identifying himself as the teacher, in "Holy War," *New York Review of Books* (6 Nov. 1969), p. 14.
84 After leaving the headmastership of the Royal Belfast Academy in 1943, Alex Foster taught as a temporary teacher at the Royal Belfast Academical Institution for the rest of the war years and then, because of his ingravescent manic-depressive syndrome, retired to County Wicklow. Annie Lynd, his first wife, died in 1946, and he married Betty Guidera and became a Catholic. Foster's career in retirement was as a constructive controversialist on both sides of the border. (He and his second wife moved back to Belfast after a time in Wicklow, and later to County Kerry.) He was especially active in anti-apartheid work and was one of the organizers of the protest against the rugby matches with the touring Springbok team of South Africa. (See obituary in *Irish Times*, 27 Aug. 1972, unsigned, but written by George Hetherington, and "An Appreciation" in the *Irish Times*, 3 Aug. 1972, by Conor.) For an indication of Foster's intellectual style, see A.R. Foster, "Derry City: Frontier Stronghold," in Owen Dudley Edwards, ed., *Conor Cruise O'Brien Introduces Ireland* (London: André Deutsch, 1969), pp. 197–200.
85 Christine Foster Hetherington interview; O'Brien interviews.
86 *T.C.D.: A College Miscellany* (9 Nov. 1939), pp. 25–26. The surmise that Conor, at that time the paper's editor, was the author of this item is confirmed by his being the butt of a satirical letter aimed at the editorial's writer (16 Nov. 1939), p. 44.
87 CCOB, Commonplace Book, entry for 24 Jan. 1940.
88 Ibid.

89 Ibid., entry for 21 May 1940.
90 Ibid. I am a touch skeptical of the reality of this entry, chiefly because of the self-dramatizing, almost fictional way it is written.
91 Ibid.
92 Ibid., undated entry [mid-summer 1940].
93 O'Toole, p. 27.
94 McDowell and Webb, p. 113.
95 *T.C.D.: A College Miscellany* (26 Oct. 1939), p. 3.
96 CCOB, *The Great Melody: A Thematic Biography and Commented Anthology of Edmund Burke* (Chicago: University of Chicago Press, 1992), p. xv.
97 Told, without identification of McDowell, in CCOB, "We Shall Be the Masters of Medicine," *Observer*, 25 Jan. 1981.
98 See Letters to the Editor in *T.C.D.: A College Miscellany* (12 June 1940), pp. 201–2, and (20 June 1940), p. 212.
99 "Irish Times Profile: Conor Cruise O'Brien."

CHAPTER 5

1   On the Department of Finance and the "Emergency," see Ronan Fanning, *The Irish Department of Finance, 1922–58* (Dublin: Institute of Public Administration, 1978), pp. 308–404.
2   O'Brien interviews.
3   "An Irish Times Profile: Conor Cruise O'Brien," *Irish Times*, 12 June 1969.
4   Joseph Hone, *W.B. Yeats, 1865–1939* (London: Macmillan, 1942).
5   O'Brien interviews; CCOB, "I became an anti-Imperialist," [forthcoming, *Atlantic*, June 1994].
6   Ibid.
7   O'Brien interviews; "An Irish Times Profile: Conor Cruise O'Brien."
8   D.H. Akenson, *The United States and Ireland* (Cambridge: Harvard University Press, 1973), p. 254.
9   Dermot Keogh, *Ireland and Europe, 1919–1948* (Dublin: Gill and Macmillan, 1988), p. 110. On treatment of Jews, see pp. 100–112, 227n32.
10 Akenson, p. 258. For Conor's analysis of Irish neutrality, see CCOB, "Ireland in International Affairs," in Owen Dudley Edwards, ed., *Conor Cruise O'Brien Introduces Ireland* (London: André Deutsch, 1969), pp. 120–24. "Partition was not the reason why the Irish people felt differently from those of the English-speaking dominions. It was not the reason, it was the symbol" (p. 122). For background, see Patrick Keating, *The Formulation of Irish Foreign Policy* (Dublin: Institute of Public Administration, 1973), and Trevor C. Salmon, *Unneutral Ireland: An Ambivalent and Unique Security Policy* (Oxford: Clarendon Press, 1989).
11 Noel Dorr interview.
12 Brian Inglis, *West Briton* (London: Faber and Faber, 1962), p. 138; Keogh, 239n16; Noel Dorr interview.
13 Vivian Mercier, "The Fourth Estate: 'The Irish Press,'" *The Bell* (March 1945), pp. 475–85; Mercier, "The Fourth Estate: Verdict on 'The Bell,'" *The Bell* (May 1945), pp. 156–64.
14 "Donat O'Donnell," "The Fourth Estate: The Irish Independent," *The Bell* (Feb. 1945), pp. 386–94.
15 "Donat O'Donnell," "The Catholic Press: A Study in Theopolitics," *The Bell* (April 1945), pp. 30–40.

16 "Donat O'Donnell," "Horizon," *The Bell* (March 1946), pp. 1030–38.

17 Mercier, "The Fourth Estate: Verdict on 'The Bell,'" p. 157.

18 "Donat O'Donnell," "A Rider to the Verdict," *The Bell* (May 1945), pp. 164–67.

19 "Donat O'Donnell," "Horizon," p. 1030.

20 Letter of "Donat O'Donnell," dated 3 Nov. 1947, to *Sunday Independent*, 9 Nov. 1947.

21 "Donat O'Donnell," "The Unfallen," *Envoy* 1 (Dec. 1949), pp. 44–50. Letter by O'Faolain, *Envoy* 1 (Jan. 1950), pp. 87–90, and reply by "Donat O'Donnell," *Envoy* 1 (Feb. 1950), pp. 89–90.

22 "Donat O'Donnell," "The Parnellism of Sean O'Faolain," *Irish Writing* 5 (July 1948), pp. 66, 69.

23 His 1948 essay on O'Faolain was republished unchanged in "Donat O'Donnell's" 1952 book, *Maria Cross: Imaginative Patterns in a Group of Modern Catholic Writers* (New York: Oxford University Press, 1952; London: Chatto and Windus, 1953), pp. 95–118. In the second edition of this book (London: Burns and Oates, 1963), Conor wrote in the preface that "Mr. O'Faolain has not, I think, extricated himself creatively from the situation which I have attempted to describe in the essay on him which follows; I have, in any case, found nothing new to say about him." Latterly, he came to appreciate O'Faolain's stature. When O'Faolain died in May 1991, Conor protested that no governmental representative attended his funeral. CCOB, "Pride in the Language," *Irish Independent*, 11 May 1991.

O'Faolain, for his part, was rather more quick to forgive. In an undated letter to Conor (from 1953–54, after the appearance of *Maria Cross*), he was more than merely courteous. "As you rightly observe there are only two urges in Ireland, nationalism and religion. ... The second is a monster. No one could handle it without satire and I am not a satirist. I am a lyric writer who cannot find enough copy." He concluded, "With many thanks for a lot of pleasure and, of course, intense discomfort in being written about at all" (O'Brien Papers, UCD). Paddy Lynch, who saw O'Faolain frequently in the late 1980s and early 1990s, when O'Faolain's health and mind were declining, reported that, in listing men or women of letters in Ireland, he included Hubert Butler, David Greene, Maurice Craig, Elizabeth Bowen, but that he had hesitations about including Conor. Patrick Lynch, "O'Faolain's Way: Pages from a Memoir," *Irish University Review* 22 (Spring-Summer, 1992), p. 144. This may have been another piece of editorial overscrupulousness on O'Faolain's part, for he thought of Conor chiefly as a scholar. As O'Faolain declined sharply, Paddy Lynch tells me, he and O'Faolain would sometimes walk along the sea front after visiting the Dalkey Island Hotel or the Killiney Court, and O'Faolain, no longer able to think of names, would point toward Howth, visible across Dublin Bay and say "That is where that genius lives." He meant Conor.

24 Elisabeth Young-Bruehl and Robert Hogan, *Conor Cruise O'Brien: An Appraisal* (Newark, Del.: Proscenium Press, 1971), p. 7.

25 CCOB to Philip Vaudrin, 29 May 1951 (UCD).

26 Margaret Nicholson to CCOB, 26 Oct. 1951 (UCD); and [Alfred A. Knopf, Inc.] to CCOB, 25 Sept. 1951 (UCD).

27 Seamus Heaney interview in "Conor Cruise O'Brien: Making a Stand, Taking a Side," Irish Television documentary, directed by Gerry Gregg, 1986.

28 CCOB to *Encounter*, 18 Sept. 1963 (UCD). Conor was replying to a review by John Weightman, "The Sexy Cross," *Encounter* (Sept. 1963), pp. 70–73. It is reprinted in John Weightman, *The Concept of the Avant-Garde: Explorations in Modernism* (London: Alcove Press), pp. 270–76.

29 "Literature and Dogma," *Times Literary Supplement* (22 Jan. 1954), pp. 49–50.

30 Tom Paulin, *Ireland and the English Crisis* (London: Bloodaxe Books, 1984), p. 29.

31 The Burns and Oates paperback edition (1963) included an article on Claudel, written shortly after his death, and reviews of two recently published Graham Greene novels, *The Quiet American* and *A Burnt-Out Case*. For Conor's later views of Greene, see "A Funny Sort of God," *New York Review of Books* (18 Oct. 1973), pp. 56–58—a review of *The Honorary Consul* and of Greene's *Collected Stories*—and "Greene's Castle," *New York Review of Books* (1 June 1978), pp. 3–5—a review of *The Human Factor*. For Conor's later view of Waugh, see "Nobs and Snobs," *New York Review of Books* (4 Feb. 1988), pp. 3–4—a review of *Evelyn Waugh: The Early Years* by Martin Stannard.

32 Philip Vaudrin to ccob (6 February 1948, ucd) apologizes for having been "an unconscionably long time in making up our mind about taking on a book about Catholic writing as suggested by your pieces."

33 National Bank Ltd. to ccob, 19 Oct. 1943 (ucd).

34 See, for example, John Lehman (editor of *New Writing*) to Christine Foster O'Brien,—1948 (ucd).

35 "Kate Cruise O'Brien, Biography," information sheet prepared for Association of Teachers of English, conference at St. Patrick's Training College, Drumcondra, c. 1990, p. 1.

36 Christine Foster Hetherington interview.

37 "Irish Times Profile: Conor Cruise O'Brien"; Fintan O'Toole, "The Life and Times of Conor Cruise O'Brien, Part I," *Magill* 9 (April 1986), p. 29; interviews with ccob and with Maire Cruise O'Brien.

38 Margaret Ward, *Maud Gonne, Ireland's Joan of Arc* (London: Pandora, 1990), p. 86. Sean had a half-brother that he never knew about. While in South Africa, fighting on the side of the Afrikaaners, John MacBride had an illegitimate baby with a "Malaysian" woman. This McBride line (the spelling changed) was officially "coloured" under apartheid. Derek McBride, John MacBride's great-grandson, was given the death penalty for a car bombing, but this was not carried out. He became a significant figure in the African National Congress (ibid., p. 87).

39 Like so much in MacBride's life, there was rich irony even here. The rooms at Mount St. Benedict's where Father Sweetman taught Sinn Fein doctrine had originally been part of an estate named "Mount Nebo." It had been the home of Hunter Gowan, one of the most notorious of the anti-Catholic vigilantes in 1798, and the home of Ogle Gowan who, in 1830, founded the Orange Order in Canada. See D.H. Akenson, *The Orangeman: The Life and Times of Ogle Gowan* (Toronto: Lorimer, 1986).

40 Noel Browne, *Against the Tide* (Dublin: Gill and Macmillan, 1986), p. 102.

41 For a very perceptive discussion of MacBride, see Michael Farrell, "The Extraordinary Life and Times of Sean MacBride, Part I," *Magill* 5 (Dec. 1982), pp. 17–30, and "Part II," *Magill* 5 (Jan. 1983), pp. 25–37. Also useful is A.M. Kehoe, *History Makers of 20th Century Ireland* (Dublin: Mentor Publications, 1989), pp. 181–97.

42 Brian Inglis, *West Briton* (London: Faber and Faber, 1962), pp. 114–15.

43 The complexities of Eire's relationship to the Marshall Plan are well analyzed in Bernadette Whelan, "Ireland and the Marshall Plan," *Irish Economic and Social History* 19 (1992), pp. 49–70.

44 The elaborate layers of deception and, later, self-deception on this matter are stripped away very effectively in Ian McCabe, *A Diplomatic History of Ireland, 1948–49: The Republic, the Commonwealth and NATO* (Dublin: Irish Academic Press, 1991). On the totally unexpected—and non-cabinet—nature of Costello's announcement of the republic, see esp. pp. 42, 55, and 149. McCabe's study confirms the fundamental lines of the story told by Noel Browne in *Against the Tide*.

45   Browne, p. 136. The interaction of the United States and Ireland on the NATO issue is succinctly scrutinized in Noel Quirke, "The Irish Refusal to Join NATO in 1949: The American Reaction," in Philip Bull, Chris McConville, and Noel McLachlan, eds., *Irish-Australian Studies: Papers Delivered at the Sixth Irish-Australian Conference, July 1990* (Melbourne: La Trobe University, 1991), pp. 185–200. See also Ronan Fanning, "The United States and Irish Participation in NATO: The Debate of 1950," *Irish Studies in International Affairs* 1 (1979), pp. 38–48.

46   The story of the Republic of Ireland Act and of the guarantees to the northern Protestant population in 1949, usually leaves out the northern Protestants both as actors and as affected parties. An excellent antidote to this is Dennis Kennedy, *The Widening Gulf: Northern Attitudes to the Independent Irish State, 1919–49* (Belfast: Blackstaff Press, 1988).

47   CCOB, *States of Ireland*, p. 139.

48   *Eire*, 14 Oct. 1949. A full set of the sheets is found in the Ministry of Foreign Affairs, Dublin, which generously made them available to me.

49   Ibid., 19 Dec. 1949.

50   Ibid., 6 March 1950.

51   See O'Toole, p. 30.

52   *Finances of Partition* was published in Dublin by Clonmore and Reynolds. *The Indivisible Island* was published in London by Victor Gollancz. If one accepts O'Toole's suggestion (p. 30) that the two books were financed as antipartition propaganda (which I do), it should be noted that the financing could have taken various forms and was not necessarily the same for the two volumes. The most obvious forms of possible subvention were direct payments to the publishers (which I find easily plausible in the case of the Clonmore and Reynolds book, but not in the case of the Gollancz volume); guarantees of governmental purchase of the book in significant quantities; money for the preparation of the manuscript, including research assistance; payment of salaries or honoraria to the authors.

53   Source for identification of Gallagher as primary author is O'Brien interviews, confirmed by article in the *Frontier Sentinel*, 3 Dec. 1949.

54   CCOB, "Who's to Blame?" *Irish Independent*, 21 Oct. 1989.

55   "Distribution of 'Ireland's Right to Unity,'" National Archives of Ireland, Dublin, Department of External Affairs Files (hereafter DFA), 305/14/64.

56   Report of CCOB of his trip to the North, 23–25 March 1953 (DFA 305/14/2/3).

57   Geoffrey Bing, *John Bull's Other Ireland*, 3d ed. (London: Tribune, 1949); Geoffrey Bing, *Set the Pubs Free: An Inquiry into the Monopoly Power of Brewers* (London: Tribune, 1952); CCOB to Patrick Lynch, 13 Jan. 1951 (DFA 305/14/167); "Distribution to date (8 Feb. 1951) 'John Bull's Other Ireland'" (DFA 305/14/167); CCOB to Frank Gallagher, 8 Feb. 1951 (DFA 305/14/64).

58   CCOB to Captain Jerome, 18 Aug. 1949 (DFA 305/14/56).

59   CCOB to Frank Gallagher, 29 Aug. 1949 (DFA 305/14).

60   Frank Gallagher to CCOB, 30 Aug. 1949 (DFA 305/14).

61   "Donat O'Donnell," "L'Unité de l'Irelande et les Irlandais d'Amérique," *Revue Générale Belge* 57 (July 1950), pp. 1–9. Andrée Sheehy-Skeffington says that Owen Sheehy-Skeffington translated this for Conor, but I doubt it. He was quite able to write in French himself. More likely, Owen went over the French. He did not agree with the argument put forward. See Andrée Sheehy-Skeffington, *Skeff: The Life of Owen Sheehy-Skeffington, 1909–1970* (Dublin: Lilliput Press, 1991), p. 146.

62   O'Brien interviews.

63   CCOB to J.D. Brennan, 27 Sept. 1949, and attached correspondence (DFA 305/14/9/2).

64 CCOB to F. Boland, 6 Feb. 1950, and attached items (DFA 305/14/9A).
65 CCOB to Sean Nunan, 30 May 1950 (DFA 305/14/56).
66 T. Woods to CCOB, 29 July 1953 (DFA 305/14/36/2).
67 *Christian Science Monitor*, 4 Dec. 1952, and DFA 305/14/9B.
68 McCabe, p. 147.
69 John Healy, *Healy, Reporter—The Early Years* (Achill: House of Healy, 1991), p. 69.
70 The other one was Conor Cruise O'Brien.
71 O'Toole, p. 29.
72 Browne, p. 92. Noel Browne's verbal sketches of politicians of the period are brilliant, if almost entirely unsympathetic.
73 O'Brien interviews; Douglas Gageby interview.
74 "The Irish News Agency," audited report of start-up expenses, and corporate structure, 19 Aug. 1950 (O'Brien Papers, UCD). See also Healy, p. 61; "An Irish Times Profile: Conor Cruise O'Brien."
75 Inglis, p. 139.
76 Healy, p. 72.
77 Ibid.
78 See "The Life and Irish Times of Douglas Gageby," *Magill* 3 (Dec. 1979), pp. 14–32.
79 Healy, p. 86.
80 O'Brien interviews; Douglas Gageby interview.
81 Healy, p. 70. Paddy Scott, the Belfast bureau chief, is lauded by Healy, pp. 100–103. His abilities were certainly recognized by Conor, who told the northern nationalist leader Eddie MacAteer, "Paddy Scott in Belfast is our bureau chief in the Six Counties and a man of proved discretion as well as enterprise." CCOB to Edward MacAteer, 4 March 1953 (DFA 305/14/108).
82 "Irish News Agency," audited report.
83 Garret FitzGerald, "A Polite Response to Conor Cruise O'Brien," *Irish Times*, 4 Sept. 1993.
84 Patrick O'Farrell, "Fair Exchange. Some Exotic Experiences at Trinity in 1972–73," *Eureka Street* 2 (July 1992), pp. 27 and 29.
85 On Moody's life and scholarly production, see F.S.L. Lyons, "T.W.M." and J.G. Simms, "The Historical Work of T.W. Moody," in F.S.L. Lyons and R.A.J. Hawkins, eds., *Ireland under the Union: Varieties of Tension. Essays in Honour of T.W. Moody* (Oxford: Clarendon Press, 1980), pp. 1–33 and 321–28.
86 O'Brien interviews. Conor's retrospective recognition of Moody's occasional pusillanimity in part comes from his observation of Moody as a member of the Irish Broadcasting Authority and as a member of the Commission on Higher Education, and of Moody's activities as an expert court witness for a variety of cases that paid well.
87 "Donat O'Donnell," "Parnell's Monument," *The Bell* (Oct. 1945), pp. 5.
88 Ibid., pp. 569–70.
89 John V. Kelleher in the *Annals of the American Academy* 314 (November 1957), p. 187. Kelleher's comment was prescient. In fact, Conor's thesis had been titled "The Irish Parliamentary Party, 1880–90."
90 O'Brien interviews.
91 O'Farrell, p. 27.
92 Cormac O'Grada, "'Making History' in Ireland in the 1940s and 1950s: The Saga of *The Great Famine*," introduction to reprint ed. of Edwards and Williams (eds.), *The Great Famine*, typescript, p. 13.
93 T.W. Moody to CCOB, 1 Dec. 1954 (UCD).
94 Davin was on his way to being one of the most influential individuals in scholarly pub-

lishing in the English-speaking world. He became director of the academic division of Oxford University Press. Born in New Zealand in 1907, he also was considered one of the major New Zealand writers of his generation. He and Conor became lifelong friends. A full Davin biography is in progress; for now see my own discussion of Davin in D.H. Akenson, *Half the World from Home: Perspectives on the Irish in New Zealand, 1860–1950* (Wellington: Victoria University Press, 1990), pp. 89–122.

95 R.F. Foster, *Modern Ireland, 1600–1972* (London: Penguin Press, 1988), p. 401.

96 See D. George Boyce, "'The Portrait of the King Is the King': The Biographers of Charles Stewart Parnell," in D. George Boyce and Alan O'Day, *Parnell in Perspective* (London: Routledge, 1991), pp. 298–302.

97 Darcy O'Brien, "Conor Cruise O'Brien," *James Joyce Quarterly* 11 (Spring 1974), p. 216.

98 CCOB, "Paradise Lost," *New York Review of Books* (25 April 1991), p. 55.

99 The sequence of residence changes can be inferred from correspondence. See Alfred Knopf to CCOB, 25 Oct. 1951 (UCD); T.W. Moody to CCOB, 23 Nov. 1951 (UCD); George Trevor Fitzwilliam and Sons to CCOB, 3 Dec. 1951 (UCD); "Irish News Agency," audited statement for 1951 (UCD). The price of "Whitewater" is found in John Silverlight, "Conor Cruise O'Brien: Irishman Extraordinary," *Observer Magazine* (2 Sept. 1973), p. 47.

100 John V. Kelleher, "Ireland ... and Where Does She Stand?" *Foreign Affairs* 35 (April 1955), p. 485.

101 O'Toole, p. 29.

102 For instance, Conor and J.P. Gallagher represented the Irish News Agency at the European Technical Conference of News Agencies held at Brussels on 14 June 1952. The big achievement of that conference was outmaneuvering Reuters, which tried to prevent the INA from receiving an invitation. CCOB to Dr. Rynne, 23 June 1952 (DFA 408/401).

103 CCOB to M. O'Muimhneachain,—Nov. 1954, and attached (DFA 305/14/2). This is after the fall of the Fianna Fail government in 1954, but the network had been a favorite activity of Aiken's.

104 For example, CCOB to Edward MacAteer, 23 Feb. 1954 (DFA 305/14/2).

105 CCOB, "Visit to Six Counties, July 21–22, 1954" (DFA 305/14/2). The visit, which occurred after Aiken left office, had been set up under his administration. This report gives one a good chance to assess Conor's historical memory, as the same incident is reported in anecdotal form in *States of Ireland*, pp. 143–45. Except for the date (which, in *States*, Conor gets wrong, as 1952), his report presented at the time and his later memory correspond.

106 CCOB, *States of Ireland*, pp. 143–45.

107 Ibid., p. 144.

108 O'Brien interviews. Another version of the story is found in CCOB, *States of Ireland*, pp. 147–48.

109 Thus, two-thirds of Conor's report "Visit to Six Counties, July 21–22, 1954" was a straight intelligence report. Much of his report on his 23–25 March 1953 visit to the North also was straight intelligence, the rest of it dealing with various propaganda efforts (DFA 305/14/2/3).

110 In a Dail Eireann debate in 1970, Conor said that he had been in the North "I should think, between 60 and 70 times over a long period beginning in 1940." (246 *Dail Eireann* 1502: 13 May 1970). Even if one assumes that he went north to see his in-laws in the years 1940–47, say, three times a year, and that he made the odd visit during the late 1950s and 1960s (most of that time he was in Africa or in New York), it is clear

that Conor must have made dozens of visits to the North from 1948 to 1954, and these in one way or another were related to intelligence.

111 In *States of Ireland* (p. 145) Conor says that from 1951 onward, he knew the propaganda campaign was futile.

112 See file report on Swedish visit, including translations of press reports (DFA 436/32, and attached).

113 CCOB, "Report on Visit to the Federal Republic of Germany, September 3rd to 17th, 1954" (DFA 436/49).

CHAPTER 6

1 Fintan O'Toole, "The Life and Times of Conor Cruise O'Brien, Part I," *Magill* 9 (April 1986), p. 29; O'Brien interviews; interviews with officials of the present Ministry of Foreign Affairs.

2 Kate Cruise O'Brien, *A Gift Horse and Other Stories* (Dublin: Poolbeg Press, 1978), pp. 10–14; Kate Cruise O'Brien interview.

3 John Silverlight, "Conor Cruise O'Brien: Irishman Extraordinary," *Observer Magazine* (2 Sept. 1973), p. 34.

4 Donat O'Donnell, "Carey Bloom," *Atlantic* 202 (Nov. 1958), pp. 142–46, and 148.

5 Information on personnel from officers of the present Ministry of Foreign Affairs.

6 Ibid.

7 O'Brien interviews.

8 149 *Dail Eireann* 127–226: 3–4 July 1956, summarized in CCOB, "Ireland in International Affairs," in Owen Dudley Edwards, ed., *Conor Cruise O'Brien Introduces Ireland* (London: André Deutsch, 1969), p. 128.

9 O'Toole, p. 29. A compressed version of the story is found in CCOB, "Maybe the World Will Find a Way," *Observer*, 28 March 1982.

10 CCOB, *Conflicting Concepts of the United Nations* (Leeds: Leeds University Press, 1964), pp. 9–11; CCOB, "Standing by at the Slaughter," *Irish Independent*, 6 April 1991.

11 CCOB, *The Siege: The Saga of Israel and Zionism* (London: Weidenfeld and Nicolson, 1986), p. 14.

12 Patrick Keating, *The Formulation of Irish Foreign Policy* (Dublin: Institute of Public Administration, 1973), pp. 88–89.

13 CCOB, *To Katanga and Back: A UN Case History* (London: Hutchinson, 1962), p. 14.

14 Ibid., p. 15.

15 For an analytical discussion of the Swedish model as it applied to Irish foreign policy, see Trevor G. Salmon, *Unneutral Ireland: An Ambivalent and Unique Security Policy* (Oxford: Clarendon Press, 1989), pp. 48–81.

16 Fintan O'Toole, "The Life and Times of Conor Cruise O'Brien, Part 2," *Magill* 9 (May 1986), pp. 26–27.

17 Ibid., p. 27.

18 This story is found in CCOB, *To Katanga and Back*, pp. 21–25, and in CCOB, "Eagle Had Landed," *Irish Independent*, 2 Sept. 1989.

19 Salmon, p. 231. This proposal was made on 10 September 1957, which was before the China debate. This reinforces the point: the China issue was only the most spectacular of a whole range of new positions, and these were not dependent on the China matter.

20 Conor's views on how Irish policy on South Africa operated in the years 1957–61 are found in CCOB, *Ireland, the United Nations, and Southern Africa* (Dublin: Irish Anti-Apartheid Movement, 1967), pp. 4–6.

21 "Afro-Irish Assembly," *Economist* (19 Dec. 1959). The anonymous article was by Andrew Boyd.

22 CCOB to Joseph Shields, 17 July 1958 (National Archives of Ireland, Dublin, Department of External Affairs Files 305/14/9B, hereafter DFA).

23 Partition was still a minor element, however. For instance, as late as 1958, one finds Conor advising Val Iremonger on the revision of an antipartition pamphlet published by the British branch of the Anti-Partition League. CCOB to Valentine Iremonger, 25 July 1958 (DFA 305/14/109/1). The pamphlet was *Ireland's Affairs Have Nothing to Do with Me—or Have They?* (London: Anti-Partition of Ireland League, Britain, n.d.).

24 "Afro-Irish Assembly," p. 1139.

25 *United Nations General Assembly, Twelfth Session, Official Records, Special Political Committee*, 54th meeting, 29 Oct. 1957, p. 57.

26 *United Nations, General Assembly, Fourteenth Session, Official Records, Special Political Committee*, 171st meeting, 8 Dec. 1959, p. 208.

27 *United Nations Official Record of the General Assembly, Fourteenth Session, Plenary Meetings, 1959*, pp. 471–72.

28 "Haughey and Collins Get It Right," *Irish Times*, 27 April 1982.

29 CCOB, "Which of You Can Make a Horse?" *Observer*, 18 March 1979.

30 CCOB, *The Siege*, p. 16.

31 Ibid., p. 14.

32 CCOB, "On Being a Jewish Wild Goose," *Observer*, 3 June 1979. The incident is obliquely referred to in CCOB, *The United Nations. Sacred Drama* (London: Hutchinson, 1968), p. 77.

33 Interviews with Maire and Conor Cruise O'Brien; Maire MacEntee to CCOB, 26 Aug. 1961 (O'Brien papers, Howth) recalls the circumstances of their first intimate encounter.

34 Information on the MacEntee family from standard biographical directories; interviews with Conor and with Maire Cruise O'Brien, and with close friends of the family.

35 "In Her Own Write," *Sunday Tribune*, 8 Sept. 1985.

36 "Critic of Ghana," *New York Times*, 29 March 1965.

37 Joseph J. Lee, *Ireland, 1912–1985: Politics and Society* (Cambridge: Cambridge University Press, 1989), p. 370.

38 Silverlight, p. 36.

39 O'Toole, "Part 2," p. 27.

40 Norman Sykes, *Church and State in England in the XVIIIth Century* (Cambridge: Cambridge University Press, 1934).

41 The plan as specified by Andrew Cordier, executive assistant to Hammarskjold, was that Conor serve six months in Katanga and at the end of that time return to the UN secretariat's executive staff in New York (CCOB, *To Katanga and Back*, p. 41).

42 There is a fairly extensive literature on the Congo crisis, not all of it distinguished. The basic items that anyone dealing with the period has to come to terms with are Conor's *To Katanga and Back* and Catherine Hoskyns, *The Congo Since Independence: January 1960-December 1961* (London: Oxford University Press, for the Royal Institute of International Affairs, 1965). Despite a great difference in tone between the two volumes—Conor's is engaged and not averse to putting a name on the guilty parties, and Hoskyns's is an establishment-financed work, very gentle on the colonial powers, especially Belgium and the United Kingdom—they agree on the fundamental facts of what happened. This is crucial, given that Conor's is an insider's account and Hoskyns's that of an external scholar.

A number of journalistic accounts went into print soon after the events: King Gordon, *The United Nations in the Congo: A Quest for Peace* (New York: Carnegie Endowment for International Peace, 1962); Colin Legum, *Congo Disaster* (Harmondsworth: Penguin Books, 1961); Smith Hempstone, *Katanga Report* (London: Faber and Faber, 1962). For later analyses see Ernest W. Lefever, *Uncertain Mandate: Politics of the U.N. Congo Operation* (Baltimore: Johns Hopkins University Press, 1967); Ernest W. Lefever, *Crisis in the Congo: A United Nations Force in Action* (Washington, D.C.: Brookings Institution, 1965); Arthur L. Gavshon, *The Last Days of Dag Hammarskjold* (London: Barrie and Rockliff, 1963); R. Simmonds, *Legal Problems Arising from the United Nations Military Operations in the Congo* (Hague: Martinus Nijhoff, 1968); Association of the Bar of the City of New York, *The Legal Aspects of the United Nations Action in the Congo* (working paper, 1962). A useful summary is found in Brian Urquhart, *Ralph Bunche: An American Life* (New York: W.W. Norton, 1993), pp. 299–360. On biographical details see G. Heinz and H. Donnay (pseudonyms), *Lumumba: The Last Fifty Days* (New York: Grove Press, 1969). A strongly anti-O'Brien stance is taken in Ian Colvin's *The Rise and Fall of Moise Tshombe* (London: Leslie Frewin, 1968). Brian Urquhart's *Hammarskjold* (New York: Alfred A. Knopf, 1973) is also critical of Conor.

43 The basis of the chronology is Catherine Hoskyns, *Chatham House Memoranda: The Congo. A Chronology of Events, January 1960-December 1961* (London: Royal Institute of International Affairs, 1962), supplemented by the sources listed in note 42.

44 O'Brien interviews; CCOB, "I became an anti-Imperialist," [forthcoming, *Atlantic*, June 1994].

45 CCOB, "The Siren Song of Mrs. Thatcher," *Observer*, 29 April 1979.

46 Maire MacEntee (hereafter cited as Maire) to CCOB, 30 May 1961 (Howth). All of the items cited in the following letter sequence are in the O'Brien papers, Howth. In trying to assess how any given letter fits into Conor's life (and especially into the stress he was experiencing), the imponderable is that we know only when they were sent, not when they arrived. (His half of the correspondence, which was the basis for *To Katanga and Back*, was, in effect, a day-to-day diary of what he was doing in the field. It has disappeared; one very much hopes that it has not been destroyed.)

47 Maire to CCOB, 31 May 1961.

48 Actually, there was another divorce in the picture, George Hetherington's from his first wife. That, though, is outside the frame of this biography of Conor.

49 Maire to CCOB, 1 June 1961.

50 Maire to CCOB, 14 June 1961.

51 Maire to CCOB, 15 June 1961.

52 Maire to CCOB, 2 Sept. 1961.

53 Ibid.

54 Maire to CCOB, 15 Sept. 1961.

55 Maire to CCOB, 16 Sept. 1961.

56 Maire to CCOB, 25 Sept. 1961.

57 Ibid.

58 Maire to CCOB, 5 Oct. 1961.

59 Maire to CCOB, 2 Oct. 1961.

60 Kate Cruise O'Brien to CCOB [Oct. 1961; probably written in the first week in October].

61 Maire to CCOB, 2 Oct. 1961.

62 Kate Cruise O'Brien to CCOB [—Oct. 1961].

63 Maire to CCOB, 5 Oct. 1961.

64 Maire to CCOB, 12 Oct. 1961.

65 Maire to CCOB, 5 Oct. 1961.

66 Donal Cruise O'Brien to Maire, 16 Oct. 1961.

67 Telex, CCOB to Walter Fulcheri, 31 Oct. 1961.

68 CCOB, *To Katanga and Back*, pp. 313–14.

69 Ibid., p. 315. Boland and his wife Judy are referred to not by name but as Mr. and Mrs. "Pump"—meaning "prominent UN personality."

70 The phrase, in Bowdlerized form, is found ibid., p. 50.

71 The events that follow are from CCOB, *To Katanga and Back*, pp. 319–30, supplemented by interviews with Conor and Maire.

72 This version of events (CCOB, *To Katanga and Back*, pp. 320–26) was written by Maire fairly soon after the events (at least within three months). It conflicts in one interesting way with the version told in 1987 by Brian Urquhart in *A Life in Peace and War* (New York: Harper and Row, 1987), pp. 179–81. His does not include the heroic actions of the Irish army private—the driver Patrick Wall, who, according to Maire, risked his life to try to keep the paras from harming Urquhart. Maire today strongly maintains her version of events and suggests that an Irish foot soldier can, indeed, be as heroic as the holder of a British knighthood.

73 O'Brien interviews; "An Irish Times Profile: Conor Cruise O'Brien," *Irish Times*, 13 June 1969.

74 Interviews with Maire Cruise O'Brien and with Christine Foster Hetherington.

75 Divorce decree, 3 Jan. 1962 (O'Brien papers, Howth).

CHAPTER 7

1 This is the appropriate point to call attention to an example of first-class journalism, a three-piece series on Conor done by Fintan O'Toole and published in *Magill* magazine (April, May, and June 1986). One of the few things about which I disagree with O'Toole (chiefly as a matter of degree) is his belief that for Conor the Congo experience "had posed a cataclysmic challenge to his liberal assumptions." Fintan O'Toole, "The Life and Times of Conor Cruise O'Brien, Part 2," *Magill* 9 (May 1986), p. 30. Cataclysmic seems to me to have the wrong connotations, since the full effect of the Congo episode did not become apparent for more than a decade.

2 Ibid., p. 30.

3 In CCOB, *To Katanga and Back. A UN Case History* (London: Hutchinson, 1962), Conor notes that this false modesty was a mistake: "The emphasis in the *Observer* article ... was due, not so much to any real modesty on my part, as to the strategy of self-deprecation which one almost instinctively adopts when writing for a certain kind of English audience. I now realize that it is foolish for a foreigner to attempt this technique. Only a true-born Englishman knows the trick of being self-deprecatory without actually doing himself any damage. I only succeeded in making people as far away as Arizona think I was 'boasting.'" (p. 42*n*). In this Conor trumps the English. An apology for excessive modesty is a nice touch.

4 CCOB, *To Katanga and Back*, p. 1.

5 See ibid., pp. 43, 139, 149, 273, 283, 299–300, 304.

6 Ibid., p. 103.

7 Ibid., p. 110.

8 Ibid., p. 124.

9 Ibid.

10 Ibid., p. 134.

11   Ibid., p. 150.

12   Ibid., p. 319.

13   Ibid., p. 330.

14   The UN denial is detailed in the *Scotsman*, which has strong UN interest, 14 Nov. 1962. There is a thick file of clippings on UN and British denials in the O'Brien papers, University College, Dublin (UCD).

15   A large collection of the reviews and other press commentary on the book is found in O'Brien papers (UCD).

16   Brian Urquhart, *A Life in Peace and War* (New York: Harper and Row, 1987), p. 174.

17   The reader who is familiar with the literature of the period will notice that I have gone directly to Urquhart's autobiography of the 1980s and have not dealt with his very problematic biography *Hammarskjold* (New York: Alfred A. Knopf, 1973), which was written while Urquhart was still a serving officer of the UN and thus has something of the character of an official history, without any particularly salient personal informa-tion about Hammarskjold. Moreover, a fair amount of animus toward Conor appears in several asides (see pp. 568n and 573–74n). This had its source in the events of the early 1960s, but it is not irrelevant that Sir Brian, as he told me in conversation, was particularly outraged that Conor, in *Murderous Angels: A Political Tragedy and Comedy in Black and White* (Boston: Little, Brown, 1968; London: Hutchinson, 1969), presented Hammarskjold as gay. In an analysis of Urquhart's biography of Hammarskjold, Conor wrote: "When Mr. Urquhart reviewed my *To Katanga and Back* in the *Times Literary Supplement*, he claimed that my account of the instructions given to me ... for ending the secession 'was a ludicrously thin story.' He does not repeat that claim here. On the contrary," continues Conor, the documents quoted by Urquhart "make it reasonably clear that Hammarskjold knew what was contemplated and that his response to it was delphic. ... He certainly knew from military reports from Elisabethville, which Mr. Urquhart ignores here, what [steps] we had in reality taken. So when Hammarskjold issued a thoroughly misleading report on the subject of Leopoldville, it was a delicate form of disavowal in the form of a defence of something other than had happened." (The draft review is in O'Brien papers, UCD. I have been unable to find the published version.) That was in 1973. In 1985, in an interview with Michael Charlton on the BBC's Radio Three, Conor backed away slightly. He restated that Khiary had given him orders (and this can be taken as no longer open to chal-lenge). "Now, who Khiary cleared it with or did not clear it with I can't know. I don't know. The rest is speculation. If I say I think Hammarskjold thought it was OK, or if I say maybe Hammarskjold knew nothing about it, both are equally speculative." "Conor Cruise O'Brien talks to Michael Charlton about the UN in the Congo," *Listener* 113 (14 March 1985), p. 7.

18   Urquhart, *A Life*, p. 174.

19   CCOB, *Conflicting Concepts of the United Nations* (Leeds: Leeds University Press, 1964), pp. 2–3.

20   Ibid., p. 4.

21   Ibid., pp. 10–11.

22   Ibid., pp. 16–17. Conor was careful in his reflection on the UN and the United States not to overstate U.S. power. See "Mission Impossible," *New York Review of Books* (21 Nov. 1968), pp. 8, 10.

23   CCOB, "Survival—and Other UN Dodges," *Observer*, 25 Oct. 1981.

24   "The Donkey, the UN and the Minaret," *Observer*, 18 April 1982.

25   CCOB, "How the UN Could End the War," *New York Review of Books* (28 March 1968), pp. 22–25.

26 The one major instance of inconsistency in Conor's views of the UN had to do with South Africa. Instead of being merely a forum for dignified retreat (as on other issues, even Vietnam), Conor believed that it would be proper for the UN to use physical force in South Africa and that, despite its enormous investments in South Africa, the United States would go along, under certain circumstances. See CCOB, *Ireland, The United Nations and Southern Africa* (Dublin: Irish Anti-Apartheid Movement, 1967), pp. 18–19.

27 Harold Harris to CCOB, 31 August 1966, O'Brien papers, New York University Archives, box 5, file 10.

28 Feliks Topolski to CCOB, 15 Oct. 1966, ibid.

29 CCOB to Feliks Topolski, 16 Oct. 1966, ibid.

30 The business details, complicated as the Treaty of Vienna, are found in O'Brien papers, UCD.

31 *Times Literary Supplement* (27 June 1968), p. 677.

32 The handwritten draft of *Sacred Drama* is in the O'Brien papers, New York University Archives, box 6, files 5, 6, 7, and 9. The typescript is in box 6, files 3 and 8, and the early mimeo copy in box 6, folder 4.

33 CCOB, in Conor Cruise O'Brien and Feliks Topolski, *The United Nations: Sacred Drama* (London: Hutchinson; New York: Simon and Schuster, 1968), p. 9.

34 Ibid., pp. 9–10.

35 Ibid., p. 10.

36 Ibid., p. 19.

37 Ibid., p. 120.

38 Ibid., p. 123.

39 See CCOB, "U.N. Theatre," *New Republic* 193 (4 Nov. 1985), pp. 17–19. See also the use of the metaphor "charade" in CCOB, "At the Shrine of Honourable Failure," *Times Literary Supplement* (6–12. 1987), pp. 1211–12.

40 CCOB to Brid Lynch, 1 Dec. 1967; CCOB to Leonard Boudine, 15 Dec. 1967 (UCD).

41 CCOB, *Murderous Angels*, pp. xvii-xviii.

42 Brian Inglis, "In Search of Morality—Conor Cruise O'Brien talks to Brian Inglis," *Listener* 90 (23 Aug. 1973), p. 234. Whether or not Conor actually had this dream (I see no reason not to believe he did) is irrelevant, for consciously as well as unconsciously, the fate of Patrice Lumumba and the possibility of moral turpitude on the part of the United Nations had been on Conor's mind for several years. See the address he made at Makerere University College, Kampala, Uganda, 11 July 1964: "The United Nations, the Congo, and the Tshombe Government," in CCOB, *Writers and Politics* (London: Chatto and Windus, 1965), pp. 215–22.

43 Dag Hammarskjold, *Markings* (London: Faber and Faber, 1964), p. 86.

44 CCOB, *Murderous Angels*, p. xxxi.

45 *Guardian*, 2 Feb. 1970.

46 For a sensible, but now highly dated, discussion of the play and of O'Brien's wanting to have it both ways, see Catharine Hughes, *Plays, Politics, and Polemics* (New York: Drama Books Specialists, 1973), pp. 165–73.

47 CCOB, *Murderous Angels*, p. 60.

48 Ibid., p. 84.

49 Ibid., p. 85.

50 On race in the drama, see Nigel Deacon, "Racial Conflicts and Related Themes in *Murderous Angels*, by Conor Cruise O'Brien," in Patrick Rafoidi, Raymonde Popot, and William Parker, eds., *Aspects of the Irish Theatre* (Paris: Editions Universitaires, 1972), pp. 245–60.

51 CCOB, *Murderous Angels*, p. 161.

52 Ibid., p. 162.

53 Ibid.

54 Ibid., pp. 177–78.

55 Conor's *Murderous Angels* was published in November 1968 to muffled reviews. Conor told Richard Hall in an interview that, when the play appeared in print in America, "it fell like a stone. There was one critical review and that was all" (*Observer*, 26 Jan. 1969). Actually, there were more (see the listing in Elisabeth Young-Bruehl and Robert Hogan, *Conor Cruise O'Brien: An Appraisal* [Newark, Del.: Proscenium Press, 1974], p. 52, and the excerpts in *Book Review Digest, 1969*). However, the American notices were mostly distant and puzzled. The most engaged comment was by Lionel Abel, who, in "The Position of Noam Chomsky," *Commentary* (May 1969), pp. 35–44, gave an extended footnote over to *Murderous Angels* and to chastising Conor as an orthodox white liberal of very gross nature. For Conor's reply, of—May 1969, see O'Brien papers, New York University Archives, box 5, file 4. When the British edition appeared in 1969, the reviewers were more attentive, and more attuned to the book-drama as a form of its own. In the Sunday *Times*, John Raymond saw it as neo-Shavian, with brilliant dialogue. Raymond Williams in the *Guardian* declared that O'Brien was one of those "who now sees imperialism in so clear a light that he is one of the few necessary voices of our time." And the anonymous reviewer in the *Times Literary Supplement* of 17 July 1969 saw it as a hatchet job, with Dag Hammarskjold as the main victim. "This is not, and does not claim to be, an objective historian's account of events. As it is in may ways deeply offensive to people alive and dead, however, one is surely entitled to doubt whether its dramatic qualities are sufficient justification for its publication. Many people may quite reasonably feel that they are not."

56 The mimeo copy of *Murderous Angels* is in the O'Brien papers, New York University Archives, box 6, files 1 and 2.

57 Telegram, CCOB to Elaine Greene, 9 April 1968; CCOB to Feliks Topolski, 12 April 1968 (UCD).

58 CCOB to Feliks Topolski, 23 April 1968 (UCD).

59 *Irish Times*, 23 Jan. 1969.

60 Ibid., 27 Jan. 1969.

61 CCOB to Nicole Boireau, 25 Aug. 1981 (O'Brien papers, Howth).

62 *Irish Times*, 27 Jan. 1969. See also 8 Oct. 1969.

63 Ibid., 27 Jan. 1969.

64 Ibid.

65 Ibid., 7 Feb. 1970. Other Los Angeles reviews are summarized in the same issue.

66 Interview with Thomas Murphy.

67 CCOB to Nicole Boireau, 25 Aug. 1981.

68 Ibid. See also *Irish Times*, 26 Feb. 1971.

69 *Irish Times*, 2 March 1971.

70 Ibid., 22 March 1971.

71 CCOB to Nicole Boireau, 25 Aug. 1981.

72 Donald Cameron, "Politics and Scholarship: A Talk with Conor Cruise O'Brien," *Humanities Association of Canada Bulletin* 21 (Fall 1970), p. 12.

CHAPTER 8

1 John Silverlight, "Conor Cruise O'Brien: Irishman Extraordinary," *Observer Magazine* (2 Sept. 1973), p. 39.

2   CCOB, "Two Addresses," in *Writers and Politics* (London: Chatto and Windus, 1965), p. 239. The addresses in draft form are found in O'Brien papers, University College, Dublin (UCD).

3   For background, see W. Scott Thompson, *Ghana's Foreign Policy, 1957–1966: Diplomacy, Ideology, and the New State* (Princeton: Princeton University Press, 1969). Less analytic, but highly revealing are the memoirs of the British expatriate who for a time commanded the Ghanaian armed forces: H.T. Alexander, *African Tightrope: My Two Years as Nkrumah's Chief of Staff* (London: Pall Mall Press, 1965). For CCOB's review of this book, see *New York Review of Books* (23 June 1966), pp. 11–12.

4   Kwame Nkrumah, *Challenge of the Congo* (New York: International Publishers, 1967), p. 175.

5   Ibid., pp. 176–77.

6   CCOB, "Two Addresses," p. 239.

7   Conor's close friend, Alex Kwapong, believes that Sir Geoffrey Bing, at one time Nkrumah's chief legal adviser, "discovered" Conor for Nkrumah. Kwapong interview.

8   CCOB, "Two Addresses," p. 239; see also CCOB, "Transcript of Talk at University of California, Berkeley, on an African University, 3 May 1965," p. 2 (UCD).

9   E.A. Boateng, *A Geography of Ghana* (Cambridge: Cambridge University Press, 1960), pp. 29, 34.

10 CCOB, "Transcript of a Talk at University of California," p. 2. Conor's same false-modest device is employed, in slightly different form, in *Writers and Politics* (p. 240): "Not only the President but also the leading members of the teaching body whom I met were in favour of my accepting the appointment—on the principle, I apprehended, that if I did not accept it somebody worse might be found."

11 "In Search of Morality—Conor Cruise O'Brien Talks to Brian Inglis," *The Listener* 90 (23 Aug. 1973), p. 234.

12 The story, without identification of the main character—Nkrumah—is printed in CCOB, *Writers and Politics*, p. xiii.

13 Ibid., pp. xiv-xv.

14 CCOB, "The Fall of Africa," *New Republic* 192 (18 March 1985), p. 33. Reprinted in CCOB, *Passion and Cunning* p. 273. Italics mine.

15 CCOB, "Northern Ireland: Its Past and Its Future," *Race* 14 (July 1972), p. 11.

16 Henry L. Bretton, *The Rise and Fall of Kwame Nkrumah: A Study of Personal Rule in Africa* (New York: Frederick A. Praeger, 1966), Table 1, p. 151. For Conor's review of this book, see "'Losing Our Cool'—in Ghana," *Nation* 204 (6 March 1967), pp. 309–11. For a good deal of material relevant to the situation in the early 1960s see A. Asiedu-Akrofi, "Education in Ghana," in A. Babs Fafunwa and J.U. Aisiku, eds., *Education in Africa: A Comparative Survey* (London: George Allen and Unwin, 1982), pp. 98–114.

17 See Eric Ashby, *African Universities and Western Tradition* (Harvard: Harvard University Press, 1964), pp. 46–53; Eric Ashby, with Mary Anderson, *Universities: British, Indian, African: A Study in the Ecology of Higher Education* (London: Weidenfeld and Nicolson, 1966), pp. 308–12; Adam Curle, *Educational Problems of Developing Societies, with case studies of Ghana, Pakistan and Nigeria*, 2d ed. (New York: Praeger Publishers, 1973), pp. 97–111. For Conor's review of the Ashby and Anderson book, see *Harvard Educational Review* 37, no. 2 (1967), pp. 281–90.

18 *Report of the Commission of Enquiry, University of Science and Technology, Kumasi* (1967), paragraphs 677–687, cited in Trevor Jones, *Ghana's First Republic, 1960–1966* (London: Methuen, 1976), p. 20.

19 Act 79, 22 Aug. 1961.

20 CCOB, "Transcript of a Talk at University of California," p. 2.

21 Curle (p. 104) estimates that as of the summer of 1960 five-sixths were expatriates. The proportion of expatriates was somewhat lower by mid-1962. The proportion certainly dropped steadily during Conor's time as vice-chancellor.

22 *Commonwealth Universities Yearbook, 1962*, p. 394.

23 Curle, p. 99.

24 *Commonwealth Universities Yearbook, 1964*, pp. 467, 469.

25 *Commonwealth Universities Yearbook, 1967*, pp. 634, 640.

26 *Commonwealth Universities Yearbook, 1964*, p. 469.

27 William Hanna and Judith L. Hanna, "Students as Elites," in William John Hanna, ed., *University Students and African Politics* (New York: Africana Publishing, 1975), Table 2–7, p. 32.

28 Later in his career, Professor Kwapong was vice-chancellor of the University of Ghana, 1966–75; vice-rector of the United Nations University in Japan, 1976–88; and professor of development studies at Dalhousie University, Nova Scotia, 1988–91. He received honorary doctorates from Warwick and Princeton universities.

29 W.B. Harvey returned to the University of Michigan until 1966, then served as dean of the law school at the University of Indiana, Bloomington, in 1966–71. He was a visiting professor at Nairobi and at Duke universities in 1972, and professor of law and political science at Boston University, 1973–88. He served also as general counsel for Boston University, 1982–87.

30 Information on Bing from Alex Kwapong. Bing wrote his memoirs: *Reap the Whirlwind: An Account of Kwame Nkrumah's Ghana, 1950–66* (London: MacGibbon and Kee, 1967).

31 See Erica Powell (private secretary to Nkrumah) to CCOB, 28 Oct. 1963 (UCD).

32 African Affairs secretary, government of Ghana, to CCOB, 25 Oct. 1962, and enclosure (UCD).

33 Ashby and Anderson, pp. 312–13, give the constitutional details. It should be noted that they did not see this actual constitution as a source of weakness to the university. This is a viewpoint that I do not share.

34 Bob Fitch and Mary Oppenheimer, *Ghana: End of an Illusion* (New York: Monthly Review Press, 1966), pp. 40–41.

35 Ibid., Table 2 and Table 6, pp. 41, 85.

36 Alex A. Kwapong, "Ghana," in James A. Perkins and Barbara B. Israel, eds., *Higher Education: From Autonomy to Systems* (New York: International Council for Educational Development, 1972), p. 191.

37 On political developments from World War II onward, see David E. Apter, *Ghana in Transition* (New York: Atheneum, 1963), a revision of *The Gold Coast in Transition* (Princeton: Princeton University Press, 1955); Dennis Austin, *Politics in Ghana, 1946–1960* (London: Oxford University Press, 1964); Dennis Austin, *Ghana Observed: Essays on the Politics of a West African Republic* (Manchester: Manchester University Press, 1976); Leslie Rubin and Pauli Murray, *The Constitution and Government of Ghana*, 2d ed. (London: Sweet and Maxwell, 1964).

38 For favorable views of Nkrumah, see Basil Davidson, *Black Star: A View of the Life and Times of Kwame Nkrumah* (London: Allen Lane, 1973); Bankole Timothy, *Kwame Nkrumah, His Rise to Power* (London: George Allen and Unwin, 1955). See also Kwame Nkrumah, *The Autobiography of Kwame Nkrumah* (Edinburgh: Thomas Nelson and Sons, 1957).

39 Bretton, pp. 97–100.

40 CCOB, "Return to Ghana," *Observer*, 24 April 1966.

41 Bretton, p. 101.

42 CCOB, letter in *Spectator*, 31 Dec. 1965. This was in response to a statement by Ian Milne that terms like "Redeemer" and "Messiah" as applicable to Kwame Nkrumah were an invention of Western reactionaries.

43 Erica Powell, *Private Secretary (Female) Gold Coast* (New York: St. Martin's Press, 1984), p. 163.

44 The story is told, without identifying the country or persons involved, in CCOB, "The Politics of Flattery," *Observer*, 4 Sept. 1977, and with identification in an interview in *Macleans* 91 (1 May 1978), p. 5. In the interview Conor prefaces the story by saying "I lived for years in Ghana and used nearly to vomit when I read the papers."

45 Kwame Nkrumah, *Consciencism: Philosophy and Ideology of Decolonialisation and Development* (London: Heinemann, 1964). For a perceptive survey, see "Nkrumah and Nkrumahism," by Jitendra Mohan, *Socialist Register, 1967*, pp. 191–228. This argues that Nkrumahism was not socialism in any meaningful sense, but "increasingly became almost a fetish, a hopeless attempt to superimpose an apparent order over a mass of contradictions, neither perceived nor resolved" (p. 211). For an attempt to define Nkrumahism, see the work of the editors of the government's ideological paper, *Some Essential Features of Nkrumahism, by the Editors of "The Spark"* (New York: International Publishers, 1964). See also Kwesi Krafona, *The Pan-African Movement: Ghana's Contribution* (London: Afroworld Publishing, 1986).

46 CCOB, "The Fall of Africa," *New Republic* 192 (18 March 1985), p. 33; reprinted in CCOB, *Passion and Cunning*, p. 273. Substantially the same story is found in CCOB, "Never Stand between a Hippo and the Water," *Observer*, 1 March 1982.

47 CCOB, "The Fall of Africa," p. 34; *Passion and Cunning*, p. 274; "Never Stand between a Hippo and the Water."

48 CCOB, "'Losing Our Cool'—in Ghana," p. 311.

49 For example, Rebecca Posner, who taught at the University of Ghana between 1963 and 1965, wrote, "As for Nkrumah's 'tyranny,' always laughter prevailed over fear: the Ghanaians are, perhaps, the most amiable and genial people in the world and, in comparison with some other countries in Africa and elsewhere, Ghana remained a pleasant and safe place to live" (Letter to *Financial Times*, 15 July 1977). Scores of relevant anecdotes, from the end of the 1950s, are found in Douglas Warner, *Ghana and the New Africa* (London: Frederick Muller, 1960). See also the Ghana sojourn described by Arnold Zeitlin, *To the Peace Corps, with Love* (Garden City, N.Y.: Doubleday, 1965).

50 J. Gustav Joahoda, *White Man: A Study of the Attitudes of Africans to Europeans in Ghana before Independence* (Oxford: Oxford University Press, for the Institute of Race Relations, 1961). Although dealing mostly with the (remarkably generous) attitude of Ghanaians to Europeans, the study also documents the intracultural value system that produced the behavior that Europeans saw as good humor and amiability.

51 CCOB, "Pain, Learning ... and the Accord," *Irish Independent*, 7 May 1988.

52 In the discussion that follows, the major primary documents are found in four sources: (1) William Burnett Harvey, "The Development of Legal Education in Ghana," unpublished report to the SAILER Project of the Institute of International Education and the Ford Foundation, 1977—hereafter the "Harvey Report"; (2) a collection of correspondence and documents in the possession of W. Burnett Harvey—hereafter Harvey Collection; (3) O'Brien papers, UCD; (4) O'Brien papers in CCOB's possession—hereafter, Howth. As will be clear, many of the items are found in more than one collection.

53 Kwame Nkrumah to CCOB, 21 Feb. 1962 (UCD).

54 Robert B. Seidman, "Letter from a Deportee," p. 28 (UCD).

55   The address is reprinted in CCOB, *Writers and Politics*, pp. 240–44. See also draft (UCD).
56   CCOB, "Autonomy and Academic Freedom in Britain and Africa," *Minerva* 4 (Autumn 1966), p. 92.
57   The full speech is found in Appendix VII to the "Harvey Report."
58   CCOB to Nkrumah, 14 April 1964; Erica Powell to CCOB, 2 May 1964, quoted in "Harvey Report," Appendix VII.
59   CCOB to James Becker, 24 Feb. 1967 (O'Brien papers, New York University Archives, box 3, folder 7).
60   Seidman, p. 8.
61   Ibid.
62   W.B. Harvey interview.
63   "Harvey Report," pp. 9, 16.
64   Ibid., p. 30.
65   "A Value Analysis of Ghanaian Legal Developments since Independence," p. 5, Harvey Collection. For Harvey's later views on African law, see *Freedom, University, and the Law: The Legal Status of Academic Freedom in the University of Black Africa. The J.I.C. Taylor Memorial Lecture for 1976* (Lagos: University of Lagos Press, 1978).
66   Harvey recalls (1992) that this inaugural lecture was the only time he and Conor had a sharp disagreement. It was not over the unfortunate sentence, but over American legal realism, with which, Harvey believed, Conor had difficulty because of his early Catholic training.
67   "Harvey Report," pp. 47–48; CCOB, "Transcript of Talk at University of California," p. 2.
68   CCOB, "Transcript of Talk at University of California," pp. 2–3.
69   "Harvey Report," p. 49.
70   Nkrumah to CCOB, 28 Feb. 1964, Harvey Collection.
71   Seidman, p. 8.
72   Depositions of CCOB and Alex Kwapong before Alexis Fitzgerald and T. Michael Williams, 29 Aug. 1967 (UCD).
73   "Harvey Report," p. 9.
74   Ibid., Appendix II, p. 5.
75   CCOB to T. Michael Williams, 19 Sept. 1967 (UCD); "Harvey Report," p. 39.
76   "Harvey Report," p. 38.
77   I am making no judgment whatsoever on these matters, merely pointing out what was believed at the time and that Ekow-Daniels later disputed the accuracy of those beliefs. Conor believed that he had been told on the evening of the address that Ekow-Daniels had told Mrs. Dorothy Hodgkin, wife of the professor who had drafted Nkrumah's speech, that Ekow-Daniels had written the passages related to the law school. (CCOB to P.R. Davies, 22 Jan. 1968, Harvey Collection; see also CCOB to Alex Kwapong, 15 Oct. 1964, Harvey Collection; Draft, CCOB to Editor, *The Observer*,—May 1966, UCD; Deposition of CCOB and Alex Kwapong, 29 Aug. 1967, UCD.) This idea was believed to be accurate by many within the university community (Seidman, pp. 9–10; "Harvey Report," p. 44; W.B. Harvey to P.R. Davies, 12 Feb. 1968, Harvey Collection). The problem is that the chief direct witness to this claim, Dorothy Hodgkin, had by 1968 forgotten the passage in question, and documentation had not been obtained earlier (CCOB to P.R. Davies, 22 Jan. 1968, Harvey Collection).
78   The minute of the meeting of 27 Oct. 1963 between CCOB and Nkrumah was distributed to the law faculty teaching staff. It is found in "Harvey Report," pp. 39–40. On the circumstances, see also CCOB to Alex Kwapong, 15 Oct. 1964 (Harvey Collection).
79   Nkrumah to CCOB, 2 Nov. 1963, quoted in "Harvey Report," p. 43.

80 The mention of political science refers to the appointment of Professor Henry L. Bretton, an expert in Ghanaian history and political science, to the headship of the Department of Political Science as of September 1964. This worried Nkrumah for Bretton was an expert scholar of Ghanaian politics. Conor, ever the shrewd civil servant, resisted Nkrumah by quoting to him the university statutes concerning appointment procedures ("Harvey Report," p. 43).

81 E.J. Okoh (secretary to the Cabinet) to CCOB, 4 Nov. 1963, quoted in "Harvey Report," p. 44.

82 CCOB to Alex Kwapong, 15 Oct. 1964 (Harvey Collection).

83 Seidman, p. 10.

84 This is clearly his view in CCOB to W.B. Harvey, marked "Confidential," 25 Nov. 1963, reproduced in "Harvey Report," pp. 56–59. At this time Conor and Harvey were close to falling out, for Harvey believed, albeit only briefly, that Conor was not defending him and the law faculty against outside intrusions with sufficient zeal. See Harvey to CCOB, 23 Nov. 1963 (reproduced in "Harvey Report," pp. 52–55), and Harvey to CCOB, 25 Nov. 1963 (reproduced in "Harvey Report," pp. 59–61).

85 "Harvey Report," pp. 34–35.

86 Ibid., pp. 34–37.

87 W.E. Abraham, The Mind of Africa (London: Weidenfeld and Nicolson, 1962), p. 10.

88 Bretton refers to Abraham as "a probable co-author of Nkrumah's Consciencism." That this was the general belief (although, of course, not necessarily an accurate one) was reported in my interviews with Kwapong and O'Brien. On the matter of authorship, Bretton refers to an article by B.G.D. Folson in the Ghanaian Times, 21 March 1966 and to Professor Abraham's testimony at the Apaloo Commission, reported in Ghana Today 10 (13 July 1966), p. 5. See Bretton, p. 211n68.

89 Seidman, p. 7.

90 W.B. Harvey to P.R. Davies, 31 Jan. 1968 (Harvey Collection); "Harvey Report," pp. 78–79.

91 Bretton, p. 128.

92 Austin, Politics in Ghana, 1946–1960, had been published in London "under the auspices of the Royal Institute of International Affairs" in 1964.

93 CCOB, "Transcript of a Talk at University of California," p. 5; CCOB, Vice-Chancellor's Address to Congregation, 27 March 1965, University of Ghana Reporter 4 (23 April 1965), p. 266. Conor did not directly name Abraham as head of the government's book-banning committee. That is done in Bretton, p. 128.

94 CCOB, "Transcript of a Talk at University of California," p. 5.

95 Seidman, p. 8. The story is from pp. 7–8.

96 Harvey interview.

97 It is possible to take apparent inconsistencies in Abraham's position, as between his political proposals and his personal actions, as indications of considerable personal integrity on his part. He was not without his admirers, even among the expatriate community. On 1 May 1966, letters of D.N. Pritt and Dennis Duerden were published in the Observer, testifying to his integrity. Duerden pointed out that in the Ghanaian Times, Abraham had courageously attacked Nkrumah's cult of personality. Abraham's article in question introduced the term "Unsober Adulation" into Ghanaian political discourse and for years it was used as an encoded joke, implying that Sober Adulation was quite enough for Osagyefo's ego. One extreme critic of Nkrumah has suggested that Abraham's Unsober Adulation article actually was written on Nkrumah's own instructions and then, in a Byzantine manipulation, Nkrumah had instructed the press to take Abraham down a peg or two, after which he placated Abraham by sending him

on a world tour (T. Peter Omari, *The Anatomy of an African Dictatorship* [New York: Africana Publications, 1970], p. 147). These suggestions seem to me to be unconvincing.

98   See "Harvey Report," pp. 63-64.

99   Kwapong interviews; CCOB, letter to *Sunday Telegraph*, 7 March 1966.

100 "Harvey Report," p. 65.

101 Burnett Harvey believed that Conor had made an error in commenting publicly as an officer of the university on the treason trial's outcome ("Harvey Report," p. 65). Conor himself, fifteen months later, was fully willing to accept that some of his colleagues (and, here he meant his allies) thought him wrong. And he was willing to admit that they might have been right. However, he did not back away from the decision he had made. See CCOB, "Transcript of Talk at University of California," pp. 3-4.

102 Bretton, p. 61.

103 Of the votes cast, 2,773,920 were in favor, 2,452 against. Since 92.8 percent of the registered electorate allegedly voted—the highest proportion by far in any Ghanaian election—the results at least indicate an enthusiastic corruption of the ballot box. An informed guess is that had the voting not been rigged, probably three-fifths of the electorate would have voted "yes" (Davidson, p. 193).

104 Omari, p. 95; Silverlight, "Conor Cruise O'Brien: Irishman Extraordinary"; O'Brien interviews.

105 Douglas Brown, "Nkrumah His Own Prison," *Sunday Telegraph*, 1 March 1964.

106 Seidman, p. 11.

107 Ibid., pp. 12-13.

108 "Harvey Report," p. 65; CCOB, "Two Addresses," p. 246.

109 CCOB, "Transcript of Talk at University of California," p. 4.

110 Nkrumah to CCOB, 27 Jan. 1964, is summarized in "Harvey Report," p. 66. CCOB to Nkrumah, 29 Jan. 1964 is reproduced in "Harvey Report," Appendix VI.

111 In the later 1960s, when Conor was in the Labour party, Fianna Fail politicians grossly misrepresented his position in Ghana. Michael Moran, minister for justice, called him "Nkrumah's lap dog." Charles Haughey, the minister for finance, stated that Conor was "the only member of this House [the Irish Parliament] who served a dictator for money." See letter by John Devine in *Irish Times*, 24 Dec. 1969.

112 "Memorandum," CCOB to Nkrumah, 29 Jan. 1964 (UCD); "Two Addresses," in *Writers and Politics*, pp. 246-47. In the "memorandum," Conor says that, concerning the possibility of malicious denunciation of Harvey and Seidman, "Mr. Mfodwa appeared to agree that such possibilities could not altogether be ruled out." In "Two Addresses," Conor said that "one of the security officers made a gesture which I interpreted as meaning I was on the right track." In public documents, Conor did not in those years give the name of Greco, a rather surprising delicacy.

113 "Two Addresses," pp. 247-48; CCOB to Nkrumah, 1 Feb. 1964 (UCD).

114 The reference of course is to W.C. Ekow-Daniels. At this point, I should emphasize that it is impossible for the historian to adjudge with confidence whether or not Ekow-Daniels was involved in malicious delation: Ghanaian security police reports are not available. Therefore, in the absence of any direct evidence to the contrary, my own opinion is that he was not. The key point for understanding the historical situation is that *at the time* Conor and others believed that Ekow-Daniels indeed had acted in the way that Conor suggests. It is this belief, among influential academic staff and many of the student body, that influenced the actions several individuals took, irrespective of the ultimate accuracy or inaccuracy of their beliefs.

Conor's own views on Ekow-Daniels's actual involvement changed over time. During the autumn of 1964, Conor attended a gathering at Mensah Sarbah Hall and said something (exactly what is unclear) associating Ekow-Daniels with the deportation of the lecturers. Ekow-Daniels wrote to Alex Kwapong saying that this was actionable (W.C. Ekow-Daniels to Alex Kwapong, 12 Oct. 1964, Harvey Collection). (About his remarks at the hall, Conor replied that

> I have never made any secret of the fact that I think Dr. Daniels' activities ... weakened the position—and the reputation with the government—of Professor Harvey and Mr. Seidman, in such a way that in a time of tension and excitement they became targets for deportation orders. Dr. Daniels—if, as I have good reasons to believe, he drafted the relevant passage in the President's address ...—had sought to bring about the departure of these gentlemen by "process of Ghanaisation." Their departure was eventually brought about in another way. I have no evidence—and never claimed to have any—that he specifically recommended the use of that other method, viz, deportation. (CCOB to Alex Kwapong, 15 Oct. 1964, Harvey Collection)

But, in "Return to Ghana," *Observer*, 24 April 1966, shortly after the coup that overthrew Nkrumah, Conor said that W.B. Harvey "had been informed against by an ambitious Ghanaian colleague (subsequently appointed to Nkrumah's Government and consequently now in protective custody)." He did not name Ekow-Daniels. However, D.N. Pritt, who had been a visiting professor in the law faculty, wrote to the *Observer* stating that the man in question was unmistakably identifiable, that he was a person of honesty and integrity and that Conor's statement was an actionable libel (Letter to Editor, 1 May 1966). Conor sent a letter back to the *Observer*, giving "my grounds for my statement about the Ghanaian lawyer whom I believe to have instigated Professor Harvey's deportation from Ghana (and that of Mr. R. Seidman)." However, he now added that "it is possible of course that this lecturer did not intend that Professor Harvey and Mr. Seidman should actually be deported" (CCOB to *Observer*, May 1966, Harvey Collection). The *Observer* did not print this letter because of its considerable length (Charles Davey to W.B. Harvey, 21 May 1966, Harvey Collection).

In 1967, Ekow-Daniels began a legal action in England against the *Observer* and Conor. The problem was with the words "informed against." That Ekow-Daniels had engaged in a campaign against Harvey and, to a lesser extent, Seidman, was incontestable, but "informed" had a narrow meaning as well as a broad one. The narrow meaning could not be proved. Conor was willing to agree that the implication of "informed" in the narrow sense "is probably without foundation" (CCOB to T. Michael Williams, 12 Dec. 1967, Harvey Collection). Conor suggested the following apology: "Nothing in the article was intended to suggest that Dr. W.C. Ekow-Daniels made criminal or treasonable charges against Professor W.B. Harvey leading to the deportation of the latter" (ibid.). Confusingly, little more than a month later, Conor's stated view was that "I still do not know whether Daniels explicitly 'denounced' Harvey" (CCOB to P.R. Davies, 22 Jan. 1968, Harvey Collection). The *Observer* eventually paid Ekow-Daniels costs, but no damages (T. Michael Williams to CCOB, 30 Jan. 1969, UCD). Conor paid neither costs nor damages and, by 1992, when I talked to him about the case, he had forgotten entirely that the *Observer* had made its own settlement.

115 CCOB to Kwame Nkrumah, 1 Feb. 1964.
116 CCOB, "Two Addresses," p. 248.
117 Seidman, p. 22.
118 Ibid.

119 O'Brien interviews.

120 O'Brien interviews; Seidman, p. 25; CCOB, "Two Addresses," p. 248.

121 Seidman, pp. 26–27.

122 Ibid., p. 27.

123 Ibid., pp. 28–29.

124 Seidman, p. 29; CCOB, "Two Addresses," p. 249.

125 Seidman, pp. 29–30; CCOB, "Two Addresses," p. 249.

126 CCOB, "Transcript of Talk at University of California," p. 5.

127 CCOB, "Two Addresses," pp. 249–50.

128 Ibid., p. 250; Kwapong interviews.

129 *Evening Post* [Ghana], 10 Feb. 1964.

130 An "attack of cold feet," he candidly admits. CCOB, "Return to Ghana," *Observer*, 24 April 1966.

131 Ibid.; Harvey interview; Seidman, pp. 30–31.

132 CCOB to W.B. Harvey, 10 April 1964 (Harvey Collection).

133 W.B. Harvey to CCOB, 25 March 1964, ibid.

134 W.B. Harvey, Letter to the Editor, *Village Voice* (15 Dec. 1966). Conor's own reply is found in Letter to Editor, *Village Voice* (24 Nov. 1966). Elsewhere ("Harvey Report," pp. 73–74), Harvey states, "I am confident that the Vice-Chancellor realized that he was almost as much under attack as any of those against whom deportation orders were actually issued. I am equally clear that if only Dr. O'Brien's personal interest had been consulted, he would have made the deportations the occasion for his own resignation from the university."

135 Seidman, p. 12.

136 CCOB, "Our Wits About Us," *New Statesman* (15 Feb. 1963), p. 237.

137 CCOB, "Chorus or Cassandra," *New Statesman* (19 April, 1963), pp. 591–92.

138 CCOB, "The Schweitzer Legend," *New York Review of Books* (20 Aug. 1964), p. 7.

139 CCOB, "A Vocation," *New Statesman* (9 Oct. 1964), p. 538.

140 CCOB, "Glimpses of Gaitskell," *New Statesman* (31 Jan. 1964), p. 172.

141 CCOB, "A New Yorker Critic," *New Statesman* (29 June 1963), pp. 972–73.

142 CCOB, "Critic into Prophet," *New Statesman* (15 May 1964), pp. 765–66.

143 CCOB, "Contemporary Forms of Imperialism," *Studies on the Left* 5 (Fall 1965), p. 20.

144 CCOB, "Varieties of Anti-Communism," *New Statesman* (13 Sept. 1963), p. 321.

145 CCOB, "Journal de Combat," *New Statesman* (20 Dec. 1963), p. 911.

146 CCOB, "The Perjured Saint," *New York Review of Books* (19 Nov. 1964), p. 3. For subsequent involvement in the Hiss-Chambers issue, see CCOB letters in the *New York Review of Books* (6 April 1967), p. 35 and (4 May 1967), p. 37.

147 William F. Buckley, Jr., "The Assault on Whittaker Chambers," *National Review* (15 Dec. 1964), pp. 1098–1102. Later, in the 1980s, Conor ceased to be convinced that Hiss was framed (O'Brien interviews).

148 Nkrumah to CCOB, 20 Feb. 1964 (UCD).

149 CCOB to Nkrumah, 22 Feb. 1964; Nkrumah to CCOB, 28 Feb. 1964, cited in CCOB to Nkrumah, 2 March 1964 (Harvey Collection).

150 CCOB to Nkrumah, 2 March 1964.

151 Ibid.

152 Nkrumah to CCOB, 12 March 1964.

153 Charles Runyon (Washington, D.C.) to W.B. Harvey, 26 March 1964 (Harvey Collection).

154 Kwapong interviews.

155 The Congregation address is found in Harvey Collection, and is printed in CCOB, *Writers and Politics*, pp. 251–59.

156 *The Spark*, 17 March 1964. For Burnett Harvey's rebuttal to the charge that he believed that apartheid laws had to be respected, see Harvey to *The Spark*, 2 April 1964 (Harvey Collection). The rebuttal was not published.

157 CCOB to *Observer*,—May 1966 (draft letter) (Harvey Collection).

158 CCOB to Nkrumah, 17 March 1964 (Harvey Collection).

159 CCOB to W.Y. Eduful (?) publicity secretary, Government of Ghana,—April 1964 (UCD).

160 CCOB to Michael Dei Anang, 10 April 1964 (Harvey Collection); O'Brien interviews; D.K. Afreh to CCOB, 9 April 1964 (UCD).

161 CCOB to W.B. Harvey, 10 April 1964 (Harvey Collection); "Memorandum" [by CCOB of meeting with Nkrumah 5 June 1964] (UCD).

162 CCOB to W.B. Harvey, 6 May 1964 (Harvey Collection); Robert Seidman to W.B. Harvey, 22 April 1964 (Harvey Collection).

163 "Harvey Report," p. 10.

164 Conor doggedly insisted on Ekow-Daniels receiving proper permission from the university before taking his additional post. See Memorandum of T.K. Impraim, re "Reopening of the Law School," 1964; CCOB to Ekow-Daniels, 5 June 1964; Ekow-Daniels to CCOB, 9 June 1964; CCOB to Enoch Okoh, 8 June 1964; CCOB to Ekow-Daniels, 19 June 1964; R.W. Prah to CCOB, 23 June 1964; Ekow-Daniels to CCOB, 25 June 1964; CCOB to Enoch Okoh, 3 July 1964; CCOB to Ekow-Daniels, 3 July 1964; CCOB to B.W. Prah, 3 July 1964; CCOB to Ekow-Daniels, 9 July 1964; CCOB to W.B. Harvey, 27 July 1964; CCOB to W.B. Harvey, 4 Sept. 1964; CCOB to Enoch Okoh, 6 Sept. 1964; Ekow-Daniels to CCOB, 12 Oct. 1964. (All items in Harvey Collection; most are also found in UCD).

165 W.B. Harvey to CCOB, 7 Aug. 1964 (Harvey Collection).

166 CCOB, *Harvard Educational Review* 37, no. 2 (1967), p. 288.

167 CCOB to Kwaku Boateng, 6 Sept. 1964; CCOB to W.B. Harvey, 18 Nov. 1964; CCOB to Kwaku Boateng, 23 March 1965; "Vice-Chancellor's Report to Congregation, 29 March 1965," pp. 1–4, 6–11 (all items in Harvey Collection).

168 CCOB to Nkrumah, 11 Nov. 1964 (UCD); CCOB to Alex Kwapong, 12 Nov. 1964 (UCD); "Vice-Chancellor's Report to Congregation, 29 March 1965," pp. 4–5, 11.

169 CCOB to David Astor, 10 May 1966 (Harvey Collection and UCD). See also draft letter, CCOB to *Observer*, April 1966 (Harvey Collection and UCD).

170 CCOB to David Astor, 10 May 1966. There is no point in naming the chief culprit. He was in the same cell as E.P. Thompson, and when, in the late 1960s, O'Brien and Thompson were at New York University, Thompson told Conor that this man was one of the reasons that he had left the Communist party (O'Brien interview). Thompson also said that "I stayed quite a long time in the Party in spite of negative aspects which I recognized, but ... was in the party *because* of the negative aspects." The quotation and a generalized comparison of E.P. Thompson and this particular party stalwart are found in CCOB, "Refined and Vulgar Marxism," *Observer*, 28 Oct. 1979.

171 CCOB to W.B. Harvey, 25 March 1965 (Harvey Collection).

172 "Vice-Chancellor's Address to Congregation, 27th March 1965," *University of Ghana Reporter* 4 (23 April 1965), pp. 261–70.

173 "Vice-Chancellor's Report to Convocation, March 29, 1965," p. 13 (Harvey Collection).

174 "Press Statement," 30 March 1965 (Harvey Collection).

175 CCOB to Harvey, 25 March 1965.
176 CCOB to W.B. Harvey, 30 March 1965 (Harvey Collection).
177 CCOB to Nkrumah, 5 July 1965 (UCD).
178 "Extract from the minutes ... of the Academic Board held on 10 July 1965," enclosed in J.N.O. Lamptey to Mr. and Mrs. Sean MacEntee, 2 Aug. 1965 (Howth).
179 Ashby and Anderson, *Universities: British, Indian, African*, p. 329.
180 The subsequent careers of Professors Kwapong and Harvey are summarized in notes 28 and 29. Kwame Nkrumah was overthrown by a coup, 24 February 1966. The coup was entirely domestic in origin. Nkrumah was in Peking at the time. The former president settled in Guinea where he broadcast frequently to Ghana and wrote pamphlets and various books. He was diagnosed as having cancer and on 27 April 1972 died in a Roumanian hospital. In 1992 his remains were removed from Roumania to be reinterred in Accra at what became Kwame Nkrumah Memorial Park. Here, in what in colonial days was the Polo Grounds, there is now a twenty-foot-high statue of Dr. Nkrumah, in flowing *kente*, his hand upraised, pointing to a glorious future.

William Emmanuel Abraham had a successful academic career. Alex Kwapong's term as pro-vice-chancellor was to expire before Conor left; however, the chairman of the University Council, Kwaku Boateng, postponed holding the election until some time after Conor's tenure had expired. Alex Kwapong was given to understand that he should step down, and the implication was that this wish came from the highest level, Osagyefo. He did so and Willie Abraham was elected in his place. When the coup of February 1966 took place, he and a number of the pro-Nkrumah set were clapped in jail by the police. Alex Kwapong (who was made acting vice-chancellor and subsequently became vice-chancellor in his own right), intervened and secured Abraham's release. He ensured that back salary (for jail time) was paid to Abraham and gave him enough money from the vice-chancellor's discretionary funds to allow him to take a scholarly leave outside the country. This was a kind way of giving Abraham the opportunity to find a post outside of Ghana. Because his credentials were very good, he had no problems. He taught first at Macalester College, St. Paul, Minnesota (1969–73), and then, from 1973 on, at the University of California, Santa Cruz, as a full professor. (Kwapong interviews; *Directory of American Schools* (New York: R.R. Bowker Co., 1982), 4:2; CCOB to *Observer*, 10 May 1966 (UCD and Harvey Collection).

William Cornelius Ekow-Daniels became deputy attorney general of Ghana and was on leave from the university when the 1966 coup took place. He spent several months in "protective custody." Released, he returned to the university in the autumn of 1967. Thereafter, he continued his unusually distinguished legal career. See Depositions of CCOB and Kwapong, 29 Aug. 1967 (O'Brien papers, UCD).

CHAPTER 9

1 CCOB, "The Fall of Africa," *New Republic* 192 (18 March 1985), p. 34. For details of the three-college arrangement for the University of East Africa, see the *Commonwealth Universities Yearbook* for the years 1964–71.
2 See Bernard Onyango to CCOB, 4 Dec. 1965; cable of Onyango to CCOB, 8 Dec. 1965; cable of CCOB to Onyango 8 Dec. 1965 (O'Brien Papers, New York University Archives—hereafter NYU —box 5, file 2).
3 Mercier had taught at Bennington College, Vermont, 1947–48, and then at City College of New York in 1948–65, rising to associate professor. In 1964–65, he was himself negotiating a change of position and in mid-1965 he became a professor of English and comparative literature at the University of Colorado in Boulder. Then, in

1974, he moved to the University of California, Santa Barbara, as a professor of English.

4   David H. Greene of the New York University English Department is not to be confused with the Celtic scholar, David W. Greene, senior professor of the Dublin Institute for Advanced Studies. It is fair to guess that Greene (of NYU), a noted Synge scholar and well connected in Irish studies, would have come to know about Conor's availability for employment, with or without a tip from Mercier. In his first letter to Conor, he mentions seeing in the *New York Times* that Conor was resigning his present post. David Greene to CCOB, 10 April 1965 (O'Brien papers, University College Dublin—hereafter, "UCD").

5   Greene to CCOB, 10 April 1965; NYU news release, 2 June 1965; CCOB to Thomas Pollack, 5 July 1965 (UCD).

6   CCOB to David Greene [late June, July], 1965 in the possession of William Burnett Harvey—hereafter Harvey Collection.

7   Ibid.

8   *New York Times*, 2 Jan. 1968.

9   "The Superstars," *Newsweek* 107 (24 March 1966), p. 68.

10 CCOB to Mary Kettle, 12 Nov. 1965 (UCD).

11 CCOB, "The Villagers," *Irish Times*, 24 Feb. 1969.

12 CCOB, "Decent People and Vigilantes," *Irish Times*, 26 April 1983.

13 D.H. Akenson, *A Protestant in Purgatory: Richard Whately, Archbishop of Dublin* (Hamden, Conn,: Conference on British Studies, Archon Books, 1981), p. 84.

14 See the correspondence of Eileen Sheerin with various university functionaries, concerning the premises at 1 Fifth Avenue (NYU, box 3, files 1 and 4).

15 CCOB, Curriculum Vitae, 1969 (UCD).

16 CCOB to William Buckler, 29 Sept. 1966 (NYU, box 4, file 3).

17 The lack of a departmental base is the reason that Conor – unlike the archetypal "research professor"—did not produce Ph.D. students. The only doctoral supervision that he undertook, as far as I can discover, was of George Alexander, whose English department thesis, "A Sinister Resonance: Conrad's View of the Absurd," passed in June 1966 (NYU, box 3, folder 6).

18 See Miguel de Capriles to CCOB, 23 Feb. 1968; CCOB to de Capriles, 26 Feb. 1968; de Capriles to CCOB, 28 Feb. 1968; CCOB to Thompson Bradley, 12 March 1968; CCOB to Jonathan Mirsky, 12 March 1968. To both Bradley and Mirsky he gave the same advice: "Bethink yourself also of the example of Mr. de Valera who in 1927 took the Oath of Allegiance to the British Crown, in order to be able to abolish the requirement of the Oath in 1933." He concluded, "So please swear (or affirm) but teach."

19 The program details are found in NYU, box 3, file 1; box 4, file 3.

20 Letter, signed by 109 NYU students, to the editor, *New York Times*,—January 1968 (NYU, box 4, file 3).

21 Peter Braunstein, of the NYU archives, who is conducting an extensive series of interviews on the Village counterculture of the 1960s, says that he frequently hears in the interviews that the Schweitzer program in general, and Conor in particular, was one of the intellectual focal points of the late 1960s in the Village.

22 Information on the various persons who taught in the Schweitzer program during Conor's administration is found in the copies of personnel documents in the O'Brien papers, NYU. The material, quite voluminous, is found mostly in boxes 1 and 4. In addition, the individuals Conor recruited are usually listed in the standard directories of notables. I am, therefore, citing only unusual aspects of the recruitment or résumé of various program members.

23 For assessments of Arden as a playwright, see Frances Gray, *John Arden* (New York: Grove Press, 1983); Albert Hunt, *Arden: A Study of His Plays* (London: Eyre Methuen, 1974).

24 "Interview with Conor Cruise O'Brien," *Maclean's* 91 (1 May 1978), p. 8.

25 CCOB to William Buckler, 4 Oct. 1965 (NYU, box 1, file 1).

26 CCOB to David Caute, 4 Oct. 1965, ibid.

27 CCOB to Buckler, 4 Oct. 1965.

28 CCOB to Karl Miller, 16 June 1965 (UCD).

29 "George Steiner Interviewed by Eleanor Wachtel," *Queen's Quarterly* 99 (Winter 1992), p. 846.

30 For a latter-day (and therefore tamer, but still pungent) indication of how the two played off each other verbally, see the transcript of a panel discussion at Skidmore College of 11 April 1985, in which O'Brien and Steiner participated: "The Responsibility of Intellectuals," *Salmagundi* 70–71 (Spring-Summer 1986), pp. 164–95.

31 Interview with NYU staff member who was present on this occasion.

32 George Steiner to CCOB, 21 Aug. 1967 (NYU, box 1, file 3).

33 George Steiner's later career is well known, a virtually intergalactic phenomenon. At present, he is an Extraordinary Fellow of Churchill College, Cambridge, professor of English and comparative literature in the University of Geneva, and the chief literary critic of the *New Yorker*.

34 CCOB to Iris Murdoch, 16 Nov. 1965 (NYU, box 1, file 1).

35 Iris Murdoch to CCOB, 26 Nov. 1965, ibid.

36 Offer to Hobsbawm mentioned in cable, CCOB to Peter Nettl, 25 Feb. 1968 (NYU, box 1, file 4).

37 CCOB to V.S. Naipaul, ibid. Two points about this offer are noteworthy: (1) the rate offered, $5,000 per semester, was two-thirds of that offered to Iris Murdoch; (2) this offer was made after Conor knew that he himself would almost certainly be leaving the Schweitzer Chair.

38 The negotiations were made difficult by the financial problems of Thompson's university, Warwick, by Thompson's understandable prickliness about U.S. immigration authorities (who already had given him difficulties about his previous Communist party membership), and by Thompson's desire to arrange things so that they did not interfere with the scholarly career of his wife, Dorothy, whose work was just then beginning to get the recognition it deserved. See NYU, box 1, file 2; box 4, file 3. For a recent assessment of Thompson's work, see Michael D. Bess, "E.P. Thompson: The Historian as Activist," *American Historical Review* 98 (Feb. 1993), pp. 19–38. More detailed and more analytical is Bryan D. Palmer, *The Making of E.P. Thompson: Marxism, Humanism and History* (Toronto: New Hogtown, 1981). In the late 1970s and early 1980s, Thompson became England's best-known antinuclear weapons campaigner. For a temperate, but pointed attack on some of his positions, see CCOB, "Peace, Freedom— and Hypocrisy (An Open Letter to Edward P. Thompson)," *Observer* 7 Feb. 1982.

39 CCOB to Herbert Weisinger, 26 May 1967 (UCD).

40 CCOB to Robert Armstrong, 28 Dec. 1967 (UCD).

41 Eileen Sheerin to Bayly Winder, 10 June 1969 (NYU, box 3, file 1).

42 The body of literature produced by the New York intellectuals is immense, and even that produced about them is large. I have found the following accounts especially helpful. Alexander Bloom, *Prodigal Sons: The New York Intellectuals and Their World* (New York: Oxford University Press, 1986); Terry Cooney, *The Rise of the New York Intellectuals* (Madison: University of Wisconsin Press, 1986); John P. Diggins, *The Rise and Fall of the American Left*, 2d ed. (New York: W.W. Norton, 1992); Alan M. Wald,

The New York Intellectuals: The Rise and Decline of Anti-Stalinist Left from the 1930s to the 1980s (Chapel Hill: University of North Carolina Press, 1987). Special mention must be made of the brilliant study by Neil Jumonville, *Critical Crossings: The New York Intellectuals in Postwar America* (Berkeley: University of California Press, 1991).

43 Irving Howe, "The New York Intellectuals," in his *Decline of the New* (New York: Harcourt, Brace and World, 1970), p. 211.

44 Ibid., pp. 210–11.

45 Diggins, p. 211.

46 On the almost mythic aspect of the old Village in the orientation of the New York intellectuals, see Cooney, p. 19.

47 The quality of anyone's teaching at the university level is notoriously difficult to assess. That Conor taught well is clearly implied in the NYU student assessment which rated his program the highest at the university (especially given that he participated in more than half the courses in most years). Early in his teaching at NYU, he wrote to Owen Sheehy-Skeffington (himself a Trinity don): "I find university teaching rather harder work than I had assessed it as being during my undergraduate days. I now find that you have actually to prepare those lectures instead of getting up, as I had always assumed and saying the first thing that came into your head. I am teaching just one undergraduate course at present—two hours a week and certainly would, in earlier days, have given the horse laugh to anyone who claimed that this would involve a substantial amount of work" (CCOB to Owen Sheehy-Skeffington, 29 Oct. 1965, NYU, box 3, file 7). A fairly extensive collection of Conor's course outlines, term paper topics, and final examinations is found in NYU, box 2, file 5. They are (from my own viewpoint as a university teacher) solid, painstaking, imaginative, the sort of thing one would expect from someone who took teaching seriously. For a reflection on his teaching experience, see CCOB, "Aspects of American Education," *Irish Times*, 17 March 1969.

48 Various NYU sources, but especially Claudia Dreifus interview. Ms. Dreifus was the lead radical at NYU in the mid-1960s (at least among those serious enough to stay formally enrolled), the head of the university's version of the Students for a Democratic Society. She became a freelance journalist with a very shrewd memory and eye. See, for example, her "Chile's Challenge," *Mother Jones* (Oct. 1990), pp. 26–28. In 1987 she won the Outstanding Article Award from the American Society of Journalists and Authors.

49 There is a considerable file of Conor's speaking engagements, NYU, box 1, file 5 and box 2, file 1. It is, however, dwarfed by the files of invitations that he declined.

50 Among the invitations that Conor turned down was Richard Ellman's to spend any quarter in 1966–67 at Northwestern University. This would have resulted in his spending Mondays and Wednesdays at NYU and Tuesdays and Thursdays at Northwestern. As Conor said to Ellman, "I do not think this would be satisfactory from your point of view. From my own it would be a bit of a strain." (CCOB to Richard Ellman, 21 Oct. 1965, NYU, box 5, file 2). When his old roommate, Vivian Mercier, arranged an endowed visitorship at the University of Colorado for four or five days sometime in 1966–67, Conor had to decline as having "no one to give my lectures in my absence" (CCOB to John R. Carnes, 3 Feb. 1966), NYU, box 5, file 2).

51 Publicity release by Bob Terte (NYU, box 4, file 7).

52 The brochures on the series, now expensively printed, are found in NYU, box 4, file 7.

53 See printed brochures, NYU, box 4, file 8. See also Eileen Sheerin to Bayly Winder, 10 June 1960 (NYU, box 3, file 1).

54 List of those to be invited to Schweitzer Program Lecture Series (1967), NYU, box 4, file 71).

55 "Donat O'Donnell," "Discipline and Self-Discipline," *Spectator* (3 Dec. 1954), p. 728.

56 "Donat O'Donnell," "Generation of Saints," *Spectator* (15 Jan. 1960), p. 80.

57 Louis MacNeice, *The Poetry of W.B. Yeats* (London: Oxford University Press, 1941), pp. 41, 174.

58 The essay, "Passion and Cunning: An Essay on the Politics of W.B. Yeats," has been printed several times (see the Bibliography in the Anthology volume for books published in 1965). Quotations here are from CCOB, *Passion and Cunning: Essays on Nationalism, Terrorism and Revolutions* (New York: Simon and Schuster, 1988). The quotation in the text is from p. 8.

59 Ibid., p. 38.

60 Ibid., p. 49.

61 *New Republic* 199 (12–19 Sept. 1988), p. 39.

62 Gerald Weales, "Homo Canadidus, Liberalis Pessimisticus," *Pennsylvania Gazette* (March 1989), p. 18.

63 See "Introduction" to *Passion and Cunning*, pp. 1–2, for Conor's acknowledgment, in response to Lyons, of one instance of overstatement.

64 W.J. McCormack, *The Battle of the Books: Two Decades of Irish Cultural Debate* (Mullingar: Lilliput Press, 1986), p. 22.

65 Patrick Cosgrave, "Yeats, Fascism and Conor O'Brien," *London Magazine* 7 (July 1967), p. 41.

66 Elizabeth Cullingford, *Yeats, Ireland and Fascism* (New York: New York University Press, 1981).

67 CCOB, "What Rough Beast?" *Observer*, 19 July 1981. I suspect Conor was so generous to Cullingford in this review because of his respect for and friendship with her mentor Richard Ellman. In private correspondence he could be more direct, as when he wrote to Stephen Miller, a young graduate student at Rutgers, who had written about what he termed "Yeats' flirtation" with fascism that "if you read much about Yeats, you will see that the prevailing tone in Yeats' commentary, both biographical and critical, is exactly in the sense of your own wording, 'flirtation,' 'few positive remarks about Mussolini,' etc. The involvement is in fact considerably deeper than that." Conor pointed out that "the Ireland in which Yeats lived was a country which could have gone fascist and could be today in the position of Salazar's Portugal or Franco's Spain. Yeats knew this and it was at the very time, in 1933, when Ireland appeared the nearest to the brink of a fascist seizure of power that Yeats' relations with the Irish fascists were closest and most enthusiastic. ... Ireland is my country and I am sickened by the thought of what it would be like if Yeats' friends had had their way in 1933." CCOB to Stephen Miller, 7 Jan. 1968 (NYU, box 5, file 4).

68 Two obscure studies do a much better job than Cullingford's in putting Yeats's politics in perspective: Mark T. Pierce, "The Political Careers of William Butler Yeats and Oliver St. John Gogarty in the Irish Free State," M.A. thesis, Queen's University, Ontario, 1974; Bernard G. Krimm, *W.B. Yeats and the Emergence of the Irish Free State 1918–1939: Living in the Explosion* (Troy, N.Y.: Whitston Publishing, 1981). The present official biographer of Yeats, Roy Foster, is one of the leading historians of Ireland, and I expect that his discussion of the matter will be definitive.

69 McCormack, p. 22. He continues, with nicely formed irony, "In short, he was the forerunner of *Field Day*, even if neither party would care to acknowledge the relationship yet."

70 CCOB, "Blueshirts and Quislings," *Magill* 4 (June 1981), p. 25.

71 George Steiner, "Cat Man," *New Yorker* (24 Aug. 1992), p. 84.

72 CCOB, "Thoughts on Commitment," *Listener* 86 (16 Dec. 1971), p. 836.

73 CCOB, *Passion and Cunning*, p. 50.

74 Ibid., p. 54.
75 The lecture, "Nietzsche and the Machiavellian Schism," is found in ccob, *The Suspecting Glance* (London: Faber and Faber 1972), pp. 51–65. It was first printed, in slightly different form, in the *New York Review of Books* (5 Nov. 1970), pp. 12–16.
76 The lecture, "Burke, Nietzsche and Yeats," is found in ccob, *The Suspecting Glance*, pp. 67–91. The phrase quoted is from p. 74.
77 Max Black, ed., *The Morality of Scholarship* (Ithaca: Cornell University Press, 1967).
78 Ibid., p. v.
79 ccob, "Politics and the Morality of Scholarship," in Black, pp. 62–63. The essay is re-printed in ccob and William Dean Vanech (eds.), *Power and Consciousness* (London: University of London Press, and New York: New York University Press, 1969), pp. 33–42.
80 Ibid., pp. 64–65.
81 Ibid., p. 65.
82 Ibid.
83 Critical to an understanding of the events which follow in the text is Christopher Lasch's *The Agony of the American Left* (New York: Alfred A. Knopf, 1969), pp. 63–114. Although written soon after the events it narrates, the study stands up very well, and has the great virtue of focusing on what happened and not letting events vapor away into theory.
84 In addition to Lasch, see Bloom, pp. 265–67; Ward, pp. 277–78; Jumonville, p. 110.
85 ccob to Claude Cockburn, 15 April 1966 (ucd), in reply to Cockburn to ccob, 5 April 1966 (ucd).
86 The classic evocation of points 2, 3, and 4 are found—as late as 1987—in the autobi-ography of Sidney Hook, *Out of Step: An Unquiet Life in the 20th Century* (New York: Harper and Row, 1987), pp. 450–60.
87 *New York Times*, 10 and 11 May 1966.
88 I have been unable to find a tape of the 1966 telecast. I have talked to half a dozen peo-ple who vividly remember seeing it (and not all are admirers of Conor) and they are in agreement that it was a complete humiliation for Schlesinger. The quotations in the text are Conor's, found in ccob, "International Episodes," *New York Review of Books* 30 (29 Sept. 1983), p. 11. I think that they are accurate, because in a letter to the editor which attempts to set the record straight (ibid., 10 Nov. 1983, p. 60), Schlesinger does not challenge the accuracy of Conor's version of the television exchange.
89 The letter exchange, under the title "Writers and Issues," was found on pp. 6 and 12, *Book Week* (11 Sept. 1965).
90 Nothing came of an attempt by Conor to meet Schlesinger and to patch over their dif-ferences (ccob to Schlesinger, Sept. 1966; ccob to William Buckler, 4 Oct. 1966, nyu, box 4, file 7). In class at nyu, Conor used some of his time to rake Schlesinger over the coals (see lecture transcript, n.d., nyu, box 5, file 8). Conor begins a lecture by referring to the previous one. "In our last class, when I was going on about Arthur M. Schlesinger, Jr., Mr. Ryan asked me a question about what kind of people I admire. It was, I suppose, clear enough what kind of people I do not admire."
    Later, in 1979 in the *Observer* ("Testing the Power of Magic Blood," 11 Nov. 1979), Conor made Schlesinger into an imaginary character who was reputed to have said "As for the Founding Fathers, if they were not in favour of heredity, why do we call them the Founding Fathers?" Later still, in 1986, Conor retold the story of the Metromedia debate, and was much gentler, for he was reflecting on the constraints on truth-telling that his time in politics had laid on him. "The point in this is that the intellectual in politics comes out with two memories, two competing statements of

fact, one belonging to the period of his government service, the other to a time when he is outside that service. ... Now at the time of the debate with Arthur Schlesinger I'm afraid that I felt quite self-righteous about my own participation in these matters. But pride cometh before a fall and at that time I had not myself been engaged in active democratic electoral politics in my own country." "The Intellectual in Power," a discussion with John Lukacs, *Salmagundi* 69 (Winter 1986), p. 260.

91 "Column," *Encounter* (Aug. 1966), pp. 42, 43.

92 CCOB, "Some Encounters with the Culturally Free," *Rights* (Spring 1967). I am here quoting from the final typescript draft (UCD), pp. 4–5.

93 CCOB to Owen Sheehy-Skeffington, 24 Oct. 1966 (UCD).

94 CCOB to Alexis Fitzgerald, 9 Nov. 1966 (UCD). A good deal of Conor's information on Rees came from Isaiah Berlin.

95 CCOB, "Some Encounters with the Culturally Free," pp. 4–5; CCOB to Owen Sheehy-Skeffington, 24 Oct. 1966.

96 The reader will notice that I am not even bothering to speculate about what the "thick dossiers" (imaginary though they were) could have contained. Financial transactions? It is no secret that Conor has never been able to balance a check book or to spend less than he earns. He does not understand elementary accounting sufficiently to be able to steal from petty cash, let alone engage in peculation on a significant scale. "Past political associations?" These included, one way or another, Sean MacBride, Moise Tshombe, Dag Hammarskjold, and Kwame Nkrumah, not a group one would have brought to one's local pub, but each, in his own way, a pillar of the community. And Conor had never flirted with the Communist party, which for the *Encounter* group usually was the real mortal sin of "past political association."

97 CCOB, "Some Encounters with the Culturally Free," p. 4.

98 CCOB to Donal Cruise O'Brien, 28 Nov. 1966 (UCD); CCOB to Mary Kettle, 1 Feb. 1967 (UCD); CCOB, "Some Encounters with the Culturally Free," p. 5.

99 CCOB, "Some Encounters with the Culturally Free," p. 6; CCOB to Frank J. Donor, 16 May 1967 (UCD).

100 CCOB to Timothy O'Keefe, 30 June 1967 (UCD).

101 Melvin Lasky, letter to *Irish Times*, 20 July 1974.

102 CCOB, "Comments on 'What's Happening to America,'" *Partisan Review* 34 (Spring 1967), p. 263.

103 Ibid.

104 CCOB, "After Manilla," speech given 5 Nov. 1966 (NYU, box 2, file 2), pp. 2–3, emphasis added.

105 See CCOB, "Satirical Pastoral," *New York Review of Books* (25 April 1968), pp. 19–20, 22.

106 CCOB, "The Counterrevolutionary Reflex," *Columbia University Forum* (Spring 1966), p. 23.

107 CCOB, *Writers and Politics*, p. xxii.

108 For comments on the way in which the "death of communism" in Europe left the American anticommunists confused, see CCOB, "Communist Castaways," *Times* 26 April 1990.

109 "In Search of Morality: Conor Cruise O'Brien talks to Brian Inglis," *Listener* 90 (23 Aug. 1973), p. 235.

110 For reports of Conor's speeches at that congress, see *The Worker* [New York], 3 Oct. 1965.

111 CCOB to Francisco V. Portela, 27 Dec. 1967 (UCD).

112 CCOB, "Not Europe Only," *Massachusetts Review* 13, no. 4 (1972), p. 529n.

113 "Questionnaire," enclosed with O'Brien to Portela, 27 Dec. 1967.

114 CCOB, "Imagination and Politics, in J.C. Laidlaw, ed., *The Future of the Modern Humanities* (New York: Modern Humanities Research Association, 1969), pp. 73–74.

115 Conor's relationship with Orwell—the relationship was intellectual, not personal— was very ambiguous. He deeply respected Orwell and sometimes mentioned him as a mentor (as in his interview with Brian Inglis cited in note 109). Each wrote prose that was wonderfully engaged, but simultaneously tight, incisive, memorable, and both fought against perceived orthodoxies, both on the right and the left. Yet Conor kept an intellectual distance from Orwell. See "Donat O'Donnell," "Raffles, Stalin and George Orwell," *The Bell* (May 1946), pp. 167–71; "Donat O'Donnell," "Orwell Looks at the World," *New Statesman* (26 May 1961), p. 80; CCOB, "Honest Men," *Listener* (12 Dec. 1968), pp. 797–98. I think that the distancing took place because Orwell at the moment when Conor first encountered him as a man in his own maturity, was already being employed by the anticommunists for their own purposes. (The first article cited above, that in *The Bell* in 1946, reviewed Orwell's *Critical Essays* and *Animal Farm*.) In 1971 Conor observed that after Orwell's death, "throughout the fifties and early sixties, his last writings, read in a narrowly anti-communist sense, became part of the arsenal of Western, cold war ideology. A smelly little orthodoxy, if ever there was one." CCOB, "Thoughts on Commitment," *Listener* (16 Dec. 1971), p. 836.

116 Diggins, pp. 218–76, is especially good on the threat that the New Left implied to the Old Left, and on their disdain for Trotskyists.

117 CCOB to All Square Club Council, 19 Oct. 1965 (NYU, box 3, file 10).

118 Claudia Dreifus interview; CCOB to Dean Moss, 4 Nov. 1965, ibid.

119 CCOB to Mr. and Mrs. W.B. Such, 15 April 1968 (UCD). For a conflicting view, namely, that the exercise at NYU was a cynical cooption of everyone by the administration, see Deirdre Levinson to the editor [of the NYU newspaper], 11 April 1968 (NYU, box 5, file 4).

120 CCOB, "Student Unrest," *Irish Times* 10 March 1969. At one point in this period, Conor encountered a tomato barrage from the more radical students (Deirdre Levinson Bergson interview).

121 CCOB, "Introduction: The Legitimation of Violence," in CCOB, *Herod: Reflections on Political Violence* (London: Hutchinson, 1978), p. 9. The play is found on pp. 189–212.

122 Ibid., p. 209.

123 CCOB to Irving Howe, 23 Nov. 1965 (NYU, box 5, file 3).

124 CCOB to Thomas M. Franck, 23 Nov. 1965, ibid.

125 The speech, "After Manilla," is found in NYU, box 7, file 11.

126 Stewart Meacham to CCOB, 9 Feb. 1967 (NYU, box 2, file 2).

127 Jeffrey Rose to CCOB, 7 Nov. 1967, ibid.

128 CCOB to Peader MacSwiney, 20 Sept. 1966 (UCD).

129 The untitled speech, in long-hand, is in UCD. The letter from Muriel MacSwiney to CCOB was of 19 Sept. 1966.

130 For a summary of the data on the status level of the Irish-Americans, see D.H. Akenson, *The Irish Diaspora: A Primer* (Belfast: Institute of Irish Studies, Queen's University of Belfast; Toronto: P.D. Meany, 1993), pp. 242–44.

131 Conor, by virtue of his nationality, received more than his fair share of abusive letters from Irish-Americans. See, for example, George M. Davis to CCOB,—1966: "My grandson is after losing his leg in South Vietnam. I am not protesting. why you? Why not return to Hyde Park and select a corner to protest?" (UCD). However, when the

letters were less than abusive, he answered with an attentiveness that he would not have granted to his academic colleagues. See, for example, Jeremiah Daly to CCOB, 11 Jan. 1967, and CCOB to Daly, 16 Jan. 1967 (UCD).

132 O'Brien interview, *Irish Times* 6 Dec. 1966. There are several items related to the incident, including an attempt to sue the City of New York, in UCD. See also "On Being Kicked by a New York Cop," *Observer*, 4 March 1979.

133 Claudia Dreifus interview.

134 Conor took part in peace conferences in Wellington, New Zealand, and in Sydney, Australia, in late March or early April of 1968. (CCOB to Mr. and Mrs. W.B. Such, 15 April 1968 in UCD; CCOB to Alistair Taylor, 24 Jan. 1968, UCD. See also CCOB, "Haigspeak: A New Guide to Power," *Observer*, 24 Jan. 1982.) He pushed the work of John Gerassi, *North Vietnam: A Commentary* (London: George Allen and Unwin, 1968), to which he wrote an introduction; and in a nice piece of theater, he and Maire, who were prominent guests at a convocation ceremony in the spring of 1968 where Vice-President Hubert Humphrey was receiving an honorary degree, staged a walk-out as a protest .gainst his complicity in the Vietnam War (O'Brien interviews, and Julian Mayfield to Eileen Sheerin, 11 May 1968, NYU, box 1, file 4).

Running against this was a counterstream. Conor had in 1965 been very keen on being one of three delegates sent to North Vietnam by antiwar leaders, the other two being Benjamin Spock, the well-known pediatrician, and Robert S. Browne, professor of economics at Fairleigh Dickinson University (Jonathan Mirsky to Pham Van Chuong, 4 Dec. 1965, NYU, box 4, file 2). Conor, worried that he might be barred from return to the United States, arranged for David Astor, editor of the *Observer*, to provide him with press credentials, which presumably would permit him to argue that he went to Vietnam not as a political participant but as a professional journalist. (CCOB to Elaine Greene, 29 Nov. 1965, UCD; and CCOB to Jonathan Mirsky, 9 Dec. 1965, NYU, box 4, file 2). After the beating, however, Conor was much less keen. Rather lack-adaisically, he wrote to a New Zealand peace activist in early 1968, "As regards the possibility of going on to North Vietnam [after doing peace work in New Zealand] I am inclined to think that I will not be able to fit it in because of the limited time I can arrange away from here" (CCOB to Alistair Taylor, 24 Jan. 1968).

135 Published by the Irish Anti-Apartheid Movement, Dublin, Sept. 1967.

136 See Berta Green to CCOB, 30 Nov. 1967 (UCD).

137 CCOB to Leo Toch, 12 May 1966 (NYU, box 5, file 4).

138 Robert Silvers interview; CCOB, "Inside Biafra," *Observer*, 8 Oct. 1967.

139 CCOB, "A Condemned People," *New York Review of Books*, 21 Dec. 1967, pp. 14–19. An interesting critical response to the views in this article are found in a typescript rejoinder found in NYU, box 5, file 6: "The View from Here: A Reply to O'Brien's Plea for Biafra," by Pauline H. Baker.

140 CCOB, "Genocide and Discretion," *Listener* 81 (30 Jan. 1969), p. 129.

141 CCOB to U Thant, 11 Oct. 1967 (UCD); U Thant to CCOB, 16 Oct. 1967 (NYU, box 5, file 4); U Thant to CCOB, 28 Oct. 1967 (UCD); CCOB to Gerald Ford, 26 Feb. 1969 (NYU, box 4, file 8).

142 CCOB, "Biafra Revisited," *New York Review of Books* (22 May 1969), pp. 15–23, 26–27. The tie with the *Observer* continued. An abridged version of the piece was preprinted there, 11 May 1969.

143 241 *Dail Eireann* 455: 9 July 1969.

144 Mid-term test, 1 Nov. 1967 (NYU, box 2, file 5).

145 Christopher Hitchens, "Creon's Think Tank: The Mind of Conor Cruise O'Brien,"

in *Prepared for the Worst: Selected Essays and Minority Reports* (London: Chatto and Windus), pp. 41–42.

146 This and subsequent quotations from "The Embers of Easter" are found in the *Irish Times*, 7 April 1966. In his writings, Conor almost never sold copyright or an exclusive and perpetual license to his material. That meant that ethically he could sell it again and again. In the case of "The Embers of Easter," the desire for multiple usage of the piece had an interesting spin. In 1966, CBS Records was putting together a package about the 1916 Easter Risings, consisting of a heavily illustrated book and a set of records of patriotic ballads, interviews, and a narration by Walter Cronkite. They signed a contract with Conor for the piece, but then refused to use the article unless he substantially toned it down into something saccharine that the Irish-American community would buy. Conor refused, so CBS told him to keep his advance for $1,000 and they got what they wanted elsewhere (see CCOB to Mrs. Haven, 12 May 1966 and Bernard Farber to CCOB—1966, UCD). The version that was finally published included essays by Thomas P. O'Neill and Benedict Kiely: *The Irish Uprising, 1916–1922* [no author or editor identified] (New York: CBS Legacy Collection, 1966).

147 Conor had not put the old inanities quite as far behind him as he here implied. In 1965, after he had arrived at NYU, he accepted a commission to write an essay "Why I Hate the English" for the *Telegraph* (O'Brien papers, Howth). He went so far as to draft a version and showed it to Deirdre Levinson. She told him it was rubbish and he should not involve himself in that sort of cheap rhetoric. At first furious with this criticism, he later agreed with her and dropped the assignment. (A more self-serving version of this transaction is found in CCOB to Elaine Greene, 15 Feb. 1966, UCD.)

148 CCOB to Dympna Magee, 5 May 1966 (NYU, box 5, file 5). After being certain that the group agreed with his four principles, he accepted the patronship (Eileen Sheerin to Dympna Magee, 16 June 1966, NYU, box 5, file 5).

149 [CCOB], "Where Orange Is White," typescript (NYU, box 7, file 10).

150 *Daily Telegraph*, 24 April 1969.

151 CCOB, "The Irish Question—1969," *Irish Times*, 21 Jan. 1969.

152 *Irish Times*, 17 March 1968.

153 Ibid.

154 *Observer* (profile of CCOB), 17 Sept. 1961.

155 CCOB to Dan Davin, 4 Jan. 1966 (UCD).

156 Dan Davin to CCOB, 26 Jan. 1966 (UCD).

157 CCOB to Elaine Greene, 2 Nov. 1966 (UCD).

158 Agreement of 13 Nov. 1965 in UCD.

159 Agreement of 13 July 1967 in UCD.

160 Deirdre Levinson Bergson interview.

161 CCOB to George Steiner, 16 Dec. 1965 (NYU, box 1, file 1).

162 CCOB (marked "private and confidential") to Herbert Weisinger, 26 May 1967 (UCD).

163 George Steiner to CCOB, 21 Aug. 1967 (NYU, box 1, file 3).

164 CCOB to George Steiner, (NYU, box 1, file 3).

165 CCOB to Asa Briggs, 15 Sept. 1967.

166 253 *Dail Eireann* 575: 27 April 1971.

167 "America First or Varieties of Americocentrism" (draft in UCD). Published, with very minor amendments as "America First," *New York Review of Books* (29 Jan. 1970), pp. 8, 10, 12–14.

168 CCOB to Asa Briggs, 15 Sept. 1967. After Conor had decided to leave the United States, he also decided to file his tax returns. That led to a comic scene in the spring of 1969,

when his administrative assistant gave him the happy news that if Conor (who was then in Dublin) would arrange to be out of the country on 15 April, he would receive an automatic extension of sixty days to file his 1968 tax form: not exactly what the rich and famous mean by tax exile. (Eileen Sheerin to CCOB, 9 April 1969, NYU, box 5, file 4).

169 William Trevor, "Field of Battle," *New Yorker* (17 May 1993), p. 84.

170 CCOB to Jonathan Mirsky, 9 Dec. 1965 (NYU, box 4, file 2).

171 CCOB to Pearl Buck, 17 Dec. 1965 (UCD).

172 CCOB to Donal Cruise O'Brien, 3 Feb. 1965 (UCD).

173 Donal's Ph.D. thesis, a distinguished piece of scholarship, was revised and published as *The Mourides of Senegal: The Political and Economic Organization of an Islamic Brotherhood* (Oxford: Clarendon Press, 1971).

174 "Kate Cruise O'Brien: Biography," prepared for the Association of Teachers of English of Ireland, meeting at St. Patrick's College, Drumcondra, 1990. Kate's stories are available in book form in *A Gift Horse and Other Stories* (Swords: Poolbeg Press, 1978) and *The Homesick Garden* (Swords: Poolbeg Press, 1991).

175 CCOB to Liz Aronicka,—March 1967 (UCD).

176 Dorothea Pechulis to Dr. and Mrs. CCOB, 1 May 1967 (NYU, box 5, file 6).

177 A sanitized version of this conversation is found in an interview with Conor by Geraldine Kennedy, "Cruise O'Brien's Crusade," *The Word* [c. 1974] (UCD).

178 Eileen Sheerin to Elaine Greene, 27 Sept. 1968 (NYU, box 4, file 8). See also "Profile: Conor Cruise O'Brien," *New Statesman* (6 Dec. 1968), p. 784. Whether the inference that there was personal malice against Conor in this matter is correct or not, I cannot ascertain. Certainly Conor had left behind in the Department of External Affairs some adamant enemies when he resigned in 1961, and his criticisms of Irish foreign policy during the 1960s—as being increasingly sycophantic to the Americans—did not make many new friends. And, undeniably, from early December 1961, when Conor went public with his discussion of the Congo affray, Aiken had been angry with Conor.

179 The outline of this meeting with de Valera is found in CCOB, "Three de Valera Memories," *Irish Times*, 19 Oct. 1982.

180 Ibid.

181 CCOB, "Black Anti-Semitism," *Irish Times*, 3 March 1969.

182 CCOB, "America: The Long Search for Innocence," *Observer*, 27 Jan. 1980. Reprinted as "Purely American," *Harper's* 260 (April 1980), pp. 32–34. The quotation is from p. 34.

183 *Observer*, 22 Dec. 1968.

184 CCOB to Eileen Sheerin, 27 Dec. 1968 (NYU, box 5, file 6).

185 CCOB to William Buckler, draft of 27 Dec. 1968 (NYU, box 5, file 4).

186 CCOB to William Buckler, draft of 27 Dec. 1968, and final copy of 7 Jan. 1969 (NYU, box 5, file 6).

187 CCOB, "What Exhortation," *Irish University Review* 1 (1970), pp. 48–61. Conor's list of four possible successors for the Schweitzer Chair is interesting. His first choice was Edward Thompson ("He is a first-rate scholar and a first-rate teacher. He is primarily a social historian but his cultural interests are wide"); Barrington Moore, one of America's leading social scientists and political observers; Eric Hobsbawm ("He has a very incisive mind and unusual capacity for inter-relating the social, economic, political, and cultural elements in history"); and Herbert Marcuse ("I am not myself an unreserved admirer of Professor Marcuse's writings but there is no doubt that he has been an extremely important and seminal influence on students"). (CCOB to Bayly

Winder, 23 April 1969, NYU, box 3, file 1). In the actual event, NYU appointed the African-American novelist Ralph Ellison.

188 "Dr. Conor Cruise O'Brien ... told me yesterday that he was resigning from his position as Albert Schweitzer Professor of Humanities at New York University to stand as a Labour candidate in the Irish Parliamentary election later this year." Alex Faulkner in (London) *Daily Telegraph*, 23 April 1969.

189 F.F. Fulton to CCOB, 29 May 1969 (NYU, box 5, file 2).

190 *New York Review of Books*, 18 Oct. 1973.

CHAPTER 10

1 Kieran Furey to CCOB, 23 April 1969, O'Brien Papers, New York University Archives (NYU), box 5, file 4.

2 Eileen Sheerin to Kieran Furey (NYU, box 5, file 4).

3 Brendan Halligan interview.

4 "The Intellectual in Power," *Salmagundi* 69 (Winter 1986), p. 260 (transcript of a panel discussion with John Lukacs and CCOB).

5 Dennis Kennedy interview.

6 Halligan interview.

7 *Irish Times* (hereafter *I.T.*), 12 June 1969; O'Brien interviews.

8 *I.T.*, 20 Dec. 1968; Fintan O'Toole, "The Life and Times of Conor Cruise O'Brien, Part 3," *Magill* 9 (June 1986), pp. 37–38.

9 Halligan interview.

10 Michael Gallagher, *The Irish Labour Party in Transition, 1957–82* (Manchester: Manchester University Press, 1982), p. 83; *I.T.*, 27 Jan. 1969.

11 *I.T.*, 20 Jan. 1969.

12 O'Toole, p. 38.

13 On party organization, in addition to Gallagher, see John Horgan, *Labour: The Price of Power* (Dublin: Gill and Macmillan, 1986). This is an often funny, always revealing insider's account.

14 Gallagher, pp. 80–82.

15 Tony Brown interview; Halligan interview.

16 *I.T.*, 20 March 1969.

17 241 *Dail Eireann* (hereafter *D.E.*) 1–2; Halligan interview.

18 *I.T.*, 28 May 1969.

19 Horgan, p. 84.

20 Interviews with Brown and with John Horgan; Gallagher, pp. 97–104; *I.T.*, May and June 1969, esp. 30 May, 4 June, 17 June; T.P. O'Mahony, *Jack Lynch: A Biography* (Dublin: Blackwater Press, 1991), pp. 103–6.

21 *I.T.*, 7 Nov. 1970.

22 Conor's speech on that occasion, quite unlike anything else of his that is in print, was published as "Not Europe Only," *Massachusetts Review* 13, no. 4 (1972), pp. 529–38.

23 *I.T.*, 10 June 1972.

24 O'Brien interviews; CCOB, "Sir Harold, Mr. Toad and History," *Observer*, 18 Feb. 1979.

25 Horgan interview. I am here leaving aside as profitless the question of whether or not the Irish Labour party of the late 1960s and the 1970s was a "true" socialist party or not. Undeniably, it labeled itself as such and in that guise presented itself to the Irish electorate.

26 *I.T.*, 2 June 1969.
27 Ibid., and 3 June 1969, 5 June 1969, 7 June 1969, 14 June 1969, 16 June 1969. See also 241 *D.E.* 47–48.
28 Interviews with Brown, Halligan, Horgan.
29 *I.T.*, 20 June 1969.
30 Halligan interview.
31 For a summary of the anti-Catholic discrimination in practice at the time, see D.H. Akenson, *The United States and Ireland* (Cambridge: Harvard University Press, 1973), pp. 218–27.
32 *I.T.*, 12 June 1969.
33 For memoirs of Thornley by Muiris MacConghail and D.R. Lysaght, see "Recollections of David Thornley," *Magill* 1 (July 1978), pp. 4–6.
34 For a thumbnail sketch of Cluskey (who probably was the most beloved member of the parliamentary Labour party), see Horgan, pp. 39–41. I have filled in other material from interviews with people who knew Cluskey.
35 O'Brien interviews. A sanitized version of the story is found in O'Toole, p. 40, and in ccob, "Saints, Sinners and Sincerity," *Magill* 4 (July 1981), p. 15.
36 Noel Browne's autobiography, *Against the Tide* (Dublin: Gill and Macmillan, 1986), is one of the most interesting of Irish memoirs. Browne has a mordant eye for his colleagues' foibles, and absolutely no sense of humor. For a review essay, see Gene Kerrigan, "Solo Swimmer," *Magill* 10 (Dec. 1986), pp. 4–8.
37 Halligan interview.
38 ccob, "Burntoilet and the Bogside," *Irish Independent*, 12 Aug. 1989.
39 Ibid.
40 ccob, *The Suspecting Glance* (London: Faber and Faber, 1972), p. 29*n*.
41 Paddy Devlin interview; Kennedy interview.
42 Devlin interview. Mr. Devlin's autobiography at present is in press. Devlin, a voracious reader, was also a shrewd political and social commentator. See Paddy [Patrick Joseph] Devlin, *Tuzo, Whitelaw and the Terror in Northern Ireland* (Belfast: Social Democratic and Labour Party, 1973), and *Yes, We Have No Bananas: Outdoor Relief in Belfast, 1920–30* (Belfast: Blackstaff Press, 1981).
43 Brian Garrett interview.
44 ccob to George Steiner, 26 Sept. 1967 (NYU, box 1, file 3). In the same letter Conor suggested that if Steiner wished to write an introduction to *Thus Spake Zarathustra*, he was sure the publishers would be interested. He referred to his own experience with a New York typing agency which, when doing the final matter for one of his UN studies, introduced a reference to *That Spade Zarathustra*. Conor noted that "this would seem to throw new light on the subject."
45 ccob, "Introduction" to *Edmund Burke: Reflections on the Revolution in France and on the proceedings in certain societies in London relative to that event* (Harmondsworth: Pelican Books, 1968), p. 23.
46 Ibid., p. 41.
47 Ibid., pp. 77–81.
48 Ibid., p. 41*n*.
49 Ibid., p. 15.
50 ccob, "Introduction" to Conor Cruise O'Brien and William Dean Vanech, eds., *Power and Consciousness* (London: University of London Press, 1969), p. 4.
51 ccob, *The Suspecting Glance*, pp. 88–90.
52 ccob, "The Gentle Nietzscheans," *New York Review of Books* (5 Nov. 1970), pp. 12–16.
53 ccob, *Camus* (London: Fontana-Collins, 1970). Space here precludes dealing ade-

quately with what is a brilliant piece of compressed analysis. For a recent discussion of Conor's reading of *L'Etranger*, see Joseph McBride, *Albert Camus: Philosopher and Littérateur* (New York: St. Martin's Press, 1993), pp. 48–54.

54   CCOB, "Still a Free Country," *I.T.*, 14 Aug. 1984.

55   Tom Paulin, *Ireland and the English Crisis* (London: Bloodaxe Books, 1984), pp. 30–31.

56   The play is found in CCOB, *Herod: Reflections on Political Violence* (London: Hutchinson, 1978), pp. 157–87. The *Irish Times* published large excerpts from it (four full newspaper pages) on 2 Dec. 1968. The play opened at the Gate Theatre on 7 Oct. 1969. For reviews, see *I.T.*, 8 Oct. 1969, and *Nation* (24 Nov. 1969), p. 581. A television version was performed on RTE with Hilton Edwards again in the title role (Maire Cruise O'Brien to G. Burne, 19 Sept. 1974, O'Brien papers, Howth).

57   O'Brien interviews. The production company provided Conor with a bundle of basic documents on Collins that he was supposed to work with, a treatment of the topic done by someone else, and an outline that he was supposed to work under (O'Brien papers, Howth). The treatment was real patriotic gore, and quite incompatible with Conor's own views. For instance, the treatment's view of the 1916 Rising was totally at odds with the views Conor expressed in "The Embers of Easter."

58   241 *D.E.* 49.

59   Ibid.

60   241 *D.E.* 119.

61   244 *D.E.* 388–94; *I.T.*, 26 Feb. 1970; Clerk of Committee on Procedures and Privileges to CCOB, 20 Feb. 1970, and "Statement made to the Committee on Procedures and Privileges, 25 February 1970" (O'Brien papers, Howth). Conor was also suspended in December 1970, but this was part of a choreographed protest by Labour deputies. The occasion was the government's threatening to introduce internment without trial in the republic, and to do so without allowing Dail debate. Brendan Corish, leader of the parliamentary Labour party, was suspended for his protest at this procedure, then Noel Browne, then Stevie Coughlan, then Conor. *I.T.*, 11 Dec. 1970; 250 *D.E.* 504ff.

62   243 *D.E.* 637–62.

63   255 *D.E.* 1483–1500.

64   257 *D.E.* 209.

65   The episode is recounted in Browne, pp. 261–64.

66   "The Intellectual in Power," p. 261.

67   For example, 247 *D.E.* 1861–2013.

68   O'Brien interviews; CCOB, "European Parliament Gets Breath of Fresh Air," *I.T.*, 27 Feb. 1973.

69   "The Intellectual in Power," p. 261.

70   O'Toole, p. 43.

71   O'Brien interviews; CCOB, *States of Ireland*, pp. 224–28.

72   See CCOB, *States of Ireland*, pp. 228–29, 235.

73   Ibid., pp. 230–33.

74   Ibid., pp. 237–42. See also the later reference in CCOB, "Our Poor Boggled Minds," *I.T.*, 19 July 1983.

75   An early discussion of many of the arrangements for the importation of arms, by one of the participants, published soon after the arms trial, was *Orders for the Captain* by James Kelly (Dublin: privately printed, 1971). A pioneering investigation, still unsurpassed, was written by Vincent Browne and published in *Magill* 3 (May 1980), pp. 33–56; see also June 1980, p. 4; July 1980, pp. 17–24; and vol. 4 (Nov. 1980), pp. 4–6. On Haughey, see Bruce Arnold, *Haughey: His Life and Unlucky Deeds* (London:

Harper Collins, 1993), pp. 80–109. On Neil Blaney, see "Neil Blaney: Past and Future," *Magill* 8 (2 May 1985), pp. 16–21. For a useful clarification of Kevin Boland's role, see "Apology to Mr. Kevin Boland," *Fortnight* (April 1992), p. 7.

76 246 *D.E.* 646.

77 246 *D.E.* 648–49.

78 246 *D.E.* 1700–1703.

79 246 *D.E.* 888.

80 246 *D.E.* 1524.

81 246 *D.E.* 1524–25.

82 In any case, as Garret FitzGerald points out, the Committee on Public Accounts had been hamstrung from the very first. "I was a member of the Committee that was given the task in December 1970 of investigating and reporting on this aspect of the arms affair. ... Our committee's inquiry went on for over eighteen months. We got little co-operation from many of those asked to give evidence to us. The Official Secrets Act was invoked to prevent publication of a memo that had been sent by the Secretary of the Department of Justice to the Secretary of the Department of Finance shortly after the Dail debates and which had identified the Finance sub-head from which the money had come. A successful Supreme Court challenge was mounted on technical grounds against the committee's power to compel the attendance of witnesses." Garret FitzGerald, *An Autobiography* (Dublin: Gill and Macmillan, 1991), p. 96.

83 CCOB, "One Step Forward, Two Steps Back," *I.T.*, 5 Oct. 1982.

84 CCOB, "The Boss," *I.T.*, 2 and 3 Jan. 1984.

85 O'Toole, p. 44. For other comments of CCOB on the arms trial episode and related events, see the following columns: "Sulphurous Charms of Charles Haughey," *Observer*, 9 Dec. 1979; "The Gath Syndrome," *I.T.*, 9 Feb. 1982; "Still a Free Country."

86 Quoted in *America* 108 (4 May 1963), p. 629. It will not escape notice that this formula is essentially the same as that which, when expressed in the U.K. statute of 1949 guaranteeing the position of Northern Ireland, had so enraged the participants in the antipartition campaign.

87 CCOB, "On the Rights of Minorities," *Commentary* 55 (June 1973), p. 48. This lecture was given to the Minority Rights Group in London in November 1972, but the research dates to mid-1970.

88 Conor went so far in his enthusiasm for the shop stewards as to nominate them in January 1970 for the Nobel Prize. (The nomination papers and correspondence are in the O'Brien papers, Howth.) Gerry Fitt, however, was not at all keen on this, pointing out that the same men who were peace makers by day, often were violent on the street at night. The nomination was not repeated.

89 CCOB, "A Marxist Sense of Ireland," *I.T.*, 22 March 1983.

90 The original discussion was published in the *Crane Bag* 1, no. 1 (1977), pp. 62–64; the quotation in the text is from 4, no. 2 (1980), p. 98. The original piece also received extensive quotation, *I.T.*, 7 May 1977.

91 W.D. Flackes and Sydney Elliot, *Northern Ireland: A Political Directory, 1968–88* (Belfast: Blackstaff Press, 1989), p. 411.

92 Garrett interview.

93 Halligan interview; Brown interview.

94 *I.T.*, 12 June 1971.

95 Ibid.

96 O'Brien interviews; CCOB, *States of Ireland*, p. 226; *I.T.*, 12 June 1971.

97 *I.T.*, 12 June 1971.

98 O'Brien interviews.

99 Ibid.

100 CCOB to Secretary, Erskine Childers Commemoration Committee, 22 July 1971, reported *I.T.*, 24 July 1971.

101 Halligan interview.

102 Brendan Halligan to CCOB, 8 Oct. 1971 (UCD).

103 CCOB to Brendan Halligan, 9 Oct. 1971, ibid.

104 Analyzed in Gallagher, pp. 139–40.

105 Conor's prepared remarks are reprinted in *States of Ireland*, pp. 317–25. See also *I.T.*, 18 Sept. and 25 Sept. 1971. On a subsequent unsuccessful attempt to arrange a debate with Michael Farrell of People's Democracy, see *I.T.*, 26 Nov. 1971 and 30 Nov. 1971.

106 See Brian Farrell, "The 1969 Generation," *Economic and Social Review* 2 (April 1971), pp. 309–28.

107 256 *D.E.* 185, quoted in Gallagher, p. 140.

108 For Conor's description of O'Leary, see CCOB, "Saints, Sinners and Sincerity," *Magill* 4 (July 1981), pp. 15–16.

109 O'Brien interviews.

110 Sometimes the caucus met in Earlsfort Terrace, across St. Stephen's Green.

111 CCOB, "Noel Browne Is Not a Saint," *Irish Independent*, 23 Jan. 1988.

112 Horgan, p. 36; *I.T.*, 10 Dec. 1971; Horgan interview.

113 For a remarkably restrained protest against this lack of consultation with his colleagues on northern issues, see David Thornley to CCOB, 31 Dec. 1971 (UCD).

114 Gallagher, pp. 143–44.

115 *I.T.*, 1 Feb. 1972.

116 258 *D.E.* 1125.

117 CCOB, *States of Ireland*, p. 283.

118 258 *D.E.* 1125–26; CCOB, *States of Ireland*, p. 283.

119 CCOB, "Different Roads to the Cemetery," *Observer*, 6 Feb. 1972.

120 258 *D.E.* 1128.

121 O'Brien interviews; CCOB, *States of Ireland*, p. 284.

122 Garrett interview; CCOB, *States of Ireland*, pp. 283–84.

123 *I.T.*, 29 Jan. 1972.

124 The reports of the annual conference which follow are drawn from a variety of sources: Judy Stone, "Ireland: 'The Killing Sickness.' Sanity Convenes at Wexford," *Nation* (27 March 1972), pp. 390–92; *I.T.*, 25, 26, 28 and 29 Feb. 1972; Gallagher, pp. 145–47; and the memories of several individuals who were present—Brian Garrett, Paddy Devlin, Brendan Halligan (the latter's recollections based on party record of proceedings), John Horgan, Tony Browne, and Conor. The major narrative line of events is agreed upon by these sources, as is the outcome. The precise sequence of some events, however, is problematical.

125 Gallagher, p. 145.

126 Ibid., pp. 145–46.

127 CCOB, *States of Ireland*, p. 285; Donal Foley (*I.T.*, 28 Feb. 1972) estimated that the split was four to one.

128 Stone, p. 392.

129 Donal Foley in *I.T.*, 28 Feb. 1972.

130 CCOB, "Celebrating Patriotic Violence," *Observer*, 12 Dec. 1971.

131 That is Conor's later analysis. CCOB, "The Spiral into Civil War," *Observer*, 26 Aug. 1979.

132 Halligan interview.

133   Barry White, *John Hume: Statesman of the Troubles* (Belfast: Blackstaff Press, 1984), pp. 94–108.

134   *Independent on Sunday*, 31 Oct. 1983.

135   I am here eliding everyday events concerning Northern Ireland that affected Conor's political life. These were three. First, in a near-comic episode, in April 1972, while doing a chat show on Radio Eireann, he had been discussing the need to do away with sectarian symbols in the south, if the northern majority were to be brought into a united Ireland. Just then the Angelus sounded, and Conor, rarely able to bite his tongue, said, "Like that, perhaps." The papers were flooded with protests about his alleged desire to take the Angelus off RTE. Second, and more serious, on 6 July 1972, he met in London with William Whitelaw, secretary of state for Northern Ireland. He already had written to Whitelaw about the need to speedily release all internees and this was discussed. He found Whitelaw "disconcerted by the extent and intensity" of the Protestant backlash. After talking about the mood in the Republic, "Mr. Whitelaw said that, if the population of the South felt that they did not want such a hot potato as Belfast is in its present state of feeling, that would be proof of good sense on their part" ("Notes of an Interview with Mr. William Whitelaw," UCD). Third, his local branch of the Labour party was strongly influenced by Sinn Fein, and as a result both he and Maire resigned from it (Agenda of the Howth and District Branch Labour party for 4 August 1972; Maire Cruise O'Brien to secretary, Howth and District Branch,—August 1972; CCOB to Terence de Vere White, 18 July 1972, UCD).

136   *I.T.*, 3 Aug. 1972.

137   *I.T.*, 2 Oct. 1972.

138   For an indication of Conor's developing thought on Northern Ireland prior to writing *States of Ireland*, see the following articles which, unlike political speeches, were nuanced, allusive, and reflective. "Holy War," *New York Review of Books* (6 Nov. 1969), pp. 9–16; "Irish Troubles: The Boys in the Back Room," *New York Review of Books* (8 April 1971), pp. 35–39; "Violence in Ireland: Another Algeria?" *New York Review of Books* (23 Sept. 1971), pp. 17–19. See also the letter exchange with Paul O'Dwyer, in *New York Review of Books* (2 Dec. 1971), pp. 34–36. Also notable in this period were "On Reading Crossman's Irish Diary," *New Statesman* (24 Sept. 1971), pp. 384–85, and "Northern Ireland: Its Past and Its Future: The Future," *Race* 14 (July 1972), pp. 11–20.

139   Roy F. Foster, *Modern Ireland, 1600–1972* (London: Allen Lane, 1988), p. 595. It is well to realize that an "anti-revisionist" rump developed in Irish studies in the later 1980s, and that Foster is one of the pet hates of those with that viewpoint. Probably the most influential of the antirevisionists are the historian Brendan Bradshaw and the literary critic Seamus Deane. The former seems to hunger for a return to Irish historical writing as Roman Catholic writing, and the latter for Irish intellectual history to be the history of the mythic Celtic mind. What all the antirevisionists share is a distrust of scholarship that is not tied to a nationalist political end, and of scholarship that results in "pluralism" or other viewpoints that imply there is more than one way to be Irish. See Tom Dunne, "New Histories: Beyond 'Revisionism,'" *Irish Review* 12 (Spring-Summer 1992), pp. 1–12.

140   "The Irresponsibility of Unionism," *Times Literary Supplement*, 10 Nov. 1972, p. 1355.

141   Suzannah Lessard, "An Ulsterman's Irishman; an Arab's Jew," *Washington Monthly* (October 1972), p. 46.

142   "The Irresponsibility of Unionism," p. 1355.

143   Stone, p. 392.

144 *I.T.*, 9 Oct. 1972. The emphasis is in Conor's original text. Hume slightly misquotes Conor (*States of Ireland*, pp. 90–92), but without distorting his meaning.

145 Ibid. Hume repeated his charge that *States of Ireland* was a defense of unionism on RTE radio's "This Week," on 15 Oct. 1972. (*I.T.*, 16 Oct. 1972), and in a 1980 interview with Seamus Deane and Barre Fitzpatrick ("Interview with John Hume," *Crane Bag* 4, no. 2 (1980), p. 41).

146 O'Brien interviews; CCOB to Frank Cluskey, 12 Oct. 1972.

147 Gallagher, p. 150. As a compromise with the SDLP, the Administrative Council of the Labour party the next day accepted the motion that O'Connell had placed before the parliamentary Labour party (Gallagher, p. 151).

148 Horgan, p. 159.

149 Kennedy interview; O'Brien interviews.

150 CCOB, "A Spring in the Right Direction," *Irish Independent*, 30 July 1988.

CHAPTER 11

1   John Horgan, *Labour: The Price of Power* (Dublin: Gill and Macmillan, 1986), p. 25.

2   *Irish Times* (hereafter *I.T.*), 17 Nov. 1972.

3   CCOB, Letter to the Editor, *I.T.*, 27 Feb. 1973.

4   Joseph J. Lee, *Ireland, 1912–1985* (Cambridge: Cambridge University Press, 1989), p. 469.

5   Horgan, p. 68.

6   Ibid., p. 116.

7   "FitzGerald Peddles No Faery Myths," *Observer*, 5 July 1981.

8   For a very perceptive profile, see "Garret FitzGerald: Profile of Expectation," *Magill* 1 (Jan. 1978), pp. 7–16.

9   Garret FitzGerald interview; Garret FitzGerald, *All in a Life: Garret FitzGerald, an Autobiography* (Dublin: Gill and Macmillan, 1991), p. 113.

10 "Haughey and Collins Get It right," *I.T.*, 27 April 1982.

11 For an analysis of Irish education in this period, see D.H. Akenson, *A Mirror to Kathleen's Face: Education in Independent Ireland, 1922–1960* (Montreal: McGill-Queen's University Press, 1975).

12 259 *Dail Eireann* (hereafter *D.E.*) 241.

13 "In Search of Morality—Conor Cruise O'Brien Talks to Brian Inglis," *Listener* 90 (23 Aug. 1973), p. 235.

14 O'Brien interviews; CCOB, "Garret Stumbles in the Soft-Shoe Shuffle," *Observer*, 18 Feb. 1986.

15 O'Brien interviews.

16 FitzGerald interview.

17 O'Brien interviews.

18 Muiris MacConghail interview; O'Brien interviews; CCOB, "Three de Valera Memories," *I.T.*, 18 Oct. 1982.

19 Horgan, p. 119.

20 *I.T.*, 28 Oct. 1975.

21 CCOB, "On Being Kicked by a New York Cop," *Observer*, 4 March 1979.

22 Donal Cruise O'Brien interview.

23 A.A. Kelly, ed., *Pillars of the House: An Anthology of Verse by Irish Women from 1690 to the Present* (Dublin: Wolfhound, 1987), pp. 110–11.

24 Maire Cruise O'Brien to L. Fairfield, 29 Oct. 1975 (O'Brien papers, Howth).

25 Documents in O'Brien papers, Howth.
26 Maire Cruise O'Brien, "One Little Boy's Africa," *Kilbarrack* (Howth: Kilbarrack Labour Party, 1975), pp. 11–17.
27 Maire Cruise O'Brien to Beryl Duoda, 5 March 1975 (Howth).
28 John Silverlight, "Conor Cruise O'Brien: Irishman Extraordinary," *Observer Magazine* (Sept. 1973), p. 47.
29 Kate Cruise O'Brien, *A Gift Horse and Other Stories* (Dublin: Poolbeg, 1978), p. 20.
30 "In Her Own Write," *Sunday Tribune*, 8 Sept. 1985.
31 *I.T.*, 21 Sept. 1970; 256 *D.E.* 2347–49.
32 "The Death of Dunquin," *I.T.*, 26 Sept. 1970.
33 *I.T.*, 14 and 15 March 1973.
34 His official travel between March 1973 and November 1976 was nineteen trips, thirteen of these to England (294 *D.E.* 1287–88). He made roughly an equal number for non-official purposes, such as giving lectures (appointment diaries, Howth).
35 MacConghail interview.
36 *I.T.*, 14 May 1965. That number, 42,000 was up from 38,000 in September 1974 (*I.T.*, 21 Sept. 1974).
37 Nicholas Simms interview; Christine Foster Hetherington interview.
38 MacConghail interview.
39 FitzGerald interview.
40 There were minor strikes in 1975 (*I.T.*, 6 Feb. 1975) and 1976 (*I.T.*, 9 Feb. 1976), but these were sectional matters and only affected parts of the system.
41 87 *Seanad Eireann* (hereafter *S.E.*) 120–21, 2 Nov. 1977; *I.T.*, 8 April 1975; 19 March 1975; 7 Dec. 1976; 14 Dec. 1976.
42 *I.T.*, 9 Oct. 1973; 24 Oct. 1973.
43 266 *DE* 1031, 21 June 1973.
44 FitzGerald, p. 197; O'Brien interviews.
45 MacConghail interview; O'Brien interviews. In the period when MacConghail was in office, there was some talk of creating an Irish News Agency Service, an idea that Conor favored. (See 265 *D.E.* 545–46; 267 *D.E.* 2192–93.)
46 This individual was not selected by Conor. "Backbencher," (*I.T.*, 19 July 1975) noted "a famous dinner when Conor let go at Provo sympathizers in the media, and left more than one under the impression that he thought the new head of the G.I.B. [meaning Government Information Office] was a snaking regarder." What Conor was hitting at, of course, was the Twenty-Six County bourgeoisie, who would say, "I am against the IRA, of course, but I have a sneaking regard for their efforts." Sneaking becomes "snaking" in some Dublin dialects, and in most forms of civilized politics.
47 Lee, p. 478.
48 *I.T.*, 3 Dec. 1973.
49 274 *D.E.* 293.
50 FitzGerald, p. 309; O'Brien interviews.
51 FitzGerald, p. 309; Horgan, p. 157.
52 These are cited in 274 *D.E.* 908–11, 11 July 1974, but were in fact passed to the press, with related studies, more than a week earlier. Conor took some high-minded criticism for having staff who were hired to advise on television broadcasting deal with this delicate issue.
53 274 *D.E.* 915–18.
54 See extensive reports in *I.T.*, 29 March 1976; 1 April 1976; 3 April 1976; 2 June 1976.
55 The division lobby drama is described in FitzGerald, p. 309.
56 O'Brien interviews.

57 W.T. Cosgrave to Richard Mulcahy, 4 March 1925, reproduced in Coimisiun na Gaeltachta, *Report* (Dublin: Stationery Office, 1926), p. 3.
58 *Times Educational Supplement*, 13 Aug. 1921.
59 Ibid., 30 Oct. 1925.
60 *The Restoration of the Irish Language* [Pr. 8061], p. 6.
61 Dick Walsh, "Dr. O'Brien and the Language," *I.T.* (supplement), 2 April 1975; *I.T.*, 25 Feb. 1974.
62 Maire Cruise O'Brien interview.
63 MacConghail interview.
64 275 *D.E.* 745, 31 Oct. 1974. See also 271 *D.E.* 950–57, 27 March 1974, and "The Year Past and the Year Ahead," *I.T.*, 28 Dec. 1974.
65 *I.T.* (supplement), 2 April 1975.
66 Speech of ccob, "Culture and Communication," given 7 July 1974 at the Oxford meeting of the British and Irish Society. Extracts distributed by Government Information Services (O'Brien papers, Howth).
67 FitzGerald, pp. 305–6.
68 Ibid., p. 306. For Conor's reflections on what these changes meant, see the speech he gave at the American Conference for Irish Studies, 25 April 1975 (O'Brien papers, University College, Dublin).
69 *Broadcasting Authority Act, 1960, Acts of the Oireachtas Passed in the Year 1960*, Section 17.
70 *I.T.*, 25 Feb. 1974.
71 *Broadcasting Authority (Amendment) Act, 1976, Acts of the Oireachtas Passed in the Year 1976*, Section 13(a).
72 *I.T.*, 1 July 1974.
73 The only other performance of which I am aware was in a double bill with *King Herod Explains* in October 1978 at the Vortex Theater, Albuquerque, New Mexico (Steven Young to ccob, 3 Aug. 1978, and attachments, O'Brien papers, Howth).
74 "In Search of Morality—Conor Cruise O'Brien Talks to Brian Inglis," p. 236.
75 ccob, "King Herod Advises," in *Herod: Reflections on Political Violence* (London: Hutchinson, 1978), p. 220.
76 Ibid., p. 224.
77 Ibid., p. 235.
78 FitzGerald, p. 198. Equally candidly, if slightly less handsomely, he continued: "I am less sure about the years that followed, for I am tempted to feel that the legitimate conviction that he had been right on that occasion may have encouraged him in a delusion of near-infallibility thereafter!"
79 Ibid., p. 126.
80 Barry White, *John Hume: Statesman of the Troubles* (Belfast: Blackstaff Press, 1984), p. 152.
81 This was "by chance," his biographer says (ibid., p. 154), a gross underestimation, one suspects, of Hume's media sense.
82 ccob, "Extremists: A Delusion," *Observer*, 14 April 1974.
83 *I.T.*, 19 June 1974.
84 *Financial Times*, 26 Sept. 1974; *I.T.*, 25 Sept. 1974; *Guardian*, 27 Sept. 1974.
85 O'Brien interviews. The story, without identification of Kevin McNamara, was printed in ccob, "Can the Army Ever Leave?" *Times*, 10 Aug. 1989.
86 Retold in John Dillon, "A Letter from Ireland: Conor Cruise O'Brien and the National Identity," *San Francisco Review of Books* (June 1977), p. 21.
87 Simms interview.

88 *I.T.*, 13 Dec. 1974.

89 An article in the *Civil Service Review* claimed Conor was abusing his office by having civil servants assist him in providing information for the National Coalition Committee on Information which was an informal committee of backbenchers who supported the government—and thus was political. Also, the article said, "We are aware that Dr. Cruise O'Brien has an entourage of non-civil servants employed in his office. We should not be distressed should Dr. Cruise O'Brien decide to employ them elsewhere" (quoted in *I.T.*, 4 April 1975).

90 On the background of Irish radio and television, see Desmond Fisher, *Broadcasting in Ireland* (London: Routledge and Kegan Paul, 1978), and Martin McLoone and John MacMahon, eds., *Television and Irish Society: 21 Years of Irish Television* (Dublin: RTE, 1984).

91 The entire address is reproduced in McLoone and MacMahon, p. 149.

92 This was Conor's second involvement with the expansion of television broadcasting. The first came in 1958–59 while he still was with the Department of External Affairs. He was part of a bizarre, but very creative, attempt to use Ireland as a broadcasting base to blanket the British mainland. This was just at the time that plans were being made final for the creation of Irish television. Most of the major players in Britain and Europe wanted a piece of the action if it turned out that the Irish government decided to allow private, rather than state, television to develop. One of these groups was a Paris-based company run by Charles Mitchelson, a Romanian, who was head of a group called Europe-1. His pitch was that if the Irish government would let his firm set up a radio superstation, commercial and pop, in Ireland, that was beamed at the British mainland (Britain, recall, did not have commercial radio at this time), he would provide an Irish television service absolutely free.

Research on this matter is at present being conducted by the American scholar Dr. Robert J. Savage, but several points already are notable. First, Europe-1 very shrewdly got the Vatican involved. What this cost is unknown, but two Vatican representatives, the prelate of the papal household and an official of the Pontifical Commission on Television, came to Ireland to lobby for this proposal. Second, they had particularly close contacts with Conor's future father-in-law, Sean MacEntee, then minister for health and social welfare, and the head of the right-wing, hyper-Catholic faction of de Valera's Cabinet. The Vatican representatives, in lobbying for the commercial broadcasting proposal, wanted their mission to be secret. The front man in arranging their visit was Conor. Of his involvement in this episode, Conor says: "It is the closest I ever came in my life to being bent." (Sources: research report of Dr. Robert Savage, interviews with CCOB, Nicholas Simms, and Donall O'Morain). In an ironic coda, the man who was largely responsible for scuttling the private projects and bringing in an Irish television service modeled on the BBC was Leon O'Broin, then secretary of the Department of Posts and Telegraphs (and known to most readers of Irish history as a very competent biographer of several of the second-line late-nineteenth and twentieth-century Irish nationalist leaders). He was very Catholic and very anticommunist. In Conor's early days in the Department of Finance, O'Broin had been Conor's immediate superior, and they did not get on. At one point O'Broin asked Conor some political question and Conor gave him a canonical Marxist answer, mostly to vex him. It did: O'Broin literally clutched his stomach and ran out of the room (O'Brien interviews). Thus, the irony: the anticlerical, alleged socialist Conor pushed for a Vatican-approved form of private broadcasting, and the strongly Catholic, and strongly anti-Marxist O'Broin fought the Vatican's wishes and pressed for a state-owned system of television broadcasting.

93 An immense amount of newsprint was used in the period 1973–75 on the open broad-

casting issue; the letters to the editor's column of the major newspapers frequently had several items on the topic. Specific quotations are cited later, but a good overview is Ulick O'Connor, "When Irish Eyes are Viewing," *Listener*, (10 July 1975), p. 41.

94 *I.T.*, 10 April 1974.

95 *I.T.*, 16 Aug. 1975.

96 The text as distributed by the Government Information Service is printed in *I.T.*, 8 July 1974. Some part of the speech must have been left out, as several days later (*I.T.*, 13 July 1974), "Backbencher" was fuming about how nasty the speech was and claiming that Maire had had a hand in the writing—"Wouldn't you recognize the MacEntee venom in it?" he asked. In fact, the printed version is quite mild.

97 *I.T.*, 9 July 1974.

98 *I.T.*, 11 May 1973.

99 Donall O'Morain interview.

100 *I.T.*, 28 Oct. 1975 and 29 Oct. 1975; 288 *D.E.* 82–83.

101 *I.T.*, 26 Aug. 1975.

102 286 *D.E.* 3491; "Opinion" by H.R.Anderson, *I.T.*, 1 June 1976.

103 *I.T.*, 1 June 1976. It should be noted that Anderson was the chairman of the Cork Multi-Channel Television Campaign Committee.

104 McLoone and MacMahon, Table 23, p. 151.

105 *I.T.*, 29 May 1976.

106 Donall O'Morain interview.

107 Fisher, p. 32.

108 Ibid., pp. 34–36; *I.T.*, 25 Nov. 1972; Donall O'Morain interview; 243 *D.E.* 1519–1634; 264 *D.E.* 60–70; P.S.L. Lyons, "T.W.M.," in F.S.L. Lyons and R.A.J. Hawkins, eds., *Ireland under the Union: Varieties of Tension. Essays in Honour of T.W. Moody* (Oxford: Clarendon Press, 1980), pp. 20–21.

109 "Broadcasting Authority (Amendment) Act, 1976, Section 3, in *Acts of the Oireachtas Passed in the Year 1976*. See also 80 *S.E.*: 1380; 81 *S.E.*: 460.

110 "Broadcasting Authority Act, 1960," Section 31 (1), in *Acts of the Oireachtas Passed in the Year 1960*.

111 "Backbencher," *I.T.*, 16 June 1973.

112 254 *D.E.* 828, 2 June 1971.

113 257 *D.E.* 324–25, 24 Nov. 1971.

114 *I.T.*, 16 Dec. 1972.

115 *I.T.*, 15 May 1973.

116 See comments of Kenneth Morgan, general secretary of National Union of Journalists, *I.T.*, 26 April 1974. Soon thereafter, the Union refused to meet with Conor to hear his explanation of Section 31. *I.T.*, 25 April 1974.

117 Simms interview.

118 *Listener*, (4 July 1974), p. 6.

119 *I.T.*, 30 Oct. 1975.

120 O'Morain interview. *I.T.*, 24 Oct. 1974, confirms that Conor condemned the program before seeing it.

121 *I.T.*, 28 Oct. 1974.

122 Quoted in *I.T.*, 9 Dec. 1974.

123 CCOB to Andrée Sheehy-Skeffington, 6 March 1975 (O'Brien papers, University College, Dublin).

124 80 *D.E.* 256. The speech is found in 79 *S.E.* 761ff.

125 The amendments to Section 31 of the 1960 Broadcasting Act are found in Section 16 of what eventually became the 1976 act.

126 *I.T.*, 9 Jan. 1976.

127 A picture of Maire and her father, Sean MacEntee, arriving at Our Lady, Queen of Peace Church, Merrion Road, for the 7 September service, is found on the front page of *I.T.*, 8 Sept. 1976.

128 O'Toole, p. 46; Tim Pat Coogan, *Disillusioned Decades: Ireland 1966–87* (Dublin: Gill and Macmillan, 1987), p. 28; O'Brien interviews.

129 Nossiter's *Washington Post* story was reprinted in its entirety, as a front-page item in *I.T.*, 6 Sept. 1976.

130 For background on Tim Pat Coogan, see Risteard O'Muirithille, "The Wide-boy," *Magill* 6 (June 1983), pp. 61–64.

131 292 *D.E.* 474.

132 Geoffrey Wheatcroft, "Terror, Law and Press Freedom: An Interview with Conor Cruise O'Brien," *Spectator* (Dec. 1976), p. 7.

133 O'Brien interviews.

134 *I.T.*, 20 Oct. 1976.

135 For Conor's continuing belief in the efficiency and necessity of Section 31, see CCOB: "The Case for Censoring Television," *Observer*, 10 Sept. 1978; "Letter to a Noble Lord," *I.T.*, 8 Nov. 1983; "And About Time Too," *Irish Independent*, 22 Oct. 1988; "I Welcome This Action," *Irish Independent*, 19 Aug. 1989.

136 For an indication of why this was the case, see Garret FitzGerald, "The Case for Section 31 Deserves a Fair Hearing," *I.T.*, 13 Nov. 1993.

137 Lee, p. 478.

CHAPTER 12

1 *Observer* (article by Mary Holland), 5 June 1977.

2 Conor did not lose touch with the academic world during his political years. He was a visiting fellow of Nuffield College, Oxford, 1972–75. He received honorary doctorates from Bradford (1972), the University of Ghana (1974), and Edinburgh (1976). He took particular pleasure in serving as pro-chancellor of his old college, the University of Dublin, from 1972 to 1992.

3 "Edmund Burke and the American Revolution," in David Noel Doyle and Owen Dudley Edwards, eds., *America and Ireland, 1770–1976: The American Identity and the Irish Connection* (Westport, Conn.: Greenwood Press), p. 4. The handwritten draft of the lecture is in the O'Brien papers, Howth.

4 Ibid., p. 4.

5 Ibid., p. 7.

6 Mark Hederman, "'The Crane Bag' and the North of Ireland," *Crane Bag* 4, no. 2 (1980), p. 98. See also report of speech, *Irish Times* (hereafter *I.T.*), 22 Feb. 1977.

7 CCOB, "The Anti-Politics of Simone Weil," *New York Review of Books* (12 May 1977), pp. 23–38. The same essay, with a new 700-word introduction, is found in George Abbott White, ed., *Simone Weil: Interpretations of a Life* (Amherst: University of Massachusetts Press, 1981), pp. 95–110.

8 Fintan O'Toole, "The Life and Times of Conor Cruise O'Brien, Part 3," *Magill* 9 (June 1986), p. 44.

9 Garret FitzGerald, *All in a Life: An Autobiography* (Dublin: Gill and Macmillan, 1991), p. 319.

10 Joseph J. Lee, *Ireland 1912–1985. Politics and Society* (Cambridge: Cambridge University Press, 1989), pp. 481–82.

11 *I.T.*, 10 June 1977.

12 Ibid., 8 Dec. 1976.

13 Ibid., 3 June 1977.

14 Tony Brown interview.

15 John Horgan interview.

16 CCOB, draft, "Mr. Haughey's Pumpkin Coach," prepared for *Magill*, 1981, pp. 1-2 (O'Brien papers, University College, Dublin [hereafter UCD]).

17 See *I.T.*, 28 Jan. 1977, 29 Jan. 1977, 31 Jan. 1977, 1 Feb. 1977. An attempt was made to set up a debate between Conor and John Hume (*I.T.*, 4 Feb. 1977), but, given Conor's fierceness as a debater, it is not surprising that it did not come off. Instead, Hume settled for a tame discussion with Brian Lenihan at UCD before a student audience. (*I.T.*, 8 Feb. 1977).

18 *I.T.*, 19 Feb. 1977.

19 Ibid., 1 March 1977.

20 CCOB, "Address to the Irish Association for Civil Liberties," 28 Feb. 1977 (distributed on behalf of the Department of Posts and Telegraphs by the Government Information Service).

21 For exceptions, see *I.T.*, 3 March 1978, 8 April 1978, 17 May 1978.

22 O'Brien interviews; Roy Bradford, "Unionism's Eire Ally," *Ulster Newsletter*, 8 June 1977, p. 14. Another trick was of little importance. Posters went up saying "Election Special from the Cruiser. Abortion on demand; Private Facilities for alcoholic TDs; Suppression of the Irish language; Easy Divorce; Legalisation of drugs; Congolese call girls.—Issued by Friends of Conor Cruise O'Brien" (*I.T.*, 16 June 1977).

23 Horgan interview; John Horgan, *Labour: The Price of Power* (Dublin: Gill and Macmillan, 1986), p. 20.

24 *I.T.*, 18 June 1977, and 20 June 1977.

25 CCOB in a panel discussion, "The Responsibility of Intellectuals," *Salmagundi* 70-71 (Spring-Summer 1986), p. 190. The panel, held 11 April 1985, included George Steiner, Leszek Kolakowski, and Robert Boyers.

26 *I.T.*, 29 June 1977.

27 87 *Seanad Eireann* (hereafter *S.E.*) 2 Nov. 1977, 119-22, and 149-51.

28 Lee, p. 486.

29 CCOB, untitled draft article for *Magill*, c. 1981 (O'Brien papers, UCD).

30 92 *S.E.* 13 June 1979.

31 Horgan, p. 58.

32 O'Brien papers (Howth).

33 The script is in O'Brien papers (Howth). On the earlier treatment, see CCOB to Eamon Andrews, 24 Feb. 1967 (O'Brien papers, UCD).

34 I cannot confidently date another television effort, this one a complete script entitled "The Trial of Roger Casement" (O'Brien papers, UCD). It is very talky; it would have been a good radio play.

35 See reviews of Tom Stoppard's *Travesties*, Bertholt Brecht's *The Mother*, and W.B. Yeats's *On Baile's Strand* in *Magill* 1 (Nov. 1977), pp. 44-45.

36 Conor was good also at recognizing new talent. He briefly carried over his theater reviewing to the *Observer*. He was one of the first to understand the brilliance of Stewart Parker's *Kingdom Come* (CCOB, "A Song of Disembafflement," *Observer*, 29 Jan. 1978). This in fact was a second review of the play to be carried in the *Observer*, the first, by the paper's drama critic, having been very flat indeed.

37 Brian Inglis, *Downstart* (London: Chatto and Windus, 1990), p. 278. Inglis suspected that the phrase "Toffs against Terrorism," was coined by Tim Pat Coogan.

38 "Editor in Excelsis," *New Statesman* (13 Jan. 1978), p. 42.

39 See *I.T.*, 20 Sept. 1977. What Conor did was compare the results of a BBC survey of

mainland opinion in 1976 with the combined results of a BBC random poll of Northern Ireland (date not given) and a 1972 *non*-random poll conducted in the Irish Republic. Not only can the two Irish surveys not be aggregated (being of different dates and asking different questions), but the 1972 survey, by Father Michael MacGreil, though very illuminating on many issues, deals only with a Dublin sample. It is certain that the attitudes of people in the metropolis are markedly different on national issues than those in the countryside and small towns.

In a lecture given at the Queen's University, Belfast, 23 June 1978, Conor wisely did not repeat his Oxford assertion, but instead pointed to a 1977 Market Research Bureau of Ireland survey that showed 63 percent were in favor of Irish unity and a Gallup poll in the Irish Republic of March 1978 showing 69 percent in favor of unity. However, the latter poll showed that only 43 percent would accept any extra taxes if unity made such taxes necessary. CCOB, *Neighbours: Four Lectures Delivered by Conor Cruise O'Brien in Memory of Christopher Ewart-Biggs* (London: Faber and Faber, 1980), pp. 41–42.

40 *I.T.*, 20 Sept. 1977.

41 Ibid., 21 Sept. 1977. Characteristically, Conor bounced back quickly. By week's end he was writing that his discussion of Dubliners' political opinions caused "considerable squawking in that backyard." CCOB, "Dublin, Downing Street, and Rome ...," *Observer*, 25 Sept. 1977.

42 "Editor in Excelsis," p. 42; David Astor interview; O'Brien interviews.

43 CCOB to Maire Cruise O'Brien, 17 Nov. 1977 (O'Brien papers, Howth).

44 His stay in Tanzania was frustrating, but Conor maintained an admiration for the way Julius Nyerere successfully played the game of "socialism as racket," running alleged model communal villages—which required a week's notice before anyone got near them—and mostly improved his nation's standard of living by "his ability to persuade foreign sponsors that his objectives were sincere." See CCOB, "The Fall of Africa," *New Republic* 192 (18 March 1985), p. 34.

45 CCOB to Maire Cruise O'Brien, 25 and 26 Nov. 1977 (O'Brien papers, Howth).

46 O'Brien interviews. Conor later wrote a review essay of Donald Wood's *Biko* (*Observer*, 30 April 1978).

47 CCOB, "Linking the Separate Tables," *Observer*, 22 Jan. 1978. Christopher Hitchens in *Prepared for the Worst* (London: Chatto and Windus, 1989), p. 46, said that "Mugabe later told a friend of mine in conversation that he had been joking about the IRA and had really wanted to ask O'Brien about Patrice Lumumba." This is plausible, as Conor in his piece notes that "Mr. Mugabe changed the subject. We discussed the downfall and death of Patrice Lumumba, a subject in which he takes a strong personal interest." It is equally plausible that Mugabe, who was both a Catholic and a revolutionary, was serious in his suggestions and that he later reinterpreted them to make him appear more acceptable to Western politicians. That aside, one must be a touch skeptical of Hitchens's analysis of Conor's development in the late 1970s. He sees 1979 as "something of a hinge year for O'Brien." He believes that 1979 was the year Conor visited Mugabe in Maputo. It was 1977.

48 Browne, p. 21.

49 CCOB to Maire Cruise O'Brien, 17 Nov. 1977.

50 CCOB to Maire Cruise O'Brien, 25 and 26 Nov. 1977.

51 Arnold Goodman, *Tell Them I'm on My Way* (London: Chapman's, 1993), pp. 378–79.

52 Inglis, pp. 198–99.

53 Goodman, pp. 378–90; Arnold Goodman interview; Tom Balstow, "Anatomy of the Observer Crisis," *New Statesman* (27 June 1975), p. 819.

54 Balstow, p. 819.
55 Goodman, p. 396.
56 Goodman interview.
57 Goodman, p. 396.
58 Ibid., p. 399; Astor interview; Tom Bower, *Tiny Rowland: A Rebel Tycoon* (London: Heinemann, 1993), pp. 393–94.
59 Astor interview.
60 Ibid.
61 "Editor in Excelsis," p. 42.
62 Astor interview; Goodman interview; Goodman, p. 400.
63 The date in "Editor in Excelsis," for the Goodman-flat meeting of 10 Nov. 1977 is wrong. The meeting occurred after Conor's return from his November African trip. Almost certainly the date was 10 December. This fits with other elements in the chronology, including the later dinner with Donald Trelford (see text).
64 Dating of Conor-Trelford dinner in Dublin from *Observer*, 18 Dec. 1977. Both Conor and David Astor in interviews say that Conor had stipulated that he would not take the post of editor in chief without Donald Trelford's approval.
65 Draft publicity release in O'Brien papers (Howth).
66 *Observer*, 18 Dec. 1977.
67 CCOB's *Observer* contract and financial details for the *Observer* years are found in O'Brien papers (Howth).
68 Henry Kelly, "Observing Conor Cruise," *Magill* 1 (April 1978), p. 6.
69 *Sunday Times*, 12 Feb. 1978.
70 One could set a chartered accountancy examination using Conor's tax situation in these years as a set-problem. He was dealing with both British and Irish taxation authorities (this, moreover, in the era before exchange controls were removed), and he still had U.S. income and some residual problems with the American authorities.
71 Geoffrey Wheatcroft, "Terror, Law and Press Freedom: An Interview with Conor Cruise O'Brien," *Spectator* (4 Dec. 1976), p. 7.
72 *I.T.*, 19 Dec. 1977.
73 "The Oldie Interview: Conor Cruise O'Brien," *Oldie* (7 Aug. 1992), p. 23. Against this sort of thing the *Observer* Foreign News Service distributed internationally a feature story by John Silverlight (OFNS Bulletin no. 36794, 20 Dec. 1977). The story said: "He was the first prominent Irish politician to come out strongly in public against the IRA, Official and Provisional" and, "altogether Dr. O'Brien's treatment of Irish nationalism has been compared to George Orwell's efforts to explode the Marxist myth in the 1940s and 1950s." It concluded: "If Ireland is spared civil war—and now, after eight years of agony, there does seem to be growing hope that peace may be in sight— Conor Cruise O'Brien will have the satisfaction of having certainly done as much as anyone, and far more than most people, to keep the peace."
74 Interviews with Conor and Maire Cruise O'Brien. Travel details from CCOB appointment diaries (O'Brien papers, Howth).
75 CCOB's appointment diaries, 1978–80, inclusive (O'Brien papers, Howth).
76 O'Brien interviews; interviews with David Astor, Adrian Hamilton (the present deputy editor), and William Keegan (at present economics editor and associate editor of the paper). Other interviewees on the *Observer* will not be identified by name.
77 Donald Trelford interview on "Conor Cruise O'Brien: Making a Stand, Taking a Side," Irish television documentary directed by Gerry Gregg, 1986.
78 Hamilton and Keegan interview.
79 *Observer*, 2 Feb. 1992.

80 Goodman interview.
81 O'Brien interviews; interview with Hamilton and Keegan, and with others.
82 Donald Trelford interview with Gerry Gregg in "Making a Stand, Taking a Side."
83 Quoted in O'Toole, p. 46. The Mary Holland affair at the *Observer* deserves detailed study as a nodal case in British journalistic history.
84 Quoted in Browne, p. 21.
85 When Mary Holland's contract came up for renewal in 1979, Trelford, out of deference to Conor, did not renew it. After Conor left the *Observer*, Trelford rehired her.
86 CCOB appointment diary for 1978.
87 Alex Kwapong interview.
88 Interviews with Conor and Maire Cruise O'Brien.
89 Kwapong interview.
90 CCOB, "Long Day's Journey into Prayer," *Observer*, 4 Feb. 1979. See also report of Conor's talk on BBC-2 on "The Light of Experience" program, *Listener* 105 (18 June 1981), p. 772; and speech given when he received the Valiant for the Truth Award, Nov. 1979 (O'Brien papers, UCD).
91 Astor interview.
92 *Observer*, 3 Feb. 1980.
93 See note 39 for details.
94 Peter Fiddick, "Dr. O'Brien's Provocation," *Listener* 101 (5 April 1979), p. 476.
95 Copy of the speech, "The Irish-Factor in Anglo-American Relations," in O'Brien papers (UCD).
96 *Irish Press*, 7 Feb. 1980.
97 On "Power, Poverty and Communication" (O'Brien papers, UCD).
98 O'Brien papers, UCD.
99 Itinerary in O'Brien papers (UCD).
100 CCOB to Alf MacLochlain, 16 Dec. 1981, O'Brien papers (UCD).
101 The entire speech is printed in *I.T.*, 16 Nov. 1979 and in *Irish Independent*, 15 Nov. 1979.
102 CCOB, "No to a Nauseous Marxist-Methodist Cocktail," *Observer*, 28 Jan. 1979.
103 E.P. Thompson, "The Great Fear of Marxism," *Observer*, 4 Feb. 1979, reprinted in E.P. Thompson, *Writing by Candlelight* (London: Merlin, 1980), pp. 181–86.
104 CCOB, "Refined and Vulgar Marxism," *Observer*, 28 Oct. 1979. The piece, like Conor's argument with Thompson, was a club sport. Conor paid handsome respect to Thompson, Eric Hobsbawm, and Christopher Hill, and then told—without identifying Thompson, so that it was an in-group reference—of Thompson's leaving the Communist party, in part because of the same "Vulgar Marxist" who had put Nazi documents on the cover of *The Spark* with the caption "What the University of Ghana is teaching your children" when Conor was vice-chancellor in Ghana (see chapter 8).
105 CCOB, "Survival, Defence and Freedom," *Observer*, 6 July 1980. I have slightly reorganized the first part of the parable, as Lermontov's last words in the original article were printed as an epigram.
106 Conor wrote an unsigned editorial in favor of maintaining the British nuclear deterrent (*Observer*, 20 July 1980) and a signed piece ("Incorporation of Western Europe," 10 Aug. 1980), which paid tribute to "Professor Edward P. Thompson, the most eloquent and the most eminent of the nuclear disarmers" but voiced a strong distrust of the Soviet Union. Thompson put an alternate case ("'In place of megatons, we offer a possible strategy of love,'" 24 Aug. 1980). The game continued with CCOB's "Terminal Ideology or Prudent Reason?" (24 Aug. 1980) and "You Could Be Red First—Then Dead," (8 Nov. 1981), with Thompson's *Beyond the Cold War: Not the*

Dimbleby Lecture (London: Merlin, 1982), and its review in an open letter by CCOB ("Peace, Freedom—and Hypocrisy," 7 Feb. 1982).

107   On the way that Northern Ireland fitted into his thinking at this time, see CCOB, "Some Problems about Minorities," a lecture given to the Institute of Jewish Affairs, London, 28 Feb. 1979 (O'Brien papers, UCD).

108   CCOB, "In All Directions Like Sour Dough," *Observer*, 3 Aug. 1980.

109   CCOB, *The Siege: The Saga of Israel and Zionism* (London: Weidenfeld and Nicolson, 1986), p. 17.

110   Bower, p. 394.

111   Ibid., p. 393; Goodman, pp. 398–99.

112   Goodman, p. 400.

113   Ibid.; Goodman interview.

114   Goodman, pp. 400–401; Goodman interview.

115   Conor had some difficulty collecting all the money owed him as an *Observer* columnist, although he eventually did so. Part of the problem was that the contract he signed for his column was never taken to the full board of directors, since, by the time it was drawn, he was *persona non grata*. See CCOB to Roger Harrison, 31 March 1983, and CCOB to—Hardiman [of the Bank of Ireland], 25 Jan. 1985 (O'Brien papers, Howth).

116   Patrick's school reports for the period (O'Brien papers, Howth) show mostly "C's" and "D's" and comments indicating that he was not working very hard; nothing serious, but the sort of thing to worry an academic family such as the O'Briens.

117   Goodman, p. 401.

118   Ibid., pp. 401–2.

119   Ibid., p. 402.

120   Bower, p. 394.

121   Goodman, p. 402.

122   Goodman interview.

123   In addition to the Bower biography of Rowland, see Suzanne Cronje, Margaret Ling, and Gillian Cronje, *The Lonrho Connection: A Multinational and Its Politics in Africa* (London: Bellwether Books, 1976).

124   Bower, p. 405.

125   Robert Anderson to CCOB, 17 July 1981 (O'Brien papers, Howth).

126   See CCOB to—Hardiman [of the Bank of Ireland], 25 Jan. 1985.

127   O'Brien interviews.

CHAPTER 13

1   CCOB, "Freeing the News Flow," *Observer*, 24 June 1979.

2   Jack Beatty to CCOB, 24 Sept. 1985 (O'Brien papers, Howth). The pieces in question were "Prophets of the Holy Land," *Harper's* 269 (Dec. 1984), pp. 42–43, and "Why Israel Can't Take 'Bold Steps' for Peace," *Atlantic* 256 (Oct. 1985), pp. 45–55. There is indeed some repetition, but this would seem to fall within the realm of the divine right of a writer to repeat himself.

3   I have been through Conor's contracts for periodicals, newspapers, and books, during this period, and believe the statement in the text to be demonstrable. However, I have no wish to help the Irish Inland Revenue Service in their efforts at redistributing his income.

4   "Montgomery Fellow. ...," *The Dartmouth* (10 Oct. 1984), pp. 6–7; Gerald Weales, "Homo Candidas, Liberalis Pessimisticus," *The Pennsylvania Gazette* (March 1989), pp. 17–22; Saul P. Steinberg interview. The importance of these and similar university

visitorships to Conor is shown by his considering legal action in 1983 when Denis Donoghue in the *London Review of Books* asked "Why does Conor Cruise O'Brien exercise his intelligence when he writes for the *Observer* and turn out such vulgar rubbish for the *Irish Times*?" (Donoghue here had it backwards, I think, being repelled, one conjectures, not by the vulgarity of the *Irish Times* columns, but that it hit rather too close to the nerve.) The interesting point, however, is that Conor was so exercised about this because the *London Review of Books* is the kind of periodical that reaches university audiences, a frequent item in senior common rooms and faculty lounges, and he believed this sort of comment could cost him a visitorship. CCOB to Michael O'Mahoney, 9 June 1983). Also relevant is CCOB to Karl Miller, 17 May 1983 (both in O'Brien papers, Howth).

5 "The Responsibility of Intellectuals," *Salmagundi* 70–71 (Spring-Summer 1986), p. 189p6 Gerry Gregg interview.

7 The *New York Times* (7 Apr. 1981) reports the speech in clinical terms. Details on audience reaction from interviews with Shula Eisner and with Teddy Kollek.

8 On the early history of the Jerusalem Committee, see "Jerusalem: A United City," in the serial publication *Out of Jerusalem* (Sept. 1980), pp. 6–24; William Dunphy interview, and notes in his possession on the early years (St. Michael's College, University of Toronto). The activities of the committee are found in *Out of Jerusalem*. For the active committee members, see Teddy Kollek to Tom Sawicki, 18 Sept. 1984 (possession of William Dunphy).

9 William Dunphy interview and draft resolutions in his possession; Teddy Kollek interview.

10 Kollek interview and O'Brien writings distributed in a letter of Kollek to Jerusalem Committee members, 5 July 1982 (in possession of William Dunphy).

11 CCOB, "Address to the President of Israel on Behalf of the Jerusalem Committee," *Out of Jerusalem* (Spring 1982), pp. 13–14.

12 CCOB to Robert Silvers, 16 March 1982. Conor asked for Silvers's help in finding certain books. Indeed, during the 1980s, Conor used the *New York Review of Books* rather as a high class book dealer, frequently asking Silvers to send his staff out to find a book available only in the United States and to charge it to Conor's fees account.

13 For instance, to Shlomo Argov, Israeli ambassador to the United Kingdom. CCOB to Shlomo Argov,—1982 (O'Brien papers, University College, Dublin).

14 Kollek interview; CCOB to Teddy Kollek, 12 May 1982 (O'Brien papers, University College, Dublin).

15 Interview with Adrian Hamilton and William Keegan.

16 Tom Sawicki, one of Israel's most skilled journalists, and a good friend of Conor by virtue of Sawicki's having served as the executive secretary of the Jerusalem Committee, describes an event that happened in about 1987, after the publication of *The Siege*, but which indicates Conor's posture in public. "One particular evening when we had dinner at the Palace Hotel restaurant in East Jerusalem," he recalled, "the rooftop restaurant was empty, except for the two of us, and a party of about a dozen American black lawyers visiting the region as guests of a Palestinian lawyers group (they talked pretty loudly so it was easy to figure out who and what they were). The sentiments they expressed among themselves were distinctly anti-Israeli and even anti-Semitic. Their Palestinian hosts kept on throwing suspicious glances at Conor and me, saying from time to time to their guests: 'Not all ears here are friendly, not all ears here are friendly.'" Sawicki says, "We found the scene very amusing and at one point Conor said, 'They must think I am a Mossad agent; I must really look like one; maybe I should go over and ask them for their names?'" (Personal communication, Tom Sawicki, 23 March 1992).

17 "Leaders Worth Respect," *I.T.*, 20 Dec. 1983.
18 O'Brien interviews; ccob to Shlomo Argov,—1982.
19 Christopher Hitchens, "Creon's Think Tank: The Mind of Conor Cruise O'Brien," in *Prepared for the Worst: Selected Essays and Minority Reports* (London: Chatto and Windus, 1989), p. 47.
20 David Astor interview.
21 Elaine Greene to ccob, 14 March 1982. The advance from Weidenfeld and Nicolson was £500 (O'Brien papers, Howth).
22 For which the advance was $2,500. Elaine Greene to ccob, 24 Aug. 1982 (Howth).
23 ccob to Alice Mayhew, 30 Nov. 1983 (Howth).
24 George Weidenfeld to Elaine Greene, 9 Sept. 1983; Elaine Greene to ccob, 12 Sept. 1983; ccob to George Weidenfeld, 25 Oct. 1983 (Howth).
25 He had been in Lebanon in September 1981, and again in July 1982. See ccob, "What un Chief Wants for Middle East," *I.T.*, 12 April 1983; ccob, "'The plo is on Israel's Borders No Longer,'" *Listener* 111 (26 April 1984), p. 29.
26 Brian Garrett interview.
27 ccob, "Timerman's War: Some Critical Notes," *Encounter* 60 (Jan. 1983), p. 52. The article (pp. 49–55) is in substance (but not all details) the same as ccob, "Unreliable Witness," *New Republic* 188 (24 Jan. 1983), pp. 37–40. For a reply, see Patrick Seale, "Timerman's Long War," *Encounter* 60 (April 1983), pp. 83–85, and a reply by ccob, pp. 85–86.
28 Edward Alexander, "Liberalism and Zionism," *Commentary* 81 (Feb. 1986), p. 29.
29 Walter Lacquer, "The Strained State," *New Republic* 194 (3 March 1986), p. 26.
30 ccob, *The Siege: The Saga of Israel and Zionism* (London: Weidenfeld and Nicolson, 1986), p. 634.
31 "The Oldie Interview: Conor Cruise O'Brien," *Oldie* 13 (7 Aug. 1992), p. 22.
32 Max Beloff, "The Israelis and Their Enemies," *Encounter* 67 (Dec. 1985), p. 30.
33 ccob, "Real Zionism and Its Irish Counterfeit," *I.T.*, 19 March 1985.
34 ccob, "Peace Need Not Pass Understanding," *Observer*, 21 March 1982.
35 The congruities between Ulster Protestantism and Israeli civil religion, and the position of the minorities within Northern Ireland and Israel are discussed in detail in D.H. Akenson, *God's Peoples: Covenant and Land in South Africa, Israel, and Ulster* (Ithaca: Cornell University Press, and Montreal: McGill-Queen's University Press, 1992).
36 ccob, "'The plo Is on Israel's Borders No Longer,'" p. 29.
37 ccob, "Liberty and Terror," *Encounter* 49 (Oct. 1977), pp. 34–41. The quotation is from p. 40.
38 ccob, "Thinking about Terrorism," *Atlantic* 257 (June 1986), p. 63.
39 Ibid., pp. 64–65.
40 The moderate nationalist case for the Anglo-Irish Agreement (as well as details of the negotiations) is found in Garret FitzGerald, *All in a Life: An Autobiography* (Dublin: Gill and Macmillan, 1991), pp. 460–575. The moderate unionist case against the aia (along with details on Protestant reactions) is found in Arthur Aughey, *Under Siege: Ulster Unionism and the Anglo-Irish Agreement* (Belfast: Blackstaff Press, 1989).
41 Aughey, p. 87. This was the analysis of the psephologist Sidney Elliot, who compensated for Sinn Fein abstentions, and who concluded that if "the overtones of a referendum were present, then the vote passed the most stringent test yet set by Parliament."
42 O'Brien interviews.
43 ccob, *Second Ian Gow Memorial Lecture* (London: Friends of the Union, 1992), p. 1.
44 Ibid., p. 2.

45   Ibid., pp. 2–3.
46   CCOB, "Thinking about Terrorism," p. 66.
47   "The Intellectual in Power" (discussion between CCOB and John Lukacs), *Salmagundi* 69 (Winter 1986), p. 259.
48   CCOB, "God and Man in Nicaragua," *Atlantic* 258 (Aug. 1986), pp. 50–72. The essay was reprinted in CCOB, *Passion and Cunning: Essays on Nationalism, Terrorism, and Revolution* (London: Weidenfeld and Nicolson, 1988), pp. 80–121. The basic propositions about the Sandinismo faith were restated in CCOB, "Sandinismo: The Nationalist Faith of Nicaragua," *Center Magazine* (July-Aug. 1987), pp. 31–34. The Nicaragua essay was based on a visit he and Maire made to the country in the spring of 1986 and on considerable research before the trip.
49   O'Brien interviews.
50   "Interview with Conor Cruise O'Brien," *Macleans* 91 (1 May 1978), p. 6.
51   Ibid.; CCOB, "Why They Made Biko a Martyr," *Observer* (30 April 1978).
52   CCOB (unsigned editorial), "Dropping the Pilot," *Observer*, 3 June 1979.
53   CCOB, "The Guilt of Afrikanerdom," *Observer*, 29 July 1979.
54   Ibid. See also the companion piece, CCOB, "Metamorphoses of Apartheid," *Observer*, 22 July 1979.
55   This ideological change—this guilt—is well documented by opinion-poll evidence for the period and by quite radical changes in the theological views of the main Dutch Reformed denomination about the proper interpretation of the Bible on racial matters. See Akenson, *God's Peoples*, pp. 297–308. Particular attention should be paid to the contrasts between *Ras, Volk en Nasie* (1974) and *Kerk en Samelewing* (1986), doctrinal statements of the Dutch Reformed Church. Conor, later, in 1989, called it right in a speech given at Haverford College, Pennsylvania, 30 April 1989, entitled "Toward Peace and Security in South Africa," in which he predicted that when the crunch came (as it in fact did in 1990) the pattern would follow that of the Second Anglo-Boer War of 1899–1902: the *hensoppers* (those who gave into reality) would far outnumber among the Afrikaners the *bittereinders* (those who would fight to the end). In fact, that is exactly what happened. (Speech in O'Brien papers, Howth.)
56   CCOB, "The Afrikaner Mentality," *Atlantic* 255 (May 1985), p. 103.
57   CCOB, "What Can Become of South Africa?" *Atlantic* 257 (March 1986), p. 61.
58   Ibid.
59   Dennis Kennedy interview.
60   Ibid.
61   O'Brien interviews.
62   CCOB to Leon Wieseltier, 22 July 1986 (O'Brien papers, Howth).
63   Conor and Patrick's joint articles were "Camouflage Apartheid," in the *New Republic* 195 (13 Oct. 1986), pp. 14–15; "Tutu's Enthronement" 195 (27 Oct. 1986), pp. 9–11; "Boycott Buster" 195 (3 Nov. 1986), pp. 12–13; "Timing Is Everything" 195 (1 Dec. 1986), pp. 9–10.
64   The account that follows relies chiefly on *The Report of the Commission of Enquiry into the events which occurred on the campus of the University of Cape Town on 7 and 8 October 1986* (internal document, University of Cape Town—hereafter *Report*), and upon several internal comments on that document and statements made during the course of events, by F.R. Bradlow, S.J. Saunders (vice-chancellor), the Students' Representative Council, and various university publicity releases, upon the reports in the *Cape Times* (hereafter *C.T.*), interviews, and the O'Briens' articles in the *New Republic*. Also useful is John Higgins, "The Scholar-Warrior Versus the Children of Mao: Conor Cruise O'Brien in South Africa," in Bruce Robbins, ed., *Intellectuals, Aesthetics, Politics,*

Academics (Minneapolis: University of Minnesota Press, 1990), pp. 290–318. Additional sources are specified below, where appropriate. Because of the importance of the *Report*, it is well to recognize its provenance. It was the result of the work of three external investigators, two of whom were very active "politically." These were S.J. ("Sonny") du Plesis, former vice-chancellor of Witswatersrand University, and two lawyers, Ismael Mohammed, who had recently defended successfully sixteen members of the United Democratic Front in a treason trial, and Arthur Chaskalon, director of the Legal Resources Centre in Johannesburg and a leader in challenging anti-apartheid legislation (*C.T.*, 16 Oct. 1986).

65 *Report*, pp. 14–15; CCOB to A.W. Stadler, 17 June 1986 (O'Brien papers, Howth).
66 Beloff, p. 30.
67 CCOB, *God Land: Reflections on Religion and Nationalism* (Cambridge: Harvard University Press, 1988).
68 *Report*, pp. 14–15, with correction of dating.
69 The university's *Report*, which is quite critical of Conor as an outside agitator, virtually concedes this. See *Report*, pp. 16–17. See also commentary on the report by F.R. Bradlow. For Conor and Patrick's perspective, see *New Republic* (27 Oct. 1986), p. 10.
70 See Gerry Gregg's excellent Irish Television documentary "Conor Cruise O'Brien: Making a Stand, Taking a Side" (1986). The video out-takes for the hour-long production are held by DBA Productions, Belfast, which kindly gave me full access to them.
71 *New Republic* 195 (3 Nov. 1986), p. 12, confirmed by video out-takes.
72 On the content of special rules, see *Report*, p. 54.
73 *C.T.*, 8 Oct. 1986; *Report*, pp. 20–21; *New Republic* 195 (3 Nov. 1986), p. 12.
74 *C.T.*, 9 Oct. 1986; the *Report*, pp. 23–24, severely underestimates the violence involved, according to the video out-takes cited in note 70.
75 *C.T.*, 9 Oct. 1986.
76 Ibid.
77 *C.T.*, 10 Oct. 1986; *Report*, p. 26; O'Brien interviews.
78 *C.T.*, 11 Oct. 1986.
79 *C.T.*, 16 Oct. 1986. Curiously, the *Report* whose chronology of events is full, does not mention this.
80 A.H. Heard column in *C.T.*, 18 Oct. 1986.
81 *Report*, p. 82.
82 Ibid., p. 26.
83 CCOB, *The Great Melody: A Thematic Biography and Commented Anthology of Edmund Burke* (London: Sinclair-Stevenson, 1992). Hereafter *GM*.
84 *GM*, p. xxx.
85 J.H. Plumb, in *Country Life* (15 Oct. 1992), p. 98.
86 Conor throughout is less generous than he might be to Thomas H.D. Mahony's *Edmund Burke and Ireland* (Cambridge: Harvard University Press, 1960). This is not as socially nuanced as is *GM*, but it deserves more courtesy, for priority of discovery on a number of matters.
87 *GM*, p. xxvi.
88 CCOB, "Introduction," to Edmund Burke, *Reflections on the Revolution in France* (Harmondsworth, Pelican Books, 1968), p. 77.
89 *GM*, p. 21.
90 Ibid., p. 9.
91 Ibid., p. 13.
92 Ibid., p. 12.
93 Ibid., p. 15.

94   Ibid., p. 20.
95   Ibid., p.22n1.
96   Ibid., pp. 21–22.
97   Interviews with Conor and Maire Cruise O'Brien. See also *GM*, p. xi.
98   Garrett interview.
99   In *GM* (p. 536n2) Conor talks about his reaction when he received from Deirdre Levinson Bergson a copy of Burke's *Letter ... to a Noble Lord*, a first edition signed by Burke. In that note he backs away a bit from describing the mystical experience he had upon reading Burke's inscription. In private, he is willing to describe it as such.
100   Paul Johnson in the *Independent on Sunday Review*, 4 Oct. 1992. Almost all of the reviews of *The Great Melody* have been strongly positive. It is worth noting two exceptions. One of these was written by the late Edward Thompson in the *Times Literary Supplement* (4 Dec. 1992), pp. 3–4, and it closes the long relationship of Edward and Conor. The review was unfair—but unfair to Thompson, who we now know was dying at the time. A healthy Edward Thompson would not have written so flaccidly, and Conor humbled him in the course of his reply (*Times Literary Supplement*, 18 Dec. 1992, p. 13). The two men should be remembered not for this debate, but for earlier days, when they were evenly matched, and among the best in the British Isles at the game they played.

The other notable negative review was Seamus Deane's in the *Irish Literary Supplement* (Spring 1993, p. 19), which talks of the book's "coarsely obsessive pursuit of a single thesis, the merits of which are degraded by the aggressive, propagandist [*sic*] approach, characteristic of tabloid journalism." The reason for mentioning this free-swinging attack is not that it has much significance itself, but it is part of a long-term war that the group associated with the *Crane Bag* had with Conor beginning in the 1970s. It is worth watching as a coming-attractions notice. I would be surprised if the war did not continue.

EPILOGUE

1   CCOB, *The Great Melody: A Thematic Biography and Commented Anthology of Edmund Burke* (London: Sinclair-Stevenson, 1992), p. 15.
2   CCOB, *To Katanga and Back: A UN Case History* (London: Hutchinson, 1962), p. 286.
3   Federation of Rhodesia and Nyasaland, *Report of the Commission on the Accident Involving SE-BDY which Occurred near Ndola Airport during the Night of 17th September 1961* (Salisbury, 1962).
4   United Nations, *Report of the Commission of Investigation into the Condition and Circumstances Resulting in the Tragic Death of Mr. Dag Hammarskjold and of Members of the Party Accompanying Him*, in *General Assembly, Official Records*, seventeenth session, Doc. No. A/5069 and Add. 1. The Rhodesian inquiry is reprinted within this UN document.
5   CCOB, *Murderous Angels: A Political Tragedy and Comedy in Black and White* (London: Hutchinson, 1969), pp. 214–16.
6   The item to which Conor frequently referred in justification of the idea that the seventeenth-man theory had merit (enough merit to justify it as a serious hypothesis; he did not publicly say he actually believed fully in it), was a collection by Roger Trinquier, Jacques Duchemin, and Jacques Le Bailly, who could charitably be described as high-class soldiers of fortune. Their book is *Notre Guerre au Katanga* (Paris: Editions de la Pensée Moderne, 1963). Here is how Conor described the book on the reading list of the course he taught on the United Nations at New York University in

the 1960s: "Reflecting the viewpoint of the French OAS mercenaries around Tshombe in 1961. The book is most remarkable for the claim that the death of Secretary-General Dag Hammarskjold ... was the result of an attempt, organized by members of this group and other mercenaries on Tshombe's behalf to hijack the Secretary-General's plane with him on board. Considering the source from which it comes, this assertion deserves more attention and examination than it seems to have received" (O'Brien papers, New York University Archives, box 5, file 7).

The book (besides giving more than one mercenary's account, mutually incompatible, of how Hammarskjold died), has the character not of a historical source, but of schizophrenic discourse. It is Duchemin, who was an adviser to Tshombe, who passes on a story he had heard, that a young Belgian Lieutenant named Robert Gheysels ("blond, disciplined ... he looked like the actor Hardy Kruger") did the hijack. The following is an indication of the "documentation" provided. "The plane, with its sixteen official passengers and the seventeenth secret one, took off on a hot and stormy afternoon. Hammarskjold would have read or gossiped with his faithful Italian secretary, a pin-up boy with slightly disturbing blue eyes." And, "Here is what must have happened [note that], the only possible explanation. At six minutes after midnight, Robert Gheysels, who was on board as we say, noticed that the plane was about to land. ... Gheysels got up, took his gun from his briefcase and placed himself between the passenger cabin and the cockpit. Watching Hammarskjold and his entourage carefully, he ordered the pilot to cut radio contact and to take the plane to Kolwezi. ... One of the UN bodyguards jumped out of his seatbelt, Gheysels fired and killed him. The pilot, hoping to help the bodyguards, gave the plane a sharp turn in an attempt to unbalance the assailant or make him drop his gun. Was it the weight of the plane that destabilized it in turning around or more simply a body falling into the cockpit? ... We will never know. In any case, the *Albertina* crashed into the trees. ... It was an accidental death, not a criminal one. He who did not wish to assassinate Hammarskjold is dead along with him. ..."

"Was it not a beautiful end for this lover of black novels ('*romans noirs*'), for this aesthete?"

"Yes, this Socrates of the North, this Plato of Stockholm, died as he would have wished to die" (pp. 136–45, translation mine).

So, we have a third-hand story, that details Hammarskjold's death, but with certain inconveniences: among them that there was no seventeenth body found, and that none of Hammarskjold's bodyguards had bullet holes in them.

7 George Ivan Smith and CCOB, *Guardian*, 11 Sept. 1992. This letter, while advancing Smith's shot-control-wire theory, also says that "O'Brien believes that they also smuggled an agent into Hammarskjold's plane as added persuasion and thinks the body-count after the crash is in doubt." So much for Ockham's razor.

8 "Mercenaries Killed UN Chief in Air Crash," *Guardian*, 11 Sept. 1992.

9 Bengt Rosio, "End Notes to 'The Ndola Disaster,'" pp. 7–9. Rosio also wrote two other papers, based on his rehearsal of all known evidence, "The Ndola Disaster," and a more informal subjective set of "Comments to 'The Ndola Disaster'" (O'Brien papers, Howth). His summary, stated in a letter to Conor (who was, after all, one of the sources that led to his study) was rather tactless. "I have not found any new evidence and did not expect to find any" (Bengt Rosio to CCOB, 4 Jan. 1993, O'Brien papers, Howth).

10 Perhaps some day there will be evidence of a Hammarskjold conspiracy, although I doubt it. What I doubt even more, is that were one to be found, it would take either of the two forms that Conor has been associated with proposing. (And yet, Conor is

one of the sharpest intellects of his time—especially if one takes Horace Barlow's definition of intelligence as the art of good guesswork, that is, the capacity to detect new,
non-chance associations—so he could still be right.) One reason for my skepticism, as
indicated already, is the evidentiary weakness of the two theories—the seventeenth-
man theory and the Belgian-pilot-shoots-control-wire theory. Neither has anything
beyond hearsay to support it. More important is the very strong case made by the technical investigators—not the judicial, the technical—in the Rhodesia investigation.
These investigators were independent forensic experts and they examined every piece
of wreckage: no explosion, no "machine gun" holes, no technical malfunctions. One
of the investigators, Paul Fournier, who was with the International Civil Aviation
Organization, and de facto head of air control in the Congo, kept the entire bank of
documents, technical reports, films, photographs, from the investigation and has allowed me access. Fournier, a Canadian, was at the time of the crash one of the world's
leading forensic investigators of airplane crashes, having made his mark in 1949 with
a famous ground-breaking investigation of a crash near Quebec City in 1949, for
which eventually three conspirators who planted a bomb went to the gallows.

Circumstantially, it is relevant to the shot-down thesis that the plane Hammarskjold
was on was large and faster than any in the area; that Ndola was beyond the range of
the only gun-equipped aircraft in central Africa; that none of the planes that could
have pursued Hammarskjold's plane was equipped with radar; that Hammarskjold's
plane flew a very indirect course that made following it impossible in any case (especially after darkness fell). For the two planes that were alleged to have shot down
Hammarskjold's plane to have been there and then disappeared was, if not impossible,
then very nearly so.

However, the really compelling evidence is the photographic assessment of the
crash site. The trees looked like a large, ever-lowering lawn mower had dropped in on
them. The flight path was straight, the descent gradual. (The wheels of the plane were
down, in preparation for landing.) It was a perfect landing, save that it was about 200
feet lower than it should have been at that point in its flight path and miles short of
the Ndola airport. A perfect landing, but in the wrong place. Had the control wire
been hit, as suggested, the plane would have hit the ground quite sharply, instead of
in the controlled landing pattern.

Given that this was a visual landing—no radar—and that the airport lights were
on, why would the pilots miss the airport? The best guess is that they lost sight of the
airport lights as they banked around the airport, because at one point, if they were
fairly low, a slight rise in the ground blacked out the airport. Thus, the speculation is,
they lost reference. That said, it is not necessary to understand why they landed too
soon, in order to accept that that is what they did. (There was no "black box" on the
plane.)

Paul Fournier remembers receiving a great deal of pressure from Swedish authorities to bring in any reason other than the one actually specified by the report: pilot
error. Given that three senior SAS pilots were in charge of ferrying Sweden's most
important citizen, the last thing they wanted was to carry the responsibility on this one.
(This Swedish pressure is referred to indirectly in the Rhodesian inquiry report, at the
beginning of the "Conclusions.") The Swedish government would have been delighted with a finding of conspiracy, of technical malfunction, hijacking, with anything
except what it got. The Swedes had more clout when it came to the UN, however, and
this, I think, explains why the UN report came to no conclusion at all, and thus avoids
accepting pilot error.

In suggesting that the technical investigation was compelling, I am not endorsing the nontechnical work of the Rhodesian inquiry. It was less than rigorous. Nor am I calling into doubt Conor's contention that, whatever the reality, the Rhodesian government and their British associates at first thought they had a case of foul play on their hands and acted as if they would like to cover it up.

Index

Abbey Theatre, 27, 31, 69, 99, 118, 212–14
Abel, Rita, 269, 273, 321, 466
Abortion. *See* Birth Control.
Abraham, William E., 241–42, 262, 265–66, 523, 528
Adam, Heribert, 476
Africa, 159, 192, 436, 438–39, 455. *See also* Algeria; Biafra; Congo; Ghana; South Africa; Zimbabwe.
Aiken, Frank, 144–46, 157, 160–61, 167–68, 172, 175, 181, 324, 351, 538
Alexander, Edward, 465
Algeria, 149, 151, 348
Amis, Kingsley, 298
Anderson, Robert, 442, 452–54
Anglo-Irish Agreement of 1985, 468–70
Apprentice Boys, 342, 355
Arafat, Yasser, 463
Arden, John, 278–79
Arendt, Hannah, 285, 287
Ashby, Sir Eric, 270
Asmal, Kadar, 475
Astor, David, 436–37, 440–43, 449, 463, 534
Auden, W.H., 203, 207, 284, 328

B Specials, 342, 345, 363
Baldwin, James, 284
Balme, David, 220, 224
Barnacle, Nora, 26, 49

Barnes, Clive, 213
Barnetson, William, 443, 452–53
Barrett, William, 284, 287
Bell, Daniel, 285
Bell, The, 118–21, 142
Bellow, Saul, 285
Beloff, Max, 466, 476
Benn, Tony, 451
Bentley, Eric, 287
Biafra, 283, 309–11, 337, 351, 452
Biko, Steve, 439, 473
Bing, Geoffrey, 133, 225
Birth control, 351, 398–400, 418
Black, Max, 292
Blackmore, Michael, 212
Blackmur, R.P., 284, 288
Blaney, Neil, 357–59
Blease, Billy, 384
Blevens, Winfred, 212
Boateng, Kwaku, 240, 246, 267, 269, 528
Boland, Frederick, 115–16, 152–55, 158–59, 161, 167–68, 171, 179, 357–58
Boone, Syvia, 283
Boudin, Leonard, 283, 287
Bourne, Laurence, 213
Boyd, Andrew, 160, 166
Bradford, Roy, 95
Bradley, Thompson, 283, 287
Bradshaw, Thornton, 443

Brennan, Robert, 136
Briggs, Asa, 315
Briscoe, Robert, 134
Broadcasting Act of 1976, 403, 415–21, 424, 548
Broadcasting Authority. See RTE.
Brokensha, David, 202
Brown, Dan, 333, 336
Browne, Father Maurice, 165, 322
Browne, Margaret (later MacEntee), 164–65, 423, 436
Browne, Michael Cardinal, 165, 176, 182
Browne, Noel, 129, 343–44, 352, 366–67, 387, 541
Browne, Patrick, 165
Buckler, Dean William, 276, 279–80, 326
Buckley, William, 261
Bunche, Ralph, 179–80, 200
Burgess, Guy, 298
Burke, Edmund, 7, 91, 98, 192, 321. See also Conor and Burke.
Burke, Richard, 7, 482–86

Callaghan, James, 447
Cameron, Donald, 214
Camus, Albert, 348
Casey, Michael Thomas, 66
Catholic Church, Irish, 8, 12, 17, 27, 63, 50, 73–75, 124, 144–45, 158, 312–13, 322–23, 334–44, 354, 356, 361, 368–77, 383, 387, 402–6, 467–72, 482, 544, 548; and birth control, 351, 398–400, 418; and education, 86–87, 110; and fascism, 97, 115, 333–34
Caute, David, 278–80, 287
Censorship, 73, 292–93, 415–21, 423, 447
Central Intelligence Agency (CIA), 260, 293–99
Chamberlain, John, 274
Chambers, Whittaker, 260–61
Chapman, Audrey, 310
Chichester-Clark, Major James, 341, 361
Childers, Erskine, 51, 364, 416
China, 156–58, 165
Chomsky, Noam, 287
Cluskey, Frank, 343–45, 353, 366, 371–72, 382, 387, 390, 435
Cockburn, Claude, 295
Colley, George, 431, 434
Collins, Gerry, 396

Collins, Michael, 128, 164, 349
Colman, Frank, 396
Colum, Padriac, 27, 29, 68
Communism, 301–9, 333–34. See also Conor and communism; Marx; Soviet Union.
Congo, Katanga, 167–82, 187–93, 197–214, 311, 355, 488–90, 515–17, 561–62. See also Hammarskjold.
Congress of Cultural Freedom, 260, 293–99
Connolly, James, 54–55, 97, 312, 338, 363, 370–71, 381
Connolly, Roddy, 370–71, 373
Conquest, Robert, 298
Coogan, Tim Pat, 423
Cooney, Patrick, 399, 422, 424, 431
Cooper, Ivan, 375–76
Corish, Brendan, 332–35, 357, 362–63, 367, 371, 382, 386–89, 407, 435, 541
Cosgrave, Liam, 148, 152, 154–56, 290, 357, 386–88, 390–91, 399–400, 407, 422
Cosgrave, M.J., 431, 434
Cosgrave, W.T., 401
Costello, Declan, 332, 375, 423
Costello, John Aloysius, 129, 148, 152
Coughlan, Stephen (Stevie), 343, 344, 366, 370, 541
Crowder, Michael, 283
Cruise O'Brien, Cathleen, 24, 60, 274
Cruise O'Brien, Conor, academic career, 459–60; and academic freedom, 219, 231–54, 269, 475–81; anti-imperialism, 196, 219, 233, 259, 301–14, 318, 339, 366, 378–79, 472; antiterrorism, 187, 346–49, 354–65, 372, 379–83, 392, 418, 421–25, 439, 447, 460, 467–72; and Burke, xv, 86, 111, 287, 311, 315, 319, 345–47, 352, 429–30, 458, 481–88, 560; and Catholicism, 124–25, 188, 203–4, 318, 339, 404; childhood and youth, 1–6, 57–62, 65, 68–82, 196; in civil service, xiv, 109, 112–47; and communism, 259, 267, 293–99, 472, 534; in Congo, 168–82, 187–214; drinking, 150–51, 223, 282, 286, 319–20, 336; education, 69–82, 85–112, 138–42; vs. Encounter, 260, 292–99; and father-figures, 94, 100, 188, 210–11, 214, 318,

324, 463, 481–90; and finances, xiv,
91, 95, 110, 113, 126, 286, 318, 327, 349,
395, 436, 444, 456–58, 555; and
Christine Foster, 104–10, 126, 143,
148–50, 163, 182; in Ghana, 188,
215–72, 288, 394, 444, 477; as historian,
140–42, 205, 255, 259, 378; humor,
117–21, 152–55, 208, 223, 256, 281,
317, 405, 544; and Jews, 61, 80, 162,
405, 451–52, 460–67, 556; and Maire,
163–83, 173–78, 318–26; and media,
395–98, 403–4, 410–21, 423, 435; in
New York, 188, 259, 272–328, 333,
336, 349; as news journalist, 95–96; and
Northern Ireland, 130–31, 147, 159,
311, 318, 389–91, 398, 424–25, 437,
466–72; at Observer, 419, 437–58; in
Paris, 149–51, 348; political career, 98,
317, 330–436; political views, 219,
300–310, 338–39, 378–82, 451–52;
Posts and Telegraphs, 387, 389, 417;
and racism, 196–97, 233, 259, 305, 309,
325, 464–65, 473–80; risk taking, 78,
215, 355, 363–64, 481; and sex, 89, 105,
110, 143, 163–64; and South Africa,
473–80; and UN, 152–82; 187–93; 318;
writing career, 78, 100–105, 109–11,
118–26, 131–32, 152–53, 188–214,
255–62, 345–49, 429–30, 436,
449–51, 458, 460–67, 472–74, 481–88
Cruise O'Brien, Donal, 110, 150, 167, 171,
173–74, 178, 202, 269, 273, 320–21,
331, 364, 392, 394, 466
Cruise O'Brien, Fedelma, 68, 126, 150,
167, 173–77, 182, 269, 321, 360, 394,
466, 483, 485
Cruise O'Brien, Francis, 34–65, 67–70,
73–77, 82, 94, 96, 485, 487–88; death
of, 1–2, 6, 23, 74, 188, 210, 214; as a
young man, 19–39
Cruise O'Brien, John, 23–24
Cruise O'Brien, Kate, 126, 143, 150,
167, 173–77, 182, 269, 313, 321, 394,
466
Cruise O'Brien, Maire MacEntee, 118,
153, 163–67, 171–77, 187, 192, 217,
239, 265–67, 269–70, 272–75, 281–82,
285–86, 306–8, 313, 315–16, 318–26,
369, 392–95, 436, 438–40, 445, 448–50,
459, 466, 485, 515

Cruise O'Brien, Margaret, 323, 394, 438,
445, 450, 459, 465
Cruise O'Brien, Patrick, 323–26, 392–93,
438–39, 445, 450, 454, 459, 465,
476–80
Cuba, 162, 205, 297, 302–3, 334, 472
Culhane, Gary, 66, 500
Culhane, John F. 26, 56
Cullingford, Elizabeth, 290, 532

Daiken, Leslie, 100, 102
Dail Eireann, 64–65, 129, 156, 316, 326,
335, 342, 350–52, 357, 359, 362, 365,
369, 386–89, 396–97, 399–400, 402,
409, 417, 421, 423–24, 435, 541
Davidson, Gordon, 212–13
Davin, Dan, 314–15, 346, 510–11
Dayal, Rajeshwar, 170, 179, 198
de Valera, Eamon, 64, 72, 81, 97, 116–17,
120, 126–29, 135, 144, 156–57,
172–73, 324, 359, 391, 401, 411, 417,
423, 450, 548
Deane, Seamus, 361
Delany, Rev. William, 28–29
Department of External Affairs, Irish, 109,
114–47, 152, 165, 167, 181, 233, 386,
538, 548
Department of Finance, Irish, 113–14, 174
Derry, 342–45, 355, 368, 375–77, 447
Desmond, Barry, 368, 372
Deutscher, Isaac, 282
Devlin, Bernadette, 344, 354, 451
Devlin, Denis, 118, 207
Devlin, Paddy, 345, 354, 373, 375, 407–8,
540, 543
Diamond, Sidney, 310
Diggins, John Patrick, 284
Dillon, James, 172
Dillon, John, 33–34, 36
Dodd, Senator Thomas, 180
Dorr, Noel, 153
Dowling, Jack, 354–55
Dreifus, Claudia, 308, 531
Dublin, strike of 1913, 49–50

Easter Rising of 1916, 53–56, 67, 312
Edwards, Owen Dudley, 311
Edwards, Robin Dudley, 140–41
Eisenhower, Dwight, 155
Ekow-Daniels, William, 235, 237–40, 242,

250–52, 262, 265–66, 522, 524–25, 528
Ellison, Ralph, 284
Ellman, Richard, xiv, 18–19, 288, 290, 292, 501, 532
Encounter, 260, 292–99, 464, 534
Erdman, David V., 282–83, 287
European Parliament, 352, 376, 395
Ewart-Biggs, Christopher, 422

Fascism, 97–98, 115, 289–92, 333, 347. *See also* Germany; Yeats.
Faulkner, Brian, 361, 407–8
Fay, William, 118, 149
Fianna Fail, 81, 126, 132, 135, 144, 148, 156, 164, 168, 323, 333–40, 350, 357–59, 373, 377–78, 383, 385–88, 398–400, 413, 415–18, 423, 431–35, 437, 471, 524
Fiedler, Leslie, 285, 287, 294
Fine Gael, 101, 129, 172, 323, 334–40, 358, 375, 385–88, 398–400, 403, 410, 424, 431–35
Fitt, Gerry, 345, 354, 375–78, 407–8
FitzGerald, Alexis, 172, 298
FitzGerald, Garret, 137–38, 332, 343, 358, 360, 375, 387–88, 396, 403, 405–7, 423, 431, 435, 468, 542
Flynn, Ed, 134
Foley, Donal, 136, 373
Foster, Alec, 106–7, 110, 126, 140, 143, 148–50, 163, 167, 173–74, 176–78, 182, 313, 345, 473, 505
Foster, Christine, 104–10, 354, 466, 504
Fournier, Paul, 562
Fox, Bill, 391
Freyer, Grattan, 287
Fulcheri, Walter, 178

Gaelic League, 19, 72, 106, 401
Gageby, Douglas, 95, 136, 174, 332
Gaitskell, Hugh, 257
Galbraith, John Kenneth, 294, 296
Gallagher, Frank, 132–33
Garrett, Brian, 361, 369–70, 464, 486, 543
Gellner, Ernest, 321
Germany, 103, 115–17, 148, 294, 347–48, 467
Ghana, 215–54, 262–72, 288, 293, 444, 448, 477, 524

Gielgud, Sir John, 212
Ginsberg, Allen, 308
Gladstone, William Ewart, 34, 141
Gonne, Maude, 81, 127
Goodman, Arnold, 437, 441–43, 452–55
Goodman, Paul, 285, 300
Gossett, Lou, 213
Graft-Johnson, J.C. de, 245–46
Great Melody, The, 346, 481–87
Greco, Gaston, 248–50, 253, 524
Green, Roger, 136
Greene, Graham, 123, 461
Greene, David H., 273–74, 276, 529
Greene, David W., 88, 529
Greene, Elaine, 315, 458

Halligan, Brendan, 331–33, 336, 342, 364–65, 373–75, 384, 389, 543
Hammarskjold, Dag, 168, 170–73, 181, 188–93, 198, 201, 203–4, 206–14, 318, 488–90, 516, 561–62; death of, 171, 175, 178–79, 261
Hampshire, Stuart, 287, 292, 328
Harrington, Stephanie, 254
Harris, Kenneth, 452–54
Hartnett, Noel, 135–36
Harvey, William Burnett, 222, 233–54, 264, 268, 520, 523–26
Haughey, Charles, 339–40, 350, 357–59, 386, 397, 423, 429, 431–34
Healy, John, 135–36, 394
Heath, Edward, 361, 406, 407
Hederman, Mark, 430
Hester, James, 276, 448
Hetherington, George, 143, 150, 163, 167, 173–74, 176–77, 182
Hillery, Dr. Patrick, 351, 356
Hiss, Alger, 261–62, 283
Hitchens, Christopher, 311, 463
Hobsbawm, Eric, 282, 538, 554
Holland, Mary, 419, 447
Holmes, Erskine, 369–70
Hook, Sidney, 274, 285, 294
Horgan, John, 382, 543
Hoskyns, Catherine, 199, 206, 513
Howe, Irving, 284–85, 287, 294
Howth, 175–77, 233, 325, 336, 339, 394, 421
Hume, John, 375–78, 380, 384,390, 407–8, 433, 436, 447

Hyams, Edward, 256
Hyde, Douglas, 402

Inglis, Brian, 128, 136, 302, 405, 441
Ireland, 1–83, 85–148, 163–65, 311–14,
  331–436; civil war, 66–68; Home
  Rule, 11, 47, 49, 51, 58–59; Northern,
  333–436, 447, 466–71; neutrality
  during World War II, 116–19, 129; partition, 129–30, 144–48, 196, 360, 406;
  and UN, 153–62, 312, 386
Iremonger, Valentine, 118, 127
Irish Agricultural Organisation Society,
  42, 44
Irish language, 19, 30, 37, 72, 76, 80–81,
  91, 108, 118, 166, 192, 393–95, 397,
  401–4, 413, 485
Irish literary renaissance, 10, 43, 74
Irish News Agency, 135–38, 145, 147, 260
IRA (Irish Republican Army), Official, 357,
  370–72, 374, 410, 418; pre-1922, 128,
  144; Provisional, 345–46, 354, 357–59,
  361–62, 365, 374, 377, 382–83, 386,
  391–92, 395, 416–25, 439, 461, 463,
  466–72, 478, 546
Irish Republican Brotherhood, 51, 53, 64
Irish Times, 95–96, 99, 102, 137, 257, 311,
  332–33, 339, 356, 378, 381, 384, 394,
  429, 431, 444–45, 456, 458
Irish Transport and General Workers'
  Union, 97, 333, 362–64, 373, 375, 416
Irish Women's Franchise League, 35, 37
Israel, 155–56, 162, 451–52, 460–67, 476,
  556

James, Henry, 276, 285
Jerusalem Committee, 461–63
Jews, 116, 134, 280, 283–84, 308, 344,
  478–79. See also Conor and Jews;
  Israel.
Johnson, Paul, 486
Joyce, James, xiv, 10, 12–21, 38, 43, 49, 76,
  286, 498
Joyce, Stanislaus, 14, 24, 26, 38

Kasavubu, Joseph, 206
Katanga. See Congo.
Kaufmann, Walter, 347
Kaunda, Kenneth, 438, 455
Kearney, Joseph, 394, 466

Keating, Justin, 332, 343–44, 365–66, 382,
  387, 389, 431, 435
Keating, Paul, 153, 298
Kelleher, John, 139, 144, 288
Kelly, John, 399
Kennan, George, 296
Kennedy, Dennis, 475
Kennedy, Eamonn, 153
Kennedy, Edward, 469
Kennedy, John E., 22–23
Kennedy, John F., 296
Kennedy, Ludovic, 392
Kermode, Frank, 294–95, 297–298
Kettle, Tom, 16, 18, 21, 23–24, 26–28,
  30–33, 37, 47–52, 55–57, 105, 499
Khiary, Mahmoud, 190–91, 198, 210, 516
Kilmartin, T., 446, 449
King, Martin Luther, 305, 325
Kissinger, Henry, 472
Kofi Edzii, E.A., 241, 253, 268
Kolakowski, Leszek, 459
Kolko, Gabriel, 283, 287
Kollek, Teddy, 461–63
Korsah, Sir Arku, 243–44
Kristol, Irving, 285, 294–95, 297
Kuma, Alex, 234
Kwapong, Alexander, 222–23, 229,
  233–41, 253, 264–65, 268, 448, 520,
  528
Kyne, Tom, 399

Labour party, Irish, 97–90, 218–19, 326,
  331–47, 452, 524
Lally, Thomas, 23
Land League, Irish, 7–8, 16
Lacquer, Walter, 465
Larkin, Denis, 336
Larkin, James, 49–50, 336, 338, 363
Lasky, Melvin J., 294–300
Lebanon, 464–66
Lecky, W.E.H., 7, 45
Lemass, Sean, 415
Lenehan, Joseph, 357
Lermontov, M.Y., 451
Levinson, Deirdre, 313, 321, 535, 560
Lindsay, John, 308
Literary and Historical Society (L. & H.),
  at St. Stephen's Green college, 14–16,
  20–21, 25, 28–34, 98
Littlewood, Joan, 213

Lloyd George, David, 58, 63
Lloyd, W.E.G., 35, 45
Lumumba, Patrice, 170, 193, 205–14, 552
Lynch, Jack, 337–38, 356–57, 359, 386, 434
Lynch, Patrick, 114, 151–52, 219, 494, 507
Lynd, Robert, 27, 55–56, 105–6
Lyons, J.B., 28
Lyons, Leland, 290–91

MacAteer, Eddie, 145
MacBride, John, 81, 127
MacBride, Sean, 127, 130, 144–45, 196, 244, 260, 312, 345, 471, 476, 508
MacConghail, Muiris, 397–98, 402
McCormack, W.J., 290
McDonagh, Robert, 153
MacDonagh, Thomas, 27, 50, 55
Macdonald, Dwight, 257–58, 284, 287, 294, 300
McDowell, R.B., 111–12, 282
MacEntee, Sean, 128, 135, 153–65, 176, 182, 337–38, 355, 395, 466, 548
McInerney, Michael, 332–33, 337, 375
McKenna, Siobhan, 163
McKeown, Sean, 178
Macmillan, Harold, 216
McNamara, Kevin, 409
MacNeice, Louis, 289
MacNeill, Eoin, 51, 55–56, 72, 401
McQuaid, John Charles, 70–71, 87, 158, 323
MacSwiney, Peader, 307
MacSwiney, Terence, 307
Madden, Thomas, 22–23
Maher, Mary, 339
Mailer, Norman, 300
Mandela, Nelson, 477
Manu, Dr. Yaw, 265–66
Marcuse, Herbert, 538
Maria Cross, 122–26, 142–43, 147, 190
Markievicz, Constance, 43, 120
Martin, David, 439–40
Marx, Karl, and Marxism, 315, 346, 405, 451, 548, 553
Maudling, Reginald, 368–69
Mauriac, Francois, 123–25
Mayfield, Julian, 283, 287, 325
Mercier, Vivian, 92–94, 98–100, 109, 118–120, 256, 273, 503, 528–29, 531

Merrigan, Matt, 373
Mirsky, Jonathan, 283, 320
Mobutu, Joseph, 172, 206
Molotsi, Peter, 283
Monteagle, Lord, 42, 51, 58, 76–77
Moody, Theodore, 138–41
Moran, D.P., 30–31, 33
Mozambique, 438
Mugabe, Robert, 438–40, 473, 552
Munongo, Godefroid, 193–94, 209
Murderous Angels, 204–14, 318, 348–49, 366, 489, 518
Murdoch, Iris, 282, 530
Murdoch, Rupert, 442
Murphy, Michael Pat, 370, 387
Murphy, Tom, 213
Murphy, William Martin, 49–50, 55, 119
Muslims, 155, 310, 452, 465. See also Palestinians.

Naipaul, V.S., 282, 530
Namier, Sir Lewis, 141–42, 482
Nationalism, Irish, 6–41, 45, 47, 51, 55, 58, 63, 128–30, 147, 288–92, 334–37, 349, 362, 378, 402, 405, 410, 425, 466, 471
Naughton, John, 446
Nazis. See Fascism; Germany.
Nealon, Ted, 398
Nettl, Peter, 283, 287
New Left, 272–328
New Statesman, 255–56, 293, 298–99, 419, 444
New York Review of Books, 255, 260–61, 299, 310, 328, 462
New York Times, 295–98
New York University, Conor's Schweitzer Chair at, 272–328, 531. See also Conor in New York.
Nicaragua, 471–72
Nietzsche, F., 292, 347–48
Nigeria. See Biafra.
Nixon, Richard, 134, 261
Nkomo, Joshua, 438
Nkrumah, Kwame, 215–54, 262–72, 521, 528
Northern Ireland. See Ireland, Northern.
Nossiter, Bernard, 423
Nowlan, David, 213
Nyerere, Julius, 272, 438

Oakeshott, Michael, 321
O'Brady, Rory, 354
O'Brien, Conor, 61
O'Brien, William, 32, 36
Observer, 189–90, 201, 257, 326, 364, 369, 419, 436–58, 461, 525, 534
O'Casey, Sean, 54, 76, 214
O'Connell, David (Daithi O'Conaill), 418
O'Connor, Frank, 289
O'Donovan, Dr. John, 366
"O'Donnell, Donat" (Conor's pseudo-nym), 100, 119–20, 134, 151, 188, 255
O'Dwyer, Paul, 313, 341
O'Faolain, Sean, 102, 118–23, 507
O'Farrell, Patrick, 140
O'Hanlon, Mary, 410
Ojukwu, Colonel, 310
O'Kelly, Phil, 212
O'Leary, Michael, 354, 366, 368, 387, 400
Olivier, Sir Laurence, 211–12
O'Morain, Donall, 413–15, 419
O'Neill, Terence, 341
Oppenheimer, Robert, 296
Orange Order, 313, 342, 352, 355
O'Reagain, Liam, 396, 410
Orwell, George, 305, 440, 535, 553
Osborne, D.G., 245–46
O'Shea, Captain William, 10, 178
O'Toole, Fintan, 132, 515

Palestinians and PLO, 460–67, 556
Parliamentary Labor party (Irish), 335–42, 354, 380, 396, 399, 424, 435, 540
Parnell, Charles, xiv, 8–11, 32–33, 138–41, 178, 333, 387
Paton, Alan, 475
Paulin, Tom, 125, 348
Pearse, Patrick, 27, 33, 52–53, 55, 312, 450
Plumb, J.H., 482
Plunkett, Horace Curzon, 41–45, 54, 58–59, 64–65, 67, 76
Posts and Telegraphs ministry, 395, 417, 435
Power and Consciousness, 287, 346
Protestants, Irish, 313, 368, 377, 383, 391, 400, 402, 405–6, 420, 424–25, 433, 469, 470, 482–86
Provos. *See* IRA.

Racism, 464–65, 473–80. *See also* Conor and racism.
Raffalovitch, Sophie, 36, 81
Reagan, Ronald, 471–72
Redmond, John, 32–34, 48, 51, 55, 58, 387
Rees, Goronwy, 297–99
Reston, James, 306
Reynolds, Albert, 397
Rhodesia, 436, 455. *See also* Zimbabwe.
Robinson, Mary, 351, 398–99, 419, 421, 435
Rosenberg, Harold, 285
Rosio, Bengt, 489–90
Rowland, Tiny, 455
Royal University, Dublin, 14, 22–23, 29, 47
RTE Broadcasting Authority, 402–4, 410–21
Rudmose-Brown, T.B., 89–91
Russell, Bertrand, 294
Russell, George, 43–45, 50, 58
Ryan, Richard (Richie), 388

Sandford Park School, 71, 74–81, 86, 89, 91, 162, 460
Sartre, Jean-Paul, 257
Saunders, Dr. Stuart, 479–80
Sawicki, Tom, 556
Schlesinger, Arthur, 274, 284, 294, 296–97, 533
Seanad Eirann, 435
Seidman, Robert, 234, 239, 248–49, 251–52, 254, 524
Sheehy, Bessie, 11, 17, 20, 24–29, 35–37, 48, 57, 66
Sheehy, David, 8–13, 17, 24–25, 29, 31, 33–38, 47, 50, 55, 57, 63, 66, 80
Sheehy, Eugene, 11, 13, 16, 22–23, 26, 29, 33, 37, 50, 52, 67, 80, 91, 95
Sheehy, Father Eugene, 7–9, 17, 56, 81, 115, 172
Sheehy, Father Nicholas, 6–7, 17
Sheehy, Kathleen (later Cruise O'Brien), 11, 18–19, 30–31, 33, 36–39, 40–59, 62, 67, 69–72, 74–78, 81; death of, 93
Sheehy, Margaret, 11, 17, 26, 33, 37, 56, 62, 66
Sheehy, Mary (later Kettle), 11, 18–19, 35–39, 47, 49, 50, 62, 66, 80–81, 98, 275

Sheehy, Richard, 11, 13, 15–16, 20, 26, 29, 32–33, 37, 61, 66

Sheehy-Skeffington, Francis, 15–17, 21, 25–26, 29, 32–35, 37–38, 45, 49–52, 54, 57, 61

Sheehy-Skeffington, Hanna, 11, 17, 25, 26, 29, 33, 37–38, 41, 45, 52, 54, 61, 62, 75–76, 80–82, 93, 127, 289

Sheehy-Skeffington, Owen, 71, 81–82, 90, 95, 97–98, 100, 297–98, 420, 481, 490, 504

Sheerin, Eileen, 276, 326, 331

Siege, The, 462–67, 476

Silvers, Robert, 299, 462

Simms, Nicholas, 321, 360, 394, 399, 410, 418, 466

Sinn Fein, Official, 365, 372, 418; Provisional, 63–65, 128, 307, 333, 354, 362, 380, 383, 390, 418, 423–24, 557

Sir George Williams University, Montreal, 327–28

Smith, George Ivan, 171, 178–80, 489–90, 561

Smith-Gordon, Lionel, 44–45

Smyllie, Robert Maire, 95–96

Social Democratic and Labour Party, Irish, 375–77, 383, 405–9, 422, 471

Solomons, Bethel, 60–61

South Africa, 197, 233, 236, 303, 438–40, 465, 473–80, 517–18

Soviet Union, 152, 155, 158, 302, 472, 475

Soyinka, Wole, 213

Spain, and Franco, 97–99, 115

Spellman, Francis Cardinal, 158, 165

Spender, Stephen, 294–95, 297

Spock, Dr. Benjamin, 308, 536

Spring, Dan, 370

Spring-Rice, Mary, 76

Spring-Rice, Tom, 58, 76–77

St. Stephen's Green college, 14–15, 20, 24–25, 27, 45

Stadler, A.W., 476

Starkie, Walter, 90–91

States of Ireland, 290, 378–82, 384

Steiner, George, 277, 278, 280–83, 287, 291, 315, 459, 530, 540

Stevenson, Adlai, 162

Stone, I.F., 287, 328

Suez Canal, 155–56, 441

Sullivan, Dan, 207

Sunningdale agreement, 405–9, 419–20, 433

Suzman, Helen, 475

Sweden, 147–48, 488–90, 562

Synge, J.M., 27, 31–32

Taylor, John, 372

Television. *See* Conor and media; RTE Broadcasting Authority.

Terrorism. *See* Conor, antiterrorism; IRA.

Thant, U, 170, 172, 179, 180–81, 192, 195, 204

Thompson, Edward, 282, 287, 527, 530, 538, 554, 560, 451

Thornley, David, 342–43, 366, 368, 380–81, 387

Thorpe, Jeremy, 368–69

Times Literary Supplement, 197–98, 202, 380

Timmerman, Jacob, 464

Tingsten, Herbert, 190

To Katanga and Back, 173, 191–200, 210, 219, 314, 488, 515–16

Tone, Wolfe, 97, 410

Topolski, Feliks, 202, 211–12

Treacy, Sean, 366, 371–74, 387

Trelford, Donald, 436, 441–47, 441–47, 450, 452–56

Trilling, Diana, 294

Trilling, Lionel, 292

Trinity College History Society, 98–99, 450

Trinity College, Dublin, 85–112, 138, 225, 296, 315, 325, 450, 465, 484

Tshombe, Moise, 170–71, 175, 194, 205, 561

Tully, James, 387, 392, 431

Tynan, Kenneth, 212

Ulster. *See* Ireland, Northern.

United Irish League, 32–35

United Kingdom, and Africa, 227, 311; and Ireland, 134, 147, 342, 345, 354, 356, 368–71, 374, 376, 405–9, 418, 422, 437–58, 468

United Nations, 152–67, 448, 452, 460; in Congo, 168–82, 187–93, 197–214, 216; and Ireland, 312, 386

United Nations: Sacred Drama, 201–10, 318

United States, and Africa, 200, 205, 208, 231; foreign policy 300–310, 471–72, 475; and Ireland, 117, 129, 130, 134, 144, 383, 469; and Nicaragua, 471–72; and UN 158, 162, 201, 208; and Vietnam, 201, 235. *See also* Conor in New York; Vietnam.
University College, Dublin (UCD), 14, 30, 47, 49, 55, 65, 86, 92, 114, 151–52, 165, 224, 388, 460, 465
Urquhart, Brian, 171, 179–80, 197–99, 515–16

Vietnam, 201, 235, 281, 283, 286, 301–9, 314, 318, 368, 472, 536
Violence. *See* Conor, antiterrorism; IRA.

Wall, Patrick, 180, 515
Walshe, Joseph P., 115–16
Weil, Simone, 429–30
Welsh, David, 476
West, Trevor, 435

Wheatcroft, Geoffrey, 290, 423
"Whitewater", 143, 163, 177
Wild Geese, Irish, 23, 60
Williams, Desmond, 140, 298
Wilson, Edmund, 258, 284, 328
Wilson, Harold, 338, 368, 383, 408
Woods, Dr. Michael, 434
World War I, 51–53, 55
World War II, 102–3, 113–19, 129, 202
Wright, Richard, 284
Writers and Politics, 255, 294

Yeats, W.B., 10, 16, 27, 31–32, 74, 81, 303–4, 481; and fascism, 255, 288–92, 532
Young Ireland Branch of United Irish League (Yibs), 32–35, 37, 46, 97

Zaire. *See* Congo.
Zambia, 438
Zimbabwe, 438, 473

This book was typeset by Typo Litho Composition Inc., Québec, in 10/12 Janson, and printed and bound by Friesen Printers, Altona, Manitoba.
Design is by Miriam Bloom, Expression Communications Inc.